Microeconometrics

D1554845

The New Palgrave Economics Collection
Editors: Steven N. Durlauf, University of Wisconsin-Madison, USA & Lawrence E. Blume,
Cornell University, USA

Also in the series:

Behavioural and Experimetal Economics
Economic Growth
Game Theory
Macroeconometrics and Time Series Analysis
Monetary Economics

Series Standing Order ISBN 978-0-230-24014-8 hardcover
Series Standing Order ISBN 978-0-230-24013-1 paperback

To receive future titles in this series as they are published quote one of the ISBNs listed above to set
up a standing order: contact your bookseller; write to Customer Services Department, Macmillan
Distribution Ltd, Houndmills, Basingstoke, Hampshire, RG21 6XS; or email orders@palgrave.com.

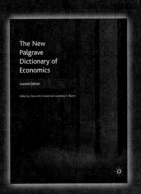

The New Palgrave Dictionary of Economics
Second Edition

Edited by Steven N. Durlauf and Lawrence E. Blume

The definitive resource for a new generation of economists

| 5.8 million words | 1,872 articles | 8 print volumes |
| 1,506 contributors | 7,680 page | 1 dynamic online resource |

Including articles by over 1,500 eminent contributors and providing a current overview of economics, this second edition of *The New Palgrave* is now available both in print and online.

The online *Dictionary* is a dynamic resource for economists which:

- Is regularly updated with new articles and updates to existing articles, along with new features and functionality

- Allows 24x7 access to members of subscribing institutions, outside library opening hours, on the move, at home or at their desk

- Offers excellent search and browse facilities, both full text and advanced, which make it possible to explore the Dictionary with great speed and ease

- Contains hyperlinked cross-references within articles, making it an indispensable tool for researchers and students

- Features carefully selected and maintained links to related sites, sources of further information and bibliographical citations

- Enables users to save searches, make personal annotations and bookmark articles they need to refer to regularly by using 'My Dictionary'

Experience the world of economics at your fingertips!

Why not see for yourself how valuable the online *Dictionary* is by encouraging your librarian to request a trial today?

Free 2 week trials of *The New Palgrave Dictionary of Economics Online* are now available to prospective institutional subscribers worldwide. Your librarian can register today at www.dictionaryofeconomics.com.

www.dictionaryofeconomics.com

Microeconometrics

Edited by
Steven N. Durlauf
University of Wisconsin-Madison, USA

Lawrence E. Blume
Cornell University, USA

First published 2010 by
PALGRAVE MACMILLAN

Palgrave Macmillan in the UK is an imprint of Macmillan Publishers Limited,
registered in England, company number 785998, of Houndmills, Basingstoke,
Hampshire RG21 6XS.

Palgrave Macmillan in the US is a division of St Martin's Press LLC,
175 Fifth Avenue, New York, NY 10010.

Palgrave Macmillan is the global academic imprint of the above companies
and has companies and representatives throughout the world.

Palgrave® and Macmillan® are registered trademarks in the United States,
the United Kingdom, Europe and other countries.

ISBN 978-0-230-23880-0   hardback
ISBN 978-0-230-23881-7   paperback

This book is printed on paper suitable for recycling and made from fully
managed and sustained forest sources. Logging, pulping and manufacturing
processes are expected to conform to the environmental regulations of the
country of origin.

A catalogue record for this book is available from the British Library.

A catalog record for this book is available from the Library of Congress.

10   9   8   7   6   5   4   3   2   1
19   18   17   16   15   14   13   12   11   10

Printed and bound in the United States of America

Contents

List of Contributors

ALBERTO ABADIE
Harvard Kennedy School, USA

JOSHUA D. ANGRIST
Massachusetts Institute of Technology, USA

BADI H. BALTAGI
University of Arizona, USA

MOSHE BUCHINSKY
University of California Los Angeles, USA

A. COLIN CAMERON
University of California Davis, USA

TIMOTHY G. CONLEY
University of Chicago, USA

JOHN DINARDO
University of Michigan, USA

JEFF DOMINITZ
Carnegie Mellon University, USA

DAVID DRAPER
University of California Santa Cruz, USA

JEAN-MARIE DUFOUR
McGill University, USA

ANDREW GELMAN
Columbia University, USA

JINYONG HAHN
University of California Los Angeles, USA

VASSILIS A. HAJIVASSILIOU
London School of Economics, UK

JERRY A. HAUSMAN
Massachusetts Institute of Technology, USA

JAMES J. HECKMAN
The University of Chicago, USA

KEISUKE HIRANO
University of Arizona, USA

CHENG HSIAO
University of Southern California, USA

GUIDO W. IMBENS
University of California Berkeley, USA

YANNIS M. IOANNIDES
Tufts University, USA

EKATERINI KYRIAZIDOU
University of California Los Angeles, USA

EDWARD E. LEAMER
University of California Los Angeles, USA

BRUCE G. LINDSAY
Penn State University, USA

OLIVER B. LINTON
London School of Economics, UK

JOHN A. LIST
University of Chicago, USA

THIERRY MAGNAC
University of Toulouse 1, France

CHARLES F. MANSKI
Northwestern University, USA

ROSA L. MATZKIN
University of California Los Angeles, USA

SALVADOR NAVARRO
University of Madison-Wisconsin, USA

JAMES L. POWELL
University of California Berkeley, USA

DAVID REILEY
University of Arizona, USA

ERIC RENAULT
University of North Carolina Chapel Hill, USA

JEAN-MARC ROBIN
University of Paris 1, France

DONALD B. RUBIN
Harvard University, USA

ROBERT P. SHERMAN
California Institute of Technology, USA

MICHAEL STEWART
University of Sydney, Australia

CHRISTOPHER TABER
The University of Wisconsin-Madison, USA

ELIE TAMER
Northwestern University, USA

PETRA E. TODD
University of Pennsylvania, USA

GERARD J. VAN DEN BERG
University of Amsterdam, The Netherlands

WILBERT VAN DER KLAAUW
Federal Reserve Bank of New York, USA

ARTHUR VAN SOEST
Tilburg University, The Netherlands

TIEMEN M. WOUTERSEN
Johns Hopkins University, USA

General Preface

All economists of a certain age remember the "little green books". Many own a few. These are the offspring of *The New Palgrave: A Dictionary of Economics*; collections of reprints from *The New Palgrave* that were meant to deliver at least a sense of the *Dictionary* into the hands of those for whom access to the entire four volume, four million word set was inconvenient or difficult. *The New Palgrave Dictionary of Economics, Second Edition* largely resolves the accessibility problem through its online presence. But while the online search facility provides convenient access to specific topics in the now eight volume, six million word *Dictionary of Economics*, no interface has yet been devised that makes browsing from a large online source a pleasurable activity for a rainy afternoon. To our delight, *The New Palgrave*'s publisher shares our view of the joys of dictionary-surfing, and we are thus pleased to present a new series, the "little blue books", to make some part of the *Dictionary* accessible in the hand or lap for teachers, students, and those who want to browse. While the volumes in this series contain only articles that appeared in the 2008 print edition, readers can, of course, refer to the online *Dictionary* and its expanding list of entries.

The selections in these volumes were chosen with several desiderata in mind: to touch on important problems, to emphasize material that may be of more general interest to economics beginners and yet still touch on the analytical core of modern economics, and to balance important theoretical concerns with key empirical debates. The 1987 Eatwell, Milgate and Newman *The New Palgrave: A Dictionary of Economics* was chiefly concerned with economic theory, both the history of its evolution and its contemporary state. The second edition has taken a different approach. While much progress has been made across the board in the 21 years between the first and second editions, it is particularly the flowering of empirical economics which distinguishes the present interval from the 61 year interval between Henry Higgs' *Palgrave's Dictionary of Political Economy* and *The New Palgrave*. It is fair to say that, in the long run, doctrine evolves more slowly than the database of facts, and so some of the selections in these volumes will age more quickly than others. This problem will be solved in the online *Dictionary* through an ongoing process of revisions and updates. While no such solution is available for these volumes, we have tried to choose topics which will give these books utility for some time to come.

Steven N. Durlauf
Lawrence E. Blume

Introduction

The 1987 edition of *The New Palgrave* came at a time of some of the most extraordinary post-war developments in microeconometrics, namely work by James Heckman on self-selection and Daniel McFadden on discrete choice. Heckman's entry from the 1987 edition is preserved as a classic in this volume and is joined by an entry on the Roy model which reflects Heckman's subsequent thinking. Coverage of discrete choice has been completely replaced with entries that are included here.

The successes of microeconometrics as of 1987 by no means imply that area has been one of comparative stasis. Much of Heckman's research, for example, has focused on exploring how one can develop inferences which avoid theoretically unmotivated assumptions, just as McFadden's research has focused on exploring how economic theory can be translated into econometric specifications of behaviour. These overarching ways of asking questions continue to generate important advances. One broad area of this type is semiparametric estimation, in which functional forms assumptions are relaxed in statistical analysis. An equally important area of this type is partial identification, which may be thought of as asking what may be learned from data under the most minimal assumptions. Further, new approaches to data acquisition such as survey analysis or the quest for finding interesting natural experiments, complement the methodological advances.

While microeconometrics is widely admired for the sustained pace of advances, there continue to be deep methodological disputes within the field. These are very much manifested in the literature on treatment effects, which now receives very extensive coverage. These disagreements reflect the different beliefs about the role of economic theory in empirical work, both in terms of how empirical exercises should be structured and in terms of the meaning of "statistical" assumptions. We believe this collection communicates the excitement of continuing research on microeconometrics.

Steven N. Durlauf
Lawrence E. Blume

categorical data

Categorical outcome models are regression models for a dependent variable that is a discrete variable recording in which of two or more categories, usually mutually exclusive, an outcome of interest lies.

Categorical outcome models are also called discrete outcome models or qualitative response models, and are examples of a limited dependent variable model. Different models specify different functional forms for the probabilities of each category. These models are binomial or multinomial models, usually estimated by maximum likelihood.

Key early econometrics references include McFadden (1974), Amemiya (1981), Manski and McFadden (1981) and Maddala (1983). For textbook treatments see Amemiya (1985), Wooldridge (2002), Greene (2003) and Cameron and Trivedi (2005). The recent econometrics literature has focused on semiparametric estimation (see Pagan and Ullah, 1999) and on simulation-based estimation of multinomial models (see Train, 2003).

Binary outcomes: logit and probit models

Binary outcomes provide the simplest case of categorical data, with just two possible outcomes. An example is whether or not an individual is employed and whether or not a consumer makes a purchase.

For binary outcomes the dependent variable y takes one of two values, for simplicity coded as 0 or 1. If $y_i = 1$ with probability p_i, then necessarily $y_i = 0$ with probability $1 - p_i$, where i denotes the ith of N observations. Regressors $\mathbf{x}_i$ are introduced by parameterizing the probability p_i, with

$$p_i = \Pr[y_i = 1 | \mathbf{x}_i] = F(\mathbf{x}_i'\beta),$$

where $F(\cdot)$ is a specified function and a single-index form is assumed.

The obvious choice of $F(\cdot)$ is a cumulative distribution function (CDF) since this ensures that $0 < p_i < 1$. The two standard models are the logit model with $p_i = \Lambda(\mathbf{x}_i'\beta) = e^{\mathbf{x}_i'\beta}/(1 + e^{\mathbf{x}_i'\beta})$, where $\Lambda(z) = e^z/(1 + e^z)$ is the logistic CDF, and the probit model with $p_i = \Phi(\mathbf{x}_i'\beta)$, where $\Phi(\cdot)$ is the standard normal CDF.

Interest usually lies in the marginal effect of a change in regressor on the probability that $y = 1$. For the rth regressor, $\partial p_i/\partial x_{ir} = F'(\mathbf{x}_i'\beta)\beta_r$ where F' denotes the derivative of F. The sign of β_r gives the sign of the marginal effect, if F is a continuous CDF since then $F' > 0$, though the magnitude depends on the point of evaluation $\mathbf{x}_i$. Common methods are to report the average marginal effect over all observations or to report the marginal effect evaluated at $\mathbf{x}$.

Parameter estimates are usually obtained by maximum likelihood (ML) estimation. Given p_i, the density can be conveniently expressed as $f(y_i) = p_i^{y_i}(1 - p_i)^{1-y_i}$. On the assumption of independence over i, the resulting log-likelihood function is

$$\ln L(\beta) = \sum_{i=1}^{N} \{y_i \ln F(\mathbf{x}_i'\beta) + (1 - y_i)\ln(1 - F(\mathbf{x}_i'\beta))\}.$$

It can be shown that consistency of the ML estimator requires only that $p_i = F(\mathbf{x}_i'\beta)$, that is, that the functional form for the conditional probability is correctly specified.

There is usually little difference between the predicted probabilities obtained by probit or logit, except for very low and high probability events. For the logit model $\ln[p_i/(1 - p_i)] = \mathbf{x}_i'\beta$, so that β_r gives the marginal effect of a change in x_{ir} on the log-odds ratio, a popular interpretation in the biostatistics literature.

A simpler method for binary data is OLS regression of y_i on $\mathbf{x}_i$, with White heteroskedastic robust standard errors used to control for the intrinsic hetero-skedasticity in binary data. A serious defect is that OLS permits predicted probabilities to lie outside the $(0, 1)$ interval. But it can be useful for exploratory analysis, as OLS coefficients can be directly interpreted as marginal effects and standard methods then exist for complications such as endogenous regressors.

When one of the outcomes is uncommon, surveys may over sample that outcome. For example, a survey of transit use may be taken at bus stops to over-sample bus riders. This is a leading example of choice-based sampling. Standard ML estimators are inconsistent and instead one must use alternative estimators such as appropriately weighted ML.

The preceding discussion presumes knowledge of F. A considerable number of semiparametric estimators that provide consistent estimates of β given unknown F have been proposed. Manski's (1975) smooth maximum score estimator was a very early example of semiparametric estimation.

Index models

Define a latent (or unobserved) variable y_i^* that measures the propensity for the event of interest to occur. If y_i^* crosses a threshold, normalized to be zero, then the event occurs and we observe $y_i = 1$ if $y_i^* > 0$ and $y_i = 0$ if $y_i^* \leq 0$. If $y_i^* = \mathbf{x}_i'\beta + u_i$, then

$$p_i = \Pr[y_i^* > 0] = \Pr[-u_i < \mathbf{x}_i'\beta] = F(\mathbf{x}_i'\beta),$$

where $F(\cdot)$ is the CDF of $-u_i$.

The logit model arises if u_i has the logistic distribution. The probit model arises if u_i has the more obvious standard normal distribution, where imposing a unit error variance ensures model identification. The probit model ties in nicely with the Tobit model, where more data are available and we actually observe $y_i = y_i^*$ when $y_i^* > 0$. And it extends naturally to ordered multinomial data.

Random utility models

In many economics applications the binary outcome is determined by individual choice, such as whether or not to work. Then the outcome should be the alternative with highest utility. The additive random utility model (ARUM) specifies the utility for individual i of alternative j to be $U_{ij} = \mathbf{x}'_{ij}\beta_j + \varepsilon_{ij}$, $j = 0, 1$, where the error term captures factors known by the decision-maker but not the econometrician. Then

$$p_i = \Pr[U_{i1} > U_{i0}] = \Pr[(\varepsilon_{i0} - \varepsilon_{i1}) \leq \mathbf{x}'_{i1}\beta_1 - \mathbf{x}'_{i0}\beta_0] = F(\mathbf{x}'_{i1}\beta_1 - \mathbf{x}'_{i0}\beta_0)$$

where F is the CDF of $(\varepsilon_{i0} - \varepsilon_{i1})$. For components x_{ir} of $\mathbf{x}_i$ that vary across alternatives (so $x_{i0r} \neq x_{i1r}$) it is common to restrict $\beta_{0r} = \beta_{1r} = \beta_r$. For components x_{ir} of $\mathbf{x}_i$ that are invariant across alternatives (so $x_{i0r} = x_{i1r}$) only the difference $\beta_{1r} - \beta_{0r}$ is identified.

The probit model arises, after rescaling, if ε_{i0} and ε_{i1} are i.i.d. standard normal. The logit model arises if ε_{i0} and ε_{i1} are i.i.d. type 1 extreme value distributed with density $f(\varepsilon) = e^{-\varepsilon}\exp(-e^{-\varepsilon})$. The latter less familiar distribution provides more tractable results when extended to multinomial models.

Multinomial outcomes

Multinomial outcomes occur when there are more than two categorical outcomes. With m outcomes the dependent variable y takes one of m mutually exclusive values, for simplicity coded as $1, \ldots, m$. Let p_j denote the probability that the jth outcome occurs. The multinomial density for y can be written as $f(y) = \prod_{j=1}^{m} p_j^{y_j}$ where y_j, $j = 1, \ldots, m$, are m indicator variables equal to 1 if $y = j$ and equal to 0 if $y \neq j$. Introducing a further subscript for the ith individual and assuming independence over i yields log-likelihood

$$\ln L(\beta) = \sum_{i=1}^{N} \sum_{j=1}^{m} y_{ij} \ln p_{ij},$$

where the probabilities p_{ij} are modelled to depend on regressors and unknown parameters β.

There are many different multinomial models, corresponding to different parameterizations of p_{ij}.

Unordered multinomial models

Usually the outcomes are unordered, such as in choice of transit mode to work. The benchmark model for unordered outcomes is the multinomial logit model. When regressors vary across alternatives (such as prices), the conditional logit (CL) model specifies $p_{ij} = e^{\mathbf{x}'_{ij}\beta} / \sum_{k=1}^{m} e^{\mathbf{x}'_{ij}\beta}$. If regressors are invariant across alternatives (such as gender), the multinomial logit (MNL) model specifies $p_{ij} = e^{\mathbf{x}'_i\beta_j} / \sum_{k=1}^{m} e^{\mathbf{x}'_i\beta_k}$, with a normalization such as $\beta_1 = 0$ to ensure identification. In practice some regressors may be a mix of invariant and varying across alternatives; such cases can be re-expressed as either a CL or MNL model.

The CL and MNL models reduce to a series of pairwise choices that do not depend on the other choices available. For example, the choice between use of car or red bus is not affected by whether another alternative is a blue bus (essentially the same as the red bus). This restriction, called the assumption of independence of irrelevant alternatives, has led to a number of alternative models.

These models are based on the ARUM. Suppose the jth alternative has utility $U_{ij} = \mathbf{x}'_{ij}\beta + \varepsilon_{ij}, \ j = 1, \ldots, m.$ Then

$$p_{ij} = \Pr[U_{ij} \geq U_{ik} \text{ for all } k] = \Pr[(\varepsilon_{ik} - \varepsilon_{ij}) \leq (\mathbf{x}'_{ij}\beta - \mathbf{x}'_{ik}\beta) \ \forall \ k].$$

The CL and MNL models arise if the errors ε_{ij} are i.i.d. type 1 extreme value distributed. More general models permit correlation across alternatives j in the errors ε_{ij}.

The most tractable model with error correlation is a nested logit model. This arises if the errors are generalized extreme value distributed. This model is simple to estimate but suffers from the need to specify a particular nesting structure.

The richer multinomial probit model specifies the errors to be m–dimensional multivariate normal with $(m + 1)$ restrictions on the covariances to ensure identification. In practice it has proved difficult to jointly estimate both β and the covariance parameters in this model. A recent popular model is the random parameters logit model. This begins with a multinomial logit model but permits the parameters β to be normally distributed. For these two models there is no closed form expression for the probabilities and estimation is usually by simulation methods or Bayesian methods.

Ordered multinomial models
In some cases the outcomes can be ordered, such as health status being excellent, good, fair or poor.

The starting point is an index model, with single latent variable, $y^*_i = \mathbf{x}'_i\beta + u_i$. As y^* crosses a series of increasing unknown thresholds we move up the ordering of alternatives. For example, for $y^* > \alpha_1$ health status improves from poor to fair, for $y^* > \alpha_2$ it improves further to good, and so on. For the ordered logit (probit) model the error u is logistic (standard normal) distributed.

An alternative model is a sequential model. For example, one may first decide whether or not to go to college ($y = 1$) and if chose college then choose either two-year college ($y = 2$) or four-year college ($y = 3$). The two decisions may be modelled as separate logit or probit models.

A special case of ordered categorical data is a count, such as number of visits to a doctor taking values 0, 1, 2, ... An ordered model can be applied to these data, but it is better to use count models. The simplest count model is Poisson regression with exponential conditional mean $\mathrm{E}[y_i|\mathbf{x}_i] = \exp(\mathbf{x}'_i\beta)$. Common procedures are to use the Poisson but obtain standard errors that relax the Poisson restriction of variance-mean equality, to estimate the richer negative binomial model, or to estimate hurdle or two-part models or with-zeroes models that permit the process determining zero counts to differ from that for positive counts.

Multivariate outcomes and panel data

Multivariate discrete data arise when more than one discrete outcome is modelled. The simplest example is bivariate binary outcome data. For example, we may seek to explain both employment status (work or not work) and family status (children or no children). The standard model is a bivariate probit model that specifies an index model for each dependent variable with normal errors that are correlated. Such models can be extended to permit simultaneity.

For panel binary data the standard model is an individual specific effects model with $p_{it} = F(\alpha_i + \mathbf{x}'_{it}\beta)$ where α_i is an individual specific effect. The random effects model usually specifies $\alpha_i \sim N[0, \sigma_\alpha^2]$ and is estimated by numerically integrating out α_i using Gaussian quadrature. The fixed effects model treats α_i as a fixed parameter. In short panels with few time periods consistent estimation of β is possible in the fixed effects logit but not the fixed effects probit model. If $\mathbf{x}_{it}$ includes $y_{i,t-1}$, a dynamic model, fixed effects logit is again possible but requires four periods of data.

A. COLIN CAMERON

See also **logit models of individual choice; maximum score methods; semiparametric estimation; simulation-based estimation.**

Bibliography

Amemiya, T. 1981. Qualitative response models: a survey. *Journal of Economic Literature* 19, 1483–536.

Amemiya, T. 1985. *Advanced Econometrics*. Cambridge, MA: Harvard University Press.

Cameron, A. and Trivedi, P. 2005. *Microeconometrics: Methods and Applications*. Cambridge: Cambridge University Press.

Greene, W. 2003. *Econometric Analysis*, 5th edn. Upper Saddle River, NJ: Prentice-Hall.

Maddala, G. 1983. *Limited-Dependent and Qualitative Variables in Econometrics*. Cambridge: Cambridge University Press.

Manski, C. 1975. The maximum score estimator of the stochastic utility model of choice. *Journal of Econometrics* 3, 205–28.

Manski, C. and McFadden, D., eds. 1981. *Structural Analysis of Discrete Data with Econometric Applications*. Cambridge, MA: MIT Press.

McFadden, D. 1974. Conditional logit analysis of qualitative choice behavior. In *Frontiers in Econometrics*, ed. P. Zarembka. New York: Academic Press.

Pagan, A. and Ullah, A. 1999. *Nonparametric Econometrics*. Cambridge: Cambridge University Press.

Train, K. 2003. *Discrete Choice Methods with Simulation*. Cambridge: Cambridge University Press.

Wooldridge, J. 2002. *Econometric Analysis of Cross Section and Panel Data*. Cambridge, MA: MIT Press.

competing risks model

A competing risks model is a model for multiple durations that start at the same point in time for a given subject, where the subject is observed until the first duration is completed and one also observes which of the multiple durations is completed first.

The term 'competing risks' originates in the interpretation that a subject faces different risks i of leaving the state it is in, each risk giving rise to its own exit destination, which can also be denoted by i. One may then define random variables T_i describing the duration until risk i is materialized. Only the smallest of all these durations $Y := \min_i T_i$ and the corresponding actual exit destination, which can be expressed as $Z := \text{argmin}_i T_i$, are observed. The other durations are censored in the sense that all is known is that their realizations exceed Y. Often those other durations are latent or counterfactual, for example if T_i denotes the time until death due to cause i.

In economics, the most common application concerns individual unemployment durations. One may envisage two durations for each individual: one until a transition into employment occurs, and one until a transition into non-participation occurs. We observe only one transition, namely, the one that occurs first. Other applications include the duration of treatments, where the exit destinations are relapse and recovery, and the duration of marriage, where one risk is divorce and the other is death of one of the spouses. More generally, the duration until an event of interest may be right-censored due to the occurrence of another event, or due to the data sampling design. The duration until the censoring is then one of the variables T_i.

Sometimes one is interested only in the distribution of Y. For example, an unemployment insurance (UI) agency may be concerned only about the expenses on UI and not in the exit destinations of recipients. In such cases one may employ standard statistical duration analysis for empirical inference with register data on the duration of UI receipt. However, in studies on individual behaviour one is typically interested in one or more of the marginal distributions of the T_i. If these variables are known to be independent, then again one may employ standard duration analysis for each of the T_i separately, treating the other variables $T_j (j \neq i)$ as independent right-censoring variables. But often it is not clear whether the T_i are independent. Indeed, economic theory often predicts that they are dependent, in particular if they can be affected by the individual's behaviour and individuals are heterogeneous. It may even be sensible from the individual's point of view to use their privately observed exogenous exit rates into destinations j as inputs for the optimal strategy affecting the exit rate into destination $i (i \neq j)$ (see, for example, van den Berg, 1990). Erroneously assuming independence leads to incorrect inference, and in fact the issue of whether the durations T_i are related is often an important question in its own right.

Unfortunately, the joint distribution of all T_i is not identified from the joint distribution of Y, Z, a result that goes back to Cox (1959). In particular, given any specific joint distribution, there is a joint distribution with independent durations T_i that generates the same distribution of the observable variables Y, Z. In other words, without additional structure, each dependent competing risks model is observationally equivalent to an independent competing risks model. The marginal distributions in the latter can be very different from the true distributions.

Of course, some properties of the joint distribution are identified. To describe these it is useful to introduce the concept of the hazard rate of a continuous duration variable, say W. Formally, the hazard rate at time t is $\theta(t) := \lim_{dt \downarrow 0} \Pr(W \in [t, t + dt))/dt$. Informally, this is the rate at which the duration W is completed at t given that it has not been completed before t. The hazard rate is the basic building block of duration analysis in social sciences because it can be directly related to individual behaviour at t. The data on Y, Z allow for identification of the hazard rates of T_i at t given that $T \geq t$. These are called the 'crude' hazard rates. If the T_i are independent, then these equal the 'net' hazard rates of the marginal distributions of the T_i.

We now turn to a number of approaches that overcome the general non-identification result for competing risks models. In econometrics, one is typically interested in covariate or regressor effects. The main approach has therefore been to specify semi-parametric models that include observed regressors X and unobserved heterogeneity terms V. With a single risk, the most popular duration model is the mixed proportional hazard (MPH) model, which specifies that $\theta(t|X = x, V) = \psi(t) \exp(x'\beta) V$ for some function $\psi(.)$. V is unobserved, and the composition of the survivors changes selectively as time proceeds, so identification from the observable distributions of $T|X$ is non-trivial. However, it holds under the assumptions that $X \perp\!\!\!\perp V$ and var$(X) > 0$ and some regularity assumptions (see van den Berg, 2001, for an overview of results). With competing risks, the analogue of the MPH model is the multivariate MPH (MMPH) model. With two risks,

$$\theta_1(t|x, V) = \psi_1(t) \exp(x'\beta_1) V_1 \quad \text{and}$$
$$\theta_2(t|x, V) = \psi_2(t) \exp(x'\beta_2) V_2.$$

where $T_1, T_2 | X, V$ are assumed independent, so that a dependence of the durations given X is modelled by way of their unobserved determinants V_1 and V_2 being dependent. Many empirical studies have estimated parametric versions of this model, using maximum likelihood estimation.

The semi-parametric model has been shown to be identified, under only slightly stronger conditions than those for the MPH model (Abbring and van den Berg, 2003). Specifically, Var$(X) > 0$ is strengthened to the condition that the vector X includes two continuous variables with the properties that (*a*) their joint support contains a non-empty open set in $\mathbb{R}^2$, and (*b*) the vectors $\widetilde{\beta}_1, \widetilde{\beta}_2$ of the corresponding elements of β_1 and β_2 form a matrix $(\widetilde{\beta}_1, \widetilde{\beta}_2)$ of full rank. Somewhat loosely, X has two continuous variables that are not perfectly collinear and that act differently on θ_1 and θ_2. Note that, with such regressors, one can manipulate $\exp(x'\beta_1)$ while keeping $\exp(x'\beta_2)$ constant. The two terms $\exp(x'\beta_i)$ are identified from the observable crude hazards at $t = 0$ because at $t = 0$ no dynamic selection due to the unobserved heterogeneity has taken place yet. Now suppose one manipulates x in the way described above. If $T_1, T_2|X$ are independent, then the observable crude hazard rate of T_2 at $t > 0$, given that $T_1 \geq t$, does not vary along. But, if $T_1, T_2|X$ are dependent, then this crude hazard rate does vary along, for the following reason. First, changes in $\exp(x'\beta_1)$ affect the distribution of unobserved heterogeneity V_1 among the survivors at t, due to the well-known fact that V_1 and X are dependent conditional on survival (i.e. conditional on $T_1 \geq t > 0$) even though they are independent unconditionally. Second, if V_1 and V_2 are dependent, this affects the distribution of V_2 among the survivors at t, which in turn affects the observable crude hazard of T_2 at t given that $T_1 \geq t$. In sum, the variation in this crude hazard with $\exp(x'\beta_1)$ for given $\exp(x'\beta_2)$ is informative on the dependence of the durations. An analogous argument holds for the crude hazard rate corresponding to cause $i = 1$.

Note that identification is not based on exclusion restrictions of the sort encountered in instrumental variable analysis, which require a regressor that affects one endogenous variable but not the other. Here, all explanatory variables are allowed to affect both duration variables – they are just not allowed to affect the duration distributions in the same way. Identification with regressors was first established by Heckman and Honoré (1989), who considered a somewhat larger class of models than the MMPH model and accordingly imposed stronger conditions on the support of X.

Although the MPH model is identified from single-risk duration data where we observe a single spell per subject, there is substantial evidence that estimates are sensitive to misspecification of functional forms of model elements (see van den Berg, 2001, for an overview). This implies that estimates of MMPH models using competing-risks data should also be viewed with caution. It is advisable to include additional data. For example, longitudinal survey data on unemployment durations subject to right-censoring can be augmented with register data or retrospective data not subject to censoring (see for example van den Berg, Lindeboom and Ridder, 1994). More in general, one may resort to 'multiple-spell competing risks' data, meaning data with multiple observations of Y, Z for each subject. For a given subject, such observations can be viewed as multiple independent draws from the subject-specific distribution of Y, Z, on the assumption that the unobserved heterogeneity terms V_1, V_2 are identical across the spells of the subject. Here, a subject can denote a single physical unit, like an individual, for which we observe two spells in exactly the same state, or it can denote a set of physical units for which we observe one spell each. Multiple-spell data allow for identification under less stringent conditions than single-spell data. Abbring and van den Berg (2003) showed that such data identify models that allow for full interactions between the elapsed durations t and x in $\theta_i(t|x, V)$, and, indeed, allow the corresponding effects to differ between the first and the second spell. The assumptions on the support of X are similar to above. Fermanian (2003) developed a nonparametric kernel estimator of the Heckman and Honoré (1989) model.

Another approach to deal with non-identification of dependent competing risks models is to determine bounds on the sets of marginal and joint distributions that are compatible with the observable data. Peterson (1976) derived sharp bounds in terms of observable quantities. They are often wide. In case of the marginal distributions of two sub-populations distinguished by a variable X, the bounds associated with the different X may overlap, whether or not X (monotonically) affects (one of) the marginal distributions. With overlap, the causal effects of X cannot even be signed.

Bond and Shaw (2006) combined bounds with regressors. In the case of a single binary regressor, the only substantive assumption made is that there exist increasing functions g and h such that $T_1, T_2|X = 0$ equals $g(T_1), h(T_2)|X = 1$ in distribution. In words, the dependence structure is invariant to the values of the regressors, so the latter affect only the marginal distributions. Specifically, the copula (and therefore Kendall's τ) of the joint distribution is invariant to the value of X. The assumption is satisfied by the aforementioned competing risks models with regressors. Clearly, by itself the assumption is insufficient for point identification. The bounds concern the regressor effects on the marginal distributions. If it is assumed that X affects the marginal distributions of T_i in terms of first-order stochastic dominance, the bounds are sufficient to sign the effect of X on at least one of the marginal distributions (so, in case of MMPH models, also on at least one of the individual marginal distributions conditional on V).

We end this article by noting some connections between competing risks models and other models. First, they are related to switching regression models, or Roy models. For example, if $T_i|X, V$ in the MMPH model have Weibull distributions, then we can write $\log T_i = x_i\alpha_i + \varepsilon_i (i = 1, 2)$ (for example, van den Berg, Lindeboom and Ridder, 1994), where we observe T_i iff $T_i < T_j (j \neq i)$. Second, competing risks models are building blocks of multivariate duration models, notably models where one of the durations is always observed (for example, T_1 captures the moment of a treatment and T_2 is the observed duration outcome of interest).

We have considered only continuous-time duration variables T_i that have different realizations with probability 1. Recently, semi-parametric and nonparametric results have been derived for discrete-time or interval-censored competing risks models and models where different risks can be realized simultaneously (see for example Bedford and Meilijson, 1997; van den Berg, van Lomwel and van Ours, 2003; Honoré and Lleras-Muney, 2006). The biostatistical literature contains many studies in which specific assumptions are made on the dependence structure of the two durations T_i, enabling inference on the marginal distributions from data on Y, Z (see for example Moeschberger and Klein, 1995, for a survey).

GERARD J. VAN DEN BERG

See also **partial identification in econometrics; proportional hazard model; selection bias and self-selection.**

Bibliography

Abbring, J. and van den Berg, G. 2003. The identifiability of the mixed proportional hazards competing risks model. *Journal of the Royal Statistical Society, Series B* 65, 701–10.

Bedford, T. and Meilijson, I. 1997. A characterization of marginal distributions of (possibly dependent) lifetime variables which right censor each other. *Annals of Statistics* 25, 1622–45.

Bond, S. and Shaw, J. 2006. Bounds on the covariate-time transformation for competing-risks survival analysis. *Life time Data Analysis* 12, 285–303.

Cox, D. 1959. The analysis of exponentially distributed life-times with two types of failure. *Journal of the Royal Statistical Society, Series B* 21, 411–21.

Fermanian, J. 2003. Nonparametric estimation of competing risks models with covariates. *Journal of Multivariate Analysis* 85, 156–91.

Heckman, J. and Honoré, B. 1989. The identifiability of the competing risks model. *Biometrika* 76, 325–30.

Honoré, B. and Lleras-Muney, A. 2006. Bounds in competing risks models and the war on cancer. *Econometrica* 74, 1675–98.

Moeschberger, M. and Klein, J. 1995. Statistical methods for dependent competing risks. *Lifetime Data Analysis* 1, 195–204.

Peterson, A. 1976. Bounds for a joint distribution function with fixed sub-distribution functions: application to competing risks. *Proceedings of the National Academy of Sciences* 73, 11–13.

van den Berg, G. 1990. Search behaviour, transitions to nonparticipation and the duration of unemployment. *Economic Journal* 100, 842–65.

van den Berg, G. 2001. Duration models: specification, identification, and multiple durations. In *Handbook of Econometrics*, vol. 5, ed. J. Heckman and E. Leamer. Amsterdam: North-Holland.

van den Berg, G., Lindeboom, M. and Ridder, G. 1994. Attrition in longitudinal panel data, and the empirical analysis of dynamic labour market behaviour. *Journal of Applied Econometrics* 9, 421–35.

van den Berg, G., van Lomwel, A. and van Ours, J. 2003. Nonparametric estimation of a dependent competing risks model for unemployment durations. Discussion Paper No. 898. Bonn: IZA.

computational methods in econometrics

1. Introduction

In evaluating the importance and usefulness of particular econometric methods, it is customary to focus on the set of *statistical* properties that a method possesses – for example, unbiasedness, consistency, efficiency, asymptotic normality, and so on. It is crucial to stress, however, that meaningful comparisons cannot be completed without paying attention also to a method's *computational* properties. Indeed the practical value of an econometric method can be assessed only by examining the inevitable interplay between the two classes of properties, since a method with excellent statistical properties may be computationally infeasible and vice versa. Computational methods in econometrics are evolving over time to reflect the current technological boundaries as defined by available computer hardware and software capabilities at a particular period, and hence are inextricably linked with determining what the state of the art is in econometric methodology.

To give a brief illustration, roughly from the late 1950s until the early 1960s we had the 'Stone Age' of econometrics, when the most sophisticated computational instrument was the slide rule, which used two rulers on a logarithmic scale, one sliding into the other, to execute approximate multiplication and division. In this Stone Age, suitably named in honour of Sir Richard Stone, winner of the 1984 Nobel Prize in Economics, the brightest Ph.D. students at the University of Cambridge were toiling for days and days in back rooms using slide rules to calculate ordinary linear regressions, a task which nowadays can be achieved in a split second on modern personal computers.

The classic linear regression problem serves to illustrate the crucial interaction between statistical and computational considerations in comparing competing econometric methods. Given data of size S, with observations on a dependent variable denoted by $S \times 1$ vector y and corresponding observations on k explanatory factors denoted by $S \times k$ matrix X ($k < X$), the linear plane fitting exercise is defined by Gauss's minimum quadratic distance problem:

$$\hat{\beta} = \arg \min_b (y - Xb)'(y - Xb) \equiv \arg \min_b \sum_{s=1}^{S} (y_s - x_s'b)^2 \tag{1}$$

where x_s' is the sth row of matrix X and b is a $k \times 1$ vector of real numbers defining the regression plane Xb. Under the assumption that X has full column rank k, the solution to this *ordinary least squares* minimization problem is the linear-in-y expression $\hat{\beta} = (X'X)^{-1}X'y$, which only requires the matrix operations of multiplication and inversion.

Suppose, however, that Gauss had chosen instead as his measure of distance the sum of absolute value of the deviations, and defined instead:

$$\tilde{\beta} = \arg\min_{b} \sum_{s=1}^{S} |y_s - x'_s b|. \tag{2}$$

The vector $\tilde{\beta}$ that solves the second minimization is known as the *least absolute deviations* (LAD) estimator and has no closed-form matrix expression. In fact, calculation of $\tilde{\beta}$ requires highly nonlinear operations for which computationally efficient algorithms were developed only in the 1970s. To give a concrete example, consider the *intercept-only* linear regression model where X is the $S \times 1$ vector of ones. Then the single $\hat{\beta}$ coefficient that solves (1) is the sample mean of y, while $\tilde{\beta}$ that solves (2) is the sample *median* of y. The latter is orders of magnitude more difficult to compute than the former since it involves sorting y and finding the value in the middle, while the former simply adds all elements of y and divides by the sample size. Clearly, it could be quite misleading if $\hat{\beta}$ and $\tilde{\beta}$ where compared solely in terms of statistical properties without any consideration of their substantially different computational requirements.

A second example in a similar vein is the following parametric estimation problem. Suppose a sample of size S is observed on a single variable y. It is believed that each observation y_s is drawn independently from the same uniform distribution on the interval $[\theta, c]$ where the lower value of the support is the single unknown parameter that needs to be estimated, while c is known. Two parametric estimation methods with particularly attractive statistical properties are the generalized method of moments (GMM) and the method of maximum likelihood (MLE). Indeed, for relatively large sample sizes these two methods are comparably attractive in terms of statistical properties, while they differ *drastically* in terms of computational requirements: the GMM solution is $\hat{\theta}_{gmm} = \frac{2}{S}\sum_{s=1}^{S} y_s - c$, thus requiring only the simple calculation of the sample mean $\bar{y}$, while the MLE involves the highly nonlinear operation of finding the minimum of the data vector y, $\hat{\theta}_{mle} = min(y_1, \ldots, y_S)$.

In the following section we discuss in turn the leading classes of methods that are of particular importance in modern econometrics, while Section 3 introduces the concept of parallel processing and describes its current value and future promise in aiding dramatically econometric computation.

2. Computational methods important for econometrics

The advancement of computational methods for econometrics relies on understanding the interplay between the disciplines of econometric theory, computer science, numerical analysis, and applied mathematics. In the five subsections below we discuss the leading classes of computational methods that have proven of great value to modern econometrics.

2.1 Matrix computation and specialized languages

To start with the fundamental econometric framework of linear regression, the *sine qua non* of econometric computation is the ability to program and perform efficiently matrix operations. To this end, specialized matrix computer languages have been developed which include Gauss and Matlab. Fundamental estimators of the linear regression coefficient vector β, like the OLS $(X'X)^{-1}X'y$ and its generalized least squares (GLS) variant $(X'\Omega^{-1}X)^{-1}X'\Omega^{-1}y$, are leading examples of the usefulness of such matrix languages, where the $S \times S$ matrix Ω is a positive definite, symmetric variance-covariance matrix of the disturbance vector $\varepsilon \equiv y - X\beta$. Matrix operations are useful even for nonlinear econometric methods discussed below, since a generally useful approach is to apply linearization approximations through the use of differentiation and Taylor's expansions.

In implementing econometric methods that involve matrix operations, special attention needs to be paid to the dimensionality of the various matrices, as well as to any special properties a matrix may posses, which can affect very substantially the feasibility and performance of the computational method to be adopted. Looking at the OLS and GLS formulae, we see three different matrices that require inversion: $X'X$, Ω, and $X'\Omega^{-1}X$. The first and the third are of dimension $k \times k$, while the second is $S \times S$. Since the number of regressors k is typically considerably smaller than the sample size S, the inversion of these matrices can involve vastly different burden in terms of total number of computer operations required as well as memory locations necessary for holding the information during those calculations. (For example, in panel data settings where multiple observations are observed in different time-periods for a cross-section of economic agents, it is not uncommon to have total sample sizes of 300,000 or more.) To this end, econometric analysts have focused on importing from numerical analysis matrix algorithms that are particularly efficient in handling sparse as opposed to dense matrices. By their very nature, sparse matrices exhibit a very high degree of compressibility and concomitantly lower memory requirements. See Drud (1977) for the use of sparse matrix techniques in econometrics. A matrix is called sparse if it is primarily populated by zeros, for example, the variance-covariance matrix of a disturbance vector following the moving-average-of-order-1 model:

$$\Omega_{ma1} = \sigma^2 \begin{pmatrix} 1 & \frac{\lambda}{1+\lambda^2} & 0 & \cdots & 0 \\ \frac{\lambda}{1+\lambda^2} & 1 & \frac{\lambda}{1+\lambda^2} & \ddots & \vdots \\ 0 & \frac{\lambda}{1+\lambda^2} & \ddots & \ddots & 0 \\ \vdots & \ddots & \ddots & 1 & \frac{\lambda}{1+\lambda^2} \\ 0 & \cdots & 0 & \frac{\lambda}{1+\lambda^2} & 1 \end{pmatrix}.$$

In contrast, a stationary autoregressive disturbance of order 1 has a dense variance-covariance matrix:

$$
\Omega_{ar1} = \sigma^2
\begin{pmatrix}
1 & \gamma & \gamma^2 & \cdots & \gamma^{S-1} \\
\gamma & 1 & \gamma & \ddots & \vdots \\
\gamma^2 & \gamma & \ddots & \ddots & \gamma^2 \\
\vdots & \ddots & \ddots & 1 & \gamma \\
\gamma^{S-1} & \cdots & \gamma^2 & \gamma & 1
\end{pmatrix}.
$$

Other matrix algebra methods especially important in econometrics are the Cholesky factorization (see Golub, 1969) of a positive definite matrix A into the product $A = R'R$ where R is an upper-triangular matrix, and the singular value decomposition that allows the calculation of pseudo-inverse of any matrix B which may be non-square, and if square, not positive definite (see Belsley, 1974).

It is important to note that on occasion a brilliant theoretical development can simplify enormously the computational burden of econometric methods that, though possessing attractive statistical properties, were thought to be infeasible with existing computation technology in the absence of the theoretical development. A case in point is the GLS/MLE estimator for the one-factor random effects model proposed by Balestra and Nerlove (1966), which is of great importance in the analysis of linear panel data models. The standard formulation gives rise to the GLS formula requiring the inversion of an equi-correlated variance covariance matrix Ω of dimension $S \times S$, where S is of the order of the product of the number of available observations in the cross-section dimension times the number available in the time dimension. For modern panel data-sets, this can exceed 300,000, thus making the calculation of Ω^{-1} infeasible even on today's super-computers, let alone with the slide rules available in 1966. Fuller and Battese (1973), however, showed that the equi-correlated nature of the one-factor random effects model made calculation of the GLS estimator equivalent to an OLS problem, where the dependent variable $\tilde{y}$ and the regressors $\tilde{X}$ are simple linear combinations of the original data $y_{it}, x_{1it}, \ldots, x_{kit}$ and its time averages $y_{i.}, x_{1i.}, \ldots, x_{ki.}$ defined by $\bar{y}_{i.} \equiv \frac{1}{T}\sum_{t=1}^{T} y_{it}$ and $\tilde{y}_{it} \equiv y_{it} - \lambda \bar{y}_{i.}$, and analogously for the regressor variables. This realization allowed the calculation of the GLS estimator without the need for inverting the usually problematically large Ω matrix.

Another important case where a theoretical development in methodology led to a dramatic lowering of the computational burden and hence allowed the calculation of models that would otherwise have had to wait perhaps for decades for sufficient advancements in computer technology is the simulation-based inference for Limited Dependent Variable models, associated with the name of Daniel McFadden (1989). See Section 2.5 below, MCFADDEN, DANIEL and SIMULATION-BASED ESTIMATION.

2.2 Optimization

Many econometric estimators with attractive statistical properties require the optimization of a (generally) nonlinear function of the form:

$$q \equiv \arg \max_{\theta} F(\theta; data) \tag{3}$$

over a vector of unknown parameters θ of dimension p, typically considerably larger than 1. Examples are: the method of maximum likelihood, minimum-distance (OLS, LAD, GMM), and other extremum estimators. (The need to optimize functions numerically is also important for certain problems in computational economics, for example, the problem of optimal control.) Algorithms for optimizing functions of many variables are a key component in the collection of tools for econometric computation. The suitability of a certain algorithm to a specific optimization econometric problem depends on the following classification:

1. *Algorithms that require the calculation of first and possibly second derivatives* Versus *algorithms that do not.* Clearly, if the function to be optimized is not twice continuously differentiable (as is the case with LAD) or even discontinuous (as is the case with the maximum score estimator for the semiparametric analysis of the binary response model – see Manski, 1975), algorithms that require differentiability will not be suitable. The leading example of an algorithm not relying on derivatives is the nonlinear simplex method of Nelder and Meade (1965).
2. *Local* Versus *global algorithms.* Optimization algorithms of the first type (for example, Gauss-Newton, Newton-Raphson, and Berndt et al. (1974)) search for an optimum in the vicinity of the starting values fed into the algorithm. This strategy may not necessarily lead to a global optimum over the full set of parameter space. This is of particular importance if the function to be optimized has multiple local optima, where typically the estimator with the desirable statistical properties corresponds to locating the overall optimum of the function. In such cases, global optimization algorithms (for example, simulated annealing and genetic optimization algorithm) should be employed instead.

Special methods are necessary for constrained optimization, where a function must be maximized or minimized subject to a set of equality or inequality constraints. These problems, in general considerably more demanding than unconstrained optimization, can be handled through three main alternative approaches: interior, exterior and re-parameterization methods.

Comprehensive reviews of optimization methods in econometrics can be found in Goldfeld and Quandt (1972), Quandt (1983), and Dennis and Schnabel (1984). These studies also discuss the related issue of the numerical approximation of derivatives and illustrate the fundamental link in terms of computation between optimization and the problem of solving linear and nonlinear equations. For similar methods used in economics, see NUMERICAL OPTIMIZATION METHODS IN ECONOMICS and NONLINEAR PROGRAMMING.

2.3 Sorting

Of special importance for computing the class of estimators known as robust or semiparametric methods is the ability to sort data rapidly and computationally efficiently. Such a need arises in the calculation of order statistics, for example, the sample median and sample minimum required by the first two estimation examples given above. The leading sorting algorithms, bubble-, heap- and quick-sort, have fundamentally different properties in terms of computation speed and memory requirements, in general depending on how close to being sorted the original data series happens to be. For a practical review of the leading sorting algorithms, see Press et al. (2001, ch. 8).

2.4 Numerical approximation and integration

Numerical approximation is necessary for any mathematical function that does not have a closed form solution, for example, exponential, natural logarithm and error functions. See Abramowitz and Stegun (1964) for an exhaustive study of mathematical functions and their efficient approximation. Judd (1996) focuses on numerical approximation methods particularly useful in economics and econometrics.

Numerical integration, also known as numerical quadrature, is a related approximation problem that is crucial to modern econometrics. There are two key fields of econometrics where integrals without a closed form must be evaluated numerically. The first is Bayesian inference where moments of posterior densities need to be evaluated, which take the form of high-dimensional integrals. See, inter alia, Zellner, Bauwens and VanDijk (1988). The second main class is classical inference in limited dependent variable (LDV) models; for example, Hajivassiliou and Ruud (1994). See Geweke (1996) for an exhaustive review of numerical integration methods in computational economics and econometrics, and Davis and Rabinowitz (1984) for earlier results.

It is important to highlight a crucial difference between the numerical integration problems in Bayesian inference and those in classical inference for LDV models, which makes various integration-by-simulation algorithms be useful to one field and not the other: in the Bayesian case, typically a single or a few high-dimensional integrals have to be evaluated accurately. In contrast, in the classical LDV inference case, quite frequently hundreds of thousands of such integrals need to be approximated.

2.5 Computer simulation

The need for efficient generation of pseudo-random numbers with good statistical properties on a computer appears very routinely in econometrics. Leading examples include:

- Statistical methods based on resampling, primarily the 'jackknife' and the 'bootstrap', as introduced by Efron (1982). These methods have proven of special value in improving the small sample properties of certain econometric estimators and test procedures, for example in reducing estimation bias. They are also used to approximate the small sample variance of estimators for which no closed form expressions can be derived.

- Evaluation of econometric estimators through Monte Carlo experiments, where hypothetical data-sets with certain characteristics are simulated repeatedly and the econometric estimators under study are calculated for each set. This allows the calculation of empirical (simulated) properties of the estimators, either to compare to theoretical mathematical calculations or because the latter are intractable.

- Calculation of frequency probabilities of possible outcomes in large-scale decision trees, for which the outcome probabilities are impossible to characterize theoretically.

- Sensitivity analyses and what-if studies, where an econometric model is 'run' on a computer under different scenarios of policy measures.

- Simulation-based Bayesian and classical inference, where integrals are approximated through computer simulation (known as Monte Carlo integration). Particularly important methods in this context are the following: frequency simulation; importance sampling; and Markov chain Monte Carlo methods (the leading exponents being Gibbs resampling and the Metropolis/Hastings algorithm). A related class of methods, known as variance-reduction simulation techniques, includes control variates and antithetics. See Geweke (1988) and Hajivassiliou, McFadden and Ruud (1996) for reviews. See also SIMULATION-BASED ESTIMATION.

3. Parallel computation

Parallel processing, where a computation task is broken up and distributed across different computers, is a technique that can afford huge savings in terms of total time required for solving particularly difficult econometric problems. For example, the simulation-based estimators mentioned in the previous section exhibit the potential of significant computational benefits by calculating them on computers with massively parallel architectures, because the necessary calculations can be organized in essentially an independent pattern. An example of such a computer is the Connection Machine CM-5 at the National Center for Supercomputing Applications in Illinois with 1,024 identical processors in a multiple-instruction/multiple-data (MIMDI) configuration. The benefits of such a parallel architecture on the problem of solving an econometric optimization classical estimator not involving simulation can also be substantial, since such estimators involve the evaluation of contributions to the criterion (for example, likelihood) function in the case of independently and identically distributed (i.i.d.) observations. Since typical applications in modern applied econometrics using cross-sectional and longitudinal data sets involve several thousands of i.i.d. observations, the potential benefits of parallel calculations of such estimators should be obvious. The benefits of a massively parallel computer architecture become even more pronounced in the case of simulation-based estimators. See Nagurney (1996) for a discussion of parallel computation in econometrics.

An alternative approach for parallel computation that does not involve a single computer with many processors has been developed recently and offers considerable promise for computational econometrics. Through the use of specialized computer languages, many separate computers are harnessed together over an organization's intranet or even over the internet, and an econometric computation task is distributed across them. The benefits of this approach depend critically on the relative burden of the overhead of communicating across the individual computers when organizing the splitting of the tasks and then collecting and processing the separate partial results. Such distributed parallel computation has the exciting potential of affording formidable super-computing powers to econometric researchers with only modest computer hardware.

VASSILIS A. HAJIVASSILIOU

See also **longitudinal data analysis; simulation-based estimation.**

Bibliography

Abramowitz, M. and Stegun, I. 1964. *Handbook of Mathematical Functions.* Washington, DC: National Bureau of Standards.

Balestra, P. and Nerlove, M. 1966. Pooling cross-section and time-series data in the estimation of a dynamic model. *Econometrica* 34, 585–612.

Belsley, D. 1974. Estimation of system of simultaneous equations and computational specifications of GREMLIN. *Annals of Economic and Social Measurement* 3, 551–614.

Berndt, E.K., Hall, B.H., Hall, R.E. and Hausman, J.A. 1974. Estimation and inference in nonlinear structural models. *Annals of Economic and Social Measurement* 3, 653–66.

Davis, P.J. and Rabinovitz, P. 1984. *Methods of Numerical Integration.* New York: Academic Press.

Dennis, J.E. and Schnabel, R.B. 1984. *Unconstrained optimization and Nonlinear Equations.* Englewood Cliffs, NJ: Prentice-Hall.

Drud, A. 1977. An optimization code for nonlinear econometric models based on sparse matrix techniques and reduced grades. *Annals of Economic and Social Measurement* 6, 563–80.

Efron, B. 1982. *The Jackknife, the Bootstrap, and Other Resampling Plans.* CBMS-NSF Monographs No. 38. Philadelphia: SIAM.

Fuller, W.A. and Battese, G.E. 1973. Transformations for estimation of linear models with nested-error structure. *Journal of the American Statistical Association* 68, 626–32.

Geweke, J. 1988. Antithetic acceleration of Monte Carlo integration in Bayesian inference. *Journal of Econometrics* 38, 73–90.

Geweke, J. 1996. Monte Carlo simulation and numerical integration. In *Handbook of Computational Economics*, vol. 1, ed. H. Amman, D. Kendrik and J. Rust. Amsterdam: North-Holland.

Golub, G.H. 1969. Matrix decompositions and statistical calculations. In *Statistical Computation*, ed. R.C. Milton and J.A. Milder. New York: Academic Press.

Goldfeld, S. and Quandt, R. 1972. *Nonlinear Methods in Econometrics.* Amsterdam: North-Holland.

Hajivassiliou, V.A. and Ruud, P.A. 1994. Classical estimation methods using simulation. In *Handbook of Econometrics*, vol. 4, ed. R. Engle and D. McFadden. Amsterdam: North-Holland.

Hajivassiliou, V.A., McFadden, D.L. and Ruud, P.A. 1996. Simulation of multivariate normal rectangle probabilities and derivatives: theoretical and computational results. *Journal of Econometrics* 72(1, 2), 85–134.

Judd, K. 1996. Approximation, perturbation, and projection methods in economic analysis. In *Handbook of Computational Economics*, vol. 1, ed. H. Amman, D. Kendrik and J. Rust. Amsterdam: North-Holland.

Manski, C. 1975. Maximum score estimation of the stochastic utility model of choice. *Journal of Econometrics* 3, 205–28.

McFadden, D. 1989. A method of simulated moments for estimation of multinomial discrete response models. *Econometrica* 57, 995–1026.

Nagurney, A. 1996. Parallel computation. In *Handbook of Computational Economics*, vol.1, ed. H. Amman, D. Kendrik and J. Rust. Amsterdam: North-Holland.

Nelder, J.A. and Meade, R. 1965. A simplex method for function minimization. *Computer Journal* 7, 308–13.

Press, W.H., Flannery, B.P., Teukolsky, S.A. and Vetterling, W.T. 2001. *Numerical Recipes in Fortran 77: The Art of Scientific Computing*. Cambridge: Cambridge University Press.

Quandt, R. 1983. Computational problems and methods. In *Handbook of Econometrics*, vol. 1, ed. Z. Griliches and M. Intriligator. Amsterdam: North-Holland.

Zellner, A., Bauwens, L. and VanDijk, H. 1988. Bayesian specification analysis and estimation of simultaneous equation models using Monte Carlo methods. *Journal of Econometrics* 38, 73–90.

control functions

The control function approach is an econometric method used to correct for biases that arise as a consequence of selection and/or endogeneity. It is the leading approach for dealing with selection bias in the correlated random coefficients model (see Heckman and Robb, 1985; 1986; Heckman and Vytlacil, 1998; Wooldridge, 1997; 2003; Heckman and Navarro, 2004), but it can be applied in more general semiparametric settings (see Newey, Powell and Vella, 1999; Altonji and Matzkin, 2005; Chesher, 2003; Imbens and Newey, 2006; Florens et al., 2007).

The basic idea behind the control function methodology is to model the dependence between the variables not observed by the analyst on the observables in a way that allows us to construct a function K such that, conditional on the function, the endogeneity problem (relative to the object of interest) disappears.

In this article I deal exclusively with the problem of identification. That is, I assume access to data on an arbitrarily large population. As a consequence, I do not discuss estimation, standard errors or inference. In the examples, I analyse how to recover parameters in a way that, I hope, shows directly how to perform estimation via sample analogues.

The Set-up

The general set-up I consider is the following two-equation structural model; an outcome equation:

$$Y = g(X, D, \varepsilon), \tag{1}$$

and an equation describing the mechanism assigning values of D to individuals:

$$D = h(X, Z, v), \tag{2}$$

where X and Z are vectors of observed random variables, D is a (possibly vector valued) observed random variable, and ε and v are general disturbance vectors not independent of each other but satisfying some form of independence of X and Z.

The problem of endogeneity arises because D is correlated with ε via the dependence between ε and v. Because eq. (2) represents an assignment mechanism in many economic models, it is generically called the 'selection' or 'choice' equation. This set-up has been applied to problems like earnings and schooling (Willis and Rosen, 1979; Cunha, Heckman and Navarro, 2005), wages and sectoral choice (Heckman and Sedlacek, 1985) and production functions and productivity (Olley and Pakes, 1996), among others.

The goal of the analysis is to recover some functional of $g(X, D, \varepsilon)$ of interest

$$a(X, D) \tag{3}$$

that cannot be recovered in a straightforward way because of the endogeneity/selection problem. As an example, when D is binary interest sometimes centres on the effect of going from $D=0$ to $D=1$ for an individual chosen at random from the population, the so-called average treatment effect: $a(X, D) = E(g(X, 1, \varepsilon) - g(X, 0, \varepsilon))$.

The key behind the control function approach is to notice that (conditional on X, Z) the only source of dependence is given by the relation between ε and v. If v was known, we could condition on it and analyse eq. (1) without having to worry about endogeneity. The main idea behind the control function approach is to recover some function of v via its relationship with the model observables so that we can now condition on it and solve the endogeneity problem.

Definition The control function approach proposes a function K (the control function) that allows us to recover a (X, D) such that K satisfies

A-1. K is a function of X, Z, D.
A-2. ε satisfies some form of independence of D conditional on ρ (X, K), with ρ a knowable function.
A-3. K is identified.

Assumption **A-2** is the key assumption of the approach. It states that, once we condition on K, the dependence between ε and D (that is, the endogeneity) is no longer a problem. To help fix ideas, consider the following example of a simple linear in parameters additively separable version of the model of eqs (1) and (2).

Example 1 *Linear regression with constant effects.* Write the outcome eq. (1) as

$$Y = X\beta + D\alpha + \varepsilon$$

and assume that our object of interest (3) is α. Assume that we can write eq. (2) as

$$D = X\rho + Z\pi + v \tag{4}$$

with v, $\varepsilon \perp\!\!\!\perp X$, Z where $\perp\!\!\!\perp$ denotes statistical independence. Such a model arises, for example, if Y is logearnings and D is years of schooling as in Heckman, Lochner and Todd (2003). If ability is unobservable since high ability is associated with higher earnings but also with higher schooling, then ε and v would be correlated.

If we let $K=v$ be the residual of the regression in (4), then we can recover α from the following regression

$$Y = X\beta + D\alpha + K\psi + \eta,$$

where it follows that $E(\eta|X, K) = 0$. It is easy to show that in this case the control function estimator and the two-stage least squares estimator are equivalent. (To my knowledge, although in a different context – a SUR model – Telser, 1964, was the first to use the residuals from other equations as regressors in the equation of interest.)

The previous case is a simple example of a control function where $K=D-E(D|X, Z)$. In this case, because of the constant effects assumption (that is, α is not random), standard instrumental variables methods and the control function approach coincide. In general, this is not the case.

In the next section I describe in detail the control function methodology for the binary choice case (Roy, 1951). This case is interesting both because it is the workhorse of the policy evaluation literature and because, by virtue of its nonlinearity, it highlights the implications of a nonlinear structure in a relatively simple context. I then briefly describe extensions to more general cases. For simplicity, I focus on the additively separable in unobservables case, but recent research provides generalizations to non-additive functions (see Blundell and Powell, 2003; Imbens and Newey, 2006, among others).

The case of a binary endogenous variable

In this section I describe how the control function approach solves the selection/ endogeneity problem when the endogenous variable is binary. This problem has a long tradition in economics going back (at least) to Roy (1951). In Roy's original version of the model (see ROY MODEL) an individual is deciding whether to become a fisherman ($D=0$) or a hunter ($D=1$).

Associated with each occupation is a payoff $Y_D = g_D(X) + \varepsilon_D$. Since we can only observe individuals in one sector at a time, the *observed* outcome for an individual is given by Y_1 if he becomes a hunter ($D=1$) and by Y_0 if he becomes a fisherman ($D=0$). That is, the observed outcome (Y) can be written as:

$$Y = DY_1 + (1-D)Y_0 = g_0(X) + D(g_1(X) - g_0(X)) + \varepsilon_0 + D(\varepsilon_1 - \varepsilon_0). \qquad (5)$$

The model is closed by assuming that individuals choose the occupation with the highest payoff. That is,

$$D = \mathbf{1}(Y_1 - Y_0 > 0) = \mathbf{1}(g_1(X) - g_0(X) + \varepsilon_1 - \varepsilon_0 > 0), \qquad (6)$$

where $\mathbf{1}(a)$ is an indicator function that takes value 1 if a is true and 0 if it is false. Endogeneity arises because the error term in choice eq. (6) contains the same random variables as the outcome eq. (5). A generalized version of the model replaces the simple income maximization rule in (6) with a more general decision rule

$$D = \mathbf{1}(h(X, Z) - v > 0). \qquad (7)$$

The model described by eqs (5) and (7) is general enough to be used in many different cases. Many questions of interest in economics fit this framework if, instead of thinking of two sectors, fishing and hunting, we think of two generic potential states, the treated state ($D=1$) and the untreated state ($D=0$) with their associated potential outcomes. The decision rule in (7) is general enough to capture not only income maximization but also utility maximization and even a deciding actor different from the agent directly affected by the outcomes (parents deciding for their children, for example). The simple income maximization rule in (6) shows why, *in general if $\varepsilon_1 \neq \varepsilon_0$*, then $\varepsilon_1 - \varepsilon_0$ is likely to be correlated with D.

The correlated random coefficients model is a special case of the model described by (5) and (7) when $\varepsilon_1 - \varepsilon_0$ is not independent of D and $g_j(X) = \alpha_j + X\beta$ for $j = 0, 1$. (For simplicity I assume $\beta_1 = \beta_0 = \beta$. The case where $\beta_1 \neq \beta_0$ follows directly.) To see why simply rewrite (5) as

$$Y = \alpha_0 + X\beta + D(\alpha_1 - \alpha_0 + \varepsilon_1 - \varepsilon_0) + \varepsilon_0 \qquad (8)$$

so that now the coefficient on D is (a) random and (b) correlated with D. In this case we have that the gains from treatment $(\alpha_1 - \alpha_0 + \varepsilon_1 - \varepsilon_0)$ are heterogeneous (that is, they are not constant even after controlling for X) and they are correlated with D. I come back to this special linear in parameters case in example 2.

Though other parameters of interest can be defined, I consider the case in which we are interested in the two particular functionals that receive the most attention in the evaluation literature – the average treatment effect and the average effect of treatment on the treated. I impose that ε_1, ε_0, v are absolutely continuous with finite means, and that ε_1, ε_0, $v \perp\!\!\!\perp X, Z$. (One could weaken the assumption to be ε_1, $\varepsilon_0 \perp\!\!\!\perp X|Z$ and $v \perp\!\!\!\perp X, Z$.)

Under these assumptions the average treatment effect is given by

$$ATE(x) = E(Y_1 - Y_0|X = x) = g_1(x) - g_0(x) = x(\beta_1 - \beta_0)$$

where the last equality follows if eq. (8) applies. $ATE(X)$ is of interest to answer questions like the average effect of a policy that is mandatory, for example. When receipt of treatment is not mandatory or randomly assigned, the average effect of treatment among those individuals who are selected into treatment is commonly the functional of interest (see Heckman, 1997; Heckman and Smith, 1998). This effect is measured by the average effect of treatment on the treated:

$$TT(x) = E(Y_1 - Y_0|X = x, D = 1) = g_1(x) - g_0(x) + E(\varepsilon_1 - \varepsilon_0|X = x, D = 1)$$
$$= \alpha_1 - \alpha_0 + E(\varepsilon_1 - \varepsilon_0|X = x, D = 1),$$

where the last equality follows for the linear in parameters case of eq. (8).

Now, suppose we ignored the endogeneity problem and attempted to recover either of these objects from the data on outcomes at hand. In particular, if we used the (observed) conditional means of the outcome

$$E(Y|X = x, D = 1) - E(Y|X = x, D = 0)$$
$$= g_1(x) - g_0(x) + E(\varepsilon_1|X = x, D = 1) - E(\varepsilon_0|X = x, D = 0)$$

we would not recover either $ATE(X)$ or $TT(x)$. Notice too that, since the endogenous variable D is binary, we cannot directly recover v and use it as a control as we did in the linear case of example 1 above. Instead, we can recover a function of v that satisfies the definition of a control function.

Let $F_v()$ denote the cumulative distribution function of v. To form the control function in this case, first take eq. (7) and write the choice probability

$$P(x, z) \equiv \Pr(D = 1|X = x, Z = z) = \Pr(v < h(x, z)) = F_v(h(x, z)),$$

which under our assumptions implies

$$h(x, z) = F_v^{-1}(P(x, z)).$$

Following the analysis in Matzkin (1992), we can recover both $h(x, z)$ and $F_v()$ nonparametrically up to normalization.

Next, take the conditional (on X, Z) expectation of the outcome for the treated group

$$E(Y|X = x, Z = z, D = 1) = g_1(x) + E(\varepsilon_1|X = x, Z = z, D = 1).$$

We can write the last term as

$$E(\varepsilon_1|X = x, Z = z, D = 1) = E(\varepsilon_1|v < h(x, z)) = E(\varepsilon_1|v < F_v^{-1}(P(x, z))).$$

That is, we can write it as a function of the known $h(x, z)$ or, equivalently, as a function of the probability of selection $P(x, z)$,

$$E(Y|X = x, Z = z, D = 1) = g_1(x) + K_1(P(x, z)),$$

where $K_1(P(X, Z))$ satisfies our definition of a control function. So, provided that we can vary $K_1(P(X, Z))$ independently of $g_1(X)$, we can recover $g_1(X)$ up to a constant. We can identify the constant in a limit set such that $P \to 1$ since $\lim_{P \to 1} K_1(P) = 0$. Provided that we have enough support in the probability of treatment – that is, provided that some people choose treatment with probability arbitrarily close to (1) –we can recover the constant. (See example 2.) Using the same argument we can form

$$E(Y|X = x, Z = z, D = 0) = g_0(x) + K_0(P(x, z))$$

and identify $g_0(X)$ (up to a constant) and the control function $K_0(P(X, Z))$. As before, we can recover the constant in $g_0(X)$ by noting that $\lim_{P \to 0} K_0(P) = 0$.

Intuitively, we need to be able to vary the $K_1(P(X, Z))$ function relative to the $g_1(X)$ function so that we can identify them from the observed variation in Y_1. One possibility is to impose that g_1 and K_1 are measurably separated functions. (That is, provided that, if $g_1(X) = K_1(P(X, Z))$ almost surely then $g_1(X)$ is a constant almost surely; see Florens, Mouchart and Rolin, 1990.) The simplest way to satisfy this restriction is by exclusion. That is, if $K_1(P(X, Z))$ is a nontrivial function of Z conditional on X and Z shows enough variation, we can vary the K_1 function by varying Z while keeping $g_1(X)$ constant. Another related possibility is to assume that g_1 and K_1 live in different function spaces. For example, g_1 a linear function and K_1 the nonlinear mills ratio term that results from assuming that $(\varepsilon_0, \varepsilon_1, v)$ are jointly normal as in the original Heckman (1979) selection correction model.

Once we have recovered $g_0(X), g_1(X), K_0(P(X, Z)), K_1(P(X, Z))$ we can now form our parameters of interest. Given $g_0(X)$ and $g_1(X)$, $ATE(X) = g_1(X) - g_0(X)$

immediately follows. To recover $TT(X)$, first notice that, by the law of iterated expectations

$$E(\varepsilon_0|X = x, Z = z) = E(\varepsilon_0|X = x, Z = z, D = 1)P(x, z)$$
$$+ E(\varepsilon_0|X = x, Z = z, D = 0)(1 - P(x, z)) = 0,$$

where $P(X, Z)$ is known from our analysis above and $E(\varepsilon_0|X = x, Z = z, D = 0) = K_0(P(x, z))$. Rewriting the expression above we get $E(\varepsilon_0|X = x, Z = z, D = 1) = -\frac{K_0(P(x,z))(1-P(x,z))}{P(x,z)}$. With this expectation in hand we can recover $TT(X, Z) = g_1(X) - g_0(X) + K_1(P(X, Z)) + \frac{K_0(P(X,Z))(1-P(X,Z))}{P(X,Z)}$. By integrating against the appropriate distribution, we can recover $TT(X) = \int TT(X, z)dF_{Z|X,D} = 1(z)$.

The following example shows how the control function methodology can be applied to recover average effects of treatment in a linear in parameters model with correlated random coefficients. This model arises when there are unobservable gains that vary over individuals and these gains are correlated with the choice of treatment (that is, when there is essential heterogeneity. See Heckman, Urzua and Vytlacil, 2006; Basu et al., 2006). The Roy model of eqs (5) and (6) in which the unobservable individual gains $(\varepsilon_1 - \varepsilon_0)$ are correlated with the choice of sector is an example of this case.

Example 2 *Correlated random coefficients with binary treatment.* Assume we can write the outcome equations in linear in parameters form,

$$Y_j = \alpha_j + X\beta_j + \varepsilon_j \quad j = 0, 1.$$

Let D be an indicator of whether an individual receives treatment $(D = 1)$ or not $(D = 0)$. We also write a linear in parameters decision rule:

$$D = 1(X\delta + Z\gamma - \nu > 0).$$

From the analysis in Manski (1988) we can recover δ, γ and F_ν (up to scale). With $P(x, z) = \Pr(D = 1|X = x, Z = z)$ in hand, we then form

$$Y_j = \alpha_j + X\beta_j + K_j(P(X, Z)) + \eta_j$$

where $E(\eta_j|X = x, K_j(P(X, Z)) = k_j) = 0$. To emphasize the problem of identification of the constant α_j we can rewrite the outcome as

$$Y_j = \tau_j + X\beta_j + \tilde{K}_j(P(X, Z)) + \eta_j$$

where $K_j(P(X, Z)) = \kappa_j + \tilde{K}_j(P(X, Z))$ and $\tau_j = \alpha_j + \kappa_j$.

The elements of the outcome equations can be recovered by various methods. One could, for example, use Robinson (1988) and use residualized nonparametric regressions to recover β_j, τ_j and $K_j(P(X, Z))$. Alternatively, one could approximate $K(P(X, Z))$ with a polynomial on $P(X, Z)$. In this case we would have

$$Y_j = \tau_j + X\beta_j + \pi_1 P(X, Z) + \pi_2 P(X, Z)^2 + \cdots + \pi_n P(X, Z)^n + \eta_j$$

where $\tilde{K}_j(P(X,Z)) = \sum_{i=1}^{n} \pi_{ji} P(X,Z)^i$. When $j=0$ then $\lim_{P\to 0} K_0(P) = 0$ and it follows that $\tilde{K}_0(P) = K_0(P)$ and $\tau_0 = \alpha_0$. For the treated case $(j=1)$ we have that $\lim_{P\to 1} K_1(P(X,Z)) = 0$. Since $\tilde{K}_1(1) = \sum_{i=1}^{n} \pi_{1i}$ it follows that $\kappa_1 = -\sum_{i=1}^{n} \pi_{1i}$ and $\alpha_1 = \tau_1 - \sum_{i=1}^{n} \pi_{1i}$.

Extensions for a continuous endogenous variable

In this section I briefly review the use of the control function approach for the case in which the endogenous variable D is continuous and we assume that $X, Z \perp\!\!\!\perp \varepsilon, v$. Following Blundell and Powell (2003) I assume that the object of interest is the average structural function

$$a(X,D) = \int g(X,D,\varepsilon) dF_\varepsilon(\varepsilon),$$

which, in the additively separable case $g(X,D,\varepsilon) = \mu(X,D) + \varepsilon$ is simply the regression function $\mu(X,D)$.

If we assume that the choice equation

$$D = h(X,Z,v)$$

is strictly monotonic in v (which would follow automatically if it were additively separable in v), we can recover $h()$ and F_v from the analysis of Matzkin (2003) up to normalization. A convenient normalization is to assume that $v \sim$ Uniform $(0,1)$ in which case we can directly recover v from the quantiles of F_v, but other normalizations are possible. From the independence assumption it follows that $E(\varepsilon|X,D,Z) = E(\varepsilon|v)$, so we can write the outcome equation as

$$Y = \mu(X,D) + E(\varepsilon|v)$$
$$= \mu(X,D) + K(v)$$

which allows us to recover $\mu(X,D)$ directly (up to normalization). In the additively separable case we analyse, we can relax the full independence assumption and instead assume directly that the weaker mean independence assumption $E(\varepsilon|X,D,Z) = E(\varepsilon|v)$ holds.

SALVADOR NAVARRO

See also **identification; Roy model; selection bias and self-selection.**

Bibliography

Altonji, J.G. and Matzkin, R.L. 2005. Cross section and panel data estimators for nonseparable models with endogenous regressors. *Econometrica* 73, 1053–102.

Basu, A., Heckman, J.J., Navarro, S. and Urzua, S. 2006. Use of instrumental variables in the presence of heterogeneity and self-selection: an application in breast cancer patients. Unpublished manuscript, Department of Medicine, University of Chicago.

Blundell, R. and Powell, J. 2003. Endogeneity in nonparametric and semiparametric regression models. In *Advances in Economics and Econometrics: Theory and Applications, Eighth World*

Congress, vol. 2, ed. L.P. Hansen, M. Dewatripont and S.J. Turnovsky. Cambridge: Cambridge University Press.

Chesher, A. 2003. Identification in nonseparable models. *Econometrica* 71, 1405–41.

Cunha, F., Heckman, J.J. and Navarro, S. 2005. Separating uncertainty from heterogeneity in life cycle earnings. *Oxford Economic Papers* 57, 191–261.

Florens, J.-P., Heckman, J.J., Meghir, C. and Vytlacil, E.J. 2007. Identification of treatment effects using control functions in models with continuous, endogenous treatment and heterogeneous effects. Unpublished manuscript, Columbia University.

Florens, J.-P., Mouchart, M. and Rolin, J.M. 1990. *Elements of Bayesian Statistics*. New York: M. Dekker.

Heckman, J.J. 1979. Sample selection bias as a specification error. *Econometrica* 47, 153–62.

Heckman, J.J. 1997. Instrumental variables: a study of implicit behavioral assumptions used in making program evaluations. *Journal of Human Resources* 32, 441–62. Addendum published in 33(1) (1998).

Heckman, J.J., Lochner, L.J. and Todd, P.E. 2003. Fifty years of Mincer earnings regressions. Technical Report No. 9732. Cambridge, MA: NBER.

Heckman, J.J. and Navarro, S. 2004. Using matching, instrumental variables, and control functions to estimate economic choice models. *Review of Economics and Statistics* 86, 30–57.

Heckman, J.J. and Robb, R. 1985. Alternative methods for evaluating the impact of interventions: an overview. *Journal of Econometrics* 30, 239–67.

Heckman, J.J. and Robb, R. 1986. Alternative methods for solving the problem of selection bias in evaluating the impact of treatments on outcomes. In *Drawing Inferences from Self-Selected Samples*, ed. H. Wainer. New York: Springer. Repr. Mahwah, NJ: Lawrence Erlbaum Associates, 2000.

Heckman, J.J. and Sedlacek, G.L. 1985. Heterogeneity, aggregation, and market wage functions: an empirical model of self-selection in the labor market. *Journal of Political Economy* 93, 1077–125.

Heckman, J.J. and Smith, J.A. 1998. Evaluating the welfare state. In *Econometrics and Economic Theory in the Twentieth Century: The Ragnar Frisch Centennial Symposium*, ed. S. Strom. New York: Cambridge University Press.

Heckman, J.J., Urzua, S. and Vytlacil, E.J. 2006. Understanding instrumental variables in models with essential heterogeneity. *Review of Economics and Statistics* 88, 389–432.

Heckman, J.J. and Vytlacil, E.J. 1998. Instrumental variables methods for the correlated random coefficient model: estimating the average rate of return to schooling when the return is correlated with schooling. *Journal of Human Resources* 33, 974–87.

Imbens, G.W. and Newey, W.K. 2006. Identification and estimation of triangular simultaneous equations models without additivity. Unpublished manuscript, Department of Economics, MIT.

Manski, C.F. 1988. Identification of binary response models. *Journal of the American Statistical Association* 83, 729–38.

Matzkin, R.L. 1992. Nonparametric and distribution-free estimation of the binary threshold crossing and the binary choice models. *Econometrica* 60, 239–70.

Matzkin, R.L. 2003. Nonparametric estimation of nonadditive random functions. *Econometrica* 71, 1393–75.

Newey, W.K., Powell, J.L. and Vella, F. 1999. Nonparametric estimation of triangular simultaneous equations models. *Econometrica* 67, 565–603.

Olley, G.S. and Pakes, A. 1996. The dynamics of productivity in the telecommunications equipment industry. *Econometrica* 64, 1263–97.

Robinson, P.M. 1988. Root-n-consistent semiparametric regression. *Econometrica* 56, 931–54.

Roy, A.D. 1951. Some thoughts on the distribution of earnings. *Oxford Economic Papers* 3, 135–46.

Telser, L.G. 1964. Iterative estimation of a set of linear regression equations. *Journal of the American Statistical Association* 59, 845–62.

Willis, R.J. and Rosen, S. 1979. Education and self-selection. *Journal of Political Economy* 87(5, Par 2), S7–S36.

Wooldridge, J.M. 1997. On two stage least squares estimation of the average treatment effect in a random coefficient model. *Economics Letters* 56, 129–33.

Wooldridge, J.M. 2003. Further results on instrumental variables estimation of average treatment effects in the correlated random coefficient model. *Economics Letters* 79, 185–91.

decision theory in econometrics

The decision-theoretic approach to statistics and econometrics explicitly specifies a set of models under consideration, a set of actions available to the analyst, and a loss function (or, equivalently, a utility function) that quantifies the value to the decision-maker of applying a particular action when a particular model holds. Decision rules, or procedures, map data into actions, and can be evaluated on the basis of their expected loss.

Abraham Wald, in a series of papers beginning with Wald (1939) and culminating in the monograph (Wald, 1950), developed statistical decision theory as an extension of the Neyman–Pearson theory of testing. It has since played a major role in statistical theory for point estimation, hypothesis testing, and forecasting, especially in the construction of 'optimal' procedures. Some textbooks such as Ferguson (1967) and Berger (1985) emphasize statistical decision theory as a foundation for statistics. But the decision theory framework is sufficiently flexible that it can be used for many empirical applications that do not fit neatly into the usual statistical set-ups. Some examples are discussed below.

Like the Neyman–Pearson theory, Wald's approach emphasizes evaluating the performance of a decision rule under various possible parameter values. There does not always exist a single rule that dominates all others uniformly over the parameter space, just as there does not always exist a uniformly most powerful test in the special case of hypothesis testing. Wald, who also made contributions to game theory, proposed to evaluate a procedure by its minmax risk – the worst-case expected loss over the parameter space. Savage (1951) discusses the minmax principle and suggests an alternative, the minmax-regret principle. Alternatively, one can place a probability measure on the parameter space, and evaluate rules by their weighted average (Bayes) risk.

Basic framework

In Wald's basic framework, we start with a set of actions $\mathscr{A}$, and a parameter space Θ, which characterizes the set of models under consideration. A loss function $L(\theta, a)$ gives the loss or disutility suffered from taking action $a \in \mathscr{A}$ when the parameter is $\theta \in \Theta$. The decision maker observes some random variable Z, distributed according to a probability measure P_θ when θ is the 'true' parameter. Here, the parameter space Θ could be finite-dimensional (corresponding to a parametric family of distributions) or infinite-dimensional (corresponding to semiparametric and nonparametric models). The observed random variable Z could be a vector, as for example in the situation of observing a random sample of size n from some distribution. Often, the set of possible probability measures $\{P_\theta : \theta \in \Theta\}$ is called a *statistical experiment*.

A decision rule or procedure $d(z)$ maps observations on Z into actions. In some cases, it is useful to allow for randomization over the actions. A randomized decision rule is a mapping from observations into probability measures over the action space. A simpler, usually equivalent formulation is to consider rules $\delta(z, u)$ which are allowed to depend on the observed value z and the value u of a random variable U, distributed standard uniform independently of Z. The *risk*, or expected loss, of a decision rule δ under θ is defined as

$$R(\theta, \delta) = E_\theta[L(\theta, \delta(Z, U))] = \int_0^1 \int L(\theta, \delta(z, u)) dP_\theta(z) du.$$

A rule δ is *admissible* if there exists no other rule δ' with

$$R(\theta, \delta') \le R(\theta, \delta), \quad \forall \theta \in \Theta,$$

and

$$R(\theta, \delta') < (\theta, \delta) \quad \text{for some } \theta.$$

Ordering decision rules

In general, there are many admissible decision rules, which may do well in different parts of the parameter space. Thus, while the admissibility criterion eliminates obviously inferior rules, it may not provide concrete guidance on how to 'solve' the decision problem. Additional criteria can help by providing a sharper partial ordering of decision rules.

One way to rank decision rules is to average their risk over the parameter space. Let Π be a probability measure on Θ. The *Bayes risk* of a decision rule δ is

$$r(\Pi, \delta) = \int R(\theta, \delta) d\Pi(\theta).$$

A rule is a *Bayes rule* if it minimizes this weighted average risk. Let the probabilities P_θ have densities p_θ with respect to some dominating measure, and let the prior Π have density π. Typically, a Bayes rule can be implemented by choosing, for any given observed data z, the action that minimizes the posterior expected loss

$$\int L(\theta, a) d\Pi(\theta|z),$$

where $\Pi(\theta|z)$ is the posterior distribution with density

$$\pi(\theta|z) = \frac{\pi(\theta) p_\theta(z)}{\int p_\theta(z) d\Pi(\theta)}.$$

There is a close connection between the admissible rules and the Bayes rules. If the parameter set is finite, a Bayes rule for a prior that places positive probability on every element of Θ is admissible. Furthermore, 'complete class theorems' give results in the opposite direction. In particular, if the parameter set is finite, any admissible rule is Bayes for some prior distribution. If Θ is not finite, some care needs to be taken to make a precise statement of the relationship between the admissible and Bayes rules; see for example Ferguson (1967).

An alternative ordering is based on the worst-case risk $\sup_{\theta\in\Theta} R(\theta, \delta)$. A *minmax* rule δ_m satisfies

$$\sup_{\theta\in\Theta} R(\theta, \delta_m) = \inf_{\delta} \sup_{\theta\in\Theta} R(\theta, \delta).$$

In general, a minmax rule need not be admissible.

A closely related criterion is the *minmax regret* criterion. The regret loss of a rule is the difference between its loss and the loss of the best possible action under θ:

$$L_r(\theta, a) = L(\theta, a) - \inf_{a\in\mathscr{A}} L(\theta, a).$$

We can then define regret risk as $R_r(\theta, \delta) = E_\theta(L_r(\theta, \delta(Z, U)))$. The *minmax regret rule* minimizes the worst-case regret risk. This rule was suggested by Savage (1951) as an alternative to the minmax criterion. He argued that in cases where the minmax criterion is unduly conservative, minmax regret rules can be reasonable.

Savage (1954) showed that a decision-maker who satisfied certain axioms of coherent behaviour would act as if she placed a prior on the parameter space and minimized posterior expected loss. Gilboa and Schmeidler (1989) showed that, under a different set of axioms, a decision-maker would follow the minmax principle.

Calculation of Bayes and minmax rules can be difficult in many applications. Bayesian posterior distributions can be calculated directly when the prior and likelihood have a conjugate form. One way to solve for a minmax rule is to guess the form of a 'least favourable' prior and solve for the associated Bayes rule. If the risk function of the Bayes rule is everywhere less than the Bayes risk, then the rule is minmax. A related method is to construct a least favourable sequence of prior distributions, and calculate the limit of the Bayes risks. If a particular rule has worst-case risk lower than the limit of Bayes risks, then the rule is minmax. Another useful technique for obtaining minmax rules makes use of invariance properties of the decision problem. If the model and loss are invariant with respect to a group of transformations, and that group satisfies a condition called amenability, then the best equivariant procedure is minmax by the Hunt–Stein theorem. These techniques are discussed in Ferguson (1967) and Berger (1985).

If Bayes and minmax rules cannot be obtained analytically, computational methods can sometimes be useful. Recently developed simulation methods such as Markov chain Monte Carlo have greatly expanded the range of settings where Bayes rules can be numerically computed. Chamberlain (2000) develops algorithms for computing minmax rules, and applies them to an estimation problem for a dynamic panel data model.

Asymptotic statistical decision theory

Despite advances in computational methods, many statistical decision problems remain intractable. In such cases, large-sample approximations may be used to show that certain rules are approximately optimal. Le Cam (1972; 1986) proposed to approximate complex statistical decision problems by simpler ones, in which optimal decision rules can be calculated relatively easily. One then finds sequences of rules in the original problem that approach the optimal rule in the limiting version of the problem.

As an example, suppose we observe n i.i.d. draws from a distribution P_θ, where $\theta \in \Theta \subset \mathbb{R}^k$ and the probability measures $\{P_\theta\}$ satisfy conventional regularity conditions with non-singular Fisher information I_θ. We can think of this as defining a sequence of experiments, where the nth experiment consists of observing an n-dimensional random vector distributed according to P_θ^n, the n-fold product of P_θ. Since, in the limit, θ can be determined exactly, we fix a centring value θ_0, and reparametrize the model in terms of local alternatives $\theta_0 + h/\sqrt{n}$, for $h \in \mathbb{R}^k$. This sequence of experiments has as its 'limit experiment' the experiment consisting of observing a single draw $Z \sim N(h, I_{\theta_0}^{-1})$, and we say that the original sequence of experiments satisfies local asymptotic normality (LAN). More precisely, according to an asymptotic representation theorem (see van der Vaart, 1991), for any sequence of procedures δ_n in the original experiments that converge in distribution under every local parameter h, these limit distributions are matched by the distributions associated with some randomized procedure $\delta(Z)$ in the limit experiment. Thus, the limit experiment characterizes the set of attainable limit distributions of procedures in the original sequence of experiments. Solving the decision problem in the limit experiment leads to bounds on the best possible asymptotic behaviour of procedures in the original problem, and often suggests the form of asymptotically optimal procedures.

Le Cam's theory underlies the classic result that in regular parametric models, Bayes and maximum likelihood point estimators of θ are 'asymptotically efficient'. In the LAN limit experiment $Z \sim N(h, I_{\theta_0}^{-1})$, a natural estimator for the parameter h is $\delta(Z) = Z$. This can be shown to be minmax and best equivariant for 'bowl-shaped' loss functions. Both the Bayes and MLE estimators in the original problem are matched asymptotically by this optimal estimator, so they are locally asymptotically minmax and best equivariant. The ideas have been extended to models with an infinite-dimensional parameter space (see Bickel et al. (1993) and van der Vaart, 1991, among others), to obtain semiparametric efficiency bounds for finite-dimensional sub-parameters. More recently, a body of work has developed limit experiment theory for nonparametric problems such as nonparametric regression and nonparametric density estimation (see Brown and Low, 1996, and Nussbaum, 1996, among others). These results show that nonparametric regression and density estimation are asymptotically equivalent to a white-noise model with drift, for which a number of optimality results are available.

Applications in economics

Portfolio choice
A number of authors have used statistical decision theory to study portfolio allocation when the distribution of returns is uncertain. Some examples include Klein and Bawa (1976), Kandel and Stambaugh (1996), and Barberis (2000), who develop Bayes rules for portfolio choice problems.

Treatment choice
Another econometric application of statistical decision theory is to treatment assignment problems, in which a social planner wishes to assign individuals to different treatments (for example, different job training programmes) to maximize some measure of social welfare. Manski (2004) develops minmax-regret results for the treatment assignment problem, Dehejia (2005) develops Bayesian rules, and Hirano and Porter (2005) obtain asymptotic minmax regret-risk bounds and show that certain simple rules are optimal according to this criterion.

Model uncertainty and macroeconomic policy
Brainard (1967) studied a macroeconomic policy problem, in which a parameter describing the effect of a policy instrument on a macroeconomic outcome is not known with certainty but is given a distribution. The policymaker has a utility function over outcomes and chooses the policy that makes expected utility. More recently, a number of authors have continued this line of work, extending the analysis to more general forms of model uncertainty and developing both Bayesian and minmax solutions. Some examples include Hansen and Sargent (2001), Rudebusch (2001), Onatski and Stock (2002), Giannoni (2002), and Brock, Durlauf and West (2003).

Instrumental variables models
Decision-theoretic ideas underlie recent work on the linear instrumental variables model in econometrics. Chamberlain (2005) develops minmax optimal point estimators in the IV model using invariance arguments. Andrews, Moreira and Stock (2004) have developed tests in the IV model that are optimal under an invariance restriction, and Chioda and Jansson (2004) have developed optimal conditional tests.

Time series models
Asymptotic statistical decision theory has been useful in studying certain time series models which do not satisfy standard regularity conditions. Jeganathan (1995) shows that a number of models for econometric time series have limit experiments that are not of the standard LAN form, but are locally asymptotically mixed normal (LAMN) or locally asymptotically quadratic (LAQ). Ploberger (2004) obtains a complete class theorem for hypothesis tests in the LAQ case, which nests the LAMN and LAN cases.

Auction and search models
Some parametric auction and search models, in which the support of the data depends on some of the model parameters, do not satisfy the LAN regularity conditions. For such models, Hirano and Porter (2003) showed that the maximum likelihood point estimator is not generally optimal in the local asymptotic minmax sense, but that Bayes estimators are asymptotically efficient.

KEISUKE HIRANO

Bibliography

Andrews, D.W.K., Moreira, M.M. and Stock, J.H. 2004. Optimal invariant similar tests for instrumental variables regression. Discussion Paper No. 1476. Cowles Foundation, Yale University.

Barberis, N.C. 2000. Investing for the long run when returns are predictable. *Journal of Finance* 55, 225–64.

Berger, J.O. 1985. *Statistical Decision Theory and Bayesian Analysis*. New York: Springer-Verlag.

Bickel, P.J., Klaasen, C.A., Ritov, Y. and Wellner, J.A. 1993. *Efficient and Adaptive Estimation for Semiparametric Models*. New York: Springer-Verlag.

Brainard, W.C. 1967. Uncertainty and the effectiveness of policy. *American Economic Review* 57, 411–25.

Brock, W.A., Durlauf, S.N. and West, K.D. 2003. Policy evaluation in uncertain economic environments. *Brookings Papers on Economic Activity* 2003(1), 235–322.

Brown, L.D. and Low, M.G. 1996. Asymptotic equivalence of nonparametric regression and white noise. *Annals of Statistics* 24, 2384–98.

Chamberlain, G. 2000. Econometric applications of maxmin expected utility. *Journal of Applied Econometrics* 15, 625–44.

Chamberlain, G. 2005. Decision theory applied to an instrumental variables model. Working paper, Harvard University.

Chioda, L. and Jansson, M. 2004. Optimal conditional inference for instrumental variables regression. Working paper, UC Berkeley.

Dehejia, R.H. 2005. Program evaluation as a decision problem. *Journal of Econometrics* 125, 141–73.

Ferguson, T.S. 1967. *Mathematical Statistics: A Decision Theoretic Approach*. New York: Academic Press.

Giannoni, M.P. 2002. Does model uncertainty justify caution? Robust optimal monetary policy in a forward-looking model. *Macroeconomic Dynamics* 6(1), 111–44.

Gilboa, I. and Schmeidler, D. 1989. Maxmin expected utility with non-unique prior. *Journal of Mathematical Economics* 18, 141–53.

Hansen, L.P. and Sargent, T.J. 2001. Acknowledging misspecification in macroeconomic theory. *Review of Economic Dynamics* 4, 519–35.

Hirano, K. and Porter, J. 2003. Asymptotic efficiency in parametric structural models with parameter-dependent support. *Econometrica* 71, 1307–38.

Hirano, K. and Porter, J. 2005. Asymptotics for statistical treatment rules. Working paper, University of Arizona.

Jeganathan, P. 1995. Some aspects of asymptotic theory with applications to time series models. *Econometric Theory* 11, 818–87.

Kandel, S. and Stambaugh, R.F. 1996. On the predictability of stock returns: an asset-allocation perspective. *Journal of Finance* 51, 385–424.

Klein, R.W. and Bawa, V.S. 1976. The effect of estimation risk on optimal portfolio choice. *Journal of Financial Economics* 3, 215–31.

Le Cam, L. 1972. Limits of experiments. *Proceedings of the Sixth Berkeley Symposium of Mathematical Statistics* 1, 245–61.

Le Cam, L. 1986. *Asymptotic Methods in Statistical Decision Theory.* New York: Springer-Verlag.

Manski, C.F. 2004. Statistical treatment rules for heterogeneous populations. *Econometrica* 72, 1221–46.

Nussbaum, M. 1996. Asymptotic equivalence of density estimation and Gaussian white noise. *Annals of Statistics* 24, 2399–430.

Onatski, A. and Stock, J.H. 2002. Robust monetary policy under model uncertainty in a small model of the U.S. economy. *Macroeconomic Dynamics* 6(1), 85–110.

Ploberger, W. 2004. A complete class of tests when the likelihood is locally asymptotically quadratic. *Journal of Econometrics* 118, 67–94.

Rudebusch, G.D. 2001. Is the fed too timid? Monetary policy in an uncertain world. *Review of Economics and Statistics* 83, 203–17.

Savage, L.J. 1951. The theory of statistical decision. *Journal of the American Statistical Association* 46, 55–67.

Savage, L.J. 1954. *The Foundations of Statistics.* New York: Wiley.

van der Vaart, A.W. 1991. An asymptotic representation theorem. *International Statistical Review* 59, 97–121.

Wald, A. 1939. Contributions to the theory of statistical estimation and testing hypotheses. *Annals of Mathematical Statistics* 10, 299–326.

Wald, A. 1950. *Statistical Decision Functions.* New York: Wiley.

difference-in-difference estimators

Motivation and definition

Difference-in-differences (DID) estimators are often used in empirical research in economics to evaluate the effects of public interventions and other treatments of interest in the absence of purely experimental data.

The usual goal of evaluation studies is to estimate the average effect of a treatment (for example, participation in a vocational training programme) on some outcome variable of interest (for example, earnings or employment). Often researchers concentrate on estimating the average effect of the treatment on the treated, that is, on those individuals exposed to the treatment or intervention (for example, the trainees). In the typical setting of an evaluation study, we observe an outcome variable, Y_i, for a sample of treated individuals and also for a sample of untreated individuals. The main challenge in evaluation research is to find an appropriate comparison group among the untreated individuals, in the sense that the distribution of the outcome variable for the untreated comparison group can be taken as an approximation to the counterfactual distribution that the outcome variable, Y_i, would have followed for the treated in the absence of the treatment.

Sometimes the sample of untreated individuals may not provide an appropriate comparison group, and therefore differences in the distribution of the outcome variable between treated and untreated reflect not only the effect of the treatment but also intrinsic differences between the two groups. To address this problem, the DID estimator uses the assumption that in the absence of the treatment the average difference in the outcome variable, Y_i, between treated and untreated would have stayed roughly constant. Then, the average difference in the outcome variable between treated and untreated before the treatment can be used to approximate the part of the difference in average outcomes after the treatment that is created by intrinsic differences between the two groups and not by the effect of the treatment.

Let $\bar{Y}_t^T$ and $\bar{Y}_t^C$ be the average outcomes in period t ($t = 1, 2$) in the treated and untreated samples, respectively. Period $t = 1$ takes place before the treatment and period $t = 2$ takes place after the treatment. The difference in average outcomes between treated and untreated after the treatment is $\bar{Y}_2^T - \bar{Y}_2^C$. The same difference for the pre-treatment period is $\bar{Y}_1^T - \bar{Y}_1^C$. Then, the DID estimator is defined as follows:

$$\hat{\alpha} = (\bar{Y}_2^T - \bar{Y}_2^C) - (\bar{Y}_1^T - \bar{Y}_1^C). \tag{1}$$

Figure 1 provides a graphical interpretation of the DID estimator. The solid lines represent the evolution in average outcomes for the treated and the untreated comparison group between the pre-treatment period ($t = 1$) and the post-treatment

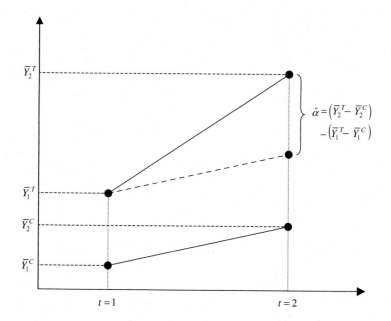

Figure 1

period ($t = 2$). The dashed line approximates the counterfactual evolution that the average outcome would have experienced for the treated in the absence of the treatment. This line is constructed under the DID assumption that, in the absence of the treatment, the difference in average outcomes between treated and untreated would have stayed roughly constant in the two periods. As reflected in Figure 1, an equivalent formulation of the DID assumption is that, in the absence of the treatment, average outcomes for treated and untreated would have followed a common trend. As a result, the untreated comparison group can be used to infer the counterfactual evolution of the average outcome for the treated in the absence of the treatment.

Difference in differences estimators have been applied to the study of a variety of issues in economics. Card and Krueger (1994) evaluate the employment effects of an increase in the minimum wage in New Jersey using a contiguous state (Pennsylvania), which did not increase the minimum wage, to approximate how employment would have evolved in New Jersey in the absence of the raise. Card (1990) applies DID estimators to evaluate the employment effects of the massive flow of Cuban immigrants to Miami during the 1980 Mariel boatlift. To estimate the effects of the boatlift, Card uses a group of four comparison cities to approximate how employment would have evolved in Miami in the absence of the 1980 immigration shock. Other applications of the DID estimator include studies of the effects of disability benefits on time out of work (Meyer, Viscusi and Durbin, 1995), the effect of anti-takeover laws on firms' leverage (Garvey and Hanka, 1999), and the effect of tax subsidies for health insurance on health insurance purchases (Gruber and Poterba, 1994).

The DID estimator has a simple regression representation. Let Y_{it} be the outcome of interest (for example, earnings) for individual i at time t, with $i = 1, \ldots, N$ and $t = 1, 2$. Let D_i be an indicator of membership to the treatment group, so $D_i = 1$ for the treated and $D_i = 0$ for the untreated. Finally, let $\Delta Y_i = Y_{i2} - Y_{i1}$ be the change in the outcome variable between the pre-treatment and the post-treatment period for individual i. The regression representation of the DID estimator is:

$$\Delta Y_i = \mu + \alpha D_i + u_i, \tag{2}$$

where u_i is a regression error, which is mean independent of D_i (that is, $E[u_i|D_i = 1] = E[u_i|D_i = 0]$). It can be easily seen that the ordinary least squares estimator of α in eq. (2) is numerical identical to the DID estimator, $\hat{\alpha}$, in eq. (1). Regression standard errors along with the point estimate, $\hat{\alpha}$, can be used to construct confidence intervals for α and perform statistical hypothesis tests. As reflected in eq. (2) and emphasized in Blundell and MaCurdy (1999), the DID estimator is a particular case of fixed effects estimators for panel data, with only two time periods and a fraction of the sample exposed to the treatment in the second time period.

Extensions
In some instances, the common trend assumption adopted for DID is not plausible because treated and untreated differ in the distribution of some variables, X_i, that are thought to affect the trend of the outcome variable. In this situation, treated and untreated may exhibit different trends in the average of the outcome variable between $t = 1$ and $t = 2$, even if the treatment does not have any impact on the outcome of interest. The regression formulation of the DID estimator is useful to compute a conditional version of the DID estimator that corrects for the effect of X_i on the trend of Y_i:

$$\Delta Y_i = \mu + \alpha D_i + X_i'\beta + u_i.$$

Abadie (2005) and Heckman, Ichimura and Todd (1997) develop semiparametric and nonparametric versions of the conditional DID estimator.

Panel data are not always necessary to apply the DID estimator. A simple inspection of eq. (1) indicates that $\hat{\alpha}$ can be estimated from repeated cross sections, using a cross-section at time $t = 2$ to estimate $\bar{Y}_2^T - \bar{Y}_2^C$ and a cross section at time $t = 1$ to estimate $\bar{Y}_1^T - \bar{Y}_1^C$. A regression formulation of the DID estimator is also available for repeated cross sections (see, for example, Meyer, 1995; Abadie, 2005). When the DID estimator is constructed using repeated cross sections, it is important to check whether there exist compositional changes in the sample between the two periods. Compositional changes may constitute a threat to the assumption that the difference in the average outcome between treated and untreated would have stayed constant in the absence of the treatment.

In general, the DID assumption cannot be tested directly with data from $t = 1$ and $t = 2$ only. However, if the common trend assumption extends to more than one pretreatment period for which data are available, preexisting differences in the trends of the outcome variable between treated and untreated can be detected by applying the DID estimator to pretreatment data. This is done by constructing ΔY_i as the difference in the outcome variable for individual i between two pretreatment periods. Then, a test of the hypothesis $\alpha = 0$ in eq. (2) is a test of the common trend assumption. In addition, the DID assumption can sometimes be rejected when the dependent variable has bounded support (for example, when Y_i is a binary variable). If the dependent variable has bounded support the DID assumption may imply that, in the absence of the treatment, the average outcome for the treated would have lain outside the support of the dependent variable (see Athey and Imbens, 2006).

For a more detailed explanation of the theory behind DID estimators, see Abadie (2005), Angrist and Krueger (1999), Ashenfelter and Card (1985), Blundell and MaCurdy (1999), Heckman, Ichimura and Todd (1997), and Meyer (1995).

ALBERTO ABADIE

See also **fixed effects and random effects; treatment effect.**

Bibliography

Abadie, A. 2005. Semiparametric difference-in-differences estimators. *Review of Economic Studies* 72, 1–19.

Angrist, J.D. and Krueger, A.B. 1999. Empirical strategies in labor economics. In *Handbook of Labor Economics*, vol. 3A, ed. O. Ashenfelter and D. Card. Amsterdam: North-Holland.

Ashenfelter, O. and Card, D. 1985. Using the longitudinal structure of earnings to estimate the effects of training programs. *Review of Economics and Statistics* 67, 648–60.

Athey, S.C. and Imbens, G.W. 2006. Identification and inference in nonlinear difference-in-difference models. *Econometrica* 74, 431–98.

Blundell, R. and MaCurdy, T. 1999. Labor supply: a review of alternative approaches. In *Handbook of Labor Economics*, vol. 3A, ed. O. Ashenfelter and D. Card. Amsterdam: North-Holland.

Card, D. 1990. The impact of the Mariel Boatlift on the Miami labor market. *Industrial and Labor Relations Review* 44, 245–57.

Card, D. and Krueger, A.B. 1994. Minimum wages and employment: a case study of the fast-food industry in New Jersey and Pennsylvania. *American Economic Review* 84, 772–93.

Garvey, G.T. and Hanka, G. 1999. Capital structure and corporate control: the effect of antitakeover statutes on firm leverage. *Journal of Finance* 54, 519–46.

Gruber, J. and Poterba, J. 1994. Tax incentives and the decision to purchase health insurance: evidence from the self-employed. *Quarterly Journal of Economics* 109, 701–33.

Heckman, J.J., Ichimura, H. and Todd, P.E. 1997. Matching as an econometric evaluation estimator: evidence from evaluating a job training programme. *Review of Economic Studies* 64, 605–54.

Meyer, B.D. 1995. Natural and quasi-experiments in economics. *Journal of Business & Economic Statistics* 13, 151–61.

Meyer, B.D., Viscusi, W.K. and Durbin, D.L. 1995. Workers' compensation and injury duration: evidence from a natural experiment. *American Economic Review* 85, 322–40.

exchangeability

Definition A sequence $y = (y_1, \ldots, y_n)$ of random variables (for $n \geq 1$) is *(finitely) exchangeable* if the joint probability distribution $p(y_1, \ldots, y_n)$ of the elements of y is invariant under permutation of the indices $(1, \ldots, n)$, and a countably infinite sequence $(y_1, y_2, \ldots)$ is *(infinitely) exchangeable* if every finite subsequence is finitely exchangeable.

The idea of exchangeability seems (Good, 1965; Bernardo and Smith, 1994) to be traceable back to Johnson (1924), who used the term *permutable*, and independently to Haag (1924). Other writers who made early use of the concept include Khintchine (1932); Fréchet (1943); Savage (1954), who called an exchangeable sequence *symmetric*; and Hewitt and Savage (1955). But the deepest implications of the idea are due to de Finetti (1930), who in (1938) still referred to exchangeable sequences as *equivalent*; by (1970) the word had been translated from the Italian as *exchangeable*, and since then usage has stabilized around this terminology under the influence of de Finetti and his translators.

The concept is important because it plays a fundamental role in the specification of statistical models from a Bayesian point of view. Following the example of Good (1950) by referring to You as a generic rational person making uncertainty assessments, suppose that You will in the future get to see a finite sequence $y = (y_1, \ldots, y_n)$ of binary observables; to illustrate the interplay between context and model, consider as an example the mortality outcomes (within 30 days of admission, say: $1 = $ died, $0 = $ lived) for a sequence of n patients with the same admission diagnosis (heart attack, say) at one particular hospital H, starting on the first day of next month. You acknowledge Your uncertainty about which elements in the sequence will be 0s and which 1s; suppose further that You find it natural (as in the Bayesian approach to statistics) to use random variables to quantify Your uncertainty. As de Finetti (1970) noted, in this situation Your fundamental imperative is to construct a *predictive* distribution $p(y_1, \ldots, y_n)$ that expresses Your uncertainty about the future observables, rather than – as is perhaps more common – to reach immediately for a standard family of *parametric* models for the y_i (that is, to posit the existence of a vector $\theta = (\theta_1, \ldots, \theta_k)$ of parameters and to model the observables by appeal to a family $p(y_i|\theta)$ of probability distributions indexed by θ).

Even though the y_i are binary, with all but the smallest values of n it still seems a formidable task to *elicit* from Yourself an n-dimensional predictive distribution $p(y_1, \ldots, y_n)$; it was while facing this challenge that de Finetti developed his version of the idea of exchangeability and its implications. As de Finetti observed, in the absence of any further information about the patients, You notice that Your uncertainty about them is exchangeable: if someone (without telling You) were to rearrange the order in which their mortality outcomes become known to You, Your predictive distribution would not change. This still seems to leave $p(y_1,\ldots,y_n)$ substantially unspecified, but de Finetti (1930) proved a remarkable theorem which shows (in effect) that all exchangeable predictive distributions for a vector of binary observables are representable as mixtures of Bernoulli sampling distributions. More formally,

Theorem 1 (representation of exchangeable predictive distributions for binary observables [de Finetti, 1930]): Suppose that You're willing to regard $(y_1,\ldots,y_n)$ as the first n terms in an infinitely exchangeable binary sequence $(y_1, y_2, \ldots)$; then, with $\bar{y}_n = \frac{1}{n}\sum_{i=1}^{n} y_i$,

- $\theta = \lim_{n\to\infty} \bar{y}_n$ must exist, and the marginal distribution (given θ) for each of the y_i must be $p(y_i|\theta) = \text{Bernoulli}(\theta) = \theta^{y_i}(1-\theta)^{1-y_i}$;
- $H(t) = \lim_{n\to\infty} P(\bar{y}_n \le t)$, the limiting cumulative distribution function (CDF) of the $\bar{y}_n$ values, must also exist for all t and must be a valid CDF, where P is Your joint probability distribution on $(y_1, y_2, \ldots)$; and
- Your predictive distribution for the first n observations can be expressed as

$$p(y_1,\ldots,y_n) = \int_0^1 \prod_{i=1}^{n} \theta^{y_i}(1-\theta)^{1-y_i}\, dH(\theta). \tag{1}$$

When (as will essentially always be the case in realistic applications) Your joint distribution P is sufficiently regular that H possesses a density (with respect to Lebesgue measure), $dH(\theta) = p(\theta)\, d\theta$, (1) can be written in a more accessible way as

$$p(y_1,\ldots,y_n) = \int_0^1 \theta^{s_n}(1-\theta)^{n-s_n}\, p(\theta)\, d\theta, \tag{2}$$

where $s_n = \sum_{i=1}^{n} y_i = n\, \bar{y}_n$.

The interpretation of (2) provides a link with non-Bayesian statistical modelling, as follows. In the frequentist (repeated-sampling) approach to statistics, to bring probability into the picture it's necessary to tell a story in which the observable y_i are either literally a random sample from some population $\mathscr{P}$ or *like* what You would get if You took a random sample from $\mathscr{P}$. This is a somewhat awkward story to tell in the medical example above, because the patients whose mortality outcomes are $(y_1,\ldots,y_n)$ are not a random sample of anything; they're simply the exhaustive list of all patients arriving at hospital H (itself not randomly chosen), with heart attack as their admission diagnosis, in a particular (not randomly chosen) window of time. In spite of this difficulty, the standard frequentist model (with the same information base as that assumed above) would define θ as the mortality rate in $\mathscr{P}$ (whatever $\mathscr{P}$ might be) and would treat the y_i as measurements on a random sample from $\mathscr{P}$ by regarding random variables Y_i (whose observed values are y_i) as independent and identically distributed (IID) draws from the Bernoulli (θ) distribution $p(Y_i = y_i) = \theta^{y_i}(1-\theta)^{1-y_i}$, which leads to the joint sampling distribution

$p(Y_1 = y_1, \ldots, Y_n = y_n) = \prod_{i=1}^{n} \theta^{y_i}(1-\theta)^{1-y_i} = \theta^{s_n}(1-\theta)^{n-s_n}$. Thus, in interpreting Theorem 1 (with reference to equation (2) above), in Your predictive modelling of the binary y_i You may as well proceed *as if*

- there is a quantity called θ, interpretable both as the marginal death probability $p(y_i = 1|\theta)$ for each patient and as the long-run mortality rate in the infinite sequence $(y_1, y_2, \ldots)$;
- conditional on θ, the y_i are IID Bernoulli (θ); and
- θ can be viewed as a realization of a random variable (this is of course how all unknown quantities are treated in the Bayesian paradigm) with density $p(\theta)$.

In other words, exchangeability of Your uncertainty about a binary process is functionally equivalent to assuming the simple Bayesian *hierarchical* model (see, for example, Draper, 2007)

$$
\begin{array}{lll}
\theta & \sim & p(\theta) \\
(y_i|\theta) & \overset{\text{IID}}{\sim} & \text{Bernoulli}(\theta).
\end{array}
\tag{3}
$$

A number of points are worth noting.

First, exchangeability is not a property of the world; it's a judgment by You concerning Your uncertainty about the world. Two reasonable people, with different knowledge bases or different views on how that knowledge should be brought to bear on the issue at hand, may consider the same set of observables, and one may judge her uncertainty about those observables exchangeable while the other may not make the same judgement about his uncertainty (for example, if I know the gender of the patients in the medical example and You do not, and if there's evidence that the mortality rate for male and female heart attack patients differs by an amount that's large in clinical terms, then You may well judge Your uncertainty about the mortality outcomes exchangeable but I would be ill-advised to adopt an exchangeable model; see partial/conditional exchangeability below). This distinction between {the world} and {Your uncertainty about the world} is sometimes blurred by terminology – I might casually say 'These patients are exchangeable' when what I mean is 'my uncertainty about these patients is exchangeable, as far as mortality is concerned' – but failing to observe the distinction can lead to what Jaynes (2003) terms the *mind projection fallacy*, with undesirable consequences for clarity of thought.

Second, in both the frequentist and Bayesian modelling approaches it's helpful to employ a fiction involving random variables, but for different purposes: in the standard frequentist approach, You regard the y_i as realizations of random variables (as a way to build a useful probability model), even though (in observational settings like the medical example above) no random sampling was performed to arrive at the observables; and in the Bayesian approach, You regard θ as random (as a way to make good predictions of observables), even though in both the frequentist and Bayesian approaches θ has the same logical status, as a fixed unknown constant.

Third, since, for any random variables X and Y for which the following symbols have meaning, the density of Y can be expressed as $p(y) = \int p(y|x)\, p(x)\, dx$ – in other words, Y can be modelled either directly or as a mixture of the conditional distribution $p(y|x)$ with $p(x)$ serving as a mixing distribution – the predictive distribution in eq. (2) can be regarded as a mixture of Bernoulli sampling distributions with $p(\theta)$ as the mixing weights.

Fourth, mathematically $p(\theta)$ is just a mixing distribution, but (of course) statistically it has a more useful interpretation. The second line of eq. (3) defines the *likelihood function* $l(\theta|y) = c\, p(y|\theta)$ (an arbitrary positive constant c times the joint sampling distribution of the data vector y, reinterpreted as a function of θ for fixed y); this is where all the information about θ internal to the data-set y is stored, and – under the logic of *Bayes's theorem* – the first line of eq. (3) defines $p(\theta)$ as the place where all the information about θ *external* to the data-set y is stored. It has become traditional to call this $p(\theta)$ a *prior distribution* for θ; this terminology is unfortunate (it sounds as though only information gathered before the data-set y arrives can go into $p(\theta)$, and this is not true), but it has been used for so long that it's unlikely it can be changed now. Equation (3) implies that (*a*) learning about θ on the basis of y can occur via Bayes's theorem: the *posterior distribution* $p(\theta|y)$, which combines the information about θ contained in the prior and the likelihood, is just a renormalized version of their product: $p(\theta|y) = c\, p(\theta)\, l(\theta|y)$, with c chosen so that $p(\theta|y)$ integrates to (1), and (*b*) predictive distributions for future data given past data may also readily be calculated (for example, for $1 < m < n$ the predictive for $(y_{m+1}, \ldots, y_n)$ based on $(y_1, \ldots, y_m)$ is

$$p(y_{m+1}, \ldots, y_n | y_1, \ldots, y_m) = \int_0^1 \theta^{s_n - s_m}(1-\theta)^{n-m-(s_n-s_m)} p(\theta|y_1, \ldots, y_m)\, d\theta, \qquad (4)$$

in which $s_m = \sum_{i=1}^m y_i$ and $p(\theta|y_1, \ldots, y_m)$ is the posterior distribution for θ based only on the first m observations.

Fifth, exchangeability evidently plays a role in Bayesian modelling that's somewhat analogous to the role of IID sampling in the frequentist approach, but exchangeability and IID are not the same: IID random variables are exchangeable, and exchangeable random variables are identically distributed, but they're not independent (for example, if You're about to observe a binary process whose tendency to yield a 1 is not known to You, and You judge Your uncertainty about future outcomes to be exchangeable, the information in the first n outcomes would definitely help You to predict outcome $(n+1)$; it's only when (somehow) the knowledge of the 'underlying' θ becomes available to You that there's no information in any of the outcomes to help predict any other outcomes – this situation might be summarized by saying that the past and the future become conditionally independent given the truth). Exchangeable observables are thus not IID, but they may often be usefully regarded as *conditionally* IID given a parameter vector θ, as in eq. (3) above.

Sixth, some awkwardness arose above in the frequentist approach to modelling the medical data, because it was not clear what population $\mathscr{P}$ the data could be regarded as *like* a random sample from. This awkwardness also arises in Bayesian modelling: even though in practice You are only going to observe $(y_1,\ldots,y_n)$, de Finetti's representation theorem requires You to extend Your judgement of finite exchangeability to the countably-infinite collective $(y_1, y_2,\ldots)$, *and this is precisely like viewing* $(y_1,\ldots,y_n)$ *as a random sample from* $\mathscr{P} = (y_1, y_2,\ldots)$. (Finite versions of de Finetti's representation theorem are available – for example, Diaconis and Freedman, 1980 – which informally say that, if You're willing to extend Your judgement of exchangeability from $(y_1,\ldots,y_n)$ to $(y_1,\ldots,y_N)$ for $N > n$, the larger N is the harder it becomes for Your predictive distribution $p(y_1,\ldots,y_n)$ to differ by a large amount from something representable by eq. (2) without violating the basic rules of probability.) The key point is that the difficulty arising from lack of clarity about the scope of valid generalizability from a given set of observational data is a fundamental scientific problem that emerges whenever purely observational data are viewed through an inferential or predictive lens, whether the statistical methods You use are frequentist or Bayesian.

The entire discussion so far has been in the context of binary outcomes y with no covariates; in practice, predictor variables x are also generally available, and extensions to non-binary data are evidently needed as well. An example involving a covariate arose in the discussion of the mind projection fallacy above: if, in the medical setting considered here, the gender x of the patients is available, and if this has a clinically meaningful bearing on mortality from heart attack, then it would be more scientifically appropriate to assert exchangeability separately and in parallel within the two gender groups {male, female}. With this in mind de Finetti (1938) defined the concept of *partial exchangeability*, which is also known as *conditional exchangeability* (Lindley and Novick, 1981; Draper et al., 1993); with this newer terminology You would say that Your uncertainty about the mortality observables for these patients is conditionally exchangeable given gender. Conditional exchangeability is related to the notion, introduced by Fisher (1956), of *recognizable subpopulations*.

Suppose now that the observable You will measure on the patients in the medical example is a severity of illness score y_i, scaled as a continuous quantity from $-\infty$ to ∞, and return temporarily to the situation with no covariate information. As before Your uncertainty about the future y_i values is (unconditionally) exchangeable, but now a representation theorem is needed for continuous real-valued outcomes; de Finetti (1937) supplied this as well.

Theorem 2 (representation of exchangeable predictive distributions for continuous observables [de Finetti, 1937]): If You're willing to regard $(y_1,\ldots,y_n)$ as the first n terms in an infinitely exchangeable sequence $(y_1, y_2,\ldots)$ of continuous values on $\mathbb{R}$, then

- $F(t) = \lim_{n\to\infty} F_n(t)$ must exist for all t and must be a valid CDF, where F_n is the *empirical CDF* based on $(y_1,\ldots,y_n)$ (i.e., $F_n(t) = \frac{1}{n}\sum_{i=1}^{n} I(y_i \leq t)$, in which $I(A)$ is the indicator function (1 if A is true, otherwise 0)), and the marginal distribution (given F) for each of the y_i must be $(y_i|F) \sim F$;

- $G(F) = \lim_{n\to\infty} P(F_n)$ must also exist, where P is Your joint probability distribution on $(y_1, y_2, \dots)$; and
- Your predictive distribution for the first n observations can be expressed as

$$p(y_1, \dots, y_n) = \int_{\mathscr{F}} \prod_{i=1}^{n} F(y_i)\, dG(F), \tag{5}$$

where $\mathscr{F}$ is the space of all possible CDFs on $\mathbb{R}$.

Equation (5) says informally that exchangeability of Your uncertainty about an observable processing unfolding on the real line is functionally equivalent to assuming the Bayesian hierarchical model

$$\begin{aligned} F &\sim & p(F) \\ (y_i|F) &\overset{\text{IID}}{\sim} & F, \end{aligned} \tag{6}$$

where $p(F)$ is a prior distribution on $\mathscr{F}$.

With binary observables, Theorem 1 (which is evidently a special case of Theorem (2) focuses attention on θ, the underlying rate of 1s in the population $\mathscr{P} = (y_1, y_2, \dots)$ from which You're in effect regarding $(y_1, \dots, y_n)$ as like a random sample; in the continuous case the analogous theorem focuses attention on F, the underlying CDF defined by $\mathscr{P}$. This makes Theorem 2 harder to implement in practice, because it's one thing to specify a prior distribution on a quantity $\theta \in (0, 1)$ and quite another to put a scientifically relevant prior distribution on the space $\mathscr{F}$ of all possible CDFs on the real line. Placing probability distributions on functions is the topic addressed by the field of *Bayesian nonparametric methods* (see, for example, Dey, Müller and Sinha, 1998), an area of statistics that has recently moved completely into the realm of day-to-day implementation and relevance through advances (since the early 1990s) in *Markov chain Monte Carlo* (MCMC) simulation-based methods of computation (see, for example, Gilks, Richardson and Spiegelhalter, 1995). Two rich families of prior distributions on CDFs about which a wealth of practical experience has recently accumulated include (mixtures of) *Dirichlet process priors* (see, for example, Ferguson, 1973) and *Pólya trees* (see, for example, Lavine, 1992).

As an example of the use of de Finetti's representation theorem for continuous outcomes, consider a randomized controlled trial or observational study with a treatment (T) and a control (C) group in which the outcome of interest y is modelled continuously on $\mathbb{R}$. A judgement of unconditional exchangeability of Your uncertainty about the y values for all subjects in the study would be equivalent to assuming that the T and C conditions had the same effect on the subjects, which (since the point of the study is presumably to see if this is true) would not be a good starting point; instead, in the absence of any other covariate information, it would be reasonable for

You to model Your uncertainty about the y values as conditionally exchangeable given the indicator variable x that identifies which group each subject is in. With F_C and F_T as the underlying control and treatment CDFs and y_i^T as the observable for subject i in the treatment group (and similarly for y_j^C), a straightforward extension of Theorem 2 then leads to the following Bayesian nonparametric model for the observables (for $i = 1, \ldots, n_T$ and $j = 1, \ldots, n_C$):

$$
\begin{aligned}
(F_C, F_T) &\sim p(F_C, F_T) \\
(y_i^T | F_C, F_T) &\overset{\text{IID}}{\sim} F_T \quad \text{and} \quad (y_j^C | F_C, F_T) \overset{\text{IID}}{\sim} F_C.
\end{aligned}
\tag{7}
$$

A nonparametric joint prior can then be placed on (F_C, F_T) using either of the Dirichlet process prior or Pólya tree methodologies mentioned above, and an appropriate functional of (F_C, F_T) (such as the difference or ratio of the underlying treatment and control means) can be monitored in the MCMC simulation. Note that this model arose solely from exchangeability considerations and (a simple extension of) Theorem 2.

Model specification has been a vexing topic in both frequentist and Bayesian statistics throughout much of the last century. Referring both to the conditional exchangeability judgements and to choices made in specifying the prior on F_C and F_T in the example above as *structural assumptions*, a popular approach to model specification (practised with equal vigour by both frequentists and Bayesians since the work of Tukey, 1962, and others on exploratory data analysis) involves (*a*) enlisting the aid of the data to conduct a search among possible structural assumptions, (*b*) choosing a single favourite structural specification S^*, and (*c*) pretending You knew all along that S^* was 'correct', even though it was arrived at via a data-driven search. From a Bayesian perspective this approach is clearly unsound, since it amounts to using the data to specify the prior distribution on the space $\mathscr{S}$ of all possible structural assumptions and then using the same data again to update the prior on $\mathscr{S}$; the result will often be inferences and predictions that are not well *calibrated*, with interval estimates that are not as wide as they need to be to fully acknowledge *model uncertainty. Bayesian model averaging* (Leamer, 1978; Draper, 1995), in which predictive distributions $p(y_f | y)$ for future observables y_f given past data y are computed by averaging over the model uncertainty uncovered by the search through $\mathscr{S}$ (rather than ignoring it), through calculations of the form

$$
p(y_f | y) = \int_{\mathscr{S}} p(y_f | y, S) \, p(S | y) \, dS,
$$

can provide one principled, satisfying and rather general method for solving the problem of Bayesian model specification in a well-calibrated manner; methods based on *cross-validation* (see, for example, Stone, 1974), in which (in effect) part of the data is used to specify the prior on $\mathscr{S}$ and the rest of the data is employed to update that prior, can provide another; and the approach illustrated above in the study with treatment and control groups – which combines conditional exchangeability judgments (driven by the context of the problem) with Bayesian nonparametric methods – can provide yet another.

DAVID DRAPER

Bibliography

Bernardo, J.M. and Smith, A.F.M. 1994. *Bayesian Theory*. New York: Wiley.

de Finetti, B. 1930. Funzione caratteristica di un fenomeno aleatorio. *Memorie della Reale Accademia dei Lincei* 4, 86–133.

de Finetti, B. 1937. La prévision: ses lois logiques, ses sources subjectives. *Annales de l'Institut H. Poincaré* 7, 1–68. Reprinted in translation as: Foresight: its logical laws, its subjective sources. In *Studies in Subjective Probability*, ed. H.E. Kyburg and H.E. Smokler. New York: Dover, 1980.

de Finetti, B. 1938. Sur la condition d'équivalence partielle. *Actualités Scientifiques et Industrielles* 739. Reprinted in translation as: On the condition of partial exchangeability. In *Studies in Inductive Logic and Probability*, ed. R.C. Jeffrey. Berkeley: University of California Press, 1980.

de Finetti, B. 1970. *Teoria delle Probabilità*, 2 vols. Turin: Eunaudi. Reprinted in translation as de Finetti B. 1974–75. *Theory of Probability*, 2 vols. Chichester: Wiley, 1974–75.

Dey, D.D., Müller, P. and Sinha, D., eds. 1998. *Practical Nonparametric and Semiparametric Bayesian Statistics*. New York: Springer.

Diaconis, P. and Freedman, D. 1980. Finite exchangeable sequences. *Annals of Probability* 8, 745–64.

Draper, D. 1995. Assessment and propagation of model uncertainty (with discussion). *Journal of the Royal Statistical Society*, Series B 57, 45–97.

Draper, D. 2007. Bayesian multilevel analysis and MCMC. In *Handbook of Multilevel Analysis*, ed. J. de Leeuw and E. Meijer. New York: Springer.

Draper, D., Hodges, J., Mallows, C. and Pregibon, D. 1993. Exchangeability and data analysis (with discussion). *Journal of the Royal Statistical Society*, Series A 156, 9–37.

Ferguson, T.S. 1973. A Bayesian analysis of some nonparametric problems. *Annals of Statistics* 1, 209–30.

Fisher, R.A. 1956. *Statistical Methods and Scientific Inference*. Edinburgh: Oliver and Boyd.

Fréchet, M. 1943. *Les Probabilités Associées à un Système d'Événements Compatibles et Dépendents*, vol. 2. Paris: Hermann et Cie.

Gilks, W.R., Richardson, S. and Spiegelhalter, D.J., eds. 1995. *Markov Chain Monte Carlo in Practice*. New York: Chapman & Hall/CRC.

Good, I.J. 1950. *Probability and the Weighing of Evidence*. London: Charles Griffin.

Good, I.J. 1965. *The Estimation of Probabilities: An Essay on Modern Bayesian Methods*. Cambridge, MA: MIT Press.

Haag, J. 1924. Sur un problème général de probabilités et ses diverses applications. *Proceedings of the International Congress of Mathematics (Toronto)* 2, 659–74.

Hewitt, E. and Savage, L.J. 1955. Symmetric measures on Cartesian products. *Transactions of the American Mathematical Society* 80, 470–501.

Jaynes, E.T. 2003. *Probability Theory: The Logic of Science*. Cambridge: Cambridge University Press.

Johnson, W.E. 1924. *Logic. III. The Logical Foundations of Science*. Cambridge: Cambridge University Press.

Khintchine, A.I. 1932. Sur les classes d'événements équivalents. *Mathematics of the USSR – Sbornik* 39, 40–3.

Lavine, M. 1992. Some aspects of Pólya tree distributions for statistical modeling. *Annals of Statistics* 20, 1222–35.

Leamer, E.E. 1978. *Specification Searches: Ad Hoc Inference with Nonexperimental Data*. New York: Wiley.

Lindley, D.V. and Novick, M.R. 1981. The role of exchangeability in inference. *Annals of Statistics* 9, 45–58.

Savage, L.J. 1954. *The Foundations of Statistics*. New York: Wiley.

Stone, M. 1974. Cross-validation choice and assessment of statistical predictions (with discussion). *Journal of the Royal Statistical Society*, Series B 36, 111–47.

Tukey, J.W. 1962. The future of data analysis. *Annals of Mathematical Statistics* 33, 1–67.

extreme bounds analysis

The analysis of economic data necessarily depends on assumptions that our weak data-sets do not allow us to test. We are forced to choose a limited number of variables in a multivariate analysis, to restrict the functional form, to limit the considered interdependence among observations to special forms, and to make special distributional assumptions. We make these assumptions, not because we believe them, but because we have to. Absent assumptions, our data-sets are utterly useless.

We sometimes put aside the discomfort that our choice of assumptions entails by doing what is conventional, like using a normal distribution, a linear functional form and the same limited set of variables studied by almost everyone else.

We sometimes pretend to treat the problem of choice of assumptions by using 'nonparametric' methods that masquerade as assumption-free. These methods are assumption-free only in Asymptopia, the land where all data-sets are unlimited. To get to the happy land of Asymptopia, we need only let the number of tested assumptions grow in the future more slowly than the number of observations. Then we can be sure to test all assumptions during our journey into the future. But here on Earth we have limited data-sets, and inevitably the way we analyse these data works well for some sets of assumptions and not so well for others. We cannot really know what we are doing unless we can draw some kind of line between the assumptions for which our inferences are valid and the assumptions for which our inferences are not valid. Thus, for example, 'heteroscedasticity-consistent' standard errors are now commonly deployed as if they were corrections for any form of heteroscedasticity. But these corrections of the standard errors, which leave the point estimates unchanged, are an appropriate treatment given the actual limited data only for some forms of heteroscedasticity, not for all. Unfortunately, with these 'nonparametric' methods, the border between the dealt-with assumptions for which the method works and the not-dealt-with assumptions is impossible to draw. Incidentally, these 'heteroscedasticity-consistent' standard errors are often called White-corrected standard errors, to which I respond rhetorically by calling the method 'White-washing'.

If conventions and nonparametric methods are not enough to soften the discomfort with the assumptions we make, we can always fantasize that the choice of assumptions doesn't really matter. We 'know' the methods we use work well under conditions that are 'close' to the assumptions that underlie them but not well if the departures are great. We hope that the neighbourhood in which the assumptions work is wide enough to encompass the problem at hand. For example, we don't really think the distribution is normal, but how much could that matter for linear regression? Isn't it enough to have symmetric unimodal distributions, shaped 'sort of like' a normal distribution?

Neither conventions, nor nonparametric sleight-of-hand, nor hope that it doesn't really matter form an adequate scientific response to doubt about the assumptions that underlie a data analysis. The correct way to deal with ambiguity in the choice of assumptions that are beyond the range of statistical tests is a sensitivity analysis that demonstrates that our assumptions do not in fact matter much. The most common sensitivity analysis involves the choice of variables in linear regression. Rather than reporting just one regression, many researchers offer a table of results, all based on different subsets of the variables. Typically, all the reported regressions have a common set of 'core' variables but differ depending on whether or not the regressions include selected 'doubtful' variables.

Although it can be comforting to discover that the coefficients of the core variables do not change much when doubtful variables are excluded, this kind of sensitivity analysis leaves open the possibility that there is some combination of doubtful variables that would radically change the result. Has the analyst worked hard enough to find the oddball estimates that these data allow? 'Extreme bounds analysis' answers this question. In an extreme bounds analysis, the computer chooses the linear combinations of doubtful variables that, when included in the regressions along with the core variables, produce the most extreme (minimum and maximum) estimates for the coefficient on a selected core variable. There is no way of fiddling with the doubtful variables that can produce an estimate outside the extreme bounds.

If the extreme bounds interval is small enough to be useful, that is the end of the story, and the result is reported to be 'sturdy'. This would occur, for example, when the core variables and the doubtful variables are 'independent', in which case the coefficients of the core variables don't change at all when doubtful variables are excluded. But quite often with highly correlated economics data these extreme bounds can be uncomfortably wide, and we are forced either to retreat in dismay or to seek some way to make the bounds narrower.

One way of restricting the range of alternative models is to allow only inclusion/ exclusion options, not the all linear combinations embodied in the extreme bounds. These inclusion/exclusion restrictions are the basis for the tables of alternative results that are commonly offered as evidence of inferential sturdiness, and the set of alternative estimates thus presented is smaller than the extreme bounds set.

But why? Why restrict to inclusion/exclusion options? Classical inference is not well suited to respond to this 'why?' question since the answer depends on the state of mind of the analyst and since classical inference presumes a researcher and an audience with a 'blank slate'. Moreover, the effect on the inferences of setting a regression coefficient to zero depends on the coordinate system for defining the parameters. (If you use x and z as explanatory variables, and I use $x + z$ and $x - z$, we get different answers.) Indeed, the extreme bounds are formed by setting coefficients to zero in an appropriately defined coordinate system, and therefore restriction to inclusion/exclusion restrictions is a meaningless restriction absent advice on how to define the coordinate system.

A Bayesian analysis can help to choose a coordinate system and can be a basis for a sensitivity analysis with a set of models that is sensibly smaller than the set of models underlying the extreme bounds. Bayesians allow the state of mind to influence the analysis by letting a researcher act as if the vector of regression coefficients on the doubtful variables, θ, comes from a normal distribution with a mean vector $\mathbf{0}$ and covariance matrix $\mathbf{V_0}$, selected by the researcher. The smaller is the covariance matrix $\mathbf{V_0}$, the more likely are the coefficients θ to hug close to zero and the more doubtful are the doubtful variables.

To parallel the decision always to include the core variables in the equation, it is natural to deploy a prior probability distribution for the core coefficients with an infinite variance – the blank-slate initial-ignorance option. Then, corresponding to each choice of covariance matrix for the coefficients of the doubtful variables are estimates of the coefficients of the core variables, $\hat{\beta}(\mathbf{V_0})$. If, for example, the covariance matrix $\mathbf{V_0}$ is set to zero, this is equivalent to assuming the coefficients of the doubtful variables are all zero, and we should be running the regression with all these doubtful variables omitted. Conversely, if the covariance matrix $\mathbf{V_0}$ is set to an 'infinitely large' matrix (unlimited variances), then this is the ignorance option for the doubtful variables, and the way to do the estimation is simply to include all the doubtful variables along with the core variables in the regression.

A 'global' sensitivity analysis in this setting is carried out by building a correspondence between sets of prior covariance matrices for the doubtful variables, $\mathbf{V_0}$, and the corresponding sets of estimates of the coefficients on the core variables, $\hat{\beta}(\mathbf{V_0})$.

Three possibilities are discussed in Leamer (1978) and Leamer and Chamberlain (1976): (a) $\mathbf{V_0}$ unrestricted, (b) $\mathbf{V_0}$ diagonal, (c) $\mathbf{V_0}$ diagonal with all diagonal elements the same.

1. The extreme bounds apply when the covariance $\mathbf{V_0}$ is any positive semi-definite matrix.
2. The 2^p regressions, found by including different subsets of the p doubtful variables, define the bound when $\mathbf{V_0}$ is a (non-negative) *diagonal* matrix. (Thus the 'right' coordinate system is the one in which the regression coefficients are a priori independent of each other in the sense that knowledge about one doesn't affect your thinking about the others.)
3. A still narrower set of bounds is found by estimating the $p+1$ 'principal component' regressions with the principal component restrictions ordered by their eigenvalues. This applies when $\mathbf{V_0}$ is proportional to the identity matrix.

Each of these three sets of prior covariance matrices includes the dogmatic priors that set certain linear combinations of the coefficients exactly to zero and also complete ignorance priors that allow certain linear combinations to be completely free. Neither of these two extremes is sensible in practice, since in the first case the data evidence is completely ignored (the restriction is imposed without testing) and in the second case the prior information is completely ignored. These can be excluded to restricting the prior covariance matrix from above and below: $\mathbf{V_L} < \mathbf{V_0} < \mathbf{V_U}$ where

$A < B$ means that the matrix $B - A$ is positive definite. The theorem that then applies comes from Leamer (1981, 1982) as is reported below. First, a statement about the posterior mean of the regression coefficient vector.

Theorem (Bayes estimate): If, conditional on the observable matrix X, and the unobservable parameters β, and σ^2, an observable vector y is normally distributed with mean $X\beta$ and covariance matrix $\sigma^2 I$, and if the coefficient vector β comes from a normal distribution with mean b_0 and covariance matrix V_0, then the conditional mean of β given y is approximately

$$b_2 = (X'X/s^2 + V_0^{-1})(X'Xb/s^2 + V_0^{-1}b_0)$$

where s^2 is the sample estimate of σ^2: $s^2 = y'(I - X(X'X)^{-1}X')y/(n-k)$, where n is the number of observations and k is the number or regression coefficients and where b is the ordinary least squares estimator (a solution to the normal equations $X'Xb = X'y$) : $b = (X'X)^{-1}X'y$.

Theorem (posterior bounds): Given $V_L < V_0 < V_U$ with V_L and V_U positive definite and with $V_L < V_0$ signifying that $V_0 - V_L$ is positive definite, then the posterior mean b_2 lies in the ellipsoid

$$(b_2 - f)'H(b_2 - f) < c$$

where

$$H = (X'X/s^2 + V_U^{-1}) + (X'X/s^2 + V_U^{-1})(V_L^{-1} - V_U^{-1})^{-1}(X'X/s^2 + V_U^{-1}) \times f$$
$$= [(X'X/s^2 + V_L^{-1})]^{-1}[X'Xb/s^2 + (V_L^{-1} - V_U^{-1})(X'X/s^2 + V_U^{-1})^{-1}X'Xb/2s^2]$$
$$c = (b'X'Xb/s^2)(X'X/s^2 + V_U^{-1})^{-1}(V_L^{-1} - V_U^{-1})(X'X/s^2 + V_L^{-1})^{-1}X'Xb/4s^2.$$

EDWARD E. LEAMER

Bibliography

Leamer, E. 1978. *Specification Searches: Ad Hoc Inference with Non Experimental Data.* New York: John Wiley and Sons.
Leamer, E. 1981. Sets of estimates of location. *Econometrica* 49, 193–204.
Leamer, E. 1982. Sets of posterior means with bounded variance priors. *Econometrica* 50, 725–36.
Leamer, E. and Chamberlain, G. 1976. Matrix weighted averages and posterior bounds. *Journal of the Royal Statistical Society,* Series B 38, 73–84.

field experiments

Field experiments occupy an important middle ground between laboratory experiments and naturally occurring field data. The underlying idea behind most field experiments is to make use of randomization in an environment that captures important characteristics of the real world. Distinct from traditional empirical economics, field experiments provide an advantage by permitting the researcher to create exogenous variation in the variables of interest, allowing us to establish causality rather than mere correlation. In relation to a laboratory experiment, a field experiment potentially gives up some of the control that a laboratory experimenter may have over her environment in exchange for increased realism.

The distinction between the laboratory and the field is much more important in the social sciences and the life sciences than it is in the physical sciences. In physics, for example, it appears that every hydrogen atom behaves exactly alike. Thus, when astronomers find hydrogen's signature wavelengths of light coming from the Andromeda Galaxy, they use this information to infer the quantity of hydrogen present there. By contrast, living creatures are much more complex than atoms and molecules, and they correspondingly behave much more heterogeneously. Despite the use of 'representative consumer' models, we know that not all consumers purchase the same bundle of goods when they face the same prices. With complex, heterogeneous behaviour, it is important to sample populations drawn from many different domains – both in the laboratory and in the field. This permits stronger inference, and one can also provide an important test of generalizability, testing whether laboratory results continue to hold in the chosen field environment.

We find an apt analogy in the study of pharmaceuticals, where randomized experiments scientifically evaluate new drugs to treat human diseases. Laboratory experiments evaluate whether drugs have desirable biochemical effects on tissues and proteins *in vitro*. If a drug appears promising, it is next tested *in vivo* on several species of animals, to see whether it is absorbed by the relevant tissues, whether it produces the desired effects on the body, and whether it produces undesirable side effects. If it remains with significant promise after those tests, it is then tested in human clinical trials to explore efficacy and measure any side effects.

Even after being tested thoroughly in human clinical trials and approved by regulators, a drug may sometimes reveal new information in large-scale use. For example, *effectiveness* may be different from the *efficacy* measured in clinical trials: if a drug must be taken frequently, for example, patients may not remember to take it as often as they are supposed to or as often as they did in closely supervised clinical trials. Furthermore, rare side effects may show up when the drug is finally exposed to a large population.

Much like this stylized example, in economics there are a number of reasons why insights gained in one environment might not perfectly map to another. Field experiments can lend insights into this question (see also Bohm, 1972; Harrison and List, 2004; Levitt and List, 2007; List, 2007). First, different types of subjects might behave differently; university students in the laboratory might not exhibit the same behaviour as financial traders or shopkeepers. In particular, the people who undertake a given economic activity have selected into that activity and market forces might have changed the composition of players as well; you might expect regular bidders to have more skill and interest in auctions than a randomly selected laboratory subject, for example.

A second reason why a field experiment might differ from a laboratory experiment is that the laboratory environment might not be fully representative of the field environment. For example, a typical donor asked to give money to charity might behave quite differently if asked to participate by choosing how much money to contribute to the public fund in a public-goods game (List, 2007). The charitable-giving context could provide familiar cognitive cues that make the task easier than an unfamiliar laboratory task. Even the mere fact of knowing that one's behaviour is being monitored, recorded, and subsequently scrutinized might alter choices (Orne, 1962).

Perhaps most important is the fact that any theory is an approximation of reality. In the laboratory, experimenters usually impose all the structural modelling assumptions of a theory (induced preferences, trading institutions, order of moves in a game) and examine whether subjects behave as predicted by the model. In a field experiment, one accepts the actual preferences and institutions used in the real world, jointly testing both the structural assumptions (such as the nature of values for a good) and the behavioural assumptions (such as Nash equilibrium).

For example, Vickrey (1961) assumes that in an auction there is a fixed, known number of bidders who have valuations for the good drawn independently from the same (known) probability distribution. He uses these assumptions, along with the assumption of a risk-neutral Nash equilibrium, to derive the 'revenue equivalence' result: that Dutch, English, first-price, and second-price auctions all yield the same expected revenue. However, in the real world the number of bidders might actually vary with the good or the auction rules, and the bidders might not know the probability distribution of values. These exceptions do not mean that the model should be abandoned as 'wrong'; it might well still have predictive power if it is a reasonable approximation to the truth. In a field experiment (such as Lucking-Reiley, 1999, for this example), we approach the real world; we do not take the structural assumptions of a theory for granted.

Such an example raises the natural question related to the actual difference between laboratory and field experiments. Harrison and List (2004) propose six factors that can be used to determine the field context of an experiment: the nature of the subject pool, the nature of the information that the subjects bring to the task, the nature of the commodity, the nature of the task or trading rules applied, the nature of the stakes, and the environment in which the subjects operate. Using these factors, they discuss a broad classification scheme that helps to organize one's thoughts about the factors that might be important when moving from the laboratory to the field.

A first useful departure from laboratory experiments using student subjects is simply to use 'non-standard' subjects, or experimental participants from the market of interest. Harrison and List (2004) adopt the term 'artefactual' field experiment to denote such studies. While one might argue that such studies are not 'field' in any way, for consistency of discussion we denote such experiments as artefactual field experiments for the remainder of this article, since they do depart in a potentially important manner from typical laboratory studies. This type of controlled experiment represents a useful type of exploration beyond traditional laboratory studies.

Moving closer to how naturally occurring data are generated, Harrison and List (2004) denote a 'framed field experiment' as the same as an artefactual field experiment but with field context in the commodity, task, stakes, or information set of the subjects. This type of experiment is important in the sense that a myriad of factors might influence behaviour, and by progressing slowly towards the environment of ultimate interest one can learn about whether, and to what extent, such factors influence behaviour in a case-by-case basis.

Finally, a 'natural field experiment' is the same as a framed field experiment but where the environment is one where the subjects naturally undertake these tasks and where the subjects do not know that they are participants in an experiment. Such an exercise represents an approach that combines the most attractive elements of the laboratory and naturally occurring data – randomization and realism. In this sense, comparing behaviour across natural and framed field experiments permits crisp insights into whether the experimental proclamation, in and of itself, influences behaviour.

Several examples of each of these types of field experiments are included in List (2006). Importantly for our purposes, each of these field experimental types represents a distinct manner in which to generate data. As List (2006) illustrates, these field experiment types fill an important hole between laboratory experiments and empirical exercises that make use of naturally occurring data. Yet an infrequently discussed question is: why do we bother to collect data in economics, or in any science?

First, we use data to collect enough facts to help construct a theory. Several prominent broader examples illustrate this point. After observing the anatomical and behavioural similarities of reptiles, one may theorize that reptiles are more closely related to each other than they are to mammals on the evolutionary tree. Watson and Crick used data from Rosalind Franklin's X-ray diffraction experiment to construct a theory of the chemical structure of DNA. Careful observations of the motions of the planets in the sky led Kepler to theorize that planets (including Earth) all travel in elliptical orbits around the Sun, and Newton to theorize the inverse-square law of gravitation. After observing with a powerful telescope that the fuzzy patches called 'spiral nebulae' are really made up of many stars, one may theorize that our solar system is itself part of its own galaxy, and the spiral nebulae are external to our Milky

Way galaxy. Robert Boyle experimented with different pressures using his vacuum pump in order to infer the inverse relationship between the pressure and the volume of a gas. Rutherford's experiments of shooting charged particles at a piece of gold foil led him to theorize that atoms have massive, positively charged nuclei.

Second, we use data to test theories' predictions. Galileo experimented with balls rolling down inclined planes in order to test his theory that all objects have the same rate of acceleration due to gravity. Pasteur rejected the theory of spontaneous generation with an experiment that showed that microorganisms grow in boiled nutrient broth when exposed to the air, but not when exposed to carefully filtered air. Arthur Eddington measured the bending of starlight by the sun during an eclipse in order to test Einstein's theory of general relativity.

Third, we use data to make measurements of key parameters. On the assumption that the electron is the smallest unit of electric charge, Robert Millikan experimented with tiny, falling droplets of oil to measure the charge of the electron. On the assumption that radioactive carbon-14 decays at a constant rate, archaeologists have been able to provide dates for various ancient artifacts. Similarly, scientists have assumed theory to be true and designed careful measurements of many other parameters, such as the speed of light, the gravitational constant, and various atomic masses.

Field experiments can be a useful tool for each of these purposes. For example, Anderson and Simester (2003) collect facts useful for constructing a theory about consumer reactions to nine-dollar endings on prices. They explore the effects of different price endings by conducting a natural field experiment with a retail catalogue merchant. Randomly selected customers receive one of three catalogue versions that show different prices for the same product. Systematically changing a product's price varies the presence or absence of a nine-dollar price ending. For example, a cotton dress may be offered to all consumers, but at prices of 34, 39, and 44 dollars, respectively, in each catalogue version. They find a positive effect of a nine-dollar price on quantity demanded, large enough that a price of 39 dollars actually produced higher quantities than a price of 34 dollars. Their results reject the theory that consumers turn a price of 34 dollars into 30 dollars by either truncation or rounding. This finding provides empirical evidence on an interesting topic and demonstrates the need for a better theory of how consumers process price endings.

List and Lucking-Reiley (2000) present an example of a framed field experiment designed to test a theory. The theory of multi-unit auctions predicts that a uniform-price sealed-bid auction will produce bids that are less than fully demand-revealing, because such bids might lower the price paid by the same bidder on another unit. By contrast, the generalized Vickrey auction predicts that bidders will submit bids equal to their values. In the experiment, List and Lucking-Reiley conduct two-person, two-unit auctions for collectible sportscards at a card trading show. The uniform-price auction awards both items to the winning bidder(s) at an amount equal to the third-highest bid (out of four total bids), while the Vickrey auction awards the items to the winning bidder(s) for amounts equal to the bids that they displaced from winning.

List and Lucking-Reiley find that, as predicted by the theory of demand reduction, the second-unit bids submitted by each bidder were lower in the uniform-price treatment than in the Vickrey treatment. The first-unit bids were predicted to be equal across treatments, but in the experiment they find that the first-unit bids were anomalously higher in the uniform-price treatment. Subsequent laboratory experiments (see, for example, Engelmann and Grimm, 2003; Porter and Vragov, 2003), have confirmed this finding.

Finally, Karlan and List (2007) is an example of a natural field experiment designed to measure key parameters of a theory. In their study, they explore the effects of 'price' changes on charitable giving by soliciting contributions from more than 50,000 supporters of a liberal organization. They randomize subjects into several different groups to explore whether solicitees respond to upfront monies used as matching funds. They find that simply announcing that a match is available considerably increases the revenue per solicitation – by 19 per cent. In addition, the match offer significantly increases the probability that an individual donates – by 22 per cent. Yet, while the match treatments relative to a control group increase the probability of donating, larger match ratios – 3:1 dollars (that is, 3 dollars match for every 1 dollar donated) and 2:1 dollar – relative to smaller match ratios (1:1 dollar) have no additional impact.

In closing, we believe that field experiments will continue to grow in popularity as scholars continue to take advantage of the settings where economic phenomena present themselves. This growth will lead to fruitful avenues, both theoretical and empirical, but it is clear that regardless of the increase in popularity, the various empirical approaches should be thought of as strong complements, and combining insights from each of the methodologies will permit economists to develop a deeper understanding of our science.

JOHN A. LIST AND DAVID REILEY

Bibliography

Anderson, E.T. and Simester, D. 2003. Effects of $9 price endings on retail sales: evidence from field experiments. *Quantitative Marketing and Economics* 1, 93–110.

Bohm, P. 1972. Estimating the demand for public goods: an experiment. *European Economic Review* 3, 111–30.

Engelmann, D. and Grimm, V. 2003. Bidding behavior in multi-unit auctions—an experimental investigation and some theoretical insights. Working paper, Centre for Economic Research and Graduate Education, Economic Institute, Prague.

Harrison, G.W. and List, J.A. 2004. Field experiments. *Journal of Economic Literature* 42, 1009–55.

Karlan, D. and List, J.A. 2007. Does price matter in charitable giving? Evidence from a large-scale natural field experiment. *American Economic Review*, forthcoming.

Levitt, S.D. and List, J.A. 2006. What do laboratory experiments measuring social preferences tell us about the real world? *Journal of Economic Perspectives* 21(2), 153–74.

List, J.A. 2006. Field experiments: a bridge between lab and naturally occurring data. *Advances in Economic Analysis & Policy* 6(2), Article 8. Abstract online. Available at: http://www.bepress.com/bejeap/advances/vol6/iss2/art8, accessed 26 May 2007.

List, J.A. and Lucking-Reiley, D. 2000. Demand reduction in a multi-unit auction: evidence from a sportscard field experiment. *American Economic Review* 90, 961–72.

Lucking-Reiley, D. 1999. Using field experiments to test equivalence between auction formats: magic on the Internet. *American Economic Review* 89, 1063–80.

Orne, M.T. 1962. On the social psychological experiment: with particular reference to demand characteristics and their implications. *American Psychologist* 17, 776–83.

Porter, D. and Vragov, R. 2003. An experimental examination of demand reduction in multi-unit versions of the uniform-price, Vickrey, and English auctions. Working paper, Interdisciplinary Center for Economic Science, George Mason University.

Vickrey, W. 1961. Counterspeculation, auctions, and competitive sealed tenders. *Journal of Finance* 16, 8–37.

fixed effects and random effects

One of the major benefits from using panel data as compared to cross-section data on individuals is that it enables us to control for individual heterogeneity. Not controlling for these unobserved individual specific effects leads to bias in the resulting estimates. Consider the panel data regression

$$y_{it} = \alpha + X'_{it}\beta + u_{it} \qquad i = 1, \ldots, N; \quad t = 1, \ldots, T \qquad (1)$$

with i denoting individuals and t denoting time. The panel data is *balanced* in that none of the observations is missing whether randomly or non-randomly due to attrition or sample selection. α is a scalar, β is $K \times 1$ and X_{it} is the itth observation on K explanatory variables. Most panel data applications utilize a one-way error component model for the disturbances, with

$$u_{it} = \mu_i + v_{it} \qquad (2)$$

where μ_i denotes the *unobservable* individual specific effect and v_{it} denotes the remainder disturbance. For example, in an earnings equation in labour economics, y_{it} will measure earnings of the head of the household, whereas X_{it} may contain a set of variables like experience, education, union membership, sex, or race. Note that μ_i is time-invariant and it accounts for any individual specific effect that is not included in the regression. In this case we could think of it as the individual's unobserved ability. The remainder disturbance v_{it} varies with individuals and time and can be thought of as the usual disturbance in the regression. If the μ_i's are assumed to be *fixed parameters* to be estimated, we get the *fixed effects (FE) model*. If the μ_i's are assumed random variables independent of X_{it} and v_{it}, for all i and t, we get the *random effects (RE) model*.

For the fixed effects model, the regression equation in (1) becomes

$$y_{it} = \alpha + X'_{it}\beta + \mu_i + v_{it} \qquad (3)$$

where the μ_i's can be estimated as coefficients of dummy variables, one for each individual. This model is also known as the least squares dummy variables (LSDV) model. Note that only $(\alpha + \mu_i)$ is estimable and that is why it is sometimes denoted by α_i. For large labour or consumer panels, where N is very large, LSDV regressions like (3) may not be feasible. In this case, one is including $(N-1)$ dummy variables in the regression and therefore inverting a huge matrix of dimension $(N+K)$ rather than $(K+1)$ as in (1). In addition, this FE regression suffers from a large loss of degrees of freedom, since we are estimating $(N-1)$ extra parameters, and too many dummies may aggravate the problem of multicollinearity among the regressors. In particular, this FE estimator cannot estimate the effect of any time-invariant variable like gender, race, religion which may be of prime interest for the researcher especially in attempting to estimate wage differentials among men and women or whites and non-whites, with other factors held constant. In fact, these time-invariant variables are spanned by the individual dummies in (3) and therefore any OLS regression attempting to estimate (3) will fail, signalling perfect multicollinearity. Averaging (3) over time yields

$$\bar{y}_{i.} = \alpha + \bar{X}'_{i.}\beta + \mu_i + \bar{v}_{i.} \tag{4}$$

Subtracting (4) from (3) gives

$$y_{it} - \bar{y}_{i.} = (X_{it} - \bar{X}_{i.})'\beta + (v_{it} - \bar{v}_{i.}). \tag{5}$$

One can show that the FE estimator of β (denoted by $\tilde{\beta}_{FE}$) obtained from the sometimes infeasible LSDV regression in (3) can be alternatively obtained from the simpler regression given in (5). The latter regression is known as the *within*-regression since it is based on the within variation in the data. Regression (4), which is a cross-section regression, is known as the *between*-regression since it is based on the between variation in the data. If (3) is the true model, FE is the best linear unbiased estimator (BLUE) as long as the remainder disturbances (the v_{it}'s) are independent and identically distributed (i.i.d.)$(0, \sigma_v^2)$. Of course, here we are assuming that the X_{it}'s are independent of the v_{it} for all i and t. The fixed effects model is deemed appropriate when one is focusing on a specific set of N countries, states, counties, regions or firms. Inference in this case is conditional on the particular N firms, countries or states that are observed. Note that, if T is fixed and $N \to \infty$ as typical in short labour panels, then only the FE estimator of β is consistent; the FE estimators of the individual effects (α_i) are not consistent since the number of these parameters increases as N increases. This is the *incidental parameter problem* discussed by Neyman and Scott (1948) and reviewed more recently by Lancaster (2000). Note that, when the true model is fixed effects as in (3), pooled OLS on (1) yields biased and inconsistent estimates of the regression parameters. This is an omission variables bias because OLS deletes the individual dummies when in fact they are relevant. One could test the joint significance of these dummies, that is, $H_0; \mu_1 = \mu_2 = \cdots = \mu_{N-1} = 0$, by performing an F-test. This is a simple Chow test with the restricted residual sums of squares (RRSS) being that of OLS on the pooled model and the unrestricted residual sums of squares (URSS) being that of the LSDV regression in (3) or equivalently the residual sum of squares from the within-regression in (5). In this case

$$F_0 = \frac{(RRSS - URSS)/(N-1)}{URSS/(NT-N-K)} \overset{H_0}{\sim} F_{N-1,N(T-1)-K}. \tag{6}$$

One computational caution for those using the within-regression computed from (5). The s^2 of this regression as obtained from a typical regression package divides the residual sums of squares by $NT - K$ since the intercept and the dummies are not included. The proper s^2, say s^{*2} from the LSDV regression in (3), would divide the same residual sums of squares by $N(T-1) - K$. Therefore, one has to adjust the variances obtained from the within-regression by multiplying the variance-covariance matrix by (s^{*2}/s^2) or simply by multiplying by $[NT - K]/[N(T - 1) - K]$. For robust estimates of the standard errors for the FE model, see Arellano (1987).

For the random effects model, $\mu_i \sim \text{IID}(0, \sigma_\mu^2)$, $v_{it} \sim \text{IID}(0, \sigma_v^2)$ and the μ_i's are independent of the v_{it}'s. In addition, the X_{it}'s are independent of the μ_i and v_{it}, for all i and t. The random effects model is an appropriate specification if we are drawing N individuals randomly from a large population, and we have no endogeneity between the regressors and the disturbances. For household panel studies, special attention is usually taken in the design of the panel to make it 'representative' of the population we are trying to make inferences about. In this case, N is usually large, and a fixed effects model would lead to an enormous loss of degrees of freedom. The individual effect is characterized as random, and inference pertains to the population from which this sample was randomly drawn. But what is the population in this case? Nerlove and Balestra (1992) emphasize Haavelmo's (1944) view that the population 'consists *not* of an infinity of individuals, in general, but of an infinity of *decisions*' that each individual might make. They argue that the fixed effects model may be more appropriate in cases where the population is sampled exhaustively (like data from geographic regions over time), whereas the random effects model is more consistent with Haavelmo's view given above. They argue that what differentiates individuals, who make the decisions with which we are concerned, is largely historical. Taking a leaf from Knight (1921), they argue that these inheritances from the past are material goods and appliances, knowledge and skill, and morale. In a dynamic context, this means that the primary reasons for heterogeneity among individuals is the different history each one has.

The random effects model implies a homoskedastic variance $\text{var}(u_{it}) = \sigma_\mu^2 + \sigma_v^2$ for all i and t, and an equi-correlated block-diagonal covariance matrix which exhibits serial correlation over time only between the disturbances of the same individual. In fact,

$$\text{cov}(u_{it}, u_{js}) = \sigma_\mu^2 + \sigma_v^2 \quad \text{for} \quad i = j, t = s$$
$$= \sigma_\mu^2 \quad \quad \text{for} \quad i = j, t \neq s$$

and zero otherwise. This also means that the correlation coefficient between u_{it} and u_{js} is

$$\rho = \text{correl}(u_{it}, u_{js}) = 1 \quad \quad \text{for} \quad i = j, t = s$$
$$= \sigma_\mu^2/(\sigma_\mu^2 + \sigma_v^2) \quad \quad \text{for} \quad i = j, t \neq s$$

and zero otherwise. In this case, the BLUE of the regression coefficients is GLS which can be obtained from a least squares regression of $y_{it}^* = y_{it} - \theta \bar{y}_{i.}$ on $X_{it}^* = X_{it} - \theta \bar{X}_{i.}$ and a constant (see Fuller and Battese, 1974). The GLS estimator of β for this random effects model will be denoted by $\hat{\beta}_{RE}$. Here $\theta = 1 - (\sigma_v/\sigma_1)$ and $\sigma_1^2 = T\sigma_\mu^2 + \sigma_v^2$. Note that (i) if $\sigma_\mu^2 = 0$ then $\theta = 0$ and $\hat{\beta}_{RE}$ reduces to $\hat{\beta}_{OLS}$ since y_{it}^* reduces to y_{it}; (ii) if $T \to \infty$, then $\theta \to 1$ and $\hat{\beta}_{RE}$ tends to $\hat{\beta}_{FE}$ since y_{it}^* reduces to $\tilde{y}_{it}$. The variance components can be estimated from the between- and within-variation of the disturbances:

$$\hat{\sigma}_1^2 = T \sum_{i=1}^{N} \hat{u}_{i.}^2 / (N - K - 1) \tag{7}$$

and

$$\hat{\sigma}_v^2 = \frac{\sum_{i=1}^{N} \sum_{t=1}^{T} \tilde{u}_{it}^2}{[N(T-1) - K]} \tag{8}$$

where $\hat{u}_{i.}$ denotes the between-residuals from (4). Note that (7) is T times the s^2 of the between-regression obtained in (4). Also, $\tilde{u}_{it}$ denotes the FE residuals from (5). So, (8) is the s^2 of the FE regression obtained in (5). Substituting these estimates for the variance components in θ and running y_{it}^* on X_{it}^* yields a feasible GLS or RE estimator suggested by Swamy and Arora (1972). For alternative estimators of the variance components, see Baltagi (2005). These are implemented using standard econometric software, including EViews, Stata, TSP, RATS and LIMDEP, to mention a few.

After this discussion of the fixed effects and the random effects models and the assumptions underlying them, the reader is left with the daunting question: which to choose? This is not as easy a choice as it might seem. In fact, the fixed versus random effects issue has generated a hot debate in the biometrics and statistics literature, which has spilled over into the panel data econometrics literature. Economists cannot perform natural experiments of, say, the effect of fertilizer brand on crop yield controlling for the effect of land and other inputs. We have to deal with human subjects whose individual effects may be correlated with the regressors even when we randomly draw these individuals. Mundlak (1961) and Wallace and Hussain (1969) were early proponents of the fixed effects model, and Balestra and Nerlove (1966) were advocates of the random effects model. The modern econometric interpretation of the μ_i's is that they are random variables but in the RE model the $E(\mu_i/X_{it}) = 0$. This implies that the individual effects are uncorrelated with the regressors. This is a strong assumption given economists preoccupation with endogeneity issues. For example, in an earnings equation, μ_i may denote the unobservable ability of the individual and this may be correlated with the schooling variable included as a regressor. In this case, $E(\mu_i/X_{it}) \neq 0$ and the RE estimator $\hat{\beta}_{RE}$ becomes biased and inconsistent for β. However, the within-transformation wipes out these μ_i's and leaves the FE estimator $\tilde{\beta}_{FE}$ unbiased and consistent for β. Hausman (1978) suggested comparing $\hat{\beta}_{RE}$ and $\tilde{\beta}_{FE}$, both of which are consistent under the null hypothesis H_0; $E(\mu_i/X_{it}) = 0$. In this case, the contrast $\hat{q} = \hat{\beta}_{RE} - \tilde{\beta}_{FE}$ will have plim $\hat{q} = 0$ under H_0. However, if H_0 is not true, plim $\hat{q} \neq 0$ and the Hausman test statistic is given by

$$m = \hat{q}'[\text{var}(\hat{q})]^{-1}\hat{q} \tag{9}$$

Under H_0 this is asymptotically distributed as χ_K^2 where K denotes the dimension of slope vector β. For significant values of m, we reject the consistency of the RE estimator. Since $\hat{\beta}_{RE}$ is the efficient estimator under the null hypothesis H_0, one can show that the $\text{cov}(\hat{q}, \hat{\beta}_{RE}) = 0$ and that the var $(\hat{q}) = \text{var}(\tilde{\beta}_{FE}) - \text{var}(\hat{\beta}_{RE})$. This makes the computation of (9) simple. Nevertheless, Hausman (1978) suggested an alternative asymptotically equivalent test to (9) that can be obtained from the augmented regression

$$y^* = X^*\beta + \widetilde{X}\gamma + w \tag{10}$$

where $y_{it}^* = y_{it} - \theta\bar{y}_{i.}$, $X_{it}^* = X_{it} - \theta\bar{X}_{i.}$ and $\widetilde{X}_{it} = X_{it} - \bar{X}_{i.}$. Hausman's test is now equivalent to testing whether $\gamma = 0$. This is a standard Wald test for the omission of the FE regressors $\widetilde{X}$ from the RE regression. For an alternative variable addition test that produces a Hausman test which is robust to autocorrelation and heteroskedasticity of arbitrary form, see Arellano (1993).

Note that the FE model allows for endogeneity of the regressors and the individual effects, whereas the RE model does not. This is why the FE model is more popular among economists. Mundlak (1978) assumed that the individual effects are a linear function of the averages of *all* the explanatory variables across time, that is,

$$\mu_i = \bar{X}_i'\pi + \varepsilon_i \tag{11}$$

where $\varepsilon_i \sim \text{IIN}(0, \sigma_\varepsilon^2)$ and $X_{i.}'$ is $1 \times K$ vector of observations on the explanatory variables averaged over time. These effects are uncorrelated with the explanatory variables if and only if $\pi = 0$. In fact, a test for $\pi = 0$ yields the Hausman (1978) test based on the contrast between the FE and the between-estimators. Mundlak (1978) shows that GLS on (3) augmented with (11) yields $\tilde{\beta}_{FE}$. Only if $\pi = 0$ does it yield $\hat{\beta}_{RE}$. This all-or-nothing choice of correlation between the individual effects and the regressors prompted Hausman and Taylor (1981) to suggest a model where *some* of the regressors are correlated with the individual effects. They proposed an instrumental variable estimator, denoted by HT, which uses both the between- and within-variation of the strictly exogenous variables as instruments. More specifically, the individual means of the strictly exogenous regressors are used as instruments for the time invariant regressors that are correlated with the individual effects (see Baltagi, 2005, for more details). The over-identification conditions are testable. In fact, this is a Hausman test based upon the contrast between the FE and the HT estimators.

Most applications in economics since the 1980s have made the choice between the RE and FE estimators based upon the standard Hausman test. If this standard Hausman test rejects the null hypothesis that the conditional mean of the disturbances given the regressors is zero, the applied researcher reports the FE estimator. Otherwise, the researcher reports the RE estimator. Unfortunately, applied researchers have interpreted a rejection as an adoption of the fixed effects model and non-rejection as an adoption of the random effects model. Chamberlain (1984) showed that the fixed effects model imposes testable restrictions on the parameters of the reduced form model and one should check the validity of these restrictions before adopting the fixed effects model (see also Angrist and Newey, 1991). For the applied researcher, performing fixed effects and random effects and the associated Hausman test, it is important to carry this analysis a step further. Test the restrictions implied by the fixed effects model derived by Chamberlain (1984) before accepting the FE estimator and check whether a Hausman and Taylor (1981) specification might be a viable alternative.

BADI H. BALTAGI

Bibliography

Angrist, J.D. and Newey, W.K. 1991. Over-identification tests in earnings functions with fixed effects. *Journal of Business and Economic Statistics* 9, 317–23.

Arellano, M. 1987. Computing robust standard errors for within-groups estimators. *Oxford Bulletin of Economics and Statistics* 49, 431–4.

Arellano, M. 1993. On the testing of correlated effects with panel data. *Journal of Econometrics* 59, 87–97.

Balestra, P. and Nerlove, M. 1966. Pooling cross-section and time-series data in the estimation of a dynamic model: the demand for natural gas. *Econometrica* 34, 585–612.

Baltagi, B.H. 2005. *Econometric Analysis of Panel Data*. Chichester: Wiley.

Chamberlain, G. 1984. Panel data. In *Handbook of Econometrics*, ed. Z. Griliches and M. Intriligator. Amsterdam: North-Holland.

Fuller, W.A. and Battese, G.E. 1974. Estimation of linear models with cross-error structure. *Journal of Econometrics* 2, 67–78.

Haavelmo, T. 1944. The probability approach in econometrics. *Econometrica* 12(Supplement), 1–118.

Hausman, J.A. 1978. Specification tests in econometrics. *Econometrica* 46, 1251–71.

Hausman, J.A. and Taylor, W.E. 1981. Panel data and unobservable individual effects. *Econometrica* 49, 1377–98.

Knight, F.H. 1921. *Risk, Uncertainty and Profit*. Boston: Houghton Mifflin.

Lancaster, T. 2000. The incidental parameter problem since 1948. *Journal of Econometrics* 95, 391–413.

Mundlak, Y. 1961. Empirical production function free of management bias. *Journal of Farm Economics* 43, 44–56.

Mundlak, Y. 1978. On the pooling of time series and cross-section data. *Econometrica* 46, 69–85.

Nerlove, M. and Balestra, P. 1992. Formulation and estimation of econometric models for panel data. In *The Econometrics of Panel Data: Handbook of Theory and Applications*, ed. L. Matyas and P. Sevestre. Dordrecht: Kluwer.

Neyman, J. and Scott, E.L. 1948. Consistent estimation from partially consistent observations. *Econometrica* 16, 1–32.

Swamy, P.A.V.B. and Arora, S.S. 1972. The exact finite sample properties of the estimators of coefficients in the error components regression models. *Econometrica* 40, 261–75.

Wallace, T.D. and Hussain, A. 1969. The use of error components models in combining cross-section and time-series data. *Econometrica* 37, 55–72.

identification

In economic analysis, we often assume that there exists an underlying structure which has generated the observations of real-world data. However, statistical inference can relate only to characteristics of the distribution of the observed variables. Statistical models which are used to explain the behaviour of observed data typically involve parameters, and statistical inference aims at making statements about these parameters. For that purpose, it is important that different values of a parameter of interest can be characterized in terms of the data distribution. Otherwise, the problem of drawing inferences about this parameter is plagued by a fundamental indeterminacy and can be viewed as 'ill-posed'.

To illustrate, consider X as being normally distributed with mean $E(X) = \mu_1 - \mu_2$. Then $\mu_1 - \mu_2$ can be estimated using observed X. But the parameters μ_1 and μ_2 are not uniquely estimable. In fact, one can think of an infinite number of pairs $(\mu_i, \mu_j), \; j = 1, 2, \ldots (i \neq j)$ such that $\mu_i - \mu_j = \mu_1 - \mu_2$. In order to determine μ_1 and μ_2 uniquely, we need additional prior information, such as $\mu_2 = 3\mu_1$ or some other assumption. Note, however, that inference about the variance of X remains feasible without extra assumptions.

More generally, *identification failures* – or situations that are close to it – complicate considerably the statistical analysis of models, so that tracking such failures and formulating restrictions to avoid them is an important problem of econometric modelling.

The problem of whether it is possible to draw inferences from the probability distribution of the observed variables to an underlying theoretical structure is the concern of econometric literature on identification. The first economists to raise this issue were Working (1925; 1927) and Wright (1915; 1928). The general formulations of the identification problems were made by Frisch (1934), Marschak (1942), Haavelmo (1944), Hurwicz (1950), Koopmans and Reiersøl (1950), Koopmans, Rubin and Leipnik (1950), Wald (1950), and many others. An extensive treatment of the theory of identification in simultaneous equation systems was provided by Fisher (1976). Surveys of the subject can be found in Hsiao (1983), Prakasa Rao (1992), Bekker and Wansbeek (2001), Manski (2003), and Matzkin (2007); see also Morgan (1990) and Stock and Trebbi (2003) on the early development of the subject.

In this article, we first define the notion of identification in general parametric models (Sections 1 and 2) and discuss its meaning in a number of specific statistical models used in econometrics, such as regression models (collinearity), simultaneous equations, dynamic models, and nonlinear models (Section 3). Identification in nonparametric models (Sections 4 and 5), weak identification (Section 6), and the statistical implications of identification failure (Section 7) are also considered.

1. Definition of parametric identification

It is generally assumed in econometrics that economic variables whose formation an economic theory is designed to explain have the characteristics of random variables. Let y be a set of such observations. A structure S is a complete specification of the probability distribution function of y. The set of all a priori possible structures, T, is called a model. In most applications, y is assumed to be generated by a parametric probability distribution function $F(y, \theta)$, where the probability distribution function F is assumed known, but the $q \times 1$ parameter vector θ is unknown. Hence, a structure is described by a parametric point θ, and a model is a set of points $A \subseteq \mathbb{R}^q$.

Definition 1 *Two structures, $S^0 = F(y, \theta^0)$ and $S^* = F(y, \theta^*)$ are said to be observationally equivalent if $F(y, \theta^0) = F(y, 0^*)$ for ('almost') all possible y. A model is identifiable if A contains no two distinct structures which are observationally equivalent. A function of θ, $g(\theta)$, is identifiable if all observationally equivalent structures have the same value for $g(\theta)$.*

Sometimes a weaker concept of identifiability is useful.

Definition 2 *A structure with parameter value θ^0 is said to be locally identified if there exists an open neighborhood of θ^0, W, such that no other θ in W is observationally equivalent to θ^0.*

2. General results for identification in parametric models

Lack of identification reflects the fact that a random variable has the same distribution for some if not all values of the parameter. R.A. Fisher's information matrix provides a sensitivity measure of the distribution of a random variable due to small changes in the value of the parameter point (Rao, 1962). It can therefore be shown that, subject to regularity conditions, θ^0 is locally identified if and only if the information matrix evaluated at θ^0 is nonsingular (Rothenberg, 1971).

It is clear that unidentified parameters cannot be consistently estimated. There are also pathological cases where identified models fail to possess consistent estimators (for example, Gabrielson, 1978). However, in most practical cases, we may treat identifiability and the existence of a consistent estimator as equivalent; for precise conditions, see Le Cam (1956) and Deistler and Seifert (1978).

3. Some specific parametric models

The choice of model structure is one of the basic ingredients in the formulation of the identification problem. In this section we briefly discuss some identification conditions for different types of models in order to demonstrate the kind of prior restrictions required.

3.1 Linear regression with collinearity

One of the most common models where an identification problem does occur is the linear regression model:

$$\mathbf{y} = X\beta + \mathbf{u} \tag{1}$$

where $\mathbf{y}$ is an $n \times 1$ vector of dependent observable variables, X is an $n \times k$ fixed matrix of observable variables, β a $k \times 1$ unknown coefficient vector, and $\mathbf{u}$ is an $n \times 1$ vector of disturbances whose components are (say) independent and identically distributed according to a normal distribution $N(0, \sigma^2)$ with unknown positive variance σ^2.

In this model, the value of β must be determined from the expected value of $\mathbf{y} : E(\mathbf{y}) = X\beta$. If the latter equation has a solution for β (that is, if the model is correct), the solution is unique if and only the regressor matrix X has rank k. If X has rank zero (which entails $X = 0$), all values of β are equivalent (β is completely *unidentifiable*). If $1 \leq \text{rank}(X) < k$, then not all the components can be determined, but some linear combinations of the components of β (say $c'\beta$) can be determined (that is, they are *identifiable*). A necessary and sufficient condition for $c'\beta$ to be estimable (identifiable) is that $c = (X'X)d$ for some vector d. Linear combinations that do not satisfy this condition are not identifiable. The typical way out of such collinearity problems consists in imposing restrictions on β (identifying restrictions) which set the values of the unidentifiable linear combinations (or components) of β.

Correspondingly, when X does not have full rank, the equation $(X'X)\hat{\beta} = X'\mathbf{y}$, which defines the least squares estimator $\hat{\beta}$, does not have a unique solution. But all solutions of the least squares problem can be determined by considering $\hat{\beta} = (X'X)^- X'\mathbf{y}$ where $(X'X)^-$ is any generalized inverse of $(X'X)$. Different generalized inverses then correspond to different identifying restrictions on β. For further discussion, see Rao (1973, ch. 4).

3.2 Linear simultaneous equations models
Consider a theory which predicts a relationship among the variables as

$$B\mathbf{y}_t + \Gamma\mathbf{x}_t = \mathbf{u}_t, t = 1, \ldots, n, \tag{2}$$

where $\mathbf{y}_t$ and $\mathbf{u}_t$ are $G \times 1$ vectors of observed and unobserved random variables, respectively, $\mathbf{x}_t$ is a $K \times 1$ vector of observed non-stochastic variables, B and Γ are $G \times G$ and $G \times K$ matrices of coefficients, with B nonsingular. We assume that the $\mathbf{u}_t$ are independently normally distributed with mean 0 and variance-covariance matrix Σ. Equations (2) are called structural equations. Solving for the endogenous variables, $\mathbf{y}$, as a function of the exogenous variables, $\mathbf{x}$, and the disturbance u, we obtain:

$$\mathbf{y}_t = -B^{-1}\Gamma\mathbf{x}_t + B^{-1}\mathbf{u}_t = \Pi\mathbf{x}_t + \mathbf{v}_t, \tag{3}$$

where $\Pi = -B^{-1}\Gamma$, $E\mathbf{v}_t = 0$, $E\mathbf{v}_t\mathbf{v}_t' = V = B^{-1}\sum(B^{-1})'$. Equations (3) are called the *reduced form* equations derived from (2) and give the conditional likelihood of $\mathbf{y}_t$ for given $\mathbf{x}_t$ that summaries the information provided by the observed $(\mathbf{y}_t, \mathbf{x}_t)$. The variables in $\mathbf{x}_t$ are often also called 'instruments'.

From (3), we see that the simultaneous equations model can be viewed as a special case of a multivariate regression model (MLR), such that the regression coefficient matrix Π satisfies the equation:

$$B\Pi = -\Gamma. \tag{4}$$

Provided the matrix $X = [x_1, \ldots, x_n]'$ has full rank K (no collinearity), the regression coefficient matrix Π is uniquely determined by the distribution of $Y = [y_1, \ldots, y_n]'$ (it is *identifiable*). The problem is then whether B and Γ can be uniquely derived from eq. (4). Premultiplying (2) by a $G \times G$ nonsingular matrix D, we get a second structural equation:

$$B^* y_t + \Gamma^* x_t = u_t^*, \tag{5}$$

where $B^* = DB$, $\Gamma^* = D\Gamma$, and $u_t^* = Du$. It is readily seen that the reduced form of (5) is also (3). So eq. (4) cannot be uniquely solved for B and Γ, given Π. Therefore, the two structures are observationally equivalent and the model is *non-identifiable*.

To make the model identifiable, additional prior restrictions have to be imposed on the matrices B, Γ and/or Σ. Consider the problem of estimating the parameters of the first equation in (2), out of a system of G equations. If the parameters cannot be estimated, the first equation is called *unidentified* or *underidentified*. If given the prior information, there is a unique way of estimating the unknown parameters, the equation is called *just identified*. If the prior information allows the parameters to be estimated in two or more linearly independent ways, it is called *overidentified*. A necessary condition for the first equation to be identified is that the number of restrictions on this equation be no less than $G - 1$ (order condition). A necessary and sufficient condition is that a specified submatrix of B, Γ and Σ be of rank $G - 1$ (rank condition) (see Fisher, 1976; Hausman and Taylor, 1983). For instance, suppose the restrictions on the first equation are in the form that certain variables do not appear. Then this rank condition says that the first equation is identified if and only if the submatrix obtained by taking the columns of B and Γ with prescribed zeros in the first row is of rank $G - 1$ (Koopmans and Reiersøl, 1950).

3.3 Dynamic models

When both lagged endogenous variables and serial correlation in the disturbance term appear, we need to impose additional conditions to identify a model. For instance, consider the following two equation system (Koopmans, Rubin and Leipnik, 1950):

$$y_{1t} + \beta_{11} y_{1,t-1} + \beta_{12} y_{2,t-1} = u_{1t}, \beta_{12} y_{1t} + y_{2t} = u_{2t}. \tag{6}$$

If (u_{1t}, u_{2t}) are serially uncorrelated, (6) is identified. If serial correlation in (u_{1t}, u_{2t}) is allowed, then

$$y_{1t} + \beta_{11}^* y_{1,t-1} + \beta_{12}^* y_{2,t-1} = u_{1t}^*,$$
$$\beta_{12} y_{1t} + y_{2t} = u_{2t}, \tag{7}$$

is observationally equivalent to (6), where $\beta_{11}^* = \beta_{11} + d\beta_{21}$, $\beta_{12}^* = \beta_{12} + d$, and $u_{1t}^* = u_{1t} + du_{2t}$.

Hannan (1971) derives generalized rank conditions for the identification of this type of model by first assuming that the maximum orders of lagged endogenous and exogenous variables are known, then imposing restrictions to eliminate redundancy in the specification and to exclude transformations of the equations that involve shifts in time. Hatanaka (1975), on the other hand, assumes that the prior information takes only the form of excluding certain variables from an equation, and derives a rank condition which allows common roots to appear in each equation.

3.4 Nonlinear models

For linear models, we have either global identification or else an infinite number of observationally equivalent structures. For models that are linear in parameters, but nonlinear in variables, there is a broad class of models whose members can commonly achieve identification (Brown, 1983; McManus, 1992). For models linear in the variables but nonlinear in the parameters, the state of the mathematical art is such that we only talk about local properties. That is, we cannot tell the true structure from any other substitute; however, we may be able to distinguish it from other structures which are close to it. A sufficient condition for local identification is that the Jacobian matrix formed by taking the first partial derivatives of

$$
\begin{aligned}
\omega_i &= \Psi_i(\theta), \quad i = 1, \ldots, n, \\
0 &= \varphi_j(\theta), \quad j = 1, \ldots, R,
\end{aligned}
\tag{8}
$$

with respect to θ be of full column rank, where the ω_i are n population moments of y and the φ_j are the R a priori restrictions on θ (Fisher, 1976).

When the Jacobian matrix of (8) has less than full column rank, the model may still be locally identifiable via conditions implied by the higher-order derivatives. However, the estimator of a model suffering from first-order lack of identification will in finite samples behave in a way which is difficult to distinguish from the behaviour of an unidentified model (Sargan, 1983).

3.5 Bayesian analysis

In Bayesian analysis all quantities, including the parameters, are random variables. Thus, a model is said to be identified in probability if the posterior distribution for θ is proper. When the prior distribution for θ is proper, so is the posterior, regardless of the likelihood function of y. In this sense unidentifiability causes no real difficulty in the Bayesian approach. However, basic to the Bayesian argument is that all probability statements are conditional, that is, they consist essentially in revising the probability of a fixed event in the light of various conditioning events, the revision being accomplished by Bayes' theorem. Therefore, in order for an experiment to be informative with regard to unknown parameters (that is, for the posterior to be different from the prior), the parameter must be identified or estimable in the classical sense and identification remains as a property of the likelihood function (Kadane, 1975).

Drèze (1975) has commented that exact restrictions are unlikely to hold with probability 1 and has suggested using probabilistic prior information. In order to incorporate a stochastic prior, he has derived necessary rank conditions for the identification of a linear simultaneous equation model.

4. Definition of identification in nonparametric models

When the restrictions of an economic model specify all functions and distributions up to the value of a finite dimensional vector, the model is said to be parametric. When some functions or distributions are left parametrically unspecified, the model is said to be semiparametric. The model is nonparametric if none of the functions and distributions are specified parametrically. The previous discussion is based on parametric specification. We now turn to the issue of whether economic restrictions such as concavity, continuity and monotonicity of functions, equilibrium conditions, the implications of optimization, and so on, may be used to guarantee the identification of some nonparametric models and the consistency of some nonparametric estimators (see Matzkin 1994).

Formally, an econometric model is specified by a vector of observable dependent and independent variables, a vector of unobservable variables, and a set of known functional relationships among the variables. When such functional relationships are unspecified, the nonparametric identification studies what functions or features of function can be recovered from the joint distribution of the observable variables.

The set of restrictions on the unknown functions and distributions in an econometric model defines the set of functions and distributions to which these belong. Let the model T denote the set of all a priori possible unknown functions and distributions. Let m denote a vector of the unknown functions and distributions in T and $P(m)$ denote the joint distribution of the observable variables under m. Then the identification of m can be defined as follows.

Definition 3 *The vector of functions m is identified in T if for any other vector, $m^* \in T$ such that $m \neq m^*$, $P(m) \neq P(m^*)$.*

Let $C(m)$ denote some feature of m, such as the sign of some coordinate of m.

Definition 4 *The feature C(m) of m is identified if $C(m) = C(m^*)$ for all m, $m^* \in T$ such that $P(m) = P(m^*)$.*

5. Examples of nonparametric identification

Contrary to the parametric model, there is no general result for nonparametric identification. We shall therefore give some examples of how restrictions can be used to identify nonparametric functions.

5.1 Generalized regression models

Economists often consider a model of the form

$$y = g(\mathbf{x}) + u. \tag{9}$$

When $E(u|\mathbf{x}) = 0$ and $g(\cdot)$ is a continuous function $g : \mathbf{x} \to \mathbb{R}$, then $g(\cdot)$ can be recovered from the joint distribution of $(y, \mathbf{x})$ because $E(y|\mathbf{x}) = g(\mathbf{x})$.

In some cases, the object of interest is not a conditional mean function $g(\cdot)$, but some 'deeper' function, such as a utility function generating the distribution of demand for commodities by a consumer. For example, $\mathbf{x}$ in (9) can be a price vector for K commodities and the income of a consumer. Mas-Colell (1977) has shown that we can recover the underlying utility function from the distribution of demand if we restrict $g(\cdot)$ to be monotone increasing, continuous, concave and strictly quasi-concave functions.

5.2 Simultaneous equations models
Suppose $(\mathbf{y}, \mathbf{x})$ satisfies the structural equations

$$\mathbf{r}(\mathbf{x}, \mathbf{y}) = \mathbf{u}, \tag{10}$$

where $\mathbf{y}$ and $\mathbf{u}$ denote $G \times 1$ vectors of observable endogenous and unobservable variables, respectively, $\mathbf{x}$ is a $K \times 1$ vector of observable exogenous variables, $\mathbf{r}$ denotes the G unknown functions, and let $p(\mathbf{r})$ and $p(\mathbf{r}^*)$ represent the joint distributions of the observables under $\mathbf{r}$ and $\mathbf{r}^*$ respectively. Assume also that: (i) $\forall (\mathbf{x}, \mathbf{y})$, $\partial \mathbf{r}/\partial \mathbf{y}$ has full rank, (ii) there exists a function $\pi(\cdot)$ such that $y = \pi(\mathbf{x}, \mathbf{u})$ (for conditions ensuring this, see Benkard and Berry, 2006), and (iii) $\mathbf{u}$ is distributed independently of $\mathbf{x}$. Then a necessary and sufficient condition guaranteeing that $p(\mathbf{r}^*) = p(\mathbf{r})$ is that

$$\text{rank} \begin{pmatrix} \frac{\partial r_i^*}{\partial(\mathbf{x},\mathbf{y})} \\ \frac{\partial r}{\partial(\mathbf{x},\mathbf{y})} \end{pmatrix} < G + 1, \tag{11}$$

for all $(\mathbf{x}, \mathbf{y})$ and $i = 1, \ldots, G$, and all, where r_i^* denotes the i-th coordinate function of $\mathbf{r}^* \in T$ (see Roehrig, 1988; Matzkin, 2007).

5.3 Latent variable models and the measurement of treatment effects
For each person i, let (y_{0i}^*, y_{1i}^*) denote the potential outcomes in the untreated and treated states, respectively. Then the treatment effect for individual i is

$$\Delta_i = y_{1i}^* - y_{0i}^*$$

and the average treatment effect (ATE) is defined as

$$E(\Delta_i) = E(y_{1i}^* - y_{0i}^*); \tag{12}$$

see Heckman and Vytlacil (2001).

Let the treatment status be denoted by the dummy variable d_i where $d_i = 1$ denotes the receipt of treatment and $d_i = 0$ denotes nonreceipt. The observed data are often in the form

$$y_i = d_i y_{1i}^* + (1 - d_i) y_{0i}^*. \tag{13}$$

Suppose $y_{1i}^* = \mu_1(\mathbf{x}_i, u_{1i})$, $y_{0i}^* = \mu_0(\mathbf{x}_i, u_{0i})$, and $d_i^* = \mu_D(\mathbf{z}_i) - u_{di}$, where $d_i = 1$ if $d_i^* \geq 0$ and 0 otherwise, $\mathbf{x}_i$ and $\mathbf{z}_i$ are vectors of observable exogenous variables and (u_{1i}, u_{0i}, u_{di}) are unobserved random variables. The average treatment effect and the complete structural econometric model can be identified with parametric specifications of $(\mu_1(\cdot), \mu_0(\cdot), \mu_D(\cdot))$ and the joint distributions of (u_{1i}, u_{0i}, u_{di}) even though we do not simultaneously observe y_{1i}^* and y_{0i}^*. In the case that neither $(\mu_1(\cdot), \mu_0(\cdot), \mu_D(\cdot))$ nor the joint distribution of (u_1, u_0, u_d) are specified, certain treatment effects may still be nonparametrically identified under weaker assumptions. For instance, under the assumption that d_i is orthogonal to (y_{1i}^*, y_{0i}^*) conditional on a set of confounders (x, z) (conditional independence or ignorable selection), the ATE is identifiable and estimable by comparing the difference of the average outcomes from the treatment group and from the untreated (control) group (Heckman and Robb, 1985; Rosenbaum and Rubin, 1985). If the focus is on the average treatment effect for someone who would not participate if $p(\mathbf{z}) \leq p(\mathbf{z}_0)$ and would participate if $p(\mathbf{z}) > p(\mathbf{z}_0)$ (the local average treatment effect (LATE)), where $p(\mathbf{z}) = \text{Prob}(d = 1|\mathbf{z})$ (propensity score), Imbens and Angrist (1994) show that under the assumptions of separability of the effects of observable factors and unobservable factors and independence between observed factors and unobserved factors, they can be estimated by the sample analogue of

$$\Delta^{LATE}(\mathbf{x}, p(\mathbf{z}), p(\mathbf{z}_0)) \equiv \frac{E(y|\mathbf{x}, p(\mathbf{z})) - E(y|\mathbf{x}, p(\mathbf{z}_0))}{p(\mathbf{z}) - p(\mathbf{z}_0)} \tag{14}$$

where, without loss of generality, we assume $p(\mathbf{z}) > p(\mathbf{z}_0)$. The limit of LATE provides the local instrumental variable (LIV) estimand (Heckman and Vytlacil, 1999):

$$\Delta^{LIV}(\mathbf{x}, p(\mathbf{z})) \equiv \frac{\partial E(y|\mathbf{x}, p(\mathbf{z}))}{\partial p(\mathbf{z})}. \tag{15}$$

Heckman and Vytlacil (2001) give conditions that suitably weighted versions of LIV identify the ATE.

6. Weak instruments and weak identification

The most common way of trying to achieve identification consists in imposing exclusion restrictions on the variables of a structural equation. In model (2), suppose that $\mathbf{y}_t$ and $\mathbf{x}_t$ are partitioned as $\mathbf{y}_t = (y_{1t}, \mathbf{y}_{2t}', \mathbf{y}_{3t}')'$ and $\mathbf{x}_t = (\mathbf{x}_{1t}', \mathbf{x}_{2t}')'$ where y_{1t} is a scalar, $\mathbf{y}_{it}$ has dimension $G_i (i = 2, 3)$ and $\mathbf{x}_{it}$ has dimension $K_i (i = 1, 2)$. If $\mathbf{y}_{3t}$ and $\mathbf{x}_{2t}$ are excluded from the first equation and the coefficient of y_{1t} is normalized to one, this yields an equation of the form:

$$y_{1t} - \mathbf{y}_{2t}'\beta_1 = \mathbf{x}_{1t}'\gamma_1 + u_{1t}, \quad t = 1, \dots, n. \tag{16}$$

Let us also rewrite the reduced equation for $\mathbf{y}_{2t}$ in terms of $\mathbf{x}_{1t}$ and $\mathbf{x}_{2t}$:

$$\mathbf{y}_{2t} = \Pi_{21}\mathbf{x}_{1t} + \Pi_{22}\mathbf{x}_{2t} + \mathbf{v}_{2t}. \tag{17}$$

Then, substituting (17) into (16), we see that the reduced form for y_{1t} is:

$$y_{1t} = \Pi_{11}\mathbf{x}_{1t} + \Pi_{12}\mathbf{x}_{2t} + \mathbf{v}_{1t}, \tag{18}$$

where $\mathbf{v}_{1t} = u_{1t} + \mathbf{v}_{2t}'\beta_1$, $\quad \Pi_{11} = \gamma_1' + \beta_1'\Pi_{21}$ and

$$\Pi_{12}' = \Pi_{22}'\beta_1. \tag{19}$$

Since γ_1 is free, Π_{11} is not restricted, but eq. (19) determines the identifiability of β_1, hence also of γ_1. Provided eq. (19) has a solution (that is, if eq. (16) is consistent with the data), the solution is unique if and only if the rank of the $G_2 \times K_2$ matrix Π_{22} is equal to G_2, the dimension of β_1:

$$\text{rank}(\Pi_{22}) = G_2. \tag{20}$$

If $\text{rank}(\Pi_{22}) < G_2$, the vector β_1 is not identifiable. However, it is completely unidentifiable only if $\text{rank}(\Pi_{22}) = 0$, or equivalently if $\Pi_{22} = 0$. If $1 < \text{rank}(\Pi_{22}) < G_2$, some linear combinations $c'\beta_1$ are identifiable, but not all of them. Failure of the identification condition means that the regressors (or the 'instruments') $\mathbf{x}_{2t}$ do not move enough to separate the effects of the different variables in $\mathbf{y}_{2t}$. Condition (20) underscores two important things: first, exclusion and normalization restrictions – which are easy to check – are not sufficient to ensure identification; second, identification depends on the way the exogenous variables $\mathbf{x}_{2t}$ excluded from the structural equation of interest (16) are related to endogenous variables $\mathbf{y}_{2t}$ included in the equation. The latter feature is determined by the matrix Π_{22} whose rows should be linearly independent. Since Π_{22} is not observable, this may be difficult to determine in practice.

A situation that can lead to identification difficulties is the one where the identification condition (20) indeed holds, but, in some sense, Π_{22} is 'close' not to have sufficient rank. In such situations, we say that we have *weak instruments*. In view of the fact that the distributions of most statistics move continuously as functions of Π_{22}, the practical consequences of being close to identification failure are essentially the same. Assessing the closeness to non-identification may be done in various ways, for example by considering the eigenvalues of the matrices which measure the 'size' of Π_{22}, such as $\Pi_{22}\Pi_{22}'$, $\Pi_{22}X_2'M(X_1)X_2\Pi_{22}'$ or a *concentration matrix* $\Sigma_{22}^{-1/2}\Pi_{22}X_2'M(X_1)X_2\Pi_{22}'\Sigma_{22}^{-1/2}$ where $X_1 = [\mathbf{x}_{11}, \ldots, \mathbf{x}_{1n}]'$, $X_2 = [\mathbf{x}_{21}, \ldots, \mathbf{x}_{2n}]'$, Σ_{22} is the covariance matrix of $\mathbf{v}_{2t}$, $\Sigma_{22}^{-1/2}$ is its square root, and $M(X_1) = I_n - X_1(X_1'X_1)^{-1}X_1'$. More generally, any situation where a parameter may be difficult to determine because we are close to a case where a parameter ceases to be identifiable may be called *weak identification*. Weak identification was highlighted as a problem of practical interest by Nelson and Startz (1990), Bound, Jaeger and Baker (1995), Dufour (1997), and Staiger and Stock (1997); for reviews, see Stock, Wright and Yogo (2002) and Dufour (2003).

7. Statistical consequences of identification failure
Identification failure has several detrimental consequences for statistical analysis:

1. Parameter estimates, tests and confidence sets computed for unidentified parameters have no clear inpt; this situation may be especially misleading if the statistical instruments used do not reveal the presence of the problem.
2. Consistent estimation is not possible unless additional information is supplied.

3. Many standard distributional results used for inference on such models are not anymore valid, even with a large sample size (see Phillips, 1983; 1989; Rothenberg, 1984).

4. Numerical problems also easily appear, due for example to the need to invert (quasi) singular matrices.

Weak identification problems lead to similar difficulties, but may be more treacherous in the sense that standard asymptotic distributional may remain valid, but they constitute very bad approximations to what happens in finite samples:

1. Standard consistent estimators of structural parameters can be heavily biased and follow distributions whose form is far from the limiting Gaussian distribution, such as bimodal distributions, even with fairly large samples (Nelson and Startz, 1990; Hillier, 1990; Buse, 1992).

2. Standard tests and confidence sets, such as Wald-type procedures based on estimated standard errors, become highly unreliable or completely invalid (Dufour, 1997).

A striking illustration of these problems appears in the reconsideration by Bound, Jaeger and Baker (1995) of a study on returns to education by Angrist and Krueger (1991). Using 329,000 observations, these authors found that replacing the instruments used by Angrist and Krueger (1991) with randomly generated (totally irrelevant) instruments produced very similar point estimates and standard errors. This result indicates that the original instruments were weak. Recent work in this area is reviewed in Stock, Wright and Yogo (2002) and Dufour (2003).

8. Concluding remarks

The study of identifiability is undertaken in order to explore the limitations of statistical inference (when working with economic data) or to specify what sort of a priori information is needed to make a model estimable. It is a fundamental problem concomitant with the existence of a structure. Logically it precedes all problems of estimation or of testing hypotheses.

An important point that arises in the study of identification is that without a priori restrictions imposed by economic theory it would be almost impossible to estimate economic relationships. In fact, Liu (1960) and Sims (1980) have argued that economic relations are not identifiable because the world is so interdependent as to have almost all variables appearing in every equation, thus violating the necessary condition for identification. However, almost all the models we discuss in econometrics are only approximate. We use convenient formulations which behave in a general way that corresponds to our economic theories and intuitions, and which cannot be rejected by the available data. In this sense, identification is a property of the model but not necessarily of the real world. It is also important to be careful about situations where identification almost does not hold (weak identification), since these are in practice as damaging for statistical analysis as identification failure itself.

The problem of identification arises in a number of different fields such as automatic control, biomedical engineering, psychology, systems science, and so on, where the underlying physical structure may be deterministic (for example, see Aström and Eykhoff, 1971). It is also aptly linked to the design of experiments (for example, Kempthorne, 1947; Bailey, Gilchrist and Patterson, 1977). Here, we restrict our discussion to economic applications of statistical identifiability involving random variables.

JEAN-MARIE DUFOUR AND CHENG HSIAO

See also **treatment effect.**

Bibliography

Angrist, J.D. and Krueger, A.B. 1991. Does compulsory school attendance affect schooling and earning? *Quarterly Journal of Economics* 106, 979–1014.
Aström, K.J. and Eykhoff, P. 1971. System identification – a survey. *Automatica* 7, 123–62.
Bailey, R.A., Gilchrist, F.H.L. and Patterson, H.D. 1977. Identification of effects and confounding patterns in factorial designs. *Biometrika* 64, 347–54.
Bekker, P. and Wansbeek, T. 2001. Identification in parametric models. In *Companion to Theoretical Econometrics*, ed. B. Baltagi. Oxford: Blackwell.
Benkard, C.L. and Berry, S. 2006. On the nonparametric identification of nonlinear simultaneous equations models: comment on Brown (1983) and Roehrig (1988). *Econometrica* 74, 1429–40.
Bound, J., Jaeger, D.A. and Baker, R.M. 1995. Problems with instrumental variables estimation when the correlation between the instruments and the endogenous explanatory variable is weak. *Journal of the American Statistical Association* 90, 443–50.
Brown, B.W. 1983. The identification problem in systems nonlinear in the variables. *Econometrica* 51, 175–96.
Buse, A. 1992. The bias of instrumental variables estimators. *Econometrica* 60, 173–80.
Deistler, M. and Seifert, H.-G. 1978. Identifiability and consistent estimability in econometric models. *Econometrica* 46, 969–80.
Drèze, J. 1975. Bayesian theory of identification in simultaneous equations models. In *Studies in Bayesian Econometrics and Statistics*, ed. S.E. Fienberg and A. Zellner. Amsterdam: North-Holland.
Dufour, J.-M. 1997. Some impossibility theorems in econometrics, with applications to structural and dynamic models. *Econometrica* 65, 1365–89.
Dufour, J.-M. 2003. Identification, weak instruments and statistical inference in econometrics. *Canadian Journal of Economics* 36, 767–808.
Fienberg, S.E. and Zellner, A., eds. 1975. *Studies in Bayesian Econometrics and Statistics.* Amsterdam: North-Holland.
Fisher, F.M. 1976. *The Identification Problem in Econometrics.* Huntington, NY: Krieger.
Frisch, R. 1934. *Statistical Confluence Analysis by Means of Complete Regression Systems.* Oslo: Universitetes Okonomiske Institutt.
Gabrielson, A. 1978. Consistency and identifiability. *Journal of Econometrics* 8, 261–3.
Griliches, Z. and Intriligator, M.D., eds. 1983. *Handbook of Econometrics*, vol. 1, Amsterdam: North-Holland.
Haavelmo, T. 1944. The probability approach in econometrics. *Econometrica* 12(Supp.), 1–115.
Hannan, E.J. 1971. The identification problem for multiple equation systems with moving average errors. *Econometrica* 39, 751–66.

Hatanaka, M. 1975. On the global identification of the dynamic simultaneous equations model with stationary disturbances. *International Economic Review* 16, 545–54.

Hausman, J.A. and Taylor, W.E. 1983. Identification, estimation and testing in simultaneous equations models with disturbance covariance restriction. *Econometrica* 51, 1527–49.

Heckman, J. and Robb, R. 1985. Alternative methods for evaluating the impact of interventions. In *Longitudinal Analysis of Labor Market Data*, ed. J. Heckman and B. Singer. New York: Cambridge University Press.

Heckman, J.J. and Vytlacil, E. 1999. Local instrumental variables and latent variables models for identifying and bounding treatment effects. *Proceedings of the National Academy of Sciences* 96, 4730–4.

Heckman, J.J. and Vytlacil, E. 2001. Local instrumental variables. In *Nonlinear Statistical Modeling Proceedings of the Thirteenth International Symposium in Economic Theory and Econometrics: Essays in Honor of Takeshi Amemiya*, ed. C. Hsiao, K. Morimune and J.L. Powell. Cambridge: Cambridge University Press.

Hillier, G.H. 1990. On the normalization of structural equations: properties of direction estimators. *Econometrica* 58, 1181–94.

Hsiao, C. 1983. Identification. In *Handbook of Econometrics*, vol. 1, ed. Z. Griliches and M.D. Intriligator. Amsterdam: North-Holland.

Hurwicz, L. 1950. Generalization of the concept of identification. In *Statistical Inference in Dynamic Economic Models*, ed. T.C. Koopmans. New York: Wiley.

Imbens, G. and Angrist, J. 1994. Identification and estimation of local average treatment effects. *Econometrica* 62, 467–76.

Kadane, J.B. 1975. The role of identification in Bayesian theory. In *Studies in Bayesian Econometrics and Statistics*, ed. S.E. Fienberg and A. Zellner. Amsterdam: North-Holland.

Kempthorne, O. 1947. A simple approach to confounding and factorial replication in factorial experiments. *Biometrika* 34, 255–72.

Koopmans, T.C. 1950. *Statistical Inference in Dynamic Economic Models*. New York: Wiley.

Koopmans, T.C. and Reiersøl, O. 1950. The identification of structural characteristics. *Annals of Mathematical Statistics* 21, 165–81.

Koopmans, T.C., Rubin, H. and Leipnik, R.B. 1950. Measuring the equation systems of dynamic economics. In *Statistical Inference in Dynamic Economic Models*, ed. T.C. Koopmans. New York: Wiley.

Le Cam, L. 1956. On the asymptotic theory of estimation and testing hypotheses. In *Proceedings of the Third Berkeley Symposium on Mathematical Statistics and Probability*. Berkeley, CA: University of California Press.

Liu, T.C. 1960. Underidentification, structural estimation, and forecasting. *Econometrica* 28, 855–65.

Manski, C. 2003. *Partial Identification of Probability Distributions*. New York: Springer.

Marschak, J. 1942. Economic interdependence and statistical analysis. In *Studies in Mathematical Economics and Econometrics*, ed. O. Lange, F. McIntyre and T.O. Yntema. Chicago: University of Chicago Press.

Mas-Collel, A. 1977. On the recoverability of consumers preferences from market demand behavior. *Econometrica* 45, 1409–30.

Matzkin, R. 1994. Restrictions of economic theory in nonparametric methods. In *Handbook of Econometrics*, vol. 4, ed. R.F. Engle and D.L. McFadden. Amsterdam: North-Holland.

Matzkin, R. 2007. Nonparametric Identification. In *Handbook of Econometrics*, vol. 6, ed. J. Heckman and E. Leamer. Amsterdam: North-Holland.

McManus, D.A. 1992. How common is identification in parametric models? *Journal of Econometrics* 53, 5–23.

Morgan, M.S. 1990. *The History of Econometric Ideas*. Cambridge: Cambridge University Press.

Nelson, C.R. and Startz, R. 1990. The distribution of the instrumental variable estimator and its *t*-ratio when the instrument is a poor one. *Journal of Business* 63, 125–40.

Phillips, P.C.B. 1983. Exact small sample theory in the simultaneous equations model. In *Handbook of Econometrics*, vol. 1, ed. Z. Griliches and M.D. Intriligator. Amsterdam: North-Holland.

Phillips, P.C.B. 1989. Partially identified econometric models. *Econometric Theory* 5, 181–240.

Prakasa Rao, B.L.S. 1992. *Identifiability in Stochastic Models: Characterization of Probability Distributions*. New York: Academic Press.

Rao, C.R. 1962. Problems of selection with restriction. *Journal of the Royal Statistical Society*, Series B 24, 401–5.

Rao, C.R. 1973. *Linear Statistical Inference and its Applications*, 2nd edn. New York: Wiley.

Roehrig, C.S. 1988. Conditions for identification in nonparametric and parametric models. *Econometrica* 56, 433–77.

Rosenbaum, P. and Rubin, D. 1985. Reducing bias in observational studies using subclassification on the propensity score. *Journal of the American Statistical Association* 79, 516–24.

Rothenberg, T.J. 1971. Identification in parametric models. *Econometrica* 39, 577–91.

Rothenberg, T.J. 1984. Approximating the distributions of econometric estimators and test statistics. In *Handbook of Econometrics*, vol. 2, ed. Z. Griliches and M.D. Intriligator. Amsterdam: North-Holland.

Sargan, J.D. 1983. Identification and lack of identification. *Econometrica* 51, 1605–33.

Sims, C. 1980. Macroeconomics and reality. *Econometrica* 48, 1–48.

Staiger, D. and Stock, J.H. 1997. Instrumental variables regression with weak instruments. *Econometrica* 65, 557–86.

Stock, J.H. and Trebbi, F. 2003. Who invented IV regression? *Journal of Economic Perspectives* 17(3), 177–94.

Stock, J.H., Wright, J.H. and Yogo, M. 2002. A survey of weak instruments and weak identification in generalized method of moments. *Journal of Business and Economic Statistics* 20, 518–29.

Wald, A. 1950. Note on the identification of economic relations. In *Statistical Inference in Dynamic Economic Models*, ed. T.C. Koopmans. New York: Wiley.

Working, E.J. 1927. What do statistical demand curves show? *Quarterly Journal of Economics* 41, 212–35.

Working, H. 1925. The statistical determination of demand curves. *Quarterly Journal of Economics* 39, 503–43.

Wright, P.G. 1915. Moore's economic cycles. *Quarterly Journal of Economics* 29, 631–41.

Wright, P.G. 1928. *The Tariff on Animal and Vegetable Oils*. New York: Macmillan.

local regression models

Local regression models are regression models where the parameters are 'localized', that is, they are allowed to vary with some or all of the covariates in a general way. Suppose that (Y, X) are random variables and let

$$E(Y|X = x) = m(x) \tag{1}$$

when it exists. The regression function $m(x)$ is of primary interest because it describes how X affects Y. One may also be interested in derivatives of m or averages thereof or in derived quantities like conditional variance $var(Y|X = x) = E(Y^2|X = x) - E^2(Y|X = x)$. In cases of heavy-tailed distributions, the conditional expectation may not exist, in which case one may instead work with other location functionals like trimmed mean or median. The conditional expectation is particularly easy to deal with but a lot of what is done for the mean can also be done for the median or other quantities.

A parametric regression model for $m(x)$ is a family of functions $M(x; \theta)$, $\theta \in \Theta \subset \mathbb{R}^p$, where for each θ, $M(x; \theta)$ is a known function. The true parameter θ_0 for which $M(x; \theta_0) = m(x)$ for all $x \in \mathcal{X}$ is unknown and has to be estimated from data. For example, $M(x; \theta) = x^\top \theta$ would correspond to the linear regression case, which is the central model of econometrics. A key concept is that of identifiability: M is identifiable when distinct parameter values lead to different values of M for at least some x values. See Rothenberg (1971) for discussion. Parametric models arise frequently in economics and are of central importance. However, such models arise only when one has imposed specific functional forms on utility or production functions. Without these ad hoc assumptions one only gets much milder restrictions on functional form like concavity, symmetry, homogeneity and so on. The nonparametric approach is based on the belief that parametric models are usually mis-specified and may result in incorrect inferences. In this approach one treats the regression function $m(x)$ as being of unknown functional form. One usually assumes that m is a continuous function or even differentiable, although there are cases of interest where $m(x)$ is, say, continuous only from the right (left) with limits on the left (right), that is, there may be jumps at certain known or unknown locations in the support $\mathcal{X}$ of X (see Delgado and Hidalgo, 2000). By not restricting the functional form one obtains valid inferences for a much larger range of circumstances. In practice, the applicability depends on the sample size and the quality of data available. The theory and methods for carrying out such estimation are well understood, and are reviewed elsewhere (Härdle and Linton, 1994). Local regression models are one way of interpreting the nonparametric approach.

A local regression model is a family of functions

$$M(x; \theta(x)), \quad \theta \in \Theta = \{\theta : \mathcal{X} \to \mathbb{R}^p\}, \tag{2}$$

where $M(x;\theta)$ is a known function of both arguments. The true (functional) parameter $\theta_0(\cdot)$ for which $M(x;\theta_0(x)) = m(x)$ for all $x \in \mathscr{X}$ is unknown. It is usually assumed to be smooth. In other words this is a standard parametric regression model except that the parameters vary with the covariate value. There are a number of special cases. At one extreme lies the parametric model in which $\theta(x) = \theta$ for all $x \in \mathscr{X} \subset \mathbb{R}^d$, but the true θ_0 is unknown. At the other extreme lies the fully nonparametric case where $\theta(\cdot)$ is not subject to any exclusion restrictions.

Many different M functions will generally do. For example, the local constant case corresponds to $M(x;\theta) = \theta$ and the local linear case corresponds to $M(x;\theta) = \theta_0 + \theta_1 x$. These cases along with higher-order polynomials have been widely studied (see, for example, Fan and Gijbels, 1996). There are also other possibilities. Consider the Cobb–Douglas parametric model

$$M(x;\theta) = \theta_0 x_1^{\theta_1} \cdots x_d^{\theta_d}, \tag{3}$$

which is widely used in studies of production. By making $\theta = (\theta_0, \theta_1, \ldots, \theta_d)$ vary freely with x one can match with any function $m(x)$ so long as the supports coincide (see, for example, Charnes, Cooper and Schinnar, 1976). For binary data where it is known that $m(x) \in [0,1]$ it is appropriate to take $M(x;\theta) = F(\theta_0 + \theta_1 x)$ for some given c.d.f. F like the normal or logit. In that case, for a given x, there exists $\theta_0(x)$, $\theta_1(x)$ such that $m(x) = F(\theta_0(x) + \theta_1(x)x)$. This example illustrates some pitfalls; for example, when $m(x) > 1$ for some x of interest. In that case, taking $M(x;\theta) = F(\theta_0 + \theta_1 x)$ will not be satisfactory.

The statistical justification for using local constant, local linear, and more generally local polynomial models is that any smooth function $m(x)$ can be approximated near the point x_0 by Taylor series expansions, so for p-times continuously differentiable scalar functions we have

$$m(x) = \sum_{j=0}^{p} \frac{1}{j!} \frac{d^j m}{dx^j}(x_0)(x - x_0)^j + R(x, x_0), \tag{4}$$

where the remainder term satisfies $R(x, x_0)/|x - x_0|^p \to 0$ as $x \to x_0$. Thus the function m is locally well approximated by a polynomial of order p, $\sum_{j=0}^{p} \alpha_j (x - x_0)^j$, where α_j can be identified with $j!^{-1} d^j m(x_0)/dx^j$. This justifies using local polynomial regression. But why should one ever work with local regression models outside the local polynomial class? First, any other local parametric model $M(x, \theta)$ that is p-times continuously differentiable in x at x_0, satisfies a similar expansion to (4), $\sum_{j=0}^{p} \beta_j (x - x_0)^j$, where β_j are functions of θ. By equating coefficients one obtains the same leading terms as long as there are 'enough' parameters in θ. Therefore, the same approximating objectives are reached by any such model. In some cases other equivalent classes may provide better approximations. Polynomials can sometimes violate some known features, like for example $m(x) \in [0,1]$. In that case, taking $M(x;\theta)$ to be a c.d.f. of a polynomial provides the same approximation (so long as the c.d.f. chosen is also smooth enough) but imposes the boundedness restriction.

Second, the local parameters may also be of interest in themselves. In the Cobb–Douglas case, the $\theta_j(x)$ can be interpreted as local elasticities. A third benefit is that the local model nests the parametric model. This leads to better statistical properties for estimators and test statistics when the model is true or approximately true, the 'home turf' case (see Hjort and Glad, 1995). When the default parametric model in the area of interest is nonlinear, as is true in many fields, there are some advantages to taking a localization of this in the nonparametric approach.

The issue of identification in local regression models is not well explored but some results are known (see Gozalo and Linton, 2000). The expansion (4) is clearly crucial for identification. If the function m is continuous but not differentiable, then only a single parameter is identifiable, which corresponds to the first term in (4); additional parameters remain unidentified. It is also necessary that there is a neighbourhood of the estimation point that contains enough observations (this is guaranteed when the marginal density exists and is positive).

Estimation of local regression models can be carried out by localization of the usual estimation criteria adopted for estimation of the corresponding parametric model like maximum likelihood or the method of moments where the localization is carried out by multiplying the contribution of observation i to the sample average objective function by the weight $w_{ni} = K((x - Xi)/h)$, where K is called the kernel and usually satisfies at least $\int K(u)du = 1$, while $h = h(n)$ is the bandwidth, a sequence designed to go to zero with sample size. The effect of the weighting factor w_{ni} is to emphasize observations close to the point of interest x and to de-emphasize observations far from x, whence the appellation 'localization'.

In the multivariate case, the expansion (4) becomes much more complicated: there are d first order partial derivatives, $d(d - 1)/2$ second order partial derivatives, and so on. With $p = 5$ and $d = 10$ the local parametric model would have over 1,000 parameters, which is too many for practical use. There are many interesting and important cases lying between the two extremes of parametric and fully nonparametric models, where some of the θ_j vary with only a subset of x. In this case, the local parametric model is imposing exclusion restrictions on the function m and the expansion is reduced. We next give some examples.

A function $m(x)$ is additively separable if

$$m(x) = \sum_{j=1}^{d} m_j(x_j)$$

for some functions m_j. In terms of the framework of the previous section $p = d$ and

$$M(x; \theta) = \sum_{j=1}^{d} M_j(x_j, \theta_j); \theta_j(x) = \theta_j(x_j).$$

The functions $\theta_j(x_j)$ are one-dimensional but of unknown form. This implies that $m(x) = \sum_{j=1}^{d} m_j(x_j)$, where $m_j(x_j) = \theta_j(x_j)$. In this case, each function $\theta_j(x)$ has $d - 1$ exclusion restrictions. This is consistent with strong separability as defined in

Goldman and Uzawa (1964). A generalization of this is to the so-called generalized additive models where $M(x;\theta) = G(\sum_{j=1}^{d} M_j(x_j, \theta_j))$, where $\theta_j(x) = \theta_j(x_j)$, in which G is a known 'link' function, while θ_j are univariate functions as before. For example, G could be the c.d.f. of a random variable like the normal or logit. Linton and Nielsen (1995) discuss estimation of additive models.

In time series one is often interested in the relationship

$$E[y_t|I_{t-1}] = m(I_{t-1}),$$

where the information set $I_{t-1} = \{y_{t-1}, \ldots\}$ includes all past variables, either for estimation or forecasting purposes. This situation is complicated because I_{t-1} contains infinitely many variables and apart from the important class of Markov models m generally depends on all of them. A common assumption here is some kind of mixing condition that guarantees that the effect of y_{t-k} on y_t dies out as $k \to \infty$. For example, an invertible $MA(1)$ process has $m(I_{t-1}) = \sum_{j=1}^{\infty} \theta^{j-1} y_{t-j}$ for some $|\theta| < 1$. A natural generalization of this is the model $m(I_{t-1}) = \sum_{j=1}^{\infty} m_j(y_{t-j})$, where m_j is a sequence of functions such that the sum is well defined, that is, $m_j(\cdot)$ must decline in importance as $j \to \infty$. This model is hard to analyse and to estimate. Instead, consider the more restrictive version

$$m(I_{t-1}) = \sum_{j=1}^{\infty} \theta^{j-1} m(y_{t-j}) \tag{5}$$

for some unknown function $m(\cdot)$ and parameter θ. When $m(y) = y$ this includes the $MA(1)$ process as a special case, but includes many other nonlinear models. By taking a local parametric model $M(y) = a_0(y) + a_1(y)y + a_2(y)y^2$ for m one can nest the GARCH(1, 1) model of Bollerslev (1986). Linton and Mammen (2005) have recently developed a theory of estimation for this class of models.

Another popular approach is the locally stationary models pioneered by Dahlhaus (1997). A locally stationary AR(1) process is $y_t = \rho(t/T)y_{t-1} + \varepsilon_t$, where ε_t is i.i.d. and $\rho(\cdot)$ is a smooth but unknown form. By taking the local parametric model $M(y) = a_0$ one can nest the conventional autoregression, although there are other possibilities. Dahlhaus actually deals with a more general class of linear processes with $y_t = \sum_{j=0}^{\infty} c_j(t/T)\varepsilon_{t-j}$, where $c_j(\cdot)$ are unknown but smooth functions.

OLIVER B. LINTON

See also **nonparametric structural models; semiparametric estimation.**

Bibliography

Bollerslev, T. 1986. Generalized autoregressive conditional heteroskedasticity. *Journal of Econometrics* 31, 307–27.

Charnes, A., Cooper, W. and Schinnar, A. 1976. A theorem on homogeneous functions and extended Cobb–Douglas forms. *Proceedings of the National Academy of Science, USA* 73, 3747–4748.

Dahlhaus, R. 1997. Fitting time series models to nonstationary processes. *Annals of Statistics* 25, 1–37.

Delgado, M. and Hidalgo, F. 2000. Nonparametric inference on structural breaks. *Journal of Econometrics* 96, 113–44.

Fan, J. and Gijbels, I. 1996. *Local Polynomial Modelling and its Applications*. London: Chapman and Hall.

Goldman, S. and Uzawa, H. 1964. A note on separability and demand analysis. *Econometrica* 32, 387–98.

Gozalo, P. and Linton, O. 2000. Local nonlinear least squares estimation: using parametric information nonparametrically. *Journal of Econometrics* 99, 63–106.

Härdle, W. and Linton, O. 1994. Applied nonparametric methods. In *The Handbook of Econometrics*, vol. 4, ed. D. McFadden and R. Engle. Amsterdam: North- Holland.

Hjort, N. and Glad, I. 1995. Nonparametric density estimation with a parametric start. *Annals of Statistics* 23, 882–904.

Linton, O. and Mammen, E. 2005. Estimating semiparametric ARCH models by kernel smoothing methods. *Econometrica* 73, 771–836.

Linton, O. and Nielsen, J. 1995. A kernel method of estimating structured nonparametric regression based on marginal integration. *Biometrika* 82, 93–100.

Rothenberg, T. 1971. Identification in parametric models. *Econometrica* 39, 577–91.

logit models of individual choice

The logit function is the reciprocal function to the sigmoid *logistic* function. It maps the interval [0,1] into the real line and is written as:

$$logit(p) = \ln(p/(1-p)).$$

Two traditions are involved in the modern theory of logit models of individual choices. The first one concerns *curve fitting* as exposed by Berkson (1944), who coined the term 'logit' after its close competitor 'probit' which is derived from the normal distribution. Both models are by far the most popular econometric methods used in applied work to estimate models for binary variables, even though the development of semiparametric and nonparametric alternatives since the mid-1970s has been intensive (Horowitz and Savin, 2001).

In the second strand of literature, models of discrete variables and discrete choices as originally set up by Thurstone (1927) in psychometrics have been known as 'random utility models' (RUM) since Marschak (1960) introduced them to economists. As the availability of individual databases and the need for tools to forecast aggregate demands derived from discrete choices were increasing from the 1960s onwards, different waves of innovations, fostered by McFadden (see his Nobel lecture, 2001) elaborated more and more sophisticated and flexible logit models. The use of these models and of simulation methods has triggered burgeoning applied research in demand analysis in recent years.

Those who wish to study the subject in greater detail are referred to Gouriéroux (2000), McFadden (2001) or Train (2003), where references to applications in economics and marketing can also be found.

Measurement models

As Berkson (1951, p. 327) put it, logit (or probit) models may be seen as 'merely a convenient way of graphically representing and fitting a function'. They are used for any empirical phenomenon delivering a binary random variable Y_i, taking values 0 and 1, to be analysed. In a logit model, it is postulated that its probability distribution conditional on a vector of covariates X_i is given by:

$$\Pr(Y_i = 1|X_i) = \frac{\exp(X_i\beta)}{1 + \exp(X_i\beta)}$$

where β is a vector of parameters. This model can also be derived from more general frameworks in statistical mechanics or spatial statistics (Strauss, 1992).

With the use of cross-sectional samples, the parameter of interest is estimated using maximum likelihood or by generalized linear models (GLM) methods where the link function is logit (McCullagh and Nelder, 1989). Under the maintained assumption that it is the true model and other standard assumptions, the maximum likelihood estimator (MLE) is consistent, asymptotically normal and efficient (Amemiya, 1985). Nevertheless, the MLE may fail to exist, or more exactly be at the bounds of the parameter space, when the samples are uniformly composed of 0 s or 1 s, for instance (Berkson, 1955).

When repeated observations are available, the method of Berkson delivers an estimator close to MLE since they are asymptotically equivalent. Observe first that the logit function of the true probability obeys the linear equation:

$$logit(\Pr(Y_c = 1|X_c)) = X_c\beta$$

where the covariates X_c now take a discrete number of values defining each cell, c. Second, use the observed frequency in each cell, $\hat{p}_c$, and contrast it with the theoretical probability, p_c, as:

$$logit(\hat{p}_c) = X_c\beta + (logit(\hat{p}_c) - logit(p_c)) = X_c\beta + \varepsilon_c.$$

The random term ε_c properly scaled by the square root of the number of observations in cell c is asymptotically normally distributed with variance equal to $1/(p_c(1 - p_c))$. The method of Berkson then consists in using minimum chi-square, that is, a method of moments, to estimate β, an instance of what is know as minimum distance or asymptotic least squares (Gouriéroux, Monfort and Trognon, 1985).

When measurements for a single individual are repeated, Rasch (1960) suspected that individual effects might be important and proposed to write:

$$logit(\Pr(Y_{it} = 1|X_{it})) = X_{it}\beta + \delta_i$$

where t indexes the different items that are measured and δ_i is an individual specific intercept or fixed effect. Items can be different questions in performance tests or different periods. In the original Rasch formulation, parameters were allowed to be different across items, β_t, and there were no covariates.

Given that the number of items is small, it is well known that the estimation of such a model runs into the problem of incidental parameters (see Lancaster, 2000). As the number of parameters δ_i increases with the cross-section dimension, the MLE is inconsistent (Chamberlain, 1984). Nevertheless, the nuisance parameters δ_i can be differenced out using conditional likelihood methods (Andersen, 1973) because:

$$logit(\Pr(Y_{it} = 1|X_{it}, Y_{it} + Y_{it'} = 1)) = (X_{it} - X_{it'})\beta.$$

The conditional likelihood estimator of β is consistent and root n asymptotically normal but it is not efficient, although no efficient estimator is known. Furthermore, when binary variables Y_{it} are independent, conditionally on X_i, the only model where a root n consistent estimator exists is a logit model (Chamberlain, 1992). Extensions of Rasch rely on the fact that root n consistent estimators exist if and only if $Y_{it} + Y_{it'}$ is a sufficient statistic for the nuisance parameters δ_i (Magnac, 2004). When the number of items or periods becomes large, profile likelihood methods where individual effects are treated as parameters seem to be accurate in Monte Carlo experiments as soon as the number of periods is four or five (Arellano, 2003).

Multinomial logit (or in disuse 'conditional logit') is to binary logit what a multinomial is to a binomial distribution (Theil, 1969). Given a vector Y_i consisting of K elements which are binary random variables and lie in the $\mathbb{R}^K-$ simplex (their sum is equal to 1), it is postulated that:

$$\Pr(Y_i^{(k)} = 1 | X_i) = \frac{\exp(X_i \beta^{(k)})}{1 + \sum_{k=2}^{K} \exp(X_i \beta^{(k)})}$$

where by normalization, $\beta^{(1)} = 0$. Ordered logit has a different flavour since it applies to rank-ordered data such as education levels (Gouriéroux, 2000).

As probits, logit models are very tightly specified parametric models and can be substantially generalized. Much effort has been exerted to relax parametric and conditional independence assumptions, starting with Manski (1975). Manski (1988) analyses the identifying restrictions in binary models, and Horowitz (1998) reviews estimation methods. In some cases, Lewbel (2000) and Matzkin (1992) offer alternatives.

Random utility models

The theory of discrete choice is directly set up in a multiple alternative framework. A choice of an alternative k belonging to a set C is assumed to be probabilistic either because preferences are stochastic or heterogenous, or because choices are perturbed in a random way. By definition, choice probability functions map each alternative and choice sets into the simplex of $\mathbb{R}^K$.

A strong restriction on choices is the axiom of Independence of Irrelevant Alternatives (IIA, Luce, 1959). The axiom states that the choice between two alternatives is independent of any other alternative in the choice set. The version that allows for zero probabilities (McFadden, 2001) states that for any pair of choice set C, C' such that $\{k, k'\} \in C$ and $C \subset C'$:

Pr(k is chosen in C') = Pr(k is chosen in C).
Pr(An element of C is chosen in C').

Under this axiom, choice probabilities take a multinomial generalized logit form.

Moreover, assume that choices are associated with utility functions, $\{u^{(k)}\}_k$ that depend on determinants X_i and random shocks:

$$u^{(k)} = X\beta^{(k)} + \varepsilon^{(k)},$$

and that the actual choice of the decision maker yields maximum utility to her. Then, the IIA axiom is verified if and only if $\varepsilon^{(k)}$ are independent and extreme value distributed (McFadden, 1974). Extensions of decision theory under IIA were proposed in the continuous case (Resnick and Roy, 1991) or in an intertemporal context (Dagsvik, 2002).

The IIA axiom is a strong restriction as in the famous red and blue bus example where, if IIA is assumed, the existence of different colours affects choices of transport between bus and other modes while introspection suggests that colours should indeed be irrelevant. Several generalizations which proceed from logit were proposed to bypass IIA. Hierarchical or tree structures were the first to be used. At the upper level, the choice set consists of broad groups of alternatives. In each of these groups, there are various alternatives which can consist themselves of subsets of alternatives, and so on. The best-known model is the two-level nested logit, where alternatives are grouped by similarities. For instance, the first level is the choice of the type of the car, the second level is the make of the car. The formula of choice probabilities for nested logit,

$$p^{(k)} = \frac{\exp(X\beta^{(k)}/\lambda_{B_s})(\sum_{j \in B_s} \exp(X\beta^{(j)}/\lambda_{B_s}))^{\lambda_{B_s}-1}}{\sum_{t=1}^{T}(\sum_{j \in B_t} \exp(X\beta^{(j)}/\lambda_{B_s}))^{\lambda_{B_t}}},$$

where alternative k belongs to B_s, is not illuminating but the logic of construction is clear. Choices at each level are modelled as multinomial logit (Train, 2003).

General extreme value distributions (McFadden, 1984) provide more extensions, although they do not generate all configurations of choice probabilities. In contrast, mixed logit does, as shown by McFadden and Train (2000). Instead of considering that parameters are deterministic, make them random or heterogeneous across agents. The result is a mixture model where individual probabilities of choice are obtained by integrating out the random elements as in

$$p^{(k)} = \int p^{(k)}(\beta)f(\beta)d\beta.$$

Integrals are computed using simulation methods (MacFadden, 2001). The same principle is used by Berry, Levinsohn and Pakes (1995) with a view to generalizing the aggregate logit choice models using market data. Logit models are still very much in use in applied settings in demand analysis and marketing, and are equivalent to a representative consumer model (Anderson, de Palma and Thisse, 1992). Mixed logits permit much more general patterns of substitution between alternatives and should probably become the standard tool in the near future.

THIERRY MAGNAC

See also **categorical data; mixture models; nonlinear panel data models.**

Bibliography

Amemiya, T. 1985. *Advanced Econometrics*. Cambridge, MA: Harvard University Press.
Andersen, E.B. 1973. *Conditional Inference and Models for Measuring*. Copenhagen: Mentalhygiejnisk Forlag.
Anderson, S.P., de Palma, A. and Thisse, J.F. 1992. *Discrete Choice Theory of Product Differentiation*. Cambridge, MA: MIT Press.

Arellano, M. 2003. Discrete choices with panel data. *Investigaciones Economicas* 27, 423–58.

Berkson, J. 1944. Application of the logistic function to bioassay. *Journal of the American Statistical Association* 39, 357–65.

Berkson, J. 1951. Why I prefer logits to probits. *Biometrics* 7, 327–39.

Berkson, J. 1955. Maximum likelihood and minimum chi-square estimates of the logistic function. *Journal of the American Statistical Association* 50, 130–62.

Berry, S.T., Levinsohn, J.A. and Pakes, A. 1995. Automobile prices in market equilibrium. *Econometrica* 63, 841–90.

Chamberlain, G. 1984. Panel data. In *Handbook of Econometrics*, vol. 2, ed. Z. Griliches and M. Intriligator. Amsterdam: North-Holland.

Chamberlain, G. 1992. Binary response models for panel data: identification and information. Unpublished manuscript, Harvard University.

Dagsvik, J. 2002. Discrete choice in continuous time: implications of an intertemporal version of IAA. *Econometrica* 70, 817–31.

Gouriéroux, C. 2000. *Econometrics of Qualitative Dependent Variables*. Cambridge: Cambridge University Press.

Gouriéroux, C., Monfort, A. and Trognon, A. 1985. Moindres carrés asymptotiques. *Annales de l'INSEE* 58, 91–121.

Horowitz, J. 1998. *Semiparametric Methods in Econometrics*. Berlin: Springer.

Horowitz, J.L. and Savin, N.E. 2001. Binary response models: logits, probits and semiparametrics. *Journal of Economic Perspectives* 15(4), 43–56.

Lancaster, T. 2000. The incidental parameter problem since 1948. *Journal of Econometrics* 95, 391–413.

Lewbel, A. 2000. Semiparametric qualitative response model estimation with unknown heteroskedasticity or instrumental variables. *Journal of Econometrics* 97, 145–77.

Luce, R. 1959. *Individual Choice Behavior: A Theoretical Analysis*. New York: Wiley.

Magnac, T. 2004. Panel binary variables and sufficiency: generalizing conditional logit. *Econometrica* 72, 1859–77.

Manski, C.F. 1975. The maximum score estimation of the stochastic utility model of choice. *Journal of Econometrics* 3, 205–28.

Manski, C.F. 1988. Identification of binary response models. *Journal of the American Statistical Association* 83, 729–38.

Marschak, J. 1960. Binary choice constraints and random utility indicators. In *Mathematical Methods in the Social Sciences*, ed. K. Arrow. Stanford: Stanford University Press.

Matzkin, R. 1992. Nonparametric and distribution-free estimation of the binary threshold crossing and the binary choice models. *Econometrica* 60, 239–70.

McCullagh, P. and Nelder, J.A. 1989. *Generalized Linear Models*. London: Chapman and Hall.

McFadden, D. 1974. Conditional logit analysis of qualitative choice behavior. In *Frontiers in Econometrics*, ed. P. Zarembka. New York: Academic Press.

McFadden, D. 1984. Econometric analysis of qualitative response models. In *Handbook of Econometrics*, vol. 2, ed. Z. Griliches and M.D. Intriligator. Amsterdam: North-Holland.

McFadden, D. 2001. Economic choices. *American Economic Review* 91, 351–78.

McFadden, D. and Train, K. 2000. Mixed MNL models for discrete responses. *Journal of Applied Econometrics* 15, 447–70.

Rasch, G. 1960. *Probabilistic Models for Some Intelligence and Attainment Tests*. Copenhagen: Denmark Paedagogiske Institut.

Resnick, S.I. and Roy, R. 1991. Random USC functions, max stable process and continuous choice. *Annals of Applied Probability* 1, 267–92.

Strauss, D. 1992. The many faces of logistic regression. *American Statistician* 46, 321–27.

Theil, H. 1969. A multinomial extension of the linear logit model. *International Economic Review* 10, 251–9.

Thurstone, L. 1927. A law of comparative judgement. *Psychological Review* 34, 273–86.

Train, K. 2003. *Discrete Choice Methods with Simulation.* Cambridge: Cambridge University Press.

longitudinal data analysis

1. Why panel data?

'Longitudinal data' (or 'panel data') refers to data-sets that contain time series observations of a number of individuals. In other words, it provides multiple observations for each individual in the sample. Compared with cross-sectional data, in which observations for a number of individuals are available only for a given time, or time-series data, in which a single entity is observed over time, panel data have the obvious advantages of more degrees of freedom and less collinearity among explanatory variables, and so provide the possibility of obtaining more accurate parameter estimates. More importantly, by blending inter-individual differences with intra-individual dynamics, panel data allow the investigation of more complicated behavioural hypotheses than those that can be addressed using cross-sectional or time-series data.

For instance, suppose a cross-sectional sample yields an average labour-participation rate of 50 per cent for married women. Given that the standard assumption for the analysis of cross-sectional data is that, conditional on certain variables, each woman is a random draw from a homogeneous population, this would imply that each woman has a 50 per cent chance of being in the labour force at any given time. Hence, a married woman would be expected to spend half of her married life in the labour force and half out of it. The job turnover would be frequent, and the expected average job duration would be just two years (Ben-Porath, 1973). However, the cross-sectional data could be drawn from a heterogeneous population in which 50 per cent of the sample was drawn from the population that always works and 50 per cent from the population that never works. In this situation, there is no turnover and a woman's current work status is a perfect predictor of her future work status. To discriminate between these two possibilities, we need information on individual labour-force histories in different sub-intervals of the life cycle, which can be provided only if information is available on the intertemporal dynamics of individual entities. On the other hand, although time series data provide information on dynamic adjustment, variables over time tend to move collinearly, hence making it difficult to identify micro-dynamic or macro-dynamic effects. Often, estimation of distributed lag models has to rely on strong prior restrictions like the Koyck or Almon lag, with very little empirical justification (for example, Griliches, 1967). With panel data, the inter-individual differences can often lessen the problem of multicollinearity and provide the possibility of estimating unrestricted time adjustment patterns (for example, Pakes and Griliches, 1984).

By utilizing information on both the intertemporal dynamics and the individuality of the entities, panel data may also allow an investigator to control the effects of missing or unobserved variables. For instance, MaCurdy's (1981) life-cycle labour supply of prime-age males with perfect foresight model assumes that the logarithm of hours worked is a linear function of the real wage rate and the logarithm of the worker's marginal utility of initial wealth, which is unobserved. Since the wage rate and the marginal utility of initial wealth are correlated, any instrument that is correlated with the wage rate will be correlated with the marginal utility of initial wealth. There is no way one can obtain a consistent estimate of the coefficient of the wage rate with cross-sectional data. But, if panel data are available and since marginal utility of initial wealth stays constant over time, one can take the difference of the labour supply model over time to get rid of the marginal utility of initial wealth as an explanatory variable. Regressing change in hour on change in wage rate and other socio-demographic variables can yield consistent estimates of the coefficient of the wage rate and other explanatory variables.

Panel data may also provide microfoundations for aggregate data analysis. Aggregate data analysis often invokes the 'representative agent' assumption. If micro units are heterogeneous, the time series properties of aggregate data may be very different from those of disaggregate data (for example, Granger, 1990; Lewbel, 1994) and policy evaluation based on aggregate data could also be grossly misleading (for example, Hsiao, Shen and Fujiki, 2005). By providing time series observations for a number of individuals, panel data are ideal for the investigation of the homogeneity issue.

Panel data involve observations of two or more dimensions. In normal circumstances, one would expect the computation and inference of panel data models to be more complicated than those of cross-section or time series data. However, in certain situations the availability of panel data actually simplifies inference. For instance, statistical inference for non-stationary panel data can be complicated (for example, Phillips, 1986). But, if observations are independently distributed across cross-sectional units, central limit theorems applied across cross-sectional units lead to asymptotically normally distributed statistics (for example, Levin, Lin and Chu, 2002; Im, Pesaran and Shin, 2003).

2. Issues of panel data analysis

Standard statistical methodology is based on the assumption that the outcomes, say y, conditional on certain variables, say $\underset{\sim}{x}$, are random outcomes from a probability distribution that is characterized by a fixed dimensional parameter vector, $\underset{\sim}{\theta}, f(y|\underset{\sim}{x}; \underset{\sim}{\theta})$. For instance, the standard linear regression model assumes that $f(y|\underset{\sim}{x}; \underset{\sim}{\theta})$ takes the form that $E(y|\underset{\sim}{x}) = \alpha + \beta'\underset{\sim}{x}$, and $\text{Var}(y|\underset{\sim}{x}) = \sigma^2$, where $\underset{\sim}{\theta}' = (\alpha, \beta', \sigma^2)$. Panel data, by their nature, focus on individual outcomes. Factors affecting individual outcomes are numerous. It is rare to be able to assume a common conditional probability density function of y conditional on $\underset{\sim}{x}$ for all cross-sectional units, i, at all time, t. If the conditional density of y given $\underset{\sim}{x}$ varies across i and over t, the fundamental theorems for statistical inference, the laws of large numbers and central limit theorems, will be difficult to implement. Ignoring the heterogeneity across i and over t that are not captured by $\underset{\sim}{x}$ can lead to severely biased inference. For instance, suppose that the data is generated by

$$y_{it} = \alpha_i + \beta' \underset{\sim}{x}_{it} + v_{it}, \qquad \begin{array}{l} i = 1,\dots,N, \\ t = 1,\dots,T. \end{array} \tag{2.1}$$

as depicted by Figure 1 in which the broken-time ellipses represent the point scatter of individual observation around the mean, represented by the broken straight lines. If an investigator ignores the presence of unobserved individual-specific effects, α_i, and mistakenly estimates a model of the form

$$y_{it} = \alpha + \beta' \underset{\sim}{x}_{it} + v_{it}^* \tag{2.2}$$

the following equation solid line in Figure 1 would depict the pooled least squares regression result which could completely contradict the individual relation between y and $\underset{\sim}{x}$.

One way to restore homogeneity across i and/or over t is to add more conditional variables, say $\underset{\sim}{z}$,

$$f(y_{it}|\underset{\sim}{x}_{it}, \underset{\sim}{z}_{it}; \theta). \tag{2.3}$$

However, the dimension of $\underset{\sim}{z}$ can be large. A model is a simplification of reality, not an exact representation of reality. The inclusion of $\underset{\sim}{z}$ may confuse the fundamental relationship between y and x, in particular when there is a shortage of degrees of freedom or multicollinearity, and so on. Moreover, $\underset{\sim}{z}$ may not be observable. If an investigator is interested only in the relationship between y and $\underset{\sim}{x}$, one approach to characterize the heterogeneity not captured by $\underset{\sim}{x}$ is to assume that the parameter vector varies across i and over t, θ_{it}, so that the conditional density of y given $\underset{\sim}{x}$ takes the form $f(y_{it}|\underset{\sim}{x}_{it}; \theta_{it})$. However, without a structure being imposed on θ_{it}, such a

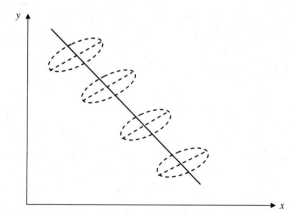

Figure 1   Scatter diagram of (y_{it}, x_{it})

model has only descriptive value; it is not possible to draw any inference on $\underset{\sim}{\theta}_{it}$ from observed data.

One primary focus of methodological panel data literature is to suggest possible structures for θ_{it}. One way to impose some structure on θ_{it} is to decompose θ_{it} into $(\beta, \underset{\sim}{\gamma}_{it})$, where β is the same across i and over t, referred to as *structural parameters*, and $\underset{\sim}{\gamma}_{it}$ as *incidental parameters* because when observations in cross-sectional units and/or time series units increase, there are rising numbers of $\underset{\sim}{\gamma}_{it}$ to be estimated. The focus then will be on how to make valid inference on β after controlling the impact of $\underset{\sim}{\gamma}_{it}$.

Without imposing structure for $\underset{\sim}{\gamma}_{it}$, again it is not possible to make any inference on $\underset{\sim}{\beta}$ because the unknown $\underset{\sim}{\gamma}_{it}$ will exhaust all available sample information. On the assumption that the impacts of observable variables, $\underset{\sim}{x}$, are the same across i and over t, represented by the structure parameters, β, the incidental parameters $\underset{\sim}{\gamma}_{it}$ represent the heterogeneity across i and over t that are not captured by $\underset{\sim}{x}_{it}$. They can be considered as composed of the effects of omitted individual time-invariant, α_i, period individual-invariant, λ_t, and individual time-varying variables, δ_{it}. The individual time-invariant variables are variables that are the same for a given cross-sectional unit through time but that vary across cross-sectional units, such as individual-firm management, ability, gender, and socio-economic background. The period individual-invariant variables are variables that are the same for all cross-sectional units at a given time but that vary though time, such as prices, interest rates, and widespread optimism or pessimism. The individual time-varying variables are variables that vary across cross-sectional units at a given point in time and also exhibit variations through time, such as firm profits, sales and capital stock. The unobserved heterogeneity as represented by the individual-specific effects, α_i and time specific effects, λ_t, or individual time-varying effects, δ_{it} can be assumed to be either random variables (referred to as the *random effects* model) or fixed parameters (referred to as the *fixed effects* model).

3. Linear static models

A widely used panel data model assumes that the effects of observed explanatory variables, $\underset{\sim}{x}$, are identical across cross-sectional units, i, and over time, t, while the effects of omitted variables can be decomposed into the individual-specific effects, α_i, time-specific effects, λ_t, and individual time-varying effects, $\delta_{it} = u_{it}$, as follows:

$$y_{it} = \underset{\sim}{\beta}' \underset{\sim}{x}_{it} + \alpha_i + \lambda_t + u_{it}, \quad \begin{array}{l} i = 1, \ldots, N, \\ t = 1, \ldots, T. \end{array} \tag{3.1}$$

In a single equation framework, individual time effects, u, are assumed random and uncorrelated with $\underset{\sim}{x}$, while α_i and λ_t may or may not be correlated with $\underset{\sim}{x}$. When α_i and λ_t are treated as fixed constants, they are parameters to be estimated, so whether they are correlated with $\underset{\sim}{x}$ is not an issue. On the other hand, when α_i and λ_t are treated as random, they are typically assumed to be uncorrelated with $\underset{\sim}{x}_{it}$.

For ease of exposition, we assume that there are no time-specific effects, that is, $\lambda_t = 0$ for all t and u_{it} are independently, identically distributed (i.i.d) across i and over t. Stack an individual's T time series observations of (y_{it}, x_{it}') into a vector and a matrix, (3.1) may alternatively be written as

$$\underset{\sim}{y}_i = X_i \beta + \underset{\sim}{e} \alpha_i + \underset{\sim}{u}_i, \quad i = 1, \ldots, N, \tag{3.2}$$

where $\underset{\sim}{y}_i = (y_{i1}, \ldots, y_{iT})'$, $X_i = (\underset{\sim}{x}_{i1}, \ldots, \underset{\sim}{x}_{iT})'$, $\underset{\sim}{u}_i = (u_{i1}, \ldots, u_{iT})'$, and $\underset{\sim}{e}$ is a $T \times 1$ vector of 1's.

Let Q be a $T \times T$ matrix satisfying the condition that $Q \underset{\sim}{e} = \underset{\sim}{0}$. Pre-multiplying (3.2) by Q yields

$$Q\underset{\sim}{y}_i = QX_i \beta + Q\underset{\sim}{u}_i, \quad i = 1, \ldots, N. \tag{3.3}$$

Equation (3.3) no longer involves α_i. The issue of whether α_i is correlated with $\underset{\sim}{x}_{it}$ or whether α_i should be treated as fixed or random is no longer relevant for (3.3). Moreover, since X_i is exogenous, $E(QX_i \underset{\sim}{u}_i' Q') = QE(X_i \underset{\sim}{u}_i')Q' = \underset{\sim}{0}$ and $EQ\underset{\sim}{u}_i \underset{\sim}{u}_i' Q' = \sigma_u^2 QQ'$. An efficient estimator of β is the generalized least squares estimator (GLS),

$$\hat{\underset{\sim}{\beta}} = \left[\sum_{i=1}^{N} X_i' Q'(QQ')^- QX_i \right]^{-1} \left[\sum_{i=1}^{N} X_i' Q'(QQ')^- Q\underset{\sim}{Y}_i \right], \tag{3.4}$$

where $(Q'Q)^-$ denotes the Moore–Penrose generalized inverse (for example, Rao, 1973).

When $Q = I_T - \frac{1}{T} \underset{\sim}{e}\, \underset{\sim}{e}'$, Q is idempotent. The Moore–Penrose generalized inverse of $(Q'Q)^-$ is just $Q = I_T - \frac{1}{T} \underset{\sim}{e}\, \underset{\sim}{e}'$ itself. Pre-multiplying (3.3) by Q is equivalent to transforming (3.1) into a model

$$(y_{it} - y_i) = \beta'(\underset{\sim}{x}_{it} - \underset{\sim}{x}_i) + (u_{it} - u_i), \quad \begin{aligned} 1 &= 1, \ldots, N, \\ t &= 1, \ldots, T. \end{aligned} \tag{3.5}$$

where $y_i = \frac{1}{T}\sum_{t=1}^{T} y_{it}$, $\underset{\sim}{x}_i = \frac{1}{T}\sum_{t=1}^{T} \underset{\sim}{x}_{it}$ and $u_i = \frac{1}{T}\sum_{t=1}^{T} u_{it}$. The transformation is called *covariance transformation*. The least squares estimator (LS) (or a generalized least squares estimator, GLS) of (3.5),

$$\hat{\underset{\sim}{\beta}}_{cv} = \left[\sum_{i=1}^{N} \sum_{t=1}^{T} (\underset{\sim}{x}_{it} - \underset{\sim}{x}_i)(\underset{\sim}{x}_{it} - \underset{\sim}{x}_i)' \right]^{-1} \left[\sum_{t=1}^{N} \sum_{t=1}^{T} (\underset{\sim}{x}_{it} - \underset{\sim}{x}_i)(y_{it} - y_i) \right], \tag{3.6}$$

is called *covariance estimator* or *within* estimator because the estimation of β only makes use of within (group) variation of y_{it} and x_{it} only. The covariance estimator of β turns out to be also the least squares estimator of (3.1) when $\lambda_t = 0$. It is the best linear unbiased estimator of β if α_i is treated as fixed and u_{it} is i.i.d.

If α_i is random, transforming (3.2) into (3.3) transforms T independent equations (or observations) into $(T-1)$ independent equations, hence the covariance estimator is not as efficient as the efficient generalized least squares estimator if $E\alpha_i \underset{\sim}{x}_{it}' = \underset{\sim}{0}'$.

When α_i is independent of $\underset{\sim}{x}_{it}$ and is independently, identically distributed across i with mean $\underset{\sim}{0}$ and variance σ_α^2, the best linear unbiased estimator (BLUE) of $\underset{\sim}{\beta}$ is GLS,

$$\hat{\underset{\sim}{\beta}} = \left[\sum_{i=1}^{N} X_i'V^{-1}X_i\right]^{-1}\left[\sum_{i=1}^{N} X_i'V^{-1}\underset{\sim}{Y}_i\right], \tag{3.7}$$

where $V = \sigma_u^2 I_T + \sigma_\alpha^2 \underset{\sim}{e}\,\underset{\sim}{e}'$, $V^{-1} = \frac{1}{\sigma_u^2}[I_T - \frac{\sigma_\alpha^2}{\sigma_u^2+T\sigma_\alpha^2}\underset{\sim}{e}\,\underset{\sim}{e}']$, Let $\psi = \frac{\sigma_u^2}{\sigma_u^2+T\sigma_\alpha^2}$, the GLS is equivalent to first transforming the data by subtracting a fraction $(1 - \psi^{1/2})$ of individual means y_i and x_i from their corresponding y_{it} and $\underset{\sim}{x}_{it}$, then regressing $[y_{it} - (1 - \psi^{1/2})\bar{y}_i]$ on $[\underset{\sim}{x}_{it} - (1 - \psi^{1/2})\bar{\underset{\sim}{x}}_i]$. (for detail, see Baltagi, 2001; Hsiao, 2003).

When α_i is treated as fixed, the covariance estimator is equivalent to applying LS to the transformed model (3.5). If a variable is time-invariant, like a gender dummy, $x_{kit} = x_{kis} = x_{ki}$, the transformation eliminates the corresponding variable from the specification. Hence, the coefficients of time-invariant variables cannot be estimated. On the other hand, if α_i is random and uncorrelated with $\underset{\sim}{x}_i$, $\psi \neq 1$, the GLS can still estimate the coefficients of those time-invariant variables.

4. Dynamic models

When the regressors of a linear model contains lagged dependent variables, say, of the form (for example, Balestra and Nerlove, 1966)

$$\underset{\sim}{y}_i = \underset{\sim}{y}_{i,-1}\gamma + X_i\beta + \underset{\sim}{e}\,\alpha_i + \underset{\sim}{u}_i = Z_i\underset{\sim}{\theta} + \underset{\sim}{e}\,\alpha_i + \underset{\sim}{u}_i, \quad i = 1,\dots,N. \tag{4.1}$$

where $\underset{\sim}{y}_{i,-1} = (y_{i0},\dots,y_{i,T-1})'$, $Z_i = (\underset{\sim}{y}_{i,-1}, X_i)$ and $\underset{\sim}{\theta} = (\gamma,\beta')'$. For ease of notation, we assume that y_{i0} are observable. Technically, we can still eliminate the individual-specific effects by pre-multiplying (4.1) by the transformation matrix $Q(Q\underset{\sim}{e} = \underset{\sim}{0})$,

$$Q\underset{\sim}{y}_i = QZ_i\underset{\sim}{\theta} + Q\underset{\sim}{u}_i. \tag{4.2}$$

However, because of the presence of lagged dependent variables, $EQZ_i\underset{\sim}{u}_i'Q' \neq 0$ even with the assumption that u_{it} is independently, identically distributed across i and over t. For instance, the covariance transformation matrix $Q = I_T - \frac{1}{T}\underset{\sim}{e}\,\underset{\sim}{e}'$ transforms (4.1) into the form

$$(y_{it} - y_i) = (y_{i,t-1} - y_{i,-1})\gamma + (\underset{\sim}{x}_{it} - \underset{\sim}{x}_i)'\,\beta + (u_{it} - u_i), \quad \begin{array}{l} i = 1,\dots,N, \\ t = 1,\dots,T. \end{array} \tag{4.3}$$

where $y_i = \frac{1}{T}\sum_{t=1}^{T}y_{it}$, $y_{i,-1} = \frac{1}{T}\sum_{t=1}^{T}y_{i,t-1}$ and $u_i = \frac{1}{T}\sum_{t=1}^{T}u_{it}$. Although, $y_{i,t-1}$ and u_{it} are uncorrelated under the assumption of serial independence of u_{it}, the covariance between $y_{i,-1}$ and u_{it} or $y_{i,t-1}$ and u_i is of order $(1/T)$ if $|\gamma| < 1$. Therefore, the covariance estimator of $\underset{\sim}{\theta}$ creates a bias of order $(1/T)$ when $N \to \infty$ (Anderson and Hsiao, 1981; 1982; Nickell, 1981). Since most panel data contain large N but small T, the magnitude of the bias can not be ignored (for example, with $T = 10$ and $\gamma = 0.5$, the asymptotic bias is -0.167).

When $EQZ_i u_i' Q' \neq \underset{\sim}{0}$, one way to obtain a consistent estimator for $\underset{\sim}{\theta}$ is to find instruments W_i that satisfy

$$EW_i \underset{\sim}{u_i'} Q' = \underset{\sim}{0},$$ (4.4)

and

$$\text{rank}(W_i QZ_i) = k,$$ (4.5)

where k denotes the dimension of $(\gamma, \beta')'$, then apply the generalized instrumental variable or generalized method of moments (GMM) estimator by minimizing the objective function

$$\left[\sum_{i=1}^{N} W_i(Q\underset{\sim}{y_i} - QZ_i \underset{\sim}{\theta}) \right]' \left[\sum_{i=1}^{N} (W_i Q \underset{\sim}{u_i} \underset{\sim}{u_i'} Q' W_i') \right]^{-1} \left[\sum_{i=1}^{N} W_i(Q\underset{\sim}{y_i} - QZ_i' \underset{\sim}{\theta}) \right],$$ (4.6)

with respect to $\underset{\sim}{\theta}$ (for example, Arellano, 2003; Ahn and Schmidt, 1995; Arellano and Bond, 1991; Arellano and Bover, 1995). For instance, one may let Q be a $(T-1) \times T$ matrix of the form

$$D = \begin{bmatrix} -1 & 1 & 0 & . & . \\ 0 & -1 & 1 & . & . \\ 0 & & . & . & . \\ . & . & . & -1 & 1 \end{bmatrix},$$ (4.7)

then the transformation (4.2) is equivalent to taking the first difference of (4.1) over time to eliminate α_i for $t = 2, \ldots, T$,

$$\Delta y_{it} = \Delta y_{i,t-1}\gamma + \Delta \underset{\sim}{x_{it}'} \underset{\sim}{\beta} + \Delta u_{it}, \quad \begin{matrix} i = 1, \ldots, N, \\ t = 2, \ldots, T, \end{matrix}$$ (4.8)

where $\Delta = (1 - L)$ and L denotes the lag operator, $Ly_t = y_{t-1}$. Since $\Delta u_{it} = (u_{it} - u_{i,t-1})$ is uncorrelated with $y_{i,t-j}$ for $j \geq 2$ and $\underset{\sim}{x_{is}}$, for all s, when u_{it} is independently distributed over time and x_{it} is exogenous, one can let W_i be a $T(T-1)[K + \frac{1}{2}] \times (T-1)$ matrix of the form

$$W_i = \begin{bmatrix} \underset{\sim}{q_{i2}} & 0 & . & . \\ \underset{\sim}{0} & \underset{\sim}{q_{i3}} & . & . \\ . & . & . & . \\ . & . & . & . \\ . & . & . & \underset{\sim}{q_{iT}} \end{bmatrix},$$ (4.9)

where $q_{it} = (y_{i0}, y_{i1}, \ldots, y_{i,t-2}, x_i'), x_i = (x_{i1}', \ldots, x_{iT}')'$, and $K = k - 1$. Under the assumption that (y_i', x_i') are independently, identically distributed across i, the Arellano–Bover (1995) GMM estimator takes the form

$$
\hat{\theta}_{AB,GMM} = \left\{ \left[\sum_{i=1}^{N} Z_i' D' W_i' \right] \left[\sum_{i=1}^{N} W_i A W_i' \right]^{-1} \left[\sum_{i=1}^{N} W_i D Z_i \right] \right\}^{-1}
$$
$$
\times \left\{ \left[\sum_{i=1}^{N} Z_i' D' W_i' \right] \left[\sum_{i=1}^{N} W_i A W_i' \right]^{-1} \left[\sum_{i=1}^{N} W_i D y_i \right] \right\},
$$

(4.10)

where A is a $(T - 1) \times (T - 1)$ matrix with 2 on the diagonal elements, -1 on the elements above and below the diagonal elements, and 0 elsewhere.

The GMM estimator has the advantage that it is consistent and asymptotically normally distributed whether α_i is treated as fixed or random because it eliminates α_i from the specification. However, the number of moment conditions increases at the order of T^2, which can create severe downward bias in finite sample (Zilak, 1997). An alternative is to use a (quasi-) likelihood approach which has the advantage of having a fixed number of orthogonality conditions independent of the sample size. It also has the advantage of making use of all the available samples, hence can yield a more efficient estimator than (4.10) (for example, Hsiao, Pesaran and Tahmiscioglu, 2002; Binder, Hsiao and Pesaran, 2005). Since there is no reason to assume the data-generating process of initial observations, y_{i0}, to be different from the rest of y_{it}, the likelihood approach has to formulate the joint likelihood function of $(y_{i0}, y_{i1}, \ldots, y_{iT})$ (or the conditional likelihood function $(y_{i1}, \ldots, y_{iT} | y_{i0})$). However, y_{i0} depends on previous values of $x_{i,-j}$ and α_i, which are unavailable. Bhargava and Sargan (1983) suggest circumscribing this missing data problem by conditioning y_{i0} on x_i and α_i if α_i is treated as random, while Hsiao, Pesaran and Tahmiscioglu (2002) propose conditioning $(y_{i1} - y_{i0})$ on the first difference of x_i if α_i is treated as a fixed constant.

5. Random vs. fixed effects specification

The advantages of random effects (RE) specifications are as follows:

1. The number of parameters stays constant when sample size increases.
2. It allows the derivation of efficient estimators that make use of both within- and between-(group) variation.
3. It allows the estimation of the impact of time-invariant variables.

The disadvantages of RE specification are that it typically assumes that the individual- and/or time-specific effects are randomly distributed with a common mean and are independent of x_{it}. If the effects are correlated with x_{it} or if there is a fundamental difference among individual units, that is, conditional on x_{it}, y_{it} cannot be viewed as a random draw from a common distribution, the common RE model is mis-specified and the resulting estimator is biased.

The advantages of fixed effects (FE) specification are that it allows the individual-and/or time-specific effects to be correlated with explanatory variables $\underset{\sim}{x}_{it}$. Neither does it require an investigator to model their correlation patterns.

The disadvantages of the FE specification are as follows:

1. The number of unknown parameters increases with the number of sample observations. In the case when T (or N for λ_t) is finite, it introduces the classical incidental parameter problem (for example, Neyman and Scott, 1948).
2. The FE estimator does not allow the estimation of the coefficients that are time-invariant.

In other words, the advantages of RE specification are the disadvantages of FE specification, and the disadvantages of RE specification are the advantages of FE specification. To choose between the two specifications, Hausman (1978) notes that the FE estimator (or GMM), $\hat{\underset{\sim}{\theta}}_{FE}$, is consistent whether α_i is fixed or random. On the other hand, the commonly used RE estimator (or GLS), $\hat{\underset{\sim}{\theta}}_{RE}$, is consistent and efficient only when α_i is indeed uncorrelated with $\underset{\sim}{x}_{it}$. If α_i is correlated with $\underset{\sim}{x}_{it}$, the RE estimator is inconsistent. Therefore, Hausman (1978) suggests using the statistic

$$\left(\hat{\underset{\sim}{\theta}}_{FE} - \hat{\underset{\sim}{\theta}}_{RE}\right)' \left[\text{cov}\left(\hat{\underset{\sim}{\theta}}_{FE}\right) - \text{cov}\left(\hat{\underset{\sim}{\theta}}_{RE}\right)\right]^{-} \left(\hat{\underset{\sim}{\theta}}_{FE} - \hat{\underset{\sim}{\theta}}_{RE}\right) \tag{5.1}$$

to test RE vs FE specification. The statistic (5.1) is asymptotically chi-square distributed with degrees of freedom equal to the rank of $[\text{cov}(\hat{\underset{\sim}{\theta}}_{FE}) - \text{cov}(\hat{\underset{\sim}{\theta}}_{RE})]$.

6. Nonlinear models

The introduction of individual-specific effects, α_i, and/or time-specific effects, λ_t, provides a simple way to capture the unobserved heterogeneity across i and over t. However, the likelihood functions are in terms of observables, $(y_i, x_i), i = 1, \ldots, N$. Therefore, we will have either to treat α_i as unknown parameters (fixed effects) and consider the conditional likelihood,

$$f(\underset{\sim}{y}_i | \underset{\sim}{x}_i, \underset{\sim}{\beta}, \alpha_i), \quad i = 1, \ldots, N, \tag{6.1}$$

or to treat α_i as random and consider the marginal likelihood

$$f(\underset{\sim}{y}_i | \underset{\sim}{x}_i, \underset{\sim}{\beta}) = \int f(\underset{\sim}{y}_i | \underset{\sim}{x}_i, \underset{\sim}{\beta}, \alpha_i) f(\alpha_i | \underset{\sim}{x}_i) d\alpha_i, \quad i = 1, \ldots, N, \tag{6.2}$$

where $f(\alpha_i | \underset{\sim}{x}_i)$ denotes the conditional density of α_i given $\underset{\sim}{x}_i$.

When the unobserved individual specific effects, α_i, (and or time-specific effects, λ_t) affect the outcome, y_{it}, linearly, one can avoid the consideration of random versus fixed effects specification by eliminating them from the specification through some linear transformation such as the covariance transformation (3.3) or first difference transformation (4.8). However, if α_i affects y_{it} nonlinearly, it is not easy to find a transformation that can eliminate α_i. For instance, consider the following binary choice model where the observed y_{it} takes the value of either 1 or 0 depending on the latent response function

$$y_{it}^* = \beta' \underset{\sim}{x}_{it} + \alpha_i + u_{it}, \tag{6.3}$$

and

$$y_{it} = \begin{cases} 1, & \text{if } y_{it}^* > 0, \\ 0, & \text{if } y_{it}^* \leq 0, \end{cases} \tag{6.4}$$

where u_{it} is independently, identically distributed with density function $f(u_{it})$. Let

$$y_{it} = E(y_{it}|\underset{\sim}{x}_{it}, \alpha_i) + \varepsilon_{it}, \tag{6.5}$$

then

$$E(y_{it}|\underset{\sim}{x}_{it}, \alpha_i) = \int_{-(\beta' \underset{\sim}{x}_{it} + \alpha_i)}^{\infty} f(u) du = [1 - F(-\beta' \underset{\sim}{x}_{it} - \alpha_i)]. \tag{6.6}$$

Since α_i affects $E(y_{it}|\underset{\sim}{x}_{it}, \alpha_i)$ nonlinearly, α_i remains after taking successive difference of y_{it},

$$y_{it} - y_{i,t-1} = [1 - F(-\beta' \underset{\sim}{x}_{it} - \alpha_i)] - [1 - F(-\beta' \underset{\sim}{x}_{i,t-1} - \alpha_i)] + (\varepsilon_{it} - \varepsilon_{i,t-1}). \tag{6.7}$$

The likelihood function conditional on $\underset{\sim}{x}_i$ and α_i takes the form,

$$\prod_{i=1}^{N} \prod_{t=1}^{T} [F(-\beta' \underset{\sim}{x}_{it} - \alpha_i)]^{1-y_{it}} [1 - F(-\beta' \underset{\sim}{x}_{it} - \alpha_i)]^{y_{it}}. \tag{6.8}$$

If T is large, a consistent estimator of β and α_i can be obtained by maximizing (6.8). If T is finite, there is only limited information about α_i no matter how large N is. The presence of incidental parameters, α_i, violates the regularity conditions for the consistency of the maximum likelihood estimator of β.

If $f(\alpha_i|\underset{\sim}{x}_i)$ is known, and is characterized by a fixed dimensional parameter vector, a consistent estimator of β can be obtained by maximizing the marginal likelihood function,

$$\prod_{i=1}^{N} \int \prod_{t=1}^{T} [F(-\beta' \underset{\sim}{x}_{it} - \alpha_i)]^{1-y_{it}} [1 - F(-\beta' \underset{\sim}{x}_{it} - \alpha_i)]^{y_{it}} f(\alpha_i|\underset{\sim}{x}_i) d\alpha_i. \tag{6.9}$$

However, maximizing (6.9) involves T-dimensional integration. Butler and Moffitt (1982), Chamberlain (1984), Heckman (1981), and others have suggested methods to simplify the computation.

The advantage of RE specification is that there is no incidental parameter problem. The problem is that $f(\alpha_i|\underset{\sim}{x}_i)$ is in general unknown. If a wrong $f(\alpha_i|\underset{\sim}{x}_i)$ is postulated, maximizing the wrong likelihood function will not yield a consistent estimator of β.

Moreover, the derivation of marginal likelihood through multiple integration may be computationally infeasible. The advantage of FE specification is that there is no need to specify $f(\alpha_i|x_i)$. The likelihood function will be the product of individual likelihood (for example, (6.8)) if the errors are assumed i.i.d. The disadvantage is that it introduces incidental parameters.

A general approach to estimating a model involving incidental parameters is to find transformations to transform the original model into a model that does not involve incidental parameters. Unfortunately, there is no general rule available for nonlinear models. One has to explore the specific structure of a nonlinear model to find such a transformation. For instance, if $f(u)$ in (6.3) is logistic, then

$$\text{Prob}(y_{it} = 1|\underset{\sim}{x}_{it}, \alpha_i) = \frac{e^{\beta'\underset{\sim}{x}_{it}+\alpha_i}}{1+e^{\beta'\underset{\sim}{x}_{it}+\alpha_i}}. \tag{6.10}$$

Since, in a logit model, the denominators of Prob $(y_{it} = 1|\underset{\sim}{x}_{it}, \alpha_i)$ and Prob $(y_{it} = 0|\underset{\sim}{x}_{it}, \alpha_i)$ are identical and the numerator of any sequence $\{y_{i1}, \ldots, y_{iT}\}$ with $\sum_{t=1}^{T}y_{it} = s$ always equal to $\exp(\alpha_i s) \cdot \exp\{\sum_{t=1}^{T}(\beta'\underset{\sim}{x}_{it})y_{it}\}$, the conditional likelihood function conditional on $\sum_{t=1}^{T}y_{it} = s$ will not involve the incidental parameters α_i. For instance, consider the simple case that $T = 2$, then

$$\text{Prob}(y_{i1} = 1, y_{i2} = 0|y_{i1} + y_{i2} = 1) = \frac{e^{\beta'\underset{\sim}{x}_{i1}}}{e^{\beta'\underset{\sim}{x}_{i1}} + e^{\beta'\underset{\sim}{x}_{i2}}} = \frac{1}{1+e^{\beta'\Delta\underset{\sim}{x}_{i2}}} \tag{6.11}$$

and

$$\text{Prob}(y_{i1} = 0, y_{i2} = 1|y_{i1} + y_{i2} = 1) = \frac{e^{\beta'\Delta\underset{\sim}{x}_{i2}}}{1+e^{\beta'\Delta\underset{\sim}{x}_{i2}}}, \tag{6.12}$$

(Chamberlain, 1980; Hsiao, 2003).

This approach works because of the logit structure. In the case when $f(u)$ is unknown, Manski (1987) exploits the latent linear structure of (6.3) by noting that, for given i,

$$\begin{aligned}
\beta'\underset{\sim}{x}_{it} > \beta'\underset{\sim}{x}_{i,t-1} & \quad E(y_{it}|\underset{\sim}{x}_{it}, \alpha_i) > E(y_{i,t-1}|\underset{\sim}{x}_{i,t-1}, \alpha_i), \\
\beta'\underset{\sim}{x}_{it} = \beta'\underset{\sim}{x}_{i,t-1} & \quad E(y_{it}|\underset{\sim}{x}_{it}, \alpha_i) = E(y_{i,t-1}|\underset{\sim}{x}_{i,t-1}, \alpha_i), \\
\beta'\underset{\sim}{x}_{it} < \beta'\underset{\sim}{x}_{i,t-1} & \quad E(y_{it}|\underset{\sim}{x}_{it}, \alpha_i) < E(y_{i,t-1}|\underset{\sim}{x}_{i,t-1}, \alpha_i),
\end{aligned} \tag{6.13}$$

and suggests maximizing the objective function

$$H_N(b) = \frac{1}{N}\sum_{i=1}^{N}\sum_{t=2}^{T}\text{sgn}(\underset{\sim}{b}'\Delta\underset{\sim}{x}_{it})\Delta y_{it}, \tag{6.14}$$

where $sgn(w) = 1$ if $w > 0$, $= 0$ if $w = 0$, and -1 if $w < 0$. The advantage of the Manski (1987) maximum score estimator is that it is consistent without the knowledge of $f(u)$. The disadvantage is that (6.13) holds for any $c\beta$ where $c > 0$. Only the relative magnitude of the coefficients can be estimated $\underset{\sim}{}$ with some normalization rule, say $\| \beta \| = 1$. Moreover, the speed of convergence is considerably slower ($N^{1/3}$) and the limiting distribution is quite complicated. Horowitz (1992) and Lee (1999) have proposed modified estimators that improve the speed of convergence and are asymptotically normally distributed.

Other examples of exploiting specific structure of nonlinear models to eliminate the effects of incidental parameters α_i include dynamic discrete choice models (Chamberlain, 1993; Honoré and Kyriazidou, 2000; Hsiao et al., 2005), symmetrically trimmed least squares estimator for truncated and censored data (tobit models) (Honoré, 1992), sample selection models (or type II tobit models) (Kyriazidou, 1997), and so on. However, often they impose very severe restrictions on the data such that not much of it can be utilized to obtain parameter estimates. Moreover, there are models that do not appear to yield consistent estimator when T is finite.

An alternative to consistent estimators is to consider bias-reduced estimators. The advantage of such an approach is that the bias-reduced estimators may still allow the use of all the sample information so that, from a mean square error point of view, the bias-reduced estimator may still dominate consistent estimators because the latter often have to throw away a lot of the sample, and thus tend to have large variances.

Following the ideas of Cox and Reid (1987), Arellano (2001) and Carro (2006) propose to derive the modified MLE by maximizing the modified log-likelihood function

$$L^*(\underset{\sim}{\beta}) = \sum_{i=1}^{N} \left[\ell_i^*(\underset{\sim}{\beta}, \hat{\alpha}_i(\underset{\sim}{\beta})) - \frac{1}{2} \log \ell_{i,\alpha_i\alpha_i}^*(\underset{\sim}{\beta}, \hat{\alpha}_i(\underset{\sim}{\beta})) \right] \tag{6.15}$$

where $\ell_i^*(\underset{\sim}{\beta}, \hat{\alpha}_i(\underset{\sim}{\beta}))$ denotes the concentrated log-likelihood function of $\underset{\sim}{y}_i$ after substituting the MLE of α_i in terms of $\beta, \hat{\alpha}_i(\beta)$ (that is, the solution of $\frac{\partial \log L}{\partial \alpha_i} = 0$ in terms of $\beta, i = 1, \ldots, N$) into the log-likelihood function and $\ell_{i,\alpha_i\alpha_i}^*(\underset{\sim}{\beta}, \hat{\alpha}_i(\beta))$ denotes the second derivative of ℓ_i^* with respect to α_i. The bias correction term is derived by noting that to the order of $(1/T)$ the first derivative of ℓ_i^* with respect to β converges to $\frac{1}{2} E[\ell_{i,\beta\alpha_i}^*(\beta, \alpha_i)] / E[\ell_{i,\alpha_i\alpha_i}^*(\beta, \alpha_i)]$. By subtracting the order $(1/T)$ bias from the likelihood function, the modified MLE is biased only to the order of $(1/T^2)$, without increasing the asymptotic variance.

Monte Carlo experiments conducted by Carro (2006) have shown that, when $T = 8$, the bias of modified MLE for dynamic probit and logit models is negligible. Another advantage of the Arellano–Carro approach is its generality. For instance, a dynamic logit model with time dummy explanatory variable does not meet the Honoré and Kyriazidou (2000) conditions for generating consistent estimators, but will not affect the asymptotic properties of the modified MLE.

7. Modelling cross-sectional dependence

Most panel studies assume that, apart from the possible presence of individual invariant but period-varying time-specific effects, λ_t, the effects of omitted variables are independently distributed across cross-sectional units. However, often economic theory predicts that agents take actions that lead to interdependence among themselves. For example, the prediction that risk-averse agents will make insurance contracts allowing them to smooth idiosyncratic shocks implies dependence in consumption across individuals. Ignoring cross-sectional dependence can lead to inconsistent estimators, in particular when T is finite (for example, Hsiao and Tahmiscioglu, 2005). Unfortunately, contrary to the time series data in which the time label gives a natural ordering and structure, general forms of dependence for cross-sectional dimension are difficult to formulate. Therefore, econometricians have relied on strong parametric assumptions to model cross-sectional dependence. Two approaches have been proposed to model cross-sectional dependence: economic distance (or a spatial approach) and a factor approach.

In regional science, correlation across cross-section units is assumed to follow a certain spatial ordering, that is, dependence among cross-sectional units is related to location and distance, in a geographic or more general economic or social network space (for example, Anselin, 1988; Anselin and Griffith, 1988; Anselin, Le Gallo and Jayet, 2006). A known spatial weights matrix, $W = (w_{ij})$, an $N \times N$ positive matrix in which the rows and columns correspond to the cross-sectional units, is specified to express the prior strength of the interaction between individual (location) i (in the row of the matrix) and individual (location) j (column), w_{ij}. By convention, the diagonal elements, $w_{ii} = 0$. The weights are often standardized so that the sum of each row, $\sum_{j=1}^{N} w_{ij} = 1$.

The spatial weight matrix, W, is often included into a model specification to the dependent variable, to the explanatory variables, or to the error term. For instance, a *spatial lag* model for the $NT \times 1$ variable $\underset{\sim}{y} = (\underset{\sim 1}{y'}, \dots, \underset{\sim N}{y'})', \underset{\sim i}{y} = (y_{i1}, \dots, y_{iT})'$, may take the form

$$\underset{\sim}{y} = \rho(W \otimes I_T)\,\underset{\sim}{y} + X\,\underset{\sim}{\beta} + \underset{\sim}{u} \tag{7.1}$$

where X and $\underset{\sim}{u}$ denote the $NT \times 1$ explanatory variables and $NT \times 1$ vector of error terms, respectively, and $\otimes$ denotes the Kronecker product. A *spatial error* model may take the form

$$\underset{\sim}{y} = X\,\underset{\sim}{\beta} + \underset{\sim}{v} \tag{7.2}$$

where $\underset{\sim}{v}$ may be specified as in a *spatial autoregressive* form,

$$\underset{\sim}{v} = \theta(W \otimes I_T)\,\underset{\sim}{v} + \underset{\sim}{u}, \tag{7.3}$$

or a spatial moving average form,

$$\underset{\sim}{v} = \gamma(W \otimes I_T)\,\underset{\sim}{u} + \underset{\sim}{u}. \tag{7.4}$$

The spatial model can be estimated by the instrumental variables (GMM estimator) or the maximum likelihood method. However, the approach of defining cross-sectional dependence in terms of 'economic distance' measure requires that the econometricians have information regarding this 'economic distance'. Another approach to model cross-sectional dependence is to assume that the error of a model, say model (7.3), follows a linear factor model,

$$v_{it} = \sum_{j=1}^{r} b_{ij} f_{jt} + u_{it},$$ (7.5)

where $f_t = (f_{1t}, \ldots, f_{rt})'$ is a $r \times 1$ vector of random factors, $b_i' = (b_{i1}, \ldots, b_{ir})$, is $r \times 1$ non-random factor loading coefficients, u_{it}, represents the effects of idiosyncratic shocks which is independent of f_t and is independently distributed across i. (for example, Bai and Ng, 2002; Moon and Perron, 2004; Pesaran, 2006). The conventional time-specific effects model is a special case of (7.5) when $r = 1$ and $b_i = b_\ell$ for all i and ℓ.

The factor approach requires considerably less prior information than the economic distance approach. Moreover, the number of time-varying factors, r, and factor load matrix $B = (b_{ij})$ can be empirically identified if both N and T are large. However, when T is large, one can estimate the covariance between i and j, σ_{ij}, by $\frac{1}{T}\sum_{t=1}^{T} \hat{v}_{it} \hat{v}_{jt}$ directly, then apply the generalized least squares method, where $\hat{v}_{it}$ is some preliminary estimate of v_{it}.

8. Large-N and large-T panels

Our discussion has been mostly focusing on panels with large N and finite T. There are panel data sets, like the Penn-World tables, covering different individuals, industries and countries over long periods. In general, if an estimator is consistent in the fixed-T, large-N case, it will remain consistent if both N and T tend to infinity. Moreover, even in the case that an estimator is inconsistent for fixed T and large N (say, the MLE of dynamic model (4.1) or fixed effects probit or logit models (6.6)), it can become consistent if T also tends to infinity. The probability limit of an estimator, in general, is identical irrespective of how N and T tend to infinity. However, the properly scaled limiting distribution may depend on how the two indexes, N and T, tend to infinity.

There are several approaches for deriving the limits of large-N, large-T panels:

1. *Sequential limits.* First, fix one index, say N, and allow the other, say T, to go to infinity, giving an intermediate limit, then let N go to infinity.
2. *Diagonal-path limits.* Let the two indexes, N and T, pass to infinity along a specific diagonal path, say $T = T(N)$ as $N \to \infty$.
3. *Joint limits.* Let N and T pass to infinity simultaneously without placing specific diagonal path restrictions on the divergence.

In many applications, sequential limits are easy to derive. However, sometimes sequential limits can give misleading asymptotic results. A joint limit will give a more robust result than either a sequential limit or a diagonal-path limit, but will also be substantially more difficult to derive and will apply only under stronger conditions, such as the existence of higher moments. Phillips and Moon (1999) have given a set of sufficient conditions that ensures that sequential limits are equivalent to joint limits.

When T is large, there is a need to consider serial correlations more generally, including both short-memory and persistent components. For instance, if unit roots are present in y and x (that is, both are integrated of order 1) but are not cointegrated, Phillips and Moon (1999) show that, if N is fixed but $T \to \infty$, the least squares regression of y on x is a non-degenerate random variable that is a functional of Brownian motion that does not converge to the long-run average relation between y and x, but it does if N also tends to infinity. In other words, the issue of spurious regression will not arise in a panel with large N (for example, Kao, 1999).

Both theoretical and applied researchers have paid a great deal of attention to the unit root and spurious regression properties of variables. When N is finite and T is large, standard time-series techniques can be used to derive the statistical properties of panel data estimators. When N is large and cross-sectional units are independently distributed across i, central limit theorems can be invoked along the cross-sectional dimension. Asymptotically normal estimators and test statistics (with suitably adjustment for finite T bias) for unit roots and cointegration have been proposed (for example, Baltagi and Kao, 2000; Im, Pesaran and Shin, 2003; Levin, Lin and Chu, 2002). They, in general, gain statistical power over their standard time series counterpart (for example, Choi, 2001).

When both N and T are large and cross-sectional units are not independent, a factor analytic framework of the form (7.5) has been proposed to model cross-sectional dependency and variants of unit root tests are proposed (for example, Moon and Perron, 2004). However, the implementation of those panel unit root tests is quite complicated. When $N \to \infty$, $\frac{1}{N}\sum_{i=1}^{N} u_{it} \to 0$, (7.5) implies that $\bar{v}_t = \underset{\sim}{b}'\underset{\sim}{f}$, where $\underset{\sim}{b}'$ is the cross-sectional average of $\underset{\sim}{b}'_i = (b_{i1}, \ldots, b_{ir})$. Approximating $\underset{\sim}{b}'_i \underset{\sim}{f}$ by its cross-sectional mean function, Pesaran (2005; 2006) suggests a simple approach to filter out the cross-sectional dependency by augmenting the cross-sectional means, $\bar{y}_t$ and $\bar{\underset{\sim}{x}}_t$ to the regression model (7.2),

$$y_{it} = \underset{\sim}{x}'_{it}\,\beta + \alpha_i + \bar{y}_t c_i + \bar{\underset{\sim}{x}}'_t \underset{\sim}{d}_1 + e_{it}, \tag{8.1}$$

or $\bar{y}_t, \Delta\bar{y}_{t-j}$ to the Dickey–Fuller (1979) type regression model,

$$\Delta y_{it} = \alpha_i + \delta_i t + \gamma_i y_{i,t-1} + \sum_{\ell=1}^{p_i} \phi_{i\ell}\Delta y_{i,t-\ell} + c_i y_{t-1} + \sum_{\ell=1}^{p_i} d_{i\ell}\Delta y_{t-\ell} + e_{it}, \tag{8.2}$$

for testing of unit root, where $\bar{y}_t = \frac{1}{N}\sum_{i=1}^{N} y_{it}, \bar{\underset{\sim}{x}}_t = \frac{1}{N}\sum_{i=1}^{N} \underset{\sim}{x}_{it}, \Delta\bar{y}_{t-j} = \frac{1}{N}\sum_{i=1}^{N} \Delta y_{i,t-j}$ and $\Delta = (1 - L), L$ denotes the lag operator. The resulting pooled estimator will again be asymptotically normally distributed.

When cross-sectional dependency is of unknown form, Chang (2002) suggests using nonlinear transformations of the lagged level variable, $y_{i,t-1}, F(y_{i,t-1})$, as instrumental variables (IV) for the usual augmented Dickey–Fuller (1979) type regression. The test static for the unit root hypothesis is simply defined as a standardized sum of individual IV t-ratios. As long as $F(\cdot)$ is regularly integrable, say $F(y_{i,t-1}) = y_{i,t-1}e^{-c_i|y_{i,t-1}|}$, where c_i is a positive constant, the product of the nonlinear instruments $F(y_{i,t-1})$ and $F(y_{j,t-1})$ from different cross-sectional units i and j are asymptotically uncorrelated, even the variables $y_{i,t-1}$ and $y_{j,t-1}$ generating the instruments are correlated. Hence, the usual central limit theorems can be invoked and the standardized sum of individual IV t-ratios is asymptotically normally distributed.

For further review of the literature on unit roots and cointegration in panels, see Breitung and Pesaran (2006) and Choi (2006).

9. Concluding remarks

In this paper we have tried to provide a summary of the advantages of using panel data and the fundamental issues of panel data analysis. Assuming that the heterogeneity across cross-sectional units and over time that is not captured by the observed variables can be captured by period-invariant individual specific and/or individual-invariant time-specific effects, we surveyed the fundamental methods for the analysis of linear static and dynamic models. We have also discussed difficulties in analysing nonlinear models and modelling cross-sectional dependence. There are many important issues, such as the modelling of joint dependence or simultaneous equations models, time-varying parameter models (for example, Hsiao, 1996; 2003; Hsiao and Pesaran, 2006), unbalanced panel, measurement errors (Griliches and Hausman, 1986; Wansbeek and Koning, 1989), and so on, that were not discussed, but can be found in Arellano (2003), Baltagi (2001) or Hsiao (2003).

Although panel data offer many advantages, they are no panacea. The power of panel data to isolate the effects of specific actions, treatments or more general policies depends critically on the compatibility of the assumptions of statistical tools with the data-generating process. In choosing the proper method for exploiting the richness and unique properties of the panel, it might be helpful to keep the following questions in mind. First, in investigating economic issues what advantages do panel data offer us over data-sets consisting of a single cross section or time series? Second, what are the limitations of panel data and the econometric methods that have been proposed for analysing such data? Third, when using panel data, how can we increase the efficiency of parameter estimates? Fourth, are the assumptions underlying the statistical inference procedures and the data-generating process compatible?

I would like to thank Steven Durlauf for helpful comments.

CHENG HSIAO

Bibliography

Ahn, S.C. and Schmidt, P. 1995. Efficient estimation of models for dynamic panel data. *Journal of Econometrics* 68, 5–27.

Anderson, T.W. and Hsiao, C. 1981. Estimation of dynamic models with error components. *Journal of the American Statistical Association* 76, 598–606.

Anderson, T.W. and Hsiao, C. 1982. Formulation and estimation of dynamic models using panel data. *Journal of Econometrics* 18, 47–82.

Anselin, L. 1988. *Spatial Econometrics: Methods and Models*. Boston: Kluwer.

Anselin, L. and Griffith, D.A. 1988. Do spatial effects really matter in regression analysis? *Papers of the Regional Science Association* 65, 11–34.

Anselin, L., Le Gallo, J. and Jayet, H. 2006. Spatial panel econometrics. In *The Econometrics of Panel Data: Fundamentals and Recent Developments in Theory and Practice*. 3rd edn, ed. L. Matyas and P. Sevestre. Dordrecht: Kluwer.

Arellano, M. 2001. Discrete choice with panel data. Working Paper No. 0101. Madrid: CEMFI.

Arellano, M. 2003. *Panel Data Econometrics*. Oxford: Oxford University Press.

Arellano, M. and Bond, S.R. 1991. Some tests of specification for panel data: Monte Carlo evidence and an application to employment equations. *Review of Economic Studies* 58, 277–97.

Arellano, M. and Bover, O. 1995. Another look at the instrumental variable estimation of error-components models. *Journal of Econometrics* 68, 29–51.

Bai, J. and Ng, S. 2002. Determining the number of factors in approximate factor models. *Econometrica* 70, 91–121.

Balestra, P. and Nerlove, M. 1966. Pooling cross-section and time series data in the estimation of a dynamic model: the demand for natural gas. *Econometrica* 34, 585–612.

Baltagi, B.H. 2001. *Econometric Analysis of Panel Data*. 2nd edn. New York: Wiley.

Baltagi, B.H. and Kao, C. 2000. Nonstationary panels, cointegration in panels and dynamic panel: a survey. In *Nonstationary Panels Panel Cointegration, and Dynamic Panels*, ed. B. Baltagi. Amsterdam: JAI Press.

Ben-Porath, Y. 1973. Labor force participation rates and the supply of labor. *Journal of Political Economy* 81, 697–704.

Bhargava, A. and Sargan, J.D. 1983. Estimating dynamic random effects models from panel data covering short time periods. *Econometrica* 51, 1635–59.

Binder, M., Hsiao, C. and Pesaran, M.H. 2005. Estimation and inference in short panel vector autoregressions with unit roots and cointegration. *Econometric Theory* 21, 795–837.

Breitung, J. and Pesaran, M.H. 2006. Unit roots and cointegration in panels. In *The Econometrics of Panel Data: Fundamentals and Recent Developments in Theory and Practice*. 3rd edn, ed. L. Matyas and P. Sevestre. Dordrecht: Kluwer.

Butler, J.S. and Moffitt, R. 1982. A computationally efficient quadrature procedure for the one factor multinomial probit model. *Econometrica* 50, 761–4.

Carro, J.M. 2006. Estimating dynamic panel data discrete choice models with fixed effects. *Journal of Econometrics* (forthcoming).

Chamberlain, G. 1980. Analysis of covariance with qualitative data. *Review of Economic Studies* 47, 225–38.

Chamberlain, G. 1984. Panel data. In *Handbook of Econometrics*, vol. 2, ed. Z. Griliches and M. Intriligato. Amsterdam: North-Holland.

Chamberlain, G. 1993. Feedback in panel data models. Mimeo, Department of Economics, Harvard University.

Chang, Y. 2002. Nonlinear IV unit root tests in panels with cross-sectional dependency. *Journal of Econometrics* 110, 261–92.

Choi, I. 2001. Unit root tests for panel data. *Journal of International Money and Finance* 20, 249–72.

Choi, I. 2006. Nonstationary panels. In *Palgrave Handbooks of Econometrics*, vol. 1, ed. T.C. Mills and K.D. Patterson. Basingstoke: Palgrave Macmillan.

Cox, D.R. and Reid, N. 1987. Parameter orthogonality and approximate conditional inference. *Journal of the Royal Statistical Society, B* 49, 1–39.

Dickey, D.A. and Fuller, W.A. 1979. Distribution of the estimators for autoregressive time series with a unit root. *Journal of the American Statistical Association* 74, 427–31.

Granger, C.W.J. 1990. Aggregation of time-series variables: a survey. In *Disaggregation in Econometric Modeling*, ed. T. Barker and M.H. Pesaran. London: Routledge.

Griliches, Z. 1967. Distributed lags: a survey. *Econometrica* 35, 16–49.

Griliches, Z. and Hausman, J.A. 1986. Errors-in-variables in panel data. *Journal of Econometrics* 31, 93–118.

Hausman, J.A. 1978. Specification tests in econometrics. *Econometrica* 46, 1251–71.

Heckman, J.J. 1981. Statistical models for discrete panel data. In *Structural Analysis of Discrete Data with Econometric Applications*, ed. C.F. Manski and D. McFadden. Cambridge, MA: MIT Press.

Honoré, B. 1992. Trimmed LAD and least squares estimation of truncated and censored regression models with fixed effects. *Econometrica* 60, 533–67.

Honoré, B. and Kyriazidou, E. 2000. Panel data discrete choice models with lagged dependent variables. *Econometrica* 68, 839–74.

Horowitz, J.L. 1992. A smoothed maximum score estimator for the binary response model. *Econometrica* 60, 505–31.

Hsiao, C. 1996. Random coefficient models. In *The Econometrics of Panel Data*. 2nd edn, ed. L. Matyas and P. Sevestre. Dordrecht: Kluwer.

Hsiao, C. 2003. *Analysis of Panel Data*, 2nd edn. Cambridge: Cambridge University Press.

Hsiao, C. and Pesaran, M.H. 2006. Random coefficients models. In *The Econometrics of Panel Data: Fundamentals and Recent Developments in Theory and Practice*. 3rd edn, ed. L. Matyas and P. Sevestre. Dordrecht: Kluwer.

Hsiao, C., Pesaran, M.H. and Tahmiscioglu, A.K. 2002. Maximum likelihood estimation of fixed effects dynamic panel data models covering short time periods. *Journal of Econometrics* 109, 107–50.

Hsiao, C., Shen, Y. and Fujiki, H. 2005. Aggregate vs disaggregate data analysis – a paradox in the estimation of money demand function of Japan under the low interest rate policy. *Journal of Applied Econometrics* 20, 579–601.

Hsiao, C., Shen, Y., Wang, B. and Weeks, G. 2005. Evaluating the effectiveness of Washington State repeated job search services on the employment rate of prime-age female welfare recipients. Mimeo, University of Southern California.

Hsiao, C. and Tahmiscioglu, A.K. 2005. Estimation of dynamic panel data models with both individual and time specific effects. Mimeo.

Im, K., Pesaran, M.H. and Shin, Y. 2003. Testing for unit roots in heterogeneous panels. *Journal of Econometrics* 115, 53–74.

Kao, C. 1999. Spurious regression and residual-based tests for cointegration in panel data. *Journal of Econometrics* 90, 1–44.

Kyriazidou, E. 1997. Estimation of a panel data sample selection model. *Econometrica* 65, 1335–64.

Lee, M.J. 1999. A root-N-consistent semiparametric estimator for related effects binary response panel data. *Econometrica* 67, 427–33.

Levin, A., Lin, C. and Chu, J. 2002. Unit root tests in panel data: asymptotic and finite sample properties. *Journal of Econometrics* 108, 21–24.

Lewbel, A. 1994. Aggregation and simple dynamics. *American Economic Review* 84, 905–18.

MaCurdy, T.E. 1981. An empirical model of labor supply in a life cycle setting. *Journal of Political Economy* 89, 1059–85.

Manski, C.F. 1987. Semiparametric analysis of random effects linear models from binary panel data. *Econometrica* 55, 357–62.

Moon, H.R. and Perron, B. 2004. Testing for a unit root in panels with dynamic factors. *Journal of Econometrics* 122, 81–126.

Neyman, J. and Scott, E.L. 1948. Consistent estimates based on partially consistent observations. *Econometrica* 16, 1–32.

Nickell, S. 1981. Biases in dynamic models with fixed effects. *Econometrica* 49, 1399–416.

Pakes, A. and Griliches, Z. 1984. Estimating distributed lags in short panels with an application to the specification of depreciation patterns and capital stock constructs. *Review of Economic Studies* 51, 243–62.

Pesaran, M.H. 2005. A simple panel unit root test in the presence of cross-section dependence. DAE Working Paper No. 0346, Cambridge University.

Pesaran, M.H. 2006. Estimation and inference in large heterogeneous panels with a multifactor error structure. *Econometrica* 74, 967–1012.

Phillips, P.C. 1986. Understanding spurious regressions in econometrics. *Journal of Econometrics* 33, 311–40.

Phillips, P.C. and Moon, H.R 1999. Linear regression limit theory for nonstationary panel data. *Econometrica* 67, 1057–111.

Rao, C.R. 1973. *Linear Statistical Inference and Its Applications*, 2nd edn. NewYork: Wiley.

Wansbeek, T.J. and Koning, R.H. 1989. Measurement error and panel data. *Statistica Neerlandica* 45, 85–92.

Zilak, J.P. 1997. Efficient estimation with panel data when instruments are predetermined: an empirical comparison of moment-condition estimators. *Journal of Business and Economic Statistics* 15, 419–31.

matching estimators

1. Introduction

Matching is a widely used non-experimental method of evaluation that can be used to estimate the average effect of a treatment or programme intervention. The method compares the outcomes of programme participants with those of matched non-participants, where matches are chosen on the basis of similarity in observed characteristics. One of the main advantages of matching estimators is that they typically do not require specifying the functional form of the outcome equation and are therefore not susceptible to misspecification bias along that dimension. Traditional matching estimators pair each programme participant with a single matched non-participant (see, for example, Rosenbaum and Rubin, 1983), whereas more recently developed estimators pair programme participants with multiple non-participants and use weighted averaging to construct the matched outcomes.

We next define some notation and discuss how matching estimators solve the evaluation problem. Much of the treatment effect literature is built on the potential outcomes framework of Fisher (1935), exposited more recently in Rubin (1974) and Holland (1986). The framework assumes that there are two potential outcomes, denoted (Y_0, Y_1) that represent the states of being without and with treatment. An individual can be in only one state at a time, so only one of the outcomes is observed. The outcome that is not observed is termed a *counterfactual outcome*. The treatment impact for an individual is

$$\Delta = Y_1 - Y_0,$$

which is not directly observable. Assessing the impact of a programme intervention requires making an inference about what outcomes would have been observed in the no-programme state. Let $D = 1$ for persons who participate in the programme and $D = 0$ for persons who do not. The $D = 1$ sample often represents a select group of persons who were deemed eligible for a programme, applied to it, got accepted into it and decided to participate in it. The outcome that is observed is $Y = DY_1 + (1 - D)Y_0$.

Before considering different parameters of interest and their estimation, we first consider what is available directly from the data. The conditional distributions $F(Y_1|X, D = 1)$ and $F(Y_0|X, D = 0)$ can be recovered from the observations on Y_1 and Y_0, but not the joint distributions $F(Y_0, Y_1|X, D = 1)$, $F(Y_0, Y_1|X)$ or the impact distribution, $F(\Delta|X, D = 1)$. Because of this missing data problem, researchers often aim instead on recovering some features of the impact distribution, such as its mean. The parameter that is most commonly the focus of evaluation studies is the *mean impact of treatment on the treated*, $TT = E(Y_1 - Y_0|D = 1)$, which gives the benefit of the programme to programme participants. (If the outcome were earnings and the TT parameter exceeded the average cost of the programme, then the programme might be considered to at least cover its costs.)

Matching estimators typically assume that there exist a set of observed characteristics Z such that outcomes are independent of programme participation conditional on Z. That is, it is assumed that the outcomes (Y_0, Y_1) are independent of participation status D conditional on Z,

$$(Y_0, Y_1) \perp\!\!\!\perp D|Z. \tag{1}$$

The independence condition can be equivalently represented as $\Pr(D = 1|Y_0, Y_1, Z) = \Pr(D = 1|Z)$, or $E(D|Y_0, Y_1, Z) = E(D|Z)$. In the terminology of Rosenbaum and Rubin, 1983, treatment assignment is 'strictly ignorable' given Z. It is also assumed that for all Z there is a positive probability of either participating $(D=1)$ or not participating $(D=0)$ in the programme: that is,

$$0 < \Pr(D = 1|Z) < 1. \tag{2}$$

This assumption is required so that matches for $D=0$ and $D=1$ observations can be found. If assumptions (1) and (2) are satisfied, then the problem of determining mean programme impacts can be solved by substituting the Y_0 distribution observed for matched on Z non-participants for the missing participant Y_0 distribution.

The above assumptions are overly strong if the parameter of interest is the mean impact of treatment on the treated (TT), in which case a weaker conditional mean independence assumption on Y_0 suffices (see Heckman, Ichimura and Todd, 1998):

$$E(Y_0|Z, D = 1) = E(Y_0|Z, D = 0) = E(Y_0|Z). \tag{3}$$

Furthermore, when TT is the parameter of interest, the condition $0 < \Pr(D = 1|Z)$ is also not required, because that condition is only needed to guarantee a participant analogue for each non-participant. The TT parameter requires only

$$\Pr(D = 1|Z) < 1. \tag{4}$$

Under these assumptions, the mean impact of the programme on programme participants can be written as

$$\begin{aligned}\Delta_{TT} &= E(Y_1 - Y_0|D = 1) = E(Y_1|D = 1) - E_{Z|D=1}\{E_Y(Y|D = 1, Z)\} \\ &= E(Y_1|D = 1) - E_{Z|D=1}\{E_Y(Y|D = 0, Z)\},\end{aligned}$$

where the second term can be estimated from the mean outcomes of the matched on Z comparison group. (The notation $E_{Z|D=1}$ denotes that the expectation is taken with respect to the $f(Z|D = 1)$ density.)

Assumption (3) implies that D does not help predict values of Y_0 conditional on Z which rules out selection into the programme directly on values of Y_0. However, there is no similar restriction imposed on Y_1, so the method does allow individuals who expect to experience higher levels of Y_1 to select into the programme on the basis of that information. For estimating the TT parameter, matching methods allow selection into treatment to be based on possibly unobserved components of the anticipated programme impact, but only in so far as the programme participation decisions are based on the unobservable determinants of Y_1 and not those of Y_0.

Second, the matching method also requires that the distribution of the matching variables, Z, not be affected by whether the treatment is received. For example, age, gender, and race would generally be valid matching variables, but marital status may not be if it were potentially affected by receipt of the programme. To see why this assumption is necessary, consider the term

$$E_{Z|D=1}\{E_Y(Y|D=0,Z)\} = \int_{z \in Z} \int_{y \in Y} y \, f(y|D=0,z)f(z|D=1)dz.$$

It uses the $f(z|D=1)$ conditional density to represent the density that would also have been observed in the no treatment $(D=0)$ state, which rules out the possibility that receipt of treatment changes the density of Z. Variables that are likely to be affected by the treatment or programme intervention cannot be used in the set of matching variables.

With non-experimental data, there may or may not exist a set of observed conditioning variables for which (1) and (2), or (3) and (4), hold. A finding of Heckman, Ichimura and Todd (1997) and Heckman et al. (1996; 1998) in their application of matching methods to data from the Job Training and Partnership Act (JTPA) programme is that (2) and (4) were not satisfied, because no match could be found for a fraction of the participants. If there are regions where the support of Z does not overlap for the $D=1$ and $D=0$ groups, then matching is justified only when performed over the *region of common support*. The estimated treatment effect must then be defined conditionally on the region of overlap. Some methods for empirically determining the overlap region are described below.

Matching estimators can be difficult to implement when the set of conditioning variables Z is large. If Z are discrete, small-cell problems may arise. If Z are continuous and the conditional mean $E(Y_0|D=0,Z)$ is estimated nonparametrically, then convergence rates will be slow due to the so-called *curse of dimensionality* problem. Rosenbaum and Rubin (1983) provide a theorem that can be used to address this dimensionality problem. They show that for random variables Y and Z and a discrete random variable D

$$E(D|Y,P(D=1|Z)) = E(E(D|Y,Z)|Y,\Pr(D=1|Z)),$$

so that

$$E(D|Y,Z) = E(D|Z) \Rightarrow E(D|Y,\Pr(D=1|Z) = E(D|\Pr(D=1|Z)).$$

This result implies that, when Y_0 outcomes are independent of programme participation conditional on Z, they are also independent of participation conditional on the probability of participation, $P(Z) = \Pr(D=1|Z)$. That is, when matching on

Z is valid, matching on the summary statistic $\Pr(D = 1|Z)$ (the *propensity score*) is also valid. Provided that $P(Z)$ can be estimated parametrically (or semiparametrically at a rate faster than the nonparametric rate), matching on the propensity score reduces the dimensionality of the matching problem to that of a univariate problem. For this reason, much of the literature on matching focuses on propensity score matching methods. (Heckman, Ichumura and Todd, 1998, and Hahn, 1998, consider whether it is better in terms of efficiency to match on $P(X)$ or on X directly.) With the use of the Rosenbaum and Rubin (1983) theorem, the matching procedure can be broken down into two stages. In the first stage, the propensity score $\Pr(D = 1|Z)$ is estimated, using a binary discrete choice model. (Options for first the stage estimation include, for example, a parametric logit or probit model or a semiparametric estimator, such as semiparametric least squares – Ichimura, 1993 – maximum score – Manski, 1973 – smoothed maximum score – Horowitz, 1992 – or semiparametric maximum likelihood – Klein and Spady, 1993. If $P(Z)$ were estimated using a fully nonparametric method, then the curse of dimensionality problem would reappear.) In the second stage, individuals are matched on the basis of their predicted probabilities of participation.

We next describe a simple model of the programme participation decision to illustrate the kinds of assumptions needed to justify matching. (This model is similar to an example given in Heckman, Lalonde and Smith, 1999.) Assume that an individual chooses whether to apply to a training programme on the basis of the expected benefits. He or she compares the expected earnings streams with and without participating, taking into account opportunity costs and net of some random training cost ε, which may include a psychic component expressed in monetary terms. The participation decision is made at time $t = 0$ and the training programme lasts for periods 1 through τ, during which time earnings are zero. The information set used to determine expected earnings is denoted by W, which might include, for example, earnings and employment history. The participation model is

$$D = 1 \ \text{if} \ E\left(\sum_{j=\tau}^{T} \frac{Y_{1j}}{(1+r)^j} - \sum_{k=1}^{T} \frac{Y_{0k}}{(1+r)^k} \middle| W\right) > \varepsilon + Y_{00}, \ \text{else} \ D = 0.$$

The terms in the right-hand side of the inequality are assumed to be known to the individual but not to the econometrician.

If $f(Y_{0k}|\varepsilon + Y_{00}, X) = f(Y_{0k}|X)$, then

$$E(Y_{0k}|X, D = 1) = E(Y_{0k}|X, \varepsilon + Y_{00} < \eta(W)) = E(Y_{0k}|X),$$

which would justify application of a matching estimator. This assumption places restrictions on the correlation structure of the earnings residuals. For example, the assumption would not be plausible if $X = W$ and $Y_{00} = Y_{0k}$, because knowing that a person selected into the programme ($D = 1$) would likely be informative about subsequent earnings. We could assume, however, a model for earnings such as

$$Y_{0k} = \phi(X) + v_{0k},$$

where v_{0k} follows an MA(q) process with $q < k$, which would imply that Y_{0k} and Y_{00} are uncorrelated conditional on X. The matching method does not require that everything in the information set be known, but it does assume sufficient information to make the selection on observables assumption plausible.

2. Cross-sectional matching methods

For notational simplicity, let $P = P(Z)$. A prototypical propensity score matching estimator takes the form

$$\hat{\alpha}_M = \frac{1}{n_1} \sum_{i \in I_1 \cap S_P} [Y_{1i} - \hat{E}(Y_{0i}|D = 1, P_i)] \tag{5}$$

$$\hat{E}(Y_{0i}|D = 1, P_i) = \sum_{j \in I_0} W(i, j) Y_{0j},$$

where I_1 denotes the set of programme participants, I_0 the set of non-participants, S_P the region of common support (see below for ways of constructing this set). n_1 is the number of persons in the set $I_1 \cap S_P$. The match for each participant $I \in I_1 \cap S_P$ is constructed as a weighted average over the outcomes of non-participants, where the weights $W(i, j)$ depend on the distance between P_i and P_j. Define a neighbourhood $C(P_i)$ for each i in the participant sample. Neighbours for i are non-participants $j \in I_0$ for whom $P_j \in C(P_i)$. The persons matched to i are those people in set A_i where $A_i = \{j \in I_0 | P_j \in C(P_i)\}$. We describe a number of alternative matching estimators below, that differ in how the neighbourhood is defined and in how the weights $W(i, j)$ are constructed.

2.1 Alternative ways of constructing matched outcomes

2.1.1 Nearest-neighbour matching

Traditional, pairwise matching, also called *nearest-neighbour matching*, sets:

$$C(P_i) = \min_j ||P_i - P_j||, \; j \in I_0.$$

That is, the non-participant with the value of P_j that is closest to P_i is selected as the match and A_i is a singleton set. The estimator can be implemented either matching with or without replacement. When matching is performed with replacement, the same comparison group observation can be used repeatedly as a match. A drawback of matching without replacement is that the final estimate will usually depend on the initial ordering of the treated observations for which the matches were selected.

Caliper matching (Cochran and Rubin, 1973) is a variation of nearest neighbour matching that attempts to avoid 'bad' matches (those for which P_j is far from P_i) by imposing a tolerance on the maximum distance $||P_i - P_j||$ allowed. That is, a match for person i is selected only if $||P_i - P_j|| < \varepsilon$, $j \in I_0$, where ε is a pre-specified tolerance. Treated persons for whom no matches can be found within the caliper are excluded from the analysis, which is one way of imposing a common support condition. A drawback of caliper matching is that it is difficult to know a priori what choice for the tolerance level is reasonable.

2.1.2 Stratification or interval matching
In this variant of matching, the common support of P is partitioned into a set of intervals, and average treatment impacts are calculating through simple averaging within each interval. A weighted average of the interval impact estimates, using the fraction of the $D = 1$ population in each interval for the weights, provides an overall average impact estimate. Implementing this method requires a decision on how wide the intervals should be. Dehejia and Wahba (1999) implement interval matching using intervals that are selected such that the mean values of the estimated P_i and P_j are not statistically different from each other within intervals.

2.1.3 Kernel and local linear matching
More recently developed matching estimators construct a match for each programme participant using a weighted average over multiple persons in the comparison group. Consider, for example, the nonparametric *kernel matching estimator*, given by

$$\hat{\alpha}_{KM} = \frac{1}{n_1} \sum_{i \in I_1} \left\{ Y_{1i} - \frac{\sum_{j \in I_0} Y_{0j} G\left(\frac{P_j - P_i}{a_n}\right)}{\sum_{k \in I_0} G\left(\frac{P_k - P_i}{a_n}\right)} \right\}$$

where $G(\cdot)$ is a kernel function and a_n is a bandwidth parameter. (See Heckman, Ichimura and Todd, 1997; 1998; and Heckman et al., 1998.) In terms of eq. (5), the weighting function, $W(i, j)$, is equal to

$$\frac{G\left(\frac{P_j - P_i}{a_n}\right)}{\sum_{k \in I_0} G\left(\frac{P_k - P_i}{a_n}\right)}.$$

For a kernel function bounded between -1 and 1, the neighbourhood is

$$C(P_i) = \left\{ \left|\frac{P_i - P_j}{a_n}\right| \leq 1 \right\}, \quad j \in I_0.$$

Under standard conditions on the bandwidth and kernel,

$$\frac{\sum_{j\in I_0} Y_{0j} G\left(\frac{P_j - P_i}{a_n}\right)}{\sum_{k\in I_0} G\left(\frac{P_k - P_i}{a_n}\right)}$$

is a consistent estimator of $E(Y_0|D=1, P_i)$. (Specifically, we require that $G(\cdot)$ integrates to one, has mean zero and that $a_n \to 0$ as $n \to \infty$ and $na_n \to \infty$. One example of a kernel function is the quartic kernel, given by $G(s) = \frac{15}{16}(s^2 - 1)^2$ if $|s| < 1$, $G(s) = 0$ otherwise.)

Heckman, Ichimura and Todd (1997) also propose a generalized version of kernel matching, called local linear matching. Recent research by Fan, 1992a; 1992b, demonstrated advantages of local linear estimation over more standard kernel estimation methods. These advantages include a faster rate of convergence near boundary points and greater robustness to different data design densities; see Fan, 1992a; 1992b.) The local linear weighting function is given by

$$W(i,j) = \frac{G_{ij}\sum_{k\in I_0} G_{ik}(P_k - P_i)^2 - [G_{ij}(P_j - P_i)]\left[\sum_{k\in I_0} G_{ik}(P_k - P_i)\right]}{\sum_{j\in I_0} G_{ij}\sum_{k\in I_0} G_{ij}(P_k - P_i)^2 - \left(\sum_{k\in I_0} G_{ik}(P_k - P_i)\right)^2}. \tag{6}$$

As demonstrated in research by Fan (1992a; 1992b), local linear estimation has some advantages over standard kernel estimation. These advantages include a faster rate of convergence near boundary points and greater robustness to different data design densities (see Fan, 1992a; 1992b). Thus, local linear regression would be expected to perform better than kernel estimation in cases where the non-participant observations on P fall on one side of the participant observations.

To implement the matching estimator given by eq. (5), the region of common support S_P needs to be determined. The common support region can be estimated by

$$\hat{S}_P = \{P : \hat{f}(P|D=1) > 0 \text{ and } \hat{f}(P|D=0) > c_q\},$$

where $\hat{f}(P|D=d)$, $d \in \{0,1\}$ are standard nonparametric density estimators. To ensure that the densities are strictly greater than zero, it is required that the densities be strictly positive (that is, exceed zero by a certain amount), determined using a 'trimming level' q. That is, after excluding any P points for which the estimated density is zero, an additional small percentage of the remaining P points is excluded for which the estimated density is positive but very low. The set of eligible matches is thus given by

$$\hat{S}_q = \{P \in \hat{S}_P : \hat{f}(P|D=1) > c_q \text{ and } \hat{f}(P|D=0) > c_q\},$$

where c_q is the density cut-off level that satisfies

$$\sup_{c_q} \frac{1}{2J} \sum_{\{i\in I_1 \cap \hat{S}_P\}} \{1(\hat{f}(P|D=1)) < c_q + 1(1(\hat{f}(P|D=0)) < c_q)\} \leq q.$$

Here, J is the cardinality of the set of observed values of P that lie in $I_1 \cap \hat{S}_P$. That is, matches are constructed only for the programme participants for which the propensity scores lie in $\hat{S}_q$.

The above estimators are representations of matching estimators and are commonly used. They can be easily adapted to estimate other parameters of interest, such as the average effect of treatment on the untreated ($UT = E(Y_1 - Y_0|D = 0, X)$), or the average treatment effect ($ATE = E(Y_1 - Y_0|X)$), which is just a weighted average of treatment on the treated (TT) and treatment on the untreated (UT).

The recent literature has also developed alternative matching estimators that employ different weighting schemes to increase efficiency. See, for example, Hahn (1998) and Hirano, Imbens and Ridder (2003) for estimators that attain the semiparametric efficiency bound. The methods are not described in detail here, because those studies focus on the ATE and not on the average effect of treatment on the treated (TT) parameter. Heckman, Ichimura and Todd (1998) develop a regression-adjusted version of the matching estimator, which replaces Y_{0j} as the dependent variable with the residual from a regression of Y_{0j} on a vector of exogenous covariates. The estimator uses a Robinson (1988) type estimation approach to incorporate exclusion restrictions: that is, that some of the conditioning variables in an equation for the outcomes do not enter into the participation equation or vice versa. In principle, imposing exclusion restrictions can increase efficiency. In practice, though, researchers have not observed much gain from using the regression-adjusted matching estimator. Some alternatives to propensity score matching are discussed in Diamond and Sekhon (2005).

2.2 When does bias arise in matching?
The success of a matching estimator depends on the availability of observable data to construct the conditioning set Z, such that (1) and (2) are satisfied. Suppose only a subset $Z_0 \subset Z$ of the required variables is observed. The propensity score matching estimator based on Z_0 then converges to

$$\alpha'_M = E_{P(Z_0)|D=1}(E(Y_1|P(Z_0), D = 1) - E(Y_0|P(Z_0), D = 0)). \tag{7}$$

The bias for the parameter of interest, $E(Y_1 - Y_0|D = 1)$, is

$$\text{bias}_M = E(Y_0|D = 1) - E_{P(Z_0)|D=1}\{E(Y_0|P(Z_0), D = 0)\}.$$

There is no way of a priori choosing the set of Z variables to satisfy the matching condition or of testing whether a particular set meets the requirements. In rare cases, where data are available on a randomized social experiment, it is sometimes possible to ascertain the bias (see, for example, Heckman, Ichimura, and Todd, 1997; Dehejia and Wahba, 1999; 2002; Smith and Todd, 2005).

3. Difference-in-difference matching estimators
The estimators described above assume that, after conditioning on a set of observable characteristics, outcomes are conditionally mean independent of programme

participation. However, for a variety of reasons there may be systematic differences between participant and non-participant outcomes, even after conditioning on observables, which could lead to a violation of the identification conditions required for matching. Such differences may arise, for example, because of programme selectivity on unmeasured characteristics or because of levels differences in outcomes that might arise when participants and non-participants reside in different local labour markets or if the survey questionnaires used to gather the data differ in some ways across groups.

A difference-in-differences (DID) matching strategy, as defined in Heckman, Ichimura and Todd (1997) and Heckman et al. (1998), allows for temporally invariant differences in outcomes between participants and non-participants. This type of estimator matches on the basis of differences in outcomes using the same weighting functions described above. The propensity score DID matching estimator requires that

$$E(Y_{0t} - Y_{0t'}|P, D = 1) = E(Y_{0t} - Y_{0t'}|P, D = 0),$$

where t and t' are time periods after and before the programme enrolment date. This estimator also requires the support condition given above, which must now hold in both periods t and t'. The local linear difference-in-difference estimator is given by

$$\hat{\alpha}_{DM} = \frac{1}{n_1} \sum_{i \in I_1 \cap S_P} \left\{ (Y_{1ti} - Y_{0t'i}) - \sum_{j \in I_0 \cap S_P} W(i,j)(Y_{0tj} - Y_{0t'j}) \right\},$$

where the weights correspond to the local linear weights defined above. If repeated cross-section data are available, instead of longitudinal data, the estimator can be implemented as

$$\hat{\alpha}_{DM} = \frac{1}{n_{1t}} \sum_{i \in I_{1t} \cap S_P} \left\{ (Y_{1ti} - \sum_{j \in I_{0t} \cap S_P} W(i,j)Y_{0tj} \right\}$$
$$- \frac{1}{n_{1t'}} \sum_{i \in I_{1t'} \cap S_P} \left\{ (Y_{1t'i} - \sum_{j \in I_{0t'}} W(i,j)Y_{0t'j} \right\},$$

where $I_{1t}, I_{1t'}, I_{0t}, I_{0t'}$ denote the treatment and comparison group data-sets in each time period.

Finally, the DID matching estimator allows selection into the programme to be based on anticipated gains from the programme in the sense that D can help predict the value of Y_1 given P. However, the method assumes that D does not help predict changes $Y_{0t} - Y_{0t'}$ conditional on a set of observables (Z) used in estimating the propensity score. In their analysis of the effectiveness of matching estimators, Smith and Todd (2005) found difference-in-difference matching estimators to perform much better than cross-sectional methods in cases where participants and non-participants were drawn from different regional labour markets and/or were given different survey questionnaires.

4. Matching when the data are choice-based sampled

The samples used in evaluating the impacts of programmes are often choice-based, with programme participants oversampled relative to their frequency in the population of persons eligible for the programme. Under choice-based sampling, weights are generally required to consistently estimate the probabilities of programme participation. (See, for example, Manski and Lerman, 1977, for discussion of weighting for logistic regressions.) When the weights are unknown, Heckman and Todd (1995) show that with a slight modification matching methods can still be applied, because the odds ratio $(P/(1 - P))$ estimated using a logistic model with incorrect weights (that is, ignoring the fact that samples are choice-based) is a scalar multiple of the true odds ratio, which is itself a monotonic transformation of the propensity scores. Therefore, matching can proceed on the (misweighted) estimate of the odds ratio (or on the log odds ratio).

5. Using balancing tests to check the specification of the propensity score model

As described earlier, the propensity score matching estimator requires the outcome variable to be mean independent of the treatment indicator conditional on the propensity score, $P(Z)$. An important consideration in implementation is how to choose Z. Unfortunately, there is no theoretical basis for choosing a particular set Z to satisfy the identifying assumptions, and the set is not necessarily the most inclusive one.

To guide in the selection of Z, there is some accumulated empirical evidence on how bias estimates depended on the choice of Z in particular applications. For example, Heckman et al. (1998), Heckman, Ichimura and Todd (1997) and Lechner (2001) show that the choice of variables included in Z can make a substantial difference to the estimator's performance. These papers found that biases tended to be higher when the participation equation was estimated using a cruder set of conditioning variables. One approach adopted is to select the set Z to maximize the percentage of people correctly classified under the model. Another finding in these papers is that the matching estimators performed best when the treatment and control groups were located in the same geographic area and when the same survey instrument was administered to both treatments and controls to ensure comparable measurement of outcomes.

Rosenbaum and Rubin (1983) suggest a method to aid in the specification of the propensity score model. The method does not provide guidance in choosing which variables to include in Z, but can help to determine which interactions and higher-order terms to include in the model for a given Z set. They note that for the true propensity score, the following holds:

$$Z \perp\!\!\!\perp D | \Pr(D = 1|Z),$$

or equivalently $E(D|Z, \Pr(D = 1|Z)) = E(D|\Pr(D = 1|Z))$. The basic intuition is that, after conditioning on $\Pr(D = 1|Z)$, additional conditioning on Z should not provide new information about D. If after conditioning on the estimated values of $P(D=1|Z)$ there is still dependence on Z, this suggests misspecification in the model used to estimate $\Pr(D=1|Z)$. The theorem holds for any Z, including sets Z that do not satisfy the conditional independence condition required to justify matching. As such, the theorem is not informative about what set of variables to include in Z.

This result motivates a specification test for $\Pr(D=1|Z)$, that is a test whether or not there are differences in Z between the $D=1$ and $D=0$ groups after conditioning on $P(Z)$. The test has been implemented in the literature a number of ways (see, for example Eichler and Lechner, 2002; Dehijia and Wahba, 1999; 2002; Smith and Todd, 2002; Diamond and Sekohn, 2005).

6. Assessing the variability of matching estimators

The distribution theory for the cross-sectional and difference-in-difference kernel and local linear matching estimators described above is derived in Heckman, Ichimura and Todd (1998). However, implementing the asymptotic standard error formulae can be cumbersome, so standard errors for matching estimators are often instead generating using bootstrap resampling methods. (See Efron and Tibshirani, 1993, for an introduction to bootstrap methods, and Horowitz, 2003, for a recent survey of bootstrapping in econometrics.) A recent paper by Abadie and Imbens (2006a) shows that standard bootstrap resampling methods are not valid for assessing the variability of nearest neighbour estimators, but can be applied to assess the variability of kernel or local linear matching estimators for a suitably chosen bandwidth. Abadie and Imbens (2006b) present alternative standard error formulae for assessing the variability of nearest neighbour matching estimators.

7. Applications

There have been numerous evaluations of matching estimators in recent decades. For a survey of many applications in the context of evaluating the effects of labour market programmes (see Heckman, Lalonde and Smith, 1999). More recently, propensity score matching estimators have been used in evaluating the impacts of a variety of programme interventions in developing countries. Jalan and Ravallion (1999) assess the impact of a workfare programme in Argentina (the *Trabajar* programme), and Jalan and Ravallion (2003) study the effects of public investments in piped water on child health outcomes in rural India. Galiani, Gertler and Schargrodsky (2005) use difference-in-difference matching methods to analyse the effects of privatization of water services on child mortality in Argentina. Other applications include Gertler, Levine and Ames (2004) in a study of the effects of parental death on child outcomes, Lavy (2004) in a study of the effects of a teacher incentive programme in Israel on student performance, Angrist and Lavy (2001) in a study of the effects of teacher training on children's test scores in Israel, and Chen and Ravallion (2003) in a study of a poverty reduction project in China.

Behrman, Cheng and Todd (2004) use a modified version of a propensity score matching estimator to evaluate the effects of a preschool programme in Bolivia on child health and cognitive outcomes. They identify programme effects by comparing children with different lengths of duration in the programme, using matching to control for selectivity into alternative durations. Also, see Imbens (2000) and Hirano and Imbens (2004) for an analysis of the role of the propensity score with continuous treatments. Lechner (2001) extends propensity score analysis for the case of multiple treatments.

PETRA E. TODD

See also **propensity score; selection bias and self-selection; semiparametric estimation; treatment effect.**

Bibliography

Abadie, A. and Imbens, G. 2006a. On the failure of the bootstrap for matching estimators. Technical Working Paper No. 325. Cambridge, MA: NBER.

Abadie, A. and Imbens, G. 2006b. Large sample properties of matching estimators for average treatment effects. *Econometrica* 74, 235–67.

Angrist, J. and Lavy, V. 2001. Does teacher training affect pupil learning? Evidence from matched comparisons in Jerusalem public schools. *Journal of Labor Economics* 19, 343–69.

Behrman, J., Cheng, Y. and Todd, P. 2004. Evaluating preschool programs when length of exposure to the program varies: a nonparametric approach. *Review of Economics and Statistics* 86, 108–32.

Chen, S. and Ravallion, M. 2003. Hidden impact? Ex-post evaluation of an anti-poverty program. Policy Research Working Paper No. 3049. Washington, DC: World Bank.

Cochran, W. and Rubin, D. 1973. Controlling bias in observational studies. *Sankyha* 35, 417–46.

Dehejia, R. and Wahba, S. 1999. Causal effects in non-experimental studies: reevaluating the evaluation of training programs. *Journal of the American Statistical Association* 94, 1053–62.

Dehejia, R. and Wahba, S. 2002. Propensity score matching methods for nonexperimental causal studies. *Review of Economics and Statistics* 84, 151–61.

Diamond, A. and Sekhon, J.S. 2005. Genetic matching for estimating causal effects: a general multivariate matching method for achieving balance in observational studies. Working paper, Department of Political Science, Berkeley.

Efron, B. and Tibshirani, R. 1993. *An Introduction to the Bootstrap.* New York: Chapman and Hall.

Eichler, M. and Lechner, M. 2002. An evaluation of public employment programmes in the East German state of Sachsen-Anhalt. *Labour Economics* 9, 143–86.

Fan, J. 1992a. Design adaptive nonparametric regression. *Journal of the American Statistical Association* 87, 998–1004.

Fan, J. 1992b. Local linear regression smoothers and their minimax efficiencies. *Annals of Statistics* 21, 196–216.

Fisher, R.A. 1935. *Design of Experiments.* New York: Hafner.

Friedlander, D. and Robins, P. 1995. Evaluating program evaluations: new evidence on commonly used nonexperimental methods. *American Economic Review* 85, 923–37.

Galiani, S., Gertler, P. and Schargrodsky, E. 2005. Water for life: the impact of the privatization of water services on child mortality in Argentina. *Journal of Political Economy* 113, 83–120.

Gertler, P., Levine, D. and Ames, M. 2004. Schooling and parental death. *Review of Economics and Statistics* 86, 211–25.

Hahn, J. 1998. On the role of the propensity score in efficient estimation of average treatment effects. *Econometrica* 66, 315–31.

Heckman, J., Ichimura, H. and Todd, P. 1997. Matching as an econometric evaluation estimator: evidence from evaluating a job training program. *Review of Economic Studies* 64, 605–54.

Heckman, J., Ichimura, H. and Todd, P. 1998. Matching as an econometric evaluation estimator. *Review of Economic Studies* 65, 261–94.

Heckman, J., Lalonde, R. and Smith, J. 1999. The economics and econometrics of active labor market programs. In *Handbook of Labor Economics*, vol. 3A, ed. O. Ashenfelter and D. Card. Amsterdam: North-Holland.

Heckman, J., Smith, J. and Clements, N. 1997. Making the most out of social experiments: accounting for heterogeneity in programme impacts. *Review of Economic Studies* 64, 487–536.

Heckman, J. and Todd, P. 1995. Adapting propensity score matching and selection models to choice-based samples. Manuscript, Department of Economics, University of Chicago.

Heckman, J., Ichimura, H., Smith, J. and Todd, P. 1996. Sources of selection bias in evaluating social programs: an interpretation of conventional measures and evidence on the effectiveness of matching as a program evaluation method. *Proceedings of the National Academy of Sciences* 93, 13416–20.

Heckman, J., Ichimura, H., Smith, J. and Todd, P. 1998. Characterizing selection bias using experimental data. *Econometrica* 66, 1017–98.

Hirano, K., Imbens, G. and Ridder, G. 2003. Efficient estimation of average treatment effects using the estimated propensity score. *Econometrica* 71, 1161–89.

Hirano, K. and Imbens, G. 2004. The propensity score with continuous treatments. In *Applied Bayesian Modeling and Causal Inference from Incomplete Data Perspectives*, ed. A. Gelman and X.L. Meng. New York: Wiley.

Holland, P.W. 1986. Statistics and causal inference (with discussion). *Journal of the American Statistical Association* 81, 945–70.

Horowitz, J.L. 1992. A smoothed maximum score estimator for the binary response model. *Econometrica* 60, 505–32.

Horowitz, J.L. 2003. The bootstrap. *Handbook of Econometrics*, vol. 5, ed. J.J. Heckman and E.E. Leamer. Amsterdam: North-Holland.

Ichimura, H. 1993. Semiparametric least squares and weighted SLS estimation of single index models. *Journal of Econometrics* 58, 71–120.

Imbens, G. 2000. The role of the propensity score in estimating dose-response functions. *Biometrika* 87, 706–10.

Jalan, J. and Ravallion, M. 1999. Efficient estimation of average treatment effects: evidence for Argentina's Trabajar program. Policy Research Working Paper. Washington, DC: World Bank.

Jalan, J. and Ravallion, M. 2003. Does piped water reduce diarrhea for children in rural India. *Journal of Econometrics* 112, 153–73.

Klein, R.W. and Spady, R.H. 1993. An efficient semiparametric estimator for binary response models. *Econometrica* 61, 387–422.

LaLonde, R. 1986. Evaluating the econometric evaluations of training programs with experimental data. *American Economic Review* 76, 604–20.

Lavy, V. 2002. Evaluating the effects of teachers' group performance incentives on pupil achievement. *Journal of Political Economics* 110, 1286–387.

Lavy, V. 2004. Performance pay and teachers' effort, productivity and grading ethics. Working Paper No. 10622. Cambridge, MA: NBER.

Lechner, M. 2001. Identification and estimation of causal effects of multiple treatments under the conditional independence assumption. In *Econometric Evaluations of Active Labor Market Policies in Europe*, ed. M. Lechner and F. Pfeiffer. Heidelberg: Physica.

Manski, C. 1973. Maximum score estimation of the stochastic utility model of choice. *Journal of Econometrics* 3, 205–28.

Manski, C. and Lerman, S. 1977. The estimation of choice probabilities from choice-based samples. *Econometrica* 45, 1977–88.

Robinson, P. 1988. Root-N consistent nonparametric regression. *Econometrica* 56, 931–54.

Rosenbaum, P. and Rubin, D. 1983. The central role of the propensity score in observational studies for causal effects. *Biometrika* 70, 41–55.

Rosenbaum, P. and Rubin, D. 1985. Constructing a control group using multivariate matched sampling methods that incorporate the propensity score. *American Statistician* 39, 33–8.

Rubin, D.B. 1974. Estimating causal effects of treatments in randomized and nonrandomized studies. *Journal of Educational Psychology* 66, 688–701.

Silverman, B.W. 1986. *Density Estimation for Statistics and Data Analysis*. London: Chapman and Hall.

Smith, J. and Todd, P. 2005. Does matching overcome Lalonde's critique of nonexperimental estimators? *Journal of Econometrics* 125, 305–53.

maximum score methods

In a seminal paper, Manski (1975) introduces the maximum score estimator (MSE) of the structural parameters of a multinomial choice model and proves consistency without assuming knowledge of the distribution of the error terms in the model. As such, the MSE is the first instance of a semiparametric estimator of a limited dependent variable model in the econometrics literature.

Maximum score estimation of the parameters of a binary choice model has received the most attention in the literature. Manski (1975) covers this model, but Manski (1985) focuses on it. The key assumption that Manski (1985) makes is that the latent variable underlying the observed binary data satisfies a linear α-quantile regression specification. (He focuses on the linear median regression case, where $\alpha = 0.5$.) This is perhaps an under-appreciated fact about maximum score estimation in the binary choice setting. If the latent variable were observed, then classical quantile regression estimation (Koenker and Bassett, 1978), using the latent data, would estimate, albeit more efficiently, the same regression parameters that would be estimated by maximum score estimation using the binary data. In short, the estimands would be the same for these two estimation procedures.

Assuming that the underlying latent variable satisfies a linear α-quantile regression specification is equivalent to assuming that the regression parameters in the linear model do not depend on the regressors and that the error term in the model has zero α-quantile conditional on the regressors. Under these assumptions, Manski (1985) proves strong consistency of the MSE. The zero conditional α-quantile assumption does not require the existence of any error moments and allows heteroskedastic errors of an unknown form. This flexibility is in contrast to many semiparametric estimators of comparable structural parameters for the binary choice model. As discussed in Powell (1994), many of these latter estimators require the existence of error moments and most require more restrictive assumptions governing the relation of errors to regressors.

The weak zero conditional α-quantile assumption comes at a price, however. Extrapolation power is limited: off the observed support of the regressors it is not possible to identify the conditional probability of the choice of interest, but only whether this probability is above or below $1 - \alpha$. See Manski (1995, pp. 149–50). There are also disadvantages associated with the estimation procedure. The maximum score criterion function is a sum of indicator functions of sets involving parameters. This lack of smoothness precludes using standard optimization routines to compute the MSE. Moreover, Kim and Pollard (1990) show that this type of discontinuity leads to a convergence rate of $n^{-1/3}$ rather than the $n^{-1/2}$ convergence rate attained by most semiparametric estimators of parameters in this model. In addition, Kim and Pollard (1990) show that the MSE has a nonstandard limiting distribution. The properties of this distribution are largely unknown, making asymptotic inference problematic. Also, Abrevaya and Huang (2005) prove that the bootstrapped MSE is an inconsistent estimator of the parameters of interest, precluding bootstrap inference.

To repair some of these shortcomings, Horowitz (1992) develops a smoothed MSE (SMSE) for the linear median regression case. This estimator retains the attractive flexibility properties of the MSE, but can be computed using standard optimization routines. In addition, the SMSE converges at a faster rate than the MSE and has a normal limit law allowing first order asymptotic inference. Horowitz (2002) proves that bootstrapped SMSE provides asymptotic refinements and in various simulations demonstrates the superiority of bootstrap tests over first-order asymptotic tests. Kordas (2006) generalizes Horowitz's (1992) SMSE to cover all α-quantiles.

In the next section, we present the multinomial choice model under random utility maximization as well as some intuition behind maximum score estimation in this context. We then discuss the relation between maximum score estimation in the binary response model and quantile regression. Next, we present Kim and Pollard's (1990) heuristic argument for the nonstandard rate of convergence of the MSE in the binary model. Finally, we discuss the method of Horowitz (1992) for smoothing the MSE.

The random utility maximization model of choice and the MSE

Manski (1975) developed the MSE for the multinomial choice model in the context of random utility maximization. Suppose the ith individual in a sample of size n from a population of interest must make exactly one of J choices, where $J \geq 2$.

For $i \in \{1, 2,\ldots, n\}$ and $j \in \{1, 2,\ldots, J\}$, let U_{ij} denote the utility to individual i of making choice j. Assume the structural form $U_{ij} = X'_{ij}\beta + \varepsilon_{ij}$ where X_{ij} is an observable $m \times 1$ vector of explanatory variables, β is a unknown $m \times 1$ parameter vector, and ε_{ij} is an unobservable random disturbance. (A more general set-up can be accommodated. For example, there can be a different parameter vector associated with each choice.)

The utilities associated with the choices an individual faces are latent, or unobservable. However, an individual's choice is observable. Suppose we adopt the maximum utility model of choice: if individual i makes choice j then $U_{ij} > U_{ik}$ for all $k \neq j$. For any event E, define the indicator function $\{E\} = 1$ if E occurs and 0 otherwise. Define

$$Y_{ij} = \{U_{ij} > U_{ik}, \text{ for all } k \neq j\} = \{X'_{ij}\beta + \varepsilon_{ij} > X'_{ij}\beta + \varepsilon_{ik}, \text{ for all } k \neq j\}. \quad (1)$$

If choice j has maximum utility, then $Y_{ij} = 1$. Otherwise, $Y_{ij} = 0$. Thus, for each individual i, we observe $X_{ij}, j = 1, 2,\ldots, J$ and $Y_{ij}, j = 1, 2,\ldots, J$.

The traditional approach to estimating β in the multinomial choice model under the assumption of random utility maximization is the method of maximum likelihood in which the errors are iid with a distribution known up to scale. The likelihood function to be maximized has the form

$$\sum_{i=1}^{n}\sum_{j=1}^{J} Y_{ij}\ \log\ P\left\{Y_{ij} = 1 | X_{i1}, X_{i2}, \ldots, X_{iJ}, b\right\}.$$

For example, when ε_{ij} has the Type 1 extreme-value cdf $F(t) = \exp(-\exp(-t))$, $t \in R$, McFadden (1974) shows that the likelihood probabilities have the multinomial logit specification $\exp\ (X'_{ij}b)[\sum_{k=1}^{J}\exp(X'_{ik}b)]^{-1}$. The corresponding likelihood function is analytic and globally concave. Despite the consequent computational advantages, this specification makes very strong assumptions about the distribution of the errors. The MSE is consistent under much weaker assumptions about the errors. Manski (1975) only assumes that the disturbances ε_{ij} are independent and identically distributed (iid) across choices and independent but not necessarily identically distributed across individuals.

Write b for a generic element of the parameter space. It follows trivially from (1) that the infeasible criterion function

$$\sum_{i=1}^{n}\sum_{j=1}^{J} Y_{ij}\{X'_{ij}b + \varepsilon_{ij} > X'_{ik}b + \varepsilon_{ik}, k \neq j\}$$

attains its maximum value of n at $b = \beta$. Since, for each i, the disturbances ε_{ij} are iid variates, this suggests estimating β with the maximizer of the so-called score function

$$\sum_{i=1}^{n}\sum_{j=1}^{J} Y_{ij}\{X'_{ij}b > X'_{ij}b, k \neq j\}\ .$$

A score for a parameter b is the number of correct predictions made by predicting Y_{ij} to be 1 whenever $X'_{ij}b$ exceeds $X'_{ij}b$ for all $k \neq j$. A maximizer of the score function is an MSE of β. The maximizer need not be unique.

The MSE in the binary choice model and quantile regression
Now consider the binary model where $J = 2$. Define $Y_i = Y_{i1}$ (implying $Y_{i2} = 1 - Y_i$) and $X_i = X_{i1} - X_{i2}$. Then the score function in (2) reduces to

$$\sum_{i=1}^{n}\left[Y_i\{X'_ib > 0\} + (1 - Y_i)\{X'_ib < 0\}\right]. \tag{3}$$

Substitute $1 - \{X'_ib > 0\}$ for $\{X'_ib < 0\}$ in (3) and expand each summand to see that maximizing (3) is equivalent to maximizing

$$S_n(b) = n^{-1}\sum_{i=1}^{n}(2Y_i - 1)\{X'_ib > 0\}. \tag{4}$$

Note that $Y_i = \{Y_i^* > 0\}$ where $Y_i^* = X'_i\beta + \varepsilon_i$ with $\varepsilon_i = \varepsilon_{i1} - \varepsilon_{i2}$. For ease of exposition, write (Y^*, Y, X, ε) for $(Y_1^*, Y_1, X_1, \varepsilon_1)$ and x for an arbitrary point in the support of X. Thus, $Y = \{Y^* > 0\}$ where $Y^* = X'\beta + \varepsilon$.

Before proceeding further, we must consider what interpretation to give to the parameter β in the last paragraph. The interpretation depends on our assumptions. For example, if we assume that β does not depend on x and that for every x, $E[Y^*|x] = x'\beta$, then β is such that the conditional mean of Y^* given $X=x$ is equal to $x'\beta$. However, if we assume that MED $(Y^*|x) = x'\beta$, then β is such that the conditional median of Y^* given $X=x$ is equal to $x'\beta$. In general, the β satisfying the conditional mean assumption will be different from the β satisfying the conditional median assumption. Similarly, if we assume that for $a \neq 0.5$, the conditional α-quantile of Y^* given x is equal to $x'\beta$, then this β will, in general, be different from the β satisfying the conditional median assumption.

With this in mind, for $\alpha \in (0,1)$, write $Q_\alpha(Y^*|x)$ for the α-quantile of Y^* given $X=x$. Fix an $\alpha \in (0,1)$ and assume the linear α-quantile regression specification. That is, assume that for each x in the support of X, there exists a unique parameter β_α, depending on α but not on x, such that $Q_\alpha(Y^*|x) = x'\beta_\alpha$. This implies a zero conditional α-quantile restriction on ε: $Q_\alpha(\varepsilon|x) = 0$ for all x.

For $\alpha \in (0,1)$, define

$$S_n^\alpha(b) = n^{-1} \sum_{i=1}^n [(2Y_i - 1) - (1 - 2\alpha)]\{X_i'b > 0\} . \tag{5}$$

Clearly, $S_n^{0.5}(b) = S_n(b)$ in (4). Assume that the linear α-quantile regression specification holds for some $\alpha \in (0,1)$. To see that it makes sense, under this assumption, to estimate β_α with the maximizer of $S_n^\alpha(b)$, consider $S^\alpha(b) = ES_n^\alpha(b)$. We see that

$$\begin{aligned}
S^\alpha(b) &= E^X[E[(2Y-1) - (1-2\alpha)]\{X'b > 0\}|X] \\
&= E^X[[(2P\{-\varepsilon < X'\beta_\alpha|X\} - 1) - (1 - 2\alpha)]\{X'b > 0\}].
\end{aligned}$$

The linear α-quantile regression specification implies a zero conditional α-quantile restriction on ε: for all x, $P\{\varepsilon \leq 0|x\} \leq \alpha$ and $P\{\varepsilon \geq 0|x\} \geq 1 - \alpha$. Thus, $x'\beta_\alpha > 0$ if and only if $P\{-\varepsilon \leq x'\beta_\alpha|x\} \geq P\{-\varepsilon \leq 0|x\} \geq 1 - \alpha$. Deduce that for each possible value of X, the term in outer brackets in the last expression is maximized at $b = \beta_\alpha$. It follows that $S^\alpha(b)$ is maximized at $b = \beta_\alpha$. The analogy principle (Manski, 1988) prescribes using a maximizer of $S_n^\alpha(b)$ to estimate β_α.

The nonstandard convergence rate

The summands of the criterion function in (5) depend on b only through indicator functions of sets. As such, each summand has a 'sharp edge', to use the terminology of Kim and Pollard (1990). These authors provide a beautiful heuristic for why estimators that optimize empirical processes with sharp-edge summands converge at rate $n^{-1/3}$, rather than the usual $n^{-1/2}$ rate. They decompose the sample criterion function into a deterministic trend plus noise. Then, for each possible parameter value, they consider how the trend and the noise compete for dominance. Only a parameter value for which the trend does not overwhelm the standard deviation of the noise has a fighting chance of being an optimizer. Sharp edges produce standard errors with nonstandard sizes leading to the nonstandard $n^{-1/3}$ rate. We now examine how their argument works for the MSE for a very simple model.

Assume the median regression specification for the model $Y = \{\beta - X - \varepsilon > 0\}$. Thus, $\beta_{0.5} = (\beta, -1)$ where the slope coefficient is known to equal -1 and the intercept β is the unknown parameter of interest. Assume that ε has median zero and is independent of X, so that the conditional median zero restriction is trivially satisfied. Also, assume that the distributions of X and ε have everywhere positive Lebesgue densities.

Refer to (4). Define $S(b) = ES_n(b) = E(2Y - 1)\{X'b > 0\}$. In the intercept example, $S(b) = E(2\{\varepsilon < \beta - X\} - 1)\{X < b\}$. Simple calculations show that

$$S(b) = 2 \int_{-\infty}^{b} F_\varepsilon(\beta - t) f_x(t) dt - F_x(b)$$

where $F_\varepsilon(\cdot)$ is the cdf of ε, $f_x(\cdot)$ is the pdf of X, and $F_X(\ )$ is the cdf of X. Write $f_\varepsilon(\cdot)$ for the pdf of ε. Again, simple calculations show that

$$S'(b) = 2F_\varepsilon(\beta - b) f_x(b) - f_x(b)$$
$$S''(b) = 2F_\varepsilon(\beta - b) f'_x(b) - f_x(b) 2f_\varepsilon(\beta - b) - f'_x(b) .$$

By the median restriction, we see that $S'(\beta) = 0$ and $S''(\beta) = -2f_x(\beta)f_\varepsilon(0) < 0$. Thus, $S(b)$ is locally maximized at $b = \beta$. In fact, the given assumptions imply that $S(b)$ is globally and uniquely maximized at $b = \beta$. The MSE maximizes $S_n(b) - S_n(\beta)$. For each b, decompose $S_n(b) - S_n(\beta)$ into a sum of a deterministic trend and a random perturbation:

$$S_n(b) - S_n(\beta) = S(b) - S(\beta) + [S_n(b) - S_n(\beta) - [S(b) - S(\beta)]] .$$

A Taylor expansion about β shows that for b near β, the trend $S(b) - S(\beta)$ is approximately quadratic with maximum value zero at $b = \beta$:

$$S(b) - S(\beta) \approx S''(\beta)(b - \beta)^2 .$$

By a central limit theorem, for large n, the random contribution $S_n(b) - S_n(\beta) - [S(b) - S(\beta)]$ is approximately normally distributed with mean zero and variance σ_b^2/n where

$$\sigma_b^2 = E[(2Y - 1)[\{X < b\} - \{X < \beta\}]]^2 - [E(2Y - 1)[\{X < b\} - \{X < \beta\}]]^2 .$$

For b near β, the second term is much smaller than the first. It is the first term that accounts for the sharp-edge effect. It equals

$$F_X(\beta) + F_X(b) - 2[F_X(\beta)\{b > \beta\} + F_X(b)\{b < \beta\}] .$$

A Taylor expansion of both $F_x(b)$ terms about β shows that this term is approximately equal to $|b-\beta|f_x(\beta)$ for b near β. Thus, near β, the criterion function $S_n(b)-S_n(\beta)$ is approximately equal to a quadratic maximized at β, namely, $-c_1(b-\beta)^2$ for $c_1 > 0$, plus a zero-mean random variable with standard deviation equal to $c_2 n^{-1/2}|b-\beta|^{1/2}$ for $c_2 > 0$. Values of b for which $-c_1(b-\beta)^2$ is much bigger in absolute value than $c_2 n^{-1/2}|b-\beta|^{-1/2}$ have little chance of maximizing $S_n(b)-S_n(\beta)$. Rather, the maximizer is likely to be among those b values for which, for some $c > 0$,

$$(b-\beta)^2 \le cn^{-1/2}|b-\beta|^{1/2} .$$

Rearranging, we see that the maximizer is likely to be among the b values for which

$$|b-\beta| \le cn^{-1/3} .$$

This is the essence of the heuristic presented by Kim and Pollard (1990) for $n^{-1/3}$ convergence rates. These authors also note that, when criterion functions are smooth, the variance of the random perturbation usually has order $|b-\beta|^2$ (instead of $|b-\beta|$) which, by the same heuristic, leads to the faster $n^{-1/2}$ convergence rate.

Smoothing the MSE

In order to remedy some of the shortcomings of the MSE, Horowitz (1992) develops a smoothed maximum score estimator (SMSE) under a linear median regression specification for the latent variable in the binary model. He replaces the indicator function in (4) with a smooth approximation. His SMSE maximizes a criterion function of the form

$$n^{-1} \sum_{i=1}^{n} (2Y_i - 1)K(X_i'b/\sigma_n)$$

where K is essentially a smooth cdf and σ_n approaches zero as the sample size increases. Thus, $K(X_i'b/\sigma_n)$ approaches the indicator function $\{X_i'b > 0\}$ as $n \to \infty$. By smoothing out the sharp-edge of the indicator function in (4), Horowitz is able to use Taylor expansion arguments to show that the SMSE, under slightly stronger conditions than those required for consistency of the MSE, converges at rate n^δ for $2/5 \le \delta < 1/2$ and has a normal limit. The exact rate of convergence depends on certain smoothness assumptions and satisfies an optimality property (see Horowitz, 1993). The normality result makes it possible to do standard asymptotic inference with the SMSE. Horowitz (2002) shows that the bootstrapped SMSE provides asymptotic refinements.

Kordas (2006) applies the smoothing technique of Horowitz (1992) to the criterion function in (5) and obtains asymptotic results similar to those of Horowitz (1992) for any $\alpha \in (0, 1)$.

ROBERT P. SHERMAN

See also **quantile regression.**

Bibliography

Abrevaya, J. and Huang, J. 2005. On the bootstrap of the maximum score estimator. *Econometrica* 73, 1175–204.

Horowitz, J.L. 1992. A smoothed maximum score estimator for the binary response model. *Econometrica* 60, 505–31.

Horowitz, J.L. 1993. Optimal rates of convergence of parameter estimators in the binary response model with weak distributional assumptions. *Econometric Theory* 9, 1–18.

Horowitz, J.L. 2002. Bootstrap critical values for tests based on the smoothed maximum score estimator. *Econometrica* 111, 141–67.

Kim, J. and Pollard, D. 1990. Cube root asymptotics. *Annals of Statistics* 18, 191–219.

Koenker, R. and Bassett, G., Jr. 1978. Regression quantiles. *Econometrica* 46, 33–50.

Kordas, G. 2006. Smoothed binary regression quantiles. *Journal of Applied Econometrics* 21, 387–407.

Manski, C.F. 1975. Maximum score estimation of the stochastic utility model of choice. *Journal of Econometrics* 3, 205–28.

Manski, C.F. 1985. Semiparametric analysis of discrete response: asymptotic properties of the maximum score estimator. *Journal of Econometrics* 27, 313–33.

Manski, C.F. 1988. *Analog Estimation Methods in Econometrics*. New York: Chapman and Hall.

Manski, C.F. 1995. *Identification Problems in the Social Sciences*. Cambridge, MA: Harvard University Press.

McFadden, D. 1974. Conditional logit analysis of qualitative choice behavior. In *Frontiers in Econometrics*, ed. P. Zarembka. New York: Academic Press.

Powell, J.L. 1994. Estimation of semiparametric models. In *Handbook of Econometrics*, vol. 4, ed. R. Engle and D. McFadden. Amsterdam: North-Holland.

mixture models

Suppose that $\mathscr{F} = \{F_\theta : \theta \in S\}$ is a parametric family of distributions on a sample space X, and let Q denote a probability distribution defined on the parameter space S. The distribution

$$F_Q = \int F_\theta \, dQ(\theta)$$

is a mixture distribution. An observation X drawn from F_Q can be thought of as being obtained in a two-step procedure: first, a random Θ is drawn from the distribution Q and then, conditional on $\Theta = \theta$, X is drawn from the distribution F_θ. Suppose we have a random sample $X_1, \ldots, X_n$ from F_Q. We can view this as a missing data problem in that the 'full data' consists of pairs $(X_1, \Theta_1), \ldots, (X_n, \Theta_n)$, with $\Theta_i \sim Q$ and $X_i | \Theta_i = \theta \sim F_\theta$, but then only the first member X_i of each pair is observed; the labels Θ_i are hidden.

If the distribution Q is discrete with a finite number k of mass points $\theta_1, \ldots, \theta_k$ then we can write

$$F_Q = \sum_{j=1}^{k} q_j F_{\theta_j},$$

where $q_j = Q\{\theta_j\}$. The distribution F_Q is called a finite mixture distribution, the distributions F_θ are the component distributions and the q_j are the component weights.

There are several reasons why mixture distributions, and in particular finite mixture distributions, are of interest. First, there are many applications where the mechanism generating the data is truly of a mixture form; we sample from a population which we know or suspect is made up of several relatively homogeneous sub-populations in each of which the data of interest have the component distributions. We may wish to draw inferences, based on such a sample, relating to certain characteristics of the component sub-populations (parameters θ_j) or the relative proportions (parameters q_j) of the population in each sub-population, or both. Even the precise number of sub-populations may be unknown to us. An example is a population of fish, where the sub-populations are the yearly spawnings. Interest may focus on the relative abundances of each spawning, an unusually low proportion possibly corresponding to unfavourable conditions one year.

Second, even when there is no a priori reason to anticipate a mixture distribution, families of mixture distributions, in particular finite mixtures, provide us with particularly flexible families of probability distributions and densities which can be used to fit to unusually (skewed, long-tailed, multimodal) shaped data which would otherwise be difficult to describe with a more conventional parametric family of densities. Also, such a fit is often comparable in flexibility to a fully nonparametric estimate but structurally simpler, and often requires less subjective input, for example in terms of choosing smoothing parameters. For example, it has been shown that the very skewed log-normal density can often by well approximated by a two- or three-component mixture of normals, each with possibly different means and variances.

Third, many problems can be recast as mixture problems. An example is the problem of estimating a decreasing density function on the positive half-line. Such a density can be expressed as a mixture of uniform distributions, and, in the nonparametric maximum likelihood estimation of mixing distributions discussed below, we see that the solution to this density estimation problem follows from the solution to the general mixture problem.

Formal interest in finite mixtures dates back to at least Karl Pearson's laborious method-of-moments fitting of a two-component normal mixture to data on physical dimensions of crabs in the late 19th century. The mathematical difficulties inherent in fitting mixtures in that time have been greatly eased with the advent of the expectation-minimization (EM) algorithm in the 1970s. This algorithm yields an iterative method for computing maximum likelihood estimates (or very accurate approximations thereof) in a general missing-data situation. As mentioned above, mixtures have a natural missing-data interpretation and so the EM algorithm, together with improved computing technology, has made the task of fitting mixtures models to data much easier, leading to a renewal of interest in them.

Fitting finite mixtures using maximum likelihood

The EM-algorithm generates a sequence of parameter estimates each of which is guaranteed to give a larger likelihood than its predecessor. It can be used whenever the original log-likelihood $\log f_X(x;\theta)$ is difficult to maximize over θ for given x, but $f_X(x;\theta)$ can be expressed as the marginal distribution of X in a pair (X, J) whose corresponding log-likelihood $\log f_{XJ}(x, j; \theta)$ is easier to maximize over θ for given x and j. Given a 'current estimate' θ_0, the next in the sequence θ_1 is defined as the maximizer of the EM-log-likelihood $\ell_{EM}(\theta; x)$ which is defined as the conditional expectation of $\log f_{XJ}(x, J; \theta)$ over the 'missing data' J given $X = x$ computed under θ_0, that is

$$\ell_{EM}(\theta; x) = E \log f(x, J; \theta) \text{ where } J \text{ has density } f_{J|X}(j|x; \theta_0) = f_{XJ}(x, j; \theta_0)/f_X(x; \theta_0).$$

It is guaranteed that $\log f_X(x; \theta_1) \geq \log f_X(x; \theta_0)$.

If we wish to fit a finite mixture

$$f(x; Q) = \sum_{j=1}^{k} q_j f(x; \theta_j)$$

where the number of components k is known, the EM-algorithm works in almost the same way for either one or both of the q_j's or θ_j's unknown. We regard the x_i's as the observed first members of random pairs $(X_1, J_1), \ldots, (X_n, J_n)$, but the J_i's are unobserved. We can write the full data log-likelihood as

$$\sum_{i=1}^{n} \sum_{j=1}^{k} 1\{J_i = j\}\{\log q_j + \log f(x_i; \theta_j)\}$$

(here $q_j = P\{J_i = j\}$). We now outline how to go from an initial set of estimates $q_{01}, \ldots, q_{0k}, \theta_{01}, \ldots, \theta_{0k}$ to the next in the EM-sequence $q_{11}, \ldots, q_{1k}, \theta_{11}, \ldots, \theta_{1k}$. If some of these values are known, then they of course remain unchanged. The first step is to compute the posterior probabilities

$$\pi_{j|i} = P\{J_i = j | X_i = x_i\} \text{ computed under the } q_{0j}\text{s and } \theta_{0j}\text{s} = \frac{q_{0j}f(x_i; \theta_{0j})}{\sum_{j=1}^{k} q_{0j}f(x_i; \theta_{0j})}.$$

The EM-log-likelihood is then obtained by replacing the $1\{J_i = j\}$'s in the full data log-likelihood with the $\pi_{j|i}$'s; note that the EM-log-likelihood thus obtained separates into a term involving the q_j's only and one involving the θ_j's only.

If the q_j's are unknown, we maximize

$$\sum_{j=1}^{k} \log q_j \left\{ \sum_{i=1}^{n} \pi_{j|i} \right\}$$

with respect to the q_j's; this is maximized at

$$q_{1j} = n^{-1} \sum_{i=1}^{n} \pi_{j|i},$$

simply the averages of the posterior probabilities over the data:

If the θ_j's are unknown, we maximize

$$\sum_{j=1}^{k} \sum_{i=1}^{n} \pi_{j|i} \log f(x_i; \theta_j)$$

with respect to the θ_j's. Differentiating with respect to each θ_j and setting to zero yields k weighted score equations:

$$\sum_{i=1}^{n} \pi_{j|i} \frac{\partial \log f(x_i; \theta_j)}{\partial \theta_j} = 0.$$

In many common models these are easily solved. For example, in one-parameter exponential families of the form $f(x; \theta) = e^{\theta x - K(\theta)} f_0(x)$, (for example, normal with known variance, Poisson, and so on) let $\hat{\theta}(t)$ be that value of θ that solves $K'(\theta) = t$.

Then for each j one can explicitly find the EM update as

$$\theta_{j1} = \hat{\theta}\left(\frac{\sum_{i=1}^{n} \pi_{j|i}\, x_i}{\sum_{i=1}^{n} \pi_{j|i}}\right),$$

a known function of a $\pi_{j|i}$-weighted average of the x_is.

Further inferences

Once the model has been fitted, further inferences may consist of confidence intervals for, or hypothesis tests concerning, the component parameters θ_j and/or the mixing proportions q_j. When the model is correctly specified (that is, there really are k components and all the q_j's are positive), the parameter estimates behave more or less in a standard fashion: they are asymptotically normal with an estimable covariance matrix, subject to the component densities $f(x; \theta_j)$ being suitably regular. Hence confidence regions can be computed in a standard fashion, bearing in mind the restrictions on the q_j's: they are non-negative and add to 1. In addition, one should be aware that, when the weights q_j are small or the parameters θ_j for two or more groups are similar, there is a sharp loss of estimating efficiency as well as good reason to be doubtful of the accuracy of asymptotic approximations. This occurs because of the near loss of identifiability of the parameters near the boundaries of the parameter space.

Hypothesis tests are perhaps not so standard, at least not for tests concerning the q_js. If one wishes to test whether an estimate $\hat{q}_j$ is significantly different from zero, the non-negativity constraints have a significant impact, at least when it comes to using large-sample χ^2 approximations to the p-values. Since such a hypothesis constrains a parameter to be on the boundary of the parameter space, the asymptotic distribution of twice the log-likelihood ratio will be a mixture of χ^2 distributions rather than a pure χ^2, on the assumption that the model is otherwise suitably regular. In such a case, a parametric bootstrap approach can be used to obtain an approximate p-value.

An unknown number of components, or completely unknown Q

If the number of components of a putatively finite mixture is unknown, we are essentially on the same footing as knowing absolutely nothing about Q, for reasons we now explain.

For any given data-set $x_1, \ldots, x_n$ with $d \le n$ distinct x_i's and any pre-specified Q, no matter it be discrete or continuous, so long as the likelihoods $f(x_i; \theta)$ are bounded in θ we can find a discrete $\tilde{Q}$ with $m \le d$ support points such that Q and $\tilde{Q}$ provide exactly the same density values at the observed data. That is, for any mixing distribution Q there is a possibly different $\tilde{Q}$ yielding a finite mixture such that Q and $\tilde{Q}$ cannot be distinguished, at least in terms of the data $x_1, \ldots, x_n$. So it suffices to restrict attention to such $\tilde{Q}$s.

An implication of this, when the likelihoods are bounded in θ, is that the maximum likelihood estimate of Q over all distributions, which we denote by $\hat{Q}$, exists and is finite with at most d (the number of distinct x_is) support points. So we never need leave the realm of finite mixtures in this setting.

This is not to say, however, that an estimate of an unknown k is readily available. The number of components in $\hat{Q}$ may be an overestimate in that some support points (respectively mixing proportions) may be so close together (small) that combining them into a single point (removing them) hardly decreases the likelihood. This and other issues related to trying to infer something about the number of components in a mixture, like hypothesis tests concerning k, are difficult problems. Some problems are still open, others have solutions that are possibly too complex to be useful.

The nonparametric estimate of Q

When the estimate $\hat{Q}$ discussed above exists, it is discrete with at most d support points. Hence a strategy for computing it is to try to fit a finite mixture with d components using the EM-algorithm. In many situations this yields a sensible result. More sophisticated algorithms exist however which are related to the following gradient function characterization.

The gradient function

$$D_Q(\theta) = \sum_{i=1}^{n} \left[\frac{f(x_i; \theta)}{f(x_i; Q)} - 1 \right]$$

measures the rate of increase in the log-likelihood if we remove a small amount of weight from the mixing distribution Q and put it at the point θ. Hence, for a candidate estimate Q, if for some θ we have $D_Q(\theta) > 0$, we know that we can increase the log-likelihood by putting some weight at θ.

In light of this the following result is not surprising: if the nonparametric maximum likelihood estimate $\hat{Q}$ exists, then $D_{\hat{Q}}(\theta) \leq 0$ for all θ, and the support points of $\hat{Q}$ are included in the set of values θ where $D_{\hat{Q}}(\theta) = 0$. The fact that $D_{\hat{Q}}(\theta) > 0$ for no θ makes sense; moving mass around from $\hat{Q}$ to any other θ cannot increase the likelihood.

The nonparametric version of the mixture model falls into the class of convex models, a subject with its own independent literature. Often convex models can be written as mixture models. For example, a distribution function that is concave on the positive half-line can also be written as a nonparametric mixture of the form $\int f(x; \theta)\, dQ(\theta)$ with component density $f(x; \theta) = 1\{0 < x < \theta\}/\theta$. One can deduce that the nonparametric likelihood estimator is the least concave majorant of the empirical distribution function using the above gradient characterization. See McLachlan and Peel (2000), Titterington, Smith and Makov (1985) or Lindsay (1995) for further examples and other references.

Mixtures and nonlinear time series

Methods related to mixtures of distributions have in recent times enjoyed a surge in popularity in finance and econometrics, in particular in the area of time series analysis. Traditional (linear) time series models, while intuitive and tractable, are well-known to be unable to capture certain features of much financial or econometric data, including variability that changes over time and marginal distributions that can be multimodal or long-tailed.

Traditional linear time series models with Gaussian innovations have marginal and conditional distributions which are Gaussian. However, in many applications both marginal and conditional distributions can be multimodal, skewed, and fat-tailed, and exhibit other non-Gaussian features. Also, series can exhibit bursts of volatility, where the variability changes in strange ways, sometimes with some dependence on past and current values of the observable series or an unobserved underlying process of 'shocks'. In several different settings, ideas of mixtures have led to new types of models that have been quite successful at capturing many of these problematic features.

One example is the mixture of autoregressive (AR) models idea. The standard autoregressive model, where the observation at time t, Y_t, has a conditional distribution, given the past $Y_{t-1}, Y_{t-2}, \ldots$ of the form

$$Y_t = \theta_0 + \sum_{\ell=1}^{L} \theta_\ell Y_{t-\ell} + sZ_t,$$

where the θ_ℓ's are fixed constants and the Z_t's are independent (often standard Gaussian) random variables. Assuming $\theta_k \neq 0$ here, the model is said to be autoregressive of order L (we abbreviate this to AR(L)). The mixture version can be represented by replacing the parameter vector $\theta = (\theta_0, \theta_1, \ldots, \theta_L, s)^T$ above at each time point t with a random version $\Theta_t = (\Theta_{0t}, \Theta_{1t}, \ldots, \Theta_{Lt}, S_t)^T$, yielding

$$Y_t = \Theta_{0t} + \sum_{\ell=1}^{L} \Theta_{\ell t} Y_{t-\ell} + S_t Z_t$$

where $P(\Theta_t = \theta^{(j)}) = q_j$, each $q_j \geq 0$ and $\sum_{j=1}^{k} q_j = 1$. For each j, we have a different AR *regime* with corresponding parameter vector $\theta^{(j)} = (\theta_0^{(j)}, \ldots, \theta_L^{(j)}, s_j)^T$ which is chosen randomly at each time point according to the probability distribution given by the q_j's, independently of Z_t and past values of the series. All regimes need not be of the same order; an AR(L') regime with $L' < L$ can be obtained by just setting $\theta_{L'+1}^{(j)} = \cdots = \theta_L^{(j)} = 0$.

This so-called mixture autoregressive (MAR) model has several appealing features. Its mathematical form means that it is relatively straightforward to derive its autocorrelation function, and indeed its stationarity properties are similarly easy to derive. An interesting point here is that it is possible to have some of the component regimes non-stationary, but, so long as their mixing proportions q_j are small enough, the overall series can still have a second-order stationarity property. In looser terms, we can have occasional explosive behaviour but still have a series that is well-behaved in the long run. For example, when the stock market becomes volatile we can have short bursts of heightened activity which eventually settle down. Such features cannot be captured by a single AR model.

Another feature of the MAR model is that the marginal as well as conditional distributions can change with time and be multimodal. Again, during a period of stock market volatility we might expect some sharp increases and/or decreases during these periods which may result in bi- or multimodal conditional distributions. Consider the following example (simplified version of fit to IBM data from Wong and Li, 2000):

$$Y_t = \begin{cases} 0.7Y_{t-1} + 0.3Y_{t-2} + 5Z_t + & \text{with prob. } 0.55; \\ 1.7Y_{t-1} - 0.7Y_{t-2} + 5Z_t + & \text{with prob. } 0.4; \\ Y_{t-1} + 20Z_t & \text{with prob. } 0.5. \end{cases}$$

If the series has been quite volatile and Y_{t-1} and Y_{t-2} are very different, say $Y_{t-1} = 200$ and $Y_{t-2} = 300$, then the conditional distribution of Y_t would be a mixture of the form

$$Y_t \sim \begin{cases} N(230, 25) & \text{with prob. } 0.55; \\ N(130, 25) & \text{with prob. } 0.4; \\ N(200, 400) & \text{with prob. } 0.05. \end{cases}$$

However, if the series had been quite stable, say with $Y_{t-1} = 200$ and $Y_{t-2} = 201$ say, then the conditional distribution would be

$$Y_t \sim \begin{cases} N(200.3, 25) & \text{with prob. } 0.55; \\ N(199.3, 25) & \text{with prob. } 0.4; \\ N(200, 400) & \text{with prob. } 0.05. \end{cases}$$

So we still have a component for increases, a component for decreases and the same component for outliers. However, the first two components are so similar that the mixture density is markedly unimodal. This example illustrates that the MAR can capture volatility as well as a changing, possibly multimodal conditional distribution.

Estimation

The mixture structure also enables maximum-likelihood estimation of unknown parameters via the EM algorithm. We briefly outline how this would work when fitting a mixture of k AR(L) regimes, although the basic steps are the same in cases where the order of each regime can differ from component to component. As in the i.i.d. case though, the question of choosing k, the number of components of the mixture, is a difficult open problem.

We can represent the mixture in terms of an unobserved label J_t at each time point which indicates which regime applies; it is equal to j with probability $q_j, j = 1, \ldots, k$. If these were known, then the full log-likelihood of observed $(y_{L+1}, \ldots, y_n)^T$

(conditional on $y_1, \ldots, y_L$) would be

$$\ell_{\text{full}}(\boldsymbol{q}, \boldsymbol{\theta}^{(1)}, \ldots, \boldsymbol{\theta}^{(k)}) = \sum_{t=L+1}^{n} \left\{ \sum_{j=1}^{k} 1\{J_t = j\}[\log q_j + \log f(y_t, \ldots, y_{t-L}; \boldsymbol{\theta}^{(j)})] \right\},$$

where $f(\cdot; \boldsymbol{\theta})$ is the conditional density of Y_t given $Y_{t-1}, \ldots, Y_{t-L}$ under a single AR(L) regime. We now show how a current set of estimates $\tilde{q}, \tilde{\boldsymbol{\theta}}^{(1)}, \ldots, \tilde{\boldsymbol{\theta}}^{(k)}$ would be updated. There are two steps, an E-step and an M-step. At the E-step the missing data is set equal to its conditional expectation, given current parameter estimates and data, which here reduce to the posterior probabilities:

$$\pi_{j|t} = P\{J_t = j | Y_t = y_t, \ldots, Y_{t-L} = y_{t-L}\}$$

$$\text{computed under current estimates} = \frac{\tilde{q}_j f(y_t, \ldots, y_{t-L}; \tilde{\boldsymbol{\theta}}^{(j)})}{\sum_{t=L+1}^{n} \tilde{q}_j f(y_t, \ldots, y_{t-L}; \tilde{\boldsymbol{\theta}}^{(j)})}$$

The M-step consists of firstly defining the EM-log-likelihood $\ell_{\text{EM}}(\boldsymbol{q}, \boldsymbol{\theta}^{(1)}, \ldots, \boldsymbol{\theta}^{(k)})$ obtained by replacing $1\{J_j = t\}$ with $\pi_{j|t}$, and then maximizing over the remaining parameters. As in the i.i.d. case, the EM-log-likelihood separates into two pieces, one involving just the q_j's, which is maximized at

$$\hat{q}_j = \frac{\sum_{t=L+1}^{n} \pi_{j|t}}{n - L}$$

and another involving the other parameters of the form

$$\sum_{j=1}^{k} \sum_{t=L+1}^{n} \pi_{j|t} \log f(y_t, \ldots, y_{t-L}; \boldsymbol{\theta}^{(j)})$$

which when differentiated partially with respect to each $\boldsymbol{\theta}^{(j)}$ yields a separate set of *weighted likelihood* equations just as in the i.i.d. case, for example,

$$\frac{\partial}{\partial \theta_0^{(j)}} \ell_{\text{EM}}(\boldsymbol{q}, \boldsymbol{\theta}^{(1)}, \ldots, \boldsymbol{\theta}^{(k)}) = \sum_{t=L+1}^{n} \pi_{j|t} \frac{\partial}{\partial \theta_0} \log f(y_t, \ldots, y_{t-L}; \boldsymbol{\theta}) \bigg|_{\boldsymbol{\theta} = \boldsymbol{\theta}^{(j)}}.$$

Thus, if one has a computational method to obtain the maximum likelihood estimate for a straight AR(L) model, it is possible to use the same computations on this weighted form in the M-step for the more general mixture case. Note that this method is not restricted to the Gaussian-Z_t case or a linear autoregression function.

As mentioned earlier, the autocorrelation structure of the MAR model is quite straightforward to analyse; in fact, it inherits much of the simplicity of the standard AR model. One thing that one cannot obtain using an AR or MAR model is a first-order stationary series whose square exhibits some autocorrelation, which is a key feature of certain time series models designed to capture time-varying volatility.

The main breakthrough in this area was the introduction of the autoregressive conditional heteroscedastic (ARCH) model for time series errors in the early 1980s by Engle, where S_t^2, the variance of the error at time t, is allowed to depend on squares of earlier errors: if Z_t's are i.i.d. mean-zero-unit-variance errors then the series $\{\varepsilon_t\}$ given by

$$\varepsilon_t = S_t Z_t; \quad S_t = \left(\beta_0 + \sum_{\ell=1}^{M} \beta_\ell \varepsilon_{t-\ell}^2 \right)$$

is an ARCH(M)-series. One can incorporate this into a mixture setting by using the same specification for the conditional mean as in the MAR case, but allowing the errors to be generated *within each regime* by a different ARCH mechanism. Hence the full specification is

$$Y_t = \Theta_{0t} + \sum_{\ell=1}^{L} \Theta_{\ell t} Y_{t-\ell} + \varepsilon_t, \varepsilon_t = S_t Z_t; \quad S_t = \left(B_0 + \sum_{\ell=1}^{M} B_\ell \varepsilon_{t-\ell}^2 \right),$$

where now (Θ_t, B_t) takes the value $(\theta^{(j)}, \beta^{(j)})$ with probability q_j.

The resulting MAR–ARCH model combines the extra flexibility of the MAR model with the superior modelling of volatility enjoyed by ARCH series. In addition, the ability to fit several different AR–ARCH regimes provides an aid to interpretation; as in the MAR case, we can have a different regime for each of several possible reactions at each time point, and furthermore the choices (that is, conditional distributions) can change with time. The EM-algorithm can be employed in essentially the same way as the MAR model, so long as weighted maximum likelihood estimation can be performed in the M-step for each AR-ARCH regime (allowing the possibility of non-normal errors).

Connection to threshold models
There is some connection between MAR and MAR-ARCH models and another class of non-linear time series known as (self-exciting) threshold autoregressive (SETAR) models. An elementary version is

$$Y_t = \begin{cases} \theta_0^{(1)} + \theta_1^{(1)} Y_{t-1} + s_1 Z_t & \text{if } Y_{t-1} < c, \\ \theta_0^{(2)} + \theta_1^{(2)} Y_{t-1} + s_2 Z_t & \text{if } Y_{t-1} \geq c, \end{cases}$$

That is, follows one of two possible AR(1) regimes, the choice depending on whether the previous value Y_{t-1} exceeds a threshold c, in contrast to the MAR model where the choice is made independently of the earlier values of the series.

It can be shown that if the Z_t's are Gaussian then the marginal distribution of the zeroth order (where $\theta_1^{(j)} \equiv 0$) is a mixture of Gaussians, permitting multimodality.

A class of models intermediate between the SETAR models and MAR involves having several AR regimes, but the choice at each time point is partly influenced by earlier values of the series, but not in a completely deterministic way. A simple version involves replacing the thresholding rule $Y_{t-1} < c$ with $Y_{t-1} + {}_t < c$ for an independent random variable η_t. In this case, we have a mixture of AR regimes where the mixing proportions $q_j = q_j(Y_{t-1}, c)$ depend on earlier values of the series and the threshold.

These models (MAR, MAR-ARCH, SETAR and intermediate versions) are still being fully developed, however an excellent introduction is provided in Tong (1990).

Summary

Mixture distributions, particularly finite mixtures, in general permit a great increase in flexibility of modelling without an overwhelming increase in computation difficulty, while also helping in interpretation by modelling heterogeneity in a natural way. In particular, if distributions within a certain model can be fitted by maximum likelihood, then finite mixtures of distributions from the same model can in general also by fitted by maximum likelihood using the EM-algorithm. Such finite mixtures can capture heterogeneity or other complex behaviour that single components (that is, when there is no mixture) cannot capture.

BRUCE G. LINDSAY AND MICHAEL STEWART

Bibliography

Lindsay, B.G. 1995. *Mixture Models: Theory, Geometry and Applications*, NSF-CBMS Regional Conference Series in Probability and Statistics, 5. Hayward, CA: Institute of Mathematical Statistics and American Statistical Association.

McLachlan, G. and Peel, D. 2000. *Finite Mixture Models*. New York: Wiley-Interscience.

Titterington, D.M., Smith, A.F.M. and Makov, U.E. 1985. *Statistical Analysis of Finite Mixture Distributions*. Chichester: John Wiley.

Tong, H. 1990. *Nonlinear Time Series: A Dynamical System Approach*. Oxford: Clarendon Press.

Wong, C.S. and Li, W.K. 2000. On a mixture autoregressive model. *Journal of the Royal Statistical Society*, Series B 62, 95–115.

natural experiments and quasi-natural experiments

The term 'natural experiment' has been used in many, often, contradictory, ways. It is not unfair to say that the term is frequently employed to describe situations that are neither 'natural' nor 'experiments' or situations which are 'natural, but not experiments' or vice versa.

It will serve the interests of clarity to initially direct most of our attention to the second term – experiment. A useful, albeit philosophically charged definition of an experiment 'is a set of actions and observations, performed in the context of solving a particular problem or question, to support or falsify a hypothesis or research concerning phenomena' (Wikipedia, 2006).

With such a broad definition in hand, it may not be surprising to observe a wide range of views among economists about whether or not they perform experiments. Vernon Smith, for example, in EXPERIMENTAL METHODS IN ECONOMICS, begins with the premise that 'historically, the method and subject matter of economics have *presupposed* that it was a *non–experimental ... science more like astronomy or meteorology than physics or chemistry*' (emphasis added). As he makes clear, his observation implies that *today*, economics is an experimental science. Bastable's article on the same subject in the first edition of *The New Palgrave* overlaps only superficially with Smith's and divides experiments along the lines suggested by Bacon: *experimenta lucifera*, in which 'theoretical' concerns dominate, and *experimenta fructifera*, which concern themselves with 'practical' matters. In sharp contrast to Smith, Bastable concludes that *experimenta lucifera* are 'a very slight resource' (1987, p. 240) in economics.

These two views of experiment, however, do not seem helpful in understanding the controversy regarding natural experiments. 'Experiment' in our context is merely the notion of putting one's view to the most 'severe' test possible. A good summary of the the spirit of experiment (natural or otherwise) comes from the American philosopher Charles Sanders Peirce (and see Mayo, 1996 for a nice exposition of this and related points):

> [After posing a question or theory], the next business in order is to commence deducing from it whatever experimental predictions are extremest and most unlikely ... in order to subject them to the *test of experiment*.
>
> The process of testing it will consist, not in examining the facts, in order to see how well they accord with the hypothesis, but on the contrary in examining such of the probable consequences of the hypothesis as would be capable of direct verification, especially those consequences which would be very unlikely or surprising in case the hypothesis were not true.
>
> When the hypothesis has sustained a testing as severe as the present state of our knowledge ... renders imperative, it will be admitted provisionally ...

subject of course to reconsideration. (Peirce, 1958, 7.182 (emphasis added) and 7.231 as cited in Mayo, 1996)

The philosophy of experimentation in natural science

In the emergence of modern natural science during the 16th century, experiments represented an important break with a long historical tradition in which observation of phenomenon was used *in* theories as a way to justify or support a priori reasoning. In Drake's (1981) view: 'The Aristotelian principle of appealing to experience had degenerated among philosophers into dependence on reasoning supported by casual examples among philosophers and the refutation of opponents by pointing to apparent exceptions not carefully examined.' In the useful historical account provided by Shadish, Cook, and Campbell (2002) it is suggested that this 'break' was twofold: first, experiments were frequently employed to correct or refute theories. This naturally led to conflict with political and religious authorities: Galileo Galilei's conflict with the Church and his fate at the hands of the Inquisition is among the best-known examples of this conflict. Second, experiments increasingly involved 'manipulation' to learn about 'causes'. Passive observation was not sufficient. As Hacking (1983, p. 149) says of early experimenter Sir Francis Bacon: 'He taught that not only must we observe nature in the raw, but that we must also "twist the lion's tale", that is, manipulate our world in order to learn its secrets.'

Indeed, at some level in the natural sciences there has been comparatively little debate about the centrality of experiment – ironically, it has typically been only philosophers of science who have downplayed the importance of experiment. Hacking (1983) makes a strong case that philosophers typically have exhibited a remarkably high degree of bias in minimizing their importance in favour of 'theory'. Until the 19th century, the term experiment was typically reserved for studies in the natural sciences.

In the low sciences such as economics and medicine, the role of experiment is been the subject of extensive debate, much tied up with the debate on whether all the types of experiments possible in real science are possible in economics as well as with debates about the many meanings of the word 'cause'.

A key distinction between much real science and economics involves the centrality of 'randomization'. No randomization is required, for example, to study whether certain actions will produce nuclear fission, since 'control' is possible: if a set of procedures applied to a piece of plutonium – under certain pre-specified experimental conditions – regularly produces nuclear fission, as long as agreement exists on the pre-specified conditions and on what constitutes plutonium, and so on, it is possible to put the implied propositions to the type of severe test that would gain widespread assent – all without randomization. Put in a different way, randomization is required only when it is difficult to put a proposition to a severe test without it.

A related issue is whether a study of 'causes' requires some notion of 'manipulation'. Most definitions of 'cause' in social science involve some notion of 'manipulation' (Heckman, 2005) – Bacon's 'twisting of the tail', so to speak.

In physics, by way of contrast, some important 'causes' do not involve manipulation per se. One might argue that Newton's law of gravitation was an example of a mere empirical regularity that became a 'cause'. Indeed, when proposed by Newton, Leibnitz objected to this new 'law': in the prevailing intellectual and scientific climate where the world was understood in terms of 'mechanical pushes and pulls', this new law seemed to require the invocation of 'occult powers' (Hacking, 1983). (There is an element of irony in Leibnitz's objection. Leibnitz is believed by some to be the object of Voltaire's satire as the character Dr Pangloss in *Candide* of whom it is said that he 'proved admirably that there is no effect without a cause ... in this the best of all possible worlds' – a very different notion of causation! Voltaire, 1759, ch. 1.)

In this article, we take the view that, even if manipulation were not necessary to *define* causality, manipulation is central to whether it is possible to discuss the idea intelligibly in social sciences and whether some kind of 'severe test' is possible (DiNardo, 2007). Some philosophers have sought to *define* science around issues related to 'control', arguing that the phenomena economists try to investigate are impossible to study scientifically at all. Philosophers have articulated numerous reasons for the difference between social and natural science. A few examples may be helpful: Nelson (1990, pp. 102–6) argues, for example, that the objects of enquiry by the economist do not constitute 'a natural kind'. Put very crudely, the issue is the extent to which all the phenomena that we lump into the category 'commodity', for example, can be refined to some essence that is sufficiently 'similar' so that a scientific theory about commodities is possible in the same way as a 'body' is in Newtonian mechanics. This is often discussed as the issue of whether the relevant taxonomy results in 'carving nature at the joints'. Hacking (2000) introduces the notions of 'indifferent kinds' – the objects in the physical science – atoms, quarks, and so on with 'interactive' kinds – the objects of study in medicine or the social sciences. We might interact with plutonium or bacteria, but neither the plutonium nor the bacteria are aware of how we are classifying them or what we are doing to them. This can be contrasted with 'interactive kinds' that are aware and for which 'looping' is possible. For example, mental retardation might lead to segregation of those so designated. This segregation might lead to new behaviours which then might not fall under the old label, and so on. Consequently, investigation of such phenomena might be likened to 'trying to hit a moving target'. Searle (1995) on the other hand, notes that the objects of interest in social science while epistemologically objective, are ontologically subjective. While the loss of 100 dollars may be very 'real' to someone, the notion of money requires groups of individual to accept money as a medium of exchange. Again the existence of atoms does not require us to recognize their existence.

Randomization: an attempt to evade the problems of imperfect 'control'

If one accepts the centrality of manipulation (or something like it), it will not be surprising that the application of principles of experimentation to humans who have free will, make choices, and so on entails a host of issues that, inter alia, sharply constrain what might be reasonable to expect of experiments, natural, or otherwise.

If it is not possible, desirable, or ethical to 'control' humans or their 'environment' as it sometimes is in the natural sciences, is it possible to learn anything at all from experiment broadly construed? *Randomization* in experiments developed in part to try to evade the usual problems of isolating the role of the single phenomenon in situations. In the 19th century, it was discovered that by the use of 'artificial randomizers' (such as a coin toss) it was possible, in principle, to create two groups of individuals which were the same 'on average' apart from a single 'treatment' (cause) which was under (at least partial) control of the experimenter. Hacking (1988, p. 427) has observed that their use began primarily in contexts 'marked by complete ignorance': the economist F. Y. Edgeworth was early to apply the mathematical logic of both Bayesian and 'classical' statistics to a randomized trial of the existence of 'telepathy'.

Although economists played an important role in the development of randomization, economists as a whole were quite slow to embrace the new tools. In an echo of debates that faced natural sciences in the 1600s, this was due in part 'because the theory [of economics] was not in doubt, applied workers sought neither to verify nor to disprove' (Morgan, 1987, pp. 171–2).

Over time, the term 'experiment' evolved to include both experiments of the 'hard sciences' where a measure of control was possible as well as situations in which artificial randomizers were used to assign individuals (or plots of land, and so on) to different 'treatments'. A key role was played by R. A. Fisher (1935) and his seminal *Design of Experiments* as well subsequent publications which discussed the theory and practice of using artificial randomizers to learn about causes.

There are at least two key limitations of randomized experiments relative to experiments where 'scientific' control is possible:

- Without real control, one only has a weak understanding of the 'cause' in question. For instance, one can do a randomized controlled trial of the effect of aspirin on heart failure while understanding nothing of the mechanism by which aspirin affects the outcome. Moreover, it is clear that the experiment is 'context specific'. One's generalization about atoms in a laboratory often extends to atoms in other contexts in a way not possible in social science.
- Any single experiment – even under the ideal situation – does not always reveal the true answer. In the logic of randomized design, the usual inference procedure is merely one that *would* give the right answer on average *if* the experiment were repeated. At best, the true answer is just a 'long-run tendency' in repeated identical experiments.

Social experiments: why not do a 'real' randomized trial?

Even without these limitations, there is a long list of reasons why economists frequently have little interest in randomized trials. The most important reason is that many of the real randomized experiments (often called 'Social experiments') of which one could conceive (or have been implemented), are immoral or unethical. At a most basic level, the decision as to who 'performs an experiment' and who 'decides' or is recruited to be experimented upon often reflects deep-seated social injustice. Even Brandeisian (see below) experiments can take on a sinister cast – state governments surely do not consider the interests of all their citizens equally.

Indeed, historically the conduct of experiments on persons has told us as much or more about the structure of society than anything else: one well-known example is the series of 'experiments' conducted by the US Public Health Service from 1932 to 1972 on about 400 poor black men who had advanced syphilis. One aim of the experiment was to determine the effect of untreated syphilis. To this end, the medical doctors misrepresented themselves to the subjects (the sons and grandsons of slaves), claiming to provide free medical care. For example, when penicillin became the standard of care, the subjects were deliberately not provided with the medication: rather, the doctors were content to observe the horrific progress of the disease as some went blind or insane.

Another set of reasons is practical – experiments are costly to administer. Another reason is attrition: often people drop out of such experiments (often in non-random ways), greatly complicating the problem of inference. A distinct, although sometimes related, reason is that the results of social experiments involving randomization are sometimes difficult to interpret. One often cited reason is that those recruited to participate in such experiments may be different from those for whom the policy is ultimately intended. In even the simplest experiments, 'compliance' is imperfect. Not everyone assigned to a treatment takes it up – indeed, it is often the case that analysis is made on an 'intent to treat' basis. That is, those 'assigned' to treatment are compared to those assigned to the control whether or not those assigned to treatment actually 'took' the treatment. Another often cited reason is that what is likely when a social experiment is conducted with a small number of persons might be very different when applied to much larger numbers of persons. Persons, unlike atomic particles, enjoy free will. In the world of persons, the 'experiment' does not necessarily stop after the experimenters have made their observations. For example, even in the context of a true randomized experiment, those denied treatment often have the opportunity to find it elsewhere (see Heckman and Smith, 1995, with references, for one discussion of the merits of randomized trials in the social science).

Types of natural experiments

Thus far we have seen that the word 'experiment' can be used in two very different senses: one to denote situations where real 'control' is possible and second involving artificial randomizers. As a consequence, the term 'natural experiment' has been used in very different senses. I now turn to the origins of the term and the different ways the term has been used, although we focus on natural experiments most frequently arising in economics.

Natural experiments in natural science
An early use of the term 'natural experiment' in English describes an investigation into the functioning of 'nature'. The term comes from a translation *Saggi di naturali*

esperienze fatte nell'Accademia del Cimento published in Italian in 1667 which appeared in an English translation by Richard Waller in 1684 as *Essayes of natural experiments made in the Academie del Cimento* (Waller, 1684). The short-lived Accademia del Cimento was founded in Florence in 1657 by the Medici brothers, Prince Leopold and Grand Duke Ferdinand II, and the *Saggi* record a small subset of the large number of experiments by the Cimento that involved such issues as 'smells do not traverse Glass', and 'the failure to confirm Existence of Atoms of cold' (1684, p. xx). Although the experiments of the Academy included trials involving humans, they did not involve randomization. Indeed, the legacy of these investigations into humans is more relevant to the study of 16th-century culture and authority relations than 16th-century science. (Tribby, 1994, for example, discusses an investigation into a 'gentler' laxative that could 'satisfy' the needs of Grand Duke Ferdinand II as well as those of the many 'delicate persons' who visited or had dealings with the court that involved experimentation on individuals described variously as 'a mercenary', 'a vagrant', 'the Little Moor', and so on.)

Over time, in the hard sciences, the term natural experiment has also come to describe both cases where 'nature' provides an experiment that resembles the controlled situation that scientists would like observe but are unable to create themselves. An unsuccessful experiment may help make the point clear: in a famous quote by Albert Einstein to Erwin Findlay Freundlich (who was attempting to assess the whether path of a ray of light was affected by gravity), Einstein wrote: 'If only we had a considerably larger planet than Jupiter! But nature has not made it a priority to make it easy for us to discover its laws.' ('Wenn wir nur einen ordentlich grösseren Planeten als Jupiter hätten! Aber die Natur hat es sich nicht angelegen sein lassen, uns die Auffindung ihrer Gesetze bequem zu machen', (as cited in Ashtekar et al., 2003; translation from the *New York Times*, 24 March 1992).

Natural experiments as serendipitous randomized trials

In contrast to the natural experiment of the hard sciences, the term natural experiment is often used by economists to denote a situation where real randomization was employed, without the intent of providing a randomized experiment. For example, between 1970 and 1972 men from specific birth cohorts were conscripted into the US military by way of a draft lottery. Each day of the year was randomly assigned a number which (in part) determined whether or not one was at risk of being inducted into the military service to fight in the US war on Indochina. As a consequence, men of specific birth cohorts born only a day apart, for example, had very different risks of serving in the military. In Hearst, Newman and Hulley (1986), the authors asked whether the war continued to kill after the warrior returned home. The authors compared, among other things, the suicide rates among individuals who on average were *ex ante* similar, but who had very different probabilities of having completed military service.

The example is sufficiently simple to make a number of points about the limitations of natural experiments. *If* one can assume that the mere fact of having such a birth date put one at high risk of military duty, and that having a birth date raised (or did not lower) any person's risk of serving in the military, then it is possible to use something akin to two stage least squares (2SLS) to estimate an 'average' effect of military service for those who were induced to serve in the military by the draft lottery. However, Hearst, Newman and Hulley (1986) are quick to observe that *whether or not* one actually served in the military, the mere fact of having been put at risk of the lottery might have had an effect on delayed mortality. In econometric terms, this would be a violation of the 'exclusion restriction' of 2SLS. If such is the case, it is apparent that a comparison of men with high-risk birthdays to those with low-risk birthdays will be an admixture of the effect of the military service on later mortality *and* any direct effect of the lottery itself. An additional problem is the possibility of non-random selection induced by men dying while at war. This was judged to be small due since the fraction of US soldiers who died while serving in action was a small fraction of the total.

Returning to how one might go from an estimate generated in this way to more general inference, one has a number of other obstacles. For example, the delayed mortality effects of military service on those *induced* to serve by an unlucky birth date might be different from the effect on those who *volunteered* to fight in the war. If the effects are very different, it would obviously be incorrect to use estimates generated by those induced to serve to extrapolate to the broader population of interest.

More generally, our ability to generalize the valid results of an experiment is much more limited when we can only manipulate the cause indirectly (as in the example above) than when we can manipulate the cause directly: there is often the possibility of important differences between persons who take up the treatment as a result of having been encouraged to participate and those who were similarly encouraged but did not take up the treatment.

The regression discontinuity design as a natural experiment
One research design that involves the 'serendipitous' randomization of individuals into a treatment is called the regression discontinuity design. Since it is a relatively 'clean' example of something that approaches a truly randomized experiment without involving explicit randomization, it provides a good illustration of the strengths and weaknesses of natural experiments. (For an analysis of the relationship between the regression discontinuity design and randomized controlled trials see Lee, 2007.) For illustration, let us consider DiNardo and Lee's (2004) analysis of the causal effect of 'unionization' on firms in the United States. The naive approach would be to compare unionized firms to non-unionized firms.

The basis of the regression discontinuity design is the existence of a 'score' or a 'vote' which assigns persons to one treatment or another. In the US context, workers at a firm can win the right to form a labour union by means of a secret ballot election. If 50 per cent plus one of the workers votes in favour of the union, the workers win the right to be represented by a union; less than that, and they are denied such rights.

To understand how this works, consider elections at two different sets of work sites that employ large numbers of workers. In one set, $0.5 + \Delta$ of the workers vote in favour of the union and win the right to bargain collectively where Δ is some small number. In another set, slightly less than 50 per cent vote in favour of the union, and are denied the right to bargain collectively. The vote share in these sites is $0.5 - \Delta$. Suppose we have large amounts of data on such elections and can accurately estimate the average outcome (say the fraction of firms that continue to exist 15 years after the vote).

Using almost exactly the same set-up as before, we compare those places where the union wins with those where the union loses:

$$E[\bar{y}_{\text{Union}} - \bar{y}_{\text{No Union}}] = E[y|\text{vote} = 0.5 + \Delta] - E[y|\text{vote} = 0.5 - \Delta]$$

If firm survival is described by the same 'model' as in å above, where now $T = 1$ denotes winning the right to bargain collectively, we get:

$$E[\bar{y}_{\text{Union}} - \bar{y}_{\text{No Union}}] = \beta + \left(\underbrace{E[f(X)|\text{vote} = 0.5 + \Delta] - E[f(X)|\text{vote} = 0.5 - \Delta]}_{\text{Observable Differences}} \right)$$

$$+ \left(\underbrace{E[\varepsilon|\text{vote} = 0.5 + \Delta] - E[\varepsilon|\text{vote} = 0.5 - \Delta]}_{\text{Unobservable Differences}} \right)$$

The 'trick' is that if we choose Δ to be small enough (that is, close to zero), then

$$E[f(X)|\text{vote} = 0.5 + \Delta] \approx E[f(X)|\text{vote} = 0.5 - \Delta] \text{ and}$$
$$E[\varepsilon|\text{vote} = 0.5 + \Delta] \approx E[\varepsilon|\text{vote} = 0.5 - \Delta]$$

and we get a 'good' estimate of the 'effect of unions' in the same sense that we get a good estimate of the effect of a treatment in a randomized controlled trial. That is, if we focus our attention on the difference in outcomes between 'near winners' and 'near losers' such a contrast is formally equivalent to a randomized controlled trial if there is at least some 'random' component to the vote share. For example, sometimes people take ill on the day of the vote – if that happens randomly in some sites, two sites that would have had the same final vote tally had everyone shown up are now different. When such differences are the difference between recognition or not, one has the practical equivalent of a randomized controlled trial. The mere existence of a 'score' that discontinuously exposes one to a treatment is not enough. This design would not be appropriate, for example, to analyse the causal effects of US Congressional votes on various issues. Substantial 'manipulation' – that is, through negotiation, and so on – of the final vote tally is common and suggests that individuals near but on opposite sides of the threshold are not otherwise similar (see REGRESSION-DISCONTINUITY ANALYSIS).

A few moments' reflection will make clear both the appeal of such experiments and their limits. Advocates of a natural experiment approach point to the fact that the implicit randomization involved in this design means that we can be more confident with such a comparison than a naive comparison that merely compares unionized to non-unionized firms. This would almost certainly confound the true 'effect' with pre-existing differences in unionized and non-unionized firms with 'unionization'. Advocates will also point to the fact that the experiment is relevant to a potential policy – say lowering the threshold required to win representation rights by a small amount.

Detractors will observe many limitations. Is the effect of a union that is set into a place by a 51 per cent vote the same as the effect of a union where the workers vote unanimously? Possibly not. Stipulating the validity of the estimate, is it reasonable to suggest that the effect of unionization would be the same if all workplaces were allowed to vote on a union? Probably not. Is it possible that a union at one work site affects other work sites? What about the effect on the firm's competitors? Indeed, it is even possible to question the premise that a union is a 'treatment' at all. Does it make sense to talk of a single effect of a labour union when there is such heterogeneity in what the notion 'labour union' represents? While the anarcho-syndicalist Industrial Workers of the World (IWW) of Joe Hill (a famous militant IWW member and subject of a well-known folksong) and the American Federation of Labor and Congress of Industrial Organizations (AFL-CIO) of George Meany (a conservative 'anti-communist' who was its president for many years) were both labour unions, they had virtually contrary aims and wildly different political structures.

More generally, 'causes', 'treatments', and so on are much more fragile objects for the types of things usually interesting to economists than the types of things interesting to natural science. The concepts of natural science are often capable of quite substantial refinement in a way that concepts in the human sciences rarely are.

'Natural natural experiments'?

As I have already mentioned, the term 'natural experiment' has been used in several different ways inconsistent with our definition. It seems pointless, however, to claim that our definition is the 'true' or correct one. We shall therefore consider some cases that use the term which do not obviously involve randomization of a treatment or something that approximates such randomization.

Rosenzweig and Wolpin (2000) for instance, have coined the expression 'natural natural experiments' to denote a wide range of studies involving the use of twins. The emphasis on the word 'natural' is intended to highlight the role of nature in providing the variation. Twins have been of inordinate interest to the social scientists since they seem to offer the possibility of 'controlling' for 'genetics'. Consider one case of interest to economists, 'returns to schooling'. Does acquiring an additional year of school result in higher wages in the labour market? How much higher? To fix ideas consider a simple model of the sort:

$$y_{ij} = \beta S_{ij} + a_j + \varepsilon_{ij}.$$

We are interested in some outcome, say hourly wages, and the causal effect of years of schooling S. It will greatly simplify the discussion if we assume that all persons 'treated' with 'schooling' experience the same increase in their wages – that is, the treatment effect is a constant across individuals. We have gathered a random sample of $j = 1, \ldots, J$ 'identical' (monozygotic) twins ($i = 1, 2$). The term a_j is not directly observable but includes everything that the twins have in common – genetics, environment, and so on. The error term ε_{ij} includes everything that the twins do not have in common and cannot be observed as well as the effects of misspecification, and so on. Though this simple set-up can be greatly elaborated (see Ashenfelter and Krueger, 1994, for a clear exposition) the essential idea is that the *difference* between the twins purges the outcome of the a_j term so that an ordinary least squares regression of the difference in wages Δy_{ij} on ΔS_{ij} yields a good estimate of

$$\hat{\beta} \text{ is a good estimate of } \beta + \frac{\mathrm{Var}(\Delta \varepsilon, \Delta S)}{\mathrm{Var}(\Delta S)}.$$

The first term is the goal of such studies. The second term points to the possibility that there are other influences which might be correlated both with schooling and that affect the outcome. The second term can be interpreted as the slope coefficient from the following hypothetical ordinary least squares (OLS) regression, where δ is the slope of the 'best-fitting' line in this expression:

$$\varepsilon = \text{constant} + S\delta + \text{error}.$$

When will $\hat{\beta}$ to be a good estimate of the returns to schooling β? The conditions are essentially the same as for the randomized controlled trial: if we can treat the assignment of schooling to the two twins as if it were determined by a random coin toss then differences in the level of schooling between the two twins – ΔS_{ij} – will be independent of differences between the two twins in unobserved influences on wages – $\Delta \varepsilon_{ij}$. Detractors of this approach doubt that such an assumption is plausible. In simple language, if the twins are so 'identical' why do they have different levels of schooling? Perhaps the parents noticed that one twin was more interested or had more 'aptitude' for schoolwork than another. If that were the case, estimates of the returns to schooling would be confounded with differences in the aptitude for schooling despite the fact that we had 'controlled' for a large number of other factors. The key difference between this case and what I have identified as a natural experiment is the lack of an obvious approximation to randomization. Bound and Solon (1999) discuss, inter alia, a host of difficulties in treating twin differences as experimental variation. I do not discuss twins studies that utilize twins as a 'surprise' to family size which have some element of randomization.

Other research designs: quasi-experiments
Finally, I should make note of the fact that some authors use the term natural experiment more broadly than I have construed it here. Meyer (1995, p. 151) for

instance, considers natural experiments the broad class of research designs 'patterned after randomized experiments' but not (generally) involving actual randomization. One term often used for such situations is 'quasi-experiment'. The relationship between these quasi-experiments and the natural experiments I have been describing is quite varied and ranges from those whose difference from the standard of randomized assignment is merely a matter of 'degree' to those in which assignment to treatment differs so much from the standard of randomization that it is really a difference in 'kind'.

Most of these quasi-experiments are variants of a 'before and after' where an observation is made before and after a treatment. Often a before–after comparison for one set of observations (the treatment – T) is compared to another set (the control – C). A typical set-up might compute a treatment effect by taking the difference in two differences:

$$\text{Treatment Effect} = \{\bar{y}_{T,\text{after}} - \bar{y}_{T,\text{before}}\} - \{\bar{y}_{C,\text{after}} - \bar{y}_{C,\text{before}}\}.$$

For this reason, such quasi-experiments are described as using 'difference-in-differences' approach to identifying a causal relationship.

In the United States, the fact that the state (or city) governments have some liberty to enact laws independently of the federal government, for example, has led to a great deal of research using 'Brandeisian' experiments. The term comes by way of US Supreme Court Justice Louis Brandeis, in the case *New State Ice* v. *Liebmann*:

> There must be power in the States and the Nation to remould, through experimentation, our economic practices and institutions to meet changing social and economic needs. ... It is one of the happy incidents of the federal system that a single courageous State may, if its citizens choose, serve as a laboratory; and try novel social and economic experiments without risk to the rest of the country. (U.S. Supreme Court *New State Ice Co.* v. *Liebmann*, 285 U.S. 262 (1932))

To give one such example, consider DiNardo and Lemieux's (2001) evaluation of the effect of changing the age at which it is legal to purchase alcohol or the consumption of marijuana. At the beginning of the 1980s states generally enforced two types of legal regimes. In one set, alcohol could not be legally sold to those under the age of 21. In another, the legal minimum drinking age (LMDA) was 18. In the mid-1980s, the federal government put a great deal of pressure on those states with LMDA of 18 to raise them to 21 and by the end of the 1980s, in all states drinking age was 21.

The assignment of drinking age statutes to the states at the beginning of the 1980s could not be considered 'approximately' random. Utah, for example, which is home to a large number of adherents to the Mormon religion – which proscribes alcohol use – had a 21-year drinking age at the beginning of the 1980s. However, due to a federal policy implemented in the mid-1980s of eventually denying federal highway funds to states with legal minimums less than 21 years old, something perhaps approximating an 'experiment' can be arrived at by comparing *changes* in alcohol or marijuana consumption during the 1980s in those states which were forced to change (and changed early) with those who were forced to but raised their drinking age later.

Let Δy_t denote the change in the fraction of 18–21 year olds who reported smoking marijuana in the previous 30 days from 1980 to 1990 in states that had 18-year-old drinking ages that were increased, and Δy_c denote the similar change in states whose drinking age was always 21. Then an estimate of the effect of the drinking age might be:

$$\Delta y_t - \Delta y_c = \text{Effect of LMDA.}$$

Although randomization is not employed per se, the credibility of these exercises can be at least partially evaluated. For instance, if the outcome of interest has been approximately constant in both the treatment and control groups for a long time preceding the change in legal regime, the estimate is generally more credible. Less credible is the case in which the outcomes in the control group and the treatment group are quite variable over time, the control group and the treatment group do not follow similar patterns *before* the proposed experiment, or when both are true.

Controversies: concluding remarks

Natural experiments and their like have been at the heart of much work in economics. Nonetheless, they are the subject of considerable debate. One of the most cited limitations of natural experiments – by both supporters and detractors – is that such experiments are context specific. Indeed, one frequently encountered 'strength' of natural experiments is that it often concerns the evaluation of an actual policy. There are limitations, however. If we assume that the experiment is 'internally valid' we still have to ask: how do we generalize from one experiment to the broader questions of policy? The foregoing has suggested that it is difficult. There are at least three broad classes of reasons:

1. While a natural experiment might provide a credible estimate of some particular serendipitous 'intervention', this may have only a weak relation to the type of interventions being contemplated as policies. Many of the potential reasons for a weak relationship are similar to those encountered in social experiments (among other things, for example, the effect of a treatment in a demonstration programme might be quite different from the outcome that would obtain if the treatment were applied more broadly or to different persons).
2. Some interesting questions are unanswerable with such an approach because serendipitous randomized experiments are few and far between. The extent to which this criticism is warranted, of course, depends on the availability of alternative ways of putting our views to a severe test.
3. More generally, without a 'theory', estimates from natural experiments are uninterpretable.

I am sympathetic with all three criticisms although (3) deserves some qualification. While it has been argued that even in the natural sciences it is impossible to have 'pre-theoretical' observations or experiments, Hacking (1983) makes a strong case that experimentation has a life of its own, sometimes suggesting ideas in advance of theory, other times the consequence of theory, and sometimes testing theories. Much of this debate in the natural sciences revolves around the notion of what constitutes a 'theory'. Whatever the validity of the view that one cannot experiment in advance of 'theory' in the natural sciences, in the social sciences, it is clear that no theory has the same standing as, say, general relativity in physics. This is the sense in which Noam Chomsky observes that 'as soon as questions of will or decision or reason or choice of action arise, human science is pretty much at a loss' (Magee, 2001, p. 184). Indeed, the standing of randomized experiments – in some fields of enquiry regarded as 'the gold standard' of evidence – is a great deal lower than the best experiments of natural science; they are most often useful in situations otherwise marked by 'complete ignorance' (Hacking, 1988). In short, while the human sciences might have the same ambition as natural science, the status of what we know will almost surely be quite limited.

Nonetheless, one does not need a 'correct' theory to hand, nor an understanding as rich as that found in some of the natural sciences to find an experiment useful. At the risk of over-using such metaphors, the fact that the Michelson–Morley experiments were in part about testing for the existence of 'ether' did not make them uninteresting. Experiments are just ways to use things we (think we) understand to learn about something we do not. And while the sorts of 'natural' experiments 'serendipitously' provided by society may be very limited and are often the product of unhappy social realities, they can sometimes perhaps serve a small role in enhancing our understanding.

Any assessment of the usefulness of natural experiments depends on how one judges the power of other methods of enquiry. Such a discussion is well beyond the scope of this article. Nonetheless, not discounting their many limitations, one benefit of natural experiments I have tried to highlight is that for some they might open up the possibility of revising their beliefs in light of evidence or suggest new ways to think about old problems, however limited. A key aspect of experiments (natural or otherwise) is the willingness to put one's ideas 'to the test'. Often, careful study of a natural experiment, however limited, may also make one aware of how complicated and difficult are the problems we call 'economics'. Even if the success we might have in generalizing natural experiments more broadly may be quite limited, if they bring nothing but humility to the claims social scientists make about much we actually understand, that alone would justify an interest in natural experiments.

J. DINARDO

See also **difference-in-difference estimators; regression-discontinuity analysis.**

Bibliography

Ashenfelter, O. and Krueger, A.B. 1994. Estimates of the economic returns to schooling from a new sample of identical twins. *American Economic Review* 84, 1157–73.

Ashtekar, A., Cohen, R.S., Howard, D. Renn, J. Sarkear, S. and Shimony, A. 2003. *Revisiting the Foundations of Relativistic Physics: Festschrift in Honor of John Stachel*. Boston Studies in the Philosophy of Science, vol. 234. Dordrecht: Kluwer Academic.

Bastable, C.F. 1987. Experimental methods in economics (i). In *The New Palgrave: A Dictionary of Economics*, vol. 2, ed. J. Eatwell, M. Milgate and P. Newman. London: Macmillan.

Bound, J. and Solon, G. 1999. Double trouble: on the value of twins-based estimation of the return to schooling. *Economics of Education Review* 18, 169–82.

DiNardo, J. 2007. Interesting questions in freakonomics. *Journal of Economic Literature*.

DiNardo, J. and Lee, D.S. 2002. The impact of unionization on establishment closure: a regression discontinuity analysis of representation elections. Working Paper No. 8993. Cambridge, MA: NBER.

DiNardo, J. and Lee, D.S. 2004. Economic impacts of new unionization on private sector employers: 1984–2001. *Quarterly Journal of Economics* 119, 1383–441.

DiNardo, J. and Lemieux, T. 2001. Alcohol, marijuana, and American youth: the unintended consequences of government regulation. *Journal of Health Economics* 20, 991–1010.

Drake, S. 1981. *Cause, Experiment, and Science: A Galilean Dialogue, Incorporating a New English Translation of Galileo's Bodies that Stay atop Water, or Move in It*. Chicago: University of Chicago Press.

Fisher, R.A. 1935. *Design of Experiments*. Edinburgh, London: Oliver & Boyd.

Hacking, I. 1983. *Representing and Intervening: Introductory Topics in the Philosophy of Natural Science*. Cambridge: Cambridge University Press.

Hacking, I. 1988. Telepathy: origins of randomization in experimental design. *Isis* 79, 427–51.

Hacking, I. 2000. *The Social Construction of What?* Cambridge, MA: Harvard University Press.

Hearst, N., Newman, T.B. and Hulley, S.B. 1986. Delayed effects of the military draft on mortality: a randomized natural experiment. *New England Journal of Medicine* 314, 620–4.

Heckman, J.J. 2005. The scientific model of causality. *Sociological Methodology* 35, 1–97.

Heckman, J.J. and Smith, J.A. 1995. Assessing the case for social experiments. *Journal of Economic Perspectives* 9(2), 85–110.

Lee, D.S. 2008. Randomized experiments from non-random selection in U.S. house elections. *Journal of Econometrics*.

Magee, B. 2001. *Talking Philosophy: Dialogues with Fifteen Leading Philosphers*. Oxford: Oxford University Press.

Mayo, D.G. 1996. *Error and the Growth of Experimental Knowledge Science and Its Conceptual Foundations*. Chicago: University of Chicago Press.

Meyer, B. 1995. Natural and quasi-experiments in economics. *Journal of Business and Economic Statistics* 13, 151–61.

Morgan, M.S. 1987. Statistics without probability and Haavelmo's revolution in econometrics. In *The Probabilistic Revolution: Ideas in the Sciences*, vol. 2, ed. L. Krüger, G. Gigerenzer and M.S. Morgan. Cambridge, MA: MIT Press.

Nelson, A. 1990. Are economic kinds natural? In *Scientific Theories of Minnesota Studies in the Philosophy of Science*, vol. 14, ed. C. Wade Savage. Minneapolis: University of Minnesota Press.

Peirce, C.S. 1958. In *Collected Papers*, vols. 7–8, ed. A. Burks. Cambridge, MA: Harvard University Press.

Rosenzweig, M.R. and Wolpin, K.I. 2000. Natural 'natural experiments' in economics. *Journal of Economic Literature* 38, 827–74.

Searle, J. 1995. *The Construction of Social Reality*. New York: Free Press.

Shadish, W.R., Cook, T.D. and Campbell, D.T. 2002. *Experimental and Quasi–Experimental Designs for Generalized Causal Inference*. Boston: Houghton Mifflin.

Tribby, J. 1994. Club Medici: natural experiment and the imagineering of 'Tuscany'. *Configurations* 2, 215–35.

Voltaire. 1759. *The History of Candide; or All for the Best*, ed. C. Cooke. London, 1796.

Waller, R. 1684. *Essayes of natural experiments made in the academie del cimento, under the protection of the most serene Prince Leopold of Tuscany*. Facsimile edn, ed. R. Hall, trans. R. Waller. New York and London, 1964.

Wikipedia. 2006. Experiment. http://en.wikipedia.org, accessed 28 September 2006.

nonlinear panel data models

1. Introduction

Panel or longitudinal data are becoming increasingly popular in applied work as they offer a number of advantages over pure cross-sectional or pure time-series data. A particularly useful feature is that they allow researchers to model *unobserved heterogeneity* at the level of the observational unit, where the latter may be an individual, a household, a firm or a country. Standard practice in the econometric literature is to model this heterogeneity as an individual-specific effect which enters additively in the model, typically assumed to be linear, that captures the statistical relationship between the dependent and the independent variables. The presence of these *individual effects* may cause problems in estimation. In particular in short panels, that is, in panels where the time-series dimension is of smaller order than the cross-sectional dimension, their estimation in conjunction with the other parameters of interest usually yields inconsistent estimators for both. (Notable exceptions are the static linear and the Poisson count panel data models, where estimation of the individual effects along with the finite dimensional coefficient vector yields consistent estimators of the latter.) This is the well-known *incidental parameters* problem (Neyman and Scott, 1948). In linear regression models, this problem may be dealt with by taking transformations of the model, such as first differences or differences from time averages ('within transformation'), which remove the individual effect from the equation under consideration. However they do not apply to nonlinear econometric models, that is, models which are nonlinear in the parameters of interest and which include models that arise frequently in applied work, such as discrete choice models, limited dependent variable models, and duration models, among others.

This article describes several estimation methods that are available for nonlinear panel data models. An approach that is available for estimating certain linear and nonlinear parametric models with individual effects is the *conditional maximum likelihood* approach. This is described in Section 2. Section 3 describes estimation techniques that have been recently developed for several semiparametric nonlinear panel data models. A common feature in the methods discussed in that section is that we do not make any assumptions about the nature of these individual effects, that is, whether they are fixed constants or random variables. Thus, we do not make any assumptions about whether they are related to the conditioning variables and, if so, in what manner. This approach is typically referred to as the *fixed effects* approach. Section 4 describes the so-called *random effects* approach in estimating nonlinear panel data models. In contrast to the fixed effects approach, the random effects approach does make assumptions about the individual effects.

The discussion distinguishes between two types of models, *static* and *dynamic*. In static models, the conditioning set includes past, present and future values of the variables. In this case the conditioning variables are said to be *strictly exogenous*. In dynamic models, the conditioning set may also include lags of the dependent variable and other endogenous variables, that is, variables that are only *weakly exogenous* or *predetermined*.

Our discussion is limited in several aspects. First, we focus only on the case when the time series dimension of the panel (T) is short so that it makes sense to consider the asymptotic properties of the estimators when the cross-sectional dimension (N) is large while T remains fixed. Second, we do not consider estimation of *random coefficient models*, that is, models where all the parameters are varying at the individual level. Finally, we do not discuss the Bayesian approach to estimating panel data models.

2. The conditional maximum likelihood (CML) approach

Suppose that a random variable y_{it} has density $f(\cdot, \theta, \alpha_i)$ where θ is the parameter of interest which is common across all units i, whereas α_i is a nuisance parameter which is allowed to differ across i. A *sufficient statistic* S_i for a_i is a function of the data such that the conditional distribution of the data given S_i does not depend on α_i. However, the conditional distribution may depend on θ. In this case, one can estimate θ by maximizing the *conditional likelihood function*, which conditions on the sufficient statistic(s). Such sufficient statistics are readily available for the exponential family that includes the normal, Poisson, gamma, logistic, and binomial distributions. The CML approach, when it exists, yields consistent and asymptotically normal estimators for parametric panel data models with individual effects (Andersen, 1970). We will next demonstrate how the CML approach works in the case of a static and a dynamic logit model with individual effects.

2.1 The static panel data logit model
Consider the binary choice logit model with individual effects

$$y_{it} = 1\{x_{it}\beta_0 + \alpha_i + \varepsilon_{it} \geq 0\} \quad i = 1, \ldots, N; \ t = 1, \ldots, T$$

where $1\{A\} = 1$ if A occurs and is 0 otherwise. Let $x_i \equiv (x_{i1}, \ldots, x_{iT})$. Here the error term ε_{it} is distributed i.i.d. over t with a logistic distribution conditional on (x_i, α_i). Note that this assumption implies that ε_{it} is in fact independent of α_i and x_{it} for all t. We can easily calculate that

$$\Pr(y_{it} = 1 | x_i, \alpha_i) = \frac{\exp(x_{it}\beta_0 + \alpha_i)}{1 + \exp(x_{it}\beta_0 + \alpha_i)}.$$

In this model it turns out that $\sum_t y_{it}$ is a sufficient statistic for α_i. Indeed, let $T = 2$. Note that

$$\Pr(y_{it} = 1 | y_{i1} + y_{i2} = 0, x_i, \alpha_i) = 0$$

$$\Pr(y_{it} = 1 | y_{i1} + y_{i2} = 2, x_i, \alpha_i) = 1$$

that is, individuals who do not switch states (i.e. who are 0 or 1 in both periods) do not offer any information about β_0. But it can be easily shown that

$$\Pr(y_{i1} = 1 | y_{i1} + y_{i2} = 1, x_i, \alpha_i) = \frac{1}{1 + \exp((x_{i2} - x_{i1})\beta_0)}$$

and

$$\Pr(y_{i1} = 0 | y_{i1} + y_{i2} = 1, x_i, \alpha_i) = \frac{\exp((x_{i2} - x_{i1})\beta_0)}{1 + \exp((x_{i2} - x_{i1})\beta_0)}.$$

In other words, conditional on the individual switching states (from 0 to 1 or from 1 to 0), the probability that y_{it} is 1 or 0 depends on β_0 (that is, contains information about β_0) but is independent of α_i.

The conditional log-likelihood is

$$\mathscr{L}_C(\beta) = \sum_{i=1}^{N} 1\{y_{i1} + y_{i2} = 1\} \ln \left(\frac{\exp((x_{i2} - x_{i1})\beta)^{(1-y_{i1})}}{1 + \exp((x_{i2} - x_{i1})\beta)} \right)$$

and may be maximized over β to produce a consistent and root-N asymptotically normal estimator of β_0. Note that the approach uses a subset of the data, since only individuals who switch states enter the likelihood. For the expression of the conditional log-likelihood in the general T case, see Chamberlain (1984).

2.2 The dynamic panel data logit model

Chamberlain (1985) noticed that the conditional maximum likelihood approach also applies to the 'AR(1)' logit model with individual effects:

$$y_{it} = 1\{\gamma_0 y_{it-1} + \alpha_i + \varepsilon_{it} \geq 0\} \qquad i = 1, \ldots, N; \ t = 1, \ldots, T$$

where the error term ε_{it} is distributed i.i.d. with a logistic distribution conditional on α_i and the initial observation of the sample y_{i0}. Note that we are not making any assumption about the distribution of the initial y_{i0}. As we will see, the approach requires at least four observations for each individual (including the initial observation). In fact, let that be the case and consider the events:

$$A = \{y_{i0} = d_0, y_{i1} = 0, y_{i2} = 1, y_{i3} = d_3\}$$

$$B = \{y_{i0} = d_0, y_{i1} = 1, y_{i2} = 0, y_{i3} = d_3\}$$

where d_0 and d_3 are either 0 or 1. It is rather easy to derive the following probabilities which condition on the individual switching states in the two middle periods

$$\Pr(A|A \cup B, \alpha_i) = \frac{1}{1 + \exp(\gamma_0(d_0 - d_3))}$$

$$\Pr(B|A \cup B, \alpha_i) = \frac{\exp(\gamma_0(d_0 - d_3))}{1 + \exp(\gamma_0(d_0 - d_3))}.$$

Note that these depend on γ_0 but are independent of α_i. The conditional log-likelihood of the model for four periods is:

$$\mathcal{L}_C(\beta) = \sum_i 1\{y_{i1} + y_{i2} = 1\} \ln\left(\frac{\exp(\gamma(y_{i0} - y_{i3}))^{y_{i1}}}{1 + \exp(\gamma(y_{i0} - y_{i3}))} \right)$$

and maximizing it with respect to γ produces a consistent and root-N asymptotically normal estimator. The approach generalizes to logit models with more than one lags of y_{it} (see Magnac, 2000).

It is important to note that the CML approach described above does *not* work in the logit model

$$y_{it} = 1\{\gamma_0 y_{it-1} + x_{it}\beta_0 + \alpha_i + \varepsilon_{it} \geq 0\} \qquad i = 1, \ldots, N; \quad t = 1, \ldots, T$$

that is, when the conditioning set also includes exogenous variables. Honoré and Kyriazidou (2000a) show that β_0 and γ_0 in the model above are in fact identified both for the case when the errors ε_{it} are logistic and when they are only assumed to have the same distribution over time conditional on (x_i, y_{i0}) (see below). In the logistic case identification is based on the fact that the following probabilities

$$\Pr(A|A \cup B, x_{i2} = x_{i3}, x_i, \alpha_i) = \frac{1}{1 + \exp((x_{i1} - x_{i2})\beta_0 + \gamma_0(d_0 - d_3))}$$

$$\Pr(B|A \cup B, x_{i2} = x_{i3}, x_i, \alpha_i) = \frac{\exp((x_{i1} - x_{i2})\beta_0 + \gamma_0(d_0 - d_3))}{1 + \exp((x_{i1} - x_{i2})\beta_0 + \gamma_0(d_0 - d_3))}$$

are independent of α_i. Note that the probabilities above condition not only on the individual switching states in the middle two periods so that $y_{i1} + y_{i2} = 1$ but also on the event that $x_{i2} = x_{i3}$. Honoré and Kyriazidou (2000a) propose estimating

β_0 and γ_0 by maximizing

$$\sum_i 1\{x_{i2} - x_{i3} = 0\}1\{y_{i1} + y_{i2} = 1\} \times \ln\left(\frac{\exp((x_{i1} - x_{i2})\beta + \gamma(y_{i0} - y_{i3}))^{y_{i1}}}{1 + \exp((x_{i1} - x_{i2})\beta + \gamma(y_{i0} - y_{i3}))}\right)$$

when $\Pr(x_{i2} = x_{i3}) > 0$. When $x_{i2} - x_{i3}$ is continuously distributed with support around 0, β_0 and γ_0 can be obtained by maximizing

$$\sum_i K\left(\frac{x_{i2} - x_{i3}}{h_N}\right)1\{y_{i1} + y_{i2} = 1\} \times \ln\left(\frac{\exp((x_{i1} - x_{i2})\beta + \gamma(y_{i0} - y_{i3}))^{y_{i1}}}{1 + \exp((x_{i1} - x_{i2})\beta + \gamma(y_{i0} - y_{i3}))}\right)$$

where $K()$ is a *kernel density function* and h_N is a *bandwidth sequence*, chosen so as to satisfy certain assumptions that guarantee consistency and asymptotic normality of the proposed estimators.

3. The fixed effects approach

The conditional maximum likelihood approach is not always available. For example, there are no sufficient statistics for the binary choice model with individual effects when the errors are normally distributed. Furthermore, like all ML approaches, the approach suffers from the fact that the distribution of the unobserved idiosyncratic errors needs to be parametrically specified. There do exist, however, methods for some *semiparametric* nonlinear panel data models with individual effects where the distribution of the underlying idiosyncratic errors is left unspecified. These include the binary choice model, the censored and truncated regression models, and the sample selection model.

3.1 The semiparametric panel data binary choice model

Manski (1987) considers the model

$$y_{it} = 1\{x_{it}\beta_0 + \alpha_i - \varepsilon_{it} \geq 0\} \qquad i = 1, \ldots, N; \ t = 1, \ldots, T$$

where ε_{it} is identically distributed over time conditional on (x_i, α_i), with distribution function F that is a continuous and strictly increasing function on $\Re$. Note that, in contrast to the models considered above, F here is not assumed to have a specific functional form, hence the characterization of the model as *semiparametric*.

He observes that for $T = 2$ the time invariance of F implies that

$$\Pr(y_{i1} = 1|x_i) \lesseqgtr \Pr(y_{i2} = 1|x_i) \qquad \text{if and only if} \quad x_{i1}\beta_0 \lesseqgtr x_{i2}\beta_0$$

or equivalently that

$$sgn(\Pr(y_{i2} = 1|x_i, \alpha_i) - \Pr(y_{i1} = 1|x_i, \alpha_i)) = sgn((x_{i2} - x_{i1})\beta_0)).$$

In fact it can be shown that, under appropriate regularity conditions on the joint distribution of $\Delta x_i \equiv (x_{i2} - x_{i1})$, β_0 uniquely (up to scale) maximizes the so-called population 'score function'

$$E[\Delta y_i \cdot sgn(\Delta x_i \beta_0)]$$

where $sgn(x)$ equals 1 if $x > 0$, equals -1 if $x < 0$ and is equal to 0 if $x = 0$. This suggests estimating β_0 by the so-called *conditional maximum score estimator* which maximizes the sample analog of the population score function

$$\hat{\beta} = \arg\max_{\beta} \sum_i \Delta y_i \cdot sgn(\Delta x_i \beta).$$

Note that only observations for which $y_{i1} \neq y_{i2}$ are used here, similarly to conditional logit. The estimator is consistent under some additional assumptions but is not asymptotically normal and its rate of convergence is not root-N.

Honoré and Kyriazidou (2000a) show that it is possible to extend the conditional maximum score approach to the dynamic binary choice model:

$$\Pr(y_{i0} = 1|x_i, \alpha_i) = p_0(x_i, \alpha_i)$$
$$\Pr(y_{it} = 1|x_i, \alpha_i, y_{i0}, \ldots, y_{it-1}) = F(x_{it}\beta_0 + \gamma_0 y_{it-1} + \alpha_i) \quad t = 1, \ldots, T$$

where y_{i0} is assumed to be observed and F is strictly increasing.

We will next demonstrate their identification scheme. Assume $T = 3$ and define the events A and B as above. Then

$$\Pr(A|x_i, \alpha_i, x_{i2} = x_{i3}) = p_0(x_i, \alpha_i)^{d_0}(1 - p_0(x_i, \alpha_i))^{1-d_0}$$
$$\times (1 - F(x_{i1}\beta_0 + \gamma_0 d_0 + \alpha_i)) \times F(x_{i2}\beta_0 + \alpha_i)$$
$$\times (1 - F(x_{i2}\beta_0 + \gamma_0 + \alpha_i))^{(1-d_3)} \times F(x_{i2}\beta_0 + \gamma_0 + \alpha_i)^{d_3}$$
$$\Pr(B|x_i, \alpha_i, x_{i2} = x_{i3}) = p_0(x_i, \alpha_i)^{d_0}(1 - p_0(x_i, \alpha_i))^{1-d_0} \times F(x_{i1}\beta_0 + \gamma_0 d_0 + \alpha_i)$$
$$\times (1 - F(x_{i2}\beta_0 + \gamma_0 + \alpha_i)) \times (1 - F(x_{i2}\beta_0 + \alpha_i))^{(1-d_3)}$$
$$\times F(x_{i2}\beta_0 + \alpha_i)^{d_3}.$$

If $d_3 = 0$, then,

$$\frac{\Pr(A|x_i, \alpha_i, x_{i2} = x_{i3})}{\Pr(B|x_i, \alpha_i, x_{i2} = x_{i3})} = \frac{(1 - F(x_{i1}\beta_0 + \gamma_0 d_0 + \alpha_i))}{(1 - F(x_{i2}\beta_0 + \alpha_i))} \times \frac{F(x_{i2}\beta_0 + \alpha_i)}{F(x_{i1}\beta_0 + \gamma_0 d_0 + \alpha_i)}$$

$$= \frac{(1 - F(x_{i1}\beta_0 + \gamma_0 d_0 + \alpha_i))}{(1 - F(x_{i2}\beta_0 + \gamma_0 d_3 + \alpha_i))} \times \frac{F(x_{i2}\beta_0 + \gamma_0 + \alpha_i)}{F(x_{i2}\beta_0 + \alpha_i)}$$

while if $d_3 = 1$, then,

$$\frac{\Pr(A|x_i, \alpha_i, x_{i2} = x_{i3})}{\Pr(B|x_i, \alpha_i, x_{i2} = x_{i3})} = \frac{(1 - F(x_{i1}\beta_0 + \gamma_0 d_0 + \alpha_i))}{(1 - F(x_{i2}\beta_0 + \gamma_0 + \alpha_i))} \times \frac{F(x_{i2}\beta_0 + \gamma_0 + \alpha_i)}{F(x_{i1}\beta_0 + \gamma_0 d_0 + \alpha_i)}$$

$$= \frac{(1 - F(x_{i1}\beta_0 + \gamma_0 d_0 + \alpha_i))}{(1 - F(x_{i2}\beta_0 + \gamma_0 d_3 + \alpha_i))} \times \frac{F(x_{i2}\beta_0 + \gamma_0 d_3 + \alpha_i)}{F(x_{i2}\beta_0 + \gamma_0 d_0 + \alpha_i)}.$$

Monotonicity of F implies that

$$sgn(\Pr(A|x_i, \alpha_i, x_{i2} = x_{i3}) - \Pr(B|x_i, \alpha_i, x_{i2} = x_{i3}) = sgn((x_{i2} - x_{i1})\beta_0 + \gamma_0(d_3 - d_0)).$$

This last equation suggests that β_0 and γ_0 can be estimated by conditional maximum score using only the observations satisfying $y_{i1} + y_{i2} = 1$ and $x_{i2} = x_{i3}$, that is, by maximizing

$$\sum_i 1\{x_{i2} - x_{i3} = 0\} \; (y_{i2} - y_{i1})$$

$$sgn((x_{i2} - x_{i1})\beta + \gamma(y_{i3} - y_{i0})).$$

Similar to the logit case, when $x_{i2} - x_{i3}$ is continuously distributed with support around 0, estimation of β_0 and γ_0 can be obtained by maximizing

$$\sum_i K\left(\frac{x_{i2} - x_{i3}}{h_N}\right) (y_{i2} - y_{i1})$$

$$sgn((x_{i2} - x_{i1})\beta + \gamma(y_{i3} - y_{i0})).$$

3.2 The semiparametric panel data censored regression model
The standard censored panel data (or Type 1 Tobit) model with individual effects is given by

$$y_{it} = \max\{x_{it}\beta_0 + \alpha_i + \varepsilon_{it}, 0\} \qquad i = 1, \ldots, N; \; t = 1, \ldots, T.$$

Estimation of this model was first considered by Honoré (1992) and later by Honoré and Kyriazidou (2000b), who extend the results of the former paper. We will present here Honoré (1992), who assumes that $(\varepsilon_{it}, \varepsilon_{is})$ are *pairwise exchangeable* conditional on (x_i, a_i). This implies that ε_{it} and ε_{is} are identically distributed conditional on (x_i, a_i) although it does not require (conditional) independence over time. (Fristedt and Gray, 1997, give the following definition of exchangeability: Let $\mathcal{I}$ be a countable set. A sequence $(X_i : i \in \mathcal{I})$, finite or infinite, of random variables on a probability space $(\Omega, \mathcal{F}, P)$ is *exchangeable* if, for every permutation ρ of $\mathcal{I}$, the distribution of $(X_{p(i)} : i \in \mathcal{I})$ and $(X_i : i \in \mathcal{I})$ are identical. Note that a finite or infinite i.i.d. sequence is exchangeable and that exchangeability allows for certain types of serial correlation. Furthermore, exchangeability implies strict stationarity although the converse is not true.)

Consider the 'pseudo-error':

$$e_{ist}(\beta) = \max\{y_{is}, (x_{is} - x_{it})\beta\} - x_{is}\beta.$$

With this definition, at the true β_0

$$
\begin{aligned}
e_{ist}(\beta_0) &= \max\{y_{is}, (x_{is} - x_{it})\beta_0\} - x_{is}\beta_0 \\
&= \max\{\max\{x_{is}\beta_0 + \alpha_i + \varepsilon_{is}, 0\}, (x_{is} - x_{it})\beta_0\} - x_{is}\beta_0 \\
&= \max\{\max\{\alpha_i + \varepsilon_{is}, -x_{is}\beta_0\}, -x_{it}\beta_0\} \\
&= \max\{\alpha_i + \varepsilon_{is}, -x_{is}\beta_0, -x_{it}\beta_0\}
\end{aligned}
$$

The conditional exchangeability assumption implies that $(e_{ist}(\beta_0), e_{its}(\beta_0))$ is distributed like $(e_{its}(\beta_0), e_{ist}(\beta_0))$ conditional on (x_{it}, x_{is}, a_i) and hence the difference $e_{its}(\beta_0) - e_{ist}(\beta_0)$ is distributed symmetrically around 0 conditional on (x_{it}, x_{is}, a_i). Since this is true for any α_i this symmetry holds conditional only on (x_{it}, x_{is}). Therefore for any odd function ξ (that is, a function ξ that satisfies $\xi(-d) = -\xi(d)$) we have

$$E[\xi(e_{ist}(\beta_0) - e_{its}(\beta_0))|x_{it}, x_{is}] = 0 \tag{3.1}$$

which also implies the following moment restriction:

$$E[\xi(e_{ist}(\beta_0) - e_{its}(\beta_0))(x_{is} - x_{it})'|x_{it}, x_{is}] = 0.$$

The left-hand side of the moment condition above may be thought of as the first order condition for the following population minimization problem

$$\min_{\beta} E[q(y_{is}, y_{it}, (x_{is} - x_{it})\beta)|x_{it}, x_{is}]$$

where

$$
q(y_i, y_j, \delta) =
\begin{cases}
\Xi(y_i) - (y_j + \delta)\xi(y_i) & \text{if} \quad \delta \leq -y_j \\
\Xi(y_i - y_j - \delta) & \text{if} \quad -y_j < \delta < y_i \\
\Xi(-y_j) - (\delta - y_i)\xi(-y_i) & \text{if} \quad y_i \leq \delta
\end{cases}
$$

and $\Xi(d) : \Re \to \Re^+$ is an even function (that is, $\Xi(-d) = \Xi(d)$) which is convex, strictly increasing for $d > 0$ and has $\Xi(0) = 0$, and $\Xi'(d) = \xi(d)$ where $\xi(0) = 0$. Note that for Ξ to be convex, ξ has to be monotone. Obvious choices for Ξ are $\Xi(d) = d^2$ (which corresponds to $\xi(d) = 2d$) and $\Xi(d) = |d|$ (which corresponds to $\xi(d) = sgn(d)$).

The fact that the true β_0 solves the population minimization problem above suggests the following estimator for β_0:

$$\hat{\beta} = \arg\min_{\beta} \sum_i \sum_{s<t} q(y_{is}, y_{it}(x_{is} - x_{it})\beta).$$

Honoré (1992) shows that the estimators corresponding to $\Xi(d) = d^2$ and $\Xi(d) = |d|$ are root-N consistent and asymptotically normal.

Honoré (1993) considers a dynamic version of the model where the lag of the *observed* (censored) dependent variable appears in the model instead of the latent one. Hu (2002) considers the case where one lag of the *latent* (unobserved) dependent variable is included along with the set of exogenous variables x_{it}.

3.3 The semiparametric panel data sample selection model

The standard panel data sample selection (or Type 2 Tobit) model is defined as:

$$y_{it}^* = x_{it}^* \beta_0 + \alpha_i^* + \varepsilon_{it}^*$$

$$y_{it} = d_{it} \cdot y_{it}^*$$

$$d_{it} = 1\{z_{it}\gamma_0 + {}_i - u_{it} \geq 0\}$$

where $i = 1, 2, \ldots, N$; $t = 1, \ldots, T$. Kyriazidou (1997) considers estimation without any parametric assumptions on the form of the joint distribution of $(\varepsilon_{it}^*, u_{it})$ or on the individual effects (α_i, η_i).

Consider the case where $T = 2$ and only those individuals for whom $d_{i1} = d_{i2} = 1$. Let $\xi_i = (z_{i1}, z_{i2}, x_{i1}^*, x_{i2}^*, \alpha_i^*, {}_i)$ denote all the information about individual i. Note that

$$E(y_{i1} - y_{i2}|d_{i1} = d_{i2} = 1, \xi_i) = (x_{i1}^* - x_{i2}^*)\beta_0 + E(\varepsilon_{i1}^* - \varepsilon_{i2}^*|d_{i1} = d_{i2} = 1, \xi_i)$$

and hence OLS estimation of the first differenced model will not yield consistent estimation of β_0 since in general the so-called 'sample selection bias term'

$$\lambda_{it} \equiv E(\varepsilon_{it}^*|d_{i1} = d_{i2} = 1, \xi_i)$$

$$= E(\varepsilon_{it}^*|u_{i1} \leq z_{i1}\gamma_0 + {}_i, u_{i2} \leq z_{i2}\gamma_0 + {}_i, \xi_i)$$

is not zero. Nor do we have in general that $\lambda_{i1} = \lambda_{i2}$, so that first differencing removes the sample selection bias along with the individual effects. Kyriazidou (1997) makes a *conditional exchangeability assumption* that $(\varepsilon_{i1}^*, \varepsilon_{i2}^*, u_{i1}, u_{i2})$ and $(\varepsilon_{i2}^*, \varepsilon_{i1}^*, u_{i2}, u_{i1})$ are identically distributed conditional on ξ_i. Under this assumption, it is easy to see that if $z_{i1}\gamma_0 = z_{i2}\gamma_0$ then

$$\lambda_{i1} = E(\varepsilon_{i1}^*|u_{i1} \leq z_{i1}\gamma_0 + {}_i, u_{i2} \leq z_{i2}\gamma_0 + {}_i, \xi_i)$$

$$= E(\varepsilon_{i2}^*|u_{i1} \leq z_{i1}\gamma_0 + {}_i, u_{i2} \leq z_{i2}\gamma_0 + {}_i, \xi_i) = \lambda_{i2}$$

so that first differencing will eliminate both α_i and λ_{it} simultaneously. So β_0 can be estimated by first difference OLS for the subsample of individuals that are observed in both periods (that is, that have $d_{i1} = d_{i2} = 1$) and also have the selection index, $z_{it}\gamma_0$, constant (that is, $z_{i1}\gamma_0 = z_{i2}\gamma_0$). Of course, this estimation scheme cannot be directly implemented since γ_0 is unknown. And it is quite possible that no observation has $z_{i1}\gamma_0 = z_{i2}\gamma_0$ if $z_{it}\gamma_0$ is continuously distributed. If, however, λ_{it} is a sufficiently smooth function and $\hat{\gamma}$ is a consistent estimator of γ_0, $z_{i1}\gamma_0 \approx z_{i2}\gamma_0$ implies $\lambda_{i1} \approx \lambda_{i2}$, and the preceding augment holds approximately. Kyriazidou proposes a two-step estimation procedure, in the spirit of Powell (2001), and Ahn and Powell (1993) who consider estimation of cross-section versions of the sample selection model. In the first step, γ_0 is consistently estimated based on the selection equation. In the second step, the estimate $\hat{\gamma}$ is used to estimate β_0 based on those pairs of observations for which $z_{i1}\hat{\gamma}$ and $z_{i2}\hat{\gamma}$ are 'close'. To this end define

$$\hat{\psi}_i = \frac{1}{h_N} K\left(\frac{\Delta z_i \hat{\gamma}}{h_N}\right)$$

where $K()$ is a kernel density function and h_N is a bandwidth sequence. The proposed estimator takes the form:

$$\hat{\beta} = \left[\sum_{i=1}^{N} \hat{\psi}_i \Delta x_i' \Delta x_i d_{i1} d_{i2}\right]^{-1} \sum_{i=1}^{N} \hat{\psi}_i \Delta x_i' \Delta y_i d_{i1} d_{i2}.$$

Under some assumptions and by appropriately choosing h_N, the estimator can be shown to be asymptotically normal although the rate of convergence is slower that the parametric $\sqrt{N}$ rate. Apart from the conditional exchangeability assumption, another important assumption that underlies the approach is that there is at least one variable in z_{it} not contained in x_{it}, which is an exclusion restriction common in semiparametric sample selection models.

A dynamic version of the panel data sample selection model, with the own lagged dependent variable appearing in each equation, is considered by Kyriazidou (2001).

4. The random effects approach

Fixed effects methods and conditional maximum likelihood methods (when they exist) estimate the coefficients of time-varying regressors consistently without making any assumptions on how the individual effects are related to the observed covariates or to the time-varying errors or to the initial observations of the sample. However, these methods do not deliver estimates of coefficients of time-invariant regressors and of the individual effects, and hence cannot be used for prediction, or for computation of marginal effects and elasticities which are often the quantities of interest. Furthermore, none of these approaches allows for non-stationary errors and hence for time-series heteroskedasticity.

These problems do not arise in the random effects approach. The approach essentially consists of treating $(\alpha_I + \varepsilon_{it})$ as a two-component error term and making assumptions about its relationship with the observed covariates and, in the case of dynamic models, with the initial conditions as well. A downside of the approach is that misspecification of any part of the model typically yields inconsistent estimates.

4.1 Static case

In the static panel data linear regression model, the traditional random effects approach (sometimes also called the *uncorrelated random effects approach*) assumes that the individual effects α_i along with the time-varying errors ε_{it} are uncorrelated with the observed covariates x_{it}. Then the coefficients of both time-varying and time-invariant regressors may be estimated consistently (albeit not efficiently) by pooled OLS. In static nonlinear models, the traditional random effects approach apart from parameterizing the conditional distribution of ε_{it} given x_{it}, also assumes that α_i is independent of x_{it} and ε_{it} for all t, and has a distribution, say H, that depends on a finite set of unknown parameters, say δ_0. For example, in the binary choice model,

$$y_{it} = 1\{x_{it}\beta_0 + \alpha_i + \varepsilon_{it} \geq 0\} \qquad i = 1,\ldots,N; \ t = 1,\ldots,T \tag{4.1}$$

assuming that ε_{it} are i.i.d. over time and independent of x_i and α_i with known distribution F (say, standard normal or logistic), we may estimate the unknown parameters (β_0, δ_0) via ML. The log-likelihood is

$$\ln L(\beta, \delta) = \sum_i \ln \int \prod_{t=1}^{T} F(x_{it}\beta + \alpha)^{y_{it}} (1 - F(x_{it}\beta + \alpha))^{1-y_{it}} \, dH(\alpha, \delta)$$

and involves a one-dimensional integral which may be calculated numerically, for example, by *quadrature procedures* (see Butler and Moffitt, 1982).

However, things become quite complicated if we want to allow for arbitrary serial correlation in the ε_{it}'s. Consider the binary choice model

$$y_{it} = 1\{x_{it}\beta_0 - u_{it} \geq 0\}$$

where $u_{it} = \alpha_I + \varepsilon_{it}$ is the composite error term. For $T = 3$ there are 2^3 possible sequences of 0's and 1's. The likelihood for an individual for whom the sequence of observed y_{it}'s is (0, 1, 0) takes the form

$$\int_{x_{i1}\beta} \int^{x_{i2}\beta} \int_{x_{i3}\beta} f(u_1, u_2, u_3) \, du_1 du_2 du_3$$

where f is the trivariate density of (u_1, u_2, u_3) conditional on x_i. The log-likelihood is

$$\ln L(\beta, \delta) = \sum_{i:(0,0,0)} \ln \int_{x_{i1}\beta} \int_{x_{i2}\beta} \int_{x_{i3}\beta} f(u_1, u_2, u_3)\, du_1 du_2 du_3$$

$$+ \sum_{i:(0,0,1)} \ln \int_{x_{i1}\beta} \int_{x_{i2}\beta} \int^{x_{i3}\beta} f(u_1, u_2, u_3)\, du_1 du_2 du_3 + \ldots$$

which requires the computation of multiple trivariate integrals. Multivariate integration is basically infeasible for large T. This is where simulation methods come in very handy.

The assumption that α_i is independent of x_i is often found unsatisfactory. A possible solution is to assume a specific functional form for the relationship of α_i with x_i. This approach (recently also called the *correlated random effects approach*) was first proposed by Chamberlain (1984). Suppose that

$$\alpha_i = \sum_{t=1}^{T} x_{it} \gamma_{0,t} + v_i$$

where v_i is independent of x_i, similarly to the time varying error component ε_{it}, and that the composite new error term $v_i + \varepsilon_{it}$ follows a specific distribution, say normal. In the case of the binary choice model, for example, assuming that $\varepsilon_{it} + v_i | x_i, \alpha_i$ is $N(0, \sigma_{0,t}^2)$ implies that

$$\Pr(y_{it} = 1 | x_i) = \Phi\left(\frac{x_{it}\beta_0 + \sum_{t=1}^{T} x_{it}\gamma_{0,t}}{\sigma_{0,t}} \right) = \Phi(x_{it}\theta_{0,t}).$$

For computational simplicity, Chamberlain proposes to estimate the unknown parameters $\theta_{0,t}$ via period-by-period probit. The 'structural parameters' β_0, $\{\sigma_{0,t}^2\}_{t=1}^{T}$, and $\{\gamma_{0,t}\}_{t=1}^{T}$ can then be recovered by *minimum distance* estimation. Note that the approach allows for time series heteroskedasticity and requires only one normalization e.g. that $\sigma_{0,t}^2 = 1$.

Newey (1994) generalizes Chamberlain's approach by postulating that

$$\alpha_i = \rho(x_{i1}, \ldots, x_{it}) + v_i$$

where $\rho()$ is an unknown function of x_i. Assuming again that v_i and ε_{it} are independent of x_i and that the composite new error term $v_i + \varepsilon_{it}$ follows a specific distribution, say F_t, we obtain

$$\pi_t = \Pr(y_{it} = 1 | x_i) = F_t(\rho(x_i) + x_{it}\beta_0)$$

which for a strictly monotonic F_t implies that

$$F_t^{-1}(\pi_t) = \rho(x_i) + x_{it}\beta_0.$$

For example in the normal case

$$\Phi^{-1}(\pi_t) = \frac{\rho(x_i) + x_{it}\beta_0}{\sigma_{0,t}}.$$

Thus for two periods t and s we obtain

$$\Phi^{-1}(\pi_t) = \frac{\sigma_{0,s}}{\sigma_{0,t}}\Phi^{-1}(\pi_s) + \frac{\sigma_{0,s}}{\sigma_{0,t}}(x_{it} - x_{is})\beta_0.$$

Normalizing $\sigma_{0,t} = 1$ and estimating π_t and π_s nonparametrically, we can recover $\sigma_{0,s}$ and β_0 from the regression of $\Phi^{-1}(\hat{\pi}_t)$ on $\Phi^{-1}(\hat{\pi}_s)$ and $(x_{it} - x_{is})$.

A criticism of all these correlated random effects approaches is that, although in the linear model writing $\alpha_i = \sum_{t=1}^{T} x_{it}\gamma_{0,t} + u_i$ where $E(u_i x_{it}) = 0$ for all t does not impose $x_{it} - x_{is}$ any restrictions on the joint distribution of α_i and x_i (apart from the requirement that it has second moments) since this is just the best linear projection of α_i on x_i, in the nonlinear model assuming $\alpha_i = \rho(x_{i1}, \ldots, x_{it}) + u_i$, even without specifying the functional form of ρ, imposes implausible restrictions in the sense that, if this relationship holds for the T observations, a similar one will *not* in general hold for $T + 1$.

4.2 Dynamic case

In the case where there are genuine dynamics in the model in the form of lags of the dependent variable or other endogenous regressors, random effects methods become even more complicated and require additional assumptions about the relationship of the individual effects with the initial observations. We next describe a general approach for estimating dynamic random effects models suggested by Wooldridge (2000). For simplicity we will drop the subscripts i.

We are interested in the conditional distribution of y_t given a vector of strictly exogenous variables $z^T \equiv (z_1, \ldots, z_T)$, own lags and lags of other endogenous variables $x^{t-1} \equiv (y_{t-1}, w_{t-1}, y_{t-2}, w_{t-2}, \ldots, y_0, w_0)$, and an unobserved scalar or vector random effect α. Here z_t is strictly exogenous in the sense that

$$F(w_t|z^T, x^{t-1}, \alpha) = F(w_t|z_t, x^{t-1}, \alpha).$$

The conditional density of $x_t \equiv (y_t, w_t)$ is

$$f_t(x_t|z^T, x^{t-1}, \alpha) = f_t(x_t|z_t, x^{t-1}, \alpha)$$
$$= f_t(y_t|w_t, z_t, x^{t-1}, \alpha) \cdot f_t(w_t|z_t, x^{t-1}, \alpha)$$

and the joint density for all T periods is

$$f(x_1, x_2, \ldots, x_T|z^T, x_0, \alpha) = \prod_{t=1}^{T} f_t(x_t|z_t, x^{t-1}, \alpha).$$

But a is unobserved. We need to integrate it out. One solution is to parameterize the distribution of α conditional on z^T and x_0, say $h(\alpha|z^T, x_0)$. Then

$$f(x_1, x_2, \ldots, x_T | z^T, x_0) = \int \prod_{t=1}^{T} f_t(x_t | z_t, x^{t-1}, \alpha) \, h(\alpha|z^T, x_0) \, d\alpha.$$

Notice that in the traditional random effects approach (in the line of Anderson and Hsiao, 1981) we would have to make assumptions about the conditional distribution of x_0 conditional on a and z^T.

EKATERINI KYRIAZIDOU

See also **fixed effects and random effects.**

Bibliography

Ahn, H. and Powell, J.L. 1993. Semiparametric estimation of censored selection models with a nonparametric selection mechanism. *Journal of Econometrics* 58, 3–29.

Andersen, E. 1970. Asymptotic properties of conditional maximum likelihood estimators. *Journal of the Royal Statistical Society,* Series B 32, 283–301.

Anderson, T. and Hsiao, C. 1981. Estimation of dynamic models with error components. *Journal of the American Statistical Association* 76(375), 598–606.

Butler, J.S. and Moffitt, R. 1982. A computationally efficient quadrature procedure for the one-factor multinomial probit model. *Econometrica* 50, 761–4.

Chamberlain, G. 1984. Panel data. In *Handbook of Econometrics,* vol 2, ed. Z. Griliches and M. Intrilligator. Amsterdam: North-Holland.

Chamberlain, G. 1985. Heterogeneity, omitted variable bias, and duration dependence. In *Longitudinal Analysis of Labor Market Data,* ed. J.J. Heckman and B. Singer. Cambridge: Cambridge University Press.

Fristedt, B. and Gray, L. 1997. *A Modern Approach to Probability Theory.* Boston: Birkhauser.

Honoré, B.E. 1992. Trimmed LAD and least squares estimation of truncated and censored regression models with fixed effects. *Econometrica* 60, 533–65.

Honoré, B.E. 1993. Orthogonality conditions for Tobit models with fixed effects and lagged dependent variables. *Journal of Econometrics* 59, 35–61.

Honoré, B.E. and Kyriazidou, E. 2000a. Panel data discrete choice models with lagged dependent variables. *Econometrica* 68, 839–74.

Honoré, B.E. and Kyriazidou, E. 2000b. Estimation of Tobit-type models with individual specific effects. *Econometric Reviews* 19, 341–66.

Hu, L. 2002. Estimation of a censored dynamic panel data model. *Econometrica* 70, 2499–517.

Kyriazidou, E. 1997. Estimation of a panel data sample selection model. *Econometrica* 65, 1335–64.

Kyriazidou, E. 2001. Estimation of dynamic panel data sample selection models. *Review of Economic Studies* 68, 543–72.

Magnac, T. 2000. Subsidised training and youth employment: distinguishing unobserved heterogeneity from state dependence in labour market histories. *Economic Journal* 110, 805–37.

Manski, C. 1987. Semiparametric analysis of random effects linear models from binary panel data. *Econometrica* 55, 357–62.

Newey, W. 1994. The asymptotic variance of semiparametric estimators. *Econometrica* 62, 1349–82.

Neyman, J. and Scott, E.L. 1948. Consistent estimation from partially consistent observations. *Econometrica* 16, 1–32.

Powell, J.L. 2001. Semiparametric estimation of bivariate latent variable models. In *Nonlinear Statistical Modeling: Proceedings of the Thirteenth International Symposium in Economic Theory and Econometrics: Essays in Honor of Takeshi Amemiya*, ed. C. Hsiao, K. Morimune and J.L. Powell. Cambridge: Cambridge University Press.

Wooldridge, J.M. 2000. A framework for estimating dynamic, unobserved effects panel data models with possible feedback to future explanatory variables. *Economics Letters* 68, 245–50.

nonparametric structural models

The interplay between economic theory and econometrics comes to its full force when analysing structural models. These models are used in industrial organization, marketing, public finance, labour economics and many other fields in economics. Structural econometric methods make use of the behavioural and equilibrium assumptions specified in economic models to define a mapping between the distribution of the observable variables and the primitive functions and distributions that are used in the model. Using these methods, one can infer elements of the model, such as utility and production functions, that are not directly observed. This allows one to predict behaviour and equilibria outcomes under new environments and to evaluate the welfare of individuals and profits of firms under alternative policies, among other benefits.

To provide an example, suppose that one would like to predict the demand for a new product. Since the product has not previously been available, no direct data exists. However, one could use data on the demand for existent products together with a structural model, as shown and developed by McFadden (1974). Characterize the new product and the existent competing products by vectors of common attributes. Assume that consumers derive utility from the observable and unobservable attributes of the products, and that each chooses the product that maximizes his or her utility of those attributes among the existent products. Then, from the choice of consumers among existent products, one can infer their preferences for the attributes, and then predict what the choice of each of them would be in a situation when a new vector of attributes, corresponding to the new product, is available. Moreover, one could get a measure of the differences in the welfare of the consumers when the new product is available.

Economic theory seldom has implications regarding the parametric structures that functions and distributions may possess. The behavioural and equilibrium specifications made in economic models typically imply shape restrictions, such as monotonicity, concavity, homogeneity, weak separability, and additive separability, and exclusion restrictions, but typically not parametric specifications, such as linearity of conditional expectations, or normal distributions for unobserved variables. Nonparametric methods, which do not require specification of parametric structures for the functions and distributions in a model, are ideally fitted, therefore, to analyse structural models, using as few a priori restrictions as possible. Nonparametric techniques have been applied to many models, such as discrete choice models, tobit models, selection models, and duration models. We will concentrate here, however, on the basic models and on those, indicate some of the latest works that have dealt with identification and estimation.

Nonparametric structural econometric models

As with parametric models, a nonparametric econometric model is characterized by a vector X of variables that are determined outside the model and are observable, a vector ε of variables that are determined outside the model and are unobservable, a vector Υ of outcome variables, which are determined within the model and are unobservable, and a vector Y of outcome variables that are determined within the model and are observable. These variables are related by functional relationships, which determine the causal structure by which Υ and Y are determined from X and ε. The functional relationships are characterized by some functions that are known and some that are unknown. Similarly, some distributions may be known, some are unknown, and the others should be derived from the functional relationships and the known and unknown functions and distributions. Let $\underline{h}^*$ denote the vector of all the unknown functions in the model, $\underline{F}^*$ denote the vector of all unknown distributions, and $\zeta^* = (\underline{h}^*, \underline{F}^*)$. In contrast to parametric models, in nonparametric models, none of the coordinates of ζ^* is assumed known up to a finite dimensional parameter. Only restrictions such as continuity or values of the conditional expectations are assumed. The specification of the model should be such that from any vector $\zeta = (\underline{h}, \underline{F})$, satisfying those same restrictions that ζ^* is assumed to satisfy, one is able to derive a distribution for the observable variables, $F_{YX}(\cdot, \zeta)$.

Nonparametric identification

When specifying an econometric model, we may be interested in testing it, or we may be interested in estimating $\zeta^* = (\underline{h}^*, \underline{F}^*)$ or some feature of ζ^*, such as only one of the elements of $\underline{h}^*$, or even the value of that element at one point. Suppose that interest lies on estimating a particular feature, $\psi(\zeta^*)$ of ζ^*. The first question one must answer is whether that feature is identified. Let Ω denote the set of all possible values that $\psi(\zeta)$ may attain, when ζ is restricted to satisfy the properties that ζ^* is assumed to satisfy. Given $\psi \in \Omega$, define $\Gamma_{Y,X}(\psi)$ to be the set of all probability distributions of (Y, X) that are consistent with ψ. This is the set of all distributions that can be generated by a ζ, satisfying the properties that ζ^* is assumed to satisfy, and with $\psi(\zeta) = \psi$. We say that two values $\psi, \psi' \in \Omega$ are *observationally equivalent* if

$$\left[\Gamma_{Y,X}(\psi) \cap \Gamma_{Y,X}(\psi') \right] \neq \varnothing,$$

that is, they are observationally equivalent if there exist a distribution of the observable variables that could have been generated by two vectors ζ and ζ' with $\psi(\zeta) = \psi$ and $\psi(\zeta') = \psi'$. The feature $\psi^* = \psi(\zeta^*)$ is said to be identified if there is no $\psi \in \Omega$ such that $\psi \neq \psi^*$ and ψ is observationally equivalent to ψ^*. That is, $\psi^* = \psi(\zeta^*)$ is identified if a change from ψ^* to $\psi \neq \psi^*$ cannot be compensated by a change in other unknown elements of ζ, so that a same distribution of observable variables could be generated by both, vectors ζ^* and ζ with $\psi^* = \psi(\zeta^*)$ and $\psi = \psi(\zeta)$.

When ψ^* can be expressed as a continuous functional of the distribution of observable variables (Y, X) one can typically estimate ψ^* nonparametrically by substituting the distribution by a nonparametric estimator for it.

Additive and nonadditive models with exogenous explanatory variables

The current literature on nonparametric econometrics methods considers additive and nonadditive models. In *additive models*, the unobservable exogenous variables ε are specified as affecting the value of Y though an additive function. Hence, for some functions m and v and some unobservable η

$$Y = m(X) + v(X, \varepsilon)$$
$$= m(X) + \eta.$$

In these models, the object of interest is typically the function m. Depending on the restrictions that one may impose on η, m may denote a conditional expectation, a conditional quantile, or some other function. Many methods exist to estimate conditional means and conditional quantiles nonparametrically. Prakasa Rao (1983), Härdle and Linton (1994), Matzkin (1994; 2007b), Pagan and Ullah (1999), Koenker (2005), and Chen (2007), among others, survey parts of this literature. Some nonparametric tests for these models include Wooldridge (1992), Yatchew (1992), Hong and White (1995), and Fan and Li (1996).

In *nonadditive models*, one is interested in analysing the interaction between the unobservable and observable explanatory variables. These models are specified, for some function m as

$$Y = m(X, \varepsilon).$$

Nonparametric identification and estimation in models of this type was studied in Roehrig (1988), Olley and Pakes (1996), Brown and Matzkin (1998), Matzkin (1999; 2003; 2004; 2005; 2006), Chesher (2003), Imbens and Newey (2003), and Athey and Imbens (2006), among others.

Dependence between observable and unobservable explanatory variables

In econometric models, it is often the case that in an equation of interest, some of the explanatory variables are endogenous; they are not distributed independently of the unobservable explanatory variables in that same equation. This typically occurs when restrictions such as agent's optimization and equilibrium conditions generate interrelationships among observable variables and unobservable variables, ε, that affect a common observable outcome variable, Y. In such cases, the distribution of the observable outcome and observable explanatory variables does not provide enough information to recover the causal effect of those explanatory variables on the outcome variable, since changes in those explanatory variables do not leave the value of ε fixed. A typical example of this is when Y denotes quantity demanded for a product, X denotes the price of the product, and ε is an unobservable demand shifter. If the price that will make firms produce a certain quantity increases with quantity, this change in ε will generate an increment in the price X. Hence, the observable effect of a change in price in demanded quantity would not correspond to the effect of changing the value of price when the value ε stays constant. Another typical example arises when analysing the effect of years of education on wages. An unobservable variable, such as ability, affects wages and also affects the decision about years of education.

Estimation techniques for additive and nonadditive functions of endogenous variables

The estimation techniques that have been developed to estimate nonparametric models with endogenous explanatory variables typically make use of additional information, which provides some exogenous variation on either the value of the endogenous variable or on the value of the unobservable variable. The common procedures are based on conditional independence methods and on instrumental variable methods. In the first set of procedures, independence between the unobservable and observable explanatory variables in a model is typically achieved by either *conditioning on observable* variables, or *conditioning on unobservable* variables. A *control function* approach (Heckman and Robb, 1985) models the unobservable as a function, so that conditioning on that function purges the dependence between the explanatory observable and unobservable variables in the model. Instrumental variable methods derive identification from an independence condition between the unobservable and an external variable (an instrument) or function, which is correlated with the endogenous variable and which might be estimable.

Conditioning on unobservable variables often requires the estimation of those unobservable variables. Two-step procedures, where they are first estimated, and then used as additional regressors in the model of interest have been developed for additive models by Ng and Pinkse (1995), Pinkse (2000), and Newey, Powell and Vella (1999), among others. Two-step procedures for nonadditive models have been developed by Altonji and Matzkin (2001), Blundell and Powell (2003), Chesher (2003), and Imbens and Newey (2003), among others. Conditional moment estimation methods or quasi-maximum likelihood estimation methods can also be used (see, for example, Ai and Chen, 2003). Altonji and Ichimura (2000), Altonji and Matzkin (2001; 2005), and Matzkin (2004), among others, considered conditioning on observables for estimation of nonadditive models with endogenous explanatory variables. Matzkin (2004) provides insight into the sources of exogeneity that are generated when conditioning on either observables or unobservables, and which allow identification and estimation in nonadditive models. In particular, if $Y = m(X, \varepsilon)$, with m strictly increasing in ε, and ε is independent of X conditional on W, she shows that there exists functions $s(W, \eta)$ and $r(W, \delta)$ such that δ is independent η conditional on W, $X = s(W, \eta)$ and $\varepsilon = r(W, \delta)$. Hence,

$$Y = m(X, \varepsilon) = m(s(W, \eta), r(W, \delta)).$$

Instrumental variable methods for additive models were considered by Newey and Powell (1989; 2003), Ai and Chen (2003), Darolles, Florens and Renault (2003), and Hall and Horowitz (2003), among others. To develop estimators for m in the model

$$Y_1 = m(Y_2) + \varepsilon \quad E[\varepsilon|Z] = 0.$$

they use the moment condition

$$E[Y_1|Z = z] = \int m(y_2) f_{Y_2|Z=z}(y_2) dy_2,$$

which depends on the conditional expectation $E[Y_1|Z=z]$ and the conditional density $f_{Y_2|Z=z}(y_2)$, which can be estimated nonparametrically. For nonadditive models, of the form

$$Y_1 = m(Y_2, \varepsilon) \quad \varepsilon \text{ independent of } Z$$

where m is strictly increasing in ε, Chernozhukov and Hansen (2005) and Chernozhukov, Imbens and Newey (2007) developed estimation methods using the moment condition that for al τ

$$\tau = E[1(\varepsilon < \tau)] = E[1(\varepsilon < \tau)|Z]$$

from which m can be estimated using the conditional moment restriction

$$E[1(Y_1 < m(Y_2, \varepsilon)) - \varepsilon|Z] = 0.$$

Matzkin (2006) considered the model

$$Y_1 = m_1(Y_2, \varepsilon)$$
$$Y_2 = m_2(Y_1, Z, \eta)$$

where Z is distributed independently of (ε, η). She established restrictions on the functions m_1 and m_2 and on the distribution of (ε, η, Z) under which

$$\left[\frac{\partial r_1(y_1, y_2)}{\partial y_2} \right]^{-1} \left[\frac{\partial r_1(y_1, y_2)}{\partial y_1} \right]$$

can be expressed as a function of the conditional density $f_{Y_1, Y_2|Z=z^*}(y_1, y_2)$, where r_1 is the inverse of m_1 with respect to ε, and the value z^* of the instrument Z is easily identified (see also Matzkin, 2005; 2007a; 2007b).

Estimation of averages and average derivatives

Nonparametric estimators are notorious by their slow rate of convergence, which worsens as the dimension of the number of arguments of the nonparametric function increases. A remedy for this is to consider averages of the nonparametric function. The average derivative method in Powell, Stock and Stoker (1989) and the partial integration methods of Newey (1994) and Linton and Nielsen (1995), for example, show how rates of convergence can increase by averaging a nonparametric function or its derivatives. This approach has been extended to cases where the explanatory variables are endogenous, using additional variables to deal with the endogeneity, and averaging over them. Examples are Blundell and Powell's (2003) *average structural function*, Imbens and Newey's (2003) *average quantile function*, and Altonji and Matzkin's (2001; 2005) *local average response* function.

Suppose, for example, that the model of interest is

$$Y_1 = m(Y_2, \varepsilon)$$

and W is such that Y_2 and ε are independent conditional on W. Then, the Blundell and Powell (2003) average structural function is

$$G(y_2) = \int m(y_2, \varepsilon) f_\varepsilon(\varepsilon) d\varepsilon$$

which can be derived from a nonparametric estimator for the distribution of (Y_1, Y_2, W) as

$$G(y_2) = \int E(Y_1 | Y_2 = y_2, W = w) f_W(w) dw.$$

Imbens and Newey's (2003) quantile structural function is defined for the τ-th quantile of $\varepsilon, q_\varepsilon(\tau)$, as

$$r(y_2, y_1) = \Pr(m(Y_2, q_\varepsilon(\tau)) \le y_1 | Y_2 = y_2)$$

which can be estimated by

$$r(y_2, y_1) = \int \Pr(Y_1 \le y_1 | Y_2 = y_2, W = w) f_W(w) dv.$$

Altonji and Matzkin's (2001; 2005) local average response function is

$$\beta(y_2) = \int \frac{\partial m(y_2, \varepsilon)}{\partial y_2} f_{\varepsilon | Y_2 = y_2}(\varepsilon) d\varepsilon$$

which can be derived from a nonparametric estimator for the distribution of (Y_1, Y_2, W) as

$$\beta(y_2) = \int \frac{\partial E(Y_1 | Y_2 = y_2, W = w)}{\partial y_2} f_{W | Y_2 = y_2}(w) dw.$$

Conclusions

The literature on nonparametric structural models has been rapidly developing in recent years. The new methods allow one to analyse counterfactuals without making use of parametric assumptions. Estimation of some features of the model rather than the functions themselves may reduce the curse of dimensionality, therefore providing improved properties and reducing the need for large data-sets.

ROSA L. MATZKIN

See also **identification; quantile regression.**

Bibliography

Ai, C. and Chen, X. 2003. Efficient estimation of models with conditional moments restrictions containing unknown functions. *Econometrica* 71, 1795–843.

Altonji, J.G. and Ichimura, H. 2000. Estimating derivatives in nonseparable models with limited dependent variables. Mimeo. Northwestern University.

Altonji, J.G. and Matzkin, R.L. 2001. Panel data estimators for nonseparable models with endogenous regressors. NBER Working Paper T0267.

Altonji, J.G. and Matzkin, R.L. 2005. Cross section and panel data estimators for nonseparable models with endogenous regressors. *Econometrica* 73, 1053–102.

Athey, S. and Imbens, G. 2006. Identification and inference in nonlinear difference-in-differences models. *Econometrica* 74, 431–97.

Blundell, R. and Powell, J.L. 2003. Endogeneity in nonparametric and semiparametric regression models. In *Advances in Economics and Econometrics, Theory and Applications, Eighth World Congress*, vol. 2, ed. M. Dewatripont, L.P. Hansen and S.J. Turnovsky. Cambridge: Cambridge University Press.

Brown, D.J. and Matzkin, R.L. 1998. Estimation of nonparametric functions in simultaneous equations models, with an application to consumer demand. Discussion Paper No. 1175, Cowles Foundation, Yale University.

Chen, X. 2007. Large sample sieve estimation of semi-nonparametric models. In *Handbook of Econometrics*, vol. 6, ed. E. Leamer and J.J. Heckman. Amsterdam: North-Holland.

Chernozhukov, V. and Hansen, C. 2005. An IV model of quantile treatment effects. *Econometrica* 73, 245–61.

Chernozhukov, V., Imbens, G. and Newey, W. 2007. Instrumental variable estimation of nonseparable models. *Journal of Econometrics* 139, 4–14.

Chesher, A. 2003. Identification in nonseparable models. *Econometrica* 71, 1404–441.

Darolles, S., Florens, J.P. and Renault, E. 2003. Nonparametric instrumental regression. IDEI Working Paper No. 228.

Fan, Y. and Li, Q. 1996. Consistent model specification tests: omitted variables and semiparametric functional forms. *Econometrica* 64, 4.

Florens, J.P. 2003. Inverse problems and structural econometrics: the example of instrumental variables. In *Advances in Economics and Econometrics, Theory and Applications*, vol. 2, ed. M. Dewatripont, L.P. Hansen and S. Turnovsky. Cambridge: Cambridge University Press.

Hall, P. and Horowitz, J.L. 2003. Nonparametric methods for inference in the presence of instrumental variables. Working Paper No. 102/03, CMMD.

Härdle, W. and Linton, O. 1994. Applied nonparametric methods. In *Handbook of Econometrics*, vol. 4, ed. R.F. Engel and D.F. McFadden. Amsterdam: North-Holland.

Heckman, J.J. and Robb, R. 1985. Alternative methods for evaluating the impact of interventions. In *Longitudinal Analysis of Labor Market Data*, ed. J.J. Heckman and B. Singer. Cambridge: Cambridge University Press.

Hong, Y. and White, H. 1995. Consistent specification testing via nonparametric series regression. *Econometrica* 63, 1133–59.

Imbens, G.W. and Newey, W.K. 2003. Identification and estimation of triangular simultaneous equations models without additivity. Mimeo, Massachusetts Institute of Technology.

Koenker, R.W. 2005. *Quantile Regression*. Cambridge: Cambridge University Press.

Linton, O.B. and Nielsen, J.B. 1995. A kernel method of estimating structured nonparametric regression based on marginal integration. *Biometrika* 82, 93–100.

Matzkin, R.L. 1994. Restrictions of economic theory in nonparametric methods. In *Handbook of Econometrics*, vol. 4, ed. R.F. Engel and D.L. McFadden. Amsterdam: North-Holland.

Matzkin, R.L. 1999. Nonparametric estimation of nonadditive random functions. Mimeo. Northwestern University.

Matzkin, R.L. 2003. Nonparametric estimation of nonadditive random functions. *Econometrica* 71, 1339–75.

Matzkin, R.L. 2004. Unobservable instruments. Mimeo, Northwestern University.

Matzkin, R.L. 2005. Identification in nonparametric simultaneous equations. Mimeo, Northwestern University.

Matzkin, R.L. 2006. Estimation of nonparametric simultaneous equations. Mimeo, Northwestern University.

Matzkin, R.L. 2007a. Heterogenous choice. Invited lecture, Ninth World Congress of the Econometric Society. In *Advanced in Economics and Econometrics, Theory and Applications, Ninth World Congress*, vol. 3, ed. R. Blundell, W. Newey, and T. Persson. Cambridge: Cambridge University Press.

Matzkin, R.L. 2007b. Nonparametric identification. In *Handbook of Econometrics*, vol. 6, ed. E. Leamer and J.J. Heckman. Amsterdam: North-Holland.

McFadden, D. 1974. Conditional logit analysis of qualitative choice behavior. In *Frontiers in Econometrics*, ed. P. Zarembka. New York: Academic Press.

Newey, W.K. 1994. Kernel estimation of partial means and a general variance estimator. *Econometric Theory* 10, 233–53.

Newey, W. and Powell, J. 1989. Instrumental variables estimation of nonparametric models. Mimeo. Princeton University.

Newey, W. and Powell, J. 2003. Instrumental variables estimation of nonparametric models. *Econometrica* 71, 1565–78.

Newey, W.K., Powell, J.L. and Vella, F. 1999. Nonparametric estimation of triangular simultaneous equations models. *Econometrica* 67, 565–603.

Ng, S. and Pinkse, J. 1995. Nonparametric two-step estimation of unknown regression functions when the regressors and the regression error are not independent. Mimeo, CIREQ.

Olley, G.S. and Pakes, A. 1996. The dynamics of productivity in the telecommunications equipment industry. *Econometrica* 64, 1263–97.

Pagan, A. and Ullah, A. 1999. *Nonparametric Econometrics*. Cambridge: Cambridge University Press.

Pinkse, J. 2000. Nonparametric two-step regression estimation when regressors and errors are dependent. *Canadian Journal of Statistics* 28, 289–300.

Powell, J.L., Stock, J.H. and Stoker, T.M. 1989. Semiparametric estimation of index coefficients. *Econometrica* 51, 1403–30.

Prakasa Rao, B.L.S. 1983. *Nonparametric Functional Estimation*. New York: Academic Press.

Roehrig, C.S. 1988. Conditions for identification in nonparametric and parametric models. *Econometrica* 56, 433–47.

Wooldridge, J. 1992. Nonparametric regression tests based on an infinite dimensional least squares procedure. *Econometric Theory* 8, 435–51.

Yatchew, A.J. 1992. Nonparametric regression tests based on an infinite dimensional least squares procedure. *Econometric Theory* 8, 435–51.

partial identification in econometrics

Suppose that one wants to use sample data to draw conclusions about a population of interest. Econometricians have long found it useful to separately study identification problems and problems of statistical inference. Studies of identification characterize the conclusions that could be drawn if one were able to observe an unlimited number of realizations of the sampling process. Studies of statistical inference characterize the generally weaker conclusions that can be drawn given a sample of positive but finite size. Koopmans (1949, p. 132) put it this way in the article that introduced the term 'identification':

> In our discussion we have used the phrase 'a parameter that can be determined from a sufficient number of observations.' We shall now define this concept more sharply, and give it the name *identifiability* of a parameter. Instead of reasoning, as before, from 'a sufficiently large number of observations' we shall base our discussion on a hypothetical knowledge of the probability distribution of the observations, as defined more fully below. It is clear that exact knowledge of this probability distribution cannot be derived from any finite number of observations. Such knowledge is the limit approachable but not attainable by extended observation. By hypothesizing nevertheless the full availability of such knowledge, we obtain a clear separation between problems of statistical inference arising from the variability of finite samples, and problems of identification in which we explore the limits to which inference even from an infinite number of observations is suspect.

For most of the 20th century, econometricians commonly thought of identification as a binary event – a parameter is either identified or it is not. Empirical researchers applying econometric methods combined available data with assumptions that yield point identification and they reported point estimates of parameters. Many economists recognized with discomfort that point identification often requires strong assumptions that are difficult to motivate. However, they saw no other way to perform inference.

Yet there is enormous scope for fruitful inference using weaker and more credible assumptions that partially identify population parameters. A parameter is partially identified if the sampling process and maintained assumptions reveal that the parameter lies in a set, its 'identification region', that is smaller than the logical range of the parameter but larger than a single point. Estimates of partially identified parameters generically are set-valued; a natural estimate of an identification region is its sample analog.

Until recently, study of partial identification was rare and fragmented. Frisch (1934) and Reiersol (1941) developed sharp bounds on the slope parameter of a linear regression with errors-in-variables, with refinement by Klepper and Leamer (1984) and others. Duncan and Davis (1953) used a numerical example to show that the ecological inference problem of political science is a matter of partial identification. Cochran, Mosteller and Tukey (1954) suggested conservative analysis of surveys with missing data due to non-response by sample members, although Cochran (1977) subsequently downplayed the idea. Peterson (1976) initiated study of partial identification of the competing risks model of survival analysis.

For whatever reason, these scattered contributions remained at the fringes of econometric consciousness and did not spawn systematic study of partial identification. However, a coherent body of research took shape in the 1990s and has grown rapidly. The new literature on partial identification emerged out of concern with traditional approaches to inference with missing outcome data. Empirical researchers have commonly assumed that missingness is random, in the sense that the observability of an outcome is statistically independent of its value. Yet this and other point-identifying assumptions have regularly been criticized as implausible. So it was natural to ask what random sampling with partial observability of outcomes reveals about outcome distributions if nothing is known about the missingness process or if assumptions weak enough to be widely credible are imposed. This question was posed and partially answered in Manski (1989), with subsequent development in Manski (1994; 2003, chs. 1 and 2), Scharfstein, Manski and Anthony (2004), Blundell et al. (2004) and Stoye (2005).

Study of inference with missing outcome data led naturally to consideration of conditional prediction and analysis of treatment response. A common objective of empirical research is to predict an outcome conditional on given covariates, using data from a random sample of the population. Often, sample realizations of outcomes and/or covariates are missing. Horowitz and Manski (1998; 2000) and Zaffalon (2002) study nonparametric prediction when nothing is known about the missingness process; Horowitz et al. (2003) and Horowitz and Manski (2006) consider the computationally challenging problem of parametric prediction. Missing data on outcomes and covariates is the extreme case of interval measurement of these variables. Manski and Tamer (2002) study conditional prediction with interval data on outcomes or covariates, while Haile and Tamer (2003) analyse an interesting problem of interval data that arises in econometric analysis of auctions.

Analysis of treatment response must contend with the fundamental problem that counterfactual outcomes are not observable; hence, findings on partial identification with missing outcome data are directly applicable. Yet analysis of treatment response poses much more than a generic missing-data problem. One reason is that observations of realized outcomes, when combined with suitable assumptions, can provide information about counterfactual ones. Another is that practical problems of treatment choice as well as other concerns motivate research on treatment response and thereby determine what population parameters are of interest. For these reasons, it has been productive to study partial identification of treatment response as a subject in its own right. This stream of research was initiated independently in Robins (1989) and Manski (1990). Subsequent contributions include Manski (1995; 1997a; 1997b), Balke and Pearl (1997), Heckman, Smith and Clements

(1997), Hotz, Mullin and Sanders (1997), Manski and Nagin (1998), Manski and Pepper (2000), Moinari (2002), and Pepper (2003). The normative problem of treatment choice when treatment response is partially identified is studied in Manski (2000; 2002; 2005a; 2005b; 2006) and Brock (2005).

Another broad subject of study has been inference on the components of finite probability mixtures. The mathematical problem of decomposition of mixtures arises in many substantively distinct settings, including contaminated sampling, ecological inference, and conditional prediction with missing or misclassified covariate data. Findings on partial identification of mixtures have application to all of these subjects and more. Research on this subject includes Horowitz and Manski (1995), Bollinger (1996), Cross and Manski (2002), Dominitz and Sherman (2004), Kreider and Pepper (2004), and Molinari (2004).

There has been other research as well. In discrete response analysis, response-based sampling poses a 'reverse regression' problem in which one seeks to learn the distribution of outcomes given covariates but the sampling process reveals the distribution of covariates given outcomes. This problem has been studied in Manski (1995, ch. 4; 2001; 2003, ch. 6) and King and Zeng (2002). In econometric analysis of multi-player games, a long-standing problem has been to infer behaviour from outcome data when the game being studied may have multiple equilibria. Ciliberto and Tamer (2004) address this problem.

Whatever the specific subject under study, a common theme runs through the new literature on partial identification. One first asks what the sampling process alone reveals about the population of interest and then studies the identifying power of assumptions that aim to be credible in practice. This conservative approach to inference makes clear the conclusions one can draw in empirical research without imposing untenable assumptions. It establishes a domain of consensus among researchers who may hold disparate beliefs about what assumptions are appropriate. It also makes plain the limitations of the available data. When credible identification regions turn out to be large, researchers should face up to the fact that the available data do not support inferences as tight as they might like to achieve.

The remainder of this article uses the problem of inference with missing outcome data and the analysis of treatment response to develop the common theme of recent research on partial identification and to give illustrative findings. Readers who aim to learn more may want to begin with two monographs that provide self-contained expositions with different audiences in mind. Manski (1995) presents basic ideas in a way intended to be broadly accessible to students and researchers in the social sciences. Manski (2003) develops the subject in a rigorous manner meant to provide the foundation for further study by econometricians.

Readers who prefer to learn about econometric methods through the study of empirical applications will find diverse case studies using observational data to analyse treatment response. Manski et al. (1992) investigate the effect of family structure on children's outcomes, and Hotz, Mullin and Sanders (1997) analyse the effect of teenage childbearing. Manski and Nagin (1998) study the effects of judicial sentencing on criminal recidivism. Pepper (2000) examines the intergenerational effects of welfare receipt. Manski and Pepper (2000) and Ginther (2002) analyse the returns to schooling.

There have also been empirical studies of problems of partial identification that arise in analysis of randomized experiments. Horowitz and Manski (2000) study a medical clinical trial with missing data on outcomes and covariates. Pepper (2003) asks what welfare-to-work experiments reveal about the operation of welfare policy when case workers have discretion in treatment assignment. Scharfstein, Manski and Anthony (2004) analyse an educational experiment with randomized assignment to treatment but non-random attrition of subjects.

Inference with missing outcome data

To formalize the missing data problem, let each member j of a population J have an outcome y, in a space Y. The population is a probability space and $y : J \to Y$ is a random variable with distribution $P(y)$. Let a sampling process draw persons at random from J. However, not all realizations of y are observable. Let the realization of a binary random variable z indicate observability; y is observable if $z = 1$ and not observable if $z = 0$.

By the Law of Total Probability

$$P(y) = P(y|z = 1)P(z = 1) + P(y|z = 0)P(z = 0). \tag{1}$$

The sampling process reveals $P(y|z = 1)$ and $P(z)$, but is uninformative regarding $P(y|z = 0)$. Hence, the sampling process partially identifies $P(y)$. In particular, it reveals that $P(y)$ lies in the identification region

$$H[P(y)] \equiv [P(y|z = 1)P(z = 1) + \gamma P(z = 0), \gamma \in \Gamma_Y], \tag{2}$$

where Γ_Y is the space of all probability distributions on Y.

The size of the identification region $H[P(y)]$ grows with $P(z = 0)$, which measures the prevalence of missing data. The region is a proper subset of Γ_Y whenever the probability of missing data is less than 1, and it is a singleton when there are no missing data. Thus, $P(y)$ is partially identified when $0 < P(z = 0) < 1$ and is point-identified when $P(z = 0) = 0$.

Means of bounded functions of y

A common objective of empirical research is to infer parameters of a probability distribution. The identification region for a parameter of $P(y)$ follows immediately from $H[P(y)]$. Let $\tau(\cdot) : \Gamma_Y \to T$ map probability distributions on Y into a parameter space T and consider inference on the parameter $\tau[P(y)]$. The identification region consists of all possible values of the parameter. Thus,

$$H\{\tau[P(y)]\} = \{\tau(\eta), \eta \in H[P(y)]\}. \tag{3}$$

Result (3) is simple but is too abstract to be useful as stated. Research on partial identification has sought to characterize $H\{\tau[P(y)]\}$ for different parameters. Manski (1989) does this for means of bounded functions of y, Manski (1994) for quantiles, and Manski (2003, ch. 1) for all parameters that respect first-order stochastic dominance. Blundell et al. (2004) and Stoye (2005) characterize the identification regions for spread parameters such as the variance, inter-quartile range, and the Gini coefficient; these authors apply their findings in empirical research assessing nationwide income inequality using surveys with missing income data.

The results for means of bounded functions are easy to derive and instructive, so I focus on these parameters here. Let R be the real line. Let $g(\cdot)$ be a function that maps Y into R and that attains finite lower and upper bounds $g_0 \equiv \min_{y \in Y} g(y)$ and $g_1 \equiv \max_{y \in Y} g(y)$. The problem of interest is to infer $E[g(y)]$.

The Law of Iterated Expectations gives

$$E[g(y)] = E[g(y)|z = 1]P(z = 1) + E[g(y)|z = 0]P(z = 0). \tag{4}$$

The sampling process reveals $E[g(y)|z = 1$ and $P(z)$, but is uninformative regarding $E[g(y)|z = 0$, which can take any value in the interval $[g_0, g_1]$. Hence, the identification region for $E[g(y)]$ is the closed interval

$$
\begin{aligned}
H\{E[g(y)]\} &= [E[g(y)|z = 1]P(z = 1) + g_0 P(z = 0), \\
&\quad E[g(y)|z = 1]P(z = 1) + g_1 P(z = 0)].
\end{aligned}
\tag{5}
$$

$H\{E[g(y)]\}$ is a proper subset of $[g_0, g_1]$ whenever $P(z=0)$ is less than one. The width of the region is $(g_1 - g_0)P(z=0)$. Thus, the severity of the identification problem varies directly with the prevalence of missing data.

Result (5) has many applications. Perhaps the most far-reaching is the identification region it implies for the probability that y lies in any non-empty, proper set $B \subset Y$. Let $g_B(\cdot)$ be the indicator function $g_B(y) \equiv 1[y \in B]$; that is, $g_B(y) = 1$ if $y \in B$ and $g_B(y) = 0$ otherwise. Then $g_B(\cdot)$ attains its lower and upper bounds on Y, these being 0 and 1. Moreover, $E[g_B(y)] = P(y \in B)$ and $E[g_B(y)|z=1] = P(y \in B|z=1)$. Hence,

$$
\begin{aligned}
H[P(y \in B)] &= [P(y \in B|z = 1)P(z = 1), \\
&\quad P(y \in B|z = 1)P(z = 1) + P(z = 0)].
\end{aligned}
\tag{6}
$$

Observe that the width $P(z = 0)$ of this interval depends only on the prevalence of missing data, not on the form of set B.

When y is real-valued, result (6) immediately yields the identification region for the distribution function of y. Given any $r \in R$, it follows from (6) that

$$
\begin{aligned}
H[P(y \leq r)] &= [P(y \leq r|z = 1)P(z = 1), \\
&\quad P(y \leq r|z = 1)P(z = 1) + P(z = 0)].
\end{aligned}
\tag{7}
$$

The feasible distribution functions are all increasing functions $F(\cdot)$ such that $F(r) \in H[P(y \leq r)]$ for all $r \in R$.

To go further still, result (7) may be used to obtain sharp bounds on quantiles of y, by inverting the bounds on the distribution function. Manski (1994) and Manski (2003, ch. 1) give alternative derivations of the results for quantiles.

Distributional assumptions
Distributional assumptions may enable one to shrink identification regions obtained using the empirical evidence alone. One type of assumption asserts that the distribution $P(y|z = 0)$ of missing outcomes lies in some set $\Gamma_{0Y} \subset \Gamma_Y$. Then the identification region shrinks from $H[P(y)]$ to

$$H_1[P(y)] \equiv [P(y|z = 1)P(z = 1) + \gamma(P(z = 0), \gamma \in \Gamma_{0Y}]. \tag{8}$$

Assumptions of this type are not refutable; after all, the empirical evidence reveals nothing about $P(y|z = 0)$. A leading example is the assumption that data are missing at random. Formally, this is the assumption that $P(y|z = 0) = P(y|z = 1)$, which implies that $H_1[P(y)]$ contains the single distribution $P(y|z = 1)$.

A different type of assumption asserts that the distribution of interest, $P(y)$, lies in a set $\Gamma_{0Y} \subset \Gamma_Y$. Then the identification region shrinks from $H[P(y)]$ to

$$H_1[P(y)] \equiv \Gamma_{0Y} \cap H[P(y)]. \tag{9}$$

Assumptions of the latter type may be refutable: if the intersection of Γ_{0Y} and $H[P(y)]$ should be empty, then $P(y)$ cannot lie in Γ_{0Y}. For example, let y be real-valued and consider the assumption that $P(y)$ is a symmetric distribution. Then $H_1[P(y)]$ is composed of all members of $H[P(y)]$ that are symmetric. If $H[P(y)]$ contains no symmetric distributions, the empirical evidence reveals that $P(y)$ is not symmetric.

Statistical inference
The fundamental problem posed by missing data is identification, so it has been convenient in the above discussion to suppose that one knows the distributions that are asymptotically revealed by the sampling process, namely, $P(y|z = 1)$ and $P(z)$. An empirical researcher observing a sample of finite size N must contend with issues of statistical inference as well as identification. I shall not dwell on these here, but merely point out that the empirical distributions $P_N(y|z = 1)$ and $P_N(z)$ almost surely converge to $P(y|z = 1)$ and $P(z)$ respectively. Hence, a consistent estimate of the identification region $H[P(y)]$ is its sample analog

$$H_N[P(y)] \equiv [P_N(y|z = 1)P_N(z = 1) + \gamma P_N(z = 0), \gamma \in \Gamma_Y]. \tag{10}$$

Moreover, a natural estimate of the identification region for a parameter τ is $\{\tau(\eta), \eta \in H_N[P(y)]\}$. Sample analogs may also be used in the presence of distributional assumptions.

Confidence intervals (CIs) may be constructed to measure the sampling variation in estimates of identification regions. Considering cases in which the identification region is an interval on the real line, Horowitz and Manski (2000) propose CIs that asymptotically cover the entire region with fixed probability. Chernozhukov, Hong and Tamer (2004) develop methods for construction of such CIs when the identification region is a general finite-dimensional set. Imbens and Manski (2004) develop a conceptually different confidence interval; rather than cover the entire identification region with fixed probability, their interval asymptotically covers the true value of the parameter with this probability.

Analysis of treatment response

Analysis of treatment response poses a pervasive and distinctive problem of missing outcomes. Studies of treatment response aim to predict the outcomes that would occur if different treatment rules were applied to a population. Treatments are mutually exclusive, so one cannot observe the outcomes that a person would experience under all treatments. At most, one can observe the outcome that a person experiences under the treatment he actually receives. The counterfactual outcomes that a person would have experienced under other treatments are logically unobservable.

For example, suppose that patients ill with a specified disease can be treated by drugs or by surgery. The relevant outcome might be lifespan. One may want to predict the lifespans that would occur if all patients were to be treated by drugs. The available data may be observations of the actual lifespans of patients in a study population, some of whom were treated by drugs and the rest by surgery.

To formalize the inferential problem, let each member j of a study population J have a response function $y_j(\,\cdot\,) : T \to Y$ mapping the mutually exclusive and exhaustive treatments $t \in T$ into outcomes $y_j(t) \in Y$. Let $z_j \in T$ denote the treatment that person j receives and $y_j \equiv y_j(z_j)$ be the outcome that he experiences. Then $y_j(t)$, $t \neq z_j$ are counterfactual outcomes.

Let $y(\cdot) : J \to Y^{|T|}$ be the random variable mapping the population into their response functions. Let $z : J \to T$ be the 'status quo treatment rule' mapping the members of J into the treatments that they actually receive. Response functions are not observable, but realized treatments and outcomes may be observable. If so, random sampling from J reveals the status quo (outcome, treatment) distribution $P(y, z)$.

The selection problem

Analysis of treatment response seeks to predict the outcomes that would occur under alternatives to the status quo treatment rule. A leading objective is to predict the outcomes that would occur if all persons were to receive the same treatment. By definition, $P[y(t)]$ is the distribution of outcomes that would occur if all persons were to receive a specified treatment t. Hence prediction of outcomes under a rule mandating uniform treatment requires inference on $P[y(t)]$. The problem of identification of this distribution from knowledge of $P(y, z)$ is commonly called the 'selection problem'.

The selection problem has the same structure as the missing-outcomes problem discussed above. To see this, write

$$P[y(t)] = P[y(t)|z = t]P(z = t) + P[y(t)|z \neq t]P(z \neq t)$$
$$= P(y|z = t)P(z = t) + P[y(t)|z \neq t]P(z \neq t). \tag{11}$$

The first equality is the Law of Total Probability. The second holds because $y(t)$ is the outcome experienced by persons who receive treatment t. The sampling process reveals $P(y|z = t)$, $P(z = t)$, and $P(z \neq t)$, but it is uninformative about $P[y(t)|z \neq t]$. Hence, the identification region for $P[y(t)]$ if we use the empirical evidence alone is

$$H\{P[y(t)]\} = \{P(y|z = t)P(z = t) + \gamma P(z \neq t), \gamma \in \Gamma_Y\}. \tag{12}$$

This identification region has the same form as the region (2) for inference on outcomes with missing data, with $P(z \neq t)$ being the probability of missing data. Hence, all of the analysis of missing outcomes discussed above applies here as well.

Distributional assumptions
A familiar 'solution' to the selection problem is to assume that the status quo treatment rule makes realized treatments statistically independent of response functions; that is,

$$P[y(\cdot)] = P[y(\cdot)|z]. \tag{13}$$

This assumption implies that $P[y(t)] = P(y|z = t)$. The sampling process reveals $P(y|z = t)$. Hence, assumption (13) point-identifies $P[y(t)]$.

Assumption (13) is credible when the status quo treatment rule calls for random assignment of treatments and all persons comply with their assignments. Indeed, the fact that (13) holds is the reason why randomized experiments are held in high esteem. However, the credibility of the assumption in settings without random assignment or full compliance almost invariably is a matter of controversy. This motivates interest in other assumptions that may be better motivated in practice.

There has been much study of assumptions that use an 'instrumental variable'; that is, an observable covariate whose value varies across the study population. Suppose that outcomes are real-valued. Manski (1990) poses the mean-independence assumption $E[y(t)] = E[y(t)|v]$. If outcomes are bounded with values normalized to lie in the unit interval, the resulting identification region for $E[y(t)]$ is

$$H\{E[y(t)]\} = [\max_{v \in V} E\{y \cdot 1[z = t]|v = v\},$$
$$\min_{v \in V} E\{y \cdot 1[z = t] + 1[z \neq t]|v = v\}]. \tag{14}$$

Manski and Pepper (2000) study identification of $E[y(t)]$ when v is real-valued and the assumption of mean independence is weakened to state that $E[y(t)|v]$ weakly increases in v. Heckman and Vytlacil (2001) combine the mean-independence assumption with some of the structure of an econometric selection model and show that the identification region for $E[y(t)]$ remains (14).

Statistical independence assumptions are stronger than mean independence. Manski (2003, ch. 7) poses the assumption $P[y(t)] = P[y(t)|v]$ and shows that it yields this identification region for $P[y(t)]$:

$$H\{P[y(t)]\} = \bigcap_{v \in V} \{P(y|v = v, z = t)P(z = t|v = v) + \gamma_v$$
$$\cdot P(z \neq t|v = v), \gamma_v \in \Gamma_Y\}. \tag{15}$$

Balke and Pearl (1997) poses the yet stronger assumption $P[y(\cdot) = P[y(\cdot)|v]$ and characterize its identifying power when outcomes are binary variables.

A different idea, developed in Manski (1995, ch. 6; 1997a) is to place assumptions on the shape of the response functions $y(\cdot)$. One may sometimes believe that treatment response is monotone, in the sense that outcomes increase with the intensity of the treatment. When the set T of treatments is ordered in terms of degree of intensity, the assumption of 'monotone treatment response' asserts that, for all persons j and all treatment pairs (s, t), $t \geq s \Rightarrow y_j(t) \geq y_j(s)$. If outcomes are bounded with values normalized to lie in the unit interval, the resulting identification region for $E[y(t)]$ is the interval

$$H\{E[y(t)]\} = [E(y|t \geq z) \cdot P(t \geq z),$$
$$P(t > z) + E(y|t \leq z) \cdot P(t \leq z)]. \tag{16}$$

A narrower interval results if treatment response is assumed to be concave as well as monotone.

Shape restrictions on the response function and assumptions using instrumental variables illustrate the vast middle ground between inference from the empirical evidence alone and analysis predicated on assumptions that are strong enough to achieve point identification. As the study of partial identification continues to broaden and deepen, empirical researchers will be able to choose from a growing menu of inferential options. One should, however, not expect one uniformly best option to emerge. The appeal of any approach to inference necessarily depends on the objectives of the research, the available data, and the assumptions that are credible to maintain.

CHARLES F. MANSKI

See also **nonparametric structural models; treatment effect.**

Bibliography

Balke, A. and Pearl, J. 1997. Bounds on treatment effects from studies with imperfect compliance. *Journal of the American Statistical Association* 92, 1171–7.

Blundell, R., Gosling, A., Ichimura, H. and Meghir, C. 2004. Changes in the distribution of male and female wages accounting for employment composition using bounds. Working Paper W04/25. London: Institute of Fiscal Studies.

Bollinger, C. 1996. Bounding mean regressions when a binary regressor is mismeasured. *Journal of Econometrics* 73, 387–99.

Brock, W. 2005. Profiling problems with partially identified structure. Mimeo. Madison, WI: Department of Economics, University of Wisconsin-Madison.

Chernozhukov, V., Hong, H. and Tamer, E. 2004. Parameter set inference in a class of econometric models. Mimeo. Evanston, IL: Department of Economics, Northwestern University.

Ciliberto, F. and Tamer, E. 2004. Evanston, IL: Market structure and multiple equilibria in airline markets. Mimeo. Evanston, IL: Department of Economics, Northwestern University.

Cochran, W. 1977. *Sampling Techniques*, 3rd edn. New York: Wiley.

Cochran, W., Mosteller, F. and Tukey, J. 1954. *Statistical Problems of the Kinsey Report on Sexual Behavior in the Human Male*. Washington, DC: American Statistical Association.

Cross, P. and Manski, C. 2002. Regressions, short and long. *Econometrica* 70, 357–68.

Dominitz, J. and Sherman, R. 2004. Sharp bounds under contaminated or corrupted sampling with verification, with an application to environmental pollutant data. *Journal of Agricultural, Biological, and Environmental Statistics* 9, 319–38.

Duncan, O. and Davis, B. 1953. An alternative to ecological correlation. *American Sociological Review* 18, 665–6.

Frisch, R. 1934. *Statistical Confluence Analysis by Means of Complete Regression Systems*. Oslo, Norway: University Institute for Economics.

Ginther, D. 2002. Alternative estimates of the effect of schooling on earnings. *Review of Economics and Statistics* 82, 103–16.

Haile, P. and Tamer, E. 2003. Inference with an incomplete model of English auctions. *Journal of Political Economy* 111, 1–51.

Heckman, J., Smith, J. and Clements, N. 1997. Making the most out of programme evaluations and social experiments: accounting for heterogeneity in programme impacts. *Review of Economic Studies* 64, 487–535.

Heckman, J. and Vytlacil, E. 2001. Localinstrumental variables. In *Nonlinear Statistical Inference: Essays in Honor of Takeshi Amemiya*, ed. C. Hsiao, K. Morimune and J. Powell. Cambridge: Cambridge University Press.

Horowitz, J. and Manski, C. 1995. Identification and robustness with contaminated and corrupted data. *Econometrica* 63, 281–302.

Horowitz, J. and Manski, C. 1998. Censoring of outcomes and regressors due to survey nonresponse: identification and estimation using weights and imputations. *Journal of Econometrics* 84, 37–58.

Horowitz, J. and Manski, C. 2000. Nonparametric analysis of randomized experiments with missing covariate and outcome data. *Journal of the American Statistical Association* 95, 77–84.

Horowitz, J. and Manski, C. 2006. Identification and estimation of statistical functionals using incomplete data. *Journal of Econometrics* 132(2), 445–59.

Horowitz, J., Manski, C., Ponomareva, M. and Stoye, J. 2003. Computation of bounds on population parameters when the data are incomplete. *Reliable Computing* 9, 419–40.

Hotz, J., Mullin, C. and Sanders, S. 1997. Bounding causal effects using data from a contaminated natural experiment: analyzing the effects of teenage childbearing. *Review of Economic Studies* 64, 575–603.

Imbens, G. and Manski, C. 2004. Confidence intervals for partially identified parameters. *Econometrica* 72, 1845–57.

King, G. and Zeng, L. 2002. Estimating risk and rate levels, ratios and differences in case-control studies. *Statistics in Medicine* 21, 1409–27.

Klepper, S. and Leamer, E. 1984. Consistent sets of estimates for regressions with errors in all variables. *Econometrica* 52, 163–83.

Koopmans, T. 1949. Identification problems in economic model construction. *Econometrica* 17, 125–44.

Kreider, B. and Pepper, J. 2004. Disability and employment: reevaluating the evidence in light of reporting errors. Mimeo. Ames, IA: Department of Economics, Iowa State University.

Manski, C. 1989. Anatomy of the selection problem. *Journal of Human Resources* 24, 343–60.

Manski, C. 1990. Nonparametric bounds on treatment effects. *American Economic Review Papers and Proceedings* 80, 319–23.

Manski, C. 1994. The selection problem. In *Advances in Econometrics, Sixth World Congress*, ed. C. Sims. Cambridge: Cambridge University Press.

Manski, C. 1995. *Identification Problems in the Social Sciences*. Cambridge, MA: Harvard University Press.

Manski, C. 1997a. Monotone treatment response. *Econometrica* 65, 1311–34.

Manski, C. 1997b. The mixing problem in programme evaluation. *Review of Economic Studies* 64, 537–53.

Partially linear models are more attractive than linear models especially in cases where the linearity assumption on a subset of the regressors is suspect. This more robust model allows for a more flexible parametrization for that part of the regression where the analyst is not convinced of the linearity. On the other hand, the main motivation for modelling the regression function as partially nonparametric, or semiparametric, as opposed to fully nonparametric, is the concern for the precision of the estimates. In particular, with more continuous regressors in the regression the 'curse of dimensionality' slows the rate of convergence, effectively reducing the usefulness of the regression in data-sets with moderate sizes. Hence, partially linear models provide another practical tool for analysts to use in regressions where linearity of part of the regression function is questionable and provides a middle ground between a completely linear regression that is less robust and one that is totally nonparametric but less practical.

There are many approaches to estimating β and g. For example, one can use a penalized spline regression similar to the one used in Engle et al. (1986), or use semiparametric sieve least squares by replacing the function f with an appropriate sieve that approximates the function space (where g lies) as sample size increases. The method we describe here uses kernel smoothing similar to the one used by Robinson (1988) and Speckman (1988). Notice that eq. (1) above implies that

$$E[y|z] = E[x'|z]\beta + g(z). \tag{2}$$

Subtracting (2) from (1) we obtain

$$y - E[y|z] = (x - E[x|z])'\beta + u. \tag{3}$$

Hence, one can consistently estimate β by regressing $(y - E[y|z])$ on $(x - E[x|z])$ if the matrix $E[(x - E[x|z])(x - E[x|z])']$ is full rank. This procedure has some similarities to a linear regression where one is interested in a subset of the slope parameters. One can obtain this by regressing the dependent variable on residuals from a regression of the regressors of interest on the nuisance regressors. It is a regression of the outcome on what remains of the regressors after purging them of their linear component that is common with other regressors.

One problem in our set-up is that the regression in (3) is unfeasible since $E[y|z]$ and $E[x|z]$ are not known. These can be consistently estimated using a variety of methods like kernels or sieves. Robinson (1988), for example, replaces the conditional expectations by appropriate Naradaya–Watson kernel estimators where for a random sample of size N,

$$\hat{E}[y|z] = \frac{1}{N}\sum_{i=1}^{N} w_{in}(z)y_i \tag{4}$$

where the weight function w_{in} is such

$$w_{in}(z) = \frac{K\left(\frac{z_i - z}{h_n}\right)}{\frac{1}{N}\sum K\left(\frac{z_i - z}{h_n}\right)}.$$ (5)

$K(.)$ is a kernel function satisfying certain conditions (see Hardle, 1991, for more on smoothing conditional expectations), and h_n is a bandwidth parameter that is positive and converges to zero as sample size increases. Conditions on the rate of convergence of this bandwidth are obtained to ensure desirable theoretical properties of the estimators (for example, on the conditional expectation case, we have $h_n = \lambda n^{-1/5}$ where $0 < \lambda < \infty$). Robinson then shows that the estimator $\hat{\beta}$ of β is normally distributed asymptotically as sample size increases. (The estimator Robinson considers requires trimming those values of z that cause instability in the estimates in the 'random denominator' of the conditional expectation.) In particular,

$$\sqrt{n}(\hat{\beta} - \beta) \to_d \mathcal{N}(0, \sigma^2 E[(x - E[x|z])(x - E[x|z])']^{-1}).$$ (6)

This is derived on the assumption of homoskedasticity ($V(u|x) = \sigma^2$), and other conditions guaranteeing well behaviour of the kernel estimators as sample size increases. As for estimating the nonparametric function $g(.)$, one can use a feasible version of eq. (2) to get

$$\hat{g}(z) = \hat{E}[y|z] - \hat{E}[x|z]'\hat{\beta}.$$ (7)

Under a set of assumptions, it can be shown that $\hat{g}(z)$ is a consistent estimator for $g(z)$. For example, in the case of scalar z that has support on $[0, 1]$, it can be shown that under appropriate assumptions,

$$sup_{t \in [0,1]} |\hat{g}(t) - g(t)| = O(n^{-2/5}\log^{2/5} n).$$

In addition, Hardle, Liang and Gao (2001) provide more consistency results for the nonparametric function $g(.)$.

In practice, to implement a partially linear regression, three additional tasks remain. First, one needs to choose a kernel function. Second, although rates of convergence for the smoothing parameter h_n were given, those provide no guidance for choosing a particular value for this smoothing parameter with a given data-set. Third, and to account for sample variability, one needs to obtain estimates for the variance covariance matrix. As for the choice of the kernel function, one can use $K(u) = (2\pi)^{-1/2}exp(-\frac{1}{2}u^2)$, $K(u) = \frac{1}{2}1[|u| \le 1]$ or a quartic kernel $15/16((1 - u^2)^2 I(|u| \le 1))$ (see Hardle, 1991, for more on kernel selection. Kernel selection does not seem to make a difference in practice). As for the choice of the smoothing parameter h_n, one method that can be used is *cross validation*. In particular, our estimators of β and the function $g(.)$ obtained from (3) and (7) can be written as $\hat{\beta}(h_n)$ and $\hat{g}(z) = \hat{g}(z; h_n)$ which are functions of the smoothing parameter h_n. So, to choose h_n in practice, one can minimize the cross-validation function $cv(h_n)$ defined as

$$cv(h_n) = \frac{1}{N} \sum_{i=1} (_i - x_i \hat{\beta}(h_n) - \hat{g}(z_i; h_n))^2. \tag{8}$$

Finally, to estimate the variance covariance matrix in the homoskedastic case, one can replace $\sigma^2 E[(x - E[x|z])(x - E[x|z]')]^{-1}$ by its sample analog. In particular, an estimator $\hat{\sigma}^2$ of σ^2 can be:

$$\hat{\sigma}^2 = \frac{1}{N} \sum_{i=1}^{N} (y_i - x_i \hat{\beta} - \hat{g}(z_i))^2.$$

However, since the conditional mean is semiparametric, a better estimator for the variance matrix is one that is heteroskedasticity robust. This estimator is similar to the heteroskedasticity robust estimator in linear regression and can be written as

$$\hat{V} = \frac{1}{N} \sum (x_i - \hat{E}(x|z_i))(x_i - \hat{E}(x|z_i))'(y_i - \hat{\beta}x_i - \hat{g}(z_i))^2.$$

One can also approximate the finite sample distribution of the estimator by a bootstrapped distribution. After estimating β and $g(.)$, one obtains a set of centred residuals $e_i^*, i = 1, \ldots, N$ with distribution F_n^* from which one can draw a bootstrap sample, and then generate a sample of y's from which one can obtain one's bootstrap estimates. Hardle, Liang and Gao (2001) contains consistency results for the bootstrap procedure in the partially linear model above.

Partially linear models are semiparametric linear regressions where the regression function contains a nonparametric function. These regressions are robust to the linear specification for part of the regressors. In addition, partially linear models provide a good alternative to fully nonparametric regression in settings where the data-set that is available is of moderate sample sizes and/or when one has to smooth over a set of continuous random variables of high dimension. Finally, one can also extend the independence (or mean independence) usually used in estimating partially linear models to conditional quantile restrictions and obtain a partially linear semiparametric quantile regression.

ELIE TAMER

See also **semiparametric estimation.**

Bibliography

Ahn, H. and Powell, J. 1993. Semiparametric estimation of censored selection models. *Journal of Econometrics* 58, 3–29.

Engle, R., Granger, C., Rice, C. and Weiss, J. 1986. Semiparametric estimates of the relation between weather and electricity sales. *Journal of the American Statistical Association* 81, 310–20.

Hardle, W. 1991. *Applied Nonparametric Regression.* New York: Cambridge University Press.

Hardle, W., Liang, H. and Gao, J. 2001. *Partially Linear Models (Contributions to Statistics).* Heidelberg: Physica-Verlag.

Heckman, J. 1974. Shadow wages, market wages and labor supply. *Econometrica* 42, 679–93.

Robinson, P. 1988. Root-n-consistent semiparametric regression. *Econometrica* 56, 931–54.

Schmalensee, R. and Stoker, T. 1999. Household gasoline demand in the United States. *Econometrica* 67, 645–62.

Speckman, P. 1988. Kernel Smoothing in partial linear models. *Journal of the Royal Statistical Society, B* 50, 413–36.

propensity score

Propensity score is an object often discussed in evaluation studies. It is defined as the conditional probability of treatment given covariates. It has attracted attention for its potential to control for the bias in the presence of high dimensional covariates.

Evaluation research typically begins by comparing the treated group with the control group. For example, estimates of the effect of training programmes on earnings compare the earnings of those who receive training with a candidate control sample of untrained people. Because typically trainees are not chosen randomly, a simple comparison of the two groups may not provide a very accurate picture of what would have happened to the trainees had they not been trained. Under some conditions, such problems can be avoided by comparing the treated and the control groups with identical covariate values.

For more formal discussion, denote the covariate vector for person i by X_i, treatment status by D_i such that $D_i = 1$ if the ith person is treated and $D_i = 0$ otherwise, and define the conditional probability of treatment, or propensity score, as $p(X_i) \equiv \Pr[D_i = 1|X_i]$. Let Y_{1i} denote the potential, or counter-factual, outcome if the ith person receives the treatment, and let Y_{0i} denote potential earnings if he or she does not receive the treatment. Note that Y_{1i} is observed only when $D_i = 1$. Likewise, Y_{0i} is observed only when $D_i = 0$. This implies that $Y_{1I} - Y_{0i}$ is not observed by the researcher, and therefore the average treatment effects, which are defined to be $\beta = E[Y_{1i} - Y_{0i}]$, cannot be estimated by the sample analog of $E[Y_{1i} - Y_{0i}]$. Because D_i is not usually assigned randomly, a simple comparison of the two groups, that is, the sample analog of $E[Y_{1i}|D_i = 1] - E[Y_{0i}|D_i = 0]$, does not provide a consistent estimate of β, either. On the other hand, if (Y_{0i}, Y_{1i}) is independent of D_i given X_i, that is,

$$Y_{0i}, Y_{1i} \perp\!\!\!\perp D_i | X_i, \tag{1}$$

then the sample analog of

$$E\{E[Y_{1i}|X_i, D_i = 1] - E[Y_{0i}|X_i, D_i = 0]\}$$

will provide a consistent estimator for β. In other words, β can be consistently estimated by 'matching' the treated and the control groups with identical covariate values.

A problem that often arises in studies of this type is the need to control for continuously distributed and/or high-dimensional covariates. In many evaluation studies, the sample sizes are small, there are many covariates, and some of the covariates are continuous. A number of variations on exact covariate-matching schemes have been developed to deal with such situations. These typically involve approximate matching, or nonparametric smoothing, of some sort.

An alternative strategy to control for covariates begins with Rosenbaum and Rubin's (1983) observation that bias can be eliminated by controlling for a scalar-valued function of the covariates, namely, the propensity score. Rosenbaum and Rubin's propensity-score theorem states that, if (1) is true, then it must also be true that conditioning on $p(X_i)$ eliminates selection bias, that is,

$$Y_{0i}, Y_{1i} \perp\!\!\!\perp D_i | p(X_i). \tag{2}$$

This implies that the β can be consistently estimated by the sample analog of

$$E\{E[Y_{1i}|p(X_i), D_i = 1] - E[Y_{0i}|p(X_i), D_i = 0]\}.$$

It is easier to estimate $E[Y_{1i}|p(X_i), D_i = 1]$ than $E[Y_{1i}|X_i, D_i = 1]$, because the former requires the nonparametric regression of Y_{1i} on a scalar object $p(X_i)$ whereas the latter requires the nonparametric regression on a multi-dimensional object X_i. (Such difficulty is often called the curse of dimensionality in the nonparametrics literature.) The value of propensity score matching is in the 'dimension reduction' generated by regions where $p(X_i)$ is constant while $E[Y_{1i}|X_i]$ or $E[Y_{0i}|X_i]$ are not constant. The value of the propensity score is not clear, though, when the applied researcher does not have any information about the treatment assignment. Without such information, the propensity score needs to be estimated, which requires a nonparametric regression of D_i on X_i. Because this estimation suffers from the curse of dimensionality, the propensity score theorem seems to have little practical value when the propensity score itself needs to be estimated nonparametrically. On the other hand, it can be quite useful when applied researchers may have more information or are willing to make stronger assumptions about treatment assignment than about the relationship between covariates and outcomes. A number of empirical examples using the propensity score suggest that this approach works reasonably well (see, for example, Rosenbaum and Rubin, 1984; 1985; Dehejia and Wahba, 1999; Imbens, Rubin and Sacerdote, 2001; Heckman, Ichimura and Todd, 1998).

This evidence of practical utility notwithstanding, from an asymptotic theory point of view propensity-score-based estimators present a puzzle. Hahn (1998) shows that the propensity score is ancillary for estimates of average treatment effects, in the sense that knowledge of the propensity score does not lower the semiparametric efficiency bound for this parameter. Moreover, covariate matching is asymptotically efficient, that is, it attains the semiparametric efficiency bound, while propensity score matching does not. These results based on conventional asymptotic arguments seem to offer no justification for anything other than full control for covariates in estimation of average treatment effects.

The propensity score may still be a useful device. First, the propensity score may enhance finite sample efficiency. Angrist and Hahn (2004) use a non-standard asymptotic argument to point out that the traditional first-order asymptotic theory misses some of the subtleties in finite sample property, and observe that an estimator based on propensity score matching may be superior to the one based on covariate matching. They note, though, that the finite sample efficiency gain becomes smaller as the sample size grows, which is in accordance with the prediction from the traditional asymptotic theory. Second, when the estimated propensity scores are used as a weight in a certain way but not as a basis of matching, the estimator of the average treatment effects based on estimated propensity score is as asymptotically efficient as the covariate matching (Hirano, Imbens and Ridder, 2003).

JINYONG HAHN

See also **matching estimators.**

Bibliography

Angrist, J. and Hahn, J. 2004. When to control for covariates? Panel-asymptotic results for estimates of treatment effects. *Review of Economics and Statistics* 86, 58–72.

Dehejia, R. and Wahba, S. 1999. Propensity score matching methods for non-experimental causal studies. *Journal of the American Statistical Association* 94, 1053–62.

Hahn, J. 1998. On the role of the propensity score in the efficient estimation of average treatment effects. *Econometrica* 66, 315–32.

Heckman, J., Ichimura, H. and Todd, P. 1998. Matching as an econometric evaluation estimator. *Review of Economic Studies* 65, 261–94.

Hirano, K., Imbens, G. and Ridder, G. 2003. Efficient estimation of average treatment effects using the estimated propensity score. *Econometrica* 71, 1161–89.

Imbens, G., Rubin, D. and Sacerdote, B. 2001. Estimating the effect of unearned income on labor supply, earnings, savings and consumption: evidence from a sample of lottery players. *American Economic Review* 91, 778–94.

Rosenbaum, P. and Rubin, D. 1983. The central role of the propensity score in observational studies for causal effects. *Biometrika* 70, 41–55.

Rosenbaum, P. and Rubin, D. 1984. Reducing bias in observational studies using subclassification on the propensity score. *Journal of the American Statistical Association* 79, 516–24.

Rosenbaum, P. and Rubin, D. 1985. Constructing a control group using multi-variate matching methods that include the propensity score. *American Statistician* 39, 33–8.

proportional hazard model

The estimation of duration models has been the subject of significant research in econometrics since the late 1970s. Cox (1972) proposed the use of proportional hazard models in biostatistics and they were soon adopted for use in economics. Since Lancaster (1979), it has been recognized among economists that it is important to account for unobserved heterogeneity in models for duration data. Failure to account for unobserved heterogeneity causes the estimated hazard rate to decrease more with the duration than the hazard rate of a randomly selected member of the population. Moreover, the estimated proportional effect of explanatory variables on the population hazard rate is smaller in absolute value than that on the hazard rate of the average population member and decreases with the duration. To account for unobserved heterogeneity Lancaster proposed a parametric mixed proportional hazard (MPH) model, a partial generalization of Cox's proportional hazard model, that specifies the hazard rate as the product of a regression function that captures the effect of observed explanatory variables, a baseline hazard that captures variation in the hazard over the spell, and a random variable that accounts for the omitted heterogeneity. In particular, Lancaster (1979) introduced the mixed proportional hazard model in which the hazard is a function of a regressor X unobserved heterogeneity v, and a function of time $\lambda(t)$,

$$\theta(t|X, v) = v e^{X\beta_0} \lambda(t). \tag{1}$$

The function $\lambda(t)$ is often referred to as the baseline hazard and $v|X$ has a gamma distribution. The popularity of the mixed proportional hazard model is partly due to the fact that it nests two alternative explanations for the hazard $\theta(t|X)$ to be decreasing with time. In particular, estimating the mixed proportional hazard model gives the relative importance of the heterogeneity, v, and genuine duration dependence, $\lambda(t)$ (see Lancaster, 1990, and Van den Berg, 2001, for overviews). Lancaster (1979) uses functional form assumptions on $\lambda(t)$, which were not required by the Cox model, and distributional assumptions on v to identify the model. Examples by Lancaster and Nickell (1980) and Heckman and Singer (1984), however, show the sensitivity to these functional form and distributional assumptions. Thus, Lancaster's MPH model is fully parametric and from the outset questions were raised about the role of functional form and parametric assumptions in the distinction between unobserved hetero-geneity and duration dependence. (Heckman, 1991, gives an overview of attempts to make this distinction in duration and dynamic panel data models.) This question was resolved by Elbers and Ridder (1982), who showed that the MPH model is semi-parametrically identified if there is minimal variation in the regression function. A single indicator variable in the regression function suffices to recover the regression function, the baseline hazard, and the distribution of the unobserved component, provided that this distribution does not depend on the explanatory variables. Semi-parametric identification means that semi-parametric estimation is feasible, and a number of semi-parametric estimators for the MPH model have been proposed that progressively relaxed the parametric restrictions.

Nielsen et al. (1992) showed that the partial likelihood estimator of Cox (1972) can be generalized to the MPH model with gamma-distributed unobserved heterogeneity. Their estimator is semi-parametric because it uses parametric specifications of the regression function and the distribution of the unobserved heterogeneity. The estimator requires numerical integration of the order of the sample size, as originally discussed by Han and Hausman (1990), which further limits its usefulness and makes it impractical for most situations in econometrics. Heckman and Singer (1984) considered the non-parametric maximum likelihood estimator of the MPH model with a parametric baseline hazard and regression function. Using results of Kiefer and Wolfowitz (1956), they approximate the unobserved heterogeneity with a discrete mixture. The rate of convergence and the asymptotic distribution of this estimator are not known. As a result, these estimators that use discrete mixture with an increasing number of support points cannot be used to test hypotheses. Another estimator that does not require the specification of the unobserved heterogeneity distribution was suggested by Honoré (1990). This estimator assumes a Weibull baseline hazard and uses only very short durations to estimate the Weibull parameter.

Han and Hausman (1990) and Meyer (1990) propose an estimator that assumes that the baseline hazard is piecewise-constant, to permit flexibility, and that the heterogeneity has a gamma distribution. Both papers find that the hazard rate, conditional on heterogeneity, is non-monotonic so that the Weibull model cannot hold. Hausman and Woutersen (2005) present simulations and a theoretical result that show that using a nonparametric estimator of the baseline hazard with gamma heterogeneity yields inconsistent estimates for all parameters and functions if the true mixing distribution is not a gamma, which limits the usefulness of the Han–Hausman–Meyer approach. Thus, Hausman and Woutersen (2005) find it important to specify a model that does not require a parametric specification of the unobserved heterogeneity.

Horowitz (1999) was the first to propose an estimator that estimates both the baseline hazard and the distribution of the unobserved heterogeneity nonparametrically. His estimator is an adaptation of the semi-parametric estimator for a transformation model that he introduced in Horowitz (1996). In particular, if the regressors are constant over the duration, then the MPH model has a transformation model representation with the logarithm of the integrated baseline hazard as the dependent variable and a random error that is equal to the logarithm of a log standard exponential minus the logarithm of a positive random variable. In the transformation model the regression coefficients are identified only up to scale. As shown by Ridder (1990), the scale parameter is identified in the MPH model if the unobserved heterogeneity has a finite mean. Horowitz (1999) suggests an estimator of the scale parameter that is similar to Honoré's (1990) estimator of the Weibull parameter and is consistent if the finite mean assumption holds so that his approach allows estimation of the regression coefficients (not just up to scale). However, the Horowitz approach permits estimation of the regression coefficients only at a slow rate of convergence and it is not $N^{-1/2}$ consistent, where N is the sample size. The reason for the slower than $N^{-1/2}$ convergence is that the information matrix of the MPH model is singular under Horowitz assumptions (see Hahn, 1994; Ishwaran, 1996a). In particular, Horowitz (1999) assumes that the first three moments of the heterogeneity distribution exist, and Ishwaran (1996b) shows that the fastest possible rate of convergence is $N^{-2/5}$ for that case and Horowitz's (1999) estimator converges arbitrarily close to that rate. In other words, the slow rate of convergence is implied by the assumptions and is not a peculiarity of the estimator.

Subsequent research has focused on strengthening the assumptions of the MPH model so that $N^{-1/2}$ convergence is possible. Ridder and Woutersen (2003) derive a $N^{-1/2}$ consistent estimator for the MPH model by assuming that the baseline hazard rate is constant over a small interval, $\lambda(t) = \lambda$ for $0 \leq t \leq \varepsilon$ for any $\varepsilon > 0$ while allowing for a nonparametric baseline hazard function for $t > \varepsilon$. For parametric baseline hazards, Ridder and Woutersen (2003) assume that $\lim_{t \downarrow 0} \lambda(t) = \lambda$ for $0 < \lambda < \infty$ and derive another $N^{-1/2}$ consistent estimator. Hausman and Woutersen (2005) derive an estimator for the mixed proportional hazard model (with heterogeneity) that allows for a nonparametric baseline hazard and uses time-varying regressors. No parametric specification of the heterogeneity distribution or nonparametric estimation of the heterogeneity distribution is necessary. Intuitively, Hausman and Woutersen (2005) condition out the heterogeneity distribution, which makes it unnecessary to estimate it. Thus, they eliminate the problems that arise with the Lancaster (1979) approach to MPH models. In this model the baseline hazard rate is nonparametric, and the estimator of the integrated baseline hazard rate converges at the regular rate, $N^{-1/2}$ where N is the sample size. This convergence rate is the same rate as for a duration model without heterogeneity. The regressor parameters also converge at the regular rate. A nice feature of the estimator is that it allows the durations to be measured on a finite set of points. Such discrete measurement of durations is important in economics; for example, unemployment is often measured in weeks. In the case of discrete duration measurements, the estimator of the integrated baseline hazard converges only at this set of points, as would be expected.

It may be argued that the bias in the estimates of the regression coefficients is small if the estimates of the MPH model indicate that there is no significant unobserved heterogeneity. The problem with this argument is that estimates of the heterogeneity distribution are usually not very accurate. Given the results in Horowitz (1999), this finding should not come as a surprise. The simulation results in Baker and Melino (2000) show that it is empirically difficult to find evidence of unobserved heterogeneity, in particular if one chooses a flexible parametric representation of the baseline hazard. However, Han and Hausman (1990) and applications of their approach have found significant heterogeneity using a flexible approach to the baseline hazard. Bijwaard and Ridder (2002) find that the bias in the regression parameters is largely independent of the specification of the baseline hazard. Hence, failure to find significant unobserved heterogeneity should not lead to the conclusion that the bias due to correlation of the regressors and the unobservables that affect the hazard is small.

Because it is empirically difficult to recover the distribution of the unobserved heterogeneity, estimators that rely on estimation of this distribution may be unreliable. Therefore, it may be advisable to avoid estimating the unobserved heterogeneity distribution and the remainder of the MPH model simultaneously. Nevertheless, after estimating the baseline hazard and regression function, one can usually identify the mixing distribution. In particular, Horowitz (1999) uses the following equation to estimate the mixing distribution,

$$\ln\{\Lambda(T)\} + X\beta - \ln(Z) = -\ln(\nu)$$

where $\Lambda(T)$ and β can be estimated and the unobserved Z has an exponential distribution with mean one. Thus, Horowitz (1999) solves a deconvolution problem and the speed of convergence depends on the assumptions on the distribution of ν.

A hazard model is a natural framework for time-varying regressors if a flow or a transition probability depends on a regressor that changes with time since a hazard model avoids the curse of dimensionality that would arise from interacting the regressors at each point in time with one another. A non-constructive identification proof for the duration model with time-varying regressors can be produced using techniques similar to Honoré (1993b), and Honoré (1993a) gives such a proof. (A non-constructive identification proof is an identification proof that does not suggest an estimator.) In particular, Honoré (1993a) does not assume that the mean of the heterogeneity distribution is finite (nor does Honoré, 1993a, assume a tail condition as in Heckman and Singer, 1984). Ridder and Woutersen (2003) argue that it is precisely the finite mean assumption that makes the identification of Elbers and Ridder (1982) 'weak' in the sense that the model of Elbers and Ridder (1982) cannot be estimated at rate $N^{-1/2}$. As in Honoré (1993a), Hausman and Woutersen (2005) do not need the finite mean $N^{-1/2}$ assumption which gives an intuitive explanation of why Hausman and Woutersen (2005) can estimate the model at rate $N^{-1/2}$.

JERRY A. HAUSMAN AND TIEMEN M. WOUTERSEN

Bibliography

Baker, M. and Melino, A. 2000. Duration dependence and nonparametric heterogeneity: a Monte Carlo study. *Journal of Econometrics* 96, 357–93.

Bijwaard, G. and Ridder, G. 2002. Efficient estimation of the semi-parametric mixed proportional hazard model. Working paper.

Cox, D. 1972. Regression models and life tables (with discussion). *Journal of the Royal Statistical Society* B, 34, 187–220.

Elbers, C. and Ridder, G. 1982. True and spurious duration dependence: the identifiability of the proportional hazard model. *Review of Economic Studies* 49, 402–09.

Hahn, J. 1994. The efficiency bound of the mixed proportional hazard model. *Review of Economic Studies* 61, 607–29.

Han, A. and Hausman, J. 1990. Flexible parametric estimation of duration and competing risk models. *Journal of Applied Econometrics* 6, 1–28.

Hausman, J. and Woutersen, T. M. 2005. Estimating a semi-parametric duration model without specifying heterogeneity. Working paper, UCL: CeMMAP, Institute for Fiscal Studies.

Heckman, J. 1991. Identifying the hand of the past: distinguishing state dependence from heterogeneity. *American Economic Review* 81, 75–9.

Heckman, J. and Singer, B. 1984. A method for minimizing the impact of distributional assumptions in econometric models for duration data. *Econometrica* 52, 271–320.

Honoré, B. 1990. Simple estimation of a duration model with unobserved heterogeneity. *Econometrica* 58, 453–73.

Honoré, B. 1993a. Identification results for duration models with multiple spells or time-varying regressors. Northwestern working paper.

Honoré, B. 1993b. Identification results for duration models with multiple spells. *Review of Economic Studies* 60, 241–6.

Horowitz, J. 1996. Semiparametric estimation of a regression model with an unknown transformation of the dependent variable. *Econometrica* 64, 103–7.

Horowitz, J. 1999. Semiparametric estimation of a proportional hazard model with unobserved heterogeneity. *Econometrica* 67, 1001–28.

Ishwaran, H. 1996a. Identifiability and rates of estimation for scale parameters in location mixture models. *Annals of Statistics* 24, 1560–71.

Ishwaran, H. 1996b. Uniform rates of estimation in the semiparametric Weibull mixture model. *Annals of Statistics* 24, 1572–85.

Kiefer, J. and Wolfowitz, J. 1956. Consistency of maximum likelihood estimator in the presence of infinitely many incidental parameters. *Annals of Mathematical Statistics* 27, 887–906.

Lancaster, T. 1979. Econometric methods for the duration of unemployment. *Econometrica* 47, 939–56.

Lancaster, T. 1990. *The Econometric Analysis of Transition Data*. Cambridge: Cambridge University Press.

Lancaster, T. and Nickell, S. 1980. The analysis of re-employment probabilities for the unemployed. *Journal of the Royal Statistical Society, A*, 143, 141–65.

Meyer, B. 1990. Unemployment insurance and unemployment spells. *Econometrica* 58, 757–82.

Nielsen, G., Gill, R., Andersen, P. and Sørensen, T. 1992. A counting process approach to maximum likelihood estimation in frailty models. *Scandanavian Journal of Statistics* 19, 25–43.

Ridder, G. 1990. The non-parametric identification of generalized accelerated failure time models. *Review of Economic Studies* 57, 167–82.

Ridder, G. and Woutersen, T. 2003. The singularity of the information matrix of the mixed proportional hazard model. *Econometrica* 71, 1579–89.

Van den Berg, G. 2001. Duration models: specification, identification, and multiple duration. In *Handbook of Econometrics*, vol. 5, ed. J. Heckman and E. Leamer. Amsterdam: North-Holland.

quantile regression

1. Introduction

The quantile regression is a semiparametric technique that has been gaining considerable popularity in economics (for example, Buchinsky, 1994). It was introduced by Koenker and Bassett (1978b) as an extension to ordinary quantiles in a location model. In this model, the conditional quantiles have linear forms. A well-known special case of quantile regression is the least absolute deviation (LAD) estimator of Koenker and Bassett (1978a), which fits medians to a linear function of covariates. In an important generalization of the quantile regression model, Powell (1984; 1986) introduced the censored quantile regression model. This model is an extension of the 'Tobit' model and is designed to handle situations in which some of the observations on the dependent variable are censored.

The quantile regression model has some very attractive features: (a) it can be used to characterize the entire conditional distribution of a dependent variable given a set of regressors; (b) it has a linear programming representation which makes estimation easy; (c) it gives a robust measure of location; (d) typically, the quantile regression estimator is more efficient than the least squares estimator when the error term is non-normal; and (e) L-estimators, based on a linear combination of quantile estimators (for example, Portnoy and Koenker, 1989) are, in general, more efficient than least squares estimators.

This article presents the basic structure of the quantile regression model. It highlights the most important features and provides the elementary tools for using quantile regressions in empirical applications. The article concentrates on cross-section applications, where the observations are assumed to be independently and identically distributed (i.i.d.).

2. The Model

2.1 Definitions and estimator

Any real-valued random variable z is completely characterized by its (right continuous) conditional distribution function $F(z) = \Pr(z \leq a)$. For any $0 < \theta < 1$, the quantity $Q_\theta(z) \equiv F^{-1}(\theta) = \inf\{a : F(a) \geq \theta\}$ is called the θth quantile of z. This quantile is obtained as a solution to a minimization problem of a particular objective function, the *check function*, given by $\rho_\theta(\lambda) = \lambda(\theta - I(\lambda < 0))$, where $I(\cdot)$ denotes the usual indicator function. That is,

$$Q_\theta(z) \equiv \arg\min_{a} E[\rho_\theta(z - a)].$$

An estimate for the θth quantile of z can be obtained from i.i.d. data z_i, $i = 1, \ldots, n$, by minimizing the sample analogue of the population objective function defined above. That is,

$$\hat{Q}_\theta(z) \equiv \arg\min_a \frac{1}{n} \sum_{i=1}^n \rho_\theta(z_i - a),$$

or alternatively

$$\hat{Q}_\theta(z) \equiv \arg\min_a \left\{ \sum_{i:z_i \geq b} \theta |z_i - a| + \sum_{i:z_i < b} (1 - \theta)|z_i - a| \right\}.$$

The last equation provides a clear intuition for the quantile estimates. The θth quantile estimate is obtained by weighting the positive residuals by θ, while the negative residuals are weighted by the complement of θ, namely, $1-\theta$.

The extension of this idea to the case of a conditional quantile is straightforward. Suppose that the θth conditional quantile of y, conditional on a $K \times 1$ vector of regressors $x = (1, x_2, \ldots, x_K)$, is

$$Q_\theta(y|x) = x'\beta_\theta.$$

This implies that the model can be written as

$$y = x'\beta_\theta + u_\theta, \tag{1}$$

and, by construction, it follows that $Q_\theta(u_\theta|x) = 0$.

This model, which was first introduced by Koenker and Bassett (1978b), can be viewed as a location model. That is,

$$\Pr(y \leq \tau|x) = F_{u_\theta}(\tau - x'\beta_\theta|x),$$

where u_θ has the (right continuous) conditional distribution function $F_{u_\theta}(\cdot|x)$, satisfying $Q_\theta(u_\theta|x) = 0$.

Similar to the unconditional case presented above, the population parameter vector β_θ is defined by

$$\beta_\theta \equiv \arg\min_\beta E[\rho_\theta(y - x'\beta)|x].$$

The sample analogue for the θth quantile conditional quantile is defined in a similar manner. Let (y_i, x_i), $i = 1, \ldots, n$, be an i.i.d. sample from the population. Then, $\hat{\beta}_\theta$, the estimator for β_θ, is defined by

$$\hat{\beta}_\theta = \arg\min_\beta \frac{1}{n} \sum_{i=1}^n \rho_\theta(u_{\theta i}), \quad \text{or alternatively} \tag{2}$$

$$\hat{\beta}_\theta = \arg\min_\beta \frac{1}{n} \left\{ \sum_{i:y_i \geq x_i'\beta} \theta|y_i - x_i'\beta| + \sum_{i:y_i < x_i'\beta} (1-\theta)|y_i - x_i'\beta| \right\}.$$

The θth quantile regression problem in (2) can be also be rewritten as

$$\hat{\beta}_\theta = \arg\min_\beta \frac{1}{n} \sum_{i=1}^n (\theta - 1/2 + 1/2 \ \text{sgn}(y_i - x_i'b))(y_i - x_i'b),$$

where $\text{sgn}(\lambda) = I(\lambda > 0) - I(\lambda < 0)$. The last equation gives, in turn, the $K \times 1$ vector of first-order conditions (F.O.C.):

$$\frac{1}{n} \sum_{i=1}^n (\theta - 1/2 + 1/2 \ \text{sgn}(y_i - x_i'\hat{\beta}))x_i = \frac{1}{n} \sum_{i=1}^n \psi(x_i, y_i, \beta) = 0, \qquad (3)$$

where $\psi(x, y, \beta) = (\theta - 1/2 + 1/2 \ \text{sgn}(y - x'\beta))x$. It is straightforward to show that under the quantile restriction $Q_\theta(u_{\theta i}|x_i) = 0$ the moment function $\psi(\cdot)$ satisfies $E[\psi(x_i, y_i, \beta_\theta)] \equiv E[\psi(x_i, y_i, \beta)]|_{\beta = \beta_\theta} = 0$. In the jargon of the generalized method of moments (GMM) framework, this establishes the validity of $\psi(\cdot)$ as a moment function. Consequently, using the methodology of Huber (1967), one can establish consistency and asymptotic normality of $\hat{\beta}_\theta$.

For illustration and discussion below, it is convenient to define the following: Let y denote the stacked vector of y_i, $i = 1, \ldots, n$, and let X denote the stacked matrix of the row vectors x_i', $i = 1, \ldots, n$.

2.2 Linear programming and quantile regression

The problem in (2) can be shown to have a linear programming (LP) representation. This feature has some important consequences from both theoretical and practical standpoints.

Let the $K \times 1$ vector β be written as a difference of two non-negative vectors β^+ and β^-, that is, $\beta = \beta^+ - \beta^-$, for $\beta^+, \beta^- \geq 0$. Similarly let the $n \times 1$ residuals vector u be written as a difference of two non-negative vectors u^+ and u^-, that is, $u = u^+ - u^-$, for $u^+, u^- \geq 0$. Furthermore, define the following quantities: $A \equiv (X, -X, I_n, -I_n)$, where I_n is an n dimensional identity matrix, $z = (\beta^{+'}, \beta^{-'}, u^{+'}, u^{-'})'$, $c = (0', 0', \theta \cdot l', (1-\theta) \cdot l')'$, $\mathbf{0}$ is a $k \times 1$ vector of zeros, and l is an $n \times 1$ vector of ones.

When written in matrix notation the problem in (2) takes the familiar *primal problem* of LP:

$$\min_z c'z$$

subject to $Az = y$, $z \geq 0$.

Furthermore, the dual problem, of LP is (approximately) the same as the F.O.C. given above, namely

$$\max_{w} w'y$$

subject to $w'A \leq c'$.

The *duality theorem* of LP implies that feasible solutions exist for both the primal and the dual problems, if the design matrix X is of full column rank, that is, rank $(X) = K$. The *equilibrium theorem* of LP guarantees then that this solution is optimal.

The LP representation of the quantile regression problem has several important implications from both computational and conceptual standpoints. First, it is guaranteed that an estimate will be obtained in a finite number of simplex iterations. Second, the parameter estimate is robust to outliers. That is, for all $y_i - x_i'\hat{\beta}_\theta > 0$, y_i can be increased toward ∞, and for all $y_i - x_i'\hat{\beta}_\theta < 0$, y_i can be decreased toward $-\infty$, without altering the solution $\hat{\beta}_\theta$. In other words, the only thing that matters is not the exact value of y, but rather on which side of the estimated hyperplane it lies. This is important for many economic applications in which y_i might be censored, at say y_i^0. For example, for the right-censored model $\hat{\beta}_\theta$ will not be affected as long as for all i we have $y_i^0 - x_i'\hat{\beta}_\theta > 0$.

2.3 Equivariance properties

The quantile regression estimator has several important equivariance properties which help facilitate the computation procedure. That is, data-sets that are based on certain transformations of the original data set lead to estimators which are simple transformations of the original estimator. Denote the set of feasible solutions to the problem defined in (2) by $B(\theta, y, X)$. Then for every $\hat{\beta}_\theta \equiv \hat{\beta}(\theta, y, X) \in B(\theta, y, X)$ we have (see Koenker and Bassett, 1978b: Theorem 3.2):

$$\hat{\beta}(\theta, \lambda y, X) = \lambda \hat{\beta}(\theta, y, X), \quad \text{for } \lambda \in [0, \infty),$$

$$\hat{\beta}(1 - \theta, \lambda y, X) = \lambda \hat{\beta}(\theta, y, X), \quad \text{for } \lambda \in (-\infty, 0],$$

$$\hat{\beta}(\theta, y + X\gamma, X) = \hat{\beta}(\theta, y, X) + \gamma, \quad \text{for } \gamma \in \Re^K,$$

$$\hat{\beta}(\theta, y, XA) = A^{-1}\hat{\beta}(\theta, y, X), \quad \text{for nonsingular } k \times k \text{ matrix } A.$$

These properties help in reducing the number of simplex iterations (of any LP algorithm) required for obtaining $\hat{\beta}_\theta$. For example, suppose that $\hat{\beta}_\theta^0$ is a good starting value for $\hat{\beta}_\theta$ (for example, the least-squares estimate from the regression of y on x, or an estimate obtained from only a small subset of the data available). Let $\hat{\beta}_\theta^R$ denote the quantile regression estimate from the θth quantile regression of $y^R = y - X\hat{\beta}_\theta^0$ on x. Then $\hat{\beta}_\theta \equiv \hat{\beta}_\theta^R + \hat{\beta}_\theta^0$. In many cases it is faster to obtain the two estimates $\hat{\beta}_\theta^R$ and $\hat{\beta}_\theta^0$ than to estimate $\hat{\beta}_\theta$ directly.

2.4 Efficient estimation

The quantile regression estimator described above is not the efficient estimator for β_θ. An efficient estimator can be obtained by solving

$$\min_{\beta} \frac{1}{n}\sum_{i=1}^{n} f_{u_\theta}(0|x)(\theta - 1/2 + 1/2 \ \text{sgn}(y_i - x_i'\beta))(y_i - x_i'\beta).$$

That is, each observation is weighted by the conditional density of its error evaluated at zero. This estimation procedure requires the use of an estimate for the unknown density $f_{u_\theta}(0|x)$. Below we provide details about the estimation of the asymptotic covariance matrix, which, in turn, also provides information about possible estimates for $f_{u_\theta}(0|x)$. (For a more complete discussion of this estimator, see Newey and Powell, 1990.)

2.5 Interpretation of the quantile regression

How can the quantile's coefficients be interpreted? Consider the partial derivative of the conditional quantile of y with respect to one of the regressors, say j, that is, $\partial Q_\theta(y|x)/\partial x_j$. This derivative may be interpreted as the marginal change in the θth conditional quantile due to a marginal change in the jth element of x. If x contains K distinct variables, then this derivative is given simply by $\beta_{\theta j}$, the coefficient on the jth variable. It is important to note that one should be cautious not to confuse this result with the location of an individual in the conditional distribution. In general, it need not be the case that an observation that happened to be in the θth quantile of one conditional distribution will also be at the same quantile if x had changed. The above derivative reflects changes in the conditional distribution but has nothing to say about the location of an observation within the conditional distribution.

Note that an estimate for the θth conditional quantile of y given x is given by $Q_\theta(y|x) = x'\hat{\beta}_\theta$. Hence, if one were to vary θ between 0 and 1 and estimate a different quantile regression estimate for each θ, one can trace the entire conditional distribution of y, conditional on x.

3. Large sample properties of $\hat{\beta}_\theta$

We denote the conditional distribution function of u_θ by $F_{u_\theta}(\cdot|x)$ and the corresponding density function by $f_{u_\theta}(\cdot|x)$.

Assumption A.1 The distribution functions $\{F_{u_{\theta i}}(\cdot|x_i)\}$ are absolutely continuous, with continuous density functions $f_{u_{\theta i}}(\cdot|x_i)$ uniformly bounded away from 0 and ∞ at the point 0, for $i = 1, 2, \ldots$

Assumption A.2 There exit positive definite matrices Δ_θ and Λ_0 such that

(i) $\lim_{n\to\infty}\frac{1}{n}\sum_{i=1}^{n}x_i x_i' = \Lambda_0$;
(ii) $\lim_{n\to\infty}\frac{1}{n}\sum_{i=1}^{n} f_{u_{\theta i}}(0|x_i)x_i x_i' = \Delta_\theta$; and
(iii) $\max_{i=1,\ldots,n}\|x\|/\sqrt{n} \to 0$.

Assumption A.3 The parameter vector β_θ is in the interior of the parameter space $\mathscr{B}_\theta$.

Assumption A.1 requires that the conditional density of $u_{\theta i}$, conditional on x_i, be bounded and that there be no mass point at the conditional θth quantile at which β_θ is estimated.

Assumptions A.2 and A.3 provide regularity conditions very similar to those used for the usual least-squares estimator. Assumptions A.1 and A.2 are sufficient for establishing that $\hat{\beta}_\theta \to \beta_\theta$ as $n \to \infty$, while Assumption A.3 is needed in addition for establishing the asymptotic normality of $\hat{\beta}_\theta$ in the following theorem.

Theorem 1 Under Assumptions A.1–A.3

(i) $\sqrt{n}(\hat{\beta}_\theta - \beta_\theta) \xrightarrow{\mathscr{L}} N(0, \theta(1-\theta)\Delta_\theta^{-1}\Lambda_0\Delta_\theta^{-1})$;

(ii) if in addition $f_{u_\theta}(0|x) = f_{u_\theta}(0)$ with probability 1, then $\sqrt{n}(\hat{\beta}_\theta - \beta_\theta) \xrightarrow{\mathscr{L}} N(0, \omega_\theta^2\Lambda_0^{-1})$, where $\omega_\theta^2 = \theta(1-\theta)f_{u_\theta}^2(0)$.

The result in (i) uses the fact that the (y_i, x_i) are independent, but need not be identically distributed. This is the case when $f_{u_\theta}(\cdot|x)$ depends on x, as is the case, for example, with heteroskedasticity. The result in (ii) simplifies the result in (i) when (y_i, x_i') are i.i.d.

3.1 Estimation of the asymptotic covariance matrix

Several estimators for the asymptotic covariance matrix are readily available. Some of the estimators are valid under Theorem 1(i), while others are valid only under the independence assumption of Theorem 1(ii). In the following, we refer to the former as the *general case*, while the latter is referred to as the *i.i.d. case*. Note that under either cases Λ_0 can be easily estimated by its sample analogue, namely, $\hat{\Lambda} = n^{-1}\sum_{i=1}^{n} x_i x_i'$.

3.1.1 The i.i.d. case

In this case the problem centers around estimating ω_θ^2, or more specifically around estimating $1/f_{u_\theta}(0)$. Let $\hat{u}_{\theta(1)}, \ldots, \hat{u}_{\theta(n)}$ be the ordered residuals from the θth quantile regression.

Order estimator: Following Siddiqui (1960), an estimator for $1/f_{u_\theta}^2(0)$ is provided by

$$\frac{1}{\hat{f}_{u_\theta}^2(0)} = \frac{\left(\hat{u}_{\theta([n(\theta+h_n)])} - \hat{u}_{\theta([n(\theta+h_n)])}\right)^2}{4h_n},$$

for some bandwidth $h_n = o_p(1)$. Bofinger (1975) provides an optimal choice for the bandwidth, that minimizes the mean squared error, based on the normal approximation for the true $f_{u_\theta}(\cdot)$:

$$h_n = n^{-1/5}\left(\frac{4.5\phi^4(\Phi^{-1}(\theta))}{\left[(2\Phi^{-1}(\theta))^2 + 1\right]^2}\right)^{1/5},$$

where Φ and ϕ denote the distribution function and density function of a standard normal variable, respectively.

Kernel estimator: The density $f_{u_\theta}(0)$ can be estimated directly by

$$\hat{f}_{u_\theta}(0) = (c_n n)^{-1} \sum_{i=1}^{n} \kappa(\hat{u}_{\theta i}),$$

where $\kappa(\cdot)$ is some kernel function $\kappa(\cdot)$ and $c_n = o_p(1)$ is the kernel bandwidth. It can be optimally chosen using a variety of cross-validation methods (for example, least-squares, log likelihood, and so on).

Bootstrap estimator for ω_θ^2: This estimator relies on bootstrapping the residual series $\hat{u}_{\theta i}$, $i = 1, \ldots, n$. Specifically, one can obtain B bootstrap estimates for q_θ, the θ's quantile of u_θ, say $\hat{q}_{\theta 1}^*, \ldots, \hat{q}_{\theta B}^*$, from B bootstrap samples drawn from the empirical distribution $\hat{F}_{u_\theta}$. An estimator for ω_θ^2 is obtained then by

$$\hat{\omega}_\theta^2 = \frac{n}{B} \sum_{j-1}^{B} (q_{\theta j}^* - q_\theta^*)^2,$$

where $q_\theta^* = \frac{1}{B} \sum_{j=1}^{B} \hat{q}_{\theta j}^*$.

3.1.2 The general case
There are several alternative estimators for the general case. Here we provide two possible estimators that have been proven accurate in a variety of Monte Carlo studies (for example, Buchinsky, 1995).

Kernel estimator: Powell (1986) considered the following kernel estimator for Δ_θ

$$\hat{\Delta}_\theta = (c_n n)^{-1} \sum_{i=1}^{n} \kappa(\hat{u}_{\theta i}) x_i x_i',$$

where $\kappa(\cdot)$ is some kernel function and $c_n = o_p(1)$ is the kernel bandwidth. Note that the top left-hand element of the matrix $\hat{\Delta}_\theta$ is an estimate of the density $f_{u_\theta}(0)$. Hence, the same cross-validation methods discussed before can be used to optimally choose c_n.

Design matrix bootstrap estimators: There are several alternative ways for employing the bootstrap method of Efron (1979). The most general method is what is termed the *design matrix bootstrapping*, whereby one re-samples from the joint distribution of (y, x). Specifically, let (y_i^*, x_i^*), $i = 1, \ldots, n$, be a randomly drawn sample from the empirical distribution of (x, y), denoted $\hat{F}_{xy}$. Let $\hat{\beta}_\theta^*$ denote the quantile regression estimate based on the bootstrap sample. If we repeat this process B times, then an estimate for $V_\theta \equiv \theta(1 - \theta)\Delta_\theta^{-1}\Lambda_0\Delta_\theta^{-1}$ is given by

$$\hat{V}_\theta = \frac{n}{B} \sum_{j=1}^{B} (\hat{\beta}_{\theta j}^* - \beta_\theta^*)(\hat{\beta}_{\theta j}^* - \beta_\theta^*)',$$

where $\beta_\theta^* = \frac{1}{B}\sum_{j=1}^B \hat{\beta}_{\theta j}^*$. The estimate $\hat{V}_\theta$ is a consistent estimator for V_θ in the sense that the conditional distribution of $\sqrt{n}(\hat{\beta}_\theta^* - \hat{\beta}_\theta)$, conditional on the data, weakly converges to the unconditional distribution of $\sqrt{n}(\hat{\beta}_\theta - \beta_\theta)$.

One important caveat about bootstrapping is in order. If one already uses the bootstrap method, it can be used more efficiently and effectively, taking advantage of the higher-order refinement properties of the method. For example, one can directly construct confidence intervals, test statistics, and so forth, based on the bootstrap estimates without having to first compute an estimate for V_θ. The number of bootstrap repetitions required for the particular application may be different. Nevertheless, the exact number of repetitions can be computed using the method proposed by Andrews and Buchinsky (2000).

4. Set of quantile regressions

The model presented in (1) considered only the estimation for a single quantile θ. In practice one would like to estimate several quantile regressions at distinct points of the conditional distribution of the dependent variable. This section outlines the estimation of a finite sequence of quantile regressions and provides its asymptotic distribution.

4.1 Estimation and large sample properties

Consider the model given in (1) (dropping the i subscript) for p alternative θ's:

$$y = x'\beta_{\theta_j} + u_{\theta_j} \quad \text{where,} \quad Q_{\theta_j}(u_{\theta_j}|x) = 0,$$

for $j = 1, \ldots, p$. Without loss of generality assume that $0 < \theta_1 < \theta_2 < \cdots < \theta_p < 1$. Estimating the p quantile regressions amounts to running p separate regressions for θ_1 through θ_p. Let the stacked vector of β's $\beta_\theta = (\beta_{\theta_1}', \ldots, \beta_{\theta_p}')'$ denote the population's true parameter vector and let $\hat{\beta}_\theta = (\hat{\beta}_{\theta_1}', \ldots, \hat{\beta}_{\theta_p}')'$ denote its corresponding estimate.

Theorem 2 under Assumptions A.1–A.3

(i) $\sqrt{n}(\hat{\beta}_\theta - \beta_\theta) \xrightarrow{\mathscr{L}} N(0, \Lambda_\theta)$, where $\Lambda_\theta = \{\Lambda_{\theta_{jk}}\}_{j,k=1,\ldots,p}$, and

(ii) $\Lambda_{\theta_{jk}} = (\min\{\theta_j, \theta_k\} - \theta_j\theta_k)\Delta_{\theta_j}^{-1}\Lambda_0\Delta_{\theta_k}^{-1}$; if in addition $f_{u_{\theta_j}}(0|x) = f_{u_\theta}(0)$ for $j = 1, \ldots, p$ with probability 1, then $\sqrt{n}(\hat{\beta}_\theta - \beta_\theta) \xrightarrow{} N(0, \Lambda_\theta)$, where $\Lambda_\theta = \Omega_\theta \otimes \Lambda_0^{-1}$ and $\Omega_{\theta_{jk}} = [\min\{\theta_j, \theta_k\} - \theta_j\theta_k]/[f_{u_{\theta_j}}(0)f_{u_{\theta_k}}(0)]$

4.2 Crossing of quantiles

Note that the estimated conditional quantiles, conditional on x, are given by $x'\hat{\beta}_{\theta_1}, \ldots, x'\hat{\beta}_{\theta_p}$. Since the estimates $\hat{\beta}_{\theta_j}$ $(j = 1, \ldots, p)$ for the p quantiles are obtained from separate quantile regressions, it is possible that for some vector x_0, $x_0'\hat{\beta}_{\theta_j} > x_0'\hat{\beta}_{\theta_k}$ even though $\theta_j < \theta_k$, that is, conditional quantiles may cross each other. This may not be of any practical consequence, since there may not be such a vector within the relevant range of plausible x's. Nevertheless, in any empirical application these potential crossing need to be examined.

4.3 Testing for equality of slope coefficients

Under the i.i.d. assumption the p coefficient vectors $\beta_{\theta_1}, \ldots, \beta_{\theta_p}$ should be the same, except for the intercept coefficients. There are a number of ways for testing the null hypothesis of i.i.d. errors. Only two testing procedures are provided here. For other alternative methods see Koenker (2005).

4.3.1 Wald-type testing

This testing procedure is based on the optimal minimum distance (MD) estimator under the null hypothesis. Denote the parameter vector under the null by β_θ^R and note that $\beta_\theta^R = (\beta_{\theta_1 1}, \ldots, \beta_{\theta_p 1}, \beta_2, \ldots, \beta_k)'$ is a $(p + K - 1) \times 1$, with p distinct intercepts $\beta_{\theta_1 1}, \ldots, \beta_{\theta_p 1}$, and $k - 1$ common slope parameters $\beta_2, \ldots, \beta_k$.

An optimal estimate for the restricted coefficient vector β_θ^R is defined by

$$\hat{\beta}_\theta^R = \arg \min_{\beta^R} (\hat{\beta}_\theta - R\beta^R)' \hat{V}_\theta^{-1} (\hat{\beta}_\theta - R\beta^R),$$

where $\hat{V}_\theta$ is a consistent estimate for the covariance matrix of $\hat{\beta}_\theta$, the unrestricted parameter estimate from the p quantile regressions, estimated under the null (that is, under Theorem 2(ii). The matrix R is simply a $(p + K - 1) \times p \cdot k$ restriction matrix which imposes the restrictions implied by the i.i.d. assumption. A test statistic for equality of the slope coefficients is provided then by

$$W_n = n(\hat{\beta}_\theta - R\hat{\beta}_\theta^R)' \hat{V}_\theta^{-1} (\hat{\beta}_\theta - R\hat{\beta}_\theta^R).$$

Under the null hypothesis $W_n \xrightarrow{D} \chi^2(pK - p - K + 1)$ as $n \to \infty$. So, the null hypothesis is rejected if $W_n > \chi_{1-\alpha}^2(pK - p - K + 1)$, where $\chi_{1-\alpha}^2(m)$ denotes the $1-\alpha$ quantile of a χ^2-distribution with m degrees of freedom.

4.3.2 GMM-type testing

An alternative testing procedure can be applied using Hansen's (1982) GMM method. Define a moment function $\psi(x, y, \beta)$ by stacking the p individual moment functions as defined in (3). While this moment function is a $pk \times 1$ vector, under the null there are only $p + K - 1$ parameters to be estimated. Hansen's GMM framework provides an estimator for β_θ^R, say $\hat{\beta}_\theta^R$, defined by

$$\hat{\beta}_\theta^R = \arg \min_b \left(\frac{1}{n} \sum_{i=1}^n \psi(x_i, y_i, b) \right)' A^{-1} \left(\frac{1}{n} \sum_{i=1}^n \psi(x_i, y_i, b) \right), \tag{4}$$

An efficient estimator can be obtained if A is chosen so that $A \xrightarrow{P} E[\psi(x, y, \beta_\theta)\psi(x, y, \beta_\theta)']$ as $n \to \infty$. This framework provides us with a straightforward testing procedure. Under the null hypothesis

$$n\left(\frac{1}{n}\sum_{i=1}^{n}\psi(x_i,y_i,\hat{\beta}_{\theta}^{R})\right)'A^{-1}\left(\frac{1}{n}\sum_{i=1}^{n}\psi(x_i,y_i,\hat{\beta}_{\theta}^{R})\right)\xrightarrow{D}\chi^2(pK-p-K+1),$$

as $n\rightarrow\infty$.

Note that, because of the linearity of the conditional quantiles, the GMM testing provides a test statistics which is (asymptotically) equivalent to that provided by the MD testing.

5. Censored quantile regression

An important extension to the quantile regression model was suggested by Powell (1984; 1986). This extension considers the case in which some of the observations are censored. This model is essentially a semiparametric extension to the well known 'Tobit' model and can be written as

$$y_i = \min\{y_i^0, x_i'\beta_{\theta} + u_{\theta i}\},$$

for $i=1,\ldots,n$, where y_i^0 is the (known) top coding value of y_i in the sample, for $i=1,\ldots,n$. (For simplicity of presentation it will be assumed that $y_i^0 = y^0$ for all $i=1,\ldots,n$.)

This model can be written as a latent variable model. That is, we have $y_i^* = x_i'\beta_{\theta} + u_{\theta i}$, where $Q_{\theta}(u_{\theta i}|x_i) = 0$ and $y_i = y_i^* I(y_i^* \le y^0)$. It is easy to see that the observed conditional θth quantile of y_i, conditional on x_i, is given by $Q_{\theta}(y_i|x_i) = \min\{y^0, x_i'\beta_{\theta}\}$.

Hence, Powell suggested the following estimator for β_{θ}

$$\hat{\beta}_{\theta} = \arg\ \min_{\beta}\frac{1}{n}\sum_{i=1}^{n}\rho_{\theta}(y_i - \min\{y^0, x_i'\beta\}), \tag{5}$$

where $\rho_{\theta}(\lambda)$ is the same check function as defined above. Note that in order to obtain a consistent estimator of β_{θ} it is necessary that $x_i'\beta_{\theta} < y^0$ for at least a fraction of the sample. Intuitively, the larger the fraction, the more precise the estimator will be.

Powell (1986) showed that, under certain regularity conditions, similar to those established by Huber (1967), the estimator is asymptotically normal. That is,

$$\sqrt{n}(\hat{\beta}_{\theta} - \beta_{\theta})\xrightarrow{D}N(0, V_{\theta}^C)\text{ as }n\rightarrow\infty,\text{ where}$$

$$V_{\theta}^C = \theta(1-\theta)\Delta_{C\theta}^{-1}\Lambda_{C\theta}\Delta_{C\theta}^{-1},$$
$$\Delta_{C\theta} = E[f_{u_{\theta}}(0|x)I(x'\beta_{\theta} \le y^0)xx'],\text{ and}$$
$$\Lambda_{C\theta} = E[I(x'\beta_{\theta} < y^0)xx'].$$

As in the basic quantile regression model, if $f_{u_\theta}(0|x) = f_{u_\theta}(0)$ with probability 1, then V_θ^C simplifies to $V_\theta^C = \omega_\theta^2 \Lambda_{C\theta}^{-1}$, where $\omega_\theta^2 = \theta(1-\theta)f_{u_\theta}^2(0)$.

It is important to note that if $x_i'\hat{\beta}_\theta \leq y^0$ for all observations, then the censored quantile regression estimate coincides with the basic quantile regression.

The simple intuition for this estimation procedure is that β_θ can be estimated only from that part of the sample for which it is observed, that is, for that fraction of the sample for which $y = y^* = x'\beta_\theta + u_\theta \leq y^0$. As a result, we note that the asymptotic covariance is 'adjusted' for that fact. That is, the term $I(x'\beta_\theta \leq y^0)$ is included in both $\Delta_{C\theta}$ and $\Delta_{C\theta}$.

A considerable drawback of the censored quantile regression model is that it does not have the attractive LP representation and the objective function is not globally convex in β.

6. Concluding remarks

The main goal of this article is to provide the basic structure of the quantile regression model. Versions of this model have been widely used in the empirical literature in a variety of situations not covered by this article. Furthermore, there have been substantial advancements in the theoretical literature as well. This literature includes quantile regression for nonlinear models, time-series models, and others. There are also a number of empirical studies that have used quantile regression extensively, in a variety of data configurations and economic contexts. For a brilliant in-depth exposition of a wide variety of topics related to quantile regression, interested readers should refer to Koenker (2005).

MOSHE BUCHINSKY

See also **semiparametric estimation.**

Bibliography

Andrews, D. and Buchinsky, M. 2000. A three-step method for choosing the number of bootstrap repetitions. *Econometrica* 68, 23–51.

Bofinger, E. 1975. Estimation of density function using order statistics. *Australian Journal of Statistics* 17, 1–7.

Buchinsky, M. 1994. Changes in the U.S. wage structure 1963–1987: application of quantile regression. *Econometrica* 62, 405–58.

Buchinsky, M. 1995. Estimating the asymptotic covariance matrix for quantile regression models: a Monte Carlo study. *Journal of Econometrics* 68, 303–38.

Efron, B. 1979. Bootstrap methods: another look at the jackknife. *Annals of Statistics* 7, 1–26.

Hansen, L. 1982. Large sample properties of generalized method of moments estimators. *Econometrica* 50, 1029–54.

Huber, P. 1967. The behavior of maximum likelihood estimates under nonstandard conditions. *Proceedings of the Fifth Berkeley Symposium on Mathematical Statistics and Probability*, vol. 1. Berkeley: University of California Press.

Koenker, R. 2005. *Quantile Regression*. Econometric Society Monograph. New York: Cambridge University Press.

Koenker, R. and Bassett, G. 1978a. The asymptotic distribution of the least absolute error estimator. *Journal of the American Statistical Association* 73, 618–22.

Koenker, R. and Bassett, G. 1978b. Regression quantiles. *Econometrica* 46, 33–50.

Newey, W. and Powell, J. 1990. Efficient estimation of linear and type I censored regression models under conditional quantile restrictions. *Econometric Theory* 6, 295–317.

Portnoy, S. and Koenker, R. 1989. Adaptive *L*-estimation for linear models. *Annals of Statistics* 17, 362–81.

Powell, J. 1984. Least absolute deviation estimation for the censored regression model. *Journal of Econometrics* 25, 303–25.

Powell, J. 1986. Censored regression quantiles. *Journal of Econometrics* 32, 143–55.

Siddiqui, M. 1960. Distribution of quantile from a bivariate population. *Journal of Research of the National Bureau of Standards* 64, 145–50.

regression-discontinuity analysis

The regression discontinuity (RD) data design is a quasi-experimental evaluation design first introduced by Thistlethwaite and Campbell (1960) as an alternative approach to evaluating social programmes. The design is characterized by a treatment assignment or selection rule which involves the use of a known *cut-off* point with respect to a continuous variable, generating a discontinuity in the probability of treatment receipt at that point. Under certain comparability conditions, a comparison of average outcomes for observations just left and right of the cut-off can be used to estimate a meaningful causal impact. While interest in the design had previously been mainly limited to evaluation research methodologists (Cook and Campbell, 1979; Trochim, 1984), the design is currently experiencing a renaissance among econometricians and empirical economists (Hahn, Todd and van der Klaauw, 1999; 2001; Angrist and Krueger, 1999; Porter, 2003). Among the main econometric contributions have been the formal derivation of identification conditions for causal inference and the introduction of semiparametric estimation procedures for the design. At the same time, a large and rapidly growing number of empirical applications are providing new insights into the applicability of the design, which have led to the development of several sensitivity and validity tests.

The popularity of the RD design in applied economic research can be linked to several of its features. First, the assignment rules in many existing programmes and procedures for allocating social resources, frequently lend themselves to RD evaluations. In many cases, programme resources are allocated based on some type of formula that has a cut-off structure. One area of economic research where the design has proven especially fruitful in recent years has been the evaluation of educational interventions. Education programmes are frequently assigned to schools or students who score below a cut-off on some scale (student performance, poverty), and school and programme funding decisions are often based on allocation formulas containing discontinuities. Similarly, the design has proven useful in evaluating the socio-economic impacts of a diverse set of government programmes and laws, many of which use eligibility cutoffs or funding formulas involving thresholds in allocating scarce resources to those potential recipients who need or deserve them most (see van der Klaauw, 2007a). A second attractive feature of the design is that it is intuitive and its results can be easily communicated, often with a visual portrayal of sharp changes in both treatment assignment and average outcomes around the cut-off value of the assignment variable (Bloom et al., 2005). Third, a researcher can choose from among several different methods to estimate effects that have credible causal interpretations (Hahn, Todd and van der Klaauw, 2001).

Consider the general problem of evaluating the impact of a binary treatment on an outcome variable, using a random sample of individuals where for each individual *i* we observe an outcome measure y_i and a binary treatment indicator t_i, equal to one if treatment was received and zero otherwise. The evaluation problem that arises in determining the effect of t on y, is due to the fact that each individual either receives or does not receive treatment and is never observed in both states. Let $y_i(1)$ be the outcome given treatment, and $y_i(0)$ the outcome in absence of treatment. Then the actual outcome we observe equals $y_i = t_i y_i(1) + (1 - t_i) y_i(0)$. A common regression model representation for the observed outcome can then be written as

$$y_i = \beta + \alpha_i t_i + u_i \tag{1}$$

where $\alpha_i = y_i(1) - y_i(0)$ and $y_i(0) = E[y_i(0)] + u_i = \beta + u_i$. Non-random assignment or selection into treatment implies that a comparison of average outcomes of treatment recipients and non-recipients ($E[y_i(1)|t_i = 1]$ and $E[y_i(0)|t_i = 0]$) would generally not provide us with a valid treatment effect estimate.

Hahn, Todd and van der Klaauw (HTV) (2001) analysed the conditions under which a discontinuity in the treatment assignment or selection rule can be exploited to solve the selection bias problem and to identify a meaningful causal effect. Following Trochim (1984) they distinguish between two different forms of the design, depending on whether the treatment assignment is related to the assignment variable by a deterministic function (*sharp design*) or a stochastic one (*fuzzy design*). In the case of a sharp RD design, individuals are assigned to or selected for treatment solely on the basis of a cut-off score on an observed continuous variable x. This variable, alternatively called the assignment, selection, running or ratings variable, could represent a single characteristic or a composite variable constructed using several characteristics. Those who fall below some distinct cutoff point $\bar{x}$ are placed in the control group ($t_i = 0$), while those on or above that point are placed in the treatment group ($t_i = 1$) (or vice versa). Thus, assignment occurs through a known and measured deterministic decision rule: $t_i = t(x_i) = 1\{x_i \geq \bar{x}\}$ where $1\{.\}$ is the indicator function. As the assignment variable itself may be correlated with the outcome variable, the assignment mechanism is clearly not random.

However, if we have reason to believe that persons close to the threshold with very similar x values are comparable, then we may view the design as almost experimental near x, suggesting that we could evaluate the causal impact of treatment by comparing the average outcome for those with ratings just above to those with ratings just below the cutoff. More formally, consider the following *local continuity* (*LC*) *assumption*:

$E[u_i|x]$ and $E[\alpha_i|x]$ are continuous in x at $\bar{x}$, or equivalently, $E[y(1)|x]$ and $E[y(0)|x]$ are continuous at $\bar{x}$,

then on the assumption that the density of x is positive in a neighbourhood containing $\bar{x}$,

$$\lim_{x \downarrow \bar{x}} E[y_i|x] - \lim_{x \uparrow \bar{x}} E[y_i|x] = \lim_{x \downarrow \bar{x}} E[\alpha_i t_i|x] - \lim_{x \uparrow \bar{x}} E[\alpha_i t_i|x] + \lim_{x \downarrow \bar{x}} E[u_i|x] - \lim_{x \uparrow \bar{x}} E[u_i|x]$$
$$= E[\alpha_i | x = \bar{x}]. \tag{2}$$

The RD approach therefore identifies the average treatment effect for individuals close to the discontinuity point. Note that the continuity assumption formalizes the idea that individuals just above and below the cut-off need to be 'comparable', requiring them to have similar average potential outcomes when receiving and when not receiving treatment. While in the absence of additional assumptions (such as a common effect assumption) one could learn about treatment effects only for a sub-population of persons near the discontinuity point, as pointed out by HTV this local effect is highly relevant to policymakers who are contemplating less restrictive eligibility rules and marginal expansions of programmes via a change in the cut-off.

The continuity assumption required for identification is not innocuous. Even if treatment receipt is determined solely on the basis of a cut-off score on the assignment variable, this is not a sufficient condition for the identification of a meaningful causal effect. The continuity assumption rules out coincidental functional discontinuities in the $x-y$ relationship such as those caused by other programmes employing assignment mechanisms based on the exact same assignment variable and cut-off. In addition, the continuity restriction generally rules out certain types of behaviour both on the part of potential treatment recipients who exercise control over their value of x and programme administrators in choosing the assignment variable and cut-off point. Lee (2007) analyses the conditions under which an ability to manipulate the assignment variable may invalidate the RD identification assumptions. He shows in the context of a sharp RD design that as long as individuals do not have *perfect* control over the position of the assignment variable relative to the cut-off score, the continuity assumption will be satisfied.

While in the sharp RD design treatment assignment is known to depend on the selection variable x in a deterministic way, in the case of a fuzzy design (Campbell, 1969), treatment assignment depends on x in a stochastic manner but in such a way that the propensity score function $\Pr(t=1|x)$ is again known to have a discontinuity at $\bar{x}$. Instead of a $0-1$ step function, the selection probability as a function of x would now contain a jump smaller than 1 at $\bar{x}$. The fuzzy design can occur in case of misassignment relative to the cut-off value in a sharp design, with values of x near the cut-off appearing in both treatment and control groups. This situation is analogous to having no-shows (treatment group members who do not receive treatment) and/or crossovers (control group member who do receive the treatment) in a randomized experiment. This could occur if in addition to the position of the individual's score relative to the cut-off value, assignment is based on additional variables observed by the administrator, but unobserved by the evaluator.

A comparison of average outcomes of recipients and non-recipients, even if near the cut-off, would not generally lead to correct inferences regarding an average treatment effect. However, as shown by HTV, one can again exploit the discontinuity in the selection rule to identify a causal impact of interest by noting that under the LC assumption and with a locally constant treatment effect ($\alpha_i = \alpha$ in a neighbourhood around $\bar{x}$), the treatment effect α is identified by

$$\frac{\lim_{x\downarrow\bar{x}}E[y_i|x] - \lim_{x\uparrow\bar{x}}E[y_i|x]}{\lim_{x\downarrow\bar{x}}E[t_i|x] - \lim_{x\uparrow\bar{x}}E[t_i|x]}, \tag{3}$$

where the denominator is always non-zero because of the known discontinuity of $E[t|x]$ at $\bar{x}$.

In the case of varying treatment effects, HTV show that under the local continuity assumption, and a local conditional independence assumption requiring t_i to be independent of α_i conditional on x near $\bar{x}$, the ratio above identifies $E[\alpha_i|x = \bar{x}]$, the average treatment effect for cases with values of x close to $\bar{x}$. The conditional independence assumption is a strong assumption which may be violated if individuals self-select into or are selected for treatment on the basis of expected gains from treatment. HTV show that, under a weaker local monotonicity assumption similar to that assumed by Imbens and Angrist (1994), the ratio (3) will instead identify a local average treatment effect (LATE) at the cut-off point, which represents the average treatment effect of the 'compliers', that is, the subgroup of individuals whose treatment status would switch from non-recipient to recipient if their score x crossed the cut-off. More recently Battistin and Rettore (2003) considered the special case where an eligibility rule divides the population into eligibles and non-eligibles according to a sharp RD design, and with eligible individuals self-selecting into treatment. In this case the LC assumption alone is sufficient for the ratio to identify $E[\alpha_i|t_i = 1, x = \bar{x}]$, the average treatment effect on the treated, for those near the cut-off.

As indicated by these identification results, estimation of treatment effects in an RD design involves estimating boundary points of conditional expectation functions. The most common empirical strategy in the literature has been to adopt parametric specifications for the conditional expectations functions. Consider the following alternative representation of outcome eq. (1) in case of a sharp RD design:

$$y_i = m(x_i) + \delta t_i + e_i, \tag{4}$$

where $e_i = y_i - E[y_i|t_i, x_i]$, $t_i = 1\{x_i \geq \bar{x}\}$, $m(x) = E[u_i|x] + (E[\alpha_i|x] - E[\alpha_i|\bar{x}])$ $1\{x \geq \bar{x}\}$. Then under the local continuity assumption $m(x)$ will be a continuous function of x at x, and $\delta = E[\alpha_i|\bar{x}]$ (the average treatment effect at x) will measure the discontinuity in the average outcome at the cut-off. This suggests that if the correct specification of $m(x)$ were known, and was included in the regression, we could consistently estimate the treatment effect for the sharp RD design. This idea of including a specification of $m(x)$ in the regression of y on t in order to correct for selection bias caused by selection on observables, is in the econometrics literature known as the *control function approach* (Heckman and Robb, 1985). A popular choice among empirical researchers has been to use global polynomials or to use splines (piecewise polynomials) which, even though globally continuous, have a knot at the cut-off (Trochim, 1984; van der Klaauw, 2002; McCrary, 2007).

In the case of a fuzzy RD design, when assuming local independence of t_i and α_i conditional on x, then in a neighbourhood of $\bar{x}$,

$$y_i = m(x_i) + \delta E[t_i|x_i] + w_i, \tag{5}$$

where $w_i = y_i - E[y_i|x_i]$ and $m(x) = E[u_i|x] + (E[\alpha_i|x] - E[\alpha_i|\bar{x}])E[t|x]$. With the local continuity assumption again implying that $m(x)$ will be continuous at the cut-off, and with $E[t_i|x_i]$ being discontinuous at $\bar{x}$, δ in this regression will measure the ratio in (3), which in this case equals the average local treatment effect $E[\alpha_i|\bar{x}]$. Similarly, δ can be interpreted as a local average treatment effect if we replaced the local independence assumption with the local monotonicity condition of Imbens and Angrist (1994).

This naturally leads to the two-stage procedure adopted by van der Klaauw (2002), where in the first stage we estimate the propensity score function specified as $t_i = E[t_i|x_i] + v_i = f(x_i) + \gamma 1\{x_i \geq \bar{x}\} + v_i$ where $f(\cdot)$ is continuous in x at x and γ measures the discontinuity in the propensity score function at x. In the second stage the control function-augmented outcome equation is then estimated with t_i replaced by the first-stage estimate of $E[t_i|x_i] = \Pr[t_i = 1|x_i]$ as in Maddala and Lee (1976). With correctly specified $f(x)$ and $m(x)$ functions, this two-stage procedure yields a consistent estimate of the treatment effect. The approach is similar in spirit to those proposed earlier in the RD evaluation literature by Spiegelman (1979) and Trochim and Spiegelman (1980). Note that in case of a parametric approach, if we assume the same functional form for $m(x)$ and $f(x)$, then the two-stage estimation procedure described here will be equivalent to two-stage least squares (in case of linear-in-parameter specifications) with $1\{x_i \geq \bar{x}\}$ and the terms in $m(x)$ serving as instruments. Because of the popularity of this particular parametrization, the RD approach is often interpreted as being equivalent to an instrumental variable approach, as it implicitly imposes an exclusion restriction by excluding $1\{x_i \geq \bar{x}\}$ as a variable in the outcome equation.

Valid parametric inference for the estimation of the treatment effect requires a correct specification of the control function $m(x)$ and of $f(x)$ in the treatment equation. To mitigate the potential for misspecification bias, several semiparametric estimation procedures have been proposed for estimating $m(x)$ and $f(x)$, or equivalently for estimating the limits $\lim_{x\downarrow\bar{x}} E[z|x]$ and $\lim_{x\uparrow\bar{x}} E[z|x]$ in (3) semiparametrically. These methods rely on less-restrictive smoothness conditions away from the discontinuity, with estimates based mainly on data in a neighbourhood on either side of the cut-off point. Asymptotically this neighbourhood needs to shrink, as with usual nonparametric estimation, implying that we should expect a slower than parametric rate of convergence in estimating treatment impacts. HTV considered the use of kernel and local linear regression estimators, while Porter (2003) proposed estimating the limits using local polynomial regression and partially linear model estimation. RD estimators based on local polynomial regression and partially linear model estimation have better boundary behaviour than the kernel-based estimator and as shown by Porter, achieve the optimal rate of convergence. This result is based on a known degree of smoothness of the conditional expectation functions.

Sun (2005) proposed an adaptive estimator to first estimate the degree of smoothness in the data prior to implementing either estimator.

The internal validity of the RD approach relies on the local continuity of conditional expectations of potential outcomes around the discontinuity point. While this assumption is fundamentally untestable, a number of validity tests have been developed to bolster the credibility of the RD design. First, economic behaviour may lead to sorting of individuals around the cut-off point, where those below the cut-off may differ on average from those just above the cut-off. Such precise sorting around the cut-off would generally be accompanied by a discontinuous jump in the density of the assignment variable at the cutoff. Several approaches have been used for assessing this possibility (McCrary, 2007; Lee, 2007; Chen and van der Klaauw, 2007; Lemieux and Milligan, 2004). Second, one can test for evidence that individuals on either side of the cut-off are observationally similar by directly comparing average characteristics (McEwan and Urquiola, 2005) or by repeating the RD analysis treating the characteristics as outcome variables (van der Klaauw, 2007b). Alternatively, one can test for an imbalance of relevant characteristics by assessing the sensitivity of RD estimates to the inclusion of observed characteristics as controls (van der Klaauw, 2002; Lee, 2007). Third, in some applications data are available from a baseline period in which the programme did not yet exist, or for a group of individuals that was not eligible for treatment. In such a case the credibility of the design can be significantly enhanced by repeating the RD analysis with such data. Finding a zero treatment effect in such a falsification test would suggest that a non-zero post-programme effect was not an artifact of the specific RD model specification, estimation approach chosen or caused by another programme using the same cut-off and assignment variable.

Finally, while this exposition has focused on the binary treatment case with a selection rule containing a single discontinuity at a known cut-off, the approach can be readily extended to one where there are multiple treatment dose levels and multiple cut-offs or 'cut-off ranges' within which the treatment dose varies continuously (van der Klaauw, 2007a). Similarly, the approach can be modified to cover cases where the assignment or selection variable is discrete instead of continuous (Lee and Card, 2006).

WILBERT VAN DER KLAAUW

See also **natural experiments and quasi-natural experiments; propensity score; selection bias and self-selection; semiparametric estimation; treatment effect.**

Bibliography

Angrist, J.D. and Krueger, A.B. 1999. Empirical strategies in labor economics. In *Handbook of Labor Economics*, vol. 3, ed. O. Ashenfelter and D. Card. Amsterdam: North-Holland.

Battistin, E. and Rettore, E. 2003. Another look at the regression discontinuity design. Working Paper No. CWP01/03, CeMMAP, Institute for Fiscal Studies.

Bloom, H.S., Kemple, J., Gamse, B. and Jacob, R. 2005. Using regression discontinuity analysis to measure the impacts of reading first. Paper presented at the Annual Conference of the American Educational Research Association, Montreal, Canada, April.

Campbell, D.T. 1969. Reforms as experiments. *American Psychologist* 24, 409–29.

Chen, S. and van der Klaauw, W. 2007. The work disincentive effects of the disability insurance program in the 1990s. *Journal of Econometrics*.

Cook, T.D. and Campbell, D.T. 1979. *Quasi-Experimentation: Design and Analysis Issues for Field Settings*. Boston: Houghton-Mifflin.

Hahn, J., Todd, P. and van der Klaauw, W. 1999. Evaluating the effect of an antidiscrimination law using a regression-discontinuity design. Working Paper No. 7131. Cambridge, MA: NBER.

Hahn, J., Todd, P. and van der Klaauw, W. 2001. Identification and estimation of treatment effects with a regression-discontinuity design. *Econometrica* 69, 201–09.

Heckman, J.J. and Robb, R. 1985. Alternative methods for evaluating the impact of interventions. In *Longitudinal Analysis of Labor Market Data*, ed. J. Heckman and B. Singer. New York: Cambridge University Press.

Imbens, G.W. and Angrist, J. 1994. Identification and estimation of local average treatment effects. *Econometrica* 62, 467–76.

Lee, D.S. 2007. Randomized experiments from non-random selection in U.S. house elections. *Journal of Econometrics*. (forthcoming).

Lee, D.S. and Card, D. 2006. Regression discontinuity inference with specification error. Technical Working Paper No. 322. Cambridge, MA: NBER.

Lemieux, T. and Milligan, K. 2004. Incentive effects of social assistance: a regression discontinuity approach. Working Paper No. 10541. Cambridge, MA: NBER.

Maddala, G.S. and Lee, L. 1976. Recursive models with qualitative endogenous variables. *Annals of Economic and Social Measurement* 5, 525–45.

McCrary, J. 2007. Testing for manipulation of the running variable in the regression discontinuity design. *Journal of Econometrics*.

McEwan, P.J. and Urquiola, M. 2005. Economic behavior and the regression-discontinuity design: evidence from class size reduction. Working paper, Columbia University.

Porter, J. 2003. Estimation in the regression discontinuity model. Unpublished manuscript, Harvard University.

Spiegelman, C.H. 1979. Estimating the effect of a large scale pretest posttest social program. *Proceedings of the Social Statistics Section, American Statistical Association*, pp. 370–3.

Sun, Y. 2005. Adaptive estimation of the regression discontinuity model. Working paper, University of California, San Diego.

Thistlethwaite, D. and Campbell, D. 1960. Regression-discontinuity analysis: an alternative to the ex post facto experiment. *Journal of Educational Psychology* 51, 309–17.

Trochim, W.K. 1984. *Research Design for Program Evaluation: The Regression-Discontinuity Approach*. Beverly Hills, CA: Sage.

Trochim, W. and Spiegelman, C.H. 1980. The relative assignment variable approach to selection bias in pretest-posttest group designs. *Proceedings of the Survey Research Section, American Statistical Association*, pp. 376–80.

van der Klaauw, W. 2002. Estimating the effect of financial aid offers on college enrollment: a regression-discontinuity approach. *International Economic Review* 43, 1249–87.

van der Klaauw, W. 2007a. Regression-discontinuity analysis: a survey of recent developments in economics. Unpublished manuscript, Federal Reserve Bank of New York.

van der Klaauw, W. 2007b. Breaking the link between poverty and low student achievement: an evaluation of title I. In *Journal of Econometrics*.

Roy model

The Roy (1951) model of self-selection on outcomes is one of the most important models in economics. It is a framework for analysing comparative advantage. The original model analysed occupational choice with heterogeneous skill levels and has subsequently been applied in many other contexts. We first discuss the model. We then summarize what is known about identification of the model. We end by describing some applications based on the model and its extensions.

Basic models

In the original Roy (1951) model, agents can pursue one of two possible occupations: hunting and fishing. They cannot pursue both at the same time. There is no interaction among agents so the choice of one agent does not affect the choice of another agent either through prices or through external effects. Let π_f and π_r be the price of fish and rabbits respectively in the village. Let F_i denote the number of fish that individual i would catch if he chooses to fish. Similarly let R_i denote the number rabbits he would catch. Then individual i's wage is

$$w_{fi} = \pi_f F_i$$

if he fishes and

$$w_{ri} = \pi_r R_i$$

if he hunts. The income that worker i receives for working in sector j is thus proportional to π_j (where $j \in \{r, f\}$). If workers are pure income maximizers, they will choose the occupation with higher income. Thus a worker chooses to fish if $w_{fi} > w_{ri}$. If F_i and R_i are continuous random variables, $\Pr(\pi_r R_i = \pi_f F_i) = 0$, so the indifference set is negligible. A fundamental aspect of the Roy model is that it allows for heterogeneity in (F_i, R_i). This heterogeneity can arise from inherent ability differences or human capital investment.

An important issue is self-selection. Under what conditions will the best workers self-select into an occupation? Will people who self-select be above average? For example, for fishing, under what conditions is the average productivity of people working in the fishing sector above the population mean productivity:

$$E[\log(F_i)|\pi_f F_i \geq \pi_r R_i] > E[\log(F_i)]?$$

Assume, as did Roy (1951), that log skills are jointly normally distributed

$$\begin{bmatrix} \log(F_i) \\ \log(R_i) \end{bmatrix} \sim N\left(\begin{bmatrix} \mu_f \\ \mu_r \end{bmatrix}, \begin{bmatrix} \sigma_{ff} & \sigma_{fr} \\ \sigma_{fr} & \sigma_{rr} \end{bmatrix} \right).$$

Then it is straightforward to show that

$$E[\log(F_i)|\pi_f F_i \geq \pi_r R_i] = \mu_f + \underbrace{\frac{(\sigma_{ff} - \sigma_{fr})}{\sigma}\lambda\left(\frac{\log(\pi_f) - \log(\pi_r) + \mu_f - \mu_r}{\sigma}\right)}_{selection\ effect}$$

where σ^2 is the variance of $\log(F_i/R_i)$ and $\lambda(\cdot)$ is the inverse Mills ratio. (See SELECTION BIAS AND SELF-SELECTION.)

The function λ is positive but decreasing in its arguments with $\lim_{\pi_f \to \infty}\lambda(\cdot) = 0$. The selection effect is the second term on the right-hand side of this expression. There is a parallel expression for $E(\log R_i|\pi_F F_i \leq \pi_R R_i)$ with the subscripts f and r interchanged.

Recall that $E[\log(F)] = \mu_f$ and that λ and σ must both be positive. Therefore, the question of whether there is positive selection into fishing depends only upon the sign of $\sigma_{ff} - \sigma_{fr}$. It does not depend on skill prices. Moreover, since

$$\sigma^2 = (\sigma_{ff} - \sigma_{fr}) + (\sigma_{rr} - \sigma_{fr}) > 0,$$

at least one of $(\sigma_{ff} - \sigma_{fr})$ and $(\sigma_{rr} - \sigma_{fr})$ must be positive. Thus, there must be positive selection into one of the occupations, and there can be positive selection into both.

If, however, there is positive selection into only one occupation, the question arises as to which occupation is most likely to have positive selection. Roy argues that relatively simple tasks (setting traps for rabbits in his case) can be described by a small standard deviation of skill. For more difficult skills (fishing in his example) the standard deviation will be relatively higher as there is a bigger difference between the most skilled and the least skilled. Thus, if fishing is the more difficult task, $\sigma_{ff} > \sigma_{rr}$, there must be positive selection into fishing (that is, $E(\log(F_i)|\pi_f F_i \geq \pi_r R_i) > E(\log(F_i))$).

Whether there is positive selection into hunting depends on the value of σ_{fr} relative to σ_{rr}. When $\sigma_{fr} < 0$, we will see positive selection into hunting. At the other extreme, if hunting and fishing are perfectly correlated, then σ_{fr} must be larger than σ_{rr}, and there is negative selection into hunting. Intuitively, since F and R are perfectly positively correlated, and F is more dispersed, persons with low values of F can avoid low incomes by using their value of R. Persons with high values of F (and R) should fish because the upper tail of F is more dispersed. For cases in between, either positive or negative selection is possible depending on the sign of $\sigma_{rr} - \sigma_{fr}$. Heckman and Honoré (1990) generalize this result to a broader class of distribution functions.

This model has been generalized in a number of ways. There can be more than two occupational choices. Following Heckman and Sedlacek (1985), one can assume that individuals possess a vector of skills S_i and that different tasks use the different skills according to the function $T_j(S_i)$. We still let π_j denote task prices so that we can write an individual's wage at task j as

$$w_{ji} = \pi_j T_j(S_i).$$

Another extension of the model allows individuals to care about aspects of the job other than just their wages (see Heckman and Sedlacek, 1985). Let $U_{ji}(w)$ be the utility that individual i would receive from performing task j under wage level w. This allows for some tasks (such as playing basketball) to be generally preferred to more unpleasant tasks (such as cleaning bathrooms). Individuals then choose the occupation that yields the highest level of utility for them $U_{ji}(w_{ij})$. This is the generalized Roy model in which the generalization comes in the agent decision rules.

The generalized Roy model can be trivially extended to a model of labour force participation by allowing non-market work to be one of the tasks. To see this, let $j = 0$ denote the home sector as in Gronau (1974) and Heckman (1974). Of course, in general, there will not be a market price for home-produced goods, but one can interpret $T_0(S_i)$ as the value of goods produced at home. One could also assume that staying at home is pure leisure in which $T_0(S_i) = 0$, but people enjoy staying at home $U_{0i}(0) > U_{ji}(0)$ for $j > 0$. The Roy model has been generalized to allow for uncertainty in agent decision making in Cunha, Heckman and Navarro (2005). See the reviews in Heckman, Lochner and Todd (2006) and Cunha and Heckman (2007).

Identification

The economics of these models is simple, but identification and estimation are considerably more difficult. Heckman and Honoré (1990) consider identification of the basic Roy model with two occupations and income maximization. They consider two different cases: (*a*) the standard Roy model, in which the two occupations represent two different sectors of the economy and the econometrician has data on wages in both sectors; and (*b*) a case motivated by labour supply in which the econometrician has wage data from one sector (the market sector) but not from the other (the home sector). It is important to keep in mind that the comparative advantage decision at the heart of the Roy Model is just one factor that can lead to selection bias. SELECTION BIAS AND SELF-SELECTION discusses the more general framework for thinking about sample selection and also discusses in some detail how the Roy model fits into this framework.

Heckman and Honoré (1990) consider identification from a single cross section. When one can observe wages in both sectors, under log normality, the Roy model is identified even without any regressors in the model. However, when one relaxes the log normality assumption, without regressors in the outcome equation the model is no longer identified. This is true despite the strong assumption of agent income maximization.

Heckman and Honoré (1990) provide conditions under which one can identify these models using variation across markets, or by using variation in observables within a market. To see the intuition behind the latter case, consider the model in which

$$\log (F_i) = g_f(Z_{fi}, X_i) + \varepsilon_{fi}$$
$$\log (R_i) = g_r(Z_{ri}, X_i) + \varepsilon_{ri},$$

and prices are normalized to 1. In this context, it is helpful for identification to have an exclusion restriction – that is, a variable Z_{fi} that varies separately from (X_i, Z_{ri}) and a variable Z_{ri} that varies separately from (X_i, Z_{fi}). As long as there is sufficient variation in the excluded variables, Heckman and Honoré (1990) show that with a location normalization the full model is identified provided that $(\varepsilon_{fi}, \varepsilon_{ri})$ are independent of (Z_{fi}, Z_{ri}, X_i), that is, they identify g_f, g_r and the joint distribution of $(\varepsilon_{fi}, \varepsilon_{ri})$. (They also establish identification when only one sector's output is observed.)

To see the intuition for why the model is identified, consider an 'identification at infinity' argument. For convenience, take the location normalization to be

$$E(\varepsilon_{fi}) = E(\varepsilon_{ri}) = 0.$$

Suppose that g_r is such that for any x, say x_0,

$$\lim_{z_r \to -\infty} g_r(z_r, x_0) = -\infty.$$

Let $J_i \in \{f, r\}$ be an indicator of the occupation that was chosen by individual i. Then

$$\lim_{z_r \to -\infty} E[\log(F_i) | J_i = f, X_i = x, Z_{fi} = z_f, Z_{ri} = z_r]$$
$$= g_f(z_f, x) + \lim_{z_r \to -\infty} E(\varepsilon_{fi} | g_f(z_f, x) + \varepsilon_{fi} > g_r(z_r, x) + \varepsilon_{ri},$$
$$X_i = x, Z_{fi} = z_f, Z_{ri} = z_r) = g_f(z_f, x).$$

By varying (z_f, x) one can trace out g_f. This occurs because conditioning on the event

$$g_f(z_f, x) + \varepsilon_f > g_r(z_r, x) + \varepsilon_r$$

becomes irrelevant as z_r becomes arbitrarily small. Identification of g_r is analogous using variation in z_f.

To identify the joint distribution of $(\varepsilon_{fi}, \varepsilon_{ri})$ note that from the data one can observe

$$\Pr(J_i = f, \log(F_i) < s | X_i = x, Z_{fi} = z_f, Z_{ri} = z_r)$$
$$= \Pr(g_f(z_f, x) + \varepsilon_{fi} > g_r(z_r, x) + \varepsilon_{ri}, g_f(z_f, x) + \varepsilon_{fi} < s | X_i = x, Z_{fi} = z_f, Z_{ri} = z_r)$$
$$= \Pr(\varepsilon_{fi} - \varepsilon_{ri} < g_f(z_f, x) - g_r(z_r, x), \varepsilon_{fi} < s - g_f(z_f, x) | X_i = x, Z_{fi} = z_f, Z_{ri} = z_r)$$

which is the cumulative distribution function of $(\varepsilon_{fi} - \varepsilon_{ri}, \varepsilon_{fi})$ evaluated at the point $(g_f(z_f, x) - g_r(z_r, x), s - g_f(z_f, x))$. By varying the point of evaluation one can identify the joint distribution of $(\varepsilon_{fi} - \varepsilon_{ri}, \varepsilon_{fi})$ from which one can derive the joint distribution of $(\varepsilon_{fi}, \varepsilon_{ri})$. Thus the model is identified. Heckman and Honoré (1989) also present conditions for identification of a competing risk version of a Roy model when there are no exclusion restrictions ($Z_r = X = Z_f$) but g_f and g_r can be independently varied. Buera (2006) makes stronger differentiability assumptions and relaxes the separability assumption in the choice equation. He also identifies a Roy model without exclusion restrictions.

Identifying the more general model where individuals choose fishing when

$$U_{fi}(w_{fi}) > U_{ri}(w_{ri})$$

is possible under a variety of assumptions. Consider the separable case in which

$$U_{fi}(w_{fi}) - U_{ri}(w_{ri}) = h(Q_i, Z_{fi}, Z_{ri}, X_i) + v_i$$

where Q_i is an additional variable that might affect the relative utilities of the two options. The function h is identified up to a normalization (see, for example, Matzkin, 1992).

Identification of parts of the model follows from the preceding reasoning. If there is a variable that affects sectoral choice, but not wages as a fisherman, we can identify g_r. Note that this exclusion restriction could be in the form of either Q_i or Z_{ri}. We can then identify the joint distribution of (v_i, ε_{ri}) using an argument analogous to the above. Using the same argument we can identify g_f and the joint distribution of (v_i, ε_{fi}). A formalization of this argument can be found in Heckman (1990) for the case in which h is linear and is extended in Heckman and Smith (1998), Carneiro, Hansen and Heckman (2003) and Heckman and Navarro (2007). One cannot, without further assumptions, identify the joint distribution of $(v_i, \varepsilon_{ri}, \varepsilon_{fi})$. (Abbring and Heckman, 2007, present conditions for identification of the joint distribution by restricting dependence relations. See also Aakvik, Heckman and Vytlacil, 2005.)

If one is interested in evaluating policies in which wages can change, this reduced form model is not enough since there is no separation of wage effects from non-wage effects in the choice model. Assume further that we can write

$$
\begin{aligned}
h(Q_i, Z_{fi}, Z_{ri}, X_i) + v_i &= \alpha_1 F_i - \alpha_2 R_i + h^*(Q_i, Z_{fi}, Z_{ri}, X_i) + v_i^* \\
&= \alpha_1 g_f(Z_{fi}, X_i) - \alpha_2 g_r(Z_{ri}, X_i) + h^*(Q_i, Z_{fi}, Z_{ri}, X_i) + \alpha_1 \varepsilon_{fi} - \alpha_2 \varepsilon_{ri} + v_i^*.
\end{aligned}
$$

Identification of this model is possible if there are exclusion restrictions in Z_{fi} and Z_{ri}, that is, if there are components of Z_{fi} and Z_{ri} that do not affect h^*. Under sufficient variation of these variables and imposing a normalization, the model is identified. An interesting special case of the model is when $\alpha_1 = \alpha_2$. In this case one needs a somewhat weaker exclusion restriction in that one could use variation in X_i. That is, we could use a variable that affects labour market outcomes, but not sectoral choice directly.

Empirical models

There are many examples that build on the Roy model, but in labour economics three stand out. The earliest empirical application of this model is to the labour supply decision (Heckman, 1974; Gronau, 1974). We refer interested readers to LABOUR SUPPLY rather than discuss these models explicitly. The second application is to occupational choice, which is most closely linked to the original Roy model. The third, and perhaps most well known, application is to education.

We start by describing the empirical applications of the model to education. Willis and Rosen (1979) consider a model in which students decide whether to attend college. Students may have a comparative advantage in either the college sector or the high school sector. Their model assumes that decisions about schooling are made in an environment of perfect certainty on the principle of income maximization. They assume access to outcome measures in two periods. The decision to attend college depends on interest rates which are not observable to the econometrician. (One could reinterpret their model as a generalized Roy model if one interprets the interest rate as representing utility differences rather than interest rates.) Semiparametric identification requires two types of exclusion restrictions: a variable that influences the decision to attend college but not directly wages, and a variable that influences wages but not the decision to attend college directly. For the former type of exclusion restriction, Willis and Rosen (1979) use family background variables, arguing that they will be correlated with interest rates but uncorrelated with wages. For the latter type they use test scores, arguing that they are related to skill as in the Roy model, but unrelated to the interest rate.

Although they discuss comparative advantage in the labour market, as did Roy, they do not present direct empirical evidence on this question because they cannot estimate the joint distribution of schooling outcomes across both choices. They present some indirect evidence on the importance of comparative advantage in the labour market because they can identify the counterfactual means of what college students would earn if they had been high school students and what high schools students would earn had they been college students.

There are many extensions of this model, including Taber (2000), Cameron and Taber (2004) and Heckman, Lochner and Todd (2006). Cunha, Heckman and Navarro (2005) and Cunha and Heckman (2007) extend the model to allow for uncertainty, to identify agent information and to directly test for comparative advantage in the labour market by identifying the joint distribution of outcomes for the two counterfactual states (college and high school).

In a series of papers, Heckman, Lochner and Taber (1998a; 1998b; 1998c) estimate a general equilibrium version of this model. That is, they allow the skill prices π_j to be endogenous. They show that accounting for equilibrium effects is essential for estimating the impact of policy on earnings inequality. In particular Heckman, Lochner and Taber (1998b) show that ignoring equilibrium effects overstates the impact of a tuition subsidy on college enrolment by an order of magnitude. They also decompose the policy effect on earnings inequality into its various components.

Other papers estimate a Roy model of occupational choice. Most notably, Heckman and Sedlacek (1985; 1990) estimate models in which workers choose between industrial sectors. In some cases they allow for non-market work. They show how to estimate the model, but reject a pure Roy model. They show instead that a more general model with utility maximization and non-participation can fit the data well.

Gould (2002) extends this framework to address the changing wage structure. He shows that workers choose sectors to maximize their comparative advantage and that this activity tends to decrease earnings inequality. However, he shows that the importance of this effect decreases over time as sectors increasingly value more similar skill sets.

Keane and Wolpin (1997) and Eckstein and Wolpin (1999) estimate dynamic discrete choice models of occupational and educational choice that extends the Roy model to a dynamic setting with uncertainty with serially independent shocks. Agents in their model make labour supply, education and occupational choice simultaneously. Heckman and Navarro (2007) present a nonparametric identification analysis of a dynamic discrete choice model with serially correlated shocks. Abbring and Heckman (2007) survey the dynamic discrete choice literature, including these papers.

JAMES J. HECKMAN AND CHRISTOPHER TABER

See also **selection bias and self-selection.**

Bibliography

Aakvik, A., Heckman, J.J. and Vytlacil, E.J. 2005. Estimating treatment effects for discrete outcomes when responses to treatment vary: an application to Norwegian vocational rehabilitation programs. *Journal of Econometrics* 125, 15–51.

Abbring, J.H. and Heckman, J.J. 2007. Econometric evaluation of social programs, part III: distributional treatment effects, dynamic treatment effects, dynamic discrete choice, and general equilibrium policy evaluation. In *Handbook of Econometrics*, vol. 6, ed. J. Heckman and E. Leamer. Amsterdam: North-Holland.

Buera, F.J. 2006. Non-parametric identification and testable implications of the Roy model. Unpublished manuscript, Department of Economics, Northwestern University.

Cameron, S.V. and Taber, C. 2004. Estimation of educational borrowing constraints using returns to schooling. *Journal of Political Economy* 112, 132–82.

Carneiro, P., Hansen, K. and Heckman, J.J. 2003. Estimating distributions of treatment effects with an application to the returns to schooling and measurement of the effects of uncertainty on college choice. 2001 Lawrence R. Klein Lecture. *International Economic Review* 44, 361–422.

Cunha, F. and Heckman, J.J. 2007. Identifying and estimating the distributions of ex post and ex ante returns to schooling: a survey of recent developments. *Labour Economics* 14, 870–93.

Cunha, F., Heckman, J.J. and Navarro, S. 2005. Separating uncertainty from heterogeneity in life cycle earnings. The 2004 Hicks Lecture. *Oxford Economic Papers* 57, 191–261.

Eckstein, Z. and Wolpin, K.I. 1999. Why youths drop out of high school: the impact of preferences, opportunities, and abilities. *Econometrica* 67, 1295–339.

Gould, E.D. 2002. Rising wage inequality, comparative advantage, and the growing importance of general skills in the United States. *Journal of Labor Economics* 20, 105–47.

Gronau, R. 1974. Wage comparisons – a selectivity bias. *Journal of Political Economy* 82, 1119–43.

Heckman, J.J. 1974. Shadow prices, market wages, and labor supply. *Econometrica* 42, 679–94.

Heckman, J.J. 1990. Varieties of selection bias. *American Economic Review* 80, 313–8.

Heckman, J.J. and Honoré, B.E. 1989. The identifiability of the competing risks model. *Biometrika* 76, 325–30.

Heckman, J.J. and Honoré, B.E. 1990. The empirical content of the Roy model. *Econometrica* 58, 1121–49.

Heckman, J.J., Lochner, L.J. and Taber, C. 1998a. Explaining rising wage inequality: explorations with a dynamic general equilibrium model of labor earnings with heterogeneous agents. *Review of Economic Dynamics* 1, 1–58.

Heckman, J.J., Lochner, L.J. and Taber, C. 1998b. General-equilibrium treatment effects: a study of tuition policy. *American Economic Review* 88, 381–6.

Heckman, J.J., Lochner, L.J. and Taber, C. 1998c. Tax policy and human-capital formation. *American Economic Review* 88, 293–7.

Heckman, J.J., Lochner, L.J. and Todd, P.E. 2006. Earnings equations and rates of return: the Mincer equation and beyond. In *Handbook of the Economics of Education*, ed. E.A. Hanushek and F. Welch. Amsterdam: North-Holland.

Heckman, J.J. and Navarro, S. 2007. Dynamic discrete choice and dynamic treatment effects. *Journal of Econometrics* 136, 341–96.

Heckman, J.J. and Sedlacek, G.L. 1985. Heterogeneity, aggregation, and market wage functions: an empirical model of self-selection in the labor market. *Journal of Political Economy* 93, 1077–125.

Heckman, J.J. and Sedlacek, G.L. 1990. Self-selection and the distribution of hourly wages. *Journal of Labor Economics* 8(1, Part 2), S329–63.

Heckman, J.J. and Smith, J.A. 1998. Evaluating the welfare state. In *Econometrics and Economic Theory in the Twentieth Century: The Ragnar Frisch Centennial Symposium*, ed. S. Strom. New York: Cambridge University Press.

Keane, M.P. and Wolpin, K.I. 1997. The career decisions of young men. *Journal of Political Economy* 105, 473–522.

Matzkin, R.L. 1992. Nonparametric and distribution-free estimation of the binary threshold crossing and the binary choice models. *Econometrica* 60, 239–70.

Roy, A. 1951. Some thoughts on the distribution of earnings. *Oxford Economic Papers* 3, 135–46.

Taber, C.R. 2000. Semiparametric identification and heterogeneity in discrete choice dynamic programming models. *Journal of Econometrics* 96, 201–29.

Willis, R.J. and Rosen, S. 1979. Education and self-selection. *Journal of Political Economy* 87(5, Part 2), S7–S36.

Rubin causal model

The Rubin Causal Model (RCM) is a formal mathematical framework for causal inference, first given that name by Holland (1986) for a series of previous articles developing the perspective (Rubin, 1974; 1975; 1976; 1977; 1978; 1979; 1980). There are two essential parts to the RCM, and a third optional one. The first part is the use of 'potential outcomes' to define causal effects in all situations – this part defines 'the science', which is the object of inference, and it requires the explicit consideration of the manipulations that define the treatments whose causal effects we wish to estimate. The second part is an explicit probabilistic model for the assignment of 'treatments' to 'units' as a function of all quantities that could be observed, including all potential outcomes; this model is called the 'assignment mechanism', and defines the structure of experiments designed to learn about the science from observed data or the acts of nature that lead to the observed data. The third possible part of the RCM framework is an optional distribution on the quantities being conditioned on in the assignment mechanism, including the potential outcomes, thereby allowing model-based Bayesian 'posterior predictive' (causal) inference. This part of the RCM focuses on the model-based analysis of observed data to draw inferences for causal effects, where the observed data are revealed by applying the assignment mechanism to the science. A full-length text that discusses estimation and inference for causal effects from this perspective is Imbens and Rubin (2006).

Implications of the RCM for research design

Before defining each of these three parts of the RCM, it is helpful to consider the implications of this structure for applied research about causal effects. The first part implies that we should always start by carefully defining all causal estimands (quantities to be estimated) in terms of potential outcomes, which are all values that could be observed in some real or hypothetical experiment that compares the results under an active treatment with the results under a control treatment. That is, causal effects are defined by a comparison of (*a*) the values that would be observed if the active treatment were applied and (*b*) the values that would be observed if, instead, the control treatment were applied. This step contrasts with the common practice of defining causal effects in terms of parameters in some model, where the manipulations defining the active versus control treatments are often left implicit and ill-defined, with the resulting causal inferences correspondingly weak and ill-defined. This first part can be completely abstract and can take place before any data are observed or even collected. In the RCM, however, there is 'no causation without manipulation' (Rubin, 1975, p. 238), where the manipulation (that is, the treatment) could be real or hypothetical. The collection of potential outcomes with and without this manipulation defines the scientific objective of causal inference in all studies, whether randomized, observational or entirely hypothetical.

The second part of the RCM, the assignment mechanism, implies that, given the defined science, we should continue by explicating the design of the real or hypothetical study being used to estimate that science. The assignment mechanism describes why some study units will be (or were) exposed to the active treatment and why other study units will be (or were) exposed to the control treatment, and the reasons are formalized by the mathematical statement of the assignment mechanism. When the study is a true experiment, the assignment mechanism may involve the consideration of background (that is, pretreatment assignment) variables for the purpose of creating strata of similar units to be randomized into treatment and control, thereby improving the balance of treatment and control groups with respect to these background variables (that is, covariates). A true experiment automatically cannot use any outcome (post-treatment) variables to influence design because they are not yet observed. If the observed data were not generated by a true experiment, but rather by non-randomized observational data, there still should be an explicit design phase. That is, in an observational study, the same guidelines as in an experiment should be followed.

More explicitly, the design step in the analysis of an observational data set for causal inference should structure the data to approximate (or reconstruct or replicate) a true randomized experiment as closely as possible. In this design step, the researcher never uses or even examines any outcome data but rather identifies subsets of units such that the treatments can be thought of as being randomly assigned within the subsets. This assumed randomness of treatment assignment is assessed by examining, within these subsets of units, the similarity of the distributions of the covariates in the treatment group and in the control group. Because this design step is focused on creating these subsets of units with balanced distributions of covariates between treatment and control groups, and never uses outcome data, the researcher cannot select a design to produce a desired answer, even unconsciously.

The third part of the RCM is optional; it derives inferences for causal effects from the observed data by conceptualizing the problem as one of imputing the missing potential outcomes. That is, once outcome data are available (that is, observations of the potential outcomes corresponding to the treatments actually received by the various units), then the modelling of the outcome data given the covariates should be structured to derive predictions of those potential outcomes that would have been observed if the treatment assignments had been different. This modelling will generate stochastic predictions (that is, imputations) for all missing potential outcomes in the study, which, when combined with the actually observed potential outcomes, will allow the calculation of any causal-effect estimand. Because the imputations of the missing potential outcomes are stochastic, repeating the process results in different values for the causal-effect estimand. This variation across the multiple imputations (Rubin, 1987; 2004a) generates interval estimates and tests for the causal estimands. Typically, in practice this third part is implemented using simulation-based methods, such as Markov chain Monte Carlo computation applied to Bayesian models.

The conceptual clarity in the first two steps of the RCM often allows previously difficult causal inference situations to be easily formulated and handled. The optional third part often extends this success by relying on modern computational power to handle analytically intractable problems. With this overview in place, we consider features of the RCM in more detail.

Potential outcomes and causal effects

For defining causal effects, there are three basic primitives – concepts that are fundamental and on which we must build: units, treatments and potential outcomes. A unit is a physical object, for example a person, at a particular point in time. A treatment is an action that can be applied or withheld from a unit. We focus on the case of two treatments, although the extension to more than two treatments is simple in principle although not necessarily so with real data. Associated with each unit are two potential outcomes: the value of an outcome variable Y at a future point in time if the active treatment is applied, and the value of Y at the *same* future point in time if instead the control treatment is applied. The objective is to learn about the causal effect of the application of the active treatment relative to the control on Y, where, by definition, the causal effect is a comparison of the two potential outcomes. For example, the unit could be a person 'now' without a job, the active treatment could be participating in a job training programme, and the control could be not participating. The outcome Y could be the total income over the next three years, with the two potential outcomes being the total income with and without job training; the causal effect of being trained versus not being trained is the comparison of the person's three-year total income with and without the training.

Notationally, let W indicate which treatment the unit receives: $W = 1$ the active treatment, and $W = 0$ the control treatment. Also let $Y(1)$ be the value of the potential outcome if the unit received the active version, and $Y(0)$ the value if the unit received the control version. The causal effect of the active treatment relative to the control is the comparison of $Y(1)$ and $Y(0)$ – typically the difference, $Y(1) - Y(0)$, or perhaps the difference in logs, $\log[Y(1)] - \log[Y(0)]$, or some other comparison, possibly the ratio. We can observe only one or the other of $Y(1)$ and $Y(0)$ as indicated by $W : Y_{obs} = WY(1) + (1 - W)Y(0)$. The 'fundamental problem facing inference for causal effects' (Rubin, 1978, p. 38) is that, for any individual unit, we observe the value of the potential outcome for this unit under only one of the possible treatments, namely, the treatment actually assigned, and the potential outcome under the other treatment is missing. Thus, inference for causal effects is a missing-data problem – the 'other' value is missing, so the nature of causal inference is that at least 50 per cent of the values of the potential outcomes are missing. Covariates have values that are unaffected by the treatments, such as age or sex of the unit in the job training example, and are denoted by X. Even when X represents a lagged Y, such as total income last year, $Y(1) - X$ is not the causal effect of training unless $Y(0) = X$, but rather a change of income across time.

To clarify the RCM set-up with potential outcomes, consider a specific difficult case: what is the causal effect of race on hiring practices? To consider this explicitly causal question in the RCM, we must consider the manipulations that define the active and control treatments. Literally changing one's race is presumably impossible given current medical technology, but one can conceptualize experiments that can plausibly capture what researchers want to know, that is, how employers react to race when all else is constant. For example, suppose that résumés are submitted by mail to groups of employers, where the treatment to be applied to each résumé (that is, each unit) is the name attached to it (see, for example, Bertrand and Mullainathan, 2004). Here, the active treatment is the use of a distinctive African-American name on the résumé, and the control treatment is the use of a traditional name. In this case, the explication of what is meant by 'the causal effect race' is through the description of the manipulations, and the causal effect to be estimated is thereby well-defined: the causal effect of having a résumé with an African-American name compared with a traditional name on the resultant hiring outcome. Whether that effect corresponds to what the investigator wants to estimate or to what others believe is relevant to policy is another issue, but the causal nature of the comparison is clear. If it is not the desired quantity estimand or is deemed not relevant, then other more appropriate manipulations should be described.

Suppose, now that there are N units rather than only one. To make the representation with only two potential outcomes for each unit adequate, must accept an assumption, the stable unit treatment value assumption (SUTVA; Rubin, 1980), which rules out interference between units (Cox, 1958) and rules out different versions of the treatments for the units (for example, no 'technical errors'; Neyman, 1935; Rubin, 1990b). SUTVA can be weakened, but still some such assumption regarding the full set of potential outcomes is required. Often, in practice, SUTVA is made more plausible by aggregating the units. For example, training some of the unemployed in a local labour market may affect job opportunities for others in that local market. Therefore changing the unit of analysis to be the local labour market in a study with many geographically separated local labour markets may make it more plausible that there is no effect of the exposure of one unit to the treatment on other units.

Under SUTVA, all causal estimands (quantities to be estimated) can be defined from the matrix of values with i^{th} row: $(X_i, Y_i(0), Y_i(1))$, $i = 1, \ldots, N$. A causal estimand involves a comparison of $Y_i(0)$ and $Y_i(1)$ on all N units, or on a common subset of units; for example, the average causal effect across all units that are female as indicated by their X_i, or the median $Y_i(1)$ minus the median $Y_i(0)$ for the set of units with X_i indicating male and $Y_i(0)$ indicating no income. By definition, all relevant scientific information that is recorded is encoded in this matrix, and so the labelling of its rows is a random permutation of $1, \ldots, N$; that is, the N-row matrix $\{X, Y(0), Y(1)\}$ is row exchangeable. For convenience, we refer to this array of values as the 'science', functions of which we wish to estimate.

Brief history of potential outcomes to define causal effects

The basic idea that causal effects are the comparisons of potential outcomes on a common set of units seems so direct that it must have ancient roots, and we can find elements of this definition of causal effects among both philosophers (for example, Mill, 1843, p. 327) and experimenters (for example, Fisher, 1918, p. 214). But apparently there was no formal notation for potential outcomes until Neyman (1923), which appears to have been the first place where a mathematical analysis is written for a randomized experiment. This notation became standard for work in randomized experiments with randomization-based inference, and was a major advance. Independently and nearly simultaneously, Fisher (1925) recommended physically randomizing treatments to units in experiments, as well as a different, but compatible, method of randomization-based inference, although Fisher apparently never used the potential outcomes notation. But despite the almost immediate acceptance in the late 1920s of Fisher's proposal for randomized experiments, and of Neyman's notation for potential outcomes in randomized experiments, and of both men's proposals for randomization-based inference, this potential outcome notation was not used for causal inference more generally for a half century thereafter, apparently not until introduced by Rubin (1974). As a result, the insights into causal inference that accompanied the use of the potential outcomes notation were entirely limited to the relatively simple setting of randomization-based inference in randomized experiments.

The approach used in nonrandomized settings, during the half-century following the introduction of Neyman's seminal notation for randomized experiments, was based on mathematical models (for example, regression models) relating the observed value of the outcome variable $Y_{obs,i}$ to X_i and W_i, and then defining causal effects as parameters (for example, regression coefficients) of these models. This was the standard approach in medical and social science, including economics, and led to substantial confusion – the role of randomization cannot even be directly stated mathematically using the observed outcome notation. Of course, there were seeds of this first part of the RCM in social science before 1974, in particular in economics, in Tinbergen (1930), Haavelmo (1944) and Hurwicz (1962), but we can find no previous use of explicit notation like Neyman's to define causal effects. The use of the idea of potential outcomes certainly did appear in discussions in economic theory, for example, in the context of supply and demand functions (for example, Haavelmo, 1944) or the Roy (1951) model, but these discussions did not lead to inference in terms of potential outcomes. Instead, inference took place in terms of the specification of simultaneous equations using observed quantities and distributional properties of error terms (for example, Heckman and Robb, 1984, in the context of program evaluation models).

Nevertheless, the potential outcome part of the RCM framework for defining causal effects, namely, a generalization of Neyman's notation to allow non-randomized data, seems to have been basically accepted and adopted by most researchers by the end of the 20th century; compare, for example, Imbens and Angrist (1994) and Heckman,

Ichimura and Todd (1998) with the earlier formulation in Heckman and Robb (1984). An article exploring whether the full potential outcomes framework can be avoided when conducting causal inference is Dawid (2000), which included discussion by others that was largely supportive of the propriety of potential outcomes for causal inference.

The assignment mechanism and assignment-based causal inference

The second part of the RCM framework is the specification of an 'assignment mechanism': a probabilistic model for how some units received the active treatment and how other units received the control – how we conceptualize the design for how some potential outcomes were revealed and others remained hidden (that is, missing). The assignment mechanism is fundamental to causal inference. It specifies the conditional probability of each vector of assignments $W = (W_1, \ldots, W_N)^T$ given the matrix of all covariates and potential outcomes:

$$\Pr(W|X, Y(0), Y(1)). \tag{1}$$

It appears that Rubin (1975) was the first place that expressed the possible dependence of the assignment vector on the potential outcomes in this direct way, which allows the statement of what makes randomized experiments special, and more generally, generates a classification of assignment mechanisms. Again, economic theory sometimes implied a specific assignment mechanism, but this theory was never explicitly stated as in the general form of (1). For example, individuals may choose the occupation that maximizes their earnings, as in the Roy model, which would lead to $W_i = \mathrm{argmax}_w(Y_i(W))$, or more generally individuals may optimize an objective function that involves expectations over the unknown components of the potential outcomes. Imbens and Rubin (2006) provide details of such examples.

Randomized experiments are special in that they have 'unconfounded' and 'probabilistic' assignment mechanisms. Unconfounded assignment mechanisms (Rubin, 1990a) are free of dependence on either $Y(0)$ or $Y(1)$:

$$\Pr(W|X, Y(0), Y(1)) = \Pr(W|X). \tag{2}$$

Assignment mechanisms are 'probabilistic' (or 'probability' as in Rubin, 1990a) if each unit has a positive probability of receiving either treatment:

$$0 < \Pr(W_i = 1|X, Y(0), Y(1)) < 1. \tag{3}$$

'Strongly ignorable' assignment mechanisms (Rosenbaum and Rubin, 1983a) satisfy (2) and (3), and thus have unit level probabilities, or 'propensity scores', $\Pr(W_i = 1|X_i)$, that are strictly between 0 and 1, and are free of all potential outcomes.

Ignorable assignment mechanisms (Rubin, 1978), are free from dependence on missing potential outcomes but may depend on observed potential outcomes $Y_{\mathrm{obs}} = \{Y_{\mathrm{obs},i}\}$

$$\Pr(W|X, Y(0), Y(1)) = \Pr(W|X, Y_{\mathrm{obs}}). \tag{4}$$

Ignorable but confounded assignment mechanisms arise in practice, especially in sequential experiments. All strongly ignorable assignment mechanisms are unconfounded, and all unconfounded assignment mechanisms are ignorable, but not the other way. Strongly ignorable assignment mechanisms allow particularly straightforward estimation of causal effects, and are the basic template for the analysis of observational studies. More generally, observational studies have possibly confounded, non-ignorable, assignment mechanisms. A confounded assignment mechanism is one that depends on the potential outcomes, and so does not satisfy (2); a non-ignorable assignment mechanism does not even satisfy (4), and thus allows treatment assignment (or, to use common economics terminology, 'selection') to depend on unobserved values, that is, the missing potential outcomes, $Y_{\text{mis}} = \{Y_{\text{mis},i}\}$, $Y = \{Y_{\text{obs}}, Y_{\text{mis}}\}$.

When the assignment is strongly ignorable, it can generally be represented as a 'regular' assignment mechanism, which is proportional to the product of the propensity scores:

$$\Pr(W|X, Y(0), Y(1)) \propto \prod_{i=1}^{N} \Pr(W_i = 1|X_i). \tag{5}$$

Regular assignment mechanisms are the basic template in the RCM for the analysis of observational data, because two units with the same propensity score but different treatments are essentially randomized into the two treatment conditions. Therefore, with regular assignment mechanisms, matching on the propensity score (for example, as in Rosenbaum and Rubin, 1984), or subclassifying on it (for example, as in Rosenbaum and Rubin, 1985), restores the assumed underlying experimental design, and inference is straightforward based only on the assignment mechanism. These assignment-based methods of inference are due to Neyman (1923) and Fisher (1925), and they involve the calculation of large-sample confidence intervals and exact significance tests for null hypotheses, respectively; both are discussed in Rubin (1990a; 1990b; 1991). For the validity of either Fisher's or Neyman's approach, the analysis must formally be defined a priori, as part of the design. But the existence of these assignment-based modes of inference helps justify the view in the RCM that the model for the assignment mechanism is more fundamental for causal inference than the model for the science, which is not needed for randomization-based inference.

Thus, in the RCM an observational study should be designed as if its data arose from a 'broken' randomized experiment, where the unknown propensity scores must be reconstructed on the basis of the covariates X prior to ever observing any potential outcomes. In such settings, it is often quite advantageous to use estimated propensity scores (for example, as in Rosenbaum and Rubin, 1984; Rubin and Thomas, 1992a; 1992b; 1996; 2000; Hirano, Imbens and Ridder, 2003). When estimated propensity scores for some units are so low that they have essentially no chance of being treated, then those units should be discarded from further consideration when estimating the treatment effect in the treated (see, for example, Peters, 1941; Belson, 1956; Cochran and Rubin, 1973; Rubin, 1973a; 1973b; 1977; Rosenbaum and Rubin, 1985; Dehijia and Wahba, 1999; Crump et al., 2005). The result of the design phase should be treatment and control groups with very similar distributions of observed Xs, because of either matching or subclassification. If a data-set does not permit similar X distributions to be constructed in treatment and control groups, it cannot be used to support causal inferences without extraneous assumptions justifying extrapolations. Rubin (2002) offers an example of such matching and subclassification in the context of the US tobacco litigation, and Rubin (2006a) is a book devoted to matched sampling.

A striking example of the applied success of the above approach to inference in observational studies is Dehijia and Wahba (1999), which reanalysed the classic Lalonde (1986) data on job-training experiments but using the assignment-based approach of the RCM. In contrast to the wild variety of contradictory, but highly significant, answers found by the traditional econometric methods, Dehijia and Wahba used matching on the propensity score to arrive at inferences that tracked those from the underlying randomized experiment in the overall sample and in a variety of subsamples (see also Abadie and Imbens, 2006).

Posterior predictive, or model-based, causal inference

The third part of the RCM involves an optional distribution on the N-row array of science, $\Pr(X, Y(0), Y(1))$, thereby allowing Bayesian, or model-based, inference as well as assignment-based inference. An important virtue of the RCM framework is that it distinctly separates the science – its definition in the first part (and a possible model for it in the third part) from the design of what is revealed about the science – the assignment mechanism in the second part, which can also involve some scientific insights as when it is assumed to be generated by equilibrium conditions, as in supply and demand models, or by optimizing behaviour, and so on.

Bayesian inference for causal effects directly and explicitly confronts the missing potential outcomes, Y_{mis}, by using the specification for the assignment mechanism and the specification for the underlying data to derive the posterior predictive distribution of Y_{mis}, that is, the distribution of Y_{mis} given all observed values:

$$\Pr(Y_{\mathrm{mis}}|X, Y_{\mathrm{obs}}, W).$$

This distribution is posterior because it conditions on all observed values (X, Y_{obs}, W) and is predictive because it predicts (stochastically) the missing potential outcomes. From this distribution and all of the observed values (the observed potential outcomes, Y_{obs}; the observed assignments, W; and observed covariates, X), the posterior distribution of any causal effect can, in principle, be calculated. This conclusion is immediate if we view the posterior predictive distribution as specifying how to take a random draw of Y_{mis}. Once a value of Y_{mis} is drawn, any causal effect can be directly calculated from the drawn value of Y_{mis} and the observed values of X and Y_{obs}, for example, the median causal effect for males: med$\{Y_i(1) - Y_i(0)|X_i$ indicate males$\}$. Repeatedly drawing values of Y_{mis} and calculating the causal effect for each draw generates the posterior distribution of the desired causal effect. Thus, we can view causal inference entirely as a missing data problem, where we multiply-impute (Rubin, 1987; 2004a) the missing potential outcomes to generate a posterior distribution for the causal effects.

For example, the treated units have $Y_i(1)$ observed and $Y_i(0)$ missing. Under ignorability, the regression of $Y_i(0)$ on X_i among treated units, for which there is no direct evidence, can be shown to be the same as the regression of $Y_i(0)$ on X_i among controls, for which we have data. Thus, this third part of the RCM tells us to build a realistic model of $Y_i(0)$ given X_i among control subjects, and use it to impute the missing $Y_i(0)$ among the treated from their X_i values, while being wary of issues of extrapolation beyond the observed range of X_i control values. Analogously, build a model of $Y_i(1)$ given X_i among the treated, and use it to impute the missing $Y_i(1)$ among controls. The general structure is outlined in Rubin (1978), and is developed in detail in Imbens and Rubin (2006); a chapter-length summary appears in Rubin (2007).

Advantages of the RCM

Because of the flexibility in the RCM for (*a*) formulating causal estimands, and (*b*) positing assignment mechanisms, it can handle difficult cases in principled ways. With observational studies, estimated propensity scores play a key role, because the initial analysis proceeds as if the assignment mechanism were unconfounded. To assess the consequences of this assumption, sensitivity analyses can be conducted under various hypothetical situations, typically with fully missing covariates, U, such that treatment assignment is unconfounded given U but not given the observed data. Assumed relationships (given X) between U and W, and between U, $Y(0)$ and $Y(1)$, are then varied, for example, as in Rosenbaum and Rubin (1983b), utilizing the third part of the RCM. Ideally, this speculation occurs at the design stage. Extreme versions of sensitivity analyses lead to large-sample bounds (for example, Manski, 2003).

A complication, common when the units are people, is non-compliance with assigned treatment. Early work related to this issue can be found in economics using the terminology of instrumental variables, and the bridge from this terminology to the basic RCM is developed in Imbens and Angrist (1994) and in Angrist, Imbens and Rubin (1996), and the connection to the full RCM approach is presented in Imbens and Rubin (1997) and in Hirano et al. (2000). Another complication is censoring due to death, where units may 'die' before the final outcome can be measured. This problem is formulated from the RCM perspective in Rubin (2006b), with bounds given in Zhang and Rubin (2003); see Zhang, Rubin and Mealli (2007) for application to the evaluation of job-training programmes. This topic is also related to 'direct' and 'indirect' causal effects (Rubin, 2004b; 2005). Combinations of such complications are considered in Barnard et al. (2003) in the context of a school choice example, as well as in Mealli and Rubin (2002; 2003), Jin and Rubin (2007) and Frangakis and Rubin

(1999; 2001) in other contexts. The above examples can all be viewed as special cases of 'principal stratification' (Frangakis and Rubin, 2002).

The references in the preceding paragraph are clearly idiosyncratic in the sense of their being specific applications of the RCM in which the authors of this article have been participants, and are not representative, but we hope they provide indications of the breadth of recent applications of the RCM.

GUIDO W. IMBENS AND DONALD B. RUBIN

See also **matching estimators; treatment effect.**

Bibliography
Abadie, A. and Imbens, G.W. 2006. Large sample properties of matching estimators for average treatment effects. *Econometrica* 74, 235–67.
Angrist, J.D., Imbens, G.W. and Rubin, D.B. 1996. Identification of causal effects using instrumental variables. *Journal of the American Statistical Association* 91, 444–72 (an Applications Invited Discussion Article with discussion and rejoinder).
Barnard, J., Hill, J., Frangakis, C. and Rubin, D. 2003. A principal stratification approach to broken randomized experiments: a case study of vouchers in New York City. *Journal of the American Statistical Association* 98, 299–323 (with discussion and rejoinder).
Bertrand, M. and Mullainathan, S. 2004. Are Emily and Greg more employable than Lakisha and Jamal? A field experiment on labor market discrimination. *American Economic Review* 94, 991–1013.
Belson, W.A. 1956. A technique for studying the effect of a television broadcast. *Applied Statistics* 5, 195–202.
Cochran, W.G. and Rubin, D.B. 1973. Controlling bias in observational studies: a review. *Sankhya*, A 35, 417–46.
Cox, D.R. 1958. *The Planning of Experiments*. New York: Wiley.
Crump, R., Hotz, J., Imbens, G. and Mitnik, O. 2005. Moving the goalposts: addressing limited overlap in estimation of average treatment effects by changing the estimand. Unpublished manuscript, Department of Economics, University of California, Berkeley.
Dawid, A.P. 2000. Causal inference without counterfactuals. *Journal of the American Statistical Association* 95, 407–24 (with discussion).
Dehijia, R. and Wahba, S. 1999. Causal effects in non-experimental studies: re-evaluating the evaluations of training programs. *Journal of the American Statistical Association* 94, 1053–62.
Fisher, R.A. 1918. The causes of human variability. *Eugenics Review* 10, 213–20.
Fisher, R.A. 1925. *Statistical Methods for Research Workers*, 1st edn. Edinburgh: Oliver and Boyd.
Frangakis, C. and Rubin, D.B. 1999. Addressing complications of intention-to-treat analysis in the combined presence of all-or-none treatment-noncompliance and subsequent missing outcomes. *Biometrika* 86, 366–79.
Frangakis, C.E. and Rubin, D.B. 2001. Addressing an idiosyncrasy in estimating survival curves using double sampling in the presence of self-selected right censoring. *Biometrics* 57, 333–42 (with discussion and rejoinder, 343–53).
Frangakis, C.E. and Rubin, D.B. 2002. Principal stratification in causal inference. *Biometrics* 58, 21–9.
Haavelmo, T. 1944. The probability approach in econometrics. *Econometrica* 15, 413–19.
Heckman, J., Ichimura, H. and Todd, P. 1998. Matching as an econometric evaluation estimator. *Review of Economic Studies* 65, 261–94.

Heckman, J. and Robb, R. 1984. Alternative methods for evaluating the impact of interventions. In *Longitudinal Analysis of Labor Market Data*, ed. J. Heckman and B. Singer. Cambridge: Cambridge University Press.

Hirano, K., Imbens, G. and Ridder, G. 2003. Efficient estimation of average treatment effects using the estimated propensity score. *Econometrica* 71, 1161–89.

Hirano, K., Imbens, G., Rubin, D.B. and Zhou, X. 2000. Estimating the effect of an influenza vaccine in an encouragement design. *Biostatistics* 1, 69–88.

Holland, P.W. 1986. Statistics and causal inference. *Journal of the American Statistical Association* 81, 945–70.

Hurwicz, L. 1962. On the structural form of interdependent systems. In *Logic, Methodology, and Philosophy of Science, Proceedings of the 1960 International Congress*, ed. E. Nagel, P. Suppes and A. Tarski. Stanford, CA: Stanford University Press.

Imbens, G.W. and Angrist, J. 1994. Identification and estimation of local average treatment effects. *Econometrica* 62, 467–76.

Imbens, G.W. and Rubin, D.B. 1997. Bayesian inference for causal effects in randomized experiments with noncompliance. *Annals of Statistics* 25, 305–27.

Imbens, G.W. and Rubin, D.B. 2006. *Causal Inference in Statistics and the Medical and Social Sciences*. Cambridge: Cambridge University Press.

Jin, H. and Rubin, D.B. 2007. Principal stratification for causal inference with extended partial compliance: application to Efron–Feldman data. *Journal of the American Statistical Association*.

Lalonde, R. 1986. Evaluating the econometric evaluations of training programs. *American Economic Review* 76, 604–20.

Manski, C.F. 2003. *Partial Identification of Probability Distributions*. New York: Springer-Verlag.

Mealli, F. and Rubin, D.B. 2002. Assumptions when analyzing randomized experiments with noncompliance and missing outcomes. *Health Services Outcome Research Methodology* 3, 225–32.

Mealli, F. and Rubin, D.B. 2003. Assumptions allowing the estimation of direct causal effects: discussion of 'Healthy, wealthy, and wise? Tests for direct causal paths between health and socioeconomic status' by Adams et al. *Journal of Econometrics* 112, 79–87.

Mill, J.S. 1843. A System of Logic. In *Collected Works of John Stuart Mill*, vol. 7, ed. J.M. Robson. Toronto: University of Toronto Press, 1973.

Neyman, J. 1923. On the application of probability theory to agricultural experiments: essay on principles, section 9. Translated in *Statistical Science* 5 (1990), 465–80.

Neyman, J. 1935. Statistical problems in agricultural experimentation. Supplement to *Journal of the Royal Statistical Society, B* 2, 107–8 (with discussion). (With cooperation of K. Kwaskiewicz and St. Kolodziejczyk.)

Peters, C.C. 1941. A method of matching groups for experiments with no loss of population. *Journal of Educational Research* 34, 606–12.

Rosenbaum, P.R. and Rubin, D.B. 1983a. The central role of the propensity score in observational studies for causal effects. *Biometrika* 70, 41–55.

Rosenbaum, P.R. and Rubin, D.B. 1983b. Assessing sensitivity to an unobserved binary covariate in an observational study with binary outcome. *Journal of the Royal Statistical Society, B* 45, 212–18.

Rosenbaum, P.R. and Rubin, D.B. 1984. Reducing bias in observational studies using subclassification on the propensity score. *Journal of the American Statistical Association* 79, 516–24.

Rosenbaum, P.R. and Rubin, D.B. 1985. Constructing a control group using multivariate matched sampling incorporating the propensity score. *American Statistician* 39, 33–8.

Roy, A.D. 1951. Some thoughts on the distribution of earnings. *Oxford Economic Papers* 3, 135–46.

Rubin, D.B. 1973a. Matching to remove bias in observational studies. *Biometrics* 29, 159–83. Correction note: 1974. *Biometrics* 30, 728.

Rubin, D.B. 1973b. The use of matched sampling and regression adjustment to remove bias in observational studies. *Biometrics* 29, 185–203.

Rubin, D.B. 1974. Estimating causal effects of treatments in randomized and nonrandomized studies. *Journal of Educational Psychology* 66, 688–701.

Rubin, D.B. 1975. Bayesian inference for causality: the importance of randomization. *Proceedings of the Social Statistics Section of the American Statistical Association*, 233–9.

Rubin, D.B. 1976. Inference and missing data. *Biometrika* 63, 581–92.

Rubin, D.B. 1977. Assignment of treatment group on the basis of a covariate. *Journal of Educational Statistics* 2, 1–26.

Rubin, D.B. 1978. Bayesian inference for causal effects: the role of randomization. *Annals of Statistics* 6, 34–58.

Rubin, D.B. 1979. Discussion of 'Conditional independence in statistical theory' by A.P. Dawid. *Journal of the Royal Statistical Society*, Series B 41, 27–8.

Rubin, D.B. 1980. Discussion of 'Randomization analysis of experimental data in the Fisher randomization test' by Basu. *Journal of the American Statistical Association* 75, 591–3.

Rubin, D.B. 1987. *Multiple Imputation for Nonresponse in Surveys*. New York: Wiley.

Rubin, D.B. 1990a. Formal modes of statistical inference for causal effects. *Journal of Statistical Planning and Inference* 25, 279–92.

Rubin, D.B. 1990b. Neyman (1923) and causal inference in experiments and observational studies. *Statistical Science* 5, 472–80.

Rubin, D.B. 1991. Practical implications of modes of statistical inference for causal effects. *Biometrics* 47, 1213–34.

Rubin, D.B. 2000. The utility of counterfactuals for causal inference. Comment on A.P. Dawid, 'Causal inference without counterfactuals'. *Journal of the American Statistical Association* 95, 435–8.

Rubin, D.B. 2002. Using propensity scores to help design observational studies: application to the tobacco litigation. *Health Services and Outcomes Research Methodology* 2, 169–88.

Rubin, D.B. 2004a. *Multiple Imputation for Nonresponse in Surveys*. New York: Wiley. Reprinted with new appendices as a Wiley Classic.

Rubin, D.B. 2004b. Direct and indirect causal effects via potential outcomes. *Scandinavian Journal of Statistics* 31, 161–70 (with discussion and reply, 196–8).

Rubin, D.B. 2005. Causal inference using potential outcomes: design, modeling, decisions. 2004 Fisher Lecture. *Journal of the American Statistical Association* 100, 322–31.

Rubin, D.B. 2006a. *Matched Sampling for Causal Effects*. Cambridge: Cambridge University Press.

Rubin, D.B. 2006b. Causal inference through potential outcomes and principal stratification: applications to studies with 'censoring' due to death. *Statistical Science* 21, 299–321.

Rubin, D.B. 2007. Statistical inference for causal effects, with emphasis on applications in epidemiology and medical statistics. In *Handbook of Statistics: Epidemiology and Medical Statistics*, ed. C.R. Rao, J.P. Miller and D.C. Rao. Amsterdam: North-Holland.

Rubin, D.B. and Thomas, N. 1992a. Affinely invariant matching methods with ellipsoidal distributions. *Annals of Statistics* 20, 1079–93.

Rubin, D.B. and Thomas, N. 1992b. Characterizing the effect of matching using linear propensity score methods with normal covariates. *Biometrika* 79, 797–809.

Rubin, D.B. and Thomas, N. 1996. Matching using estimated propensity scores: relating theory to practice. *Biometrics* 52, 249–64.

Rubin, D.B. and Thomas, N. 2000. Combining propensity score matching with additional adjustments for prognostic covariates. *Journal of the American Statistical Association* 95, 573–85.

Tinbergen, J. 1930. Determination and interpretation of supply curves: an example. *Zeitschrift fur Nationalokonomie.* Reprinted in *The Foundations of Econometric Analysis*, ed. D.F. Hendry and M.S. Morgan. Cambridge: Cambridge University Press, 1997.

Zhang, J. and Rubin, D.B. 2003. Estimation of causal effects via principal stratification when some outcomes are truncated by 'death'. *Journal of Educational and Behavioral Statistics* 28, 353–68.

Zhang, J., Rubin, D. and Mealli, F. 2007. Evaluating the effects of job training programs on wages through principal stratification. *Advances in Econometrics* 21.

selection bias and self-selection

The problem of selection bias in economic and social statistics arises when a rule other than simple random sampling is used to sample the underlying population that is the object of interest. The distorted representation of a true population as a consequence of a sampling rule is the essence of the selection problem. Distorting selection rules may be the outcome of decisions of sample survey statisticians, self-selection decisions by the agents being studied, or both.

A random sample of a population produces a description of the population distribution of characteristics that has many desirable properties. One attractive feature of a random sample generated by the *known rule* that all individuals are equally likely to be sampled is that it produces a description of the population distribution of characteristics that becomes increasingly accurate as sample size expands.

A sample selected by any rule not equivalent to random sampling produces a description of the population distribution of characteristics that does not accurately describe the true population distribution of characteristics no matter how big the sample size. Unless the rule by which the sample is selected is known or can be recovered from the data, the selected sample cannot be used to produce an accurate description of the underlying population. For certain sampling rules, even knowledge of the rule generating the sample does not suffice to recover the population distribution from the sampled distribution.

This entry defines the problem of selection bias and presents conditions required to solve the problem. Examples of various types of commonly encountered sampling frames are given and specific economic selection mechanisms are presented. Assumptions required to use selected samples to determine features of the population distribution are discussed.

The analytical framework developed to understand the inferential problems raised by selection bias is also fruitful in understanding the economics of self-selection. The prototypical choice theoretic model of self-selection is that of Roy (1951). In his model, agents choose among a variety of discrete 'occupational' opportunities. Agents can pursue only one 'occupation' at a time. While every person can, in principle, do the work in each 'occupation', at least at some level of competence, self-interest drives individuals to choose that 'occupation' which produces the highest income (utility) for them. As in the statistical selection bias problem, there is a latent population (of skills). Observed (utilized) skill distributions are the outcome of a selection rule by agents. The relationship between observed and latent skill distributions is of considerable interest and underlies recent work on worker hierarchies (see Willis and Rosen, 1979). The 'occupations' can be: (a) market work or non-market work (b) unemployed and searching or working at the offered wage (c) working in one province or working in another, or (d) any choice among a set of mutually exclusive opportunities.

Because the insights in the Roy model underlie much recent research, we present a brief exposition of it and demonstrate how it can be or has been fruitfully extended to a variety of settings. An important issue, closely linked to the problem of identifying population parameters from selected sample distributions, is the empirical content of economic models of self-selection and worker hierarchies. Are they artefacts of distributional assumptions for unobservable skills or are they genuine behavioural hypotheses?

1. A definition and some examples of selection bias

Any selection bias model can be described by the following set-up. Let $\mathbf{Y}$ be a vector of outcomes of interest and let $\mathbf{X}$ be a vector of 'control' or 'explanatory' variables. The population distribution of $(\mathbf{Y}, \mathbf{X})$ is $F(\mathbf{y}, \mathbf{x})$. To simplify the exposition we assume that the density is well defined and write it as $f(\mathbf{y}, \mathbf{x})$.

Any sampling rule can be interpreted as producing a non-negative weighting function $\omega(\mathbf{y}, \mathbf{x})$ that alters the population density. Let $(\mathbf{Y}^*, \mathbf{X}^*)$ denote the sampled random variables. The density of the sampled data $g(\mathbf{y}^*, \mathbf{x}^*)$ may be written as

$$g(\mathbf{y}^*, \mathbf{x}^*) = \omega(\mathbf{y}^*, \mathbf{x}^*) f(\mathbf{y}^*, \mathbf{x}^*) / \int \omega(\mathbf{y}^*, \mathbf{x}^*) f(\mathbf{y}^*, \mathbf{x}^*) d\mathbf{y}^* d\mathbf{x}^* \tag{1.1}$$

where the denominator of the expression is introduced to make the density $g(\mathbf{y}^*, \mathbf{x}^*)$ integrate to one as is required for proper densities.

Alternatively, the weight may be defined as

$$\omega^*(\mathbf{y}^*, \mathbf{x}^*) = \frac{\omega(\mathbf{y}^*, \mathbf{x}^*)}{\int \omega(\mathbf{y}^*, \mathbf{x}^*) f(\mathbf{y}^*, \mathbf{x}^*) d\mathbf{y}^* d\mathbf{x}^*}$$

so that

$$g(\mathbf{y}^*, \mathbf{x}^*) = \omega^*(\mathbf{y}^*, \mathbf{x}^*) f(\mathbf{y}^*, \mathbf{x}^*). \tag{1.2}$$

Sampling schemes for which $\omega(\mathbf{y}, \mathbf{x}) = 0$ for some values of $(\mathbf{Y}, \mathbf{X})$ create special problems. For such schemes, not all values of $(\mathbf{Y}, \mathbf{X})$ are sampled. Let indicator variable $i(\mathbf{x}, \mathbf{y}) = 0$ if a potential observation at values $\mathbf{y}, \mathbf{x}$ cannot be sampled and let $i(\mathbf{y}, \mathbf{x}) = 1$ otherwise. Let $\Delta = 1$ record the occurrence of the event 'a potential observation is sampled, i.e. the value of $\mathbf{y}, \mathbf{x}$ is observed' and let $\Delta = 0$ if it is not. In the population, the proportion that is sampled is

$$\Pr(\Delta = 1) = \int i(\mathbf{y}, \mathbf{x}) f(\mathbf{y}, \mathbf{x}) d\mathbf{y} \, d\mathbf{x}. \tag{1.3}$$

while

$$\Pr(\Delta = 0) = 1 - \Pr(\Delta = 1).$$

For samples in which $\omega(\mathbf{y},\mathbf{x})=0$ for a non-negligible proportion of the population $(\Pr(\Delta=0)>0)$ it is clarifying to consider two cases. A *truncated sample* is one for which $\Pr(\Delta=1)$ is not known and cannot be consistently estimated. For such a sample, (1.1) is the density of all of the sampled $\mathbf{Y}$ and $\mathbf{X}$ values. A *censored sample* is one for which $\Pr(\Delta=1)$ is known or can be consistently estimated. The sampling rule in this case is such that values of $\mathbf{y},\mathbf{x}$ for which $\omega(\mathbf{y},\mathbf{x})=0$ are not known but it is known whether or not $i(\mathbf{y},\mathbf{x})=0$ for all values of $\mathbf{Y},\mathbf{X}$. In this case it is notationally convenient to define $(\mathbf{Y}^*,\mathbf{X}^*)=(\mathbf{0},\mathbf{0})$ for values of $\mathbf{y},\mathbf{x}$ such that $\omega(\mathbf{y},\mathbf{x})=i(\mathbf{y},\mathbf{x})=0$. Such a definition is innocuous provided that in the population there is no point mass (concentration of probability mass) at $(\mathbf{0},\mathbf{0})$. (Any value other than $(\mathbf{0},\mathbf{0})$ can be selected provided that there is no point mass at that value.) Given $\Delta=0$ the distribution of $\mathbf{Y}^*,\mathbf{X}^*$ is

$$G(\mathbf{y}^*,\mathbf{x}^*)=1 \quad \text{for} \quad \Delta=0$$

at

$$\mathbf{Y}^*=\mathbf{0} \quad \text{and} \quad \mathbf{X}^*=\mathbf{0}.$$

The joint density of $\mathbf{Y}^*,\mathbf{X}^*,\Delta$ for the case of a censored sample is obtained by combining (1.1) and (1.3). Thus

$$g(\mathbf{y}^*,\mathbf{x}^*,\delta)=\left[\frac{\omega(\mathbf{y}^*,\mathbf{x}^*)f(\mathbf{y}^*,\mathbf{x}^*)}{\int\omega(\mathbf{y}^*,\mathbf{x}^*)f(\mathbf{y}^*,\mathbf{x}^*)d\mathbf{y}^*\,d\mathbf{x}^*}\right]^\delta\left[\int i(\mathbf{y},\mathbf{x})f(\mathbf{y},\mathbf{x})d\mathbf{y}\,d\mathbf{x}\right]^\delta$$
$$\times [1]^{1-\delta}\left[\int(1-i(\mathbf{y},\mathbf{x}))f(\mathbf{y},\mathbf{x})d\mathbf{y}\,d\mathbf{x}\right]^{1-\delta}. \tag{1.4}$$

The first term on the right-hand side of (1.4) is the conditional density of $\mathbf{Y}^*,\mathbf{X}^*$ given $\Delta=1$. The second term is the probability that $\Delta=1$. The third term is the conditional density of $\mathbf{Y}^*,\mathbf{X}^*$ given $\Delta=0$. This density assigns unit mass to $\mathbf{y}^*=0$, $\mathbf{x}^*=0$ when $\Delta=0$. The fourth term is the probability that $\Delta=0$. Notice that in the case in which $\omega(\mathbf{y},\mathbf{x})>0$ for all $\mathbf{y},\mathbf{x}$, $\Delta=1$ and (1.4) is identical to (1.1).

In a random sample $\omega(\mathbf{y}^*,\mathbf{x}^*)=1$ (and so $\omega^*(\mathbf{y}^*,\mathbf{x}^*)=1$). In a selected sample, the sampling rule weights the data differently. Values of $(\mathbf{Y},\mathbf{X})$ are over-sampled or under-sampled relative to their occurrence in the population. In the case of truncated samples, the weight is zero for certain values of the outcome.

In many problems in economics, attention focuses on $f(\mathbf{y}|\mathbf{x})$, the conditional density of $\mathbf{Y}$ given $\mathbf{X}=\mathbf{x}$. In such problems knowledge of the population distribution of $\mathbf{X}$ is of no direct interest. If samples are selected solely on the $\mathbf{x}$ variables ('selection on the exogenous variables'), $\omega(\mathbf{y},\mathbf{x})=\omega(\mathbf{x})$ and there is no problem about using selected samples to make valid inference about the population conditional density.

This is so because in the case of selection on the exogenous variables

$$g(\mathbf{y}^*, \mathbf{x}^*) = f(\mathbf{y}^*|\mathbf{x}^*) \frac{\omega(\mathbf{x}^*)f(\mathbf{x}^*)}{\int \omega(\mathbf{x}^*)f(\mathbf{x}^*)d\mathbf{x}}$$

and

$$g(\mathbf{x}^*) \frac{\omega(\mathbf{x}^*)f(\mathbf{x}^*)}{\int \omega(\mathbf{x}^*)f(\mathbf{x}^*)d\mathbf{x}^*}.$$

Thus

$$g(\mathbf{y}^*|\mathbf{x}^*) = \frac{g(\mathbf{y}^*, \mathbf{x}^*)}{g(\mathbf{x}^*)} = f(\mathbf{y}^*|\mathbf{x}^*).$$

For such problems, sample selection distorts inference only if selection occurs on **y** (or **y** and **x**). Sampling on both **y** and **x** is termed *general stratified sampling*.

From a sample of data, it is not possible to recover the true density $f(\mathbf{y}, \mathbf{x})$ without knowledge of the weighting rule. On the other hand, if the weighting rule is known $(\omega(\mathbf{y}^*, \mathbf{x}^*))$ the density of the sampled data is known $(g(\mathbf{y}^*, \mathbf{x}^*))$, the support of $(\mathbf{y}, \mathbf{x})$ is known and $\omega(\mathbf{y}, \mathbf{x})$ is non-zero, then $f(\mathbf{y}, \mathbf{x})$ can always be recovered because

$$\frac{g(\mathbf{y}^*, \mathbf{x}^*)}{\omega(\mathbf{y}^*, \mathbf{x}^*)} = \frac{f(\mathbf{y}^*, \mathbf{x}^*)}{\int \omega(\mathbf{y}^*, \mathbf{x}^*)f(\mathbf{y}^*, \mathbf{x}^*)d\mathbf{y}^* \, d\mathbf{x}^*} \tag{1.5}$$

and by hypothesis both the numerator and denominator of the left-hand side are known. From the requirement that $(\mathbf{y}^*, \mathbf{x}^*)$ has a well defined density

$$\int f(\mathbf{y}^*, \mathbf{x}^*)d\mathbf{y}^* \, d\mathbf{x}^* = 1.$$

Integrating the left-hand side of (1.5) it is possible to determine $\int \omega(\mathbf{y}^*, \mathbf{x}^*)f(\mathbf{y}^*, \mathbf{x}^*)d\mathbf{y}^* \, d\mathbf{x}^*$ and hence to use (1.5) to recover the population density of the data.

The requirements that (a) the support of $(\mathbf{y}, \mathbf{x})$ is known and (b) $\omega(\mathbf{y}, \mathbf{x})$ is nonzero are not innocuous. In many important problems in economics requirement (b) is not satisfied: the sampling rule excludes observations for certain values of **y, x** and hence it is impossible without invoking further assumptions to determine the population distribution of $(\mathbf{Y}, \mathbf{X})$ at those values. If neither the support nor the weight is known, it is impossible, without invoking strong assumptions, to determine whether the fact that data are missing at certain **y, x** values is due to the sampling plan or that the population density has no support at those values. We now turn to some specific sampling plans of interest in economics.

Example 1

Data are collected on incomes of individuals whose income Y exceeds a certain value c (for cut-off value). The rule is to observe Y if $Y > c$. Thus $\omega(y) = 1$ if $y > c$ and

$\omega(y) = 0$ if $y \le c$. Because the weight is zero for some values of y, we know that knowledge of the sampling rule does *not* suffice to recover the population distribution. From a random sample of the entire population, the social scientist knows or can consistently estimate (a) the sample distribution of Y above c and (b) the proportion of the original random sample with income below c ($F(c)$ where F is the distribution function of Y). The social scientist does not observe values of Y below c.

In this example, observed income is a *truncated random variable*. The point of truncation is c. The *sample* of observed income is said to be *censored*. If the proportion of the original random sample with income below c is not known and cannot be consistently estimated, the *sample is truncated*. In a truncated sample, nothing is known about the proportion of the underlying population that can appear in the sample. A sample is truncated only if $\omega(\mathbf{y}) = 0$ for some intervals of $\mathbf{y}$ (for $\mathbf{y}$ continuous) or if $\omega(\mathbf{y}) = 0$ at values of $\mathbf{y}$ at which there is finite probability mass. In a censored sample, the proportion of the underlying population that can appear in the sample is known, at least to an arbitrarily high degree of approximation, as sample size increases.

Let $Y^* = Y$ if $Y > c$. Define $Y^* = 0$ otherwise (the choice of the value for Y^* when Y is not observed is inessential and any value can be used in place of 0 provided that the true distribution places no mass at the selected value). Define an indicator variable $\Delta = 1$ if $Y > c$. $\Delta = 0$ otherwise. Then the distribution of Y^* is

$$G(y^*|Y>0) = F(y^*|Y>c) = F(y^*|\delta = 1) = \frac{F(y^*)}{1 - F(c)}, \quad y^* > c. \tag{1.6a}$$

$$G(y^*|Y^*>0) = 1 \quad \text{for} \quad Y^* = 0(\Delta = 0). \tag{1.6b}$$

Observe that (1.6a) is obtained from (1.1) by setting $\omega(y^*) = 1$ if $y > c$, and $\omega(y^*) = 0$ otherwise, and integrating up with respect to y^*. The distribution of Δ is

$$\text{pr}(\Delta) = [1 - F(c)]^\delta [F(c)]^{1-\delta}.$$

The joint distribution of (Y^*, Δ) is

$$F(y^*, \delta) = F(y^*|\delta)\text{Pr}(\delta) = \left\{ \frac{F(y^*)}{(1 - F(c))} \right\}^\delta [1 - F(c)]^\delta (1)^{1-\delta} [F(c)]^{1-\delta} \tag{1.7}$$

$$= [F(y^*)]^\delta [F(c)]^{1-\delta}.$$

Note that (1.7) is obtained from (1.4) by setting $\omega(y) = 0, y < c, \omega(y) = 1$ otherwise, by setting $i(y) = \omega(y)$ and by integrating up with respect to y^*. For normally distributed Y, (1.7) is the 'Tobit' distribution.

The difference between the information in a truncated sample and the information in a censored sample is encapsulated in the contrast between (1.6a) and (1.7). Clearly there is more information in a censored sample than in a truncated sample because one can obtain (1.6a) from (1.7) (by conditioning on $\Delta = 1$) but not vice versa.

Inferences about the population distribution based on assuming that $F(y^*|Y>c)$ closely approximates $F(y)$ are potentially very misleading. A description of population income inequality based on a subsample of high income people may convey no information about the true population distribution.

Without further information about F and its support, it is not possible to recover F from $G(y^*)$ from either a censored or a truncated sample. Access to a censored sample enables the analyst to recover $F(y)$ for $y>c$ but obviously does not provide any information on the shape of the true distribution for values of $y \leq c$.

This problem is routinely 'solved' by assuming that F is of a known functional form. This solution strategy does not always work. If F is normal, then it can be recovered from a censored or truncated sample (Pearson, 1901). If F is Pareto, F cannot be recovered from either a truncated or a censored sample (see Flinn and Heckman, 1982). If F is real analytic (i.e. possesses derivatives of all order) and the support of Y is known, then F can be recovered (Heckman and Singer, 1985).

Example 2

Expand the discussion in the previous example to a linear regression setting. Let

$$Y = X\beta + U \tag{1.8}$$

be the population earnings function where Y is earnings, X is a regressor vector assumed to be distributed independently of mean zero disturbance U. 'β' is a suitably dimensioned parameter vector. Conventional assumptions are invoked to ensure that ordinary least squares applied to a random sample of earnings data consistently estimates β.

Data are collected on incomes of persons for whom Y exceeds c. Again the weight depends solely on y, i.e. $\omega(y, x) = 0, y \leq c, \omega(y, x) = 1, y>c$. The social scientist knows or can consistently estimate (a) the sample distribution of Y above c (b) the sample distribution of the X for Y above c and (c) the proportion of the original random sample with income below c. The social scientist does not observe values of Y below c.

As before, let $Y^* = Y$ if $Y>c$. Define $Y^* = 0$ otherwise. $\Delta = 1$ if $Y>c$, $\Delta = 0$ otherwise. The probability of the event $\Delta = 1$ given $X = x$ is

$$\Pr(\Delta = 1|X = x) = \Pr(Y>c|X = x) = \Pr(Y>c - x\beta|X = x).$$

Invoking independence between U and X and letting F_u denote the distribution of U,

$$\Pr(\Delta = 1|X = x) = 1 - F_u(c - x\beta) \tag{1.9a}$$

and

$$\Pr(\Delta = 0 | \mathbf{X} = \mathbf{x}) = F_u(c - \mathbf{x}\boldsymbol{\beta}). \tag{1.9b}$$

The distribution of Y^* conditional on $\mathbf{X}$ is

$$G(y^* | Y > 0, \mathbf{X} = \mathbf{x}) = F(y^* | \mathbf{X} = \mathbf{x}, Y > c) = F(y^* | \mathbf{X} = \mathbf{x}, \Delta = 1)$$

$$= \frac{F_u(y^* - \mathbf{x}\boldsymbol{\beta})}{1 - F_u(c - \mathbf{x}\boldsymbol{\beta})}, \quad y^* > c. \tag{1.10a}$$

$$G(y^* | Y \leq 0) = 1 \quad \text{for} \quad Y^* = 0 (\Delta = 0). \tag{1.10b}$$

The joint distribution of (Y^*, Δ) given $\mathbf{X} = \mathbf{x}$ is

$$F(y^*, \delta | \mathbf{X} = \mathbf{x}) = F(y^* | \delta, \mathbf{x}) \Pr(\delta | \mathbf{x}).$$

$$= \{F_u(y^* - \mathbf{x}\boldsymbol{\beta})\}^{\delta} \{F_u(c - \mathbf{x}\boldsymbol{\beta})\}^{1-\delta}. \tag{1.11}$$

In particular,

$$E(Y^* | \mathbf{X} = \mathbf{x}, \Delta = 1) = \mathbf{x}\boldsymbol{\beta} + E(U | \mathbf{X} = \mathbf{x}, \delta = 1)$$

$$= \mathbf{x}\boldsymbol{\beta} + \int_{c - \mathbf{x}\boldsymbol{\beta}}^{\infty} \frac{z \, dF_u(z)}{(1 - F_u(c - \mathbf{x}\boldsymbol{\beta}))} \tag{1.12}$$

where z is a dummy variable of integration. In contrast, the population mean regression function is

$$E(Y | \mathbf{X} = \mathbf{x}) = \mathbf{x}\boldsymbol{\beta}. \tag{1.13}$$

The contrast between (1.12) and (1.13) is illuminating. Many behavioural theories in social science produce empirical counterparts of (1.8) with population conditional expectations like (1.13). Such theories sometimes restrict the signs, permissible values and other relationships among the coefficients in $\boldsymbol{\beta}$. When the theoretical model is estimated on a selected sample ($\Delta = 1$) the true conditional expectation is (1.12) not (1.13). The conditional mean of U depends on $\mathbf{x}$. In terms of conventional omitted variable analysis, $E(U | \mathbf{X} = \mathbf{x}, \Delta = 1)$ is omitted from the regression. Since this term is a function of $\mathbf{x}$ it is likely to be correlated with $\mathbf{x}$. Least squares estimates of $\boldsymbol{\beta}$ obtained on selected samples which do not account for selection are biased and inconsistent.

To illustrate the nature of the bias, it is useful to draw on the work of Cain and Watts (1973). Suppose that X is a scalar random variable (e.g. education) and that its associated coefficient is positive ($\beta > 0$). Under conventional assumptions about U (e.g. mean zero, independently and identically distributed and distributed independently of X), the population regression of Y on X is a straight line. The scatter about the regression line and the regression line are given in Figure 1. When $Y > c$ is imposed

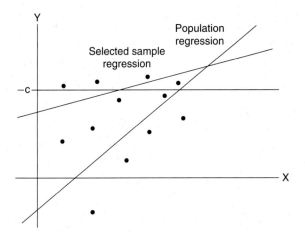

Figure 1

as a sample inclusion requirement, lower population values of U are excluded from the sample in a way that systematically depends on x ($Y > c$ or $U > c - x\beta$). As x increases, the conditional mean of $U[E(U|X = x, \Delta = 1)]$ decreases. Regression estimates of β that do not correct for sample selection (that is, include $E(U|X = x, \Delta = 1)$ as a regressor) are downward biased because of the negative correlation between x and $E(U|X = x, \Delta = 1)$. See the flattened regression line for the selected sample in Figure 1.

In models with more than one regressor, no sharp result on the sign of the bias in the regression estimate that results from ignoring the selected nature of the sample is available except when the **X** variables are from certain distributions (e.g. normal, see Goldberger, 1983). None the less, the key result – that conventional least squares estimates of $\boldsymbol{\beta}$ obtained from selected samples are biased and inconsistent – remains true.

As in example 1, it is fruitful to distinguish between the case of a truncated sample and the case of a censored sample. In the truncated sample case, no information is available about the fraction of the population that would be allocated to the truncated sample [$\Pr(\Delta = 1)$]. In the censored sample case, this fraction is known or can be consistently estimated. In the censored sample case it is fruitful to distinguish two further cases: (a) the case in which **X** is not observed when $\Delta = 0$ and (b) the case in which it is. Case (b) is the one most fully developed in the literature (Heckman and MaCurdy, 1981).

Note that the conditional mean $E(U|X = \mathbf{x}, \Delta = 1)$ is a function of $c - \mathbf{x}\beta$ solely through $\Pr(\Delta = 1|\mathbf{x})$. Since $\Pr(\Delta = 1|\mathbf{x})$ is monotonic in $c - \mathbf{x}\beta$ the conditional mean depends solely on $\Pr(\Delta = 1|\mathbf{x})$ and the parameters F_{u} i.e. since

$$F_{\mathrm{u}}^{-1}(1 - \Pr(\Delta = 1|\mathbf{x})) = c - \mathbf{x}\beta,$$

$$E(U|\mathbf{X} = \mathbf{x}, \Delta = 1) = \int_{F_{\mathrm{u}}^{-1}[1 - \Pr(\Delta = 1|\mathbf{x})]}^{\infty} \frac{z \, dF_{\mathrm{u}}(z)}{\Pr(\Delta = 1|\mathbf{x})}.$$

This relationship demonstrates that the conditional mean is a function of the probability of selection. As the probability of selection goes to 1, the conditional mean goes to zero. For samples chosen so that the values of $\mathbf{x}$ are such that the observations are certain to be included in the sample, there is no problem in using ordinary least squares on selected samples to estimate β. Thus in Figure 1, ordinary least squares regressions fit on samples selected to have large $\mathbf{x}$ values closely approximate the true regression function and become arbitrarily close as $\mathbf{x}$ becomes large. The condition mean in (1.12) is a surrogate for $\Pr(\Delta = 1|\mathbf{x})$. As this probability goes to one, the problem of sample selection in regression analysis becomes negligibly small.

Heckman (1976) demonstrates that β and F_u are identified if U is normally distributed and standard conditions invoked in regression analysis are satisfied. Gallant and Nychka (1984) and Cosslett (1984) establish conditions for identification for non-normal U. In their analyses, F_u is consistently non-parametrically estimated.

Example 3

The next example considers *censored random variables*. This concept extends the notion of a truncated random variable by letting a more general rule than truncation on the outcome of interest generate the selected sample. Because the sample generating rule may be different from a simple truncation of the outcome being studied, the concept of a censored random variable in general requires at least two distinct random variables.

Let Y_1 be the outcome of interest. Let Y_2 be another random variable. Denote observed Y_1 by Y_1^*. If $Y_2 < c$, Y_1 is observed. Otherwise Y_1 is not observed and we can set $Y_1^* = 0$ or any other convenient value (assuming that Y_1 has no point mass at $Y_1 = 0$ or at the alternative convenient value). In terms of the weighting function ω, $\omega(y_1, y_2) = 0$ if $y_2 > c$, $\omega(y_1, y_2) = 1$ if $y_2 \leq c$.

Selection rule $Y_2 < c$ does not necessarily restrict the range of Y_1. Thus Y_1^* is not in general a truncated random variable. Define $\Delta = 1$ if $Y_2 < c$; $\Delta = 0$ otherwise. If $F(y_1, y_2)$ is the population distribution of (Y_1, Y_2), the distribution of Δ is

$$\Pr(\Delta = \delta) = [1 - F_2(c)]^{1-\delta}[F_2(c)]^{\delta}, \quad \delta = 0, 1,$$

where F_2 is the marginal distribution of Y_2. The distribution of Y_1^* is

$$G(y_1^*) = F(y_1^*|\delta = 1) = \frac{F(y_1^*, c)}{F_2(c)}, \quad \Delta = 1, \tag{1.14a}$$

$$G(y_1^* = 0) = 1, \quad \Delta = 0. \tag{1.14b}$$

Note that (1.14a) is the distribution function corresponding to the density in (1.1) when $\omega(y_1, y_2) = 1$ if $y_2 \leq c$ and $\omega(y_1, y_2) = 0$ otherwise.

The joint distribution of (Y_1^*, Δ) is

$$G(y_1^*, \delta) = [F(y_1^*, c)]^{\delta}[1 - F_2(c)]^{1-\delta}. \tag{1.15}$$

This is the distribution function corresponding to density (1.4) for the special weighting rule of this example. In a censored sample, under general conditions it is possible to consistently estimate $\Pr(\Delta = \delta)$ and $G(y_1^*)$. In a truncated sample, only conditional distribution (1.14a) can be estimated. A degenerate version of this model has $Y_1 \equiv Y_2$. In that case, censored random variable Y_1 is also a truncated random variable. Note that a censored random variable may be defined for a truncated or censored sample.

Example 3 and variants of it have wide applicability in economics. Let Y_1 be the wage of a woman. Wages of women are observed only if women work. Let Y_2 be an index of a woman's propensity to work. In Gronau (1974) and Heckman (1974), Y_2 is postulated as the difference between reservation wages (the value of time at home determined from household preference functions) and potential market wages Y_1. Then if $Y_2 < 0$, the woman works. Otherwise, she does not. $Y_1^* = Y_1$ if $Y_2 < 0$ is the observed wage.

If Y_1 is the offered wage of an unemployed worker, and Y_2 is the difference between reservation wages (the return to searching) and offered market wages, $Y_1^* = Y_1$ if $Y_2 < 0$ is the accepted wage for an unemployed worker (see Flinn and Heckman, 1982). If Y_1 is the potential output of a firm and Y_2 is its profitability, $Y_1^* = Y_1$ if $Y_2 > 0$. If Y_1 is the potential income in occupation one and Y_2 is the potential income in occupation two, $Y_1^* = Y_1$ if $Y_1 - Y_2 < 0$ while $Y_2^* = Y_2$ if $Y_1 - Y_2 \geq 0$. We develop this example at length in section 2 where we consider explicit economic models of self-selection. There we discuss the identifiability of this model.

Example 4

This example builds on example 3 by introducing regressors. This produces the *censored regression model* (Heckman, 1976; 1979). In example 3 set

$$Y_1 = \mathbf{X}_1 \boldsymbol{\beta}_1 + U_1 \tag{1.16a}$$

$$Y_2 = \mathbf{X}_2 \boldsymbol{\beta}_2 + U_2 \tag{1.16b}$$

where $(\mathbf{X}_1, \mathbf{X}_2)$ are distributed independently of (U_1, U_2), a mean zero, finite variance random vector. Conventional assumptions are invoked to ensure that if Y_1 and Y_2 can be observed, least squares applied to a random sample of data on $(Y_1, Y_2, \mathbf{X}_1, \mathbf{X}_2)$ would consistently estimate $\boldsymbol{\beta}_1$ and $\boldsymbol{\beta}_2$. $Y_1^* = Y_1$ if $Y_2 < 0$. If $Y_2 < 0$, $\Delta = 1$. Then the regression function for the selected sample is

$$E(Y_1^* | \mathbf{X}_1 = \mathbf{x}_1, Y_2 < 0) = E(Y_1^* | \mathbf{X}_1 = \mathbf{x}_1, \Delta = 1) = \mathbf{X}_1 \boldsymbol{\beta}_1 + E(U_1 | \mathbf{X}_1 = \mathbf{x}_1, \Delta = 1) \tag{1.17}$$

and the regression function for the population is

$$E(Y_1 | \mathbf{X}_1 = \mathbf{x}_1) = \mathbf{X}_1 \boldsymbol{\beta}_1. \tag{1.18}$$

As in the regression analysis of truncated random variables, there is an illuminating contrast between the conditional expectation for the selected sample (1.17) and the population regression function (1.18). The two functions differ by the conditional mean of $U_1[E(U_1|\mathbf{X}_1 = \mathbf{x}_1, \Delta = 1)]$. In the regression analysis of truncated random variables, ordinary least squares estimates of $\boldsymbol{\beta}$ (in equation (1.14)) are biased and inconsistent because the conditional mean is improperly omitted from the selected sample regression. The same analysis applies to the regression analysis of censored random variables. The conditional mean is a surrogate for the probability of selection $[\Pr(\Delta = 1|\mathbf{x}_2)]$. As $\Pr(\Delta = 1|\mathbf{x}_2)$ goes to one, the problem of sample selection bias becomes negligible. However, in the censored regression case, a new phenomenon appears. If there are variables in $\mathbf{X}_2$ not in $\mathbf{X}_1$, such variables may appear to be statistically important determinants of Y_1 when ordinary least squares is applied to data generated from censored samples.

As an example, suppose that survey statisticians use some extraneous (to $\mathbf{X}_1$) variables to determine sample enrolment. Such variables may appear to be important determinants of Y_1 when in fact they are not. They are important determinants of Y_1^*. In an analysis of self-selection, let Y_1 be the wage that a potential worker could earn were he to accept a market offer. Let Y_2 be the difference between the best non-market opportunity available to the potential worker and Y_1. If $Y_2 < 0$, the agent works. The conditional expectation of observed wages ($Y_1^* = Y$ if $Y_2 < 0$) given $\mathbf{x}_1$ and $\mathbf{x}_2$ will be a non-trivial function of $\mathbf{x}_2$. Thus variables determining non-market opportunities will determine Y_1^*, even though they do not determine Y_1. For example, the number of children less than six may appear to be significant determinants of Y_1 when inadequate account is taken of sample selection, even though the market does not place any value or penalty on small children in generating wage offers for potential workers.

Heckman (1976) develops the analysis of this model when (U_1, U_2) is normally distributed. Gallant and Nychka (1984) and Cosslett (1984) demonstrate that under mild restrictions on $F(u_1, u_2)$, if there is one continuous valued variable in $\mathbf{X}_2$ not in $\mathbf{X}_1$ (so that there is no exact linear dependence between $\mathbf{X}_2$ and $\mathbf{X}_1$), $\boldsymbol{\beta}_1, \boldsymbol{\beta}_2$ and $F(u_1, u_2)$ can be consistently non-parametrically estimated. Heckman and MaCurdy (1986) develop this class of models at length.

Example 5

This example demonstrates how self-selection bias affects the interpretation placed on estimated consumer demand functions when there is self-selection. We postulate a population of consumers with a quasi-concave utility function $U(\mathbf{Z}, E)$ which depends on the consumption of goods and preference shock E which represents heterogeneity in preferences among consumers. The support of E is $\mathbf{E}$. For price vector $\mathbf{P}$ and endowment income M, the consumer's problem is to

$$\text{Max } U(\mathbf{Z}, E) \quad \text{subject to} \quad \mathbf{P}'\mathbf{Z} \leq M.$$

In the population **P** and M are distributed independently of E. First-order conditions for this problem are

$$\frac{\partial U(\mathbf{Z}, E)}{\partial \mathbf{Z}} \le \lambda \mathbf{P}, \tag{1.19}$$

where λ is the Lagrange multiplier associated with the budget constraint. Focusing on the demand for the first good, Z_1, none of it is purchased if at zero consumption of Z_1

$$\frac{\partial U(\mathbf{Z}, E)}{\partial Z_1}\bigg|_{Z_1=0} \le \lambda P_1. \tag{1.20}$$

that is, marginal valuation is less than marginal cost in utility terms. Conventional interior solution demand functions for Z_1 are defined for a given **P**, M only for values of E such that

$$\frac{\partial U(\mathbf{Z}, E)}{\partial Z_1}\bigg|_{Z_1=0} \ge \lambda P_1. \tag{1.21}$$

Let the set of E for which conventional interior solution consumer demand functions for Z_1 are defined be denoted by $\underline{E}$. Then

$$\underline{E} = \left\{ E \ \text{such that} \frac{\partial U(\mathbf{Z}, E)}{\partial Z_1}\bigg|_{Z_1=0} \ge \lambda P_1 \ \text{for given} \ \mathbf{P}, M \right\}.$$

Let $\Delta_1 = 0$ if the consumer does not purchase Z_1. Let $\Delta_1 = 1$ otherwise. If $F(\varepsilon)$ is the population distribution of E, the proportion purchasing none of good Z_1 given $\mathbf{P}, M$ is

$$\Pr(\Delta_1 = 0 | \mathbf{P}, M) = 1 - \int_{\underline{E}} dF(\varepsilon).$$

Provided inequality (1.21) is satisfied, $\Delta_1 = 1$ and interior solution demand function

$$Z_1 = Z_1(\mathbf{P}, M, E) \tag{1.22}$$

is well defined and $Z_1 = Z_1^*$. When $\Delta_1 = 0$, observed $Z_1 = Z_1^* = 0$.

Equation (1.22) is the conventional object of interest in consumer theory. Partial derivatives of that function *holding E and the other arguments constant* have well defined economic interpretations. Suppose that some non-negligible proportion of the population buys none of good Z_1. Regression estimates of the parameters of (1.22) using Z_1^* approximate the conditional expectation

$$E(Z_1 | \Delta_1 = 1, \mathbf{P}, M) = \int_{\underline{E}} Z_1(\mathbf{P}, M, \varepsilon) dF(\varepsilon). \tag{1.23}$$

The derivatives of (1.23) are different from the derivatives of (1.22). In order to define these derivatives, it is helpful to define $I_{\underline{E}}(E)$ as an indicator function for set $\underline{E}$ which equals one if $E \in \underline{E}$ and equals zero otherwise. When prices or income change, the set of values of E that satisfy inequality (1.21) changes. Let $\underline{E} + \Delta \underline{E}_{\mathbf{P}}$ be the set of E values that satisfy (1.21) when there is a finite price change $\Delta \mathbf{P}$. $I_{\underline{E} + \Delta \underline{E}_P}(E)$ is an indicator function which equals one when $E \in \underline{E} + \Delta \underline{E}\mathbf{P}$. Then the derivatives of (1.23) are, for the jth price

$$
\frac{\partial E(Z_1 | \Delta = 1, \mathbf{P}, M)}{\partial P_j} = \int_{\underline{E}} \frac{\partial Z_1(\mathbf{P}, M, \varepsilon)}{\partial P_j} dF(\varepsilon)
$$
$$
+ \lim_{\Delta P_j \to 0} \int_{\underline{E}} \frac{[(I_{\underline{E} + \Delta \underline{E}_{P_j}}(\varepsilon) - I_{\underline{E}}(\varepsilon)) Z(\mathbf{P}, M, \varepsilon)]}{\Delta P_j} dF(\varepsilon). \tag{1.24}
$$

When the limit in the second term does not exist, the derivative does not exist. We assume for expositional convenience that the limit is well defined.

The first expression on the right-hand side of (1.24) is the average effect of price change on commodity demand. The second term on the right-hand side of (1.24) arises from the change in sample composition of E as the proportion of non-purchasers changes in response to price change. This term generates the selection bias.

Neither term is the same as the price derivative of (1.22) for an arbitrary value of $E = \varepsilon$ although the first term on the right-hand side of (1.24) approximates the price derivative of (1.22) for some value of $E = \varepsilon$.

A similar decomposition of the derivatives of the conditional demand function can be performed if it is defined solely for a sample of non-zero purchasers (see Heckman and MaCurdy, 1981; 1986).

Just as in the statistical sample selection bias problem, there is a population of interest. In this case, the population parameters of interest are the distribution of E and the parameters of $U(\mathbf{Z}, E)$. Those who buy Z_1 are a self-selected sample of the population. Estimates of population parameters estimated on self-selected samples are biased and inconsistent. There is a population distribution of $Z_1(\mathbf{P}, M, E)$ generated by the distribution of E. Observations of Z_1 are obtained only if $E \in \underline{E}(\omega(E) = 1$ if $E \in \underline{E}$, $\omega(E) = 0$ otherwise). Alternatively one can express the inclusion criteria in terms of the latent population distribution of Z_1 induced by E (given $\mathbf{P}$ and M) *and write* $\omega(z_1) = 1$ if $z_1 > 0, \omega(z_1) = 0$ if $z_1 \le 0$.

Heckman (1974) and Heckman and MaCurdy (1981) provide further discussion of this type of model which is widely used in applied economics and consider issues of identifiability for such models.

Example 6. Length biased sampling

Let T be the duration of an event such as a completed unemployment spell or a completed duration of a job with an employer. The population distribution of T is $F(t)$ with density $f(t)$. The sampling rule is such that *individuals* are sampled at random. Data are recorded on a completed spell *provided that at the time of the interview the individual is experiencing the event*. Such sampling rules are in wide use in many national surveys of employment and unemployment.

In order to have a sampled completed spell, a person must be in the state at the time of the interview. Let '0' be the date of the survey. Decompose any completed spell T into a component that occurs before the survey T_b and a component that occurs after the survey T_a. Then $T = T_a + T_b$. For a person to be sampled, $T_b > 0$. The density of T given $T_b = t_b$ is

$$f(t|t_b) = \frac{f(t)}{1 - F(t_b)}, \quad t \geq t_b. \tag{1.25}$$

Suppose that the environment is stationary. The population entry rate into the state at each instant of time is k. From each vintage of entrants into the state distinguished by their distance from the survey date t_b, only $1 - F(t_b) = \Pr(T > t_b)$ survive. Aggregating over all cohorts of entrants, the population proportion in the state at the date of the interview is P where

$$P = \int_0^\infty k(1 - F(t_b))dt_b \tag{1.26}$$

which is assumed to exist. The density of T_b^*, sampled pre-survey duration, is

$$g(t_b^*|t_b^* > 0) = \frac{k(1 - F(t_b^*))}{P}. \tag{1.27}$$

The density of sampled completed durations is thus

$$g(t^*) = \int_0^{t^*} f(t^*|t_b^*)g(t_b^*|t_b^* > 0)dt_b^* = k\frac{f(t^*)}{1 - F(t_b^*)}\frac{1 - F(t_b^*)}{P}\int_0^{t^*} dt_b^* = k\frac{t^* f(t^*)}{P}.$$

Observe from (1.26) that by a standard integration by parts argument

$$P = k\int_0^\infty (1 - F(z))dz = k\int_0^\infty z\, dF(z) = kE(T).$$

Note that

$$g(t^*) = \frac{t^* f(t^*)}{E(T)}. \tag{1.28}$$

In this form (1.28) is equivalent to (1.1) with $\omega(t) = t$. Hence the term 'length biased sampling'. Intuitively, longer spells are oversampled when the requirement is imposed that a spell be in progress at the time the survey is conducted ($T_b > 0$). Suppose, instead, that individuals are randomly sampled and data are recorded on the *next* spell of the event (after the survey date). As long as successive spells are independent, such a sampling frame does not distort the sampled distribution because no requirement is imposed that the sampled spell be in progress at the date of the interview. It is important to notice that the source of the bias is the requirement that $T_b > 0$, not that only a fraction of the population experiences the event $(P < 1)$.

The simple length weight $(\omega(t) = t)$ that produces (1.28) is an artefact of the stationarity assumption. Heckman and Singer (1985) consider the consequences of non-stationarity and un-observables when there is selection on the event that a person be in the state at the time of the interview. They also demonstrate the bias that results from estimating parametric models on samples generated by length biased sampling rules when inadequate account is taken of the sampling plan. Vardi (1983, 1985) and Gill and Wellner (1985) consider nonparametric identification and estimation of models with densities of the form (1.28).

It is unfortunate that the lessons of length biased sampling are not adequately appreciated in economics. Two widely cited studies by Clark and Summers (1979) and Hall (1982) use length biased data to prove, respectively, that unemployment and employment spells are 'surprisingly long'. Whether their findings are artefacts of sampling plans remains to be determined.

Example 7. Choice based sampling

Let D be a discrete valued random variable which assumes a finite number of values I. $D = i$, $i = 1, \ldots, I$ corresponds to the occurrence of state i. States are mutually exclusive. In the literature the states may be modes of transportation choice for commuters (Domencich and McFadden, 1975), occupations, migration destinations, financial solvency status of firms, schooling choices of students, etc. Interest centres on estimating a population choice model

$$\Pr(D = i | \mathbf{X} = \mathbf{x}), \quad i = 1, \ldots, I. \tag{1.29}$$

The population density of $(D, \mathbf{X})$ is

$$f(d, \mathbf{x}) = \Pr(D = d | \mathbf{X} = \mathbf{x})h(\mathbf{x}) \tag{1.30}$$

where $h(\mathbf{x})$ is the density of the data.

In many problems, plentiful data are available on certain outcomes while data are scarce for other outcomes. For example, interviews about transportation preferences conducted at train stations tend to over-sample train riders and under-sample bus riders. Interviews about occupational choice preferences conducted at leading universities over-sample those who select professional occupations.

In choice based sampling, selection occurs solely on the D coordinate of $(D, \mathbf{X})$. In terms of (1.1) (extended to allow for discrete random variables), $\omega(d, \mathbf{X}) = \omega(d)$. Then sampled $(D^*, \mathbf{X}^*)$ has density

$$g(d^*, \mathbf{x}^*) = \frac{\omega(d^*)f(d^*, \mathbf{x}^*)}{\sum\limits_{i=1}^{I} \int \omega(i)f(i, x^*)\mathrm{d}x^*} \tag{1.31}$$

Notice that the denominator can be simplified to

$$\sum_{i=1}^{I} \omega(i) f(i)$$

where $f(d^*)$ is the marginal distribution of D^* so that

$$g(d^*, \mathbf{x}^*) = \frac{\omega(d^*) f(d^*, \mathbf{x}^*)}{\sum_{i=1}^{I} \omega(i) f(i)} \tag{1.32}$$

Also, integrating (1.31) with respect to $\mathbf{x}$ using (1.32) we obtain

$$g(d^*) = \frac{\omega(d^*) f(d^*)}{\sum_{i=1}^{I} \omega(i) f(i)} \tag{1.33}$$

which makes transparent how the sampling rule causes the sampled proportions to deviate from the population proportions. Note further that as a consequence of sampling only on D, the population conditional density

$$h(\mathbf{x}^* | d^*) = \frac{f(d^*, \mathbf{x}^*)}{f(d^*)} \tag{1.34}$$

can be recovered from the choice-based sample. The density of $\mathbf{x}$ in the sample is thus

$$g(\mathbf{x}^*) = \sum_{i=1}^{I} h(\mathbf{x}^* | i) g(i). \tag{1.35}$$

Then using (1.32)–(1.35) we reach

$$g(d^* | \mathbf{x}^*) = f(d^* | \mathbf{x}^*) \times \left\{ \left[\frac{\omega(d^*)}{\sum_{i=1}^{I} \omega(i) f(i)} \right] \left[\frac{1}{\sum_{i=1}^{I} f(i | \mathbf{x}^*) \frac{g(i)}{f(i)}} \right] \right\}. \tag{1.36}$$

The bias that results from using choice based samples to make inference about $f(d^* | \mathbf{x}^*)$ is a consequence of neglecting the terms in braces on the right-hand side of (1.36). Notice that if the data are generated by a random sampling rule, $\omega(d^*) = 1$, $g(d^*) = f(d^*)$ and the term in braces is one.

    Manski and Lerman (1977), Manski and McFadden (1981) and Cosslett (1981) provide illuminating discussions of choice based sampling.

Example 8. Size biased sampling

Let N be the number of children in a family. $f(N)$ is the density of discrete random variable N. Suppose that family size is recorded only when at least one child is interviewed. Suppose further that each child has an independent and identical chance β of being interviewed. The probability of sampled family size of $N^* = n^*$ is

$$g(n^*) = \frac{\omega(n^*)f(n^*)}{E[\omega(N^*)]} \tag{1.37}$$

where $\omega(n^*) = 1 - (1 - \beta)^{n^*}$ (the probability that at least one child from a family of size n^* will be sampled) and

$$E[\omega(N^*)] = \sum_{n^*}(1 - (1 - \beta)^{n^*})f(n^*)$$

is the probability of observing a family. In a large population $\beta \to 0$ with increasing population size. Using l'Hospital's rule, and assuming that passage to the limit under the summation sign is valid

$$\lim_{\beta \to 0} g(n^*) = \frac{n^*f(n^*)}{E(N^*)} \tag{1.38}$$

Thus the limit form of (1.37) is identical to (1.28). Larger families tend to be oversampled and hence a misleading estimate of family size will be produced from such samples. Since the model is formally equivalent to the length biased sampling model, all references and statements about identification given in example 6 apply with full force to this example. See the discussion in Rao (1965).

2. Economic models of self-selection

We begin our analysis by expositing the Roy model of self-selection for workers with heterogeneous skills. The statistical framework for this model has been outlined in examples 3 and 4. Following Roy, we assume that there are two market sectors in which income-maximizing agents can work. Agents are free to enter the sector that gives them the highest income. However, they can work in only one sector at a time.

Each sector requires a unique sector-specific task. Each agent has two skills, T_1 and T_2, which he cannot use simultaneously. The model is short run in that aggregate skill distributions are assumed to be given. There are no costs of changing sectors, and investment is ignored. Because of this assumption, the model presented here applies to environments with certain or uncertain prices for sector-specific tasks. For simplicity and without any loss of generality (given the preceding assumptions), we assume an environment of perfect certainty.

Let T_i be the amount of sector i specific task a worker can perform. The price of task i is π_i. An agent works in sector 1 if his income is higher there, that is

$$\pi_1 T_1 > \pi_2 T_2 \tag{2.1}$$

Indifference between sectors is a negligible probability event if the $T_i = 1,2$ are assumed to be continuous nondegenerate random variables. Throughout we assume that prices are positive ($\pi_i > 0$).

The log wage in task i of an individual with endowment T_i is

$$\ln W_i = \ln \pi_i + \ln T_i \qquad (2.2)$$

The proportion of the population working at task i is the proportion of the population for whom

$$T_1 > \frac{\pi_2}{\pi_1} T_2.$$

Roy assumes that ($\ln T_1$, $\ln T_2$) is normally distributed with mean (μ_1, μ_2) and covariance matrix Σ. Letting (U_1, U_2) be a mean zero normal vector, agents in the Roy model choose between two possible wages:

$$\ln W_1 = \ln \pi_1 + \mu_1 + U_1$$

or

$$\ln W_2 = \ln \pi_2 + \mu_2 + U_2.$$

Workers enter sector 1 if $\ln W_1 > \ln W_2$. Otherwise they enter sector 2.

Letting

$$\sigma^* = \sqrt{\text{var}(U_1 - U_2)}$$

and

$$c_i = (\ln(\pi_i/\pi_j) + \mu_i - \mu_j)/\sigma^*, \quad i \neq j,$$

$$\Pr(i) = P(\ln W_i > \ln W_j) = \Phi(c_i), \quad i \neq j, \quad i,j = 1,2$$

where $\Phi(\ )$ is the cumulative distribution function of a standard normal variable. When standard sample selection bias formulae are used (see, e.g. Heckman, 1976), the mean of log wages observed in sector i is

$$E(\ln W_i | \ln W_i > \ln W_j) = \ln \pi_i + \mu_i + \frac{\sigma_{ii} - \sigma_{ij}}{\sigma^*} \lambda(c_i), \quad i,j = 1,2, \ i \neq j, \qquad (2.3)$$

where

$$\lambda(c) = \frac{\frac{1}{\sqrt{2\pi}} \exp\left(-\tfrac{1}{2}c^2\right)}{\Phi(c)}$$

is a convex monotone decreasing function of c with $\lambda(c) \geq 0$ and

$$\lim_{c \to \infty} \lambda(c) = 0, \ \lim_{c \to -\infty} \lambda(c) = \infty.$$

Convexity is proved in Heckman and Honoré (1986).

The variance of log wages observed in sector i

$$\text{var}(\ln W_i | \ln W_i > \ln W_j) = \sigma_{ii}\{\rho_i^2[1 - c_i\lambda(c_i) - \lambda^2(c_i)] \\ + (1 - \rho_i^2)\}, \ i \neq j \tag{2.4}$$

where $\rho_i = \text{correl}(U_i, U_i - U_j), i \neq j = 1, 2$. The variance of the log of observed wages never exceeds σ_{ii}, the population variance, because the term in braces in (2.4) is never greater than unity. In general, sectoral variances decrease with increased selection. For example, if ρ_1 and ρ_2 do not equal zero, as π_1 increases with π_2 held fixed so that people shift from sector 2 to sector 1, the variance in the log of wages in sector 1 increases while the variance in the log of wages in sector 2 decreases.

Using the fact that $W_i = \pi_i T_i$, we may use (2.3) to write

$$E(\ln T_1 | \ln W_1 > \ln W_2) = \mu_1 + \frac{\sigma_{11} - \sigma_{12}}{\sigma^*} \lambda(c_1), \tag{2.5a}$$

$$E(\ln T_2 | \ln W_1 > \ln W_2) = \mu_2 + \frac{\sigma_{22} - \sigma_{12}}{\sigma^*} \lambda(c_2). \tag{2.5b}$$

Focusing on (2.5a) and noting that λ is positive for all values of c_1 (except $c_1 = \infty$), the mean of log task 1 used in sector 1 exceeds, equals, or falls short of the population mean endowment of log task 1 as $\sigma_{11} - \sigma_{12}$ is greater than, equal to, or less than zero. If endowments of tasks are uncorrelated ($\sigma_{12} = 0$) self-selection always causes the mean of $\ln T_1$ employed in sector 1 to be above the population mean μ_1. The opposite case occurs when $\sigma_{11} - \sigma_{12}$ is negative. This case can arise only when values of $\ln T_1$ and $\ln T_2$ are sufficiently positively correlated. If this occurs, the mean of log task 1 used in sector 1 falls below the population mean μ_1. Since covariance matrices must be positive semi-definite, $\sigma_{11} + \sigma_{22} - 2\sigma_{12} \geq 0$. Thus if $\sigma_{11} - \sigma_{12} < 0, \sigma_{22} - \sigma_{12} > 0$ so the mean of log task 2 employed in sector 2 necessarily lies above the population mean μ_2. In the Roy model the unusual case can arise in at most one sector. Notice from (2.5) that only if $\sigma_{11} - \sigma_{12} = 0$ (so $\rho_1^2 = 0$) is the variance of log task 1 employed in sector 1 identical to the variance of log task 1 in the population. Otherwise, the sectoral variance of observed log task 1 is less than the population variance of log task 1.

To gain further insight into the effect of self-selection on the distribution of earnings for workers in sector 1, it is helpful to draw on some results from normal regression theory. The regression equation for $\ln T_2$ conditional on $\ln T_1$ is

$$\ln T_2 = \mu_2 + \frac{\sigma_{12}}{\sigma_{11}}(\ln T_1 - \mu_1) + \varepsilon_2, \tag{2.6}$$

where $E(\varepsilon_2) = 0$ and $\text{var}(\varepsilon_2) = \sigma_{22}[1 - (\sigma_{12}^2/\sigma_{11}\sigma_{22})]$.

Figure 2 plots regression function (2.6) for the case $\sigma_{12} = \sigma_{11}$ and $\mu_2 > \mu_1 > 0$. For each value of $\ln T_1$, the population values of $\ln T_2$ are normally distributed around the regression line. Individuals with high values of $\ln T_1$ also tend to have a high value of $\ln T_2$. Assuming $\pi_1 = \pi_2$, individuals with $(\ln T_1, \ln T_2)$ endowments above the 45° line of equal income shown in Figure 1 choose to work in sector 2, while those individuals with endowments below this line work in sector 1. Because $\sigma_{12} = \sigma_{11}$, the regression function is parallel to the line of equal income.

The distribution of ε_2 about the regression line is the same for all values of $\ln T_1$. When individuals are classified on the basis of their $\ln T_1$ values the same proportion of individuals work in sector 1 at all values of $\ln T_1$. For this reason the distribution of $\ln T_1$ employed in sector 1 is the same as the latent population distribution. If π_1 is raised (or π_2 is lowered) so that the 45° equal income line is shifted upward, the same proportion of people enter sector 1 at each value of $T_1 = t_1$. Figure 3 plots regression function (2.6) for the case $\sigma_{12} > \sigma_{11}$ and $\mu_2 > \mu_1 > 0$.

As before we set $\pi_1 = \pi_2$. Individuals with endowments above the 45° line choose to work in sector 2, while those with endowments below this line work in sector 1. When individuals are classified on the basis of their T_1 values, the fraction of people working in sector 1 decreases the higher the value of T_1. Self-selection causes the mean of log task 1 employed in sector 1 to be less than the mean of log task 1 in the total population. People with high values of T_1 are under-represented in sector 1 and low T_1 values are over-represented. In the extreme, when $\ln T_1$ and $\ln T_2$ are perfectly positively correlated, all high-income individuals are in sector 2, while all the

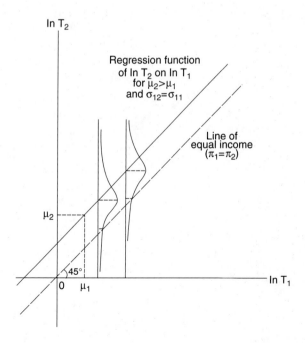

Figure 2

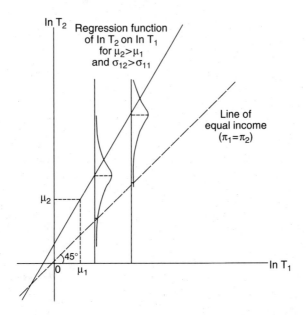

Figure 3

low-income individuals are in sector 1. The highest-paid sector 1 worker earns the same as the lowest-paid sector 2 worker (Roy, 1951; Willis and Rosen, 1979). In this case there is really only one skill dimension and individuals can be unambiguously ranked along this scale.

If π_1 is raised (or π_2 is lowered) so that the line of equal income is shifted upward, the mean of ln T_1 employed in sector 1 must rise. The only place left to get T_1 is from the high end of the T_1 distribution. Unlike the case of $\sigma_{12} = \sigma_{11}$ in which a 10 per cent increase in π_1 results in a 10 per cent increase in measured average earnings in sector 1, when $\sigma_{12} > \sigma_{11}$ a 10 per cent increase in π_1 results in a greater than 10 per cent increase in the measured average earnings in sector 1 as the average quality of the sector 1 workforce increases. The variance of log wages in sector 1 increases.

If $\sigma_{11} < \sigma_{12}$ then $\sigma_{12} < \sigma_{22}$ in order for Σ to be a covariance matrix. In the population, log task 2 must have greater variability than log task 1. Individuals with high T_1 values tend to have high T_2 values. But the population distribution of log task 2 has more mass in the tails. The higher an agent's value of T_1, the more likely it is that he will be able to get higher income in sector 2. At the lower end of the distribution, the process works in reverse: lower T_1 individuals on average have poor T_2 values. Self-selection causes the ln T_1 distribution in sector 1 to have an evacuated right tail, an exaggerated left tail, and a lower mean than the population mean of ln T_1.

If $\sigma_{12} < \sigma_{11}$ (a case not depicted graphically), the proportion of each T_1 group working in sector 1 increases, the higher the value of T_1. The mean of the log task employed in sector 1 exceeds μ_1. A 10 per cent increase in π_1 produces an increase of less than 10 per cent in the average earnings of workers in sector 1 as the mean of ln T_1 employed in sector 1 declines. In fact if $\sigma_{12} > \sigma_{22}$ it is possible for an increase in π_1 to cause measured sector 1 wages to decline. Thus through a selection phenomenon it is possible for the average wage of people working in sector 1 to decline even though the price per unit skill increases there.

How robust are these conclusions if the normality assumption is relaxed? Heckman and Sedlacek (1985) show that many propositions derived from assumed normality of skills do not hold up for more general distributions. For example, increasing selection need not decrease sectoral variances. The effects of selection on mean employed skill levels are ambiguous. Heckman and Honoré (1986) demonstrate that in a single cross-section of data, it is possible to identify all of the parameters of the model from the data if the normality assumption is invoked. However, in a single cross-section many other models can explain the data equally well. In particular, intuitive notions about the degree of correlation or dependence among skills have no empirical content and so models of skill 'hierarchies' based on the extent of such dependence have no content for single cross-sections of data with all individuals facing common prices.

To show this, write the density of skills as $f(t_1, t_2)$. Let

$$Z_1 = \begin{cases} T_1 & \text{if } T_1 > T_2 \\ 0 & \text{otherwise} \end{cases} \qquad Z_2 = \begin{cases} T_2 & \text{if } T_2 > T_1 \\ 0 & \text{otherwise} \end{cases}$$

Prices are normalized to unity ($\pi_1 = \pi_2 = 1$). Then the density of Z_1 is

$$Q_1'(z_1) = \int_{\{t_2 | t_2 < z_1\}} f(z_1, t_2) \, dt_2 = \int_0^{z_1} f(z_1, t_2) \, dt_2.$$

The density of Z_2 is

$$Q_2'(z_2) = \int_0^{z_2} f(t_1, z_2) \, dt_1.$$

Note that $Q_1'(n)$ and $Q_2'(n)$ summarize all of the available data on observed earnings. Now if T_1, T_2 are independent with cdf's F_1^* and F_2^* respectively

$$Q_1'(n) = f_1^*(n) F_2^*(n)$$

$$Q_2'(n) = F_1^*(n) f_2^*(n).$$

Define

$$Q(n) = \int_0^n [Q_1'(l) + Q_2'(l)] \, dl = F_1^*(n) F_2^*(n).$$

Then

$$\int_\phi^\infty \frac{Q_1'(n)}{Q(n)} \, dn = \int_\phi^\infty \frac{f_1^*(n)}{F_1^*(n)} \, dn = -\ln F_1^*(\phi).$$

Thus we can write

$$F_i^*(\phi) = \exp -\left(\int_\phi^\infty \left[\frac{Q_i'(n)}{Q(n)} \right] dn \right) \quad i = 1, 2$$

so that we can always rationalize the data on wages in a single cross-section by a model of skill independence, and economic models of skill hierarchies have no empirical content for a single cross-section of data.

Suppose, however, that the observing economist has access to data on skill distributions in different market settings i.e. settings in which relative skill prices vary. To take an extreme case, suppose that we observe a continuum of values of π_1/π_2 ranging from zero to infinity. Then it is possible to identify $F(t_1, t_2)$ and it is possible to give empirical content to models based on the degrees of dependence among latent skills.

This point is made most simply in a situation in which Z is observed but the analyst does not know Z_1 or Z_2 (i.e. which occupation is chosen). When $\pi_1/\pi_2 = 0$ everyone works in occupation two. Thus we can observe the marginal density of t_2. When $\pi_1/\pi_2 = \infty$ everyone works in occupation one. As π_1/π_2 pivots from zero to infinity it is thus possible to trace out the full joint distribution of (T_1, T_2).

To establish the general result, set $\sigma = \pi_2/\pi_1$. Let $F(t_1, t_2)$ be the distribution function of T_1, T_2. Then

$$\Pr(Z \le n) = \Pr(\max(T_1, \sigma T_2) \le n) = \Pr\left(T_1 \le n, T_2 \le \frac{1}{\sigma} n \right) = F\left(n, \frac{n}{\sigma} \right).$$

As σ varies between 0 and ∞ the entire distribution can be recovered since N is observed for all values in $(0, \infty)$. Note that it is not necessary to know which sector the agent selects.

This proposition establishes the benefit of having access to data from more than one market. Heckman and Honoré (1986) show how access to data from various market settings and information about the choices of agents aids in the identification of the latent skill distributions.

The Roy model is the prototype for many models of self-selection in economics. If T_1 is potential market productivity and T_2 is non-market productivity (or the reservation wage) for housewives or unemployed individuals, precisely the same model can be used to explore the effects of self-selection on measured productivity. In such a model, T_2 is never observed. This creates certain problems of identification discussed in Heckman and Honoré (1986). The model has been extended to allow for more general choice mechanisms. In particular, selection may occur as a function of variables other than or in addition to T_1 and T_2. Applications of the Roy model include studies of the union–non-union wage differential (Lee, 1978), the returns to schooling (Willis and Rosen, 1979), and the returns to training (Bjorklund and Moffitt, 1986, and Heckman and Robb, 1985). Amemiya (1984) and Heckman and

Honoré (1986) present comprehensive surveys of empirical studies based on the Roy model and its extensions.

JAMES J. HECKMAN

Bibliography

Amemiya, T. 1984. Tobit models: a survey. *Journal of Econometrics* 24, 3–61.

Bjorklund, A. and Moffitt, R. 1986. Estimation of wage gains and welfare gains from self selection models. *Review of Economics and Statistics* 24, 1–63.

Cain, G. and Watts, H. 1973. Toward a summary and synthesis of the evidence. In *Income Maintenance and Labor Supply*, ed. G. Cain and H. Watts. Madison: University of Wisconsin Press.

Clark, K. and Summers, L. 1979. Labor market dynamics and unemployment: a reconsideration. *Brookings Papers on Economic Activity*, 13–60.

Cosslett, S. 1981. Maximum likelihood estimation from choice based samples. *Econometrica*.

Cosslett, S. 1984. Distribution free estimator of regression model with sample selectivity. Unpublished manuscript, University of Florida.

Domencich, T. and McFadden, D. 1975. *Urban Travel Demand*. Amsterdam: North-Holland.

Flinn, C. and Heckman, J. 1982. New methods for analyzing structural models of labor force dynamics. *Journal of Econometrics* 18, 5–168.

Gallant, R. and Nychka, R. 1984. Consistent estimation of the censored regression model. Unpublished manuscript, North Carolina State.

Gill, R. and Wellner, J. 1985. Large sample theory of empirical distributions in biased sampling models. Unpublished manuscript, University of Washington.

Goldberger, A. 1983. Abnormal selection bias. In *Studies in Econometrics, Time Series and Multivariate Statistics*, ed. S. Karlin, T. Amemiya and L. Goodman. Wiley, NY. Gronau, R. 1974. Wage comparisons – a selectivity bias. *Journal of Political Economy* 82(6), 1119–1144.

Hall, R. 1982. The importance of lifetime jobs in the US economy. *American Economic Review* 72, September, 716–724.

Heckman, J. 1974. Shadow prices, market wages and labor supply. *Econometrica* 42(4), 679–94.

Heckman, J. 1976. The common structure of statistical models of truncation, sample selection and limited dependent variables and a simple estimator for such models. *Annals of Economic and Social Measurement* 5(4), 475–92.

Heckman, J. 1979. Sample selection bias as a specification error. *Econometrica* 47(1), 153–62.

Heckman, J. and Honoré, B. 1986. The empirical content of the Roy model. Unpublished manuscript, University of Chicago.

Heckman, J. and MaCurdy, T. 1981. New methods for estimating labor supply functions. In *Research in Labor Economics*, Vol. 4, ed. R. Ehrenberg. Greenwich, Conn.: JAI Press.

Heckman, J. and MaCurdy, T. 1986. Labor econometrics. In *Handbook of Econometrics*, vol. 3, ed. Z. Griliches and M. Intriligator. Amsterdam: North-Holland.

Heckman, J. and Robb, R. 1985. Alternative methods for evaluating the effect of training on earnings. In *Longitudinal Analysis of Labor Market Data*, ed. J. Heckman and B. Singer. Cambridge: Cambridge University Press.

Heckman, J. and Sedlacek, G. 1985. Heterogeneity, aggregation and market wage functions. *Journal of Political Economy* 93, December, 1077–125.

Heckman, J. and Singer, B. 1985. Econometric analysis of longitudinal data. In *Handbook of Econometrics*, Vol. III, ed. Z. Griliches and M. Intriligator. Amsterdam: North-Holland.

Lee, L.F. 1978. Unionism and wage rates: a simultaneous equations model with qualitative and limited dependent variables. *International Economic Review* 19, 415–33.

Manski, C. and Lerman, S. 1977. The estimation of choice probabilities from choice based samples. *Econometrica* 45, 1977–88.

Manski, C. and McFadden, D. 1981. Alternative estimates and sample designs for discrete choice analysis. In *Structural Analysis of Discrete Data with Econometric Applications*, ed. C. Manski and D. McFadden. Cambridge: MIT Press.

Pearson, K. 1901. Mathematical contributions to the theory of evolution. *Philosophical Transactions*, 195, 1–47.

Rao, C.R. 1965. On discrete distributions arising out of methods of ascertainment. In *Classical and Contagious Distributions*, ed. G. Patil. Calcutta: Pergamon Press.

Roy, A.D. 1951. Some thoughts on the distribution of earnings. *Oxford Economic Papers*, 3, 135–46.

Vardi, Y. 1983. Nonparametric estimation in the presence of length bias. *Annals of Statistics* 10, 616–20.

Vardi, Y. 1985. Empirical distributions in selection bias models. *Annals of Statistics*, 13, 178–203.

Willis, R. and Rosen, S. 1979. Education and self selection. *Journal of Political Economy* 87, S7–S36.

semiparametric estimation

Introduction

Semiparametric estimation methods are used to obtain estimators of the parameters of interest – typically the coefficients of an underlying regression function – in an econometric model, without a complete parametric specification of the conditional distribution of the dependent variable given the explanatory variables (regressors). A structural econometric model relates an observable dependent variable y to some observable regressors x; some unknown parameters β, and some unobservable 'error term' ε, through some functional form $y = g(x, \beta, \varepsilon)$; in this context, a semiparametric estimation problem does not restrict the distribution of ε (given the regressors) to belong to a parametric family determined by a finite number of unknown parameters, but instead imposes only broad restrictions on the distribution of ε (for example, independence of ε and x, or symmetry of ε about zero given x) to obtain identification of β and construct consistent estimators of it.

Thus the term 'semiparametric estimation' is something of a misnomer; the same estimator can be considered a parametric, semiparametric or nonparametric estimator depending upon the restrictions imposed upon the economic model. For example, if a random sample of dependent variables $\{y_i\}$ and regressors $\{x_i\}$ are assumed to satisfy a linear regression model $y_i = x_i'\beta + \varepsilon_i$, the classical least squares estimator can be considered a 'parametric' estimator of the regression coefficient vector β if the error terms $\{\varepsilon_i\}$ are assumed to be normally distributed and independent of $\{x_i\}$. It could alternatively be considered a 'nonparametric estimator' of the best linear predictor coefficients $\beta = [E(x_i\, x_i')]^{-1} E(x_i, y_i)$ if only the weak condition $E(x_i\, \varepsilon_i)$ is imposed (implying that β is a unique function of the joint distribution of the observations). And the least squares estimator would be 'semiparametric' under the intermediate restriction $E(\varepsilon_i|x_i) = 0$, which imposes a parametric (linear) form for the conditional mean $E(y_i|x_i) = x_i'\beta$ of the dependent variable but imposes no further restrictions on the conditional distribution. So the term 'semiparametric' is a more suitable adjective for models which are partly (but not completely) parametrically specified than it is for the estimators of those parameters.

Nevertheless, while most econometric estimation methods that do not explicitly specify the likelihood function of the observable data (for example, least squares, instrumental variables, and generalized method-of-moments estimators) could be considered semiparametric estimators, 'semiparametric' is sometimes used to refer to estimators of a finite number of parameters of interest (here, β) that involve explicit nonparametric estimators of unknown nuisance functions (for example, features of the distribution of the errors ε). Such 'semiparametric estimators' use nonparametric estimators of density or regression functions as inputs to second-stage estimators of regression coefficients or similar parameters. Occasionally terms like 'semi-nonparametric', 'distribution-free' and even 'nonparametric' have been used to describe such estimation methods, with the latter terms referring to the treatment of the error terms in an otherwise-parametric structural model.

The primary objective of semiparametric methods is to identify and consistently estimate the unknown parameter of interest β by determining which combinations of structural functions $g(x, \beta, \varepsilon)$ and weak restrictions on the distribution of the errors ε permit this. Given identification and consistent estimation, the next step in the statistical theory is determination of the speed with which the estimator $\hat{\beta}$ converges to its probability limit β. The rate of convergence for estimators for standard parametric problems is the square root of the sample size n, while nonparametric estimators of unknown density and regression functions (with continuously distributed regressors) generically converge at a slower rate; if a semiparametric estimator can be shown to converge at the parametric rate, that is, if it is 'root-n consistent', then its relative efficiency to a parametric estimator (for a correctly specified parametric model) will not tend to zero as n increases. For inference, it is also useful to demonstrate the asymptotic (that is, approximate) normality of the distribution of $\hat{\beta}$ in large samples, so that asymptotic confidence regions and hypothesis tests can be constructed using normal sampling theory. Finally, for problems where existence of root-n consistent, asymptotically normal semiparametric estimators can be shown, the question of efficient estimation arises. The solution to this question has two parts – determination of the efficiency bound for the semiparametric estimation problem and construction of a feasible estimator that attains that bound.

Econometric applications

In econometrics, most of the attention to semiparametric methods dates from the late 1970s and early 1980s, which saw the development of parametric models for discrete and *limited dependent variable (LDV)* models. Unlike the linear regression model, those models are not additive in the underlying error terms, so the validity (specifically, the consistency) of maximum likelihood and related estimation methods depends crucially on the assumed parametric form of the error distribution. As shown for particular examples by Arabmazar and Schmidt (1981; 1982) and Goldberger (1983), failure of the standard assumption of normally distributed error terms makes the corresponding likelihood-based estimators inconsistent. This is in contrast to the linear regression model, where the maximum likelihood (classical least squares) estimator is consistent under much weaker assumptions than normally (and identically) distributed errors.

Much of the early literature on semiparametric estimation concentrated on a particular limited dependent variable model, the *binary response model*, which arguably presents the most challenging setting for identification and estimation of the underlying regression coefficients. Early examples of semiparametric identification assumptions and estimation methods for this model give a flavour of the approaches used for other econometric models, among them the *censored regression* and *sample selection* models. The discussion here treats only selected assumptions and estimators for these models, and not their numerous variants; more complete surveys of semiparametric models and estimation methods are given by Manski (1989), Powell (1994), Newey (1994), and Pagan and Ullah (1999).

Semiparametric binary response models
The earliest semiparametric estimation methods in the econometrics literature on LDV models concerned the *binary response model*, in which the dependent variable y assumed the values zero or 1 depending upon the sign of some underlying latent (unobservable) dependent variable y^* which satisfies a linear regression model $y^* = x'\beta + \varepsilon$; that is,

$$y_i = 1\{x_i'\beta - \varepsilon_i > 0\},$$

where '$1\{A\}$' denotes the indicator function of the event A; that is, it is 1 if A occurs and is zero otherwise. For a parametric model, in which the errors ε_i are assumed to be independent of x_i and distributed with a known marginal cumulative distribution function $F(\varepsilon)$, the average log-likelihood function takes the form

$$L_n(\beta) = \frac{1}{n} \sum_{i=1}^{n} [y_i \ln F(x_i'\beta) + (1 - y_i) \ln (1 - F(x_i'\beta))]$$

for a random sample of size n, and consistency of the corresponding the maximum likelihood estimator $\hat{\beta}_{ML}$ requires correct specification of F unless the regressors satisfy certain restrictions (as discussed by Ruud, 1986). When F is unknown, a scale normalization on β is required, and a constant (intercept) term will not be identified no normalization on the location of ε is imposed.

Manski (1975; 1985) proposed a semiparametric alternative, termed the 'maximum score' estimator, which defined the estimator to maximize the number of correct matches of the value of y_i with an indicator function $1\{x_i'\beta > 0\}$ of the positivity of the regression function. That is, the maximum score estimator $\hat{\beta}_{MS}$ maximizes the average 'score' function

$$S_n(\beta) = \frac{1}{n} \sum_{i=1}^{n} [y_i \cdot 1\{x_i'\beta > 0\} + (1 - y_i) \cdot 1\{x_i'\beta \le 0\}]$$

over β. Unlike the maximum likelihood estimator $\hat{\beta}_{ML}$, consistency of $\hat{\beta}_{MS}$ requires only that the median of the error terms was zero given the regressors, that is, the conditional cumulative $F(\varepsilon|x)$ of given $x_i = x$ had $F(\lambda|x) > 1/2$ when $\lambda > 0$, and $F(\lambda|x) < 1/2$ when $\lambda < 0$. However, the estimation approach is generally not root-n consistent (as shown by Chamberlain, 1986). A variant of the maximum score estimator, proposed by Horowitz (1992), essentially 'smoothed' the indicator functions for positivity of $x_i'\beta$ in the minimand $S_n(\beta)$ using a continuous approximation to it, similar to the smoothing used in nonparametric kernel estimators of regression and density functions. The rate of convergence of the resulting 'smoothed maximum score' estimator can be made arbitrarily close to the root-n rate if the distribution of the regressors is sufficiently smooth.

To obtain root-n consistent estimators of the unknown β, the assumption on the error term ε can be strengthened to independence of ε and x. Han (1987) proposed an alternative to the maximum score estimator, termed the 'maximum rank correlation' estimator, which compared the sign of the difference $y_i - y_j$ of the dependent variable to the corresponding difference $(x_i - x_j)'\beta$ in the regression functions across all distinct pairs of observations i and j. The estimator $\hat{\beta}_{MRC}$ maximizes

$$M_n(\beta) = \binom{n}{2}^{-1} \sum_{i=1}^{n-1} \sum_{j=i+1}^{n} sgn(y_i - y_j) \cdot sgn((x_i - x_j)'\beta)$$

$\Leftrightarrow$ over β, where $sgn(u) \equiv 1\{u > 0\} - 1\{u < 0\}$. The rationale for this estimator is based upon the monotonicity of $\Pr\{y_i = 1|x\} = F(x_i'\beta)$ in $x_i'\beta$ so that, given $y_i \neq y_j$, $\Pr\{y_i > y_j | x_i, x_j\}$ exceeds $1/2$ when $x_i'\beta > x_j'\beta$. Han's article gave conditions under which $\hat{\beta}_{MRC}$ was shown to be consistent, and Sherman (1993) showed that this estimator was root-n consistent and asymptotically normal.

An alternative estimation approach for β under the assumption of independence of u and x combines estimation of the parameter vector β with nonparametric estimation of the unknown distribution function F. Cosslett (1983) proposed a 'nonparametric maximum likelihood' estimator $\hat{\beta}_{NPML}$ obtained by simultaneously maximizing the likelihood function $L_n(\beta) = L_n(\beta; F)$ over both β and F, where the latter function is restricted to be nondecreasing with values in the unit interval. While consistency of this estimator could be established, its rate of convergence could not. An alternative estimation method, proposed by Klein and Spady (1993), used kernel regression methods to estimate the unknown distribution function F in the likelihood function. The resulting estimator was shown to be root-n consistent and asymptotically normally distributed under additional regularity conditions; furthermore, the estimator was shown to achieve the semiparametric efficiency bound for this problem, that is, its asymptotic covariance matrix is the smallest possible among regular estimators of β which impose only the independence restriction between x and u.

Still other estimators for β when u and x are independent exploit the single index regression structure of this model, since the conditional expectation of y_i given x_i only depends upon the 'single index' $x_i'\beta$:

$$E[y_i|x_i] \equiv g(x_i) = F(x_i'\beta).$$

If the vector of regressors x_i is continuously distributed with joint density function $f_X(x)$ which is continuous for all x, Stoker (1986) noted that the vector of slope parameters β is proportional to the expectation of the derivative of $g(x)$,

$$E\left[\frac{\partial g(x_i)}{\partial x}\right] = E[F'(x_i'\beta)] \cdot \beta.$$

Using integration-by-parts, this 'average derivative' can in turn be expressed as the expected value of the product of $-y_i$ and the derivative of the logarithm of the density f_X of the regressors,

$$E\left[\frac{\partial g(x_i)}{\partial x}\right] = -E\left[y_i \frac{\partial \log[f_X(x_i)]}{\partial x}\right].$$

Härdle and Stoker (1989) proposed a semiparametric estimator of this representation of β (up to scale) using nonparametric (kernel) estimators of f_X and its gradient, while Powell, Stock and Stoker (1989) constructed a similar estimator of the 'density-weighted average derivative'

$$E\left[f_X(x_i)\frac{\partial g(x_i)}{\partial x}\right] = E\left[f_X(x_i)F'(x_i'\beta)\right] \cdot \beta = -2E\left[y_i \frac{\partial f_X(x_i)}{\partial x}\right],$$

which is also proportional to β under the single index restriction.

Though the motivation given here was based upon the binary response model under independence of the errors and regressors, the average derivative and weighted average derivative estimators apply to other models with a single index structure, for example, any *transformation model* with

$$y_i = T(x_i'\beta + \varepsilon_i),$$

for T a nondegenerate function (possibly unknown) and with ε_i continuously distributed and independent of x_i. The same is true for the 'single index regression' estimator proposed by Ichimura (1993), defined to minimize

$$R_n(\beta) = \frac{1}{n}\sum_{i=1}^n (y_i - \hat{F}(x_i'\beta; \beta))^2 t_n(x_i);$$

in this expression, $\hat{F}(u; \beta)$ represents a nonparametric regression estimator of $E[y_i|x_i'\beta = u]$ and $t_n(x_i)$ represents a 'trimming' term which is zero whenever x_i lies outside a set for which F is sufficiently precisely estimated. Unlike the average derivative $\hat{\beta}_{AD}$ and weighted average derivative $\hat{\beta}_{WAD}$ estimators, which require the regressors to be jointly continuously distributed, root-n consistency and asymptotic normality of the single index regression estimator $\hat{\beta}_{SIR}$ require only that $x_i'\beta$ has a continuous distribution, so that some of the regressors can be discrete. The criterion function $R_n(\beta)$ is the nonlinear least squares analogue of the maximand for the Klein and Spady (1993) estimator (which also involved a similar trimming term $t_n(x_i)$). The asymptotic covariance matrices for both estimators have the same general form as the corresponding nonlinear least squares and maximum likelihood estimators with F known, except for the replacement of the cross product of the regressors x_i with the cross product of $x_i - E[x_i|x_i'\beta]$, adjusting the asymptotic covariance matrices upward to account for the nonparametric estimation of the unknown function F.

The problem of consistent estimation of β in binary response models is compounded for *panel data* models with *fixed effects* (that is, individual-specific intercept terms), written as

$$y_{it} = 1\{x'_{it}\beta + \alpha_i - \varepsilon_{it} > 0\}$$

for individuals i ranging from 1 to n and time periods t from 1 to T. For this model, even if the distribution function F of the error terms ε_{it} is known, the maximum likelihood estimators of β and the fixed effects $\{\alpha_i\}$ will generally be inconsistent if the number of time periods T is fixed as N increases. A consistent semiparametric estimation strategy using a variant of the maximum rank correlation estimator was proposed by Manski (1987); for the special case $T=2$ (that is, two time periods), the estimator $\hat{\beta}_{BPD}$ can be defined as the maximizer of the criterion

$$P_{(n)}(\beta) = \frac{1}{n}\sum_{i=1}^{n} sgn(y_{i2} - y_{i1}) \cdot sgn((x_{i2} - x_{i1})'\beta),$$

which is analogous to $M_n(\beta)$, except that the differencing is across time periods rather than across individuals. While consistency of $\hat{\beta}_{BPD}$ was established under weak conditions on the error terms, it is not possible to obtain a root-n consistent estimator unless the errors are logistic (Chamberlain, 1993) or other restrictive assumptions (for example, independence of the fixed effect α_i and the regressors x_{it}, or the conditions in Honoré and Lewbel, 2002; Lee, 1999) are imposed.

Other semiparametric econometric models

Many of the identifying assumptions imposed on semiparametric binary response models give identification and yield consistent estimators for other limited dependent variable models, though these models can sometimes be identified and consistently estimated using assumptions that are uninformative for binary response. Consider, for example, the censored regression ('Tobit') model, in which the dependent variable y_i satisfies a linear regression model if it is nonnegative, and is zero otherwise:

$$y_i = \max\{0, x'_i\beta + \varepsilon_i\}.$$

For this model, as for the binary response model, the dependent variable is a monotonic function of the error term ε_i; since monotone transformations by definition preserve orderings, the median (or any other percentile) of this monotonic transformation of ε_i is the monotonic transformation evaluated at the median. Thus the assumption that the errors ε_i have conditional median zero given x_i implies that the conditional median of y_i given x_i takes the form $\max\{0, x'_i\beta\}$, depending only on the unknown coefficients β and not on the shape of the distribution of ε_i. Using this fact, and the characterization of medians as minimizers of a least absolute deviations criterion, Powell (1984) proposed estimation of the unknown β vector by the minimizer $\hat{\beta}_{CLAD}$ of

$$Q_n(\beta) = \frac{1}{n}\sum_{i=1}^{n} |y_i - \max\{0, x'_i\beta\}|$$

for this model; it is analogous to the maximum score estimator $\hat{\beta}_{MS}$ for the binary response model, which can be defined as the minimizer of the sample average absolute deviation of y_i from its conditional median function $1\{x_i'\beta > 0\}$ for binary response with median zero errors. (The maximum rank correlation estimator $\hat{\beta}_{MRC}$ and binary panel data estimator $\hat{\beta}_{BPD}$ can also be expressed as solutions to least absolute deviations problems.) Unlike $\hat{\beta}_{MS}$, though, the censored median estimator $\hat{\beta}_{CLAD}$ is root-n consistent and asymptotically normally distributed under weak regularity conditions, without need for a scale normalization. An alternative estimator for this model, which involved a nonparametric estimator of the probability that y_i equals zero given x_i, was proposed by Buchinsky and Hahn (1998).

A stronger restriction on the error distribution is conditional symmetry about zero given the regressors; while this restriction is no more informative than the implied zero median restriction for binary response, it yields different identification approaches for censored regression. Specifically, the 'symmetrically censored' residual

$$u_i(\beta) \equiv \min\{y_i - x_i'\beta, x_i'\beta\} = \min\{\max\{-x_i'\beta, \varepsilon_i\}, x_i'\beta\}$$

is an even function of ε_i when the regression function $x_i'\beta$ is positive, and thus is itself conditionally symmetric about zero. This implies a population moment restriction

$$0 = E[1\{x_i'\beta > 0\}\psi(\tilde{u}_i(\beta)) \cdot x_i],$$

for $\psi(u) = -\psi(-u)$ an odd function of its argument. Powell (1986) proposed a 'symmetrically censored least squares' estimator of β based upon this restriction with $\psi(u) = u$; like the censored median estimator $\hat{\beta}_{CLAD}$ – which exploits the same moment condition with $\psi(u) = sgn(u)$ – the estimator $\hat{\beta}_{SCLS}$ is root-n consistent and asymptotically normally distributed under weak assumptions. Neither estimator involves explicit nonparametric estimation of the error distribution, a feature shared by the maximum score estimator $\hat{\beta}_{MS}$ and its relatives $\hat{\beta}_{MRC}$ and $\hat{\beta}_{BPD}$ for binary response.

As for the binary response model or most limited dependent variable models, consistent estimation of slope coefficients using panel data with fixed effects is challenging, with maximum likelihood estimators for β being inconsistent when the number of time periods is fixed and the number estimated fixed effects increases. For the special case $T = 2$, writing

$$y_{it} = \max\{0, x_{it}'\beta + \alpha_i + \varepsilon_{it}\},$$

Honoré (1992) noted that the difference in 'identically trimmed' residuals

$$\tilde{u}_i(\beta) = \max\{-x_{i1}'\beta, y_{i2} - x_{i2}'\beta\} - \max\{-x_{i2}'\beta, y_{i1} - x_{i1}'\beta\}$$

$$= \max\{-x_{i1}'\beta, -x_{i2}'\beta, \alpha_i + \varepsilon_{i2}\} - \max\{-x_{i1}'\beta, -x_{i2}'\beta, \alpha_i + \varepsilon_{i2}\}$$

would be symmetrically distributed about zero if the error terms ε_{i1} and ε_{i2} were identically distributed given x_{i1} and x_{i2} and value of the fixed effect α_i. This implies population moment conditions of the form

$$0 = E[\psi(\tilde{u}_i(\beta)) \cdot (x_{2i} - x_{i1})],$$

again with $\psi(u)$ an odd function of its argument. Setting $\psi(u) = sgn(u)$ and $\psi(u) = u$ yields root-n consistent and asymptotically normal estimators which are similar to the censored least absolute deviations estimator $\hat{\beta}_{CLAD}$ and symmetrically-censored least squares estimator $\hat{\beta}_{SCLS}$, respectively.

Other estimation approaches for censored regression involve explicit nonparametric estimation of features of the distribution of the error terms, which is common for other semiparametric econometric models. One such model is the *semiparametric regression* (or *semilinear regression*) model, for which some regressors enter linearly while others enter nonparametrically. The model can be written algebraically as

$$y_i = x_i'\beta + \lambda(w_i) + \varepsilon_i \equiv x_i'\beta + u_i,$$

where the error terms ε_i are restricted to satisfy $E[\varepsilon_i|x_i,w_i] = 0$, or, equivalently, $E[u_i|x_i,w_i] = E[u_i|w_i] \equiv \lambda(w_i)$; the regressors x_i and w_i thus enter parametrically (linearly) or nonparametrically in the conditional mean of y_i. Robinson (1988) exploited the fact that

$$y_i - E[y_i|w_i] = (x_i - E[x_i|w_i])'\beta + \varepsilon_i$$

to construct a root-n consistent, asymptotically-normal estimator of β by applying least squares estimation to this equation, replacing the unknown quantities $E[y_i|w_i]$ and $E[x_i|w_i]$ by nonparametric (kernel) estimators. For the parameters β to be identified for this model, the covariance matrix of the 'residual regressors' must be nonsingular, ruling out functional dependence of x_i on w_i.

Though the semilinear regression model is not itself a limited dependent variable model, it arises as a consequence of 'selectivity bias' in a bivariate limited dependent variable model, the *censored selection model*, in which a linear latent 'outcome' variable $y_i^* = x_i'\beta + \varepsilon_i$ is observed only if some related binary 'selection' variable d_i equals 1:

$$d_i = 1\{w_i'\delta - _i > 0\},$$

$$y_i = d_i \cdot (x_i'\beta + \varepsilon_i),$$

where the regressors x_i and w_i are observed and the unobserved error terms η_i and ε_i need not be mutually independent. Heckman (1979) showed that, for the uncensored ($d_i = 1$) subsample from this model, the dependent variable satisfied a semilinear regression model, since

$$E[y_i|d_i = 1, x_i, w_i] = x_i'\beta + \lambda(w_i'\delta);$$

when the errors are jointly normal, as Heckman assumed, the function $\lambda(u)$ has a known parametric form, but is nonparametric if the error distribution is not in a parametric family. Cosslett (1991) developed a consistent two-step estimator for the regression parameters β in the outcome equation, computing a binary nonparametric maximum likelihood estimator $\hat{\delta}_{NPML}$ of δ in the first step and using a step-function approximation to $\lambda(u)$ in a least squares fit of the outcome equation for the uncensored observations. Ahn and Powell (1993) proposed a root-n consistent two-step estimator of β for the related semilinear model

$$E[y_i|d_i = 1, x_i, w_i] = x_i'\beta + \lambda^*(p(w_i)),$$

where the 'propensity score' $p(w_i) \equiv E[d_i|w_i]$ is first estimated by a nonparametric regression method; this semilinear model is implied by a generalization of the original censored selection model, replacing the linear form of the regression function $w_i'\delta$ in the selection equation with an unknown function of the regressors w_i.

Some variations of the censored selection model admit other semiparametric identification strategies. For example, if the selection equation is censored rather than binary, for example, if

$$d_i = \max\{0, w'\delta + {}_i\},$$

$$y_i = 1\{d_i > 0\} \cdot (x_i'\beta + \varepsilon_i),$$

then Honoré, Kyriazidou and Udry (1997) construct a root-n consistent two-step estimator of β under the assumption that the errors η_i and ε_i are jointly symmetric about zero given the regressors w_i and x_i, using a symmetrically censored least squares estimator of δ in the first step and exploiting the symmetry of $y_i - x_i'\beta$ about zero given that $0 < d_i < 2w_i'\delta$ in the second step. In contrast, estimation of censored selection models for panel data with fixed effects is no less challenging than for binary panel data models; Kyriazidou (1997) proposes a consistent (but not root-n consistent) two-step estimator for the panel data selection model

$$d_{it} = 1\{w_{it}'\delta + v_i - {}_{it} > 0\},$$

$$y_{it} = d_{it} \cdot (x_{it}'\beta + \alpha_i + \varepsilon_{it}),$$

using Manski's (1987) binary panel data estimator to estimate δ in the first step and a semilinear regression estimator similar to the Ahn and Powell (1993) approach in the second step.

JAMES L. POWELL

See also **nonlinear panel data models; nonparametric structural models; quantile regression; selection bias and self-selection; Tobit model.**

Bibliography

Ahn, H. and Powell, J.L. 1993. Semiparametric estimation of censored selection models with a nonparametric selection mechanism. *Journal of Econometrics* 58, 3–29.

Arabmazar, A. and Schmidt, P. 1981. Further evidence on the robustness of the Tobit estimator to heteroscedasticity. *Journal of Econometrics* 17, 253–8.

Arabmazar, A. and Schmidt, P. 1982. An investigation of the robustness of the Tobit estimator to non-normality. *Econometrica* 50, 1055–63.

Buchinsky, M. and Hahn, J. 1998. An alternative estimator for the censored quantile regression model. *Econometrica* 66, 653–72.

Chamberlain, G. 1986. Asymptotic efficiency in semiparametric models with censoring. *Journal of Econometrics* 32, 189–218.

Chamberlain, G. 1993. Feedback in panel data models. Unpublished manuscript, Department of Economics, Harvard University.

Cosslett, S.R. 1983. Distribution-free maximum likelihood estimator of the binary choice model. *Econometrica* 51, 765–82.

Cosslett, S.R. 1991. Distribution-free estimator of a regression model with sample selectivity. In *Nonparametric and Semiparametric Methods in Econometrics and Statistics*, ed. W.A. Barnett, J.L. Powell and G. Tauchen. Cambridge: Cambridge University Press.

Goldberger, A.S. 1983. Abnormal selection bias. In *Studies in Econometrics, Time Series, and Multivariate Statistics*, ed. S. Karlin, T. Amemiya and L. Goodman. New York: Academic Press.

Han, A.K. 1987. Non-parametric analysis of a generalized regression model: the maximum rank correlation estimator. *Journal of Econometrics* 35, 303–16.

Härdle, W. and Stoker, T.M. 1989. Investigating smooth multiple regression by the method of average derivatives. *Journal of the American Statistical Association* 84, 986–95.

Heckman, J.J. 1979. Sample selection bias as a specification error. *Econometrica* 47, 153–62.

Honoré, B.E. 1992. Trimmed LAD and least squares estimation of truncated and censored regression models with fixed effects. *Econometrica* 60, 533–65.

Honoré, B.E., Kyriazidou, E. and Udry, C. 1997. Estimation of type 3 Tobit models using symmetric trimming and pairwise comparisons. *Journal of Econometrics* 76, 107–28.

Honoré, B.E. and Lewbel, A. 2002. Semiparametric binary choice panel data models without strictly exogenous regressors. *Econometrica* 70, 2053–63.

Horowitz, J.L. 1992. A smoothed maximum score estimator for the binary response model. *Econometrica* 60, 505–31.

Ichimura, H. 1993. Semiparametric least squares (SLS) and weighted SLS estimation of single index models. *Journal of Econometrics* 58, 71–120.

Klein, R.W. and Spady, R.H. 1993. An efficient semiparametric estimator for discrete choice models. *Econometrica* 61, 387–421.

Kyriazidou, E. 1997. Estimation of a panel data sample selection model. *Econometrica* 65, 1335–64.

Lee, M-J. 1999. A root-n consistent semiparametric estimator for related effect binary response panel data. *Econometrica* 60, 533–65.

Manski, C.F. 1975. Maximum score estimation of the stochastic utility model of choice. *Journal of Econometrics* 3, 205–28.

Manski, C.F. 1985. Semiparametric analysis of discrete response, asymptotic properties of the maximum score estimator. *Journal of Econometrics* 27, 205–28.

Manski, C.F. 1987. Semiparametric analysis of random effects linear models from binary panel data. *Econometrica* 55, 357–62.

Manski, C.F. 1989. *Analog Estimation Methods in Econometrics*. New York: Chapman & Hall.

Newey, W.K. 1994. The asymptotic variance of semiparametric estimators. *Econometrica* 62, 1349–82.

Pagan, A.P. and Ullah, A. 1999. *Nonparametric Econometrics*. Cambridge: Cambridge University Press.

Powell, J.L. 1984. Least absolute deviations estimation for the censored regression model. *Journal of Econometrics* 25, 303–25.

Powell, J.L. 1986. Symmetrically trimmed least squares estimation of Tobit models. *Econometrica* 54, 1435–60.

Powell, J.L. 1994. Estimation of semiparametric models. In *Handbook of Econometrics*, vol. 4, ed. R.F. Engle, and D.L. McFadden. Amsterdam: North-Holland.

Powell, J.L., Stock, J.H. and Stoker, T.M. 1989. Semiparametric estimation of weighted average derivatives. *Econometrica* 57, 1403–30.

Robinson, P. 1988. Root-N-consistent semiparametric regression. *Econometrica* 56, 931–54.

Ruud, P. 1986. Consistent estimation of limited dependent variable models despite misspecification of distribution. *Journal of Econometrics* 32, 157–87.

Sherman, R.P. 1993. The limiting distribution of the maximum rank correlation estimator. *Econometrica* 61, 123–37.

Stoker, T.M. 1986. Consistent estimation of scaled coefficients. *Econometrica* 54, 1461–81.

simulation-based estimation

Simulation-based estimation is an application of the general Monte Carlo principle to statistical estimation: any mathematical expectation, when unavailable in closed form, can be approximated to any desired level of accuracy through a generation of (pseudo-) random numbers. Pseudo-random numbers are generated on a computer by means of a deterministic method. (For convenience, we henceforth delete the qualification 'pseudo'.) Then a well-suited drawing of random numbers (or vectors) $Z_1, Z_2, \ldots, Z_H$ provides the Monte Carlo simulator $(1/H)\sum_{h=1}^{H} g(Z_h)$ of $E[g(Z)]$. Of course, one may also want to resort to many simulators improving upon this naive one in terms of variance reduction, increased smoothness and reduced computational cost. A detailed discussion of simulation techniques is beyond the scope of this article. Nor are we going to study Monte Carlo experiments, which complement a given statistical procedure by the observation of its properties on simulated data. Rather, our focus of interest is to show how Monte Carlo integration may directly help to compute estimators that would be unfeasible without resorting to simulators.

The article is organized as follows. Section 1 is devoted to the most natural use of Monte Carlo integration for estimation, which is finite sample bias correction. It encompasses the parametric bootstrap. More generally, we use throughout the framework of a fully parametric econometric model with possibly latent variables, as defined in Section 1. Section 2 emphasizes that the simulation tool actually provides at least an asymptotic bias correction in much more general settings, such as simultaneity bias, bias due to errors in variables or any kind of misspecification bias. The general approach is dubbed *simulation-based indirect inference* (SII). Instead of using SII only for bias correcting a poor initial estimator, we can actually take advantage of any instrumental piece of information, insofar as it (over)identifies the structural parameters of interest. Section 3 is devoted to the *simulated method of moments* (SMM) and its *simulated-score-matching* version. With an asymptotic point of view, it can be seen as a particular asymptotic case of SII when instrumental parameters are some well-chosen moments. Besides computation of moments to match, Monte Carlo integration can also be used for the direct assessment of the criterion to maximize for M-estimation, when it is not available in closed form. The objective of asymptotic efficiency in the context of a parametric model leads us to put forward the *simulated maximum likelihood* (SML) or a *simulated score* technique, both described in Section 4. Some alternative simulated M-estimators, convenient though inefficient, are also reviewed. Concluding remarks in Section 5 are mainly focused on the trade-off between efficiency and robustness to misspecification; the fact that the structural model is also providing a simulator raises new issues for this classical trade-off.

The exposition in this article of simulation-based estimation methods relevant for econometric applications is selective in several respects. We do not present Markov chain Monte Carlo methods and data augmentation techniques. These are especially popular in Bayesian statistics and econometrics, but also relevant for some applications in a classical inference setting. Generally speaking, any kind of random drawing in the parametric space is beyond the scope of this article. Finally, it should be borne in mind throughout that all the simulation-based estimation methods have a non-simulation-based counterpart. While it is well known that SMM and SML are the simulation-based counterparts of GMM (generalized method of moments) and MLE (maximum likelihood estimation) respectively, it may be less known that the approaches of bootstrap and indirect interface make sense even without simulations. The essential characteristic of these techniques is to insert a consistent estimator of the data generating process in a functional of the true data distribution. Simulations are only a tool to evaluate the resulting estimated functional which, more often than not, is not available in closed form. There are, however, interesting exceptions like linear indirect least squares. Moreover, even though we always refer to the general concept of Monte Carlo integration, it does not necessarily involve a large number of simulated paths. Asymptotic theory of simulation-based estimation techniques will be considered when the length of the observed sample path goes to infinity. Depending on the techniques, the number of simulated paths may or may not be constrained to tend to infinity to get consistent estimators.

1. General framework and simulation-based bias correction

Let us denote by θ a vector of p unknown parameters. We want to build an accurate estimator $\hat{\theta}_T$ of θ from an observed sample path of length T. Let us assume that we have at our disposal some initial estimator, denoted by $\hat{\beta}_T$. Note that we purposely use a letter β different from θ to stress that the estimator $\hat{\beta}_T$ may give a very inaccurate assessment of the true unknown θ^0 we want to estimate. In particular this estimator is potentially severely biased: its expectation $b_T(\theta^0)$ does not coincide with θ^0. The notation $b_T(\theta^0)$ refers to the so-called binding function (Gourieroux and Monfort, 1995) and depends on at least two things: not only on the true unknown value of the parameters of interest but also on the sample size. The bootstrap is a method for estimating the distribution of an estimator, and in particular its expectation, by re-sampling the data. We refer the reader to Hall (1992) and Horowitz (1997) for surveys from which we borrow here. Since the bootstrap estimate is built upon an estimator of the data distribution, it is always recommended to use a parametric estimator of it when available. This is why, since this article is about estimation in parametric models, we focus on the parametric bootstrap, which was first considered in econometrics for the linear regression model with Gaussian errors:

$$y_i = z_i'b + \sigma\varepsilon_i, \qquad \varepsilon_i \sim \text{IIN}(0, 1).$$

Of course, bootstrapping is not very useful in such a simple context but it may become relevant if for instance the dependent variable is replaced by its Box–Cox transformation with some unknown parameters (Horowitz, 1997). More generally we allow for any kind of non-linear transformation and also for dynamic models in reduced form, possibly including lagged endogenous variables among the explanatory variables (see Monfort and Van Dijk, 1995 for a thorough exposition of the general framework presented below):

$$y_t = r[z(1,t), y(0, t-1), \varepsilon_t; \theta], \qquad t = 1, \ldots, T \tag{1}$$

where (ε_t) is a white-noise process whose marginal distribution P_ε is known, (z_t) is a process which is independent of (ε_t), $z(1,t) = (z_\tau)_{1 \leq \tau \leq t}$, $y(0, t-1) = (y_\tau)_{1 \leq \tau \leq t-1}$ and $r(\cdot)$ is a known function. Model (0) defines the conditional pdf $f[y_t | x_t; \theta]$ where x_t includes the realization of all the predetermined variables $z(1,t)$ and $y(0, t-1)$. Then, by drawing independently from P_ε, it is possible to simulate values ε_t^h, $t = 1, \ldots, T$ and $h = 1, \ldots, H$ and to compute:

$$y_t^h(\theta) = r[z(1,t), y(0, t-1), \varepsilon_t^h; \theta], \qquad t = 1, \ldots, T, \quad h = 1, \ldots, H.$$

The pdf of $y_t^h(\theta)$ is precisely $f[y_t | x_t; \theta]$. In other words, it is possible to perform *conditional simulations*, that is, to draw, for each t, from the conditional distribution whose pdf is $f[y_t | x_t; \theta]$ for any given value θ of the unknown parameters and for the observed value of x_t. Note that, in all simulation-based estimation methods considered below, the basic drawings ε_t^h will be kept fixed when θ changes.

For the purpose of SMM, it will actually be worthwhile making a distinction between such *conditional simulations* and (unconditional) *path simulations*, which may be the only ones feasible in the more general case of a non-linear state-space model defined as:

$$y_t = r_1[z(1,t), y(0, t-1), y^*(0,t), \varepsilon_{1t}; \theta], \qquad t = 1, \ldots, T$$
$$y_t^* = r_2[z(1,t), y(0, t-1), y^*(0, t-1), \varepsilon_{2t}; \theta], \qquad t = 1, \ldots, T \tag{2}$$

where $\varepsilon_t = (\varepsilon_{1t}', \varepsilon_{2t}')'$ is a white-noise process whose marginal distribution P_ε is known, (z_t) is independent of (ε_t), (y_t^*) is a process of latent variables and r_1 and r_2 are two known functions. The big difference between models (1) and (2) is that the latter only recursively defines the observed endogenous variables through a path of latent ones, making conditional simulation impossible. More precisely, from independent random draws ε_t^h, $t = 1, \ldots, T$ and $h = 1, \ldots, H$ in P_ε we can now compute recursively:

$$y_t^{*h}(\theta) = r_2[z(1,t), y^h(0, t-1)(\theta), y^{*h}(0, t-1)(\theta), \varepsilon_{2t}^h; \theta],$$
$$t = 1, \ldots, T; \quad h = 1, \ldots, H.$$
$$y_t^h(\theta) = r_1[z(1,t), y^h(0, t-1)(\theta), y^{*h}(0,t)(\theta), \varepsilon_{1t}^h; \theta],$$
$$t = 1, \ldots, T; \quad h = 1, \ldots, H.$$

In other words, while each simulated path $y^h(0, T)(\theta)$, $h = 1, \ldots, H$ has been correctly drawn from its distribution given the observed path $z(1, T)$ of exogenous variables for each possible value of θ, the draw of $y_t^h(\theta)$ at each given t is conditional to past *simulated* $y^h(0, t-1)(\theta)$ and not to past *observed* $y(0, t-1)$: hence the terminology *path simulations*. Note, however, that the model does not specify the probability distribution of exogenous variables and thus, all simulations are conditional to the observed path $z(1, T)$ of exogenous variables.

In both cases, model (1) or (2), since the spirit of bootstrap is re-sampling from a preliminary estimator, $\hat{\beta}_T$ gives rise to H bootstrap samples $y^h(0, T)(\hat{\beta}_T)$, $h = 1, \ldots, H$. For each bootstrap sample, the same estimation procedure can be applied to get H estimators denoted as $\beta_T^h(\hat{\beta}_T)$, $h = 1, \ldots, H$. These H estimations characterize the bootstrap distribution of $\hat{\beta}_T$ and allow us for instance to approximate the expectation $b_T(\theta^0)$ by $b_T(\hat{\beta}_T)$. Of course, $b_T(\hat{\beta}_T)$ is not known in general but may be approximated at any desired level of accuracy, from the Monte Carlo average $(1/H)\sum_{h=1}^{H}\beta_T^h(\hat{\beta}_T)$, for H sufficiently large. As already mentioned, one may imagine non-simulation based versions of bootstrap when the binding function is available in closed form. In any case, the bias-corrected bootstrap estimator is then defined as:

$$\hat{\theta}_T = \hat{\beta}_T - [b_T(\hat{\beta}_T) - \hat{\beta}_T] \tag{3}$$

It is worth mentioning however that this parametric bootstrap procedure requires that we sufficiently trust the initial estimator $\hat{\beta}_T$ to consider that the estimated bias $[b_T(\hat{\beta}_T) - \hat{\beta}_T]$ gives a correct assessment of the true bias $[b_T(\theta^0) - \theta^0]$. This is the reason why Gourieroux, Renault and Touzi (2000) have rather proposed an iterative procedure which, at step j, improves upon an estimator $\hat{\theta}_T^j$ by computing $\hat{\theta}_T^{j+1}$ as:

$$\hat{\theta}_T^{j+1} = \hat{\theta}_T^j + \lambda[\hat{\beta}_T - b_T(\hat{\theta}_T^j)] \tag{4}$$

for some given updating parameter λ between 0 and 1. In other words, at each step, a new set of simulated paths $y^h(0, T)(\hat{\theta}_T^j)$, $h = 1, \ldots, H$ is built and it provides a Monte Carlo assessment $b_T(\hat{\theta}_T^j)$ of the expectation of interest. It is worth noting that this does not involve new random draws of the noise ε. Note that (3) corresponds to the first iteration of (4) in the particular case $\lambda = 1$ with a starting value $\hat{\theta}_T^1 = \hat{\beta}_T$. While this preliminary estimator is indeed a natural starting value, the rationale for considering λ smaller than 1 is to increase the probability of convergence of the algorithm, possibly at the cost of slower convergence (if faster update would also work). If the algorithm converges, its limit will define an estimator $\hat{\theta}_T$ solution of:

$$b_T(\hat{\theta}_T) = \hat{\beta}_T \tag{5}$$

Gourieroux, Renault and Touzi (2000) study more generally the properties of the estimator (5), which is actually a particular case of SII estimators developed in the next section. The intuition is quite clear. Let us call $\hat{\beta}_T$ the naive estimator. Our preferred estimator $\hat{\theta}_T$ is the value of unknown parameters θ, which, if it had been the true one, would have generated a naive estimator which, in average, would have coincided with our actual naive estimation. In particular, if the bias function $[b_T(\theta) - \theta]$ is linear with respect to θ, we deduce $b_T[E(\hat{\theta}_T)] = E(\hat{\beta}_T) = b_T(\theta^0)$ and thus our estimator is unbiased. Otherwise, unbiasedness is only approximately true to the extent a linear approximation of the bias is reasonable. Since, in the context of stationary first order autoregressive processes, the negative bias of the OLS estimator of the correlation coefficient becomes more severely non-linear in the near unit root case, Andrews (1993) has put forward a median-unbiased estimator based on the principle (5) with median replacing expectation. The advantage of median is to be immune to nonlinear monotonic transformations. However, its generalization to multivariate parameters is problematic.

Another well-documented advantage of bootstrap is to provide asymptotic refinements when the initial procedure is not too bad. Gourieroux, Renault and Touzi (2000) have shown that SII does as well as bootstrap in this respect.

2. Simulation-based indirect inference

Let us start from the simple textbook example of a just-identified supply–demand system in equilibrium:

$$Q_t^s = \theta_1 p_t + \theta_2 z_{1t} + u_{1t}$$
$$Q_t^d = \theta_3 p_t + \theta_4 z_{2t} + u_{2t}$$
$$Q_t^s = Q_t^d = Q_t.$$

Then the reduced form can obviously be written as a bivariate regresssion of (Q_t, p_t) on (z_{1t}, z_{2t}) and the reduced form regression coefficients β are given as a function $\beta = b(\theta)$ of the structural parameters:

$$\theta = (\theta_1, \theta_2, \theta_3, \theta_4)b(\theta) = (\theta_1 - \theta_3)^{-1}(-\theta_2\theta_3, \theta_1\theta_4, -\theta_2, \theta_4).$$

Under standard assumptions, the vector β of reduced form parameters can be consistently estimated by its OLS counterpart $\hat{\beta}_T$. Moreover, the binding function $\beta = b(\theta)$ relating the vector β of reduced form parameters to the vector θ of structural parameters is clearly one-to-one. Inverting the binding function is a straightforward exercise and suggests computing a consistent estimator $\hat{\theta}_T$ of the structural parameters as $\hat{\theta}_T = b^{-1}(\hat{\beta}_T)$. This estimator has been known since the early days of the simultaneous equations literature as the *indirect least squares* estimator. We conclude from this example that defining an indirect estimator $\hat{\theta}_T$ of the parameters of interest from an initial estimator $\hat{\beta}_T$ and a binding function $b_T(\cdot)$ by solving the equation:

$$b_T(\hat{\theta}_T) = \hat{\beta}_T \tag{6}$$

may be worthwhile in many situations other than the bias-correction setting of Section 1. The vector β of the so-called *instrumental parameters* must identify the *structural parameters* θ but does not need to bear the same interpretation. However, the example of *indirect least squares* is too simple to display all the features of *indirect inference* as more generally devised by Smith (1993) and Gourieroux, Monfort and Renault (1993). Two complications may arise.

First, the binding function is not in general available in closed form and can be characterized only thanks to Monte Carlo integration. Moreover, by contrast with the simple linear example, the binding function does depend in general on the sample size T.

Second, most interesting examples allow for over-identification of the structural parameters, for instance through a bunch of instrumental variables in the simultaneous equation case. This is the reason why we refer henceforth to the auxiliary parameters β as instrumental parameters.

The key idea is that, as already explained in Section 1, our preliminary estimation procedure for instrumental parameters not only gives us an estimation $\hat{\beta}_T$ computed from the observed sample path but can also be applied to each simulated path $y^h(0, T)(\theta)$, $h = 1, \ldots, H$, always associated to the observed path $z(1, T)$ of exogenous variables. Thus, we end up, for any fixed value of θ, with a set of H 'estimations' $\beta_T^{(h)}(\theta)$. Averaging them, we get a Monte Carlo binding function:

$$\beta_{T,H}(\theta) = (1/H) \sum_{h=1}^{H} \beta_T^{(h)}(\theta).$$

The exact generalization of what we did in Section 1 amounts to defining the binding function $b_T(\theta)$ as the probability limit (w.r.t. the random draw of the process ε) of the sequence $\beta_{T,H}(\theta)$ when H goes to infinity. However, for most non-linear models, the instrumental estimators $\beta_T^{(h)}(\theta)$ are not reliable for finite T but only for a sample size T going to infinity. It is then worth realizing that when T goes to infinity, for any given $h = 1, \ldots, H$, $\beta_T^{(h)}(\theta)$ should tend towards the so-called *asymptotic binding* function $b(\theta)$ which is also the limit of the *finite sample binding* function $b_T(\theta)$.

Therefore, as far as consistency of estimators when T goes to infinity is concerned, a large number H of simulations is not necessary and we will define more generally an *indirect estimator* $\hat{\theta}_T$ as solution of a minimum distance problem:

$$\text{Min}_\theta [\hat{\beta}_T - \beta_{T,H}(\theta)]' \Omega_T [\hat{\beta}_T - \beta_{T,H}(\theta)] \tag{7}$$

where Ω_T is a positive definite matrix converging towards a deterministic positive definite matrix Ω. In case of a completed Monte Carlo integration (H large) we end up with an approximation of the exact binding function-based estimation:

$$\text{Min}_\theta [\hat{\beta}_T - b_T(\theta)]' \Omega_T [\hat{\beta}_T - b_T(\theta)] \tag{8}$$

which generalizes the bias-correction procedure of Section 1. As in Section 1, we may expect good finite sample properties of such an indirect estimator since, intuitively, the finite sample bias is similar in the two quantities, which are matched against each other and thus should cancel out in the matching process.

In terms of asymptotic theory, the main results under standard regularity conditions (see Gourieroux, Monfort and Renault, 1993) are:

(i) the indirect inference estimator $\hat{\theta}_T$ converges towards the true unknown value θ^0 insofar as the asymptotic binding function identifies it:

$$b(\theta) = b(\theta^0) \Rightarrow \theta = \theta^0;$$

(ii) the indirect inference estimator $\hat{\theta}_T$ is asymptotically normal insofar as the asymptotic binding function first order identifies the true value:

$$\frac{\partial b}{\partial \theta'}(\theta^0) \text{ is of full} - \text{column rank};$$

(iii) we get an indirect inference estimator with a minimum asymptotic variance if and only if the limit-weighting matrix is proportional to the inverse of the asymptotic variance Σ_H of $\sqrt{T}[\hat{\beta}_T - \beta_{T,H}(\theta^0)]$;

(iv) the asymptotic variance of the efficient indirect inference estimator is the inverse of

$$\frac{\partial b'}{\partial \theta}(\theta^0)(\Sigma_H)^{-1}\frac{\partial b}{\partial \theta'}(\theta^0)$$

with

$$\Sigma_H = [1 + \frac{1}{H}]\Sigma_\infty.$$

An implication of these results is that, as far as asymptotic variance of the indirect inference estimator is concerned, the only role of a finite number H of simulations is to multiply the optimal variance (obtained with $H = \infty$) by a factor $(1 + 1/H)$. Actually, when computing the indirect inference estimator (7), one may be reluctant to use a very large H since it involves, for each value of θ along a minimization algorithm, computing H instrumental estimators $\beta_T^{(h)}(\theta)$, $h = 1, \ldots, H$. We will see in Section 3 several ways to replace these H computations by only one. However, this will come at a price, which is the probable loss of the nice finite sample properties of (7) and (8).

As a conclusion, let us stress that indirect inference is able, beyond finite sample biases, to correct for any kind of misspecification bias. The philosophy of this method is basically to estimate a simple model, possibly wrong, to get easily an instrumental estimator $\hat{\beta}_T$ while a direct estimation of structural parameters θ would have been a daunting task. Therefore what really matters is to use an instrumental parameter that captures the key features of the parameters of interest, while being much simpler to estimate. For instance, Pastorello, Renault and Touzi (2000) and Engle and Lee (1996) have proposed to first estimate a GARCH model as an instrumental model to indirectly recover an estimator of the structural model of interest, a stochastic volatility model much more difficult to estimate directly. Other natural examples are models with latent variables such that an observed variable provides a convenient proxy. An estimator based on this proxy suffers from a misspecification bias, but we end up with a consistent estimator by applying the indirect inference matching. Examples of this approach are:

(i) Pastorello, Renault and Touzi (2000), who use Black and Scholes implied volatilities as a proxy of realizations of the latent spot volatility process.
(ii) Li (2006), who, following a suggestion of Renault (1997), uses observed bids in an auction market as a proxy of latent private values.

3. Simulated method of moments

SMM, as introduced by Ingram and Lee (1991) and Duffie and Singleton (1993), is the simulation-based counterpart of GMM to take advantage of the informational content of some conditional moment restrictions:

$$E\{K[y_t, z(1, t)]|z(1, t)\} = k[z(1, t); \theta^0]. \tag{9}$$

The role of simulations in this context is to provide a Monte Carlo assessment of the population conditional moment function $k[z(1, t); \theta]$ when it is not easily available in closed form. Typically, with $y_t^h(\theta)$ drawn as above for $h = 1, \ldots, H$ (model (1) or (2)), a convenient Monte Carlo counterpart is: $(1/H)\sum_{h=1}^{H} K[y_t^h(\theta), z(1, t)]$. Even though we will mainly present SMM in this simple setting, two possible extensions are worth mentioning.

1. First, in dynamic settings, one may want to consider conditional moment restrictions given not only past and current exogenous variables but also past endogenous variables:

$$E\{K[y_t, z(1, t), y(0, t - 1)]|z(1, t), y(0, t - 1)\} = k[z(1, t), y(0, t - 1); \theta^0].$$

SMM can still be applied to this kind of dynamic moment insofar as one is able to draw simulated values $y_t^h(\theta)$ in the conditional probability distribution (corresponding to the value θ of parameters) of y_t given $x_t = [z(1, t), y(0, t - 1)]$. In other words, we need conditional simulations and not only path simulations. As explained above, such conditional simulations are not feasible when the structural model is only defined through a recursive form (2). By contrast, either path simulations or conditional simulations work for static moment conditions (9).

2. Second, the introduction of latent variables paves the way for many other Monte Carlo assessments of the population expectation $E\{K[y_t, z(1, t)]|z(1, t)\}$. Let us assume to simplify that $y_t = r_1(y_t^*)$ with i.i.d. latent variables y_t^* endowed with a probability distribution with fixed support (independent of the unknown parameters θ). Of course, the density function $f[y_t^*|z(1, t); \theta]$ does depend on θ but one may also

pick, as a sampling tool called importance function, another distribution with a given density function $\varphi(u_t)$ on the same support. Then, instead of assessing the population expectation with its naive Monte Carlo counterpart

$$(1/H) \sum_{h=1}^{H} K[r_1(y_t^{*h}(\theta)), z(1, t)].$$

one may prefer to resort to

$$(1/H) \sum_{h=1}^{H} K[r_1(u_t^h), z(1, t)] \frac{f[u_t^h | z(1, t); \theta]}{\varphi(u_t^h)}$$

where the u_t^h, $h = 1, \ldots, H$, are independently drawn from the distribution with density function $\varphi(u_t)$. This kind of *importance sampling* may be helpful, for instance, for removing some nasty lack of smoothness with respect to the unknown parameters.

As far as static conditional moment restrictions like (9) are concerned, the natural way to extend GMM with a Monte Carlo assessment of the population moment is to minimize with respect to the unknown parameters θ a norm of the sample mean of:

$$Z_t \left\{ K[y_t, z(1, t)] - (1/H) \sum_{h=1}^{H} K[y_t^h(\theta), z(1, t)] \right\}$$

where Z_t is a matrix of chosen instruments, that is a fixed matrix function of $z(1, t)$. It is then clear that the minimization programme which is considered is a particular case of (7) above with:

$$\hat{\beta}_T = (1/T) \sum_{t=1}^{T} Z_t K[y_t, z(1, t)]$$

and $\beta_{T,H}(\theta)$ defined accordingly. In other words, we reinterpret SMM as a particular case of *indirect inference*, when the instrumental parameters to match are simple moments rather than themselves defined through some structural interpretations. Note, however, that the moment conditions for SMM could be slightly more general since the function $K[y_t, z(1, t)]$ itself could depend on the unknown parameters θ. In any case, the general asymptotic theory sketched above for SII is still valid. It may be a little more involved when using importance sampling, since then the variance of the simulator no longer coincides with the variance of the initial moments, and then computing the asymptotic variance of the SMM estimator is no longer simply akin to multiplying standard formulas by a factor $[1 + 1/H]$. However, we still note that the number H of simulated paths does not need to be large for getting consistent and rather accurate estimators.

In contrast with general SII as presented above, an advantage of SMM is that the instrumental parameters to match, as simple moments, are in general easier to compute than estimated auxiliary parameters $\beta_T^{(h)}(\theta)$, $h = 1, \ldots, H$, derived from some computationally demanding *extremum* estimation procedure. Gallant and Tauchen (1996) have taken advantage of this remark to propose a practical computational strategy for implementing indirect inference when the estimator $\hat{\beta}_T$ of the instrumental parameters is obtained as an M-estimator solution of:

$$\text{Max}_\beta (1/T) \sum_{t=1}^{T} q_t[y(0,t), z(1,t); \beta].$$

The key idea is then to define the moments to match through the (pseudo)-score vector of this M-estimator. Let us denote

$$K[y(0,t), z(1,t); \beta] = \frac{\partial q_t}{\partial \beta}[y(0,t), z(1,t); \beta]$$

and consider an SMM estimator of θ obtained as a minimizer of the norm of a sample mean of:

$$K[y(0,t), z(1,t); \hat{\beta}_T] - (1/H) \sum_{h=1}^{H} K[y^h(0,t)(\theta), z(1,t); \hat{\beta}_T].$$

For a suitable GMM metric, such a minimization defines a so-called *simulated-score matching* estimator $\hat{\theta}_T$ of θ. In the spirit of Gallant and Tauchen (1996), the objective function that defines the initial estimator $\hat{\beta}_T$ is typically the log-likelihood of some auxiliary model. However, this feature is not needed for the validity of the asymptotic theory sketched below. Several remarks are in order:

1. By contrast with a general SMM criterion, the minimization above does not involve the choice of any instrumental variable. Typically, over-identification will be achieved by choosing an auxiliary model with a large number of instrumental parameters β rather than by choosing instruments.
2. By definition of $\hat{\beta}_T$, the sample mean of $K[y(0,t), z(1,t); \beta]$ takes the value zero for $\beta = \hat{\beta}_T$. In other words, the minimization programme above amounts to:

$$\text{Min}_\theta \left\| (1/TH) \sum_{t=1}^{T} \sum_{h=1}^{H} \frac{\partial q_t}{\partial \beta}[y^h(0,t)(\theta), z(1,t); \hat{\beta}_T] \right\| \Omega_T \tag{10}$$

for a suitable GMM metric Ω_T.
3. It can be shown (see Gourieroux, Monfort and Renault, 1993) that under the same assumptions as for the asymptotic theory of SII, the *score-matching* estimator is consistent asymptotically normal. We get a score-matching estimator with a minimum asymptotic variance if and only if the limit-weighting matrix Ω is proportional to the inverse of the asymptotic conditional variance of

$$\sqrt{T} \sum_{t=1}^{T} \frac{\partial q_t}{\partial \beta}[y(0,t), z(1,t); b(\theta^0)]$$

given the exogenous variables z. Then the resulting *efficient score-matching estimator* is asymptotically equivalent to the *efficient indirect inference estimator*.

4. Owing to this asymptotic equivalence, the score-matching estimator can be seen as an alternative to the efficient SII estimator characterized in Section 2. This alternative is often referred to as *efficient method of moments* (EMM) since, when $q_t[y(0, t), z(1, t); \beta]$ is the log-likelihood $f^a[y_t|z(1, t), y(0, t-1); \beta]$ of some auxiliary model, the estimator is as efficient as maximum likelihood under correct specification of the auxiliary model. More generally, the auxiliary model is designed to approximate the true data generating process as closely as possible and Gallant and Tauchen (1996) propose the *semi-nonparametric* (SNP) modelling to this end. These considerations and the terminology EMM should not lead us to believe that *score-matching* is more efficient than *indirect inference*. The two estimators are asymptotically equivalent even though the score-matching approach makes more transparent the required spanning property of the auxiliary model to reach the Cramer Rao efficiency bound of the structural model.

5. Another alleged advantage of the *score-matching* with respect to *parameter-matching* in SII is its low computational cost. The fact is that with a large number of instrumental parameters β, as will typically be the case with a SNP auxiliary model, it may be costly to maximize H times the log-likelihood of the auxiliary model (for each value of θ along an optimization algorithm) with respect to β to compute $\beta_T^{(h)}(\theta)$, $h = 1, \ldots, H$. By contrast, the programme (10) minimizes only once the norm of a vector of derivatives with respect to β. One must realize, however, that not only is this cheaper computation likely to lose the expected nice finite sample properties of SII put forward in the previous section, but also that the point is not really about a choice between matching (instrumental) parameters β or matching the (instrumental) score $\sum_{t=1}^{T} \frac{\partial q_t}{\partial \beta}$. The key issue is rather the way to use H simulated paths of size T each as explained below.

6. It is worth realizing that the sum of TH terms considered in the definition (10) of the score-matching estimator is akin to consider only one simulated path $y^1(0, TH)(\theta)$ of size TH built from random draws as above (conditional simulations or path simulations) from a fictitious path $z^*(1, TH)$ of exogenous variables defined in the following way:

$$z_1^* = z_1, \ldots, z_T^* = z_T, z_{T+1}^* = z_1, \ldots,$$
$$z_{2T}^* = z_T, z_{2T+1}^* = z_1, \ldots, z_{TH}^* = z_T.$$

If for instance (z_t) is Markov of order 1, such a fictitious path is a correct draw except possibly for H values, which is immaterial when T goes to infinity. From such a simulated path, estimation of instrumental parameters would have produced a vector $\beta_{TH}^{(1)}(\theta)$ that could have been used for *indirect inference*, that is to define an estimator $\hat{\theta}_T$ solution of:

$$\text{Min}_\theta [\hat{\beta}_T - \beta_{TH}^{(1)}(\theta)]' \Omega_T [\hat{\beta}_T - \beta_{TH}^{(1)}(\theta)]. \tag{11}$$

This *parameter-matching* estimator is not more computationally demanding than the corresponding *score-matching* estimator computed from the same simulated path as solution of:

$$\text{Min}_\theta \left\| (1/TH) \sum_{t=1}^{TH} \frac{\partial q_t}{\partial \beta} [y^1(0,t)(\theta), z^*(1,t); \hat{\beta}_T] \right\| \Omega_T. \tag{12}$$

Actually, (11) and (12) are numerically identical in the case of just-identification (dim θ = dim β). Then the choice of a GMM metric is immaterial and both estimators are basically the solution $\hat{\theta}_T$ of:

$$(1/TH) \sum_{t=1}^{TH} \frac{\partial q_t}{\partial \beta} [y^1(0,t)(\hat{\theta}_T), z^*(1,t); \hat{\beta}_T] = 0.$$

More generally, the four estimators (7), (10), (11) and (12) are asymptotically equivalent when T goes to infinity and the GMM weighting matrix is efficiently chosen accordingly. However, it is quite obvious that only (7) performs the right finite sample bias correction by matching instrumental parameters values estimated on both observed and simulated paths of lengths T. The trade-off is thus between giving up finite sample bias correction or paying the price for computing H estimated instrumental parameters.

4. Simulated M-estimators

Even though well-chosen moments to match may allow one to get accurate estimators, it is somewhat contradictory to resort to a fully parametric model to perform simulations needed for SMM while Hansen's (1982) GMM was semi-parametric in spirit. *Simulated maximum likelihood* (SML) methods aim at exploiting the whole parametric structure for efficient estimation. The key role of simulations would then be to provide an unbiased simulator of each conditional p.d.f. $f[y_t|z(1,t), y(0,t-1); \theta]$ (also denoted $f[y_t|x_t; \theta]$) because it is not available in closed form. This is typically the case in a model with latent variables, and then conditioning may provide a convenient simulator. The simplest example comes from model (2) when latent variables are exogenous. Let us write it without observed exogenous variables for sake of expositional simplicity:

$$y_t = r_1[y(0,t-1), y^*(0,t), \varepsilon_{1t}; \theta], \quad t = 1, \ldots, T$$
$$y_t^* = r_2[y^*(0,t-1), \varepsilon_{2t}; \theta], \quad t = 1, \ldots, T. \tag{13}$$

Then $f[y_t|x_t; \theta]$ is nothing but the expectation with respect to the probability distribution of $y^*(0,t)$ of $f[y_t|x_t, y^*(0,t); \theta]$. While the latter is easily deduced from the pdf of ε_{1t} through the measurement equation (the first equation above), the former is in general easy to compute from the evolution equation (the second equation above). Then

Monte Carlo integration provides an unbiased estimate of $f[y_t|x_t; \theta]$ with $(1/H)\sum_{h=1}^{H} f[y_t|x_t, y^{*h}(0,t)(\theta); \theta]$ where $y^{*h}(0,t)(\theta)$, $h=1,\ldots,H$, are independent draws obtained from independent draws in the known distribution of ε_{2t}. Of course, importance sampling must also be relevant in this context. Moreover, for a general model (2), when y does cause y^*, this naive approach may be very inefficient (in terms of speed of convergence of the variance towards zero) and one may want to refer to either accelerated versions of importance sampling (Danielsson and Richard, 1993), simulated expectation maximization algorithm (SEM, see for example Shephard, 1993) and other more sophisticated simulators, which are beyond the scope of this article.

Irrespective of the choice of the simulator, the main difficulty with SML is that the logarithm of an unbiased simulator of the likelihood is not an unbiased simulator of the log-likelihood. Therefore, in contrast with SMM, SML is consistent only when both H and T go to infinity. Note, however, that asymptotic bias corrections are possible (see Gourieroux and Monfort, 1996). Under standard regularity conditions, SML is asymptotically efficient insofar as T goes to infinity slower than H^2. Another version of the SML method is the *simulated score* method (see Hajivassiliou, 1993). This is basically a version of SMM where the latent score is used as a simulator for the score of the model on observables, while the later is not tractable analytically. This method should not be confused with *simulated score matching* of the former section, where the score to match was not something to simulate to get it in closed form.

Finally, it is worth mentioning that simulation-based estimation methods are not always to be recommended, even in some fully parametric modelling situations with latent variables making standard maximum likelihood unfeasible. Such situations typically occur with structural econometric models where equilibrium of a market or of a game implies a deterministic relationship between latent variables and observed ones. Then, not only is the above SML theory no longer valid but any other simulation based method will in general be highly inefficient because the dependence between the two blocks of unknown 'parameters', namely, structural parameters and latent variables, is sharp. In such contexts, some authors have, however, considered some simulated non-linear least squares methods (Laffont, Ossard and Vuong, 1995 for auction markets) or more generally simulated pseudo-likelihood methods (Laroque and Salanie, 1993). While the focus of interest of Laroque and Salanie (1993) on a disequilibrium model raised more involved issues due to non-differentiability, it is rather clear that some implied state GMM methods (Pan, 2002; Pastorello, Patilea and Renault, 2003) are more efficient than SMM in the contexts of smooth equilibrium relationships like those produced by option pricing theory. The key issue is to take advantage of the deterministic relationship between y_t and y_t^* (for a given value of the parameters θ) to track what would have been an efficient estimation if latent variables had been observed.

5. Concluding remarks

The econometrician's search for a well-specified parametric model ('quest for the Holy Grail' as stated by Monfort, 1996) and associated efficient estimators' even remain popular when MLE becomes intractable due to highly non-linear dynamic structure including latent variables. The efficiency properties of SML, EMM and more generally of SMM and SII when the set of instrumental parameters to match is sufficiently large to span the likelihood scores are often advocated as if the likelihood score is well specified. However, the likely misspecification of the structural model requires a generalization of the theory of SII as recently proposed by Dridi, Guay and Renault (2007). As for MLE with misspecification (see White, 1982; Gourieroux, Monfort and Trognon, 1984) such a generalization entails two elements.

First, asymptotic variance formulas are complicated by the introduction of sandwich formulas. Ignoring this kind of correction is even more detrimental than for QMLE since two types of sandwich formulas must be taken into account, one for the data generating process (DGP) and one for the simulator (based either on model (1) or model (2)) which turns out to be different from the DGP in case of misspecification.

Secondly, and even more importantly, misspecification may imply that we consistently estimate a pseudo-true value, which is poorly related to the true unknown value of the parameters of interest. Dridi, Guay and Renault (2007) put forward the necessary (partial) encompassing property of the instrumental model (through instrumental parameters β) by the structural model (with parameters θ) needed to ensure consistency towards true values of (part of) the components of θ in spite of misspecification. The key issue is that, since structural parameters are recovered from instrumental ones by inverting a binding function $\beta = b(\theta)$, all components are interdependent. The requirement of encompassing typically means that, if one does not want to proceed under the maintained assumption that the structural model (1) or (2) is true, one must be parsimonious with respect to the number of moments to match or more generally to the scope of empirical evidence that is captured by the instrumental parameters β. In other words, robustness to misspecification requires an instrumental model choice strategy opposite to that commonly used for a structural model: the larger the instrumental model, the larger the risk of contamination of the estimated structural parameters of interest by what is wrong in the structural model. Of course, there is no such thing as a free lunch: robustness to misspecification through a parsimonious and well-focused instrumental model comes at the price of efficiency loss. Efficiency loss means not only lack of accuracy of estimators of structural parameters but also lack of power of specification tests.

ERIC RENAULT

Bibliography

Andrews, D. 1993. Exactly median unbiased estimation of first order autoregressive/unit root models. *Econometrica* 61, 139–65.

Danielsson, J. and Richard, J.F. 1993. Accelerated Gaussian importance sampler with application to dynamic latent variables models. *Journal of Applied Econometrics* 8, S153–73.

Dridi, R., Guay, A. and Renault, E. 2007. Indirect inference and calibration of dynamic stochastic general equilibrium models. *Journal of Econometrics* 136, 397–430.

Duffie, D. and Singleton, K. 1993. Simulated moments estimation of Markov models of asset prices. *Econometrica* 61, 929–52.

Engle, R.F. and Lee, G.G.J. 1996. Estimating diffusion models of stochastic volatility. In *Modeling Stock Market Volatility: Bridging the Gap to Continuous Time*, ed. P.E. Rossi. New York: Academic Press.

Gallant, A.R. and Tauchen, G. 1996. Which moments to match? *Econometric Theory* 12, 657–81.

Gourieroux, C. and Monfort, A. 1995. Testing, encompassing, and simulating dynamic econometric models. *Econometric Theory* 11, 195–228.

Gourieroux, C. and Monfort, A. 1996. Simulation-based econometric methods. *Core Lectures.* Oxford: Oxford University Press.

Gourieroux, C., Monfort, A. and Renault, E. 1993. Indirect inference. *Journal of Applied Econometrics* 8, S85–118.

Gourieroux, C., Monfort, A. and Trognon, A. 1984. Pseudo-maximum likelihood methods theory. *Econometrica* 52, 681–700.

Gourieroux, C., Renault, E. and Touzi, N. 2000. Calibration by simulation for small sample bias correction. In *Simulation-Based Inference in Econometrics*, ed. R. Mariano, T. Schuerman and M.J. Weeks. Cambridge: Cambridge University Press.

Hajivassiliou, V.A. 1993. Simulation estimation methods for limited dependent variable models. In *Handbook of Statistics*, vol. 11, ed. G.S. Maddala, C.R. Rao and H. Vinod. Amsterdam: North-Holland.

Hall, P. 1992. *The Bootstrap and Edgeworth Expansion.* New York: Springer.

Hansen, L.P. 1982. Large sample properties of generalized method of moments. *Econometrica* 50, 1029–54.

Horowitz, J.L. 1997. Bootstrap methods in econometrics: theory and numerical performance. In *Advances in Econometrics, seventh world congress*, ed. D. Kreps and K. Wallis. Cambridge: Cambridge University Press.

Ingram, B.F. and Lee, B.S. 1991. Estimation by simulation of time series models. *Journal of Econometrics* 47, 197–207.

Laffont, J.J., Ossard, H. and Vuong, Q. 1995. Econometrics of first-price auction. *Econometrica* 63, 953–80.

Laroque, G. and Salanie, B. 1993. Simulation based estimation of models with lagged latent variables. *Journal of Applied Econometrics* 8, S119–33.

Li, T. 2006. Indirect inference in structural econometric models. *Journal of Econometrics*, forthcoming.

Monfort, A. 1996. A reappraisal of misspecified econometric models. *Econometric Theory* 12, 597–619.

Monfort, A. and Van Dijk, H.K. 1995. Simulation-based econometrics. In *Econometric Inference Using Simulation Techniques*, ed. H.K. Van Dijk, A. Monfort and B.W. Brown. New York: Wiley.

Pan, J. 2002. The jump-risk premia implicit in options: evidence from an integrated time-series study. *Journal of Financial Economics* 63, 3–50.

Pastorello, S., Patilea, V. and Renault, E. 2003. Iterative and recursive estimation in structural non-adaptive models. Invited Lecture with discussion. *Journal of Business, Economics and Statistics* 21, 449–509.

Pastorello, S., Renault, E. and Touzi, N. 2000. Statistical inference for random-variance option pricing. *Journal of Business and Economic Statistics* 18, 358–67.

Renault, E. 1997. Econometric models of option pricing errors. In *Advances in Econometrics, Seventh World Congress*, ed. D. Kreps and K. Wallis. Cambridge: Cambridge University Press.

Shephard, N. 1993. Fitting nonlinear time series with applications to stochastic variance models. *Journal of Applied Econometrics* 8, S134–52.

Smith, A. 1993. Estimating nonlinear time series models using simulated vector autoregressions. *Journal of Applied Econometrics* 8, S63–84.

White, H. 1982. Maximum likelihood estimation of mis-specified models. *Econometrica* 50, 1–25.

social interactions (empirics)

The empirical economics literature on social interactions addresses the significance of the social context in economic decisions. Decisions of individuals who share a social milieu are likely to be interdependent. Recognizing the nature of such interdependence in a variety of conventional and unconventional settings and measuring empirically the role of social interactions poses complex econometric questions. Their resolution may be critical for a multitude of phenomena in economic and social life and of matters of public policy. Questions like why some countries are Catholic and others Protestant, why crime rates vary so much across cities in the same country, why fads exist and survive, and why there is residential segregation and neighbourhood tipping are all in principle issues that may be examined as social interactions phenomena.

The social context enters in a variety of ways. One is that individuals care not only about their own purely private outcomes – for example, the kinds of cars they drive or the education they acquire – but also about outcomes of others, such as the kinds of cars or the education of their friends. This type of interpersonal effect is known as *endogenous* social effect (or interaction), because it depends on *decisions* of others in the same social milieu. Individuals may also care about personal characteristics of others, that is, whether they are young or old, black or white, rich or poor, trendy or conventional, and so on, and about other attributes of the social milieu that may not be properly characterized as deliberate decisions of others. The latter is known as exogenous social or *contextual* effect. In addition, individuals in the same or similar social settings tend to act similarly because they share common unobservable factors. Such an interaction pattern is known as *correlated* effects. This terminology is due to Manski (1993).

Emergence of social interdependencies is natural if individuals share a common resource or space in a way that is not paid but still generates constraints on individual action. This is also known as pecuniary externalities. Individuals who try to form expectations about future outcomes of current decisions, like occupational choice, may rely on lessons from the actions of others and therefore end up mimicking their behaviour. Endogenous social interactions are a case of real externalities, a pervasive feature of economic behaviour.

Theorizing in this area must lie in the interface of economics, sociology and psychology, and often is imprecise. Terms like social interactions, neighbourhood effects, social capital and peer effects are often used as synonyms, although they may have different connotations. Empirical distinctions between endogenous, contextual and correlated effects are critical for policy analysis because of the 'social multiplier,' as we see further below.

Joint dependence among individuals' decisions *and* characteristics within a social milieu is complicated further by the fact that in many interesting circumstances individuals in effect choose the social context. For example, individuals choose their friends and their neighbourhoods and thus their neighbourhood effects as well. Such choices involve information that is in part unobservable to the analyst, and therefore require making inferences among the possible factors which contribute to decisions (Brock and Durlauf, 2001; Moffitt, 2001). The present article focuses on highlighting the significance of key empirical findings and owes a lot to Durlauf (2004), the most comprehensive review to date that examines the methodological basis, statistical reliability and conceptual and empirical breadth of the neighbourhood effects literature.

Empirical framework

Let individual *i*'s outcome ω_i, a scalar, be a linear function of a vector of observable individual characteristics, X_i, of a vector of contextual effects, $Y_{n(i)}$, which describe *i*'s neighbourhood $n(i)$, and of the expected value of the ω_j's of the members of neighbourhood $n(i)$, $j \in n(i)$. It is straightforward to incorporate social interactions into economic models in a manner that is fully compatible with economic reasoning, that is, by positing that individuals maximize a utility function subject to constraints and obtain a behavioural equation such as:

$$\omega_i = k + cX_i + dY_{n(i)} + Jm_{n(i)} + \varepsilon_i, \tag{1}$$

where ε_i is a random error and k a constant. Ignore for the moment the fact that individual *i* may have deliberately chosen neighborhood $n(i)$. The assumption that the expectation of ε_i in (1) is zero, conditional on individual characteristics, on contextual effects and on the event that *i* is a member of neighbourhood $n(i)$, allows us to focus on the estimation of the model. The critical next step for translating theoretical models into empirical applications is to assume *social equilibrium* and that individuals hold *rational expectations* over $m_{n(i)}$. That is, individuals' expectations are confirmed in that they are exactly equal to what the model predicts on average. So, taking the expectation of ω_i and setting it equal to $m_{n(i)}$ allows us to solve for $m_{n(i)}$. Substituting back into (1) yields a *reduced form equation*, an expression for individual *i*'s outcome in terms of all observables:

$$\omega_i = \frac{k}{1-J} + cX_i + \frac{J}{1-J} cX_{n(i)} + \frac{d}{1-J} Y_{n(i)} + \varepsilon_i. \tag{2}$$

This simple linear model obscures the richness that nonlinear social interactions models make possible, like multiplicity of equilibria (Brock and Durlauf, 2001). Yet it does facilitate studying other aspects. For example, it does confirm that endogenous social effects generate feedbacks which magnify the effects of neighbourhood characteristics. That is, the effect of a unit increase in $Y_{n(i)}$ is $\frac{d}{1-J}$, and not just d, as one would expect from (1). It also confirms why it is tempting for empirical researchers to study individual outcomes as functions of all observables. Following the pioneering work of Datcher (1982), a great variety of individual outcomes have been studied in the context of different neighbourhoods and typically significant effects have been found. Deriving causal results requires suitable data.

Manski (1993) emphasized that the practice of including neighbourhood averages of individual effects as contextual effects, $Y_{n(i)} = X_{n(i)}$, may cause failure of identification of endogenous as distinct from exogenous interactions, that is, to estimate J separately from d. That is, if the neighbourhood attributes *coincide* with the neighbourhood averages of its inhabitants' characteristics, or $Y_{n(i)} = X_{n(i)}$, then regressing individual outcomes on neighbourhood averages of individual characteristics as contextual effects allows us to estimate a function of the parameters of interest, $\frac{Jc+d}{1-J}$, the coefficient of $X_{n(i)}$ in a regression according to (2). A statistically significant estimate of this coefficient implies that at least one type of social interaction is present, either J or d or both are non-zero. This is known as Manski's *reflection problem*, which is specific to *linear* models: the equilibrium value of the outcome $m_{n(i)}$ is linearly related to the neighbourhood attributes, and therefore its effect on individual outcomes may not be distinguishable from their 'reflection'.

Complicating the basic model in natural ways, as by assuming correlated effects – like group members sharing group-specific unobservable effects, that is, the performance of students in the same class is affected by the quality of their teacher, which is unobservable, over and above peer effects from classmates – introduces additional difficulties with identification, even if individuals are randomly assigned to groups. Brock and Durlauf (2007) provide an exhaustive analysis of the various possibilities in binary choice situations with unobserved group effects. When more than two choices are available, there may be additional possibilities for identifying choice-specific effects by working with subsets of choices (Brock and Durlauf, 2005). Graham (2006), discussed further below, offers a promising approach for continuous outcomes when individuals are randomly assigned to groups, but is not focusing on the distinction between exogenous and endogenous interactions. Yet more possibilities appear when panel data (that is, repeated observations over time on the same decision-making units) are available. If contextual effects take time to make their impact on the endogenous social effect, the linear dependence is broken and the lack of identification – Manski's reflection problem – is mitigated. Sometimes, and depending upon the nature of the data as well, it may be impossible, especially in linear models, to identify social interactions in the presence of unobserved group effects. Moving from linear models to binary and other non-linear choice models improves identification even with cross-section data (Brock and Durlauf, 2007).

If it is plausible to exclude some neighbourhood averages of individual covariates, then identification may be possible. Also, if nonlinearities are inherent in the basic model specification, identification again may be possible, even in the case where the contextual effects coincide with neighbourhood averages of individual characteristics. Nonlinearities may eliminate the reflection problem. A noteworthy case in point here is Drewianka (2003), who studies two-sided matching in the marriage market and finds that it allows identification of endogenous *and* exogenous social interactions. The logic of the model requires that the two sides of the market contain an additional source of variation: the greater the number of potential marriage partners, the higher is the probability that a match will occur. There is an inherent multiplier effect at work here. One's prospects of finding a marriage partner depends on the rate at which other people match up, an endogenous social effect. Drewianka's results show that a ten per cent increase in the fraction of the population that is unmarried causes the marriage rate of never-married men to fall by ten per cent and that of never-married women by seven per cent.

An interesting consequence of endogenous social interactions is the amplification of differences in average neighbourhood behaviour across neighbourhoods. In fact, Glaeser, Sacerdote and Scheinkman (2003) use directly such patterns in the data to estimate a *social multiplier*. This is defined for a change in a particular fundamental determinant of an outcome as the ratio of a total effect, which includes a direct effect on an individual outcome plus the sum total of the indirect effects through the feedback from the effects on others in the social group, to the direct effect. It is easy to see it as the ratio of the 'group level' coefficient, the coefficient of $Y_{n(i)}$ in eq. (2), to the 'individual level' coefficient, the coefficient of $Y_{n(i)}$ in eq. (1): $\frac{d}{1-J}\frac{1}{d} = \frac{1}{1-J}$. It follows that a social multiplier greater than 1 implies endogenous social interactions, $0 < J < 1$. This approach must deal, in practice, with dependence across decisions of individuals belonging to the same group, which is implied by non-random sorting in terms of unobservables. It is particularly useful in delivering ranges of estimates for the endogenous social effect and when individual data are hard to obtain.

This is the case with crime data. Glaeser, Sacerdote and Scheinkman (1996) motivate their study of crime and social interactions by the extraordinary variation in incidence of crime across US metropolitan areas over and above differences in fundamentals. If social interactions are present, variations in observed outcomes are larger than would be expected from variations in underlying fundamentals. Glaeser, Sacerdote and Scheinkman (2003) regress actual crime rates against predicted crime rates, which are formed by multiplying percentages of US individuals in each of eight age categories by the crime rate of persons in that category. They perform such regressions at the level of county and state cross-sectionally and for the entire United States over time. Their results imply large social multipliers, which increase with the level of aggregation exactly as their basic theory would predict.

It is possible to modify this basic model in order to study several other areas involving economic decisions akin to social interactions. For example, diffusion of innovations, herding and adoption of norms or other institutions by a population involve ideas that are conceptually related to social interactions. Transmission of job-related information is of particular relevance (see Ioannides and Loury, 2004). Also, *J*, the endogenous social effect, may be negative, as in the case of land development, which is conceivably due to congestion.

Identification of social interactions using observational data on 'natural experiments'

Several researchers have sought to identify social interactions by exploiting uniquely suitable features of observational data, which are often referred to as 'natural experiments'. For example, consider outcomes for children from families with several children who share the common influence of unobservable family factors, such as parental values and competence, taste for education and time spent with children, and other unobservables that affect the upbringing of household members living in close proximity. They also share the variation in neighbourhood effects that is produced by families' residential moves. By using observations on several children from the same family who are separated in age by at least three years, Aaronson (1998) controls for family-specific characteristics. This obviates the need to control for the impact of self-selection in terms of unobservable neighbourhood characteristics. Aaronson uses data from the Panel Study of Income Dynamics and finds large and statistically significant contextual neighbourhood effects, but his models exclude endogenous social effects. His results are robust to changes in estimation techniques and in sample and variable definitions, but are sensitive to the formulation of neighbourhood characteristic proxy. Incomplete specification of family characteristics is an important concern, and its consequences for the robustness of estimated relationships are aptly demonstrated by Ginther, Haveman and Wolfe (2000).

Grinblatt, Keloharju and Ikaheimo (2004) use data for *all* residents of two large Finnish provinces – amounting to millions of observations – and establish that automobile purchase decisions by close residential neighbours influence one another. The measured endogenous neighbourhood effects are strongest among individuals belonging to the same 'social class' (especially if they belong to lower-income classes), or when the cars they purchase are of the same make or even the same model. These findings militate in favour of information sharing rather than 'keeping up with the Joneses'. We note that excluding neighbourhood averages of demographics as contextual effects is reasonably plausible in this case: there is no reason why the average *age* of my neighbours should affect directly my taste in *cars*. Conceptually related is the study of Aizer and Currie (2004), who use data from more than 3.5 million birth certificates from California to examine 'information sharing effects' in the utilization of publicly funded prenatal care. They conclude that it is not information sharing, but is, instead, differences in the behaviour of institutions that explain the established correlations between neighbourhood and ethnic group membership in prenatal care use.

Luttmer (2005) uses data from the US National Survey of Families and Households, augmented with census data from the Public Use Microdata Areas, and examines how self-reported well-being varies with own and neighbours' incomes and with other characteristics. He interprets his findings as direct evidence that people have preferences regarding their neighbours' incomes. That is, after an individual's own income is controlled for, higher earnings of neighbours are associated with lower levels of self-reported happiness on a variety of measures.

Sacerdote (2001) exploits the fact that at Dartmouth College freshman-year room-mates and dorm-mates are randomly assigned, thus producing a natural quasi-experimental setting for studying peer effects. Sacerdote posits that an individual's grade point average is a function of an individual's own academic ability prior to college entrance, of social habits, and of the academic ability and grade point average of his room-mates. Sacerdote finds that peers have an impact on each others' grade point average and on decisions to join social groups such as fraternities. He does not, however, find residential peer effects in other major college decisions, such as choice of college major. He finds peer effects in grade point average at the individual room level – you keep up with your room-mates! – whereas peer effects in fraternity membership occur at both the room level and the entire dorm level – dorms are conformist! These data provide strong evidence for the existence of peer effects in student outcomes, even among highly selected college students who may be otherwise quite homogeneous albeit in close proximity to one another. Peer effects are smaller the more directly a decision is related to labour market activities.

Peer effects in classrooms and schools

Social interactions in classrooms – peer effects – are particularly interesting in understanding schooling as an economic activity and its consequences for inequality of social outcomes. Whether students benefit from classmates with different characteristics and academic performance and whether the effect is different depending upon whether one's classroom peers are more or less able are important for education policy and the actual functioning of schools. In other words, deciding whether or not students should be 'tracked' – that is, administratively segregated in terms of different characteristics – is the sort of policy question which rests on understanding peer effects quantitatively.

Hoxby (2001) posits a relationship between individual academic achievement by a male student in a particular school and grade as the sum of what the mean achievement among males would have been in the absence of peer effects, of a term that is proportional to the percentage of females in the classroom, plus an error. She extends such a relationship to the case of several racial groups, which is particularly appropriate for the Texas Schools Project data that she uses. Her identification strategy involves exploring the panel structure of the data under the plausible assumption that there is natural idiosyncratic variation across successive cohorts in terms of gender, race and other individual attributes. Hoxby finds that students are affected by the achievement levels of their peers: an exogenous one-point increase in peers' reading scores raises a student's own score between 0.14 and 0.4 points. Peer effects are stronger intra-race, and there is evidence of contextual effects: both male and female students perform better in classrooms that are more female despite the fact that females' math performance is about the same as that of males.

The role of gender is corroborated by research by Arcidiacono and Nicholson (2005), who use data on the universe of students admitted to US medical schools for a particular year. One positive peer effect in US medical schools that they find pertains to female students, who benefit from attending medical schools that have other female students with relatively high scores on the verbal reasoning section of the Medical College Admission Test.

Of particular interest have been studies of the impact of school racial integration in the US on student performance. Consider Boston's Metropolitan Council for Educational Opportunities (METCO) programme, a voluntary desegregation programme. The programme allows mainly black inner-city kids from Boston public schools to commute to mainly white suburban communities in the Boston area that accommodate them in their public schools. Angrist and Lang (2004) show that, although the receiving districts, which tend to have higher mean academic performance, experience a mean decrease due to the programme, the effects are merely 'compositional', and there is little evidence of statistically significant effects of METCO students on their non-METCO classmates. Analysis with micro data from a particular receiving district (Brookline, Massachusetts) generally confirms this finding, but also produces some evidence of negative effects on *minority* students in the receiving district. METCO is a noteworthy social experiment, which was initiated by civil rights activists seeking to bring about de facto desegregation of schools. Lack of evidence of negative peer effects is particularly useful for informing desegregation policy. Still, there is self-selection in the participants on both sides.

Estimation of social interactions in experimental settings

Experimental data used by social interactions studies come from two types of deliberate experiments: field and laboratory experiments. A well-known field experiment is Project STAR, an experimental programme in the US state of Tennessee that randomly assigned entering kindergarten students into three different class sizes and then randomly assigned teachers to them. A recent study that utilizes Project STAR data is Graham (2006). He seeks to estimate a relationship like (1) by measuring 'excess' variance patterns across groups of exogenously given, but varying, sizes of classrooms that are associated with randomly assigned students and teachers in the presence of correlated effects in the form of unobservable group effects. Graham compares excess variance across small and large classrooms and finds social multipliers between 1.07 and 2.31, and 1.05 to 3.07, for math and reading achievement, respectively. Studies of this type aim at distinguishing excess between-classroom variance that is due to social interactions from that due to group-level heterogeneity.

Duflo and Saez (2003), using experimental data, study how social interactions among employees of a large US university may influence participation in a tax-deferred retirement account plan. The experiment more than tripled the attendance rate of those who received a small monetary reward for participating, doubled that of those not thus 'treated' but who belonged to the same departments as the treated, and significantly increased participation in the target programme by individuals from treated departments, and did so by almost as much as those who did not receive direct encouragement. While clearly the effect of social interactions may coexist with differential treatment and motivational reward effects, social interactions are also relevant for the effects of treatment on attendance and of attendance on participation. The authors conclude that the role of social interactions in amplifying the effect of treatment is unambiguous, in spite of the fact that they cannot distinguish unambiguously between the three different effects.

Moving to Opportunity (MTO) is a set of large randomized field experiments that were conducted by the US Department of Housing and Urban Development in several large US cities. The experiments offered poor households (who were chosen by lottery from among residents of high-poverty public housing projects) housing vouchers and logistical assistance through non-governmental organizations for the purpose of relocating to precisely defined 'better' neighborhoods. Several studies based on data from these experiments show that outcomes after relocation improved for children, primarily for females, in terms of education, risky behaviour and physical health, but the effects on male youth were adverse. Regarding outcomes for adults, such as economic self-sufficiency or physical health, the picture is more mixed. Kling, Ludwig and Katz (2005) find that four to seven years after relocation families (primarily female-headed ones with children) lived in safer neighbourhoods that had lower poverty rates than those of a control group that were not offered vouchers. Unfortunately, there is serious controversy over how to interpret these findings in the context of policy design for large-scale policy interventions (Sobel, 2006).

As for laboratory experiments, a notable study is by Ichino and Falk (2006). The experiment involves workers in pairs stuffing envelopes, with control being provided by subjects working alone in a room. These authors find that standard deviations of output are significantly smaller within pairs than between pairs, that is individuals keep up with their neighbours. They also find that social interactions raise productivity: average output per person is greater when subjects work in pairs. They also show that social interactions are asymmetric: low-productivity workers are more sensitive to the behaviour of high-productivity workers. Their setting does reduce some of the noise associated with 'natural' experiments but does not allow for contextual effects.

Identification of social interactions with self-selection to groups and sorting

The presence of non-random sorting on unobservables is a major challenge for the econometric identification of social interactions models. The critical role of local public finance in education in the United States has been studied extensively as a link between sorting into residential communities and socio-economic outcomes. Brock and Durlauf (2001) turned adversity into advantage by recognizing that self-selection itself, that is that individuals choose their neighbourhoods making $n(i)$ in eq. (1) endogenous, may provide additional evidence on identification. That is, if it is possible to estimate a neighbourhood selection rule, then correction for selection bias via the mean estimated bias, the so-called Heckman correction term, introduces an additional regressor in the right-hand side of (1) whose neighbourhood average is not a causal effect. Ioannides and Zabel (2002) implement this method successfully using micro data for a sample of households and their ten closest residential neighbours from the American Housing Survey and contextual information for the census tracts in which these individuals reside.

Endogeneity of the average of one's neighbours housing demands, an endogenous social effect, is instrumented by treating housing demands by a group of close neighbours as a simultaneous system of equations. By choosing neighbourhoods, census tracts in this application, individuals choose desirable social interactions. Ioannides and Zabel work with an otherwise standard housing demand model and find a very significant and large endogenous social effect along with very significant contextual effects in the form of unobservable group effects. Several other studies have sought to use instrumental variables to account for self-selection. Still, the identification of valid instruments is often quite hard and requires deep understanding of the actual setting.

Conclusions

Social interactions are ubiquitous. Interest in estimating their effects is expanding rapidly in numerous areas of economics and is motivating important methodological advances. For econometricians, key challenges include social interactions effects on market outcomes coexisting with feedbacks from the characteristics of individual market participants via their impacts on prices, consequences of self-selection and the attendant role of the presence of individual and group unobservables. Fundamentally, and in the light of ever-improving data availability, social interactions empirics will rely increasingly critically on careful theorizing that involves precise definitions of social interactions and justifies stochastic specification, possibly by calling on psychology and sociology to define appropriate boundaries, and must facilitate use of data from different sources. The likely payoff is enormous: better understanding of social forces in the modern economy, with individuals sharing information while self-selecting into social groups and living and working in close proximity to one another, as in firms and cities, the hallmark of modern economic life, and informed design of policy interventions.

YANNIS M. IOANNIDES

See also **natural experiments and quasi-natural experiments.**

Bibliography

Aaronson, D. 1998. Using sibling data to estimate the impact of neighborhoods on children's educational outcomes. *Journal of Human Resources* 23, 915–46.

Aizer, A. and Currie, J. 2004. Networks or neighborhoods? Interpreting correlations in the use of publicly funded maternity care in California. *Journal of Public Economics* 88, 2573–85.

Angrist, J. and Lang, K. 2004. Does school integration generate peer effects? Evidence from Boston's METCO Program. *American Economic Review* 94, 1613–34.

Arcidiacono, P. and Nicholson, S. 2005. Peer effects in medical school. *Journal of Public Economics* 89, 327–50.

Brock, W. and Durlauf, S. 2001. Interaction-based models. In *Handbook of Econometrics*, vol. 5, ed. J. Heckman and E. Leamer. Amsterdam: North-Holland.

Brock, W. and Durlauf, S. 2005. A multinomial choice model with social interactions. In *The Economy as an Evolving Complex System III*, ed. L. Blume and S. Durlauf. Oxford and New York: Oxford University Press.

Brock, W. and Durlauf, S. 2007. Identification of binary choice models with social interactions. *Journal of Econometrics* 140, 52–75.

Datcher, L. 1982. Effects of community and family background on achievement. *Review of Economics and Statistics* 64, 32–41.

Drewianka, S. 2003. Estimating social effects in matching markets: externalities in spousal search. *Review of Economics and Statistics* 85, 408–23.

Duflo, E. and Saez, E. 2003. The role of information and social interactions in retirement plan decisions: evidence from a randomized experiment. *Quarterly Journal of Economics*, 118, 815–42.

Durlauf, S. 2004. Neighbourhood effects. In *Handbook of Urban and Regional Economics, Volume 4: Cities and Geography*, ed. J. Henderson and J.-F. Thisse. Amsterdam: North-Holland.

Ginther, D., Haveman, R. and Wolfe, B. 2000. Neighborhood attributes as determinants of children's outcomes: how robust are the relationships? *Journal of Human Resources* 35, 603–42.

Glaeser, E., Sacerdote, B. and Scheinkman, J. 1996. Crime and social interactions. *Quarterly Journal of the Economics* 112, 508–48.

Glaeser, E., Sacerdote, B. and Scheinkman, J. 2003. The social multiplier. *Journal of the European Economic Association* 1, 345–53.

Graham, B. 2006. Identifying social interactions through conditional variance restrictions. Working paper, Department of Economics, University of California, Berkeley.

Grinblatt, M., Keloharju, M. and Ikaheimo, S. 2004. Interpersonal effects in consumption: evidence from the automobile purchases of neighbors. Working Paper No. 10226. Cambridge, MA: NBER.

Hoxby, C. 2001. Peer effects in the classroom: learning from gender and race variation. Working Paper No. 7867. Cambridge, MA: NBER.

Ichino, A. and Falk, A. 2006. Clean evidence on peer effects. *Journal of Labor Economics* 24, 39–57.

Ioannides, Y. and Loury, L. 2004. Job information networks, neighborhood effects, and inequality. *Journal of Economic Literature* 42, 1056–93.

Ioannides, Y. and Zabel, J. 2002. Interactions, neighborhood selection, and housing demand. Working paper, Department of Economics, Tufts University.

Kling, J., Ludwig, J. and Katz, L. 2005. Neighborhood effects on crime for female and male youth: evidence from a randomized housing experiment. *Quarterly Journal of the Economics* 120, 87–130.

Luttmer, E. 2005. Neighbors as negatives: relative earnings and well-being. *Quarterly Journal of Economics* 120, 963–1002.

Manski, C. 1993. Identification of endogenous social effects: the reflection problem. *Review of Economic Studies* 60, 531–42.

Moffitt, R. 2001. Policy interventions, low-level equilibria and social interactions. In *Social Dynamics*, ed. S. Durlauf and H. Peyton Young. Cambridge, MA: MIT Press.

Sacerdote, B. 2001. Peer Effects with random assignment: results for Dartmouth roommates. *Quarterly Journal of Economics* 116, 681–704.

Sobel, Ml. 2006. Spatial concentration and social stratification: does the clustering of disadvantage 'beget' bad outcomes?' In *Poverty Traps*, ed. S. Bowles, S. Durlauf and K. Hoff. Princeton, NJ: Princeton University Press.

spatial econometrics

Spatial econometrics is concerned with models for dependent observations indexed by points in a metric space or nodes in a graph. The key idea is that a set of locations can characterize the joint dependence between their corresponding observations. Locations provide a structure analogous to that provided by the time index in time series models. For example, near observations may be highly correlated but, as distance between observations grows, they approach independence. However, while time series are ordered in a single dimension, spatial processes are almost always indexed in more than one dimension and not ordered. Even small increases in the dimension of the indexing space permit large increases in the allowable patterns of interdependence between observations. The primary benefit of this modelling strategy is that complicated patterns of interdependence across sets of observations can be parsimoniously described in terms of relatively simple and estimable functions of objects like the distances between them.

The fundamental ingredients in any spatial model are the index space and locations for the observations. In contrast to the typical time series situation where calendar observation times are natural indices and immediately available, the researcher will often need to decide upon an index space and acquire measurements of locations/distances. The role of measured locations/distances is to characterize the inter-dependence between economic agents' variables, particularly those that are unobservable – for example, regression error terms. The appropriate index space depends on the economic application, and its choice is inherently a judgement call by the researcher. Fortunately, the economics of the application often provide considerable guidance and the index space/metric(s) can be tailored to promote a good fit between the economic model and the empirical work. For example, when local spillovers or competition are the central economic features, obvious candidate metrics are measures of transaction/travel costs limiting the range of the spillovers or competition. If productivity measurement were the focus, distances between observed firms or sectors could be based upon economic mechanisms that might generate co-movement in productivity – for example, measures of similarity between production technologies. Index spaces are not limited to the physical space or times inhabited by the agents and can be as abstract as required by the economics of the application.

Locations/distances are almost never perfectly measured, and this puts a premium on empirical methods that are robust to their mismeasurement. Even if the ideal metric were physical distance, usually agents' physical locations are imprecise, known only within an area – for example, census tract or county. At best this will result in imprecise distance information between agents, and if inter-agent distances are approximated with measurements based on these areas, such as distance between centroids, errors result. Moreover, in the great majority of applications the ideal metric is *not* physical distance and must be either estimated or approximated, inevitably resulting in some amount of measurement error.

There are two main approaches to modelling a spatial data generation process (DGP). The first is to model explicitly a population residing in an underlying metric space and the process of drawing an observed sample from this population. The second is to model the data-set of observed agents' outcomes as being determined by a system of simultaneous equations. In the remainder of this article, I discuss each of these approaches in turn for the simplest case of cross-sectional data. It is important to note, however, that the methods in the following section – covariance and generalized method of moments (GMM) estimation, spatial correlation robust inference – can be directly applied to panel or repeated cross-section data by simply including time as one of the components in the spatial index (s defined below). Most if not all cluster/group effect models can be considered a special case of spatial models with a binary metric indicating common group/cluster membership. See Wooldridge (2003) for an excellent review of these models. I do not discuss them here because their associated empirical techniques and sampling schemes do not translate well to more general spatial models. I conclude with a brief discussion of areas of econometrics where links to spatial econometrics are perhaps underappreciated.

1. Models for samples from a population

This section discusses spatial econometric models that view the data as being a sample from some arbitrarily large population (see, for example, Conley, 1999, for a more formal treatment). The population of individuals is assumed to reside in some metric space, typically $\Re^k$ or an integer lattice, with each individual i located at a point s_i.

The basic model of dependence characterizes dependence between agents' random variables via their locations. The data are assumed to be weakly dependent (perhaps after de-trending). (Andrews, 2005, is an important exception that explicitly considers strong cross sectional dependence arising from common shocks.) If two agents' locations s_i and s_j are close, then their random variables ϕ_{s_i} and ϕ_{s_j} may be highly dependent. As the distance between s_i and s_j grows large, ϕ_{s_i} and ϕ_{s_j} become essentially independent. Notions of weak dependence can be formalized in essentially the same manner as for time series, for example, with mixing coefficients. Under regularity conditions limiting the strength of dependence, laws of large numbers and central limit results can be obtained for properly normalized averages of ϕ_s. See, for example, Takahata (1983) or Bolthausen (1982). These approximations almost always use what is called an increasing domain approach to limits, with the corresponding thought experiment being that, as the sample size grows, an envelope containing the locations would be growing without bound.

When one works within this framework, it is often useful to approach an empirical problem in two steps. First, decide upon a (small) set of metrics based on the economics of the application, and then consider statistical modelling of dependence as a function of the metrics. It is much easier to conduct statistical modelling given a metric than to try to simultaneously vary both the model specification and the metric itself.

Statistics that describe spatial correlation patterns are simple to construct. Any statistic relating co-variation of ϕ_{s_i} and ϕ_{s_j} to some measure of their proximity could be used to characterize patterns in dependence. Classic references are Moran (1950) and Geary (1954), and the text by Cliff and Ord (1981) contains a good treatment. One useful approach is based on nonparametric estimation of a covariance function (see for example Conley and Topa, 2002, or Conley and Ligon, 2002). The ϕ_s process is covariance stationary if its expectation is the same at all locations and $cov(\phi_s, \phi_{s+h})$ depends only on the relative displacement h. For high-dimensional h, it is useful to consider a special case called isotropy where covariances depend only on the length of h; covariance depends upon distance but not direction. Take an isotropic covariance stationary ϕ_s with expectation zero for simplicity. Its covariance function f can be expressed in a regression equation involving distances $d_{i,j}$:

$$E(\phi_{s_i}\phi_{s_j}|s_i, s_j) = f(d_{i,j}). \tag{1}$$

The function f in eq. (1) can be estimated parametrically or, as is particularly useful in preliminary data analysis, via a nonparametric regression of $\phi_{s_i}\phi_{s_j}$ on $d_{i,j}$. Investigation of correlation patterns when there is more than one candidate metric can by done by simply letting f be a function of more than one distance measure.

In cases where ϕ_s is not isotropic or non-stationary, f can still be interpretable as a measure of average co-movement. If the process is covariance stationary but not isotropic, an estimate at a given distance d_0, call it $\hat{f}(d_0)$, will converge to a weighted average of $cov(\phi_s, \phi_{s+h})$ for displacements h that have length d_0. The relative weights of different directions h will depend on their frequency of sampling. An analogous interpretation of f is available when ϕ_s is non-stationary, $cov(\phi_s, \phi_{s+h})$ depends on s, but still weakly dependent with averages of $cov(\phi_s, \phi_{s+h})$ across s remaining convergent. In this case, $\hat{f}(d_0)$ will converge to a weighted average of $cov(\phi_s, \phi_{s+h})$ across those h with length d_0 and across all s. Typically, this is still a valuable measure of co-movement. If non-stationarity is suspected, it is also very useful to construct localized versions of measures of spatial correlation. Localized f estimates for subregions of the locations can easily be constructed by just confining the observations used to estimate (1); see Anselin (1995) for extensive treatment of localized versions of Moran (1950) and Geary (1954) measures of spatial correlation.

Estimates of f can also be viewed directly as test statistics for the null hypothesis of independence. Under the null hypothesis of independence, the sampling distribution of an f estimator can be approximated and compared to the realized value of f estimates to test the hypothesis of independence. Such tests for independence remain valid even with measurement errors in distances (see Conley and Ligon, 2002).

Parameter estimation via moment conditions
In most econometric applications, the parameters of interest can be estimated using GMM. GMM estimation with weakly spatially dependent data is straightforward, and

the spatial dependence is relevant for inference and efficiency (see Conley, 1999). Consider instrumental variables (IV) estimation in the linear model with outcome y_{s_i}, regressors x_{s_i}, and instruments z_{s_i}

$$y_{s_i} = x'_{s_i}\beta + u_{s_i}$$
$$\text{and}$$
$$Ez_{s_i}u_{s_i} = 0 \tag{2}$$

The IV estimator is identified by the moment condition (2): that the instruments are not correlated with the error term. Since this is a moment condition with respect to the marginal distribution of the data across agents, it is valid with or without spatial dependence. The familiar solution remains: $\beta = (Ez_{s_i}x'_{s_i})^{-1}Ez_{s_i}y_{s_i}$. Consistent estimates of β can be obtained using sample averages to approximate these expectations since a law of large numbers applies to weakly dependent spatial data. Thus, the usual IV estimator, $\hat{\beta}_N = (\frac{1}{N}\sum_{i=1}^{N}z_{s_i}x'_{s_i})^{-1}\frac{1}{N}\sum_{i=1}^{N}z_{s_i}y_{s_i}$, remains consistent with weak spatial dependence. It is of course feasible to construct $\hat{\beta}_N$ without any knowledge of locations/distances, so it is trivially robust to measurement error in them. The impact of such spatial dependence is only upon inference, getting correct standard errors or testing.

This logic carries over to any GMM estimator of a parameter θ_0 that is identified from a moment condition involving a (potentially nonlinear) function g:

$$Eg(\phi_s; \theta_0) = 0.$$

The majority of econometric models with nonlinearity or limited dependent variables can be estimated via some choice for g. Under mild regularity conditions, θ_0 can be consistently estimated by minimum distance methods using $\frac{1}{N}\sum_{i=1}^{N}g(\phi_{s_i}; \cdot)$ to approximate $Eg(\phi_s; \cdot)$. A GMM estimator is the argument minimizing the criterion function, $J_N(\theta)$, which takes the same form as with time series or independent data:

$$J_N(\theta) = \left[\frac{1}{N}\sum_{i=1}^{N}g(\phi_{s_i}; \theta)\right]'\Omega\left[\frac{1}{N}\sum_{i=1}^{N}g(\phi_{s_i}; \theta)\right],$$

where Ω is some positive definite matrix. Just as for the time series case (Hansen, 1982), an efficient GMM estimator can be obtained by taking Ω to be a consistent estimator of the limiting variance-covariance matrix of $\frac{1}{\sqrt{N}}\sum_{i=1}^{N}g(\phi_{s_i}; \theta_0)$, whose form depends on the spatial covariance structure of the data. One such covariance matrix estimator is described in the following subsection.

Inference
The usual approach to inference using large sample approximations can be employed with weakly spatially dependent data. Returning to the IV model, the typical

approximation for the distribution for $\hat{\beta}_N$ is based on the expression:

$$\sqrt{N}(\hat{\beta}_N - \beta) = \left(\frac{1}{N}\sum_{i=1}^{N} z_{s_i} x'_{s_i}\right)^{-1} \left[\frac{1}{\sqrt{N}}\sum_{i=1}^{N} z_{s_i} u_{s_i}\right]. \tag{3}$$

Under regularity conditions, the first term in the product converges to the matrix $Ez_{s_i} x'_{s_i}$. The second term in brackets has a limiting normal distribution:

$$\frac{1}{\sqrt{N}}\sum_{i=1}^{N} z_{s_i} u_{s_i} \Rightarrow N(0, V) \tag{4}$$

where V is the limiting variance-covariance matrix of

$$\frac{1}{\sqrt{N}}\sum_{i=1}^{N} z_{s_i} u_{s_i}.$$

V contains terms of the form $Ez_{s_i} u_{s_i} z'_{s_i} u_{s_i}$ and cross-covariance terms, $Ez_{s_i} u_{s_i} z'_{s_j} u_{s_j}$, that will be non-zero for at least some i, j pairs. With weak dependence, the covariance between variables indexed i and j will eventually vanish as the distance between s_i and s_j grows.

In some cases, V has a nice form. For example, suppose locations were on an integer lattice, Z^k; samples consist of all integer coordinates in a region (assumed to grow as $N \to \infty$); and variables are covariance stationary. In this case, V can be expressed as an infinite sum of a covariance function:

$$V = \sum_{h \in Z^k} Cov(z_s u_s, z_{s+h} u_{s+h}). \tag{5}$$

With integer locations on the line, this expression coincides with its analog for covariance stationary time series.

With a consistent estimate of V, call it $\hat{V}_N$, the approximate distribution implied by (3) and (4) can be used for inference:

$$\sqrt{N}(\hat{\beta}_N - \beta) \overset{Approx}{\sim} N\left(0, \left(\frac{1}{N}\sum_{i=1}^{N} z_{s_i} x'_{s_i}\right)^{-1} \hat{V}_N \left(\frac{1}{N}\sum_{i=1}^{N} z_{s_i} x'_{s_i}\right)^{-1'}\right).$$

There are of course many ways V could be estimated. If it were assumed to have a parametric form, for example, by parameterizing the covariance function in (5), then consistent estimates could be obtained by GMM. Perhaps the most popular approach has been nonparametric estimation of V following Conley (1996; 1999). This approach is analogous to time series heteroskedasticity and autocovariance (HAC) consistent covariance matrix estimation, and can be viewed as a smoothed periodogram spectral density estimator. (See Priestley, 1981, for a discussion of the vast literature on spectral methods in time series and some extensions to spatial processes. Spectral methods for spatial processes date back to at least the 1950s; for example, Whittle, 1954; Bartlett, 1955; Grenander and Rosenblatt, 1957; Priestley, 1964). With the use of residuals $\hat{u}_{s_i}$ to approximate u_{s_i}, V can be estimated as a weighted sum of cross products $z_{s_i}\hat{u}_{s_i}z'_{s_j}\hat{u}_{s_j}$:

$$\hat{V}_N = \frac{1}{N}\sum_{i=1}^{N}\sum_{j=1}^{N} K_N(s_i, s_j) \cdot z_{s_i}\hat{u}_{s_i}z'_{s_j}\hat{u}_{s_j}.$$

$K_N(\cdot, \cdot)$ is a kernel used to weight pairs of observations, with close observations receiving a weight near 1 and those far apart receiving weights near zero. $K_N(s_i, s_j)$ is commonly specified to be uniform kernel that is 1 if s_i and s_j are within a cut-off distance and zero otherwise. (This indicator function K_N is not guaranteed to provide positive definite (PD) covariance matrix estimates; however, this is very rarely a problem in practice. PD estimates can be insured by an alternate choice of kernel; see Conley, 1999.) $\hat{V}_N$ will be consistent if as $N \rightarrow \infty$, $K_N(s, s + h) \rightarrow 1$ for any given displacement h, but slowly enough so that the variance of $\hat{V}_N$ collapses to zero.

In practice, this estimator will require a decision about the exact form of $K_N(\cdot, \cdot)$. With a uniform kernel, this is just an operational definition of which observations are near and which are far. A conservative distinction between near and far observations can be made even with multiple candidate metrics by assigning a far classification only when all metrics agree. There is no need for the data to be covariance stationary, nor is the specific sampling framework here necessary. Analogous HAC methods can be applied to weakly dependent but non-stationary data, including that generated by simultaneous equations DGPs like those discussed in the following section 2 (see Pinkse, Slade and Brett, 2002; Kelejian and Prucha, 2007).

The main reason nonparametric estimators like $\hat{V}_N$ are often preferred to parametric models for V is their robustness to measurement errors in locations/ distances. Parametric V estimators are generally inconsistent with such errors, while $\hat{V}_N$ remains consistent under mild conditions. $\hat{V}_N$ can be consistent with spatially correlated and even endogenous errors; a sufficient condition is simply that they be bounded (Conley, 1999). With location/distance errors, the weight assigned to pair i, j can be altered relative to the weight $K_N(\cdot, \cdot)$ would assign with exact locations. But $\hat{V}_N$ remains consistent, because the altered weights will still satisfy the necessary conditions for consistency of $\hat{V}_N$: the weight on observations at any true displacement will still converge to 1, slowly enough. Even when working with parametric models of V, $\hat{V}_N$ remains of interest since the discrepancy between it and a parametric V estimator can provide a useful joint test for the absence of location/distance errors and proper parametric specification (Conley and Molinari, 2007).

More important than $\hat{V}_N$ remaining consistent is its robustness in practice to moderate amounts of location error. Consider the impact of introducing location error for $\hat{V}_N$ defined with a kernel $K_N(s_i, s_j)$ equal to 1 if s_i and s_j are within L_N units, and zero otherwise. If the magnitude of measurement error is moderate relative to L_N, then the weights on most pairs of points would be unchanged if erroneously measured locations were used in place of true locations. Changes in weights occur only for those points whose true distance is near enough to the cut-off L_N that location errors result in measured and true distances being on opposite sides of L_N. With moderate amounts of location error, these pairs of observations with true distance near L_N will usually not be a large portion of the sample, so $\hat{V}_N$ will tend to be close to its value with true locations. Similar results obtain for other kernels as weights arising from moderately mismeasured locations remain close to those received with true locations (see Conley and Molinari, 2007).

2. Population simultaneous equation models

The second approach to modelling spatial data is with a simultaneous equations model, most directly interpretable as a model for a *population* of N agents. This approach explicitly specifies a joint model for the population, in contrast to typical models in Section 1, where the joint determination of outcomes in the population is not explicitly treated. These simultaneous equation models are directly applicable to situations where the entire population of agents is observed, like all US states or counties or even all firms in an industry. Typical applications include studies of games being played among these agents or of spillovers across agents; see, for example, Case, Hines and Rosen (1993) and Pinkse, Slade and Brett (2002).

The most common type of model is a simultaneous spatial autoregression (SAR). Its simplest formulation for an $N \times 1$ outcome vector Y_N is:

$$Y_N = \rho W_N Y_N + \varepsilon_N, \tag{6}$$

with scalar parameter ρ and IID shocks ε_N (typically Gaussian). The $N \times N$ matrix W_N is commonly referred to as a 'spatial weights' matrix and assumed known. W_N has zero main-diagonal elements, and its off-diagonal elements reflect some notion of interaction. Typical W_N contain (i, j) elements that are non-zero only if locations i and j are adjacent on a graph or elements inversely related to distances between locations. W_N is usually row-standardized so that its rows sum to 1. The parameter space is restricted so that $(I - \rho W_N)^{-1}$ exists and the model has reduced form:

$$Y_N = (I - \rho W_N)^{-1} \varepsilon_N.$$

Thus Y_N is a linear combination of the ε_N IID shocks. Though SAR models are finite (usually) irregular lattice models, their origins date to at least the infinite regular lattice models of Whittle (1954). Textbook treatment of SARs can be found in Anselin (1988).

Typical specifications for W_N imply a great deal of heterogeneity across observations. Variances will typically differ across the elements of Y_N by construction unless $\rho = 0$. Unconditional heteroskedasticity is thus coupled with spatial dependence. Covariances between pairs of agents will differ in patterns that are of course determined by W_N but will depend on the entire structure of this matrix and will not generally follow a simple pattern in terms of some metric. For example, with W_N defined based upon a graph, covariance between agents i and j will not be a function of their graph distance, though it can be characterized in terms of properties of the graph (Martellosio, 2004). A given graph will 'hard-wire' patterns in correlations across agents. For example Wall (2004) notes, with model (6) for US states with W_N based on adjacency, that Missouri and Tennessee are constrained to be the least spatially correlated states, while relative correlations between other pairs of states change depending on ρ. Even with a more flexible parameterization – for example, specifying the elements of W_N to be flexible functions of distance, as in Pinkse, Slade and Brett (2002) – there is still a tendency for heterogeneity in the implied joint distribution to be difficult to anticipate. While this complicates their use as statistical models, as discussed below, it is in my view likely to be a desirable property in a structural model. For example, if the model's joint distribution is to be taken seriously as capturing equilibrium outcomes for N asymmetric agents playing a game, then one would expect 'hard-wired' heterogeneity depending on the exact structure of the game.

Though the population of agents is observed, large sample approximations taking limits as $N \to \infty$ are still potentially useful. However, the requisite limit theorems technically differ from those referenced in Section 1. Since the DGP is changing as N grows, triangular array limit results are required. Consistency and distribution results for Gaussian maximum likelihood estimators (MLEs) with spatial dependence have existed at least since Mardia and Marshall (1984). An extensive set of SAR limiting distribution results is obtained by Lee (2004a) for likelihood-based estimators under a variety of conditions upon 'spatial weights' matrices like W_N. Quite useful limit theorem results can also be found in Kelejian and Prucha (2001). Correct specification of W_N is essential for these results, as SAR estimators will generally be inconsistent when there is measurement error in locations/distances used to specify this matrix (the same holds true for other parametric models of dependence structure).

A great deal of the literature has focused on computational issues involving MLEs. Non-trivial W_N matrices make computation of normalizing constants challenging. Substantial progress has been made in techniques for computing MLEs by exploiting sparseness or specific structure of 'spatial weights' matrices and re-parameterization to facilitate computation (see Pace and Barry, 1997; Barry and Pace, 1999; LeSage and Pace, 2007). These numerical techniques allow likelihood-based inference for even very large data-sets in certain applications or specifications. It is also feasible, of course, to estimate SAR parameters without computing MLEs, by using only a subset of the implications of the model to obtain method of moments estimates (see Kelejian and Prucha, 1999, and Lee, 2007, and subsequent work by these authors). This literature has been successful in addressing most computational issues with SAR models.

The key remaining difficulties in using SAR models are in terms of model specification and interpretation. Even for the simplest SAR model (6), it is hard to characterize implications of different ρ without explicitly calculating their implied joint distributions. The parameter ρ is not a simple correlation coefficient; in general it is not comparable across different specifications for W_N. In my experience, explicit calculations of descriptive measures of the implied joint distributions for many different ρ are required to understand whether varying this parameter will trace out a useful path through the space of joint distributions.

Unless one has access to virtually complete data on a population, SAR models are very difficult to properly specify as structural models. To take an optimistic case, suppose model (6) with Gaussian ε applied to a population of N agents, but a subset of agents were sampled. The likelihood of such a sample is well-defined, and in principle its form could be found by integrating out all the unobserved variables. But this calculation requires the exact form of W_N, which depends on all the unobserved agents, a full structure which will rarely be observed if only a small fraction of the agents are sampled. Proper specification of W_N is perhaps feasible only if the vast majority of the population is sampled – for example, if only a few states or counties are missing.

Even with complete data on a population, SARs are difficult to specify because they are inherently fragile. Changing a single element of W_N will in general influence the entire joint distribution of Y and it is difficult to intuitively understand the impact of a given change in W_N. Increasing flexibility by parameterizing W_N by taking its elements to be a series expansion in distance(s), as in Pinkse, Slade and Brett (2002), is of limited help. There remains only an indirect link between the series expansion and the implied joint distribution. It is hard to see how much additional flexibility in, for example, allowed covariance structure is gained by adding another term in the expansion.

I think these difficulties should be considered a consequence of modelling a large-dimensional system of structural simultaneous equations rather than SAR-specific problems. It seems likely to be difficult to anticipate changes in equilibrium outcomes resulting from changes in individual agents' decision rules or best-response functions in any modelling framework. In my view, SARs remain a useful first step towards the goal of constructing good large-dimensional structural simultaneous equation models.

Of course SAR models need not be intended as structural models; they can be viewed, for instance, as tools to incorporate spatial dependence into forecasting models. A mis-specified but parsimonious model might still forecast well. However, the cumbersome relation between specification of 'spatial weights' and the implied joint distribution makes it hard to fashion parsimonious SAR models. This seems ample reason to avoid their use in forecasting. Directly specifying measures of dependence like covariances as a parsimonious function of distance appears far easier, even if the true DGP were an SAR.

3. Links between spatial econometrics and other areas

Work on interactions-based models has much in common with simultaneous equations-style spatial models (see Brock and Durlauf, 2001, for an extensive review).

In these models, the behaviour of individuals is influenced by the characteristics and/ or behaviour of others. Insofar as the relevant set of 'others' can be described in a spatial framework, they can be thought of as spatial econometric models. Much of this work is theory, taking the approach of specifying conditional probability measures to capture individuals' behaviours and then deriving the implied properties of the compatible joint distribution(s). Empirical work with these models has just begun and will share many of the same challenges described above; some can even be cast directly as SARs (see Lee, 2004b).

Spatial models are potentially very useful in modelling high-dimensional vector time series. Limited degrees of freedom with typical length samples require substantial restrictions upon the DGP to make progress. The potential of spatial models to capture complicated interdependence with a small number of parameters (given auxiliary location/distance information) makes them well suited for use in characterizing a variety of restrictions upon high-dimensional vector DGPs. Good examples of the benefits of spatial approaches to this type of time series modelling are Chen and Conley (2001), Giacomini and Granger (2004), and Bester (2005a; 2005b).

TIMOTHY G. CONLEY

See also **social interactions (empirics).**

Bibliography

Andrews, D. 2005. Cross-section regression with common shocks. *Econometrica* 73, 1551–85.
Anselin, L. 1988. *Spatial Econometrics: Methods and Models.* Boston: Kluwer Academic Publishers.
Anselin, L. 1995. Local indicators of spatial association. *Geographical Analysis* 27, 93–115.
Barry, R. and Pace, R. 1999. A Monte Carlo estimator of the log determinant of large sparse matrices. *Linear Algebra and its Applications* 289, 41–54.
Bartlett, M. 1955. *An Introduction to Stochastic Processes.* Cambridge: Cambridge University Press.
Bester, C. 2005a. Random field and affine models for interest rates: an empirical comparison. Working paper, University of Chicago.
Bester, C. 2005b. Bond and option pricing in random field models. Working paper, University of Chicago.
Bolthausen, E. 1982. On the central limit theorem for stationary mixing random fields. *Annals of Probability* 10, 1047–50.
Brock, W. and Durlauf, S. 2001. Interactions-based models. In *Handbook of Econometrics* 5, ed. J. Heckman and Leamer. Amsterdam: North-Holland.
Case, A., Hines, J. and Rosen, H. 1993. Budget spillovers and fiscal policy interdependence: evidence from the states. *Journal of Public Economics* 52, 285–307.
Chen, X. and Conley, T. 2001. A new semiparametric spatial model for panel time series. *Journal of Econometrics* 105, 59–83.
Cliff, A. and Ord, J. 1981. *Spatial Processes.* London: Pion Limited.
Conley, T. 1996. Econometric modeling of cross-sectional dependence. Ph.D. thesis, University of Chicago.
Conley, T. 1999. GMM estimation with cross sectional dependence. *Journal of Econometrics* 92, 1–45.
Conley, T. and Ligon, E. 2002. Economic distance, spillovers, and cross country comparisons. *Journal of Economic Growth* 7, 157–87.

Conley, T. and Molinari, F. 2007. Spatial correlation robust inference with errors in location or distance. *Journal of Econometrics* 140(1), 76–96.

Conley, T. and Topa, G. 2002. Socio-economic distance and spatial patterns in unemployment. *Journal of Applied Econometrics* 17, 303–27.

Geary, R. 1954. The contiguity ratio and statistical mapping. *Incorporated Statistician* 5, 115–45.

Giacomini, F. and Granger, C. 2004. Aggregation of space–time processes. *Journal of Econometrics* 118, 7–26.

Grenander, U. and Rosenblatt, M. 1957. Some problems in estimating the spectrum of a time series. *Proceedings of the Third Berkeley Symposium on Mathematical Statistics and Probability* 7, 77–93.

Hansen, L. 1982. Large sample properties of generalized method of moments estimators. *Econometrica* 50, 1029–54.

Kelejian, H. and Prucha, I. 1999. A Generalized moments estimator for the autoregressive parameter in a spatial model. *International Economic Review* 40, 509–33.

Kelejian, H. and Prucha, I. 2001. On the asymptotic distribution of the Moran I test statistic with applications. *Journal of Econometrics* 104, 219–57.

Kelejian, H. and Prucha, I. 2007. HAC estimation in a spatial framework. *Journal of Econometrics* 140(1), 131–54.

Lee, L. 2004a. Asymptotic distributions of quasi-maximum likelihood estimators for spatial autoregressive models. *Econometrica* 72, 1899–925.

Lee, L. 2004b. Identification and estimation of spatial econometric models with group interactions, contextual factors and fixed effects. Working paper, Ohio State University.

Lee, L. 2007. GMM and 2SLS estimation of mixed regressive, spatial autoregressive models. *Journal of Econometrics* 140(1), 155–89.

LeSage, J. and Pace, R. 2007. A matrix exponential spatial specification. *Journal of Econometrics* 140(1), 190–214.

Mardia, K. and Marshall, R. 1984. Maximum likelihood estimation of models for residual covariance in spatial regression. *Biometrika* 71, 135–46.

Martellosio, F. 2004. The correlation structure of spatial autoregressions. Working paper, University of Southampton.

Moran, P. 1950. Notes on continuous stochastic phenomena. *Biometrika* 37, 17–23.

Pace, R. and Barry, R. 1997. Quick computation of regressions with a spatially autoregressive dependent variable. *Geographical Analysis* 29, 232–47.

Pinkse, J., Slade, M. and Brett, C. 2002. Spatial price competition: a semiparametric approach. *Econometrica* 70, 1111–53.

Priestley, M. 1964. Analysis of two-dimensional processes with discontinous spectra. *Biometrika* 51, 195–217.

Priestley, M. 1981. *Spectral Analysis and Time Series*, 2 vols. New York: Academic Press.

Takahata, H. 1983. On the rates in the central limit theorem for weakly dependent random fields. *Zeitschrift fur Wahrscheinlichkeitstheorie und verwandte Gebiete* 64, 445–56.

Wall, M. 2004. A close look at the spatial structure implied by the CAR and SAR models. *Journal of Statistical Planning and Inference* 121, 311–24.

Whittle, P. 1954. On stationary processes on the plane. *Biometrika* 2, 434–49.

Wooldridge, J. 2003. Cluster-sample methods in applied econometrics. *American Economic Review* 93, 133–8.

survey data, analysis of

When economists analyse survey data, they must confront characteristics of the data-generating process that may distinguish these data from other types, such as administrative records.

Discussions of survey data analysis, such as the text by Chambers and Skinner (2003), typically consider problems caused by response errors, non-response, partially censored responses and complex sampling schemes. These problems are not unique to survey data: administrative records may not perfectly capture the phenomena of interest, may be incomplete, may be 'masked' to preserve confidentiality, and may be generated by something very different from simple random sampling or stratified sampling. Detailed discussions of methods for addressing such problems are included elsewhere in this dictionary and in standard econometrics texts.

In this article, we focus on survey data on subjective phenomena. Such data cannot be found among administrative records but are commonly reported in surveys. We discuss methods for interpreting subjective data and utilizing them in econometric analysis of individual behaviour, highlighting recent innovations in the measurement of expectations and preferences. The collection and analysis of subjective data was an important component of mainstream economic research until the mid-20th century, when it fell out of favour. Since then, the standard empirical method for the study of choice behaviour has been one of revealed preference analysis exclusively utilizing data on observed choices and attributes in combination with strong assumptions on expectations and preferences.

Yet the empirical basis for rejecting the use of subjective data was very limited (see, for example, Dominitz and Manski, 1997a; 2004). In fact, Tobin (1959, p. 11) concluded his generally negative analysis of expectations and attitudes data with a call to 'investigate the questions [of] which attitudes are the most important ones to investigate in periodic surveys and what is the best way to use these data in combination with other economic information'. But this call went unheeded by economists, who 'are taught early in their careers to believe only what people do, not what they say' (Manski, 1990).

The prevailing scepticism has recently been challenged by researchers who seek to use data on subjective phenomena to weaken assumptions made on individual behaviour and to assess the credibility of maintained assumptions. To be viable, this approach requires careful design and administration of the survey instrument and proper interpretation of survey responses. Of particular concern are loosely worded survey questions that are subject to multiple interpretations by respondents and researchers alike. These concerns apply to the collection and analysis of all forms of survey data but are particularly salient in the context of subjective data. Importantly, even if subjective data suffer more severe response problems than do other forms of data, researchers must confront the limitations of the main alternative to directly measuring expectations and preferences, that is, making strong assumptions on the form of expectations and preferences in order to infer them from realizations data alone.

In this article, we demonstrate that the existing literature provides good reasons to believe that data on expectations and preferences reported in carefully designed household surveys can greatly enhance the empirical content of models of economic decisions and choices. In so doing, we endorse Manski's (2004) argument in favour of combining subjective data with other data to estimate models of choice behaviour, and we reiterate Tobin's (1959) call to determine the circumstances under which this combination is most fruitful.

Expectations

Published reports on consumer confidence indices are almost certainly the best-known output from analyses of household survey data on expectations. We begin by summarizing the history of consumer confidence measurement, an important component of the broader history of expectations data collection (see also Dominitz and Manski, 2004). We then discuss recent developments in the analysis of such qualitative expectations data and in methods for eliciting quantitative expectations in the form called for by modern economic theory – that is, subjective probability distributions.

Measures of consumer confidence were developed during the mid-20th century by George Katona and his colleagues at the University of Michigan's Survey Research Center, where much pioneering work in economic surveys has been conducted. The Index of Consumer Sentiment aggregates responses to expectations and attitudes questions asked in the monthly Survey of Consumers, with ordered categories that are coded as positive, neutral, or negative. Responses to the following question, for instance, were and still are included:

> Now looking ahead – do you think that a year from now you (and your family living there) will be better off financially, or worse off, or just about the same as now?

The Federal Reserve Board formed a committee to assess the value of expectations and attitudes data soon after initiation of the Michigan surveys, which the Board funded. The committee produced negative findings on the ability of these and other consumer sentiment data to predict individual savings and consumption reported in follow-up interviews (Tobin, 1959). Katona (1957) and others argued that the indices predict aggregate economic outcomes. Over the next half-century, consumer confidence measures would become widely discussed indicators of the state of the economy and would find some use in macroeconomic studies of aggregate economic behaviour (Ludvigson, 2004). The qualitative data on expectations and attitudes that form the basis for these measures, however, were generally not thought to be of value for use in microeconomic studies of individual behaviour. Recent research has highlighted limitations that are generic to traditional, qualitative questions eliciting expectations.

The form of these expectations questions necessarily limits the predictive value of individual responses. Manski (1990) formally modelled respondents who report best predictions (that is, minimize expected loss) when asked yes/no expectations questions concerning future binary outcomes. These respondents say 'yes' if the subjective probability that the outcome will occur exceeds some threshold. Tobin (1959) and Juster (1966) had previously posited similar models of survey response. Manski derives sharp bounds on the correspondence between reported expectations and outcomes in a best-case scenario, where all respondents form rational expectations and minimize symmetric loss functions. The latter condition yields a threshold probability of 0.5. Even then, in the absence of an aggregate shock, all we would expect to find in a follow-up interview is that the outcome will occur for (*a*) more than half of all 'yes' respondents and (*b*) less than half of all 'no' respondents. Das, Dominitz, and van Soest (1999) extended Manski's model to ordered-category expectations of the form used in the consumer confidence questions and conducted a test of rational expectations using income expectations and realizations in a panel survey.

Dominitz and Manski (1997b) emphasize that the vague wording of many expectations questions further limits the interpersonal comparability and hence the predictive value of responses, as respondents must determine which possible outcomes would, for instance, constitute being 'better off financially', 'worse off', or 'about the same'. Still, many researchers have formally modelled such qualitative responses, under strong identifying assumptions, and used the data to learn about expectations formation and the relationship between expectations and realizations. Pesaran and Weale (2006) review work that analyses the qualitative and quantitative reports of expectations.

The limitations generic to qualitative survey data on expectations need not apply to quantitative expectations data. Some surveys use questions of the 'What do you expect…?' form to elicit point expectations of continuous variables. This question format is typical in surveys of professional forecasters (see Keane and Runkle, 1990), but has also been used in household surveys. Bernheim (1989; 1990) studied expectations of retirement age and Social Security benefits reported in the Retirement History Survey, a survey that followed about 11,000 Americans aged 58–63 in 1969 through the 1970s. Lancaster and Chesher (1983) used point expectations of wage offers, in addition to individual reports of the subjective reservation wage, to identify a structural model of job search.

These point expectations are typically interpreted as the mean of the subjective distribution, but other models of survey response are certainly plausible. Bernheim (1989), for instance, presents evidence that respondents report the mode of the subjective distribution of retirement age rather than the mean. To clarify the expectations of interest and to obtain information on uncertainty about prospective outcomes, economists designing surveys in the early 1990s began eliciting expectations in the form of subjective probabilities, as previously proposed by Juster (1966). Early examples are found in the Health and Retirement Study (HRS) survey, of which Tom Juster was the Principal Investigator, as well as the Survey of Economics Expectations (SEE), the Bank of Italy's Survey of Household Income and Wealth (SHIW), and the Dutch Center panel.

When the outcome of interest is binary, the probability of its occurrence summarizes the subjective probability distribution. Dominitz and Manski (1997b), for example, use SEE data to study economic insecurity arising from the prospective loss of a job or of health insurance coverage. When the outcome of interest takes on many values, a sequence of probabilities may be elicited to describe the subjective probability distribution. For instance, Hurd and McGarry (2002) use HRS data to study survival probabilities, which they find to be predictive of mortality. Dominitz (2001) demonstrates how SEE income expectations data can be fruitfully combined with income realizations data to estimate income expectations models of the type commonly adopted in research on consumption and savings, but allowing for greater heterogeneity. Guiso, Jappelli and Terlizzese (1992) use SHIW income expectations data to study the relationship between subjective uncertainty and precautionary savings. In each case, the authors impose parametric assumptions on the subjective probability distribution to identify the entire distribution from a handful of subjective probabilities.

Preferences

Standard econometric analysis of behaviour reported in a household survey combines data on household attributes and observed choices to make inferences on preference parameters and to generate predictions of choices not observed in the data. This application of *revealed preference* (RP) analysis typically requires strong assumptions on the expectations, choice sets, and preferences of households. In some cases, the data on choices and household attributes are sufficiently rich so as to yield credible inferences and predictions under weak assumptions. Many other situations, however, will require strong, untestable, and perhaps untenable assumptions. This may be the case, for instance, if the set of available alternatives varies considerably across households but the survey collects data only on the alternative selected by each household. The restrictiveness of the maintained assumptions may become particularly problematic when choices are made in a life cycle context with uncertainty, where subjective distributions of the future consequences of current choices are important.

The addition of survey questions on subjective phenomena may allow researchers to test and relax the maintained assumptions. First, questions on future expectations can be used, as discussed above. Second, respondents can be asked to make choices in hypothetical situations or to evaluate hypothetical opportunities, thereby providing *stated preference* (SP) data. Analysis of SP data has been commonplace for quite a long time in marketing research and transportation studies, but considerable scepticism remains in economics. Louviere, Hensher and Swait (2000) review the advantages and drawbacks of using SP data in place of or in combination with data on actual behaviour.

Consider hypothetical choice questions in which respondents are offered a number of alternatives and asked to choose one. Strong assumptions on choice sets required for analysing RP data can be avoided because the alternatives are explicitly given and thus observed by the researcher. This even applies to choices in a life cycle context where the question may specify the distribution of future outcomes associated with each alternative (for example, Barsky et al., 1997); therefore, the researcher may not need to elicit expectations or infer them from realizations data. Moreover, the range of offered alternatives can be manipulated to extract maximal information on preferences and to estimate preference parameters more efficiently than would be possible with RP data.

As with revealed preference analysis of discrete choice behaviour, hypothetical choices may be modelled using a random utility framework in which the utility of each alternative depends upon its specified attributes and an idiosyncratic disturbance term (see McFadden, 1986). For empirical implementation, the multinomial logit model has been the standard (McFadden, 1973), but more general models are available, such as multinomial probit to avoid the assumption of independence of irrelevant alternatives or mixed logit to account for unobserved heterogeneity across respondents (for example, Revelt and Train, 1998).

Still, even with hypothetical choice data some assumptions on choice sets or preference structures will be required, because it is not generally possible to fully specify the characteristics of each alternative. If so, then one may assume that unobserved attributes enter utility additively and are the same for all choice alternatives, so that they do not matter for the choice. Another possibility is to assume that the respondent takes an expectation over the distribution of unobserved attributes, given the information that is provided (Manski, 1999).

Much of the scepticism about SP data seems to arise from the extensive literature on problems with contingent valuation (CV) studies that seek to measure willingness to pay (WTP) for or willingness to accept in exchange for a non-market good, a frequent subject of analysis in environmental economics. In one type of CV survey, respondents get information about the current state (for example, of the environment) and a proposed change (for example, a quality improvement). They are then asked whether they would vote in favour of the change, given that this change would require a certain monetary cost (such as a tax increase). Survey responses are used to estimate the population distribution of the subjective valuation of the good at issue (see Mitchell and Carson, 1989).

Research has shown that CV studies can yield systematically misleading assessments of the value of a good (for example, Diamond and Hausman, 1994). Hanemann (1994) argues that many of the problems with CV arise from the way in which the survey is conducted. He concludes that the existing criticism is often justified but not valid in all circumstances: a well-designed and rigorously conducted CV study can yield reliable estimates of WTP. Note that some criticisms of the collection and analysis of these data actually question the basic assumptions of revealed preference analysis rather than simply the elicitation of preferences (for example, Ariely, Prelec and Loewenstein, 2003).

The problems with CV studies can also apply to SP experiments. For example, they can be sensitive to framing effects because respondents tend to choose the middle category, to anchoring or status quo bias if one of the alternatives is clearly specified as the benchmark, or to yea-saying if questions have a yes or no format (Schwarz et al., 1985). Recent evidence suggests, however, that serious problems can largely be avoided by a careful and precise wording of the questions (Louviere, Hensher and Swait, 2000).

An obvious way to test and validate SP data is to compare them with RP data (see Louviere, Hensher and Swait, 2000). Among economic studies, Euwals, Melenberg and van Soest (1998) show that stated preferences for changes in working hours are predictive of changes in actual hours, and Kapteyn (1994) compares data on actual expenditures on certain commodities with data on subjective income evaluations, and finds that the two types of data are consistent with a common underlying utility function. The conclusion from studies such as these seems to be that RP and SP data are often consistent with each other, once an appropriate model is used to allow for different sources of idiosyncratic noise. In such a case, SP data can lead to more efficient estimates than RP data, and opportunities for combining the two data sources can be exploited to more accurately estimate parameters of interest.

Louviere, Hensher and Swait (2000) focus on static models of consumer choice, but the potential advantages of SP data also apply to dynamic models of consumer behaviour under uncertainty. Models of intertemporal choice have become increasingly important in many areas of empirical economics as researchers have gained access to rich panel data on households in the Panel Study of Income Dynamics and many subsequent national surveys in the United States and Europe.

Two central parameters of interest describe the agent's time preference and risk aversion. Standard RP analysis would yield inferences on these preference parameters based solely on, for example, observed savings and investment decisions. The rate of time preference indicates how the utility of current consumption is traded off for future consumption (for example, paid for with current savings). Risk aversion parameters indicate how risky alternatives (such as risky assets) are valued relative to less risky ones (such as risk-free assets). A standard identifying assumption in econometric models of intertemporal choice requires that time preferences and risk preferences be invariant across households.

In recent years, economists have used SP data to estimate the distribution of time and risk preference parameters in heterogeneous populations. Frederick, Loewenstein and O'Donoghue (2002) summarize empirical measures of rates of time preference (by economists and others) via RP and SP methods and use this to argue that the standard model of intertemporal choice (a single discount rate) is misspecified. Barsky et al. (1997) use SP data from an experimental module of the HRS. For risk preferences, the survey asks respondents to choose between two jobs, either the current job with the current income or a new job with higher expected income but also with some income risk. For time preferences, the survey asks respondents to make a sequence of choices over alternative consumption profiles across time. Their results show that SP data can be usefully applied to economic choices in a life cycle context, but they also pay attention to the potential pitfalls of using SP data with incompletely specified alternatives, such as the tendency to prefer the current job for reasons other than income.

Similar survey methods have been introduced in the Netherlands. Kapteyn and Teppa (2003) use SP data from the Dutch Center panel to estimate a structural model with habit formation in which preference parameters vary with individual attributes. Donkers, Melenberg and van Soest (2001) use SP data on choices between hypothetical lotteries to identify a structural model that generalizes a standard expected utility model by allowing for reference-dependent utility, loss aversion, and probability weighting.

Conclusion

We have described recent developments in the collection of subjective data on expectations and preferences and the estimation of behavioural models using these data. Combining data on expectations and preferences with each other and with data on actual choice behaviour is an important goal of this endeavour. An ambitious example is Erdem, Keane and Strebel (2005), who estimate a dynamic structural model of information acquisition and purchase decisions by consumers who choose among brands of personal computer. To identify the model, they utilize reports of price change expectations and stated assessments of brand quality in combination with data on actual purchase behaviour.

It is far too early to conclude that the general scepticism among economists about data on subjective phenomena has been overcome. However, we strongly believe that recent innovations in the measurement and analysis of expectations and preferences are enriching the empirical content of economic models and hold great promise for the future.

JEFF DOMINITZ AND ARTHUR VAN SOEST

See also **categorical data; longitudinal data analysis; nonlinear panel data models; partial identification in econometrics; propensity score; selection bias and self-selection.**

Bibliography

Ariely, D., Prelec, D. and Loewenstein, G. 2003. Coherent arbitrariness: stable demand curves without stable preferences. *Quarterly Journal of Economics* 118, 73–105.

Barsky, R., Juster, F., Kimball, M. and Shapiro, M. 1997. Preference parameters and behavioral heterogeneity: an experimental approach in the health and retirement survey. *Quarterly Journal of Economics* 112, 537–80.

Bernheim, B. 1989. The timing of retirement: a comparison of expectations and realizations. In *The Economics of Aging*, ed. D. Wise. Chicago: NBER and University of Chicago Press.

Bernheim, B. 1990. How do the elderly form expectations? An analysis of responses to new information. In *Issues in the Economics of Aging*, ed. D. Wise. Chicago: NBER and University of Chicago Press.

Chambers, R. and Skinner, C. 2003. *Analysis of Survey Data*. Hoboken, NJ: Wiley.

Das, M., Dominitz, J. and van Soest, A. 1999. Comparing predictions and outcomes: theory and application to income changes. *Journal of the American Statistical Association* 94, 75–85.

Diamond, P. and Hausman, J. 1994. Contingent valuation: is some number better than no number? *Journal of Economic Perspectives* 8(4), 45–64.

Dominitz, J. 2001. Estimation of income expectations models using expectations and realizations data. *Journal of Econometrics* 102, 165–95.

Dominitz, J. and Manski, C. 1997a. Using expectations data to study subjective income expectations. *Journal of the American Statistical Association* 92, 855–67.

Dominitz, J. and Manski, C. 1997b. Perceptions of economic insecurity: evidence from the Survey of Economic Expectations. *Public Opinion Quarterly* 61, 261–87.

Dominitz, J. and Manski, C. 2004. How should we measure consumer confidence? *Journal of Economic Perspectives* 18(2), 51–66.

Donkers, B., Melenberg, B. and van Soest, A. 2001. Estimating risk attitudes using lotteries – a large sample approach. *Journal of Risk and Uncertainty* 22, 165–95.

Erdem, T., Keane, M. and Strebel, J. 2005. Learning about computers: an analysis of information search and technology choice. *Quantitative Marketing and Economics* 3, 207–46.

Euwals, R., Melenberg, B. and van Soest, A. 1998. Testing the predictive value of subjective labour supply data. *Journal of Applied Econometrics* 13, 567–86.

Frederick, S., Loewenstein, G. and O'Donoghue, T. 2002. Time discounting and time preference: a critical review. *Journal of Economic Literature* 40, 351–401.

Guiso, L., Jappelli, T. and Terlizzese, D. 1992. Earnings uncertainty and precautionary saving. *Journal of Monetary Economics* 30, 307–37.

Hanemann, W. 1994. Valuing the environment through contingent valuation. *Journal of Economic Perspectives* 8(4), 19–43.

Hurd, M. and McGarry, K. 1995. Evaluation of the subjective probabilities of survival in the HRS. *Journal of Human Resources* 30, S268–S292.

Hurd, M. and McGarry, K. 2002. The predictive validity of subjective probabilities of survival. *Economic Journal* 112, 966–85.

Juster, F. 1966. Consumer buying intentions and purchase probability: an experiment in survey design. *Journal of the American Statistical Association* 61, 658–96.

Kapteyn, A. 1994. The measurement of household cost functions: revealed preference versus subjective measures. *Journal of Population Economics* 7, 333–50.

Kapteyn, A. and Teppa, F. 2003. Hypothetical intertemporal consumption choices. *Economic Journal* 113, C140–C152.

Katona, G. 1957. Federal Reserve Board Committee reports on consumer expectations and savings statistics. *Review of Economics and Statistics* 39, 40–6.

Keane, M. and Runkle, D. 1990. Testing the rationality of price forecasters: new evidence from panel data. *American Economic Review* 80, 714–34.

Lancaster, T. and Chesher, A. 1983. An econometric analysis of reservation wages. *Econometrica* 51, 1661–76.

Louviere, J., Hensher, D. and Swait, J. 2000. *Stated Choice Methods*. Cambridge: Cambridge University Press.

Ludvigson, S. 2004. Consumer confidence and consumer spending. *Journal of Economic Perspectives* 18(2), 29–50.

Manski, C. 1990. The use of intentions data to predict behavior: a best-case analysis. *Journal of the American Statistical Association* 85, 934–40.

Manski, C. 1999. Analysis of choice expectations in incomplete scenarios. *Journal of Risk and Uncertainty* 19, 49–65.

Manski, C. 2004. Measuring expectations. *Econometrica* 72, 1329–76.

McFadden, D. 1973. Conditional logit analysis of qualitative choice behavior. In *Frontiers of Econometrics*, ed. P. Zarembka. New York: Academic Press.

McFadden, D. 1986. The choice theory approach to market research. *Marketing Science* 5, 275–97.

Mitchell, R. and Carson, R. 1989. *Using Surveys to Value Public Goods: The Contingent Valuation Method*. Baltimore: John Hopkins University Press.

Pesaran, M. and Weale, M. 2006. Survey expectations. In *Handbook of Economic Forecasting*, vol. 1, ed. G. Elliott, C. Granger and A. Timmermann. Amsterdam: North-Holland.

Revelt, D. and Train, K. 1998. Mixed logit with repeated choices: households' choices of appliance efficiency level. *Review of Economics and Statistics* 80, 647–57.

Schwarz, N., Hippler, H.-J., Deutsch, B. and Strack, F. 1985. Response scales: effects of category range on reported behavior and comparative judgments. *Public Opinion Quarterly* 49, 388–95.

Tobin, J. 1959. On the predictive value of consumer intentions and attitudes. *Review of Economics and Statistics* 21, 1–11.

Tobit model

The Tobit model, or censored regression model, is useful to learn about the conditional distribution of a variable y^* given a vector of regressors x, when y^* is observed only if it is above or below some known threshold (censoring). In the original model of Tobin (1958), for example, the dependent variable was expenditures on durables, and values below zero are not observed.

Censoring models state that the observed dependent variable y follows from the latent variable y^* as

$$y = \max\{y^*, 0\},$$

where we have assumed a censoring of the form $y^* > 0$ without loss of generality because, for any given top or bottom threshold a, it is always possible to change y^* into $\pm(y^* - a)$.

Censoring may either be a property of the sample or a property of the population. For example, top-coding of earnings in the Current Population Survey (CPS) generates censoring in a way that is independent of individual decisions. In contradistinction, the zero purchases of Tobin's households *are* individual decisions. This type of censoring is usually modelled as a corner solution of a decision-theoretic model. For example, the labour supply model predicts that the number of hours worked by a person is equal to the interior solution of the consumption-and-leisure utility maximization problem, if it is greater than zero; it is zero otherwise. (See Pudney, 1989, for a survey of the economics and econometrics of corner solutions.)

The relationship between the latent variable y^* and regressors x is assumed linear:

$$y^* = x^{\mathrm{T}}\beta + u,$$

where β is a vector of parameters, $x^{\mathrm{T}}\beta$ denotes the scalar product of x and β (^{T} is the transpose operator), and u is a residual component with cumulative distribution function (cdf) F conditional on x. We assume that the distribution of u given x, that is F, is continuous. It hence has a density $f = F'$.

The Tobit model corresponds to the particular case of $F(u) = \Phi(\frac{u}{\sigma})$, where Φ denotes the cdf of the standard normal distribution $N(0,1)$, and σ^2 is the variance of u (that is $u \sim N(0, \sigma^2)$).

The distribution of y given x

Let $G(y|x)$ denote the cdf of the observation y given x. The distribution of y is not continuous. It has a mass point at 0. The probability mass at 0 is

$$G(0|x) \equiv \Pr\{y = 0|x\} = \Pr\{y^* \leq 0|x\}$$

$$= \Pr\{u \leq -x^{\mathrm{T}}\beta|x\} = F(-x^{\mathrm{T}}\beta).$$

Notice that $F(-x^T\beta) = 1 - F(x^T\beta)$ if u has a symmetric distribution.

Any positive observation $y > 0$ is necessarily such that $y = x^T\beta + u$. Therefore, the cdf of the observed outcome at $y > 0$ given x is equal to the cdf of u at $y - x^T\beta$:

$$G(y|x) = F(y - x^T\beta), \quad \forall y > 0.$$

The density of any observation $y > 0$ given x is

$$g(y|x) = \frac{\partial G(y|x)}{\partial y} = f(y - x^T\beta).$$

Notice that, since 0 is a mass point of the distribution of y, its density at 0 can be defined as

$$g(0|x) = G(0|x) - G(0^-|x) = G(0|x),$$

where $G(0^-|x) = lim_{y \to 0^-} G(y|x) = 0$. (The probability density function, pdf, of a distribution or random variable is defined relative to a particular measure. Continuous variables admit a density with respect to the Lebesgue measure. Discrete distributions admit a density with respect to the counting measure. One can also define a density function for mixed discrete-continuous distributions with respect to mixtures of the Lebesgue measure and the counting measure.)

In the case of the Tobit model, $f(u) = \frac{1}{\sigma}\varphi(\frac{u}{\sigma})$, where $\varphi(v) = \Phi'(v) = \frac{1}{\sqrt{2\pi}} e^{-\frac{v^2}{2}}$ is the density of the standard normal distribution. So,

$$g(0|x) = G(0|x) = F(-x^T\beta) = \Phi\left(\frac{x_i^T\beta}{\sigma}\right),$$

$$g(y|x) = f(y - x^T\beta) = \frac{1}{\sigma}\varphi\left(\frac{y - x^T\beta}{\sigma}\right), \quad \forall y > 0.$$

Moments of y given x

Two conditional moments of y are of particular interest: $\mathbb{E}(y|x)$ and $\mathbb{E}(y|x, y > 0)$. First, notice that

$$y = \max\{y^*, 0\} \geq y^*$$

implies that

$$\mathbb{E}[y|x] \geq \mathbb{E}[y^*|x]$$

and

$$\mathbb{E}[y|x, y > 0] = \frac{\mathbb{E}[y|x]}{\Pr\{y > 0|x\}} \geq \mathbb{E}[y|x].$$

So both $\mathbb{E}(y|x)$ and $\mathbb{E}(y|x, y>0)$ overestimate the first moment of the variable of interest, that is $\mathbb{E}(y^*|x)$.

Specifically,

$$
\begin{aligned}
\mathbb{E}[y|x] &= \mathbb{E}[\max\{y^*, 0\}|x] = \mathbb{E}[\max\{x^{\mathrm{T}}\beta + u, 0\}|x] \\
&= \int_{-x^{\mathrm{T}}\beta}^{+\infty} (x^{\mathrm{T}}\beta + u)f(u)\,du \\
&= x^{\mathrm{T}}\beta(1 - F(-x^{\mathrm{T}}\beta)) + \int_{-x^{\mathrm{T}}\beta}^{+\infty} uf(u)\,du
\end{aligned}
$$

and

$$
\mathbb{E}[y|x, y>0] = \frac{\mathbb{E}[y|x]}{\Pr\{y>0|x\}} = x^{\mathrm{T}}\beta + \lambda(x^{\mathrm{T}}\beta)
$$

with

$$
\lambda(z) = \frac{\int_z^{+\infty} uf(u)\,du}{1 - F(z)}.
$$

In the particular case of the Tobit model, $\varphi'(v) = -v\varphi(v)$. It thus follows that $\lambda(v) = \sigma\frac{\varphi(\frac{v}{\sigma})}{\Phi(\frac{v}{\sigma})}$. Notice that $\frac{\varphi}{\Phi}$ is the inverse Mills ratio of the standard normal distribution.

Ordinary least squares

Let $\{(y_i, x_i), i = 1, \ldots, N\}$ be an i.i.d. random sample of observations. Regressing y_i on x_i for the uncensored observations i such that $y_i > 0$ does not yield a consistent estimator of β because of the omitted variable $\lambda(x_i^{\mathrm{T}}\beta)$ which is correlated with the regressors x_i.

For the Tobit model, a two-stage estimation procedure can be devised.

1. First, estimate a Probit model for $d_i \equiv 1\{y_i > 0\}$ ($= 1$ if $y_i > 0$ and $= 0$ otherwise):

$$
\Pr\{d_i = 1|x_i\} = \Phi(x_i^{\mathrm{T}}c),
$$

with $c = \frac{\beta}{\sigma}$. Let $\hat{c}$ be the Probit estimator of c.
2. Regress y_i on x_i and the inverse Mills ratio $\frac{\varphi(x_i^{\mathrm{T}}\hat{c})}{\Phi(x_i^{\mathrm{T}}\hat{c})}$ by OLS. This yields a consistent estimator of β and σ.

Two remarks are in order. First, as any multi-stage estimation procedure, the OLS estimator of the second stage has $\frac{\varphi(x_i^{\mathrm{T}}\hat{c})}{\Phi(x_i^{\mathrm{T}}\hat{c})}$ instead of $\frac{\varphi(x_i^{\mathrm{T}}c)}{\Phi(x_i^{\mathrm{T}}c)}$. The measurement error $\frac{\varphi(x_i^{\mathrm{T}}\hat{c})}{\Phi(x_i^{\mathrm{T}}\hat{c})} - \frac{\varphi(x_i^{\mathrm{T}}c)}{\Phi(x_i^{\mathrm{T}}c)}$ tends to 0 when N tends to infinity. So the OLS estimator of (β, σ) is asymptotically unbiased and consistent. However, its asymptotic variance has to be corrected for the statistical error on parameter c.

Second, the first stage requires knowing the entire distribution of u_i. It is therefore not clear why one would want to use this two-stage procedure instead of maximum likelihood (ML), which is efficient.

Maximum likelihood

The likelihood of one observation y_i conditional on x_i is $g(y_i|x_i)$. The conditional sample log-likelihood is then

$$L_N = \sum_{i=1}^{N} \ln g(y_i|x_i) = \sum_{i=1}^{N} \{d_i \ln f(y_i - x_i^T \beta) + (1 - d_i) \ln F(-x_i^T \beta)\}.$$

Under standard regularity conditions, the values of β and any other parameters of F that maximize the log-likelihood L_N are root-N consistent and asymptotically normal and efficient.

For the Tobit model, we obtain

$$L_N = \sum_{i=1}^{N} (1 - d_i) \ln \left(1 - \Phi\left(\frac{x_i^T \beta}{\sigma}\right)\right) - N_+ \ln \sigma - \frac{1}{2\sigma^2} \sum_{i=1}^{N} d_i(y_i - x_i^T \beta)^2$$

where $N_+ = \sum_{i=1}^{N}(1 - d_i)$ is the number of uncensored observations.

It is useful to change (β, σ) into $(c, s) = (\frac{\beta}{\sigma}, \frac{1}{\sigma})$ because

$$L_N = \sum_{i=1}^{N} (1 - d_i) \ln (1 - \Phi(x_i^T c)) + N_+ \ln s - \frac{1}{2} \sum_{i=1}^{N} d_i(sy_i - x_i^T c)^2$$

is strictly concave with respect to (c, s). Maximizing L_N with respect to (c, s) is easy and fast using standard gradient algorithms. One can then use the delta method to recover an estimate of the asymptotic variance of $(\hat{\beta}, \hat{\sigma}) = (\frac{\hat{c}}{\hat{s}}, \frac{1}{\hat{s}})$.

Consistency of ML obviously rests on the model being well specified. Non-normal errors and heteroskedasticity (when homoskedastic, normal errors are assumed) lead to inconsistent estimates.

Trimmed least squares

Powell's (1986) symmetrically trimmed least squares is a simple consistent estimator that is consistent under the assumption that the distribution of u_i is symmetric. It can yet be non-normal or heteroskedastic.

The idea is to replace y_i by $2x_i'\beta$ when $y_i \geq 2x_i'\beta$, if $x_i'\beta > 0$, and drop all observations such that $x_i'\beta \leq 0$ from the sample, as no symmetric trimming is possible in this case. In effect, let

$$\tilde{y}_i = \min\{y_i, 2x_i^T \beta\} = x_i^T \beta + \tilde{u}_i$$

where

$$\tilde{u}_i = \begin{vmatrix} -x_i^T \beta & \text{if } u_i \leq -x_i^T \beta \\ u_i & \text{if } -x_i^T \beta < u_i \leq x_i^T \beta \\ x_i^T \beta & \text{if } x_i^T \beta < u_i \end{vmatrix}$$

As u_i has a symmetric distribution conditional on x_i, then so does $\tilde{u}_i$. Hence,

$$\mathbb{E}[\tilde{y}_i | x_i] = x_i^T \beta.$$

The trimmed least squares estimator is obtained by iterating the following sequential procedure until convergence. Start with an initial value β_0 for β. For example, regress y_i on x_i on the uncensored sample. If, at iteration p, one has obtained a value β_p for β, then compute β_{p+1} by regressing $\tilde{y}_i(\beta_p) = \min\{y_i, 2x_i^T \beta_p\}$ on x_i using the sample of observations i such that $x_i'\beta_p > 0$.

Endogenous regressors

In the standard labour supply model, the observed dependent variable y_i is the actual number of hours worked by individual i, and the latent variable y_i^* is the interior solution to a utility maximization problem. This interior solution depends on the individual's wage, w_i, and other variables x_i such as non-labour income or education and age:

$$y_i^* = x_i^T \beta + \alpha w_i + u_i.$$

The residual u_i captures unobserved heterogeneity factors influencing the trade-off between consumption and leisure. It is usually understood that wages w_i and unobserved taste shifters u_i are correlated across individuals: $\text{Cov}(w_i, u_i) \neq 0$.

Suppose that w_i and x_i are both observed when $y_i = 0$. The following simple control-function procedure can apply to solve the endogeneity problem. Suppose that there exists a vector z_i of instruments such that

$$w_i = z_i^T \gamma + v_i,$$

with $\text{Cov}(z_i, v_i) = 0$. Suppose also that

$$u_i = \rho v_i + \varepsilon_i,$$

with ε_i normal $N(0, \sigma^2)$ conditional on x_i, z_i and v_i. This will be the case in particular if u_i and v_i are jointly normal conditional on x_i and z_i.

Then, the following two-stage procedure produces consistent estimators of β, α and ρ.

1. Regress w_i on z_i by OLS and compute residuals $\hat{v}_i$.
2. Estimate the Tobit model

$$y_i = \max\{x_i^T \beta + \alpha w_i + \rho \hat{v}_i + {}_i, 0\},$$

assuming $_i = \varepsilon_i - \rho(\hat{v}_i - v_i)$ normally distributed, by ML or other appropriate method.

One can test for the exogeneity of w_i by testing for $\rho = 0$ with a standard t-test. If the null hypothesis is rejected, then this two-stage procedure yields consistent estimates, but correct asymptotic standard errors, accounting for the approximation of v_i by $\hat{v}_i$, require a specific calculation.

Finally, if w_i is not observed when $y_i = 0$, which is the case for wages of not employed individuals, this procedure does not work. Heckman (1974) assumed joint normality of (u_i, v_i) and applied maximum likelihood to (y_i, w_i), $i = 1, \ldots, N$, conditional on exogenous variables.

JEAN-MARC ROBIN

See also **logit models of individual choice; selection bias and self-selection.**

Bibliography

Blundell, R.W. and Smith, R.J. 1986. An exogeneity test for a simultaneous equation Tobit model with an application to labor supply. *Econometrica* 54, 679–86.

Blundell, R.W. and Smith, R.J. 1989. Estimation in a class of simultaneous equation limited dependent variable models. *Review of Economic Studies* 56, 37–57.

Heckman, J.J. 1974. Shadow prices, market wages, and labor supply. *Econometrica* 42, 679–94.

Powell, J.L. 1986. Symmetrically trimmed least squares estimation for Tobit models. *Econometrica* 54, 1435–60.

Pudney, S. 1989. *Modelling Individual Choice: the Econometrics of Corners, Kinks and Holes.* Oxford: Blackwell.

Tobin, J. 1958. Estimation for relationships with limited dependent variables. *Econometrica* 26(2), 24–36.

treatment effect

A 'treatment effect' is the average causal effect of a binary (0–1) variable on an outcome variable of scientific or policy interest. The term 'treatment effect' originates in a medical literature concerned with the causal effects of binary, yes-or-no 'treatments', such as an experimental drug or a new surgical procedure. But the term is now used much more generally. The causal effect of a subsidized training programme is probably the mostly widely analysed treatment effect in economics (see, for example, Ashenfelter, 1978, for one of the first examples, or Heckman and Robb, 1985 for an early survey). Given a data-set describing the labour market circumstances of trainees and a non-trainee comparison group, we can compare the earnings of those who did participate in the programme and those who did not. Any empirical study of treatment effects would typically start with such simple comparisons. We might also use regression methods or matching to control for demographic or background characteristics.

In practice, simple comparisons or even regression-adjusted comparisons may provide misleading estimates of causal effects. For example, participants in subsidized training programmes are often observed to earn less than ostensibly comparable controls, even after adjusting for observed differences (see, for example, Ashenfelter and Card, 1985). This may reflect some sort of omitted variables bias, that is, a bias arising from unobserved and uncontrolled differences in earnings potential between the two groups being compared. In general, omitted variables bias (also known as selection bias) is the most serious econometric concern that arises in the estimation of treatment effects. The link between omitted variables bias, causality, and treatment effects can be seen most clearly using the potential-outcomes framework.

Causality and potential outcomes

The notion of a causal effect can be made more precise using a conceptual framework that postulates a set of potential outcomes that could be observed in alternative states of the world. Originally introduced by statisticians in the 1920s as a way to discuss treatment effects in randomized experiments, the potential outcomes framework has become the conceptual workhouse for non-experimental as well as experimental studies in many fields (see Holland, 1986, for a survey and Rubin, 1974; 1977, for influential early contributions). Potential outcomes models are essentially the same as the econometric *switching regressions* model (Quandt, 1958), though the latter is usually tied to a linear regression framework. Heckman (1976; 1979) developed simple two-step estimators for this model.

Average causal effects

Except in the realm of science fiction, where parallel universes are sometimes imagined to be observable, it is impossible to measure causal effects at the individual level. Researchers therefore focus on average causal effects. To make the idea of an average causal effect concrete, suppose again that we are interested in the effects of a training programme on the post-training earnings of trainees. Let Y_{1i} denote the potential earnings of individual i if he were to receive training and let Y_{0i} denote the potential earnings of individual i if not. Denote training status by a dummy variable, D_i. For each individual, we observe $Y_i = Y_{0i} + D_i(Y_{1i} - Y_{0i})$, that is, we observe Y_{1i} for trainees and Y_{0i} for everyone else.

Let $E[\cdot]$ denote the mathematical expectation operator, i.e., the population average of a random variable. For continuous random variables, $E[Y_i] = \int yf(y)dy$, where $f(y)$ is the density of Y_i. By the law of large numbers, sample averages converge to population averages so we can think of $E[\cdot]$ as giving the sample average in very large samples. The two most widely studied average causal effects in the treatment effects context are the average treatment effect (ATE), $E[Y_{1i} - Y_{0i}]$, and the average treatment effect on the treated (ATET), $E[Y_{1i} - Y_{0i}|D_i = 1]$. Note that the ATET can be rewritten

$$E[Y_{1i} - Y_{0i}|D_i = 1] = E[Y_{1i}|D_i = 1] - E[Y_{0i}|D_i = 1].$$

This expression highlights the counter-factual nature of a causal effect. The first term is the average earnings in the population of trainees, a potentially observable quantity. The second term is the average earnings of trainees had they not been trained. This cannot be observed, though we may have a control group or econometric modelling strategy that provides a consistent estimate.

Selection bias and social experiments

As noted above, simply comparing those who are and are not treated may provide a misleading estimate of a treatment effect. Since the omitted variables problem is unrelated to sampling variance or statistical inference, but rather concerned with population quantities, it too can be efficiently described by using mathematical expectation notation to denote population averages. The contrast in average outcomes by observed treatment status is

$$E[Y_i|D_i = 1] - E[Y_i|D_i = 0] = E[Y_{1i}|D_i = 1] - E[Y_{0i}|D_i = 0]$$

$$= E[Y_{1i} - Y_{0i}|D_i = 1] + \{E[Y_{0i}|D_i = 1] - E[Y_{0i}|D_i = 0]\}$$

Thus, the naive contrast can be written as the sum of two components, ATET, plus selection bias due to the fact that the average earnings of non-trainees, $E[Y_{0i}|D_i = 0]$, need not be a good stand-in for the earnings of trainees had they not been trained, $E[Y_{0i}|D_i = 1]$.

The problem of selection bias motivates the use of random assignment to estimate treatment effects in social experiments. Random assignment ensures that the potential earnings of trainees had they not been trained – an unobservable quantity – are well-represented by the randomly selected control group. Formally, when D_i is randomly assigned, $E[Y_i|D_i = 1] - E[Y_i|D_i = 0] = E[Y_{1i} - Y_{0i}|D_i = 1] = E[Y_{1i} - Y_{0i}]$. Replacing $E[Y_i|D_i = 1]$ and $E[Y_i|D_i = 0]$ with the corresponding sample analogs provides a consistent estimate of ATE.

Regression and matching

Although it is increasingly common for randomized trials to be used to estimate treatment effects, most economic research still uses observational data. In the absence of a randomized experiment, researchers rely on a variety of statistical control strategies and/or natural experiments to reduce omitted variables bias. The most commonly used statistical techniques in this context are regression, matching and instrumental variables.

Regression estimates of causal effects can be motivated most easily by postulating a constant-effects model, where $Y_{1i} - Y_{0i} = \alpha$ (a constant). The constant-effects assumption is not strictly necessary for regression to estimate an average causal effect, but it simplifies things to postpone a discussion of this point. More importantly, the only source of omitted-variables bias is assumed to come from a vector of observed covariates, X_i, that may be correlated with D_i. The key assumption that facilitates causal inference in regression models (sometimes called an identifying assumption), is that

$$E[Y_{0i}|X_i, D_i] = X_i'\beta, \tag{1}$$

where β is a vector of regression coefficients. This selection-on-observables assumption has two parts. First, Y_{0i} (and hence Y_{1i}, given the constant-effects assumption) is mean-independent of D_i conditional on X_i. Second, the conditional mean function for Y_{0i} given X_i is linear. Given eq. (1), it is straightforward to show that

$$E\{Y_i(D_i - R[D_i|X_i])\}/E\{D_i(D_i - R[D_i|X_i])\} = \alpha, \tag{2}$$

where $R[D_i/X_i]$ are the fitted values from a regression of D_i on X_i. This is the coefficient on D_i from the population regression of Y_i on D_i and X_i (that is, the regression coefficient in an infinite sample). Again, the law of large numbers ensures that sample regression coefficients estimate this population regression coefficient consistently.

Matching is similar to regression in that it is motivated by the assumption that the only source of omitted variables or selection bias is the set of observed covariates, X_i. Unlike regression, however, matching estimates of treatment effects are constructed by matching individuals with the same covariates instead of through a linear model for the effect of covariates. Instead of (1), the selection-on-observables assumption becomes

$$E[Y_{ji}|X_i, D_i] = E[Y_{ji}|X_i], \quad \text{for } j = 0, 1. \tag{3}$$

This implies

$$E[Y_{1i} - Y_{0i}|D_i = 1] = E\{E[Y_{1i}|X_i, D_i = 1] - [Y_{0i}|X_i, D_i = 1]|D_i = 1\}$$
$$= E\{E[Y_{1i}|X_i, D_i = 1] - [Y_{0i}|X_i, D_i = 0]|D_i = 1\} \tag{4a}$$

and, likewise,

$$E[Y_{1i} - Y_{0i}] = E\{E[Y_{1i}|X_i, D_i = 1] - [Y_{0i}|X_i, D_i = 0]\} \tag{4b}$$

In other words, we can construct ATET or ATE by averaging X-specific treatment-control contrasts, and then reweighting these X-specific contrasts using the distribution of X_i for the treated (for ATET) or using the marginal distribution of X_i (for ATE). Since these expressions involve observable quantities, it is straightforward to construct consistent estimators from their sample analogs.

The conditional independence assumption that motivates the use of regression and matching is most plausible when researchers have extensive knowledge of the process determining treatment status. An example in this spirit is the Angrist (1998) study of the effect of voluntary military service on the civilian earnings of soldiers after discharge, discussed further below.

Regression and matching details

In practice, regression can be understood as a type of weighted matching estimator. If, for example, $E[D_i|X_i]$ is a linear function of X_i (as it might be if the covariates are all discrete), then it is possible to show that eq. (2) is equivalent to a matching estimator that weights cell-by-cell treatment-control contrasts by the conditional variance of treatment in each cell (Angrist, 1998). This equivalence highlights the fact that the most important econometric issue in a study that relies on selection-on-observables assumptions to identify causal effects is the validity of these conditional independence assumptions, not whether regression or matching is used to implement them.

A computational difficulty that sometimes arises in matching models is how to find good matches for each possible value of the covariates when the covariates take on many values. For example, beginning with Ashenfelter (1978), many studies of the effect of training programmes have shown that trainees typically experience a period of declining earnings before they go into training. Because lagged earnings is both continuous and multidimensional (since more than one period's earnings seem to matter), it may be hard to match trainees and controls with exactly the same pattern of lagged earnings. A possible solution in this case is to match trainees and controls on the *propensity score*, the conditional probability of treatment given covariates. Propensity-score matching relies on the fact that, if conditioning on X_i eliminates selection bias, then so does conditioning on $P[D_i = 1|X_i]$, as first noted by Rosenbaum and Rubin (1983). Use of the propensity score reduces the dimensionality of the matching problem since the propensity score is a scalar, though in practice it must still be estimated. See Dehejia and Wahba (1999) for an illustration.

Regression and matching example

Between 1989 and 1992, the size of the military declined sharply because of increasing enlistment standards. Policymakers would like to know whether the people – many of them black men – who would have served under the old rules but were unable to enlist under the new rules were hurt by the lost opportunity for service. The Angrist (1998) study attempts to answer this question. The regression and matching assumptions seem plausible in this context because soldiers are selected on the basis of a few well-documented criteria related to age, schooling and test scores and because the control group used in the study also applied to enter the military.

Naive comparisons clearly overestimate the benefit of military service. This can be seen in Table 1, which reports differences-in-means, matching and regression estimates of the effect of voluntary military service on the 1988–91 Social Security-taxable earnings of men who applied to join the military between 1979 and 1982. The matching estimates were constructed from the sample analog of (4a), that is, from covariate-value-specific differences in earnings, weighted to form a single estimate using the distribution of covariates among veterans. The covariates in this case are the age, schooling and test-score variables used to select soldiers from the pool of applicants. Although white veterans earn $1,233 more than non-veterans, this difference becomes negative once the adjustment for differences in covariates is made. Similarly, while non-white veterans earn $2,449 more than non-veterans, controlling for covariates reduces this to $840.

Table 1 also shows regression estimates of the effect of voluntary military service, controlling for the same covariates used for matching. These are estimates of α_r in the equation

$$Y_i = \sum_X d_{iX}\beta_X + \alpha_r D_i + e_i,$$

Table 1   *Matching and regression estimates of the effects of voluntary military service in the United States*

Race	Average earnings in 1988–91 (1)	Differences in means (2)	Matching estimates (3)	Regression estimates (4)	Regression minus matching (5)
Whites	14,537	1,233.4	−197.2	−88.8	108.4
		(60.3)	(70.5)	(62.5)	(28.5)
Non-whites	11,664	2,449.1	839.7	1,074.4	234.7
		(47.4)	(62.7)	(50.7)	(32.5)

Notes: Figures are in nominal US dollars. The table shows estimates of the effect of voluntary military service on the 1988–91 Social Security-taxable earnings of men who applied to enter the armed forces during 1979–82. The matching and regression estimates control for applicants' year of birth, education at the time of application, and Armed Forces Qualification Test (AFQT) score. There are 128,968 whites and 175,262 non-whites in the sample. Standard errors are reported in parentheses.
Source: Adapted from Angrist (1998, Tables II and V).

where β_X is a regression-effect for $X_i = X$ and α_r is the regression parameter. This corresponds to a saturated model for discrete X_i. The regression estimates are larger than (and significantly different from) the matching estimates. But the regression and matching estimates are not very different economically, both pointing to a small earnings loss for White veterans and a modest gain for Non-whites.

Instrumental variables estimates of treatment effects

The assumptions required for regression or matching to identify a treatment effect are often implausible. Many of the necessary control variables are typically unmeasured or simply unknown. Instrumental variables (IV) methods solve the problem of missing or unknown controls, much as a randomized trial also obviates the need for regression or matching. To see how this is possible, begin again with a constant effects model without covariates, so $Y_{1i} - Y_{0i} = \alpha$. Also, let $Y_{0i} = \beta + \varepsilon_i$, where $\beta \equiv E[Y_{0i}]$. The potential outcomes model can now be written

$$Y_i = \beta + \alpha D_i + \varepsilon_i, \tag{5}$$

where α is the treatment effect of interest. Because D_i is likely to be correlated with ε_i, regression estimates of eq. (5) do not estimate α consistently.

Now suppose that in addition to Y_i and D_i there is a third variable, Z_i, that is correlated with D_i, but unrelated to Y_i for any other reason. In a constant-effects world, this is equivalent to saying Y_{0i} and Z_i are independent. It therefore follows that

$$E[\varepsilon_i|Z_i] = 0, \tag{6}$$

a conditional independence restriction on the relation between Z_i and Y_{0i}, instead of between D_i and Y_{0i} as required for regression or matching strategies. The variable Z_i is said to be an IV or just 'an instrument' for the causal effect of D_i on Y_i.

Suppose that Z_i is also a 0–1 variable. Taking expectations of (5) with Z_i switched off and on, we immediately obtain a simple formula for the treatment effect of interest:

$$\frac{E[Y_i|Z_i = 1] - E[Y_i|Z_i = 0]}{E[D_i|Z_i = 1] - E[D_i|Z_i = 0]} = \alpha. \tag{7}$$

The sample analog of this equation is sometimes called the Wald estimator, since it first appear in a paper by Wald (1940) on errors-in-variables problems. There are other more complicated IV estimators involving continuous, multi-valued, or multiple instruments. For example, with a multi-valued instrument, we might use the sample analog of $Cov(Z_i, Y_i)/Cov(D_i, Y_i)$. This simplifies to the Wald estimator when Z_i is 0–1. The Wald estimator captures the main idea behind most IV estimation strategies since more complicated estimators can usually be written as a linear combination of Wald estimators (Angrist, 1991).

IV example

To see how IV works in practice, it helps to use an example, in this case the effect of Vietnam-era military service on the earnings of veterans later in life (Angrist, 1990). In the 1960s and early 1970s, young men were at risk of being drafted for military service. Concerns about fairness led to the institution of a draft lottery in 1970 that was used to determine priority for conscription in cohorts of 19-year-olds. A natural instrumental variable for the Vietnam veteran treatment effect is draft-eligibility status, since this was determined by a lottery over birthdays. In particular, in each year from 1970 to 1972, random sequence numbers (RSNs) were randomly assigned to each birth date in cohorts of 19-year-olds. Men with lottery numbers below an eligibility ceiling were eligible for the draft, while men with numbers above the ceiling could not be drafted. In practice, many draft-eligible men were still exempted from service for health or other reasons, while many men who were draft-exempt nevertheless volunteered for service. So veteran status was not completely determined by randomized draft eligibility; eligibility and veteran status are merely correlated.

For white men who were at risk of being drafted in the 1970–71 draft lotteries, draft-eligibility is clearly associated with lower earnings in years after the lottery. This can be seen in Table 2, which reports the effect of randomized draft-eligibility status on average Social Security-taxable earnings in column (2). Column (1) shows average annual earnings for purposes of comparison. For men born in 1950, there are significant negative effects of eligibility status on earnings in 1970, when these men were being drafted, and in 1981, ten years later. For example, the 1981 estimate for whites is −436 dollars. In contrast, there is no evidence of an association between eligibility status and earnings in 1969, the year the lottery drawing for men born in 1950 was held but before anyone born in 1950 was actually drafted.

Because eligibility status was randomly assigned, the claim that the estimates in column (2) represent the causal effect of *draft eligibility* on earnings seems

Table 2   *Instrumental variables estimates of the effects of military service on US white men born 1950*

Earnings year	Earnings		Veteran status		Wald estimate of veteran effect
	Mean (1)	Eligibility effect (2)	Mean (3)	Eligibility effect (4)	(5)
1981	16,461	−435.8 (210.5)	0.267	0.159 (0.040)	−2,741 (1,324)
1970	2,758	−233.8 (39.7)			−1,470 (250)
1969	2,299	−2.0 (34.5)			

Notes: Figures are in nominal US dollars. There are about 13,500 observations with earnings in each cohort. Standard errors are shown in parentheses.
Sources: Adapted from Angrist (1990, Tables 2 and 3), and unpublished author tabulations. Earnings data are from Social Security administrative records. Veteran status data are from the Survey of Income and Program Participation.

uncontroversial. An additional assumption embodied in equation (6) is that the only reason eligibility affects earnings is military service. Given this, the only information required to go from draft-eligibility effects to veteran-status effects is the denominator of the Wald estimator, which is the effect of draft-eligibility on the probability of serving in the military. This information is reported in column (4) of Table 2, which shows that draft-eligible men were 0.16 more likely to have served in the Vietnam era. For earnings in 1981, long after most Vietnam-era servicemen were discharged from the military, the Wald estimates of the effect of military service reported in column (5) amount to about 15 percent of earnings. Effects were even larger in 1970, when affected soldiers were still in the army.

IV with heterogeneous treatment effects

The constant-effects assumption is clearly unrealistic. We'd like to allow for the fact that some men may have benefited from military service while others were undoubtedly hurt by it. In general, however, IV methods fail to capture either ATE or ATET in a model with heterogeneous treatment effects. Intuitively, this is because only a subset of the population is affected by any particular instrumental variable. In the draft lottery example, many men with high lottery numbers volunteered for service anyway (indeed, most Vietnam veterans were volunteers), while many draft-eligible men nevertheless avoided service. The draft lottery instrument is not informative about the effects of military service on men who were unaffected by their draft-eligibility status. On the other hand, there is a sub-population who served solely because they were draft-eligible, but would not have served otherwise. Angrist, Imbens and Rubin (1996) call the population of men whose treatment status can be manipulated by an instrumental variable the set of *compliers*. This term comes from an analogy to a medical trial with imperfect compliance. The set of compliers are those who 'take their medicine', that is, they serve in the military when draft-eligible but they do not serve otherwise.

Under reasonably general assumptions, IV methods can be relied on to capture the causal effect of treatment on compliers. The average causal effect for this group is called a local average treatment effect (LATE), and was first discussed by Imbens and Angrist (1994). A formal description of LATE requires one more bit of notation. Define potential treatment assignments D_{0i} and D_{1i} to be individual i's treatment status when Z_i equals 0 or 1. One of D_{0i} or D_{1i} is counterfactual since observed treatment status is

$$D_i = D_{0i} + Z_i(D_{1i} - D_{0i}).$$

The key identifying assumptions in this setup are (*a*) conditional independence, that is, that the joint distribution of $\{Y_{1i}, Y_{0i}, D_{1i}, D_{0i}\}$ is independent of Z_i; and (*b*) monotonicity, which requires that either $D_{1i}D_{0i}$ for all i or vice versa. Monotonicity requires that, while the instrument might have no effect on some individuals, all of those who are affected should be affected in the same way (for example, draft eligibility can only make military service more likely, not less). Assume without loss of generality that monotonicity holds with $D_{1i} \geq D_{0i}$. Given these two assumptions, the Wald estimator consistently estimates LATE, written formally as $E[Y_{1i} - Y_{0i}|D_{1i} > D_{0i}]$. In the draft lottery example, this is the effect of military service on those veterans who served because they were draft eligible but would not have served otherwise. In general, LATE compliers are a subset of the treated. An important special case where LATE = ATET is when D_{0i} equals zero for everyone. This happens in a social experiment with imperfect compliance in the treated group and no one treated in the control group.

IV Details

Typically, covariates play a role in IV models, either because the IV identification assumptions are more plausible conditional on covariates or because of statistical efficiency gains. Linear IV models with covariates can be estimated most easily by two-stage least squares (2SLS), which can also be used to estimate models with multi-valued, continuous, or multiple instruments. See Angrist and Imbens (1995) or Angrist and Krueger (2001) for details and additional references.

JOSHUA D. ANGRIST

See also **matching estimators; regression-discontinuity analysis; selection bias and self-selection.**

Bibliography

Angrist, J. 1990. Lifetime earnings and the Vietnam era draft lottery: evidence from social security administrative records. *American Economic Review* 80, 313–35.

Angrist, J. 1991. Grouped-data estimation and testing in simple labor-supply models. *Journal of Econometrics* 47, 243–266.

Angrist, J. 1998. Estimating the labor market impact of voluntary military service using Social Security data on military applicants. *Econometrica* 66, 249–88.

Angrist, J. and Imbens, G. 1995. Two-stage least squares estimates of average causal effects in models with variable treatment intensity. *Journal of the American Statistical Association* 90, 431–42.

Angrist, J., Imbens, G. and Rubin, D. 1996. Identification of causal effects using instrumental variables. *Journal of the American Statistical Association* 91, 444–55.

Angrist, J. and Krueger, A. 2001. Instrumental variables and the search for identification: from supply and demand to natural experiments. *Journal of Economic Perspectives* 15(4), 69–85.

Ashenfelter, O. 1978. Estimating the effect of training programs on earnings. *Review of Economics and Statistics* 6, 47–57.

Ashenfelter, O. and Card, D. 1985. Using the longitudinal structure of earnings to estimate the effect of training programs. *Review of Economics and Statistics* 67, 648–60.

Dehejia, R. and Wahba, S. 1999. Causal effects in nonexperimental studies: reevaluating the evaluation of training programs. *Journal of the American Statistical Association* 94, 1053–62.

Heckman, J. 1976. The common structure of statistical models of truncation, sample selection, and limited dependent variables and a simple estimator for such models. *Annals of Economic and Social Measurement* 5, 475–92.

Heckman, J. 1979. Sample selection bias as a specification error. *Econometrica* 47, 153–61.

Heckman, James J. and Robb, R. 1985. Alternative methods for evaluating the impact of interventions. In *Longitudinal Analysis of Labor Market Data*, ed. J. Heckman and B. Singer. New York: Cambridge University Press.

Holland, P. 1986. Statistics and causal inference. *Journal of the American Statistical Association* 81, 945–70.

Imbens, G. and Angrist, J. 1994. Identification and estimation of local average treatment effects. *Econometrica* 62, 467–75.

Quandt, R. 1958. The estimation of the parameters of a linear regression system obeying two separate regimes. *Journal of the American Statistical Association* 53, 873–80.

Rosenbaum, P. and Rubin, D. 1983. The central role of the propensity score in observational studies for causal effects. *Biometrika* 70, 41–55.

Rubin, D. 1974. Estimating causal effects of treatments in randomized and non-randomized studies. *Journal of Educational Psychology* 66, 688–701.

Rubin, D. 1977. Assignment to a treatment group on the basis of a covariate. *Journal of Educational Statistics* 2, 1–26.

Wald, A. 1940. The fitting of straight lines if both variables are subject to error. *Annals of Mathematical Statistics* 11, 284–300.

variance, analysis of

1. Introduction

Analysis of variance (ANOVA) represents a set of models that can be fit to data, and also a set of methods for summarizing an existing fitted model. We first consider ANOVA as it applies to classical linear models (the context for which it was originally devised; Fisher, 1925) and then discuss how ANOVA has been extended to generalized linear models and multilevel models. Analysis of variance is particularly effective for analysing highly structured experimental data (in agriculture, multiple treatments applied to different batches of animals or crops; in psychology, multi-factorial experiments manipulating several independent experimental conditions and applied to groups of people; industrial experiments in which multiple factors can be altered at different times and in different locations).

At the end of this article, we compare ANOVA with simple linear regression.

2. Analysis of variance for classical linear models

2.1 ANOVA as a family of statistical methods

When formulated as a statistical model, analysis of variance refers to an additive decomposition of data into a grand mean, main effects, possible interactions and an error term. For example, Gawron et al. (2003) describe a flight-simulator experiment that we summarize as a 5×8 array of measurements under five treatment conditions and eight different airports. The corresponding two-way ANOVA model is $y_{ij} = \mu + \alpha_i + \beta_j + \varepsilon_{ij}$. The data as described here have no replication, and so the two-way interaction becomes part of the error term. (If, for example, each treatment $\times$ airport condition were replicated three times, then the 120 data points could be modelled as $y_{ijk} = \mu + \alpha_i + \beta_j + \gamma_{ij} + \varepsilon_{ijk}$, with two sets of main effects, a two-way interaction, and an error term.)

This is a linear model with $1 + 4 + 7$ coefficients, which is typically identified by constraining the $\sum_{i=1}^{5} \alpha_i = 0$ and $\sum_{j=1}^{8} \beta_j = 0$. The corresponding ANOVA display is shown in Table 1:

1. For each source of variation, the degrees of freedom represent the number of effects at that level, minus the number of constraints (the five treatment effects sum to zero, the eight airport effects sum to zero, and each row and column of the 40 residuals sums to zero).
2. The total sum of squares – that is, $\sum_{i=1}^{5}\sum_{j=1}^{8}(y_{ij} - y_{..})^2$ – is $0.078 + 3.944 + 1.417$, which can be decomposed into these three terms corresponding to variance described by treatment, variance described by airport, and residuals.

Table 1 *Classical two-way analysis of variance for data on five treatments and eight airports with no replication*

Source	Degrees of freedom	Sum of squares	Mean square	F-ratio	p-value
Treatment	4	0.078	0.020	0.39	0.816
Airport	7	3.944	0.563	11.13	< 0.001
Residual	28	1.417	0.051		

Note: The treatment-level variation is not statistically distinguishable from noise, but the airport effects are statistically significant.
Sources for all examples in this article: Gelman (2005) and Gelman and Hill (2006).

3. The mean square for each row is the sum of squares divided by degrees of freedom. Under the null hypothesis of zero row and column effects, their mean squares would, in expectation, simply equal the mean square of the residuals.
4. The F-ratio for each row (except for the last) is the mean square, divided by the residual mean square. This ratio should be approximately 1 (in expectation) if the corresponding effects are zero; otherwise we would generally expect the F-ratio to exceed 1. We would expect the F-ratio to be less than 1 only in unusual models with negative within-group correlations (for example, if the data y have been renormalized in some way, and this had not been accounted for in the data analysis).
5. The p-value gives the statistical significance of the F-ratio with reference to the F_{v_1, v_2}, where v_1 and v_2 are the numerator and denominator degrees of freedom, respectively. (Thus, the two F-ratios in Figure 1 are being compared to $F_{4,28}$ and $F_{7,28}$ distributions, respectively.) In this example, the treatment mean square is lower than expected (an F-ratio of less than 1), but the difference from 1 is not statistically significant (a p-value of 82 per cent), hence it is reasonable to judge this difference as explainable by chance, and consistent with zero treatment effects. The airport mean square is much higher than would be expected by chance, with an F-ratio that is highly statistically significantly larger than 1; hence we can confidently reject the hypothesis of zero airport effects.

More complicated designs have correspondingly complicated ANOVA models, and complexities arise with multiple error terms. We do not intend to explain such hierarchical designs and analyses here, but we wish to alert the reader to such complications. Textbooks such as Snedecor and Cochran (1989) and Kirk (1995) provide examples of analysis of variance for a wide range of designs.

2.2 ANOVA to summarize a model that has already been fitted
We have just demonstrated ANOVA as a method of analysing highly structured data by decomposing variance into different sources, and comparing the explained variance at each level with what would be expected by chance alone. Any classical analysis of variance corresponds to a linear model (that is, a regression model, possibly with

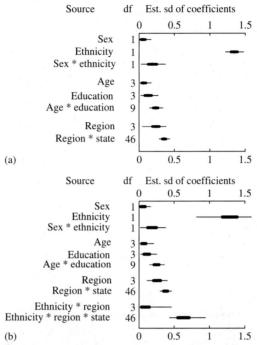

Figure 1 ANOVA display for two logistic regression models of the probability that a survey respondent prefers the Republican candidate for the 1988 US presidential election. *Notes*: Point estimates and error bars show median estimates, 50% intervals and 95% intervals of the standard deviation of each batch of coefficients. The large coefficients for ethnicity, region and state suggest that it might make sense to include interactions, hence the inclusion of ethnicity × region and ethnicity × state interactions in the second model. *Source*: data from seven CBS News polls.

multiple error terms); conversely, ANOVA tools can be used to summarize an existing linear model.

The key is the idea of 'sources of variation', each of which corresponds to a batch of coefficients in a regression. Thus, with the model $y = X\beta + \varepsilon$, the columns of X can often be batched in a reasonable way (for example, in Table 1, a constant term, four treatment indicators, and seven airport indicators) and the mean squares and F-tests then provide information about the amount of variance explained by each batch.

Such models could be fitted without any reference to ANOVA, but ANOVA tools could then be used to make some sense of the fitted models, and to test hypotheses about batches of coefficients.

2.3 Balanced and unbalanced data

In general, the amount of variance explained by a batch of predictors in a regression depends on which other variables have already been included in the model. With *balanced data*, however, in which all groups have the same number of observations (for example, each treatment applied exactly eight times, and each airport used for exactly five observations), the variance decomposition does not depend on the order in which the variables are entered. ANOVA is thus particularly easy to interpret with balanced data. The analysis of variance can also be applied to unbalanced data, but then the sums of squares, mean squares and F-ratios will depend on the order in which the sources of variation are considered.

3. ANOVA for more general models

Analysis of variance represents a way of summarizing regressions with large numbers of predictors that can be arranged in batches, and a way of testing hypotheses about batches of coefficients. Both these ideas can be applied in settings more general than linear models with balanced data.

3.1 F-tests
In a classical balanced design (as in the example in Table 1), each F-ratio compares a particular batch of effects to zero, testing the hypothesis that this particular source of variation is not necessary to fit the data.

More generally, the F-test can compare two nested models, testing the hypothesis that the smaller model fits the data adequately (so that the larger model is unnecessary). In a linear model, the F ratio is $\frac{(SS_2 - SS_1)/(df_2 - df_1)}{SS_1/df_1}$, where SS_1, df_1 and SS_2, df_2 are the residual sums of squares and degrees of freedom from fitting the larger and smaller models, respectively.

For generalized linear models, formulas exist using the *deviance* (the log-likelihood multiplied by -2) that are asymptotically equivalent to F-ratios. In general, such models are not balanced, and the test for including another batch of coefficients depends on which other sources of variation have already been included in the model.

3.2 Inference for variance parameters
A different sort of generalization interprets the ANOVA display as inference about the variance of each batch of coefficients, which we can think of as the relative importance of each source of variation in predicting the data. Even in a classical balanced ANOVA, the sums of squares and mean squares do not exactly do this, but the information contained therein can be used to estimate the variance components (Cornfield and Tukey, 1956; Searle, Casella and McCulloch, 1992). Bayesian simulation can then be used to obtain confidence intervals for the variance parameters. As illustrated in this article we display inferences for standard deviations (rather than variances) because these are more directly interpretable. Compared with the classical ANOVA display, our plots emphasize the estimated variance parameters rather than testing the hypothesis that they are zero.

3.3 Generalized linear models
The idea of estimating variance parameters applies directly to generalized linear models as well as unbalanced data-sets. All that is needed is that the parameters of a regression model are batched into 'sources of variation'. Figure 1 illustrates with a multilevel logistic regression model, predicting vote preference given a set of demographic and geographic variables.

3.4 Multilevel models and Bayesian inference

Analysis of variance is closely tied to multilevel (hierarchical) modelling, with each source of variation in the ANOVA table corresponding to a variance component in a multilevel model (see Gelman, 2005). In practice, this can mean that we perform ANOVA by fitting a multilevel model, or that we use ANOVA ideas to summarize multilevel inferences. Multilevel modelling is inherently Bayesian in that it involves a potentially large number of parameters that are modelled with probability distributions (see, for example, Goldstein, 1995; Kreft and De Leeuw, 1998; Snijders and Bosker, 1999). The differences between Bayesian and non-Bayesian multilevel models are typically minor except in settings with many sources of variation and little information on each, in which case some benefit can be gained from a fully Bayesian approach which models the variance parameters.

4. Related topics

4.1 Finite population and super-population variances

So far in this article we have considered, at each level (that is, each source of variation) of a model, the standard deviation of the corresponding set of coefficients. We call this the *finite-population* standard deviation. Another quantity of potential interest is the standard deviation of the hypothetical *super-population* from which these particular coefficients were drawn. The point estimates of these two variance parameters are similar – with the classical method of moments, the estimates are identical, because the super-population variance is the expected value of the finite-population variance – but they will have different uncertainties. The inferences for the finite-population standard deviations are more precise, as they correspond to effects for which we actually have data.

Figure 2 illustrates the finite-population and super-population inferences at each level of the model for the flight-simulator example. We know much more about the five treatments and eight airports in our data-set than for the general populations of treatments and airports. (We similarly know more about the standard deviation of the 40 particular errors in out data-set than about their hypothetical super-population, but the differences here are not so large because the super-population distribution is fairly well estimated from the 28 degrees of freedom available from these data.)

There has been much discussion about fixed and random effects in the statistical literature (see Eisenhart, 1947; Green and Tukey, 1960; Plackett, 1960; Yates, 1967; LaMotte, 1983; and Nelder, 1977; 1994, for a range of viewpoints), and unfortunately the terminology used in these discussions is incoherent (see Gelman, 2005, sec. 6). Our resolution to some of these difficulties is to always fit a multilevel model but to summarize it with the appropriate class of estimand – super-population or finite population – depending on the context of the problem. Sometimes we are interested in the particular groups at hand; at other times they are a sample from a larger population of interest. A change of focus should not require a change in the model, only a change in the inferential summaries.

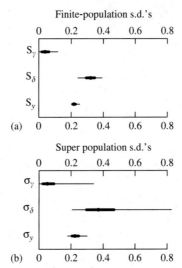

Figure 2   Median estimates, 50% intervals and 95% intervals for (a) finite population and (b) super-population standard deviations of the treatment-level, airport-level and data-level errors in the flight-simulator example from Table 1. *Note*: The two sorts of standard deviation parameters have essentially the same estimates, but the finite-population quantities are estimated much more precisely. (We follow the general practice in statistical notation, using Greek and Roman letters for population and sample quantities, respectively.)

4.2 Contrast analysis

Contrasts are a way to structuring the effects within a source of variation. In a multilevel modelling context, a contrast is simply a group-level coefficient. Introducing contrasts into an ANOVA allows a further decomposition of variance. Figure 3 illustrates for a 5×5 latin square experiment (this time, not a split plot): the left plot in the figure shows the standard ANOVA, and the right plot shows a contrast analysis including linear trends for the row, column and treatment effects. The linear trends for the columns and treatments are large, explaining most of the variation at each of these levels, but there is no evidence for a linear trend in the row effects.

Figure 4 shows the estimated effects and linear trends at each level (along with the raw data from the study), as estimated from a multilevel model. This plot shows in a different way that the variation among columns and treatments, but not among rows, is well explained by linear trends.

4.3 Non-exchangeable models

In all the ANOVA models we have discussed so far, the effects within any batch (source of variation) are modelled exchangeably, as a set of coefficients with mean 0 and some variance. An important direction of generalization is to non-exchangeable models, such as in time series, spatial structures (Besag and Higdon, 1999), correlations that arise in particular application areas such as genetics (McCullagh, 2005), and dependence in multi-way structures (Aldous, 1981; Hodges et al., 2005). In these

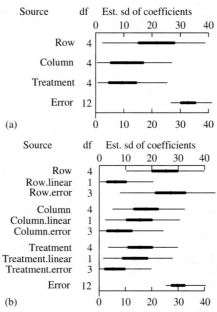

Figure 3   ANOVA displays for a 5 × 5 latin square experiment (an example of a crossed three-way structure): (a) with no group-level predictors, (b) contrast analysis including linear trends for rows, columns and treatments. *Note*: See also the plots of coefficient estimates and trends in Figure 4.

settings, both the hypothesis-testing and variance-estimating extensions of ANOVA become more elaborate. The central idea of clustering effects into batches remains, however. In this sense, 'analysis of variance' represents all efforts to summarize the relative importance of different components of a complex model.

5. ANOVA compared with linear regression

The analysis of variance is often understood by economists in relation to linear regression (for example, Goldberger, 1964). From the perspective of linear (or generalized linear) models, we identify ANOVA with the structuring of coefficients into batches, with each batch corresponding to a 'source of variation' (in ANOVA terminology).

As discussed by Gelman (2005), the relevant inferences from ANOVA can be reproduced by using regression – but not always least-squares regression. Multilevel models are needed for analysing hierarchical data structures such as 'split-plot designs', where between-group effects are compared with group-level errors, and within-group effects are compared with data-level errors.

Given that we can already fit regression models, what do we gain by thinking about ANOVA? To start with, the display of the importance of different sources of variation is a helpful exploratory summary. For example, the two plots in Figure 1 allow us to quickly understand and compare two multilevel logistic regressions, without getting overwhelmed with dozens of coefficient estimates.

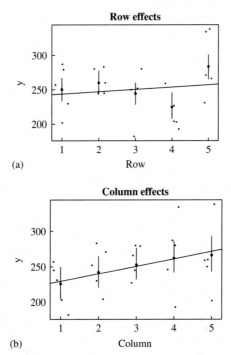

(a)

(b)

Figure 4 Estimates ± 1 standard error for the row, column and treatment effects for the latin square experiment summarized in Figure 3. *Note*: The five levels of each factor are ordered, and the lines display the estimated linear trends.

More generally, we think of the analysis of variance as a way of understanding and structuring multilevel models – not as an alternative to regression but as a tool for summarizing complex high-dimensional inferences, as can be seen, for example, in Figure 2 (finite-population and super-population standard deviations) and Figures 3 and 4 (group-level coefficients and trends).

ANDREW GELMAN

We thank Jack Needleman, Matthew Rafferty, David Pattison, Marc Shivers, Gregor Gorjanc, and several anonymous commenters for helpful suggestions and the National Science Foundation for financial support.

Bibliography

Aldous, D. 1981. Representations for partially exchangeable arrays of random variables. *Journal of Multivariate Analysis*, 581–98.

Besag, J. and Higdon, D. 1999. Bayesian analysis of agricultural field experiments (with discussion). *Journal of the Royal Statistical Society B*, 691–746.

Cochran, W. and Cox, G. 1957. *Experimental Designs*, 2nd edn. New York: Wiley.

Cornfield, J. and Tukey, J. 1956. Average values of mean squares in factorials. *Annals of Mathematical Statistics*, 907–49.

Eisenhart, C. 1947. The assumptions underlying the analysis of variance. *Biometrics* 3, 1–21.

Fisher, R.A. 1925. *Statistical Methods for Research Workers*. Edinburgh: Oliver and Boyd.

Gawron, V., Berman, B., Dismukes, R. and Peer, J. 2003. New airline pilots may not receive sufficient training to cope with airplane upsets. *Flight Safety Digest* (July–August), 19–32.

Gelman, A. 2005. Analysis of variance: why it is more important than ever (with discussion). *Annals of Statistics* 33, 1–53.

Gelman, A. and Hill, J. 2006. *Data Analysis Using Regression and Multilevel/Hierarchical Models*. New York: Cambridge University Press.

Gelman, A., Pasarica, C. and Dodhia, R. 2002. Let's practice what we preach: using graphs instead of tables. *American Statistician* 56, 121–30.

Goldberger, A. 1964. *Econometric Theory*. New York: Wiley.

Goldstein, H. 1995. *Multilevel Statistical Models*, 2nd edn. London: Edward Arnold.

Green, B. and Tukey, J. 1960. Complex analyses of variance: general problems. *Psychometrika* 25, 127–52.

Hodges, J., Cui, Y., Sargent, D. and Carlin, B. 2005. Smoothed ANOVA. Technical report, Department of Biostatistics, University of Minnesota.

Kirk, R. 1995. *Experimental Design: Procedures for the Behavioral Sciences*, 3rd edn. Pacific Grove, CA: Brooks/Cole.

Kreft, I. and De Leeuw, J. 1998. *Introducing Multilevel Modeling*. London: Sage.

LaMotte, L. 1983. Fixed-, random-, and mixed-effects models. In *Encyclopedia of Statistical Sciences*, ed. S. Kotz, N. Johnson and C. Read. New York: Wiley.

McCullagh, P. 2005. Discussion of Gelman (2005). *Annals of Statistics* 33, 33–8.

Nelder, J. 1977. A reformulation of linear models (with discussion). *Journal of the Royal Statistical Society A* 140, 48–76.

Nelder, J. 1994. The statistics of linear models: back to basics. *Statistics and Computing* 4, 221–34.

Plackett, R. 1960. Models in the analysis of variance (with discussion). *Journal of the Royal Statistical Society B* 22, 195–217.

Searle, S., Casella, G. and McCulloch, C. 1992. *Variance Components*. New York: Wiley.

Snedecor, G. and Cochran, W. 1989. *Statistical Methods*, 8th edn. Ames: Iowa State University Press.

Snijders, T. and Bosker, R. 1999. *Multilevel Analysis*. London: Sage.

Yates, F. 1967. A fresh look at the basic principles of the design and analysis of experiments. *Proceedings of the Fifth Berkeley Symposium on Mathematical Statistics and Probability* 4, 777–90.

Index